THE MOVIE BOOK OF THE WESTERN

The Movie Book of
THE WESTERN

edited by
Ian Cameron
and
Douglas Pye

STUDIO
VISTA

First published in 1996 by
Studio Vista
a Cassell imprint
Wellington House
125 Strand
London WC2R 0BB

Produced by Cameron Books
PO Box 1, Moffat
Dumfriesshire DG10 9SU, Scotland

Distributed in Australia
by Capricorn Link (Australia) Pty Ltd
2/13 Carrington Road
Castle Hill
NSW 2154

British Library Cataloguing-in-Publication Data
A catalogue record for this book is available from the British Library

ISBN 0-289-80140-0 (hardback)
ISBN 0-289-80168-0 (paperback)

A Movie Book
Text editing by Ian Cameron and Jill Hollis
Designed by Ian Cameron
Index by Jill Hollis

Filmset by Cameron Books, Moffat
Halftone reproduction by Hilite, Southampton
Printed and bound in Britain by
Hartnolls, Bodmin, Cornwall

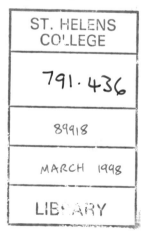
Frontispiece: James Stewart with his burnt wagons at the beginning of Anthony Mann's The Man from Laramie *(1955).*

Acknowledgements

Richard Maltby's article is a revised and expanded version of an essay originally published under the title 'John Ford and the Indians: or, Tom Doniphon's History Lesson' in *Representing Others: White Views of Indigenous People*, ed. Mick Gidley, University of Exeter Press, 1992.

An earlier draft of David Lusted's article was presented at a conference on Melodrama organised by Christine Gledhill and Jim Cook of the British Film Institute Education Department at University of London Institute of Education in 1992. David Lusted is grateful to Douglas Pye and Martin Pumphrey for advice and support while rewriting it for publication. He is also indebted to Alec Lusted and his hero, Tom Mix, for the original idea.

Peter Stanfield thanks Dr Anne Massey and staff on the Media/Film courses at Southampton Institute for creating enough time and space for him to write his article.

Martin Pumphrey's article originally appeared in *Critical Quarterly*, vol.31, no.3.

Douglas Pye's 'Genre and History' is based on articles that appeared in *Movie* 22 (Spring 1976) and 25 (Winter 1977/78).

Douglas Pye's article on Mann is a revised version of that published in *CineAction!* in 1992. It was first presented at a colloquium on the Western at the Institute of United States Studies, London, in March 1992.

Robin Wood's article on *Drums Along the Mohawk* was first published in *CineAction!*, Spring 1987.

Andrew Britton's 'Notes on *Pursued*' is extracted from a much longer article in *Framework* 4, Summer 1976. This was written in answer to the view of the film presented in Paul Willemen's book on Raoul Walsh, but contained a substantial account of the film which is reprinted here.

Douglas Pye's article on *Ulzana's Raid* first appeared in *Movie* 27/28, Winter 1980/Spring 1981.

Stills by courtesy of BFI Stills, Posters and Designs, Columbia, MGM, Paramount, Twentieth Century-Fox, United Artists, Universal, Warner Brothers.

CONTENTS

FOREWORD

This book follows the same general pattern as *The Movie Book of Film Noir* (*The Book of Film Noir* in North America). The differences are an expression of the particular nature of the Western.

For *film noir*, defining the genre seemed important, while its fashionable status was, and is, incontestable – since the 'seventies, it has been the cinematic face of the taste for retro. The Western, on the other hand, has no need of definition. Anyone can sketch out enough of its salient features for it to be identifiable. The introduction to the book is therefore concerned not with definition, but with the Western's place in film criticism, which is to say, in fashion.

Quintessentially American, the Western appears in every narrative art form from pulp fiction to ballet and is represented in painting, photography and sculpture. Within its ambit in the cinema comes a great range of work that can equally be defined by other labels: romance, comedy, musical, adventure, thriller, even horror film. The sheer variety of Western film production means that almost any generalisation about what makes a Western must be qualified by exceptions. It is not difficult to find Westerns that lack one or more of the following: cowboys, Indians, gunfighters, sheriffs, settlements, the open range, the frontier, honour, gunplay, shoot-outs, not to mention still more optional items like chases, cattle drives, wagon trains, campfires and coffee.

If there is a single feature that characterises Westerns, it is setting, and even this has to be defined negatively: the setting is not the East, whether urban and industrialised or rural and agricultural. In the relatively few Westerns set before the Civil War, not-the-East does not have to be very far west (or south); overall, the territory covered by films that are very definitely Westerns extends in a broad sweep from Alaska down to Mexico and across to Florida.

In the cinema, the sheer quantity of Westerns produced over the past ninety or so years makes any attempt at comprehensiveness liable to defeat, particularly in a volume aiming at criticism rather than cataloguing. In part, the limits have been drawn by the availability of films, as much to the book's readers as to its contributors. We have concentrated on the period since 1939 and the definitive arrival of the Western in mainstream A-feature production. Within this temporal limit, there are strands of Western production that have been excluded: series and serials, singing cowboy movies, and Westerns that are primarily musicals or comedies. Also excluded are Westerns produced in Europe, whether nourished on spaghetti or paella.

As in the *film noir* volume, the contents here are split between general articles and detailed analyses of specific films, again with the aim of covering the field in both depth and breadth. Among the general topics that have seemed most rewarding in relation to the Western are history, race, gender (particularly masculinity) and social class.

Of these, race raises particular problems of terminology. At least until the 1950s, Hollywood in general had felt able to play fast and loose with the depiction of the races and saw little problem, for example, in the idea of having Chinese characters played by Katharine Hepburn or Peter Lorre. Nowhere was Hollywood's racism more acute than in the case of Native Americans. On the whole, Whites were played by Whites, Blacks by Blacks and Native Americans by almost anyone. Given this situation, we have opted to use the word Indian to describe characters within movies, while being, I hope, scrupulous in using Native American in descriptions of real people.

The choice of films dealt with in the latter half of the book has emerged largely from the enthusiasms of the contributors. Rather than trying systematically to cover the most important Westerns – a recipe likely to produce an arid result and to be composed of some very stale ingredients – we have tried to achieve a balance between the most famous Westerns and less obvious choices. It would not be difficult to fill a second volume of at least the same size with films no less deserving of inclusion.

Of the thirty articles in this book, only six have previously appeared in print in any form, and these have to various degrees been revised and re-edited for publication here. I am grateful to the 22 contributors for their co-operation. Above all, I am indebted to Douglas Pye, for his good-natured and perceptive input as co-editor at all stages in the conception and editing of this volume.

This book is dedicated, in the year of his eightieth birthday, to Budd Boetticher, the last of the directors responsible for the unequalled richness of the Westerns made in the decade or so before 1960.

Ian Cameron
February 1996

REFERENCES

The following list includes books and articles on the Western referred to in the text, where they are cited by author/editor (or, if appropriate, title) and date. Other references are given in full on their first citation in any article.

Bazin, André 'Evolution of the Western' and 'The Western, or the American Film par excellence' in *What Is Cinema?* volume II, translated by Hugh Gray, University of California Press, Berkeley, 1971

Buscombe, Edward, ed. *The BFI Companion to the Western*, André Deutsch/BFI Publishing, London, 1988; revised edition 1993

Calder, Jenni *There Must Be a Lone Ranger: The Myth and Reality of the American Wild West*, Hamish Hamilton, London, 1974

Cawelti, John G. *The Six-Gun Mystique*, Bowling Green University Popular Press, Ohio, 1971

Cawelti, John G. *Adventure, Mystery and Romance: Formula Stories as Art and Popular Culture*, University of Chicago Press, 1976

French, Philip *Westerns*, Secker & Warburg, London, 1973, revised edition 1977

Hardy, Phil *The Aurum Film Encyclopedia: The Western*, Aurum Press, London, 1983, revised edition 1991

Fiedler, Leslie *Return of the Vanishing American*, New York, 1968, reprinted by Paladin Books, London, 1972 (page references to this edition)

Kitses, Jim *Horizons West*, Thames and Hudson, London, 1969

Nachbar, Jack, ed. *Focus on the Western*, Prentice Hall, Englewood Cliffs, New Jersey, 1974

Nash Smith, Henry *Virgin Land: The American West as Symbol and Myth*, Harvard University Press, 1950

Pumphrey, Martin 'Why Do Cowboys Wear Hats in the Bath? Style Politics for the Older Man', Critical Quarterly, vol.31, no.3, 1989, reprinted in this book

Slotkin, Richard *The Fatal Environment: The Myth of the Frontier in the Age of Industrialization*, Wesleyan University Press, Middletown, Connecticut, 1985

Tompkins, Jane *West of Everything*, Oxford University Press, New York, 1992

Tuska, Jon *The Filming of the West*, Doubleday, Garden City, New York, 1976

Warshow, Robert 'Movie Chronicle: The Westerner', *Partisan Review*, March/April 1954, reprinted in *The Immediate Experience*, Doubleday, Garden City, New York, 1962, and in Nachbar (1974)

Wright, Will *Six Guns and Society: A Structural Study of the Western*, University of California Press, Berkeley, 1975

INTRODUCTION
Criticism and the Western

Douglas Pye

The Western has been in the critical wilderness in recent years. After being at the heart of the wave of genre criticism that developed between about 1965 and 1975, it then disappeared from the main stage of film criticism almost as completely as it did from Hollywood production. After 1975, books on the Western and a trickle of articles continued to appear, but debate became muted, and few commentators significantly developed existing approaches. Symptomatic of the paralysis in critical writing on the Western film is the fact that the major publications in recent years have been reference books – Phil Hardy's *The Aurum Film Encyclopedia: The Western* (1983) and *The BFI Companion to the Western* (1988). Useful as they are, they have the feeling of tombstones marking the passing of the genre. The Phil Hardy volume lists and describes films year by year; *The BFI Companion to the Western* contains many excellent short essays in its 'Culture and History' section, entries that cut into the representation of the West from a variety of perspectives – geographical, historical, biographical, conceptual. It is a mine of information about the genre and its contexts. Its critical content, on the other hand, is much more meagre – confined to brief and inevitably limited entries on individual films and film-makers. It is hardly reasonable to criticise the volume for not being something it did not set out to be, but it offers an eloquent symptom of the Western's uneasy place in recent film criticism.

One possible explanation for the marginalisation of the genre in criticism might lie in the huge decline in the production of Westerns for cinema and television in the 'seventies and 'eighties. But this is not a sufficient cause – action movies generally were marginal to criticism in the late 'seventies and 'eighties, and this was clearly not because action cinema flagged – quite the reverse.

The gangster film, which was almost as significant as the Western in 'sixties and early 'seventies genre criticism, also largely vanished from critical attention, although crime movies and TV series were a growth area in 'eighties production. Genres of male action as a whole, in fact, were displaced from their central role in film criticism and have only recently begun once more to receive (selective) attention.

There are good reasons for looking at the Western again. In the most basic terms, it is absurd that a form which has been so hugely important to Hollywood cinema and which across a variety of media

in its various manifestations is perhaps the paradigmatic American narrative should have become marginal to film criticism. One purpose of this book is to re-open the territory in the hope that it can be made habitable once again.

As a starting point, it is instructive to look back at the very considerable interest in the Western between 1965 and 1975. Several studies of the genre had appeared in France during the 'sixties, and they were joined by a range of work in English. The books alone make up a substantial body of critical writing:

1968 Leslie Fiedler *The Return of the Vanishing American* (USA)
1969 Jim Kitses *Horizons West* (UK)
1971 John G. Cawelti *Six Gun Mystique* (USA)
1973 Philip French *Westerns* (UK)
1974 Jenni Calder *There Must Be a Lone Ranger* (UK)
      Jack Nachbar (ed.) *Focus on the Western* (USA)
1975 Will Wright *Six Guns and Society* (USA)
1976 John G. Cawelti *Adventure, Mystery and Romance* (USA)

In addition, some of the formative articles on genre in the American cinema that appeared in journals during the same period focused on the Western.

Frequently drawing on a number of key earlier publications, notably essays on the Western by André Bazin and Robert Warshow and Henry Nash Smith's *Virgin Land* (1950), these books and articles developed new and productive analytical approaches to the Western (or at least to some aspects of it). For all these writers, the Western was central to American cinema (indeed to American culture), although as Kitses commented in the first sentence of *Horizons West*, the genre had 'yet received scant critical attention'.

In fact, the emphasis on genre was itself relatively new to English-language writing on film, and it became a key concept in extending debates about popular cinema beyond authorship, the approach that had so productively opened up Hollywood cinema to systematic critical study. To Alan Lovell, for instance, in his 1967 British Film Institute seminar paper on the Western, genre was fundamental to analysing the mass media, to countering the widespread rejection of popular arts in British culture and to focusing study of the relationships between 'the artist, the structure he works in, and the society of which both the artist and the institution are a part' (reprinted in *Movies and Methods*, edited by Bill Nichols, University of California Press, Berkeley, 1976, p.175).

Even so, it is difficult to account with confidence for the Western's domination of genre discussions in this period. Its prominence, and to a lesser extent that of the gangster movie, could be due partly to their apparent visual coherence and their amenability to analysis in terms of iconography, an approach borrowed from art history that was applied to movies by a number of writers at this time. The Western was perhaps the obvious starting point, too, in terms of its sheer scale of production, covering the whole history of American cinema and massively outnumbering any other identifiable genre. But the late 'sixties were also the last period in which the Western had a major place in Hollywood film and television production. In 1967, there were twenty Western series on television in America; a decade later (the number fell relentlessly each year) there were four. Production of feature films dropped less dramatically, but the last year in which over 50 Westerns was made was 1958 (with 54); from 1960 to 1976 the highest number in any year was 28 (1960), and numbers were generally between 15 and 25. In 1977 only seven Western features were made. Perhaps as significant was the 'end of the West' theme which became increasingly emphatic during the 'sixties, the climax of a growing self-consciousness in the genre which many critics observed developing during the post World War II period. In other words, the critical visibility of the Western may owe a good deal to the way in which, against a background of declining production, contemporary film-makers foregrounded and subverted the familiar conventions. A key film in this process, Sam Peckinpah's *Ride the High Country/Guns in the Afternoon* (1962) is, for instance, a major reference point for early genre pieces by Alan Lovell and Ed Buscombe (*Screen*, vol.11, no 2, March/April 1970, pp.33-45) and, on a larger scale, Peckinpah is the last of the three directors analysed in Jim Kitses's influential book, *Horizons West* (1969).

More speculatively still, it is difficult in retrospect to resist the view that these relatively young, White male – Jenni Calder is the sole exception – critics and teachers were in a sense making peace with, as well as critical capital out of, a genre in which as boys in the postwar period they had a substantial emotional investment. The acknowledgement of such pleasure as material for criticism and theory came, on the whole, later, but Martin Pumphrey's article in this book, from a more recent critical context, suggests, at least to me, that more was going on in those earlier explorations of the Western than always met the eye.

Of the approaches developed at this time, the most productive analytical frameworks for discussion of the Western came from a combination of Kitses's approach to the genre via thematic oppositions – an approach taken at the same time by Peter Wollen in his account of John Ford in *Signs and Meaning in the Cinema* (Thames and Hudson, 1969) – and John G. Cawelti's accounts of the Western in his two books (1971 and 1976). Kitses and Wollen were among the early writers to appropriate structuralist forms of analysis in terms of binary oppositions, and both also drew on images of the West as Garden of the World and Great American Desert which structured much of Henry Nash Smith's *Virgin Land*, the single most important source in writing on the Western for ideas about the cultural meanings of America's long preoccupation with images and narratives of the West. Kitses's table of oppositions under the master terms of Civilisation and Wilderness and his stress on the inherent ambivalence of attitudes to westward expansion in the genre offered a rich and flexible conceptual framework. A number of perspectives in Cawelti's two studies, along with those of Kitses, make up a powerful analytical paradigm: the Western is set on the frontier at a time when the forces of social order and anarchy are still in tension; the 'formula', to use Cawelti's term, is an adventure story with its apotheosis of the hero who stands between the opposing forces in a symbolic landscape; the plot generally involves some form of pursuit, almost invariably ending in a moment of transcendent and heroic violence; the characters can be divided into three main groups: the townspeople or settlers; hero or heroes; villain or villains.

What is most useful about the Kitses and Cawelti approaches is their dynamism: they present a number of central terms in relation, the terms themselves and their relationships being capable of many inflections. It is important to note, however, that these approaches deal most fruitfully with those films that strongly animate the ideological field around civilisation and wilderness rather than with the bulk of the genre, which consists largely of formulaic adventure stories or films that have no great interest in the civilisation/wilderness issues as such. This inevitably places at the heart of the genre films with a pronounced social or historical dimension – films in which the representation of White westward expansion, settlement and social development is central. In the postwar period, this has tended to highlight the familiar tradition of major Western directors – John Ford, Anthony Mann, Delmer Daves, Budd Boetticher, Sam Peckinpah, Clint Eastwood – although, of course, many movies by other directors are amenable to analysis using aspects of the paradigm.

An acknowledgement of these limitations is important, not to criticise Kitses or Cawelti for failing to deal with the whole of the genre, but precisely to acknowledge that the Western is too huge and diverse to allow a comprehensive approach. Jon Tuska offers a salutary warning in this respect: 'A survey of the Western is no longer possible for me. I have seen 8,000 Westerns. I would not recommend that anyone else do it . . . I do not think it is possible to generalise about Westerns as so many have done' (Tuska, 1976, p.xviii). The Western is, in Philip French's words, 'a rag bag of a form' (French, 1973, p.24), capable of being inflected in a huge variety of ways. The best that can be achieved in genre criticism is to identify and analyse tendencies within

Still: Lyle Gorch (Warren Oates) and Tector Gorch (Ben Johnson) in the final battle of The Wild Bunch.

the tradition and to consider the variations developed by particular films or groups of films in relation to the tendencies that link them. In this respect Kitses and Cawelti are indispensable guides to central aspects of the Western.

Their other limitations are the product of the time in which they were writing – just before issues of representation and spectatorship emerged strongly in writing on cinema. In some ways the genre debates I have referred to can now seem remarkably blind to what have become 'obviously' crucial matters. Again there is little point in criticising or, even worse, rejecting them for not making use of discourses which were not then widely available. Rather, their insights need to be synthesised with more recent perspectives.

Among the key changes to the analysis of popular cinema in the mid 'seventies were those associated with gender and spectatorship, particularly in the work of feminist critics interested in exploring the place of women – as characters, directors, stars, audiences – in the Hollywood of the studio period. As this work developed, it focused on melodrama and *film noir* rather than the genres of male action, and with the emphasis on the exploration of fields relatively untouched by previous criticism and the reconceptualisation of whole areas of representation and of generic form, the Western was largely abandoned – it became in effect the ghost town of genre criticism.

The politics of representation therefore created one significant context for the relative marginalisation of male action genres in film studies during the period. The Western, apparently dominated by images of traditional masculinity and containing largely

demeaning roles for women was not obviously fertile ground for feminist analysis. Simultaneously the Western itself was in massive decline, and increased consciousness of what was implied in representations of gender and of race made it extraordinarily difficult to use many of the basic character types of the genre in the traditional ways. In a number of respects, for critics, audiences and, perhaps, for filmmakers, the conventions of the Western's generic world became embarrassing.

The Western now needs to be reconnected both to the new strands of genre criticism which displaced it and to other aspects of genre production. As Robin Wood argued in 'Ideology, Genre, Auteur' (*Film Comment*, January/February 1977, reprinted in *Film Genre Reader,* edited by Barry K. Grant, University of Texas Press, 1986), 'one of the greatest obstacles to any fruitful theory of genre has been the tendency to treat the genres as discrete. An ideological approach might suggest why they can't be, however hard they may appear to try: at best, they represent different strategies for dealing with the same ideological tensions' (*Film Comment*, p.47). In the post-1939 period with which this book is largely concerned, the Western needs to be seen in relation, for instance, to the traditions of melodrama, especially for the ways in which the films explore the social and political contradictions in the United States of the 'fifties and expose the fraught nature of gender roles and relationships. Michael Walker's idea of melodrama as a field divided between melodramas of action and those of passion ('Melodrama and the American Cinema', *Movie* 29/30, 1982) is one way of conceiving the links. Another is to examine the Western as a genre in which the crisis in masculinity explored in *film noir* and domestic melodrama is also played out. If the Western once seemed too dominated by wholly recalcitrant images of traditional masculinity to be of much interest in the context of the politics of representation, it now tends to look very different.

At the same time, other areas of representation which once seemed transparent and unproblematic have become visible and can now be subjected to historical analysis. It is difficult to make a case for the complexity of representations of race and ethnicity in the Western comparable to that which can be mounted for masculinity. But new writing inevitably has to negotiate recognition of the genre's inherent racism, even if, as with Jane Tompkins in *West of Everything* (Tompkins, pp.7-10), this recognition leads to a regretful setting aside of the subject in order to analyse other things. Much less studied in critical writing but making a further link with traditions of melodrama is the representation of social class, which is of considerable interest in the nineteenth-century Western novel and in recent analyses of the frontier myth (*see*, for instance, Slotkin, 1985), but so little discussed in terms of movies that it effectively constitutes virgin territory.

In 1980, Steve Neale briefly considered the presentation of the Western hero in terms of the debates initiated by Laura Mulvey on gender and spectatorship and wrote of the Western's 'obsession with definitions of masculinity' (*Genre*, British Film Institute, 1980, p.59). But more detailed work along these lines has only recently begun to appear; indeed the only recent writing to extend the terms of debate about the Western significantly centres on gender and especially on masculinity. Jane Tompkins argues that 'what is most interesting about Westerns at this moment in history is their relation to gender, and especially the way they create a model for men who came of age in the twentieth century' (Tompkins, 1992, p.17; *see also* Robert Murray Davis, *Playing Cowboys*, University of Oklahoma Press, 1992), Tompkins's history of the rise of the popular literary Western in the wake of Owen Wister's *The Virginian* (1902) is couched in a dialectic of forms centred on gender. In a stimulating argument, she suggests that: 'The Western *answers* the domestic novel. It is the antithesis of the cult of domesticity that dominated American Victorian culture' (p.39). At every point and in every way, Tompkins argues, the characteristics of the Western narrative respond to and reject the conventions and values of the nineteenth-century domestic novel within which women were pivotal: 'If the Western deliberately rejects evangelical Protestantism and pointedly repudiates the cult of domesticity, it is because it seeks to marginalise and suppress the figure who stood for those ideals' (p.39). And she goes further: 'The Western doesn't have anything to do with the West as such. It isn't about the encounter between civilisation and the frontier. It is about men's fear of losing their mastery, and hence their identity, both of which the Western tirelessly reinvents' (p.45).

The desire to make the Western monolithically about gender pushes a brilliant argument to a polemical extreme. However central gender now seems to be, the cultural meanings of the Western cannot be restricted to a single theme. Gender needs to be mapped on to precisely the earlier paradigms that Tompkins wants to reject. This corresponds much more to the approach Martin Pumphrey takes in 'Why Do Cowboys Wear Hats in the Bath?' (reprinted in this book), the first article to reflect on masculinity and the Western in the light of recent cultural theory. Taking his cue from Laura Mulvey, Pumphrey argues that 'the Western has coded civilisation and wilderness in gendered terms. The town that stands for the social order the hero must save and then settle into or reject and leave is characterised . . . essentially by the presence of women. The wilderness is a sphere for masculine action.' The hero is therefore faced with bridging the divide between two 'frontiers', one separating civilisation and savagery and the other between masculinity and femininity. The gendered geography of the Western is, as Pumphrey notes, not a new perception, but its implications have not before been extensively explored.

One of these implications is that the Western is not just, as I wrote in *Movie 22* (1976), a triumphalist White genre but a White *male* genre, its terms of representation dominated by that fact and the ideological viewpoint it implies. The heroes of Westerns straddle the gendered frontier of the genre's symbolic geography, torn between opposing principles which are both aspects of themselves and fantasies about what they might become. In Leslie Fiedler's words: 'Women and Indians make . . . a . . . home-grown [i.e. American as opposed to European] definition of what we consider the Real West, the West of the West, as it were; a place to which White male Americans flee from their own women into the arms of Indian males, but which those White women, in their inexorable advance from coast the coast, destroy' (Fiedler, 1968, p.49). Women and Indians are key terms in the generic equation, as it were, but with their representation largely constrained by their roles in a symbolic drama dominated by the fantasies of White men.

'There are no "real" "Indians" – no Iroquois, no Lakotas, no Navajos – in the Hollywood Western, only Hollywood Indians with different names", writes Richard Maltby (in 'A Better Sense of History' in this book), and Jane Tompkins, Jon Tuska and others make the same point. In some ways, it is difficult not to feel that such perceptions put an end to discussion – what more is there to say? Certainly, even the most honourably intended representations of Native Americans can seem risible and degrading. There is, for instance, a wonderful scene in Tony Hillerman's crime novel *Sacred Clowns* (Michael Joseph, London, 1993) in which a largely Navajo audience watch John Ford's *Cheyenne Autumn* (1964) at a drive-in in order to laugh at the film's use of Navajos to play Cheyennes and at the obscene or comic lines that, unknown to White film-makers or audience, are delivered by Navajo actors, speaking in Navajo but representing Cheyenne characters speaking their own language. The joke, as it were, is on Ford and the White audience. Such a shift of cultural viewpoint, even if Hillerman has elaborated the truth for his own narrative purposes, is salutary.

But there is nevertheless a struggle, especially in the postwar Western, over the representation of 'Indians' and their historical treatment by Whites. The fundamental terms of the genre (reinforced by conventions of casting in Hollywood movies of the period) remained deeply racist, but there are historical variations in the ways in which movies engage with their material, and these need to be examined. The problems encountered in developing a 'liberal' project in the genre, as in some of Daves's Westerns, or the fundamental contradictions that emerge in the exploration of racism in White society in Ford's *The Searchers* (1956) are significant aspects of a cultural history that should not simply be set aside.

The Western's racism has rightly been referred to very largely in terms of representation of Native Americans, and a corresponding case can be made about the exclusion and/or representation of Hispanics, African Americans and immigrants of Asian origin. But if the Western is a White genre, it is also far from inclusive and even-handed in the range of White ethnic groups it tends to represent. Irish characters are familiar enough and Scandinavian settlers not infrequent, but the focus is emphatically Anglo-Saxon, with relatively little representation of other European immigrant groups which played significant parts in the settlement of the West. Most Hollywood cinema could of course be accused of a similar suppression of difference, but there is a good case to be made that the modern Western created by Wister and the emerging attitudes to the frontier in the same period were closely bound up with hostility to the waves of immigration into the United States in the late nineteenth and early twentieth century (*see*, for instance, the discussion of Wister in Tompkins, 1992, especially pp.145-149, and Richard Maltby's article in this book). The firmly Anglo-Saxon focus may indeed have been central to the ideological power of the Western and its nostalgic appeal in an age of pluralism and contested images of American identity. (One of the distinctions of Michael Cimino's *Heaven's Gate*, 1980, is its representation of the battle for land as rooted in a conflict between wealthy Anglo-Saxon cattle interests and poor, predominantly East European settlers: an economic, class and ethnic battle for the American future.)

It is generally accepted that the Western's representation of women is also massively skewed. In one of very few feminist essays on the Western, Jacqueline Levitkin writes: '[Women] are the symbols, illustrations of the conflict that confronts the hero, and thus are the character types that have been pointed out by a number of critics. If they come from the East, they are school marm, minister's wife or pioneer woman. Identified with the West, they are the farmer's daughter, the Indian or Mexican woman and, at times, the prostitute. Eastern or Western, these women may be solid or courageous or binding and restrictive. If the woman character representing civilisation is defined positively, the woman representing wilderness, by contrast, is defined negatively, and vice versa. Generally. women characters are seen to be in conflict with one another because

they define choices of the hero. The narrative revolves around his choice' (*Film Reader* 5, 1982, p.97). David Thomson makes parallel points about the conventional representations of women in his critical overview of the limitations of the Western: 'So many of the genre's women are there as stooges or excuses. They are allowed to die, or worse; they are placid, smiling, and obedient reward when ordeal is over. But for them to think or speak is more dangerous than Chief Scar in the moonlight' (*Film Comment*, March/April 1990, p.8). And yet, as with race, this is not the end of the story – all sorts of dust, to use Laura Mulvey's image in her essay 'Sirk and Melodrama' (*Movie* 25, 1977/ 78, p.54), gets raised along the road (*see*, for instance, Peter William Evans's essay in this book on *Westward the Women*).

The whole history of the Western is therefore, at one level, inescapably bound up with reducing Native Americans and women to functions in a symbolic world centring on White male characters and embodying White (and particularly Anglo-Saxon) male visions of national and gender identity. White heroes occupy a narrative space between the opposing claims and threats of Woman and Indian. At the manifest level the hero is a figure of confident identity and charismatic authority, his detached social position dignified by the mission of making the West safe for White settlement. It would be foolish to deny the inherent problems of representation in the tradition but equally foolish to reduce the Western simply to its schematic central terms. As I implied above, the interest and value of Westerns lie not in the conventions themselves (loathsome as some of them may be) but in their varied historical uses. Andrew Britton wrote about this issue in 'A New Servitude, Bette Davis, *Now Voyager*, and the Radicalism of the Woman's Picture' (*CineAction!* 26/27, Winter 1992), and it is worth quoting him at length:

'There is no such thing as an intrinsically radical genre: the woman's film is no more progressive *per se* than the Western is *per se* conservative. A genre is produced in historical circumstances in which a cluster of related values, practices and discourses on the maintenance and reproduction of which a given culture depends undergoes a crisis of consent, such that the values and practices in question are experienced at once as necessary, unavoidable, even natural, but also as a source of conflict, friction, unhappiness and disharmony. Genres presuppose an ambivalence and uncertainty about a set of dominant values and institutions which is sufficiently profound and sufficiently generalised as to create an audience for narratives in which the crisis of these values is repeatedly acted through, with the most minute variations and inflections, and in which the terms of the status quo whose institutions are at stake are continually re-negotiated and re-secured.'

The ambivalence which Kitses identified in the Western is echoed here and needs to be considered in relation to gender and race as much as to the discourses around civilisation and wilderness. Within and around the manifest narratives all sorts of other stories are simultaneously told.

Still: the death of Jimmy Ringo (Gregory Peck) in The Gunfighter, *with Helen Westcott and Millard Mitchell.*

However limiting their representations may therefore be as terms in the generic equation, women and Indians (or their ideologically less charged alternatives, White villains) are indispensable. Much as I longed as a boy in the 'fifties for Westerns without that endless parade of bar-girls, school teachers and ranchers' daughters, the movies refused to oblige; in Anthony Mann's words, quoted by Raymond Bellour (*Camera Obscura* 3/4, 1979, p.87), 'without women a Western wouldn't work.'

This also implies something that is both obvious and frequently overlooked: romance is central rather than marginal to the twentieth-century Western. (André Bazin goes so far as to declare, 'Love is to all intents and purposes foreign to the Western' – Bazin, 1971, p.151). Romance had been present from the beginning of Western narratives, but in James Fenimore Cooper's Leatherstocking series, it almost invariably involved secondary characters – the hero, Natty Bumppo, generally stands apart from the love intrigue (even when Cooper tried to involve Natty in romance in *The Pathfinder* (1840), the experiment couldn't be made to work). Part of the triumph of *The Virginian*, the founding text of the twentieth-century Western, is to make the Western hero (originally in Cooper incapable of social integration) compatible with settlement via marriage and with social success via business. *The Virginian* is many things but it is centrally a romance. It is as though the ending of the frontier as a clear line of settlement in the late nineteenth century and the

consequent end of an unsettled West to feed the imagination meant that the twentieth-century Western story must finally be about the integration into society that had become inevitable. Wister dramatised the incompleteness of the hero without a wife. The self-containment of the hero and his escape into the West are, after 1902, definitively regressive fantasies – though fantasies that retain great power (perhaps all the greater for being so obviously threatened) in the later tradition.

(One of Jane Tompkins's themes in *West of Everything* is the way in which the Western dramatises male fears, rooted in the relationship with the mother, of not having a separate existence. Tompkins presents a suggestive case study of Wister in these terms but it is an approach clearly capable of wider development. A wider discussion of male development which considers these issues at length and discusses them in relation to a number of recent films is to be found in Jonathan Rutherford's *Men's Silences*, Routledge, London, 1992.)

The Western in the twentieth century plays endless variations on the fundamental theme of settlement, with the tensions in the idea of its inevitability constantly and variously negotiated. The hero's in-between position enacts a battle between the pulls of isolation and separateness and of relationship and community, a conflict which can have no definitive resolution but which has a number of conventional narrative closures:

1) The hero rides off into the West to have further adventures (The Lone Ranger, juvenile version) or to turn his back on settlement and accept isolation – the melancholic or semi-tragic variation, as in *Shane* (George Stevens, 1953), or *The Searchers*.
2) The hero dies. This is relatively rare, but probably occurs most often in the postwar period in which 'end of the trail' or even 'end of the West' motifs (from *The Gunfighter*, Henry King, 1950, through *Ride the High Country* to *The Shootist*, Don Siegel, 1976) become more overt.
3) The couple is formed and integration into community/society is implied or promised (*The Virginian* ending). This is probably the most frequent ending in Western movies.
4) The couple is formed but they leave community/society to live in isolation (*Stagecoach*, John Ford, 1939, is a central example).

I do not mean to suggest that these are the only possible endings for Westerns, although they form the central tendencies; as with all conventions, many variations are possible, including, for instance, those in which the hero is already married and settled (*3.10 to Yuma*, Delmer Daves, 1957; *Man of the West*, Anthony Mann, 1958) – but these seem clearly to be *variations* on the major motifs.

All four endings (but particularly the last two) raise questions not just about gender roles and relationships but also about the films' view of society. White social groupings take two main forms in Westerns – small communities (groups of settlers and farmers, a wagon train, isolated small towns) and larger settlements, mainly towns, which dramatise more complex social relationships and more developed institutions and which imply the wider society spreading from the East. The fundamental social values in Westerns tend to be associated with community, images of which are also frequently central to positively presented towns (such as those which have been 'tamed'). But towns can be tipped various ways – nice place to live and bring up kids, or more threatening and corrupt, or over-civilised.

This is to touch on another central feature of the Western, its utopianism, part of what Andrew Britton described as 'a defining characteristic of American art . . . The attempt to find a non-repressive social group . . . which can accommodate active individual energy' (*Framework* 4, Autumn 1976, p.23). Images of such groups are common in the Western, and it is the pretence of many movies which end with the social integration of the hero that such a community is possible. Frequently, though, the images are no more than moments that embody the desire for the non-repressive social groups which Britton evokes but which are only too fragile, temporary and vulnerable to wider destructive forces. This seems to me the case, for instance, in most of Ford's Westerns from *Stagecoach* onwards, as well as in those of Anthony Mann. In fact, from early in the century, Westerns repeatedly pose the problem of the nature of society and whether it can be seen positively in relation to the future of the couple. The locus classicus of that doubt is probably Zane Grey's *Riders of the Purple Sage* (1912, first filmed in 1918 and remade at least three times, including the version with Tom Mix in 1925), in which the hero and heroine escape pursuit in a hidden valley that is finally sealed from the outside world by a great fall of rock – an Eden which is also (though this is not the book's implication) an inescapable trap. It is an escape from history paralleled, if in much less mystical terms, in *Stagecoach*, when Ringo (John Wayne) and Dallas (Claire Trevor) are sent off to Ringo's farm over the border in Mexico, 'saved', as Doc Boone (Thomas Mitchell) says, 'from the blessings of civilisation'. Thus although, as Cawelti suggests, the great majority of Westerns between 1900 and 1930 'follow Wister's *The Virginian* in creating plots of romantic synthesis' (Cawelti, 1971, p.72), the relationship with society varies considerably. The theme of the settlement of the West as the development of a new and affirmed American civilisation comes and goes in tension with much more sceptical views. Overall, in fact, the twentieth-century Western is haunted not just by the dream of male separateness and escape, but by the idea of a utopia it cannot really believe in.

This implies that the central terms of the Western are essentially those of the nineteenth-century tale of Western adventure with its social primitivism and utopian dreams given an intense new power by the realities of twentieth-century America. Wister constructs America in *The Virginian* in terms of an opposition between the West (incorporating some associations of the old South – the hero is, after all, The Virginian) and an East defined via the heroine's origins in an old New England family. Totally

suppressed in this scheme of things and in the later tradition is the other America of growing cities, industrialisation and immigration, but Wister's story (and what follows) it takes much of its meaning from this suppression.

As all accounts of the Western recognise, the handling of generic conventions became increasingly complex in the post-World War II period; tensions inherent in the tradition surfaced more explicitly, notably around the identity and agency of the hero. One way of conceiving this process is in terms of a greater awareness of the mid-twentieth-century present forcing itself into the genre, with a consequent sense of crisis around the blocked dreams that the Western ceaselessly attempted to negotiate. The synthesis of Kitses's and Cawelti's approaches outlined above is particularly useful in analysing the shifting representation of the central generic terms and especially for highlighting the changing attitudes to civilisation and the hero's position in relation to it. It is in the representation of civilisation that the Western's implicit images of contemporary America – the relationship between the imagined past of the genre and the moment of production – are clearest. It is more possible at some times than at others to draw such links with confidence – for example, the immediately postwar moment of *My Darling Clementine* (John Ford, 1946), *High Noon* (Fred Zinnemann, 1952) and the period of anti-communist hysteria; or the 'Vietnam Westerns' of the late 'sixties and early 'seventies – but increasingly in the postwar period the inherent instability of the generic terms and particularly the contradictions in the hero's position are exposed. The concern with social transition – the emergence of modern America – which Cawelti identifies as increasingly evident in this period, produces more critical images of developing civilisation, together with a sense of a hero hopelessly torn between opposing principles in his nature – those pulling him to settlement and those to wilderness. (*See* John H. Lenihan, *Showdown*, University of Illinois, 1980, for reflections on the relationship between Westerns and modern America.) The opposed tendencies can neither be chosen between nor resolved. The hero's kinship with the villain, a fundamental but often suppressed implication of the symbolic structure of the Western is made increasingly explicit. In the 'sixties and 'seventies, the magnetic field of the Western in which wilderness and civilisation were held in significant though often complex opposition, with the hero ambiguously in the middle, largely loses its force and all the familiar values of the tradition are effectively overturned.

In the form in which he emerged in *The Virginian* and developed through the century, the hero was a brilliant ideological construction contradictorily committed to incompatible values of wilderness and civilisation, using his power to pave the way for Westward expansion. He was the central device which enabled the Western and its audiences – in all sorts of ways – to have its cake and eat it, simultaneously endorsing selected Western and eastern values without having fully to confront the contradictions this implied. From the late 'forties onwards,

it is as though the generic programming begins to break down – like the robot gunman played by Yul Brynner in *Westworld* (Michael Crichton, 1973) running amok. Conflicts always present in the Western hero are recast in much more problematic terms, as psychic division, neurosis, flawed moral identity (*see* the article on Anthony Mann in this book).

While it would be unhistorical and inaccurate to claim that the Western was always in some sense 'about' masculinity, much of the appeal of the genre for male audiences must have lain in the fantasy it constantly re-enacted, in dramas full of varied male types, of what being a man might be. For much of its life, however, whatever ideological functions in terms of the mediation of gender roles it was acting out, the Western seems to have been largely unreflective about the implications of its male images. Even when the hero was not a superhero like the Lone Ranger but more, as Cawelti puts it, 'one of

Still: Yul Brynner as the robot gunman in Westworld.

us', (Cawelti, 1976, p.40) his characterisation was essentially straightforward – a mode I shall call 'declarative'. That is to say that moral standing declared itself more or less transparently through action and appearance. Similarly, identity, motive and nature could be articulated unproblematically in language. Deception and disguise were frequently motifs of the narrative but what was at stake there was perception rather than identity; in the tradition of melodrama, character could be definitively *revealed*. The simplest index of this form of characterisation is the deep-rooted view that in early Western films heroes wore white hats and villains wore black. However inaccurate this is as a view of Western conventions, it points clearly to a fundamental characteristic of the genre. When Robert Warshow discusses the nature of the Western hero, he implies such a form of characterisation: 'By the time we see him, he is already "there"; he can ride a horse faultlessly, keep his countenance in the face of death, and draw his gun a little faster and shoot it a little straighter than anyone he is likely to meet. These are sharply defined acquirements, giving to the figure of the Westerner an apparent moral clarity which corresponds to the clarity of his physical image against his bare landscape . . .' Or as Warshow writes tellingly later in his article: 'A hero is one who looks like a hero.'

In the post-World War II period, this mode of characterisation was increasingly undermined. When Warshow writes of the hero of *The Gunfighter* as someone who 'no longer believes in [the drama of the gunfight] but nevertheless will continue to play his *role* perfectly' (my emphasis), he hints at what is happening. Identity, and the traditional forms of action which validated it, are being questioned. The hero's identity becomes 'performative' (to take up a term from debates about the concept of masquerade and its applicability to male images – *see*, for instance, *Screening the Male*, ed. Steven Cohan and Ena Rae Hark, Routledge, London, 1993) or 'assertive' rather than declarative. What previously were largely unquestioned aspects of a confidently held identity often become assertions which signal not confidence but insecurity, not stable but unstable identity and internal division. In *My Darling Clementine* the hero, Wyatt Earp (Henry Fonda), perfectly embodies the declarative style of the traditional Western hero, but he is shadowed by the divided and doomed Doc Holliday (Victor Mature) whose identity in Mature's splendid performance is all gesture and assertion – the attempted embodiment of a style. Doc is defined in a sense precisely as a performer, the consciousness of whose gestures and manner signal the uneasiness of his identity. Wyatt, in contrast, is at ease with himself. For him elements of a performative mode (his new haircut, the 'sweet smelling stuff' with which the barber sprays him, his 'gentlemanly' gestures as he accompanies Clementine to the dance) are marked by awkwardness and embarrassment on his part: they express a *social* unease – significantly associated with a feminising of his appearance and his contact with Clementine, and hinting at a future conflict between ways

Stills: My Darling Clementine. *Opposite – Wyatt (Henry Fonda) and Clementine (Cathy Downs). Below – Chihuahua (Linda Darnell), Doc Holliday (Victor Mature) and the barman (J. Farrell McDonald).*

of life – rather than a crisis in identity. Even so, this social uneasiness, while being little more than charming comedy in *My Darling Clementine*, does hint at what becomes a recurrent issue in the postwar Western: the accommodation the hero must make to enter society. Wyatt's adjustment of his hat in the window after his visit to the barber and his throwing it to one side as he prepares uneasily to ask Clementine to dance (a gesture which echoes that of Alan Mowbray as the actor before reciting 'to be or not to be' earlier in the film) are created as moments of *performance*, the tentative trying on of a new persona. The contrast between these modes is at work in a different way in Ford's *Fort Apache* (1948), in which Captain York (John Wayne) is presented through most of the film in the familiar declarative mode of the Westerner, while Colonel Thursday (Henry Fonda) has a rigidity and assertiveness that signal a character built on the maintenance of performance, the holding of a role. One way of looking at the ending is that York has adopted the performative mode – a much more conscious, even forced, playing of a part. In his case it signals precisely the movement into a more troubled world in which conditions dictate a less direct expression of self, a more layered and nuanced sense of identity.

The film that seems particularly significant in this movement between modes of characterisation is Howard Hawks's *Red River* (1948), in which the nature of the postwar hero and of John Wayne's mature persona are simultaneously defined. Tom Dunson is marked by losing the woman he loved and characterised by being wrong ('You're wrong,

'Mr Dunson' is a major motif of the film). Borden Chase, who wrote the script, may be a key figure in this development of the Western hero. Certainly, his heroes in the films he later wrote for Anthony Mann have similar characteristics, scarred often by loss of or deception by a woman and covering the scar and the pain, like Dunson, by obsessive purpose and perverse denial of human need. These 'heroes' are frequently monomaniacs, almost Ahab-like. Once established, this pattern became remarkably consistent, inflected in various ways by most of the major Western directors up to and including Clint Eastwood. This is not simply to do with the arrival in the Western of a more complex conception of character psychology, although the genre was clearly affected, as others were, by developments in characterisation which followed the impact of psychoanalysis on Hollywood movies. The power and control (over himself, others, the narrative) of the Western hero are also increasingly challenged in these decades. This is at its most extreme in Peckinpah's films, in which the protagonists are subject to the destructive and anonymous forces of a changing American society, their range of action finally limited in some cases to a choice of how to die, but Peckinpah has plenty of less extreme antecedents. There is less and less sense of the West offering freedom or escape – because of the encroachment of civilisation and/or because there can be no escape from the contradictions of the self. The hero becomes subject to social and historical change and, in those cases in which he is made psychologically complex, he becomes humanised; he becomes the

Stills: Red River. *Above – John Wayne as Tom Dunson and Montgomery Clift as Matthew Garth. Opposite – the first grave in the early days of the Red River D ranch.*

product of a social past, not the asocial, archetypal world of the 'West'. Two conceptions of the hero are at work here, as throughout the tradition – the ahistorical or mythic and the historical and human. Much of the intensity of the postwar Western comes from the constant negotiation of this opposition.

Writing at this level of generality inevitably simplifies a complex and varied field. Perhaps only at the top end of the production pyramid were these changes emphatically felt, with heroes uneasily occupying narrative and social positions that their ancestors in the genre and their cousins in the B feature and the television Western on the whole had occupied or continued to occupy unproblematically. Two themes constantly intertwine – emotional damage (as in 'trusted a woman once' or a murdered loved one) and social change. To return to *Fort Apache*, we might interpret York's change partly as an acknowledgement that the social world he lives in is other than he previously thought. It is not a world in which truth can be simply articulated or human value confidently communicated. Rather, it is a world in which the self has become fractured, and public and private separated in the service of what are seen as the wider interests of army and nation. The hero adopts a persona.

The social dimensions of these changes are crucial, the encroachment of civilisation bringing not

just a challenge to wilderness ways but the need to negotiate more specific social contexts in which differences in manners and mores, in class and social position become central to questions of identity. Emphasis on the mythic and archetypal dimensions of the Western has tended, perhaps, to block analysis in these terms. In this respect André Bazin and Robert Warshow have cast surprisingly long shadows. Warshow presented more eloquently than anyone else the image of the Western hero's perfected identity as apparently independent of social position and criticised attempts (such as *High Noon*) to embed him in social drama. Tellingly, he saw the effect of this in *High Noon* as lessening the hero's stature, making him a figure of pathos, not tragedy – a precise, though in Warshow's terms pejorative, way of describing one effect of the tendency I am considering here. In a parallel way, Bazin disapproved of films which added sociological, moral, aesthetic or other 'extrinsic' qualities to the traditional identity of the genre. Both writers clearly identified but deplored aspects of the changes that were taking place.

Bazin also, however, claims as examples of 'real Westerns' in the postwar period (films that had in his terms nothing 'baroque or decadent' – Bazin, 1971, pp.154-156 – about them) the Westerns of Anthony Mann and Howard Hawks's *Red River*, among others, and these films seem now to embody many of the changes to the genre that Bazin disliked. Looked at in a different way, these are films that are centrally concerned with social questions and explore the consequences of embedding the fantasy figure of the hero in contexts of social and historical

change. In a way, the question they ask is how (or whether) such a figure can enter history. As he does and is given a social past, the residual accretions of the old fantasy are increasingly seen as desperate assertions of an impossible identity (*The Searchers* is a key example).

As I was writing this section, Michael Walker drew my attention to Robert Sklar's excellent analysis of *Red River* ('*Red River*, Empire to the West', *Cineaste* vol.IX, no.1, Fall 1978), which develops precisely these perspectives. The reception of *Red River*, Sklar argues, including Bazin's account of it, stripped the film of content, of its 'ideological project': 'No one observed that *Red River* is rich in social significance . . . It is a film about the issue of Empire . . . about the territorial expansion of one society by the usurpation of land from others, and the consequences arising therefrom . . . the human themes . . . subordinate to the even more fundamental issues of economic survival, of commodity production, above all of the need to find a market for one's goods' (p.15).

Sklar's argument is that these contexts are not merely background to the personal drama, on which we tend primarily to focus, but that personal and social are inseparable. Dunson's initial identity is based on the assertion of self-interest (his leaving the wagon train) and of inflexible will (his refusal to change his mind and take Fen, the woman he loves, with him when he leaves). Following Fen's death, the denial of human need which is central to what I have called the performative dimensions of his persona is already presented as perverse, but it is crucial to his ruthless establishment of the cattle empire (the process is elided after the shooting of the Mexican who represents the land's previous owner but we are shown the graves that presumably mark successive challenges to Dunson). The context of the main action, the cattle drive, is given, however, by the South's defeat in the Civil War and the need to find new markets for beef in the North. Dunson's claim of self-sufficiency is challenged by the need for money and therefore by the necessity of developing economic relationships with the wider United States. But, equally, it is important to the film that Dunson's assertion of a tyrannical, transcendent authority acknowledging no human claims should be seen as a perverse refusal of the social and personal relationships to which Hawks and his writers give such importance.

How significant the influence of *Red River* was in itself is difficult to say. But after *Red River*, Dunson-like heroes became more and more common – anachronistic, morally problematic figures stranded in some sense by historical change, whose assertions of identity are increasingly undermined. In the 'sixties, Peckinpah made explicit the earlier tendency. *Ride the High Country* seems to juxtapose, for instance, the authenticity of the old Westerner, Steve Judd (Joel McCrea), with the fraudulent performance of Gil (Randolph Scott) as 'The Oregon Kid'. It becomes evident, however, that the distinction is not a simple one between authentic and inauthentic identities but rather between two modes of performance: Steve's rigid and unbending attempt, in the face of the social realities that confront him, to maintain his *role* as Western lawman; and Gil's performance as a Buffalo Bill look-alike, the show-biz incarnation of the Westerner. In the context of social change, the hero's identity is constituted by performance. *Major Dundee* (1965), although its historical setting is the Civil War, is a further exploration of the same theme, with Dundee (Charlton Heston) and Tyreen (Richard Harris) almost competing with each other in terms of the gestures designed to assert their chosen roles.

David Lusted's discussion (in this book) of class in a number of 'fifties movies adds a further dimension to analysis of social relationships in Westerns and opens a field which has been almost wholly ignored or, as Sklar suggests about the social issues in *Red River*, largely taken for granted. Perhaps, again, our familiar conception of the Western hero is too mythic or archetypal readily to admit a notion of class identity. Yet as soon as we think about it, the Western can be seen clearly to be soaked in issues of class: social and economic differences between individuals and groups are at the heart of the genre, even though the forlorn dream of community might express a longing to escape from social hierarchy and unequal economic relationships. David Lusted reminds us how little significance we have recently attached to these issues and how a focus on class can both shift our readings of familiar movies and inform our sense of the genre's appeal and cultural meaning.

What this approach also does is to reconnect analysis of movies to aspects of the genre's nineteenth-century history dealt with in *Virgin Land* but largely ignored in the appropriation of Nash Smith by film criticism. In Book II of *Virgin Land*, 'The Sons of Leatherstocking', Nash Smith traces developments rooted on the one hand in problems of literary decorum and on the other in opposing attitudes to the life of the frontier. Writing of the nineteenth-century historian Francis Parkman's antithetical attitudes to backwoods farmers and the hunters and trappers of the wilderness, Nash Smith comments: '. . . for Americans of that period there were two distinct Wests: the commonplace domesticated area within the agricultural frontier, and the Wild West beyond it. The agricultural West was tedious; its inhabitants belonged to a despised social class. The Wild West was by contrast an exhilarating region of adventure and comradeship in the open air. Its heroes bore none of the marks of degraded status. They were in reality not members of society at all, but noble anarchs owning no master, free denizens of a limitless wilderness' (Nash Smith, 1950, p.55). The Wild West could produce heroes of romance – adventure heroes – while the settled West could not. But as Cooper developed his frontier tales on the model of the sentimental novel he had to deal with having created a hero in Leatherstocking who, because of his inferior class position and his association with the wilderness, could not occupy the role of the hero in the love story which was so essential to the literary form Cooper was drawing on. Leatherstocking could not become a suitable partner for the genteel heroine (*Virgin Land*, pp.70ff.). In order to become a viable hero of this kind the Westerner's class identity had to be inflected upwards and his 'theoretical hostility to civilisation' (p.76) had to be reduced. One aspect of the tradition Nash Smith traces is the uniting of the figures of the well-bred young eastern hero and the old Western hunter by means of disguise in the dime novel, *Seth Jones* (1860). A second is the creation of a man of the Wild West whose 'natural' sensibility made him a suitable mate for the heroine (*Virgin Land*, Chapter IX). The development of these and related motifs is far from straightforward but the convolutions speak eloquently of the tensions generated for writers and audiences around the appropriate class identity of a figure who can combine the roles of action hero in the Wild West and romantic lover – a dual identity as mythic hero and inhabitant of a social world. This is a major theme of the literary Western up to and including *The Virginian*, in which the appropriateness of a marriage between the cowboy and the lady is a central narrative issue.

It is striking, in fact, how powerful the grip of class categories on literary convention was, even in American popular fiction, and how long it continued. It seems to have taken until the 1880s for the fantasy of 'the self-made man . . . a hero, presumably humble in origins and without formal education or inherited wealth', who was both a man of action and romantic lead, to emerge fully in the figure of Deadwood Dick (*Virgin Land* III). The 'presumably' is significant here – the hero's origins are tacitly acknowledged rather than dramatised, so that he can

to an extent float free of specific class location. Much of the energy of the tradition lies in the protracted and ingenious struggle that results in a hero whose origins can be acknowledged but transcended – or rather, acknowledged *and* transcended, both being essential to the fantasy. In other words, the construction of the hero involves, in however muted a form, questions of social position as well as the issues of personal identity which have tended to dominate accounts of the Western. It is a pretence of the Western that under certain circumstances (the instability of the frontier) a figure of low social status (the hero) can exercise decisive social power. As consciousness of change forced itself into the genre it may be that the social implications of this pattern became more explicit. In the 1950s the hero is frequently a hired man and a good deal is made of the economic relationship and the balance of power it implies. In the 1960s, part of the meaning of Ford's *The Man Who Shot Liberty Valance* (1962) is in its 'explanation' of a transfer of authority not just between one man and another – from Tom (John Wayne) to Ranse (James Stewart) – but from one class to another.

All this inevitably aligns the Western once again with melodrama and the ways in which it has been

Still: Gil Westrum (Randolph Scott) and Steve Judd (Joel McCrea) in Ride the High Country.

discussed in recent years. Although the characteristic milieus, preoccupations and narrative patterns seem very different, the more focused the Western became on the identity of the hero and the tensions within masculinity and social role, the more it was inflected towards the traditional terrain of melodrama. Thomas Schatz in *Hollywood Genres* (Temple University Press, Philadelphia, 1981) distinguishes between genres of contested and of uncontested space: those, like the Western and some other action genres, in which control of the setting is largely what is at stake, and those, like melodrama and the musical, in which a stable cultural setting exists, and established society exerts a powerful and constricting grip on the characters. While the Western of course remained a genre of contested space, the contest for control of the setting in many 'fifties and 'sixties Westerns is more apparent than real. Historically, all that is long over. The real battle is elsewhere, within the hero and in his relationship to the constantly increasing pressures of settlement and society.

COUNTRY MUSIC AND THE 1939 WESTERN

From Hillbillies to Cowboys

Peter Stanfield

'By the eve of the war the Western had reached a definitive stage of perfection . . . Let us list some names and titles for 1939-40: King Vidor: *North-west Passage* (1940), Michael Curtiz: *The Santa Fe Trail* (1940), *Virginia City* (1940); Fritz Lang: *The Return of Frank James* (1940), *Western Union*, (1940, actually released in 1941); John Ford: *Drums Along the Mohawk* (1939); William Wyler: *The Westerner* (1940); George Marshall: *Destry Rides Again*, with Marlene Dietrich, (1939)' (Bazin, 1971).

The Westerns that André Bazin canonised, alongside his formulation of *Stagecoach* (John Ford, 1939) as *the* classic Western, remain crucial to our understanding of the genre. Yet little has been written about why such films appeared at this particular juncture in American history.

This essay attempts to deal with some of the reasons behind the major studios' renewed interest in the Western in 1939/40, using a contextual gambit that examines the emergent Country and Western music industry in the 1930s and maps out how and why previously marginalised forms of vernacular American music appropriated the image of the cowboy and were thereby able to move into the mainstream of America's broadcasting, recording and film industries. This will make it clearer why the Western proved so popular with the major studios and audiences at a time when the United States was undergoing a period of introspection brought about by the Depression and the escalating conflict in Europe.

The 1930s are something of a black hole in criticism of Western films. The reasons for this are fairly obvious: between 1931 and 1939, the major studios all but abandoned the genre and left the field clear for the Poverty Row studios, which concentrated their efforts on the B Western and the Singing Cowboy, areas that have hitherto held little appeal for the academic critic. In part, this is because there has been less interest in marking out the history of the genre than in establishing a critical canon. Moreover, the ongoing neglect of the silent cinema of the 1920s means that most critical accounts of the Western don't begin until 1939. (The early silent Western is covered to some extent in Robert Anderson, 'The Role of the Western Film Genre in Industry Competition 1907-11', *Journal of the University Film Association* vol.XXXI, no.2, Spring 1979, in Peter Stanfield, 'The Western 1909-14: A Cast of Villians', *Film History* vol.1, no.2, 1987, and in Ellen Bowser, *The Transformation of Cinema 1907-*

15, Scribners, New York, 1990, pp.169-177, but this only begins to scratch the surface. The 'twenties are dealt with fairly comprehensively in Jean-Louis Leutrart, *L'Alliance brisée*, Presses Universitaires de Lyon, 1985, which, scandalously, is unavailable in translation. Tuska, 1976, remains the best general history of the pre-1940s Western. Packy Smith and Ed Hulse, eds., *Don Miller's Hollywood Corral – A Comprehensive B Western Roundup*, Riverwood Press, Burbank, California, 1993, is a reprint of Don Miller's survey of the B Western with 16 supplementary essays by various writers.) Most critics also ignore Western production in areas other than film, despite the evident popularity of the genre during the 1930s in music, literature, radio, and comics.

The presumption is that the Western film was the dominant form and that the genre as it was constituted elsewhere took its lead from the movies. This solipsistic, as opposed to syncretic, approach to the study of Western films constitutes a gross misunderstanding, diminishing the influence of other media on film to the point of invisibility and inevitably limits our concept of the cultural function of the genre. What follows is an attempt to rectify this situation by considering the role the Western played in the commercialisation of Country music and how that music's popularity suggests ways to reread the Western films of 1939/40.

Stetsons in Nashville

The Great Depression witnessed an unprecedented movement of rural workers from the South to urban centres, with migration increasing as American defence industries geared up to meet the demands of the War in Europe, and continuing unabated until the end of World War II. The sense of dislocation faced by rural workers was by all accounts immense, but was alleviated, if only momentarily, by a nostalgic and sentimental reckoning with the recent past, powered in no small part by music. But whilst the past was evoked by familiar strains it was also being transformed.

Vernacular music of the American South, as it moved with its performers and audiences (according to Colin Escott, *Hank Williams: The Biography*, Little Brown, New York, 1994, p.45, the greatest concentration of country musicians in 1946 was in Chicago), had to accommodate itself to the commercial imperatives of the recording and radio industries and to the changed economic and social circumstances of its original practitioners and listeners. The sense of regionalism, the coarseness and vulgarity in performance and often in lyrical content began to be lost. Regional accents were smoothed out, risqué lyrics were dropped, stage presentations and musical accompaniment became standardised. The means of achieving this was an appropriation of Western motifs. This meant, so the suggestion goes, that listeners could wallow in nostalgic reverie for a lost agrarian past whilst effacing the pejorative connotations attached to such a past by the urban middle-classes.

'Hillbillies have the intelligence of morons', wrote *Variety* in 1926 (quoted in P. Kingswood, A. Axelrod and S. Costello, eds., *Country: The Music and Musicians*, Abbeville, New York, second edition, 1994, p.335). Given that this was a fairly widespread attitude towards rural workers from the American South, it's no wonder they wanted to rid themselves of any negative associations. No performer better exemplifies this desire than Gene Autry. His early performing and recording career was heavily influenced by Jimmie Rodgers – 'The Singing Brakeman' and a yodeller without equal. Rodgers's repertoire was vast and ranged from gutbucket blues to the more popular idioms of the day such as crooning. This eclecticism allowed him to use musicians as diverse as Louis Armstrong, Lani McIntyre's Hawaiians and the Carter Family. He recorded seven cowboy songs, but more often he sang of a boy's love for his mother, of a working man's or drifter's life, and of the price paid for a wild Saturday night with another man's wife; whatever style he performed in or whatever he sang about, he was always unmistakably addressing a rural America. He started his recording career in Tennessee, but later moved to Texas to help alleviate the tuberculosis that was to kill him in 1933, at the height of his career. During the later years of his life, Rodgers become identified with Texas, but his image, like his music, resisted easy categorisation.

Early publicity photographs of Autry show him not as a cowboy, but as a slicked-up and suited singer, displaying all the signs of a man desperately trying to escape the confines of his class. Where the suit failed him, the stetson saved him: as a cowboy, Autry transcended any notion of class. His early repertoire of songs, like Rodgers's, ran the gamut of the sentimental and the downright obscene. In the song 'Do Right Daddy Blues' (1931), recorded before he became an actor, Autry sang 'You can feel of my legs, you can feel of my thighs. But if you feel my legs, you got to ride me high.' Later he was to tell his audience in 'Cowboy's Commandment #8' that they should '. . . always [be] clean in thought, word, deed and personal grooming'. But Autry never forgot how to yodel.

'Cowboys were known to belch frequently, and to produce other uncomely sounds, but to yodel? *Nein*', writes Nick Tosches in his irreverent but factual account of country music (*Country*, Secker & Warburg, London, 1977, revised edition 1985. You should own this book!). The roots of yodelling were in vaudeville and the blackface minstrel, as you can hear if you take a listen to Goebel Reeves's 1934 recording, 'The Yodelling Teacher' on *Hobo's Lullaby* (Bear Family, BCD 15680 AH, 1994) or to Emmett Miller & His Georgia Crackers's 1928 recording, 'Lovesick Blues' on *Okeh Western Swing* (Epic, EPC 22124, 1982). Both singers assume the persona of a Black character and give object lessons in how yodelling can tear your soul apart. Reeves, a contemporary and friend of Jimmie Rodgers (who had also performed in Blackface), takes on any number of characters across the 26 recordings he made, from drifter, to Wobbly, to henpecked husband, to soldier, to wayward son, to, of course, cowboy. In 'The Yodelling Teacher' he explicitly links the art (and it is an art) of yodelling to travelling tent shows (presumably medicine shows) and not to cowboys:

'Hey boy, what in the world do you think you're doin'?'
'I'm yodelling. What do you think I'm doin'?'
'You doing what?'
'I said I was yodelling'
'I heard it called you-delling'
'Well, you heard wrong, 'cause it's called yodelling. That's what it is. I was doing it and I reckon I know.'
'What is that anyway?'
'Well it's a musical thing that was discovered over in the Alps somewhere. Where the Swiss people live, you know. Where they make that Swiss cheese.'
'Man, you know everthing don't you?'
'Well sure. I'd worked for the White folks, in a, in a tent one time. In a show in a tent.'

Goebel Reeves's recording documents an American tradition – the Blackface Minstrel – that had long since lost popularity in urban areas, but that had somehow survived in rural America, due in no small part to its presence in travelling medicine shows, where images and the costumes of cowboys and Indians sat alongside caricatures of the Plantation South, working hand in hand for the poor man's dollar. (*See* Brooks McNamara, *Step Right Up: An Illustrated History of the Medicine Show*, Doubleday, Garden City, New York, 1976. To hear the diversity of styles displayed by Southern rural musicians, both Black and white, before attempts to standardise Country music, listen to *Roots N' Blues: The Retrospective (1925-1950)*, Columbia Legacy, C4k 47911, 1992. A variety of non-cowboy yodelling styles can be found on *White Country Blues (1926-1938)*, Columbia Legacy, Col 472886 2.)

Yodelling may never have been heard on the range, but it was omnipresent within the performances of the 'thirties singing cowboys, whose vocal gymnastics were as important to their image as their flamboyant costumes, trick riding and flirt-and-run romances. With Gene Autry's film debut in 1934, yodelling and the Western rode hand in hand. (The best career profile of Gene Autry is by Douglas B. Green and can be found in *Stars of Country Music*, edited by Bill C. Malone and Judith McCulloh, Da Capo Press, New York, 1975.) The country historian Bill C. Malone adds:

'After signing his Hollywood contract (1934), Autry made a radical shift in his repertory from "country" themes to western motifs. Instead of singing songs about the mountains, he came increasingly to perform songs with such titles as 'Riding Down the Canyon' and 'Empty Cot in the Bunkhouse'. Both in Autry's singing and in the instrumentation which accompanied him, one hears a distinctly measurable change in the records he made from 1929 to 1939. There was a definite smoothing out of presentation – a lower vocal pitch, well-rounded tones, honey-coated articulation – as the one-time hillbilly singer reached out to a larger audience. (*Country Music, USA*, Equation, Wellingborough, Northamptonshire, 1985, pp.142-143).

This transformation wasn't just to accommodate Hollywood. This was not a consideration for country stars such as Roy Acuff, who, more than anyone, began to hone the Nashville image of the conservative straight-laced country star that we have today. Like Autry, he dropped the ribald songs, put on a ten-gallon hat and changed his band's name from The Crazy Tennesseans to The Smoky Mountain Boys. By the early to mid 1940s, this trend was so firmly established that Hank (originally Hiram) Williams dressed in cowboy duds and called his band The Drifting Cowboys, despite the fact that his music and words paid barely a passing reference to the Old West. By the time Elvis Presley had made his first film, a Western with a Civil War backdrop, *Love Me Tender* (Robert D. Webb, 1956), the process of the Southern musician ridding himself of any derogatory connotations by reconstructing himself as a cowboy appeared, as it does today, totally unremarkable.

The process of incorporating country music into the mainstream of American culture began in the early 'thirties. For the most part, this move was driven by the fairly new recording and radio industries. Network radio was firmly established by 1928 and, together with records and jukeboxes, meant that it was now possible for musicians to reach a vast market. But this wasn't going to happen unless they could construct an identity able cut across regional, racial and class barriers.

The standardisation and categorisation of Southern vernacular music was officially sanctioned in June 1949 when *Billboard* first used 'Country & Western' to head up the charts that had previously been titled 'American Folk Tunes.' The impact of this standardisation can be measured to a large extent by the listening figures for *The Grand Ole Opry*, which 'by July 1940 was networked coast to coast on more than 150 stations and attracted around ten million listeners every Saturday night' (Escott, 1994, p.105). This success was achieved in no small part by the appropriation of cowboy motifs:

'The embracing of western-style music in the 1930s was, in part, merely one facet of the larger retreat to popular culture – to gangster movies, Busby Berkeley musicals, big band jazz, radio serials – undertaken by Americans as a means of coping with hard times. The resurgence of interest in the cowboy, in both his musical and non-musical guise, surely also must have its source in the renewed consciousness of and search for roots inspired by the Great Depression. In their search to regain a sense of purpose, many Americans may have found comfort in identifying with a reassuring symbol of independence and mastery, a collection of traits that the nation had once possessed and might once again assert. It is no wonder that word would go out of the White House that President Roosevelt's favourite song was "Home on the Range" ' (Bill C. Malone, *Singing Cowboys and Musical Mountaineers: Southern Culture and the Roots of Country Music*, University of Georgia Press, 1993, p.91).

There's no doubt that a great many found 'comfort' in the image of the cowboy, though I would suggest that this reassurance is found in a more complex understanding of the cowboy's identity than one based just on ideas of 'independence and mastery'.

Jane Tompkins has made a very strong case for understanding the popularity of the Western in terms of gender, arguing that the Western as a form of popular culture appeared as a patriarchal response to the women's movements of the late nineteenth and early twentieth centuries. Her argument, though persuasive, eventually has the effect of reducing the Western to the playing out of gender stereotypes (Tompkins, 1992, Chapters 1-3). Rather than dismiss her thesis, I think it more appropriate to build upon it by suggesting two further readings to accompany it. These are not, I hasten to add, all-encompassing, but are areas that have been sadly neglected in the study of the Western: race and ethnicity, and the Western as the pre-eminent form of populist discourse. Both are crucial to understanding Hollywood's response to the Great Depression and its tentative engagement with the unfolding war in Europe. (Another significant area for research is the Western as a response to industrialisation, which is subsumed here under the rubric of populism.)

The question of race as a key factor in American popular music cannot be overstated. In 1949, when *Billboard* changed its 'Folk' chart to 'Country & Western', it also changed the 'Race' chart to 'Rhythm & Blues'. Both moves attempted to give a veneer of respectability to genres that (regardless of sales) were seen as at best marginal and at worst vulgar. But, whatever the name given to these charts and musical forms, the fact remains that a recording was marketed to either a Black or a White audience. Despite the industry's construction of racially separate forms of music and audiences, these divisions meant little to the musicians, whose shared stock of influences constantly challenges our idea of racial segregation in the American South. The common sources of blues and country music only increased the industry's desire to keep them separate in radio programming, the marketing of records and the selection of discs for jukeboxes, exemplifying the contradiction of integration and separation that lies at the heart of race relations in America, and particularly in the American South (*see*, especially, Tosches, 1977, which carefully details the shared influences of blues and country music).

In the 'thirties, part of the cowboy's appeal was that he carried none of the overt race or class connotations of the hillbilly or his White Trash cousin, yet through deed and action he supported the concept of Anglo-Saxon superiority whilst also being incontestably of American origin. In other words, the cowboy was neither a Georgia peckerwood nor an Englishman. He was, as Walt Whitman had it in *Leaves of Grass*, beyond those concerns:

'The vulgar and the refined . . . . what you call sin and what you call goodness . . to think how wide a difference;

To think the difference will still continue to others, others, yet we lie beyond the difference.'

The appropriation of the cowboy by White Southern musicians, then, was partly brought about by that figure's commitment to a rural lifestyle and his uncontested Anglo-Saxon heritage. In this sense, the initial (precinematic) popularisation of the cowboy was not only a response to the women's movement, as Tompkins suggests, but also to industrialisation and the mass migration of Latin and Eastern Europeans to America at the turn of the century.

Interest in the cowboy's musical heritage first gained academic credibility in the early part of the century with the publication of Nathan Howard Thorp's *Songs of the Cowboy* in 1908 and with John Lomax's *Cowboy Songs and Other Frontier Ballads* in 1910. Interest continued to grow throughout the 1920s, and in the early 1930s, Tex Ritter, soon to be Grand National's latest all-riding, all-singing sensation, was much in demand for lecture and song recitals in Eastern colleges. But as the hillbillies began systematically to appropriate and commercialise the image of the cowboy, interest waned amongst the intelligentsia and shifted to 'folk' music from the Appalachians and figures such as Bradley Kincaid, who, according to Bill Malone 'spoke disparagingly of "hillybilly [sic] and bum songs", and extolled the mountain folk from whom he obtained his songs as "a people in whose veins runs the purest strain of Anglo-Saxon blood" ' (Malone, 1993, p.83).

Kincaid's popularity with the intelligentsia would fade, but in his place came performers like Woody Guthrie who wedded 'folk' to 'protest':

'The urban folk movement's radical origins have always affected public perceptions of it, and the linking of 'protest' and 'folk song' has contributed to false impressions about the nature of the folk and the music they have made. Furthermore, a regrettable distinction between 'folk' and 'hillbilly' music developed in the popular mind. 'Folk' music, which had become largely the province of intellectuals and reformers, became increasingly removed from the folk, while 'hillbilly' music, the creation of the folk, developed in its own independent fashion' (Malone, 1985, p.130).

In this way, 'folk' took on the mantle of radicalism and authenticity and 'country' that of commercialism and conservatism. But such a straightforward opposition misrepresents the two forms, just as surely as it is wrong to see country and blues as two mutually exclusive forms. Both are equally capable of criticising or supporting the status quo.

If we understand the Western in terms of syncreticity, rather than as a hermetically sealed ahistorical concept, then it is possible to understand how it became accepted as definitively American, which meant that it could be called upon to appeal over and above partisanship and party politics: Roosevelt's favourite song – 'Home on the Range', Woody Guthrie singing 'Jesse James' and Gene Autry's 'Don't Fence Me In' represent three very disparate agendas.

If we take Owen Wister's *The Virginian*, published in 1902, as a benchmark, the Western as a genre (across a wide variety of media) had been established for over 30 years by the mid-1930s. Its identification with country music, however, was a relatively recent phenomenon: its appropriation, as I have suggested, is specifically linked to the events brought about by the Depression and by the need for performers and audiences to transcend their present circumstances, whilst still identifying wholeheartedly with the American ideal. The Western proved to be solid and familiar enough to be understood by all and fluid enough to contain all kinds of contradictory messages. More than anything, the Western provided a home for those who felt dispossessed and dislocated.

Hollywood's Return to the West

With regard to Western film production during the 1930s, Edward Buscombe has this to offer:

'. . . between the mid-1920s and the late 1950s . . . Westerns . . . comprise(d) between a fifth and a quarter of all films made in Hollywood . . . This is an astonishingly high proportion for one kind of film. What we have to remember, though, is that all but a few Westerns were small-scale productions. Indeed, big budget or so-called A-feature Westerns . . . were a rarity. Of the 1,336 Westerns made by all producers between 1930 and 1941, only 66, or a mere 5 per cent, could be classed as A features' (Buscombe, 1988, revised edition 1993, pp.38-39).

And, it's worth adding, 31 of those A features fall within the years 1939-41. Buscombe continues: 'There can be no simple explanation of why so few A-Westerns should have been produced in the middle years of the 1930s.' To underpin his point he outlines and dismisses the two most commonly offered determinants: the introduction of sound (fairly rapidly overcome as a problem), and the demand for a 'realist' response to the problems raised by the Depression and the rise of fascism in Europe (which he disqualifies because of the popularity of 'escapist' entertainment such as Busby Berkeley spectaculars and the screwball comedy). He then adds his own determinant: the failure of two big-budget Westerns – *The Big Trail* (Raoul Walsh, 1930) and *Cimarron* (Wesley Ruggles, 1931). 'Eventually', he concludes, 'things picked up; not solely as legend has it, because of the success of *Stagecoach* in 1939, though that undoubtedly helped' (Buscombe, pp.42-43).

I would add that the major studios, having turned away from the Western with the introduction of sound and the failure of *The Big Trail* and *Cimarron*, saw no reason to reinvest in it until its popularity from the mid-'thirties onwards, with the inexorable rise in B Western production and in other areas such as music, showed without doubt that there was a market to be exploited. Furthermore, the B Western's link with the emergent Country and Western music industry and that music's increasingly high profile in radio programming meant that the studios were taking little or no risk with the move back to A-feature Western production. The potential market was very large indeed.

The major studios did not simply replicate the format of the B Western and the Singing Cowboy. (An exception is *The Return of the Cisco Kid*, Herbert I. Leeds, 1939, where Fox upped the production values and script quality, though the plot is still unbelievably hackneyed – daughter with ageing father is conned out of ranch on which gold is discovered – and Warner Baxter as the Cisco Kid rides, sings and romances his way through the film.) As Edward Buscombe has pointed out in his study of *Stagecoach* (BFI Publishing, London, 1992), the producers of the film were keen to promote it to as wide an audience as possible, hence the heavy emphasis on the film's female stars and its production values. However, the B Western did supply the A Westerns with thematic concerns. The 1930s B Western is marked by an obsession with ownership of the land, which in plot terms is often, and this *is* a generalisation, under threat of being repossessed by an underhand representative of capitalist interests,

Stills: Jesse James. *Above – Major Rufus Cobb (Henry Hull) tells the farmers, Jesse (Tyrone Power) and Frank (Henry Fonda), 'Don't you understand, you haven't got a chance . . .' Opposite – Jesse before his transformation into a Western outlaw.*

the land, unbeknown to the rightful owners, having some hidden value like gold or oil. The B Western appears to us today as highly simplistic and excessively concerned with plot at the expense of character, and no doubt it did to an urban middle-class audience in the 1930s, but it spoke eloquently to a rural population who also perceived themselves to be under threat from Northern business conglomerates.

The A-feature Western that thematically most closely echoes the B Western is *Jesse James* (Henry King, 1939). The film evinces an acute schizophrenia, never being sure from one scene to the next whether it is a full-blooded Western or a Jeffersonian paean to the agrarian ideal of the self-sufficient farmer. As such it manages to speak directly about the Depression, whilst simultaneously addressing itself to a mythological past.

In this, it works in a very similar way to *Gone With the Wind* (Victor Fleming et al, 1939). In a comparative analysis of *Gone With the Wind* and *The Grapes of Wrath*, Thomas H. Pauly has written:

'Though it was less daring and less accomplished than Ford's work as an artistic creation, *Gone With the Wind* was similarly preoccupied with the problem of survival in the face of financial deprivation and social upheaval. Both movies also demonstrate a nostalgic longing for the agrarian way of life which is ruthlessly being replaced by the fearful new economic forces of capitalism and industrialisation. By way of extension, both reflect an intense concern for the devastating consequences of these conditions upon self-reliant individualism and family unity, two of America's most cherished beliefs. In each case, however, serious concern for these implications is dissipated into indulgent sentimentalism so that the audience's anxieties are alleviated rather than aggravated' (Thomas H. Pauly, '*Gone With the Wind* and *The Grapes of Wrath* as Hollywood Histories of the Depression' in *Gone with the Wind as Book and Film*, edited by Richard Harwell, University of South Carolina Press, 1992).

It takes little effort to slip *Jesse James* into the paradigm constructed by Pauly. While images of the West are deeply inscribed in the film's title and the rolling script (which celebrates the role played by the railroads in opening up the West at the same time as condemning the manner in which this was achieved), they are confounded by the opening scenes, linked together by a sleazy railroad employee (Brian Donlevy) conning farmers out of their land. What is striking about these scenes is how free they are of Western iconography. Instead we are shown the front of neat wooden cabins occupied by salt-of-the-earth types, cast to approximate to Hollywood's idea of Dorothea Lange's or Walker Evans's Dust Bowl migrants. From an old couple with young children, to a mother and adolescent, to the Jameses. In each case, there is a marked absence of a strong patriarchal figure. It is images like these rather than the presence of Henry Fonda, John Carradine and Jane Darwell, who also starred in *The Grapes of Wrath*, that links the film so conclusively to the Depression.

As in *The Grapes of Wrath* and *Gone With the Wind*, the underlying theme is one of loss: loss of land, home, family, community, a way of life. The characters must struggle against almost insurmountable odds to reassert their values and needs, and in so doing they emerge more resilient than ever. According to Pauly, the Civil War functioned during this period as a way of addressing the problems of the Depression without having to allude to it directly. The idea is that Hollywood, by looking back to a

time when America was divided against itself, and suggesting how the country dealt with these divisions, could offer up a palliative for contemporary tensions. All the Westerns dealt with here (with the exception of *Drums Along the Mohawk*) use the repercussions of the Civil War as a factor in their dramatic conflicts.

One of the keys to defining populist discourses is how they present the promise of a prosperous future through an idealisation of the past: *back to the future*. This helps explain the otherwise gratuitous presence in *Jesse James* of the character Pinky (Ernest Whitman). the James's 'faithful darkie', an Uncle Tom and Mammy rolled into one. Pinky, as a pliant symbol of slavery and the Antebellum South without its heinous connotations, is crucial to the populist construction of American history, because he suggests an unproblematic past. The problems faced by the Jameses and their community are external (large corporations in the guise of the railroad) not internal (race). As such, the multifaceted conflicts of post-Civil-War America are reduced to a set of uncontroversial and simplistic oppositions, where it becomes possible for the community to galvanise itself into action and to overcome the common enemy. The film's didactic message is simple: if the conflicts of the past can be resolved, then so can those of the present.

Like Scarlett and the Joads, the Jameses are faced by overwhelming and impersonal odds: 'Don't you understand you haven't got a chance. The St Louis-Midland's got this whole State hog-tied. They got the police, they got the courts, they got everything. A trial right now would be a joke. The railroad's got too much at stake to let two little farmer's boys like you bollocks things up.'

With the Jameses forced into a life of crime, the film switches from a rural melodrama to a Western (note the use of Southern vernacular, as opposed to Western dialect in the above speech). The Jameses' fate is sealed, and however much the film wants to recuperate these outlaws as heroes, it also recognises that they are outside the law, and even if the law is an ass in its corrupt dealings with the railroads, it is also a necessary prerequisite for a stable society. Enter Randolph Scott as Marshall Will Wright.

His function is to balance the extremes of Jesse James (Tyrone Power) and James's father-in-law, Major Rufus Cobb (Henry Hull), the newspaper editor. 'If we are ever to have law and order in the West', says Cobb, 'first thing we gotta do is take out all the lawyers and shoot them down like dogs.' Scott, playing against type, works up his credentials as a man of the people by smoking a corn-cob pipe and pronouncing 'deaf' as 'deef'. Will Wright is the future, Jesse James is the past, despite Jesse's rebirth as a farmer – after the film's brilliant set-piece raid on Northfield Minnesota, he enters head-first, back into the world, from a womb made of hay.

The problem for Jesse James is that he loses sight of the community and its greater needs and becomes self-obsessed, driven by selfish needs and desires. This is mapped out through his increasing criminality and his literal and figurative distance from

Still: The Return of Frank James – *Frank (Henry Fonda) learns that the Governor has pardoned the Ford brothers; with Pinky (Ernest Whitman) and Clem (Jackie Cooper).*

his home and family. When he wants to return it's too late.

The ambivalence displayed towards Jesse as hero/villain and over whether or not the film is a rural melodrama or a Western is pretty much absent from *The Return of Frank James* (Fritz Lang, 1940), which was Fox's attempt to cling both to the shirt tails of *Jesse James* (the most successful box office Western of 1939, after *Drums Along the Mohawk*) and to *Gone With the Wind*. The film opens where its precursor closed with the death of Jesse and then cuts to find Frank (Henry Fonda) back on the land steering a plough through rocky Ozark soil. This Arcadian dream is again vanquished when the Governor pardons the Ford brothers. For the greater part of the second act, the film is set in the Rocky Mountains, and Frank takes his trouser legs out of his boot tops and stops looking like a farmer and more like a gunfighter. This is the west and as if to make this point, the editorials in Frank's home town paper now run along the line: 'If we are ever to have law and order in this place . . .' Colorado is the West and Missouri is now the Old South, though at times an audience could be forgiven for confusing the two, as there are more Blacks working in subservient positions in Denver, Colorado, than in Liberty, Missouri.

The connection with the Old South is more fully developed in *Frank James* and is particularly apparent when the Civil War is metaphorically refought in the courtroom scene, after Frank has given himself up to the law (which is still in the employ of the railroad) in order to save an innocent Pinky from hanging. Here Frank's innate goodness is fully established (he gives up his freedom to save a 'Negro'), and the nature of the railroad as a pack of Yankee carpetbaggers is comprehensively demonstrated.

As Frank, unlike Jesse, never gives up his commitment to community and the idea of the family, he finally makes it back into society after the Governor makes an unexplained volte-face and pardons him. Wrongs have been made right, and with Gene Tierney's character as an inducement, he might just finally move west permanently.

In Universal's *Destry Rides Again* (George Marshall, 1939) the drive of the narrative is to turn the graveyard that is the town of Bottleneck at the beginning of the film, into the orchard it has become at the end. The film thus falls easily into Jim Kitses's series of antinomies headed by Wilderness/Civilisation (Kitses, 1969). But like most Westerns, it turns out, on close scrutiny, to have a much more complex set of equations. Kitses's paradigm suggests an ahistorical approach to the Western through grouping together antinomies that appear to be eternal in their application. However, *Destry* makes much more sense if its antinomies are linked to social tensions current at the time of its production.

On one side of the divide stands Tom Jefferson Destry (James Stewart), peaceable, full of corn-pone humour and homespun homilies – the best of the South. On the other side stands Kent (Brian Donlevy), violent, a gambler and land-grabber who cheats families out of their homes (we've been here before) – a corrupt capitalist. Alongside Destry stands a reformed Wash[ington] (Charles Winniger) and a Russian immigrant, Boris 'Callahan' (Mischa Auer). Alongside Kent stands crooked Judge Slade (Samuel S. Hinds) and Gyp and Bugs Watson (Allen Jenkins and Warren Hymer) – the worst of the South: two hoods who owe more to White Trash stereotypes than to the stereotype of the evil gunslinger (which would be played to perfection by Jack Palance in *Shane*, George Stevens, 1953). In this way the film's antinomies are linked to the conflicts brought on by the Depression and to a North/South rather than East/West divide, with the overarching

Stills. Below: the old South meets the new West – Judge Roy Bean (Walter Brennan) and Cole Hardin, the Westerner (Gary Cooper) in The Westerner. *Opposite: Destry (James Stewart), the best of the South, and Frenchy (Marlene Dietrich), a symbol of a decadent South that must be expelled from the West in* Destry Rides Again.

antinomy as Industrial/Rural, rather than Civilisation/ Wilderness.

Thought of in this manner, *The Westerner* (William Wyler, 1940), like *Jesse James*, *The Return of Frank James* and *Destry Rides Again*, is not so much concerned with the frontier, as with the establishment and defence of a Jeffersonian pastoral idyll. Gregg Toland's photography manages powerfully to evoke the destruction of homes, families, crops and the ever-present threat to the land, as Judge Roy Bean (Walter Brennan), the self-appointed Law West of the Pecos, does all he can to drive out the homesteaders.

The Westerner again places its emphasis on commitment to community above individualism. Gary Cooper (Cole Hardin – the Westerner), who gets to share a bed with Walter Brennan, speaks poetically of his need to be alone, but in the end he has no choice but to become part of a family. After all, under his buckskin jacket he wears a shirt made of that most homely of textiles, gingham. The Judge, on the other hand, reveals his old Civil War colours in the final scenes in the theatre where he at last gets to see his impossible dream, Lily Langtry, and dies as he began – alone. The West is where you leave the past behind; if you take it with you, you die. This lesson is also learnt by the ex-Confederate Hatfield, played by John Carradine, in *Stagecoach* and in *Destry Rides Again* by Frenchy (Marlene Dietrich), whose allegiance to the Old South is implied through her bringing her Black maid (Lillian Yarbo) with her from New Orleans.

A counter-reading to this may be that these elements are always present as Westerns endlessly play out the conflict between cattle barons and homesteaders – *Shane*, for example. But the difference is one of degree. *Shane*, in its highly affected self-reflexivity, doesn't give the same weight to the issue of farming and land that *The Westerner* does, instead displacing the audience's attention more firmly on to the hero. And the scenes of destruction wrought by the cattlemen on the land are nothing compared to the apocalyptic vision that Gregg Toland's camera creates. The sense of loss in *The Westerner* is palpable and the heroine's determination not to give up is every bit as convincing as Scarlett O'Hara's. After the crops and homes have been devastated, we witness a long procession of wagons leaving the territory. The homesteaders' possessions are piled high on the wagons – rocking chairs in evidence – and it takes little imagination to see an analogy here with the Dust Bowl migrants heading towards

California. *The Westerner* closes with the return of the wagons and an image of lush, fertile land waiting to be harvested. The West is where the wounds of the Depression can be healed and a new Arcadia founded. America has done it before and it can do it again.

Warner Bros made two Westerns in 1939, *The Oklahoma Kid* (Lloyd Bacon) and *Dodge City* (Michael Curtiz). In the former, the story kicks off with the opening of the Cherokee Strip to settlers, and some fine visionary words from one of the would-be founders of Tulsa City: 'All around are thousands of acres of the richest land in Oklahoma and it will all be peopled by this time tomorrow, by folks that'll need doctors, lawyers, merchants. It's a new start for all of us. But it's gonna mean a lot of hard work and it's gonna mean sticking together for the common good.' The irony of this speech and one given earlier by the President, about Oklahoma having the finest farming land in the country, wouldn't have passed by a contemporary audience. Intriguingly, the film has no truck whatsoever with farmers, concentrating instead on a city built on a compromise with crime. The good citizens become forced to fight a battle that they can't possibly win against the forces of evil, led by a malevolent Whip McCord (Humphrey Bogart). With surprising haste, McCord and his men turn from outlaws into 'The McCord Corporation', allowing the film to draw on Bogart's gangster credentials and also to suggest a form of malign capitalism that has corrupted the agrarian dream.

The man in the middle is the Oklahoma Kid (James Cagney), who proves as surely as the whole cast of *Terror of Tiny Town* (Sam Newfield, 1938) that the vertically challenged do not make convincing cowboys, and also that heroes shouldn't wear heavy eye make-up and that he can't even yodel! Nevertheless, Cagney plays his part with no little

Still: The Oklahoma Kid – *James Cagney in the title role stands tall and alone against the city's forces of corruption.*

charisma and for the most part with his tongue firmly in his cheek. To him initially falls the role of the cynic – in an early bar-room scene, the Judge challenges his patriotism, and the Kid retorts: 'In the first place, the White people steal the land from the Indians. Right. They get paid for it, yeah, a measly dollar and forty cents an acre, price agreed at the point of a gun. Then the immigrants sweat and strain and break their hearts carving out a civilisation. Fine, great. Then, when they all get pretty and prosperous, along come the grafters, land grabbers and politicians, and with one hand skim off the cream and with the other scoop up the gravy.' It's a marvellous scene and is topped (and to some extent undercut) by the Kid outwitting two deputies and mounting his horse in best B-Western fashion.

At every point, the good citizens are thwarted in their attempts to gain control of events, and it's only when the government intervenes by imposing martial law that some semblance of order is maintained. Even then, it is up to the Kid to use extra-legal methods to bring Whip and his corporation to book. By the end of the film, you know that the Kid with his girl by his side has reconciled his individualism with the greater need for commitment to family and community. But not in Oklahoma. They're off to 'empire build' in Arizona.

Movement in America is always seen as beneficial, however illusory this is in reality. Don't look back, look forward is the contradictory message to an audience looking at the past in a Western to make sense of today. While films like *Gone With the Wind* are left only with the *hope* of a better future after the ravages of war and the breakdown of order –

'After all, tomorrow is another day' – Westerns almost always fulfil their promise of a better world.

The Oklahoma Kid worked hard, and not particularly successfully, to accommodate two stars who had no Western credentials, whilst Destry's non-Western persona (it was, after all, Stewart's first Western part) creates a similar generic tension to that found in *Jesse James*, but it is to a large extent disguised by the heavy emphasis on comedy. *Dodge City* also had this problem with Errol Flynn, who was better known for playing swashbuckling Englishmen than rugged frontiersmen. In recognition of this fact, the film casts him as an Irishman (all mangled grammar and repeated use of the phrase 'faith now'), ex-British officer and Civil War veteran. His cultural sophistication (represented by a number of references to Shakespeare) is levelled some-what by his two side-kicks, played by Alan Hale and Guinn 'Big Boy' Williams (who also can't yodel worth a damn), who represent his coarser side.

'The civil war has ended. Armies disband – the nation turns to the building of the west. Kansas – 1866.' The railroad is reaching west, and Colonel Dodge stops long enough to give a new town his name. He hopes that one day it will blossom to become the 'flower of the prairie'. Wade Hatton (Errol Flynn) turns down his offer of becoming the town's policeman and heads south to Texas to get into the cattle business. Nine years elapse, and Dodge City has been turned into a den of sin and

Still: Dodge City – *Wade Hatton (Errol Flynn) and Rusty Hart (Alan Hale) follow the cattlemen into the saloon.*

Still: Drums Along the Mohawk – *Lana (Claudette Colbert) marries Gil Martin before moving West to a life she is ill prepared for.*

vice – where honest ranchers are duped, and families are, at best, forced to move on to Wichita, or, at worst, all but destroyed. When the film isn't re-enacting the Civil War – this time not in court but through the mother of all saloon punch-ups – it's obsessed with the plight of the middle classes (the film is full of Victorian parlours, old men and old maids). Wade Hatton again refuses the badge of sheriff – his business is cattle – but eventually he finds a sense of social obligation, when the town's 'sheriff', played by a little boy, is killed. Time and again the message is reinforced that the West needs men like Flynn – strong men for desperate times – to accept responsibility.

A year later, in 1940, Flynn would play a part in the renowned anti-isolationist and pro-British costume drama, *The Sea Hawk* (he also made a much less spectacular Western, *Virginia City*, again directed by Michael Curtiz). If *The Sea Hawk* is explicit in its support for Britain standing alone against the tyranny of Germany (with Spain as the stand-in), then *Dodge City* is no less explicit in its call to intervention and preparedness. Its address, however, is to domestic concerns rather than to the international arena. This is because the Western is so thoroughly wrapped up in the construction of an American identity that it precludes ready analogies with international conflicts.

Flynn's character is a standardised 'reluctant hero', but his move from isolation to intervention is not contained by the story's conclusion. His next stop is Virginia City (with wife in tow). Having put on the tin star, he is not about to relinquish his role as policeman. He's got a job to do. In this, Virginia City is a very different proposition to Arizona in

The Oklahoma Kid and Ringo Kid's over-the-border ranch in *Stagecoach*. The latter two frontiers suggest resolution, whilst the former suggests a need for vigilance and involvement.

If *Dodge City* is certain of the need for intervention, *Destry Rides Again* is less convinced: the town is forced to bring in an outsider to help sort out its troubles, but rather than do the job through violence, Destry chooses to ingratiate himself with the town's womenfolk and thereby align himself with the real force and source of the community – he doesn't stay an outsider for long. Behind the localised conflicts of Bottleneck is always the assumption that the federal government remains uncorrupted, but the film just never gives the federal judge the chance to turn up, the town preferring, after much prevarication, to solve its own problems. Galvanised by the death of Wash, the townsfolk of Bottleneck clear up their own mess; the citizens of Dodge City have the outsider, played by Errol Flynn, do it for them – the two films mirror the wider political debates over government intervention as against self reliance that marked the Depression years.

All the films so far discussed deal with communities threatened by outside forces which, against great odds, they eventually overcome. But the film that dealt most comprehensively with this, and was also the biggest box-office success of them all, was *Drums Along the Mohawk*. Set during the War of Independence, the film manages to combat any accusations of sabre rattling, or fears of upsetting the British authorities and audience, by calling the opposing forces 'Tories' and having the major opposing combatants played by Indians. This takes the film out of the historical costume drama department and into the Western, where any accusations of anti-British sentiment can be effaced: this is about America, not Britain. Furthermore, it concentrates the drama on the defence of the community and stays at home when the militia march off to war.

The concentration on the domestic sphere of engagement means that the women in the film are given a prominent role – indeed it is arguable that their concerns are dominant – and the emphasis is on the suffering and sacrifice that the women go through in order to establish the community. To a lesser extent, this is also true of *Jesse James*. The audience is consistently reminded of the suffering caused to Jesse's wife, Zee (Nancy Kelly), by his absence and his increasingly criminal lifestyle. *The Westerner*, too, foregrounds the woman's role, as does *Stagecoach*, with its central dramatic device of the birth of a child to Lucy Mallory (Louise Platt) and the mothering role assumed by Dallas (Claire Trevor). And in *Destry Rides Again*, what is most significant about the resolution of the conflict between Destry and Kent is not so much Destry's eventual move towards violent confrontation, but the women's move to become the major force in clearing out the corrupt. As the gingham hoard march on the Last Chance Saloon, with farm implements raised high, they appear to be a wholly unstoppable force – well temporarily anyway. With order restored, Boris can finally enforce his authority over his wife and throw out the picture of Callahan, her previous husband, that hung above their bed, and replace it with his own portrait – Boris as a born-again cowboy and fully-paid-up American.

Drums Along the Mohawk opens with the marriage of Gilbert and Lana Martin (Henry Fonda and Claudette Colbert). The splendour and comfort of her premarital lifestyle is immediately contrasted with the primitiveness of Gil's farm, and the film revolves around Lana's problems. Gil is given a stick by the Indian Blueback (Arthur Aylesworth) to beat her with, but he never has to use it, as it soon becomes evident that it is her strength that will see them through the difficulties ahead.

After their farm is wiped out by the first Indian attack, it is Lana who finds work and cajoles Gil into accepting it. His protestation about being 'hired help' is levelled by the audience's recognition that this is a far longer fall on the social scale for Lana than it is for Gil. The point is made clear when the couple return in the winter to their burnt-out farm and Lana picks up the teapot that is a link to her past. The teapot is broken, and she lets it lie and looks forward to the future. Although they may temporarily no longer be their own masters, their plight is relieved somewhat by the tacit recognition that there is always someone lower down the scale than them: the black maid or slave – her position is never revealed – Daisy (Beulah Hall Jones).

Before the final climactic battle at the fort, Lana will lose her home again, and a child, but still she endures. When Gil makes up his mind to seek help from a neighbouring fort by running through the Indian lines, it is Lana's strength that he looks to for sustenance.

After the battle and the surrender of the British, the community is given the symbol under which they can unite: the Stars and Stripes. Cut into the scenes of celebrating white faces are two emblematic shots of Daisy and Blueback, by this means brought into the community, but also kept separate from it – a wholly appropriate image for the construction of an American identity that presumes to offer sanctuary for all, whilst constantly marginalising those who don't fit the Anglo-Saxon ideal.

Music, like comedy, is an omnipresent part of the Western, but is little commented upon. Individual performances, community dances, and saloon stage shows fill an important dramatic space within all the films discussed here. Yet intriguingly, the music has little in common with either contemporary country music in general, beyond the odd hoedown, or more specifically with the Singing Cowboy. Instead the films' musical directors reach much further back in time to the first wholly American art form: the Blackface Minstrel. Most of the musical pieces, both diegetic and extradiegetic, owe an overwhelming debt to the songs of Stephen Foster: 'Oh! Susanna' rings out time and again. In part, this can be explained by these Westerns' constant recall of the Civil War. But the music signals to the audience a common heritage, one that is indisputably American, albeit highly regionalised, an idealisation of plantation life, where all was harmony – a picture also to be seen in *Swanee River* (Sidney Lanfield, 1939), a musical bio-pic on Stephen Foster.

One of the great underlying tensions in American culture is between diversity and unity. The Western offers a way to resolve this conflict. It allows space for individualism *and* community. Characters are constantly aligning themselves to specific regions – Texas, Oklahoma, Missouri and so on. Their loyalty to their home state allows them contradictorily to foreground their individuality, while at the same time committing them to the Union through their State's membership. Hence, these films' tacit reprise of the debates engendered by post-Civil-War reconstruction. Similarly, country music's move into Western imagery meant that it was able to suggest the importance of regional identity whilst simultaneously defining itself as unimpeachably American.

The cowboy 'is a patriot (above all)' reads 'Commandment #10' in the book of Gene Autry, which is not that far from 'Well, I reckon we better be getting back to work. There's going to be a heap to be doing from now on' – Gil Martin's closing comments in *Drums Along the Mohawk*. By using the past as constructed through the Western, Americans were given the opportunity to define themselves both as Americans and as individuals, which in turn helped them to transcend the social and geopolitical tensions of the time. The ways in which the Western was able to negotiate the contradictions and conflicts of what it meant to be an American made it the most potent dramatic form for its times.

A BETTER SENSE OF HISTORY

John Ford and the Indians

Richard Maltby

'No-one goes to the Western for a history lesson' (Kevin Brownlow, *The War, the West and the Wilderness*, Secker & Warburg, London, 1979, p.223).

There is a moment, not quite at the climax of John Ford's *Two Rode Together* (1961), in which the contradictions of Hollywood's representation of the American Indian are encapsulated. It is a woodland night on a studio set; the lawman/Indian trader hero sits with the woman whom he has ransomed back from Comanche captivity. To the crashing accompaniment of Indian drums, brass and strings, the chief, villainously resplendent in eagle-feather warbonnet and brandishing a knife, bursts into the circle of light around the camp fire. He embodies the magnificent, threatening, ignoble animal of savagism, his intentions violence, rapine and despoliation. Calmly, belying the dramatic potential of the confrontation, the hero shoots him.

In this archetypal confrontation between savage Indian and frontiersman over the fate of feminine civilisation, we witness a paradox: the divergence between the terrifying image of the Indian and his actual impotence in the sights of the White hero's gun – the threat vanishes as soon as it becomes visible. This encapsulates a condition of the Western: the Indian constitutes an immediate physical threat to the hero and his charges, yet he cannot but be

vanquished, wiped out by the vanguard of civilisation. However, little in this particular archetype is pure: its details of characterisation and casting make it carry undercurrents of every racial tension in American history. The white man's motivations are mercenary and cynical, the woman is Mexican, and the Indian is personified by an African American, Woody Strode. We lack only an immigrant to complete the cultural capsule, and Ford himself performs that function: 'Who better than an Irishman could understand the Indians, while still being stirred by the tales of the US Cavalry? We were on both sides of the epic' (quoted in Tag Gallagher, *John Ford, The Man and his Films*, University of California Press, Berkeley, 1986, p.341). Ford's comment, made during the production of his last Western, *Cheyenne Autumn* (1964), is echoed in that film by Sergeant Wichowsky, played by Mike Mazurki as a revised version of the Victor McLaglen character in Ford's cavalry trilogy. Wichowsky expresses the Indians' plight in the terms of a White history:

'I'm a Pole. You know what they have in Poland besides Poles. Cossacks. You know what a Cossack

Still: Two Rode Together – *watched by Elena de la Madriaga (Linda Cristal), Guthrie McCabe (James Stewart) shoots Stone Calf (Woody Strode).*

is? A Cossack is a man on a horse with a fur cap on his head and a sabre in his hand. Now he kills Poles just because they're Poles, like we're trying to kill Indians just because they're Indians. I was proud to be an American soldier. But I ain't proud to be a Cossack.'

Ford's Indians, then, are to be understood in terms of one or other White historical paradigm, but whoever these characters are supposed to be, it is evident that they make no attempt adequately to represent the tribal nations whose names they appropriate. In the Hollywood Western, there are no 'real' 'Indians' – no Iroquois, no Lakotas, no Navajos, only Hollywood Indians with different names. With hardly an exception throughout its history, the Hollywood Western has obliterated the ethnic and cultural distinctions between the many indigenous peoples of North America, and imposed on them a stereotype, itself derived from the earlier traditions of the dime novel, the historical romance, and the captivity narrative.

(In February 1911, during the American cinema's first cycle of Westerns with Indian characters and themes, the industry trade paper, *The Moving Picture World*, reported that 'two Chippewa delegations and Indians from other sections have joined in an uprising against the moving pictures. They charge that the moving picture promoters, in order to get thrilling pictures of wild western life, have used white men costumed as Indians in depicting scenes that are not true pictures of the Indians, and are in fact grossly libellous.' The paper offered editorial support. 'Truthfulness in pictures has previously been advocated in these columns, and it is well that this timely and authoritative protest should come. While we still have the real Indians with us, why cannot thoroughly representative films be produced, making them at once illustrative and historic recorders of this noble race of people, with their splendid physique and physical powers? It is to be hoped that some of our Western manufacturers will yet produce a series of films of REAL Indian life, doing so with the distinct object in view that they are to be of educational value, both for present and future use. Such a certified series will be of great value.' In practice, however, 'truthfulness' appeared to mean authenticity in costume and avoiding plot clichés. Reviewing Pathé's *The Unwilling Bride*, directed by James Youngdeer, in August 1912, the paper appreciated that 'there were no burnings, no scalpings; no portrayal of the red man as always bad, the white man as always good. It was a picture that would extract a grunt of satisfaction from the genuine aborigine – and it is a fact that the Indian is a moving picture follower second to none in his steadfastness. *The Unwilling Bride* depicts the Indian as he is understood by those whose knowledge of the red man is gained from sources more authoritative and reliable than the average Indian drama . . . To watch [George Gebhart in the leading Indian role] mount and dismount a pony, to see him running – stealthily, catlike, swift – is to open a book of Fenimore Cooper. He is a wonder at Indian portrayal.')

The Hollywood Indian represents an Other defined in relation to White American experience. It seems almost too banal to mention, but as an account of Native American culture, *Two Rode Together* is, quite typically for the Hollywood Western, irredeemable, worse than worthless. Near the end of the film, Elena de la Madriaga (Linda Cristal) and Guthrie McCabe (James Stewart) describe the gendered division of labour among the Comanche to a group of Army officers and their wives:

Elena: For five years I was the woman of the Comanche Stone Calf. He treated me like a wife. The work was hard, the scoldings frequent, and occasionally he beat me. I did not bear him any children . . . I know that many of you regard me as a degraded woman, degraded by the touch of a savage Comanche, by having had to live as one of them.
McCabe: . . . The Comanche, he don't know when Sunday comes. And cooking's sort of the recreation for their women. And then in their spare time they chew the glue out of buffalo hides so that their men can have a nice soft pair of moccasins. Well, you can judge for yourself what kind of a life it is by the number of survivors we brought back.

From such ethnology we can learn only a White story, that is, a story of White fears, desires and neuroses, in which are inscribed the three dominant terms of the Western mythos, the Three Rs of the Western: Racism, Rape and Repression. The act of representation is here an act of appropriation, a racism undertaken, according to Jack Nachbar ('*Ulzana's Raid*' in *Western Movies*, edited by William T. Pilkington and Don Graham, University of New Mexico Press, 1979, p.140), 'for purposes of creating mythic narrative.' Justifications such as this abound in the body of Western criticism, but there is among them a curious reluctance to discuss what substance

Still: Two Rode Together – *Elena mourning the dead Stone Calf.*

35

the Western as myth has, and it is often difficult to tell what White male writers mean when they deploy the term 'myth' in such contexts. Jon Tuska is suitably scathing: '[What] apologists really mean by a "mythic" dimension in a Western film is that part of it which they know to be a lie but which, for whatever reason, they still wish to embrace' (Tuska, *The American West in Film: Critical Approaches to the Western*, Greenwood, Westport, Connecticut, 1985). The Western is, as Douglas Pye says (*Movie 22*, 1976, p.42), 'at root a triumphalist white genre', its White triumphalism, its ideological purpose, its remorseless racism deeply embedded in its structures, long predating the movies themselves.

Invoking the Western as Nachbar does amounts to pleading a mythic version of the First Amendment: the right to rewrite history in the name of free mythopoeia. At the same time, the myth is 'really about' something else, something determined by external historical forces. A 'mythic' Western, not content just to be itself, must busy itself with themes and subject matter. Critical interpretation of the postwar Western has made much of the idea that the genre and its signs, and the sign of the Indian in particular, are highly mutable and open for transfer to a variety of other contexts. André Bazin called the Superwestern 'ashamed to be just itself', and looking for 'some additional interest to justify its existence – an aesthetic, sociological, moral, psychological, political or erotic interest' (Bazin, 1971, p.151). By such an analogy, William T. Pilkington and Don Graham announce that, 'in the late 1960s and early 1970s many Westerns . . . were not about the old West at all; they were really about the American involvement in Vietnam' (Pilkington and Graham, 1979, p.10). Philip French practises a more evasive piece of critical legerdemain in arguing that: 'from around 1950 the Indian in the contemporary allegory can stand for the Negro when the implications are social or for the Communist when the implications are political, though generally the identification is somewhat woolly' (French, 1973, p.81). Indeed. But where does the woolliness in this process lie? By such critical devices the Indian becomes simply an empty signifier of the Other in search of a conveniently relevant signified. At its most innocent, this idea of semantic malleability is an attempt to explain the durability of the Western myth through its capacity to adapt to changing cultural conditions. But in the process, the 'myth' is effectively left with no specific content of its own. Now 'standing in' for this, now for that, the Hollywood Indian is never himself, not even as the victim of a racism in which he is not only the signifier but also the referent. Precisely because, as Roland Barthes says, 'Myth is constituted by the loss of the historical quality of things', it is necessary to write the history of myth to decipher how and what it signifies. If the Indian is not himself, who is he?

As William Truettner puts it, 'Myth functions to control history, to shape it in text or image as an ordained sequence of events. The word is rendered pure in the process, complexity and contradictions give way to order, clarity, and direction. Myth, then,

can be understood as an abstract shelter restricting debate' (*The West as America: Reinterpreting Images of the Frontier, 1820-1920*, edited by William H. Truettner, Smithsonian Institution Press, Washington, DC, 1991, p.40).

In *The Rise and Fall of the White Republic: Class Politics and Mass Culture in Nineteenth Century America* (Verso, London, 1990), Alexander Saxton has examined the parallel development of blackface minstrelsy and the Western vernacular hero in the nineteenth century in terms of their common function in the maintenance of White racism as a theory of history. Richard Slotkin has noted that after the Civil War, newspapers developed a rhetoric to report and interpret the three prolonged confrontations of the period: the racial strife in the South, the labour struggles in the North, and the Indian Wars. The analogies made across this rhetoric were mutually reinforcing: the riotous urban poor were described as 'Indians'; the Indians interpreted as pauper-proletarians; Sioux government was described as 'communistic'. Slotkin argues that what was being established through the frontier myth was a racial metaphor for understanding class in American society, a metaphor which insisted on the absolute differences of kind established by racial 'gifts' or qualities, rather than the differences of degree which a European understanding of class might have proposed:

'These three terms – "savage", "slave" and "pauper" – would provide the metaphors through which Americans conceived the development of a proletariat: that is, a class of workers without property, and without the prospect of acquiring property' (Slotkin, 1985, p.302).

In his analysis of the innumerable 'Last Stand' paintings by Frederic Remington and others around the turn of the century, Alex Nemerov enlarges on a related observation of Slotkin's, that the last stand served as an allegory of the plight of capitalism in an era of frequent conflict between labour and management, and equally as an allegory of Anglo-Saxon America 'defending an imperilled stockade' against the immigrant horde. More generally, Nemerov proposes that 'the iconography of cowboys and Indians that arose so vigorously around the turn of the century is best understood in relation to the urban, industrial culture in which this iconography was produced' (Nemerov, 'Doing the "Old America": The Image of the American West, 1880-1920," in Truettner, 1991, pp.287, 303, 341).

Truettner's book accompanied the 1991 Smithsonian Institution exhibition, *The West as America*, which not only offered a revisionist account of Western imagery, but also drew attention away from the dominant perspective of the legend's central protagonist, the White male self, to the Other figures created to support that self-creation. The exhibition aroused extreme hostility: the *Washington Post* denounced it for 'effectively trash[ing] not only the integrity of the art it presents but most of our national history as well, reducing the saga of America's Western pioneers to little more than victimization,

Still: 'Anything historical is mine' – Paul Newman in
Buffalo Bill and the Indians: or, Sitting Bull's
History Lesson.

disillusion and environmental rape' – something substantial is still at stake in this reinterpretation of representations of history. The furore over the Smithsonian exhibition suggests that the persistence of the Western 'myth' as part of what the *Washington Post* called 'the nation's cultural patrimony' relies on a combination of its attestable allegorical relevance to the present and a denial that the 'myth,' as discourse, has an ideological history. In much the same terms, in his recent historiography, *Creating the West: Historical Interpretations, 1890-1990* (University of New Mexico Press, 1991), Gerald Nash has castigated the revisionism of Slotkin (1985) and Richard Drinnon (*Facing West: The Metaphysics of Indian-Hating and Empire-Building*, New American Library, New York, 1980) as 'shrill', 'ideological', 'pessimistic', but above all, irresponsible, in that to 'teach America's youth exclusively about the alleged depravity of the Western experience . . . can serve the function of destroying the very fabric of national identity' (pp.239-241). What is actually at stake, of course, has to do with what, and who, constitute the national identity that is being forged at the same time as the individual identity of the protagonist.

Nash acknowledges an ideological project in Frederick Jackson Turner's synoptic account of American history: Turner, like Theodore Roosevelt, Remington and Owen Wister, 'viewed the rise of the cities with distrust and expressed his distaste for the ways of the new immigrants who poured into them, particularly from southern and eastern Europe'. Nash identifies the closing of the frontier as a symbolic rite of passage, signalling the transition from an Anglo-Saxon agrarian society to a multicultural and multiethnic state. The West of Turner's frontier hypothesis appealed to progressives as a palliative, symbolising a past that was simpler, more primitive and more pristine, less dominated by the city, the immigrant, and worker. Nash argues that the writing of Western history took other directions from 1920, as an increasing number of historians discounted the significant impact of the frontier on American life, but that the Western, as artefact of popular culture, as 'myth,' continued to flourish as a nostalgic site at which a simpler WASP America could be represented (Nash, 1991, pp.5, 7, 21, 199, 206). From a different perspective, that is to say that the Western remained the primary site in which Hollywood could maintain a racist discourse, in which racism was offered and enacted as a theory of history.

This essay is, I hope, a contribution to the revisionism Nash deplores. My title is a line from Robert Altman's *Buffalo Bill and the Indians: or, Sitting Bull's History Lesson* (1976), a movie that not only aggressively revises the conventional mythology but is also frequently concerned with the possession of history. 'Anything historical is mine', proclaims Cody (Paul Newman), and when Annie Oakley (Geraldine Chaplin) threatens to quit the show because Cody will not let Sitting Bull (Frank Kaquitts) re-enact the McLaren massacre, she tells him, 'he wanted to show the truth to the people. Why can't you accept that just once?' 'Because I got a better sense of history than that', he replies. Yet Altman's own attitude to history – at least as articulated in interviews – echoes Cody's: 'Altman claims he and [co-writer Alan] Rudolph boned up by reading biography and chronicles of the frontier . . . before . . . dispensing with facts.' 'The history', declared Altman, 'is correct philosophically, but not actually' (Patrick McGilligan, *Robert Altman: Jumping Off the Cliff*, St Martin's Press, New York, 1989, pp.442-443). It is unclear whether Sitting Bull's history lesson is one he imparts or one he learns. It might be, as he is quoted by his interpreter, William Halsey (Will Samson) as saying, that 'history is nothing but disrespect for the dead', because 'the white man has stolen the truth'. Or else it is Cody's assertion in his concluding monologue that 'truth is whatever gets the loudest applause'. 'The only difference between Injuns and whites in a situation like this', he suggests, 'is whites already know how it's gonna come out . . . In a hundred years . . . I'm still goin' to be Buffalo Bill – star! You're still gonna be The Injun!'

'This is the West, sir', says Maxwell Scott (Carleton Young), editor of the Shinbone Star, in John Ford's *The Man Who Shot Liberty Valance* (1962). 'When the legend becomes fact, print the legend.' This is Tom Doniphon's History Lesson: the inevitable confusion of history and myth in the Western. It is announced by Scott, to whom Senator

Ransom Stoddard (James Stewart) has just told his revisionist history of the man who shot Liberty Valance. That man, in legend, is Stoddard, the lawyer, civiliser of the West and archetypal embodiment of Ford's populist dream, the bringer of the Book of Law who can uphold it with the gun, a figure who occupies a place in clear line of descent from Ford's Henry Fonda in *My Darling Clementine* (1946) and *Young Mr Lincoln* (1939) – and, for that matter, from Edward Ellis's *Seth Jones* (1860). In the 'true story', the man who shot Liberty Valance is Tom Doniphon (John Wayne), physical archetype of the Western hero but too tainted by the wilderness to resist the descent into anarchic violence and alcoholic degeneracy on the loss of his girl, the Cactus Rose, Hallie (Vera Miles), to Stoddard. These two characters represent polar alternatives for the hero's fate, Senator or scapegoat, the lawyer hero of legend which has become history, or the vanishing hero of a revisionist history which is, of course, myth.

'When the legend becomes fact, print the legend.' We should recognise that Editor Scott does not construct a binary opposition out of his two terms; he is no kind of structuralist. 'Legend' can become 'fact', and still be recorded as 'legend'. We learn that the 'legend' of the Easterner who learns Western ways and ends up more skilful than the Western badman misrepresents events. Instead, we witness a 'legend' of Western hero and Western badman/outlaw in a symbiotic relationship, in which the deadly encounter between them is ultimately fatal to both. The John Wayne legend becomes 'fact' by being enacted in *The Man Who Shot Liberty Valance*, as the James Stewart legend is held to have become fact by Editor Scott. Ford presents us with both myth and history and explains their relationship. As in *My Darling Clementine*, we are presented with the ideological construct that is the West of legend/mythology, and told that it is history. But in *The*

Still: The Man Who Shot Liberty Valance – *watched by Pompey (Woody Strode), Tom Doniphon (John Wayne) gives the cactus rose to Hallie (Vera Miles). Ransom Stoddard (James Stewart) washes up; the Ericsons (John Qualen and Jeanette Nolan) cook.*

Man Who Shot Liberty Valance we are also presented with the process by which legend becomes fact, history becomes myth, and ideology is constructed. This essay proposes a similar strategy to that of Editor Scott. It presumes that the 'legend' of Western expansion has become the 'fact' of the various print and film texts that it takes as its source material. Those texts themselves have a history, but they also contain an idea of history, and of the West as history, which is itself 'legend' rather than 'fact' – mythology. The subject of my enquiry is mythology rather than history; to be more precise, it is the history of a mythology which masquerades as history but, like the Senator, knows itself to be lying.

Legend becoming fact is a description of the process of history being written, for Ford and for empiricist historians alike – although, of the two, Ford might well feel happier with the definition. In this, Ford follows tradition. The Western is always a story of vanishing Americans. The frontier is always closing, having encountered History and retreated West. By the time we get to tell stories about the frontier, it has gone. The frontier was inscribed as History into fiction almost at the moment of its happening, and that inscription involved a recognition that what was being inscribed had passed. Wayne Michael Sarf offers two versions of a similar story: 'In 1849 the famous mountain man and guide Kit Carson . . . had an odd experience when he sought to free a white woman held captive by some Apaches, who, however, killed her and escaped: in their camp Carson found a paperback novel, its cover showing him rescuing a fair maiden from fiendish red men. In one possibly apocryphal tale, Carson, shown a journal cover that had him protecting a terrified female while dead Indians littered the surrounding countryside, is quoted as remarking: "That there might be true but I hain't got no reckerlection of it." ' (Sarf, *God Bless You, Buffalo Bill: A Layman's Guide to History and the Western Film*, Fairleigh Dickinson University Press, Rutherford, New Jersey, 1983, p.253).

Implicit in Sarf's remark that one anecdote is 'possibly apocryphal' is an idea that history is inherently verifiable, authentic. But Western history – and particularly the history of 1860-90 that has become the dominant subject-matter of Westerns – has been constructed as a form of mythology, which is not susceptible to rules of evidence. On the localised scale, the fictional account of the gunfight at the OK Corral, for instance, existed as a piece of public cultural property before the historically accurate version of it was written. The corrective, revisionist history can never be free of the legend because historically the only consequential element in those events is their legendary status. The formulation of the myth of the frontier preceded the events that would provide its content, and the ideological framework provided by the myth governed the choice of material for Western history. Then the procedures of narrative fiction operated on the now-legendary events to transform them into the material of Western myth, which wrote itself as history, and identified the time of its occurrence as a moment of vanishment. The legend is inescapable. The history exists because the legend exists. The history of the West is in a sense a subgenre of the Western, and revisionist history a subgenre of that.

This essay treats Ford's films as typical instances of a generic discourse, rather than exceptional cases to be revered for their merits or their internal coherence. I want neither to make nor attack an auteurist assessment of Ford; my justification for using such familiar material is largely that, in the synthesis of *auteur* and genre studies, the critical historiography of the Western has accorded Ford an institutional status comparable only to that of James Fenimore Cooper. The auteurist approach to Hollywood has taken Ford as its archetype, and his Westerns are on the whole the most highly regarded of his films, the paradigms used by auteurists to explain such apparent aberrations as *Donovan's Reef* (1963). Within the canons of film criticism, Monument Valley came to represent the landscape of the West and to encourage by the extremes of its appearance a view of Westerns as abstracted and allegorical. Because of the Western's paradigmatic status in genre theory, students taking introductory courses with titles like '*Auteur* and Genre: Two Critical Approaches to Hollywood' discover, year after year, that the Western is where Hollywood discusses American History, in which the wilderness becomes a garden, and that the Western looks like *Stagecoach* or *My Darling Clementine* or *The Searchers*.

Despite critical claims to the contrary, there is little that is 'original' in Ford's synthesis, but this observation should not be understood as denigratory. The point of comparing *The Searchers* to *Nick of the Woods* (1837), or *The Man Who Shot Liberty Valance* to 'The Big Bear of Arkansaw' (1854) is not to

Still: My Darling Clementine – *the West as an ideological construct.*

counter acclamation of Ford's creative originality or canonic vision, or to suggest derivations, but to examine the persistence of archetypes and discursive frameworks in an attempt to interrogate the kind of cultural discourse that takes place within the framework of the Western. Variation and modulation have long been all that is possible in the Western, and to worry about originality is to display a profound misunderstanding of the workings of the genre or of myth. Every Western is a palimpsest, a manuscript written on the pages of an earlier, now partially erased, book which carries traces of its previous inscriptions.

John Ford's work is permeated with a sense of History, existing both as an external force on the films' narratives and, within the films, as an agency of motivation for his characters. *Wagon Master* (1950) begins with a song whose opening line is 'A hundred years have come and gone since 1849.' *She Wore a Yellow Ribbon* (1949) begins with the impact of the news of Custer's defeat at Little Big Horn – the event fictionalised in *Fort Apache* (1948). In talking about *My Darling Clementine*, Ford insisted on the historical accuracy of his depiction of the gunfight at the OK Corral, claiming conversations with Wyatt Earp as his primary source. Placing his films in history is not, however, limited to this external referencing. In describing the process of writing *Fort Apache*, Frank Nugent relates that Ford made him produce a biography for every character in the picture, accounting for what had brought him or her to the point where they enter the story:

'He gave me a list of about fifty books to read – memoirs, novels, anything about the period. Later he sent me down into the Old Apache country to nose around, get the smell and feel of the land. When I got back, Ford asked if I thought I had enough research. I said yes. "Good," he said. "Now just forget everything you've read and we'll start writing a movie" ' (Lindsay Anderson, *About John Ford*, Plexus, London, 1981, pp.243-244).

The process of learning and forgetting which Nugent describes is recurrent in Ford's films and to be understood as part of the revision of history, 'printing the legend'. The most conspicuous device by which it is introduced is through Ford's graveside scenes. In *She Wore a Yellow Ribbon*, the personal history of Captain Nathan Brittles (John Wayne) and the military history of Custer's Last Stand are tied together through reminiscence at the graveside of his wife Mary: 'We had some sad news today, Mary. George Custer was killed, with his whole command. Miles Keogh. You remember Miles, happy-go-lucky Irishman, who used to waltz so well with you. Yeah, I know, I guess I was a little jealous. I never could waltz myself.' Ford's films are consciously retrospective in that a sense of the past as an active force in the present is ingrained in them. The films, too, reverberate among themselves, echoing each other in ways of which we and they are always at least half-conscious. There is, for example, a remarkable consistency in the characters John Wayne plays: Tom Doniphon is a tragic version of

the Ringo Kid from *Stagecoach* (1939), and both of them, like Ethan Edwards in *The Searchers* (1956), Kirby York in *Fort Apache* and Nathan Brittles, are excluded from history.

Ford spoke of his last Western, *Cheyenne Autumn*, as somewhere between an apologia and an apology to the Navajos playing the Cheyenne extras:

'I had wanted to make it for a long time. I've killed more Indians than Custer, Beecher and Chivington put together, and people in Europe always want to know about the Indians. There are two sides to every story, but I wanted to show their point of view for a change' (Peter Bogdanovich, *John Ford*, Studio Vista, London, 1967, p.104).

In *Cheyenne Autumn*, motifs from previous films, particularly *She Wore a Yellow Ribbon*, are transferred from Whites to Indians. Ben Johnson's escape from Indian pursuit in that film is repeated across the same scenery by an Indian escaping from Whites. Only the screen direction is reversed. Where, in *She Wore a Yellow Ribbon*, the Seventh Cavalry are consigned with 'only a cold page in the history books to mark their passage', in *Cheyenne Autumn*, the Cheyennes' trek is described as 'a footnote in history'. More significant to Ford's rhetoric is the sense in which the Chief's funeral echoes that of 'Trooper Clay'. In *Cheyenne Autumn*, the values inherent in these motifs are transferred wholesale from their previous location in the small Western community or the Cavalry to the Indians. In the process, Ford provides a new critique of White Western figures in James Stewart's gambling, knockabout version of Wyatt Earp, and of White motivations, when a newspaper editor tells his staff:

'In the *Sun*, *Times*, *Chronicle*, take your pick, they're all saying the same thing we're saying: burning, killing, violating beautiful white women. It's not news any more. We're going to take a different tack. From now on, we're going to grieve for the noble Red man. We'll sell more papers that way.'

But the depiction of the Cheyennes remains couched firmly in the rhetoric of Ford's previous communities, and is mediated through the film's White stars: Richard Widmark, Carroll Baker, Mike Mazurki, and Edward G. Robinson as Secretary of the Interior Carl Schurz – who celebrates the end of the Cheyennes' trek by offering them cigars in place of their empty peace-pipes, in effect reproducing the image of the cigar-store Indian.

Learning and forgetting, making legend fact, are as much part of the critical history of the Western as they are part of the genre's work. The notion of the Western as heroic events set in a time which has just passed into legend, of the West as an era which is ending or has just ended, is something which has also been passed on to the Western itself. Almost never in its history has the death of the Western not been predicted. That demise, however, might more appropriately be seen as a displaced acknowledgement that the cultural contradictions implicit in the Western narrative are not susceptible to resolution. It is notable that the Western has

Still: Little Wolf (Ricardo Montalban) and Dull Knife (Gilbert Roland) in Cheyenne Autumn.

received particular academic attention at moments of its apparent demise. Frederick Jackson Turner wrote 'The Significance of the Frontier in American History' (1893) in the wake of the declaration by the Bureau of the Census that a frontier line no longer existed. The Western myth made available a rhetoric, a discursive framework by which a national self-image of the self-righteousness of Manifest Destiny could be maintained. That rhetoric was kept as currency by the culture industries and interrogated as historical evidence by academics, but the ideological trade was conducted by others. As in the 1840s and the 1890s, in the early 1960s, at the moment of nostalgic regret at the death of frontier values, a New Frontier was manufactured. Its frontiersman, too, became the sacrificed hero of a tragic optimism.

A reductive version of the twentieth-century myth would suggest that the Western triangle, of Indian, Westerner and woman – of savagery, heroism and civilisation – is shaped so that the hero has to interpose himself between the other two terms, conventionally to save the woman from the corruption of a fate worse than death, less frequently to protect the Indian from what Doc Boone, in the last line of *Stagecoach*, calls 'the blessings of civilisation'. As codified by James Fenimore Cooper, this narrative might be summarised as: The hero goes outside civilisation to protect it from savagery. He does not return.

Cooper's centrality to the development of Western mythology comes from the originality of his synthesis in the Leatherstocking series, in which the frontiersman ceases to be merely the guide and comic acolyte of the light hero of romance and becomes the dramatic protagonist in narratives of tragic optimism or optimistic tragedy. In Cooper's version of the myth, the minor, peripheral characters are saved to continue their optimistic work of natural destruction by the tragic death of the American hero, the 'Saint of the woods'. However noble he may be, Leatherstocking is made to recognise over and over again that he may never settle in the settlements he has made possible, and thus, like the Indian who is his companion and his enemy, he is driven ever westward in dread of the end of the frontier. The inheritor of Indian skills, he is the Indian's nemesis and he shares the Indian's destiny as America's most popular tragic hero. Although Leatherstocking never doubts the incompatibility of the two cultures, part of his contradiction is that the scout is nevertheless a 'medium . . . a link between them [the Indians] and civilised life', explaining each to the other (*The Last of the Mohicans*, 1826). It is, centrally, in the contradictions constructed around the frontiersman hero, the Indian fighter as cultural broker, the hunter who explains what he kills to those for whom he kills it, that the rich overdeterminations of the Western have been able to flourish. For while such contradictions cannot be resolved within the narrative, they provide opportunities for inflecting a given plot either to a comic celebration of the entry into marriage, or to a tragic meditation upon the cost of such an optimistic outcome.

One cultural function of the post-Civil-War Western was to provide a meeting ground for Southern codes of chivalry and Northern, commercial versions of Manifest Destiny. The optimistic version of this encounter was the transcendent Western hero eulogised by Robert Warshow in his essay on the Westerner (Warshow, 1954) as 'the last gentleman', personified in Owen Wister's *The Virginian, A Horseman of the Plains* (1902) as the civiliser who lives by the code of the West and settles down to run his ranch with his Eastern schoolmarm bride.

In the tragic account, however, the white Southerner is a scapegoat hero. Having refused either to surrender or to resign his allegiance to the Confederate States of America at the end of the Civil War, Ethan Edwards is the Western hero as displaced Southerner, in search of a new site for his racist anxieties. The Comanches who have captured his niece represent only one of the targets for the misanthropic intensity of his racial hatred. 'Our racial prejudice and our guilt for it', says Brian Henderson, 'are placed on his shoulders, then he is criticized, excluded, or lampooned, mythically purging us of them . . . Ethan is excluded for our sins; that is why we find it so moving' (Henderson, 1985, p.447). Henderson perceives *The Searchers* as offering a liberal commentary on White/Black relations, but in order to achieve the necessary structural parallelism to make his case, he finds it necessary to propose that the secondary hero of the film, Martin Pawley (Jeffrey Hunter), who is one-eighth Cherokee, functions 'in the unconscious symbolics of the film as pure

Still: Two Rode Together – *Guthrie watches as Elena experiences the reactions of the army wives.*

Indian'. The 'unconscious symbolics', therefore, equate with the overt racism of Ethan Edwards, the hero, whose horror of miscegenation casts him in the mould of Leatherstocking, the 'man without a cross' in his blood. As Henderson points out, Ethan's concern for racial purity is inconsistent; he seems unconcerned by either of Martin's prospective marriages, to Look (Beulah Archuletta) or Laurie Jorgensen (Vera Miles), to Indian or White. One might hypothesise a number of options from Ethan's inconsistency: that his concern is exclusively with family, from which he repeatedly excludes Martin; that, despite his superficial racist aggression to Martin, he in fact regards him as White and therefore a suitable marriage partner for Laurie, while having no more objection to Martin's taking a squaw than Generals Crook or Custer had to their soldiers raping Indian women; or, perhaps, that Martin's one-eighth Cherokee blood was on the female side, and therefore culturally acceptable.

Ethan Edwards is Ford's most rabid Indian-hater, and it is a commonplace in critical discussion of *The Searchers* that Chief Scar (Henry Brandon) is Ethan's dark, libidinous id. Throughout the film, they are closely paralleled. Ethan's arrival at the farm precedes Scar's by a day; Scar seeks revenge for the death of his two sons, while Ethan seeks revenge for his lost family. If Scar is the despoiler of the family, the home and centre of ritual in Ford, Ethan, too, disrupts ceremonies – Laurie's wedding, and, in a different sense, the home ceremonies of Martha (Dorothy Jordan) and Aaron (Walter Coy). He more violently disrupts Ford's most sacred ceremony, the funeral, not once, but twice. Ethan and Scar are locked in combat over the possession of women, Martha and Debbie (Natalie Wood): the Indian enacts what is, by force of social taboo, proscribed to the White man. Their combat is timeless: time passes in *The Searchers* without being accounted

for. The story covers perhaps seven years, but only Debbie, to whom the passing of time means the threat of sexual maturity, grows any older.

Critical recognition of the parallel in *The Searchers* between White hero and Indian villain derives from responses to Ethan's psychological extremism. Where attitudes similar to Ethan's are expressed by the eminently balanced Guthrie McCabe in *Two Rode Together*, critics have shown no inclination to identify either Quanah Parker (like Scar, played by Henry Brandon) or Stone Calf (Woody Strode) as 'unseen, ungovernable forces of the libido' (Joseph McBride and Michael Wilmington, *John Ford*, Secker & Warburg, London, 1974, p.154). While the casting of Woody Strode might be expected to function as a device for making the allegory explicit (the African-American, who is the true subject of the movie's discourse on racism, is disguised as an Indian), racism instead appears as a social convention, institutionalised and quite acceptable. In comparison with *The Searchers*, *Two Rode Together* reads poorly as a civil rights allegory; it asks for sympathy and cultural acceptance only for the White women who have been tainted by Indian life, not for the Indians. But when Elena describes to McCabe how Whites look at her –

'These people . . . their eyes are all on my body, like dirty fingers, as if they would turn their backs, I would leap upon them and my touch would have to be washed off like filth . . . Now I see the silent questions. How many braves has she known? How many mestizo children carry her blood in their veins? Why didn't I kill myself when I took a Comanche?'

– his response is to force her into an embrace and kiss her. Elena is the impossible object, the unsullied victim of atrocity. The transparency of her skin, her perfect teeth, the conventions of Hollywood's presentation of female beauty as object of the male gaze, belie her and McCabe's description of life among the Comanches. For the audience, her spiritual virtue shines out of her physical appearance. But the other characters, bound by restrictions of plot and convention, perceive the survival of her beauty quite differently, as itself a sign of her degradation. The female survivors of Ford's captivity narratives are dark women, physically unmarked by their ordeal, unlike their fair counterparts. To survive as a woman in the wilderness, to be degraded and yet unblemished, is to embody a contradiction in patriarchy's construction of true womanhood: to indicate, perhaps, a forbidden desire. The return of the captive woman now lacking a proper social place is precisely the Return of the Repressed. Of no worth and highly valued, an object of pity and of desire, Elena generates McCabe's libidinous desire because she has no property value, because having already been degraded and rendered valueless, she cannot be further defiled. The sign of Elena's beauty must be understood in its ambiguity. The White woman who has 'lived as one of them', become 'Comanch', now embodies the appeal of 'the forbidden, the beautiful-horrible "other"' . . . an alternative world and culture, erotically and socially freer than our own, antithetical to and an escape from the civilisation that both sustains and discomforts us' (Slotkin, 1985, p.95). *Two Rode Together* makes no attempt to resolve these contradictions. They are merely stated, and ended by a conclusion that imposes gratuitous romance on frontier tragedy.

Women, whose structural function is to elevate men to a higher plane of civilisation, can themselves be reduced to a lower plane by the consequences of capture. The Western's division of heroines into light and dark – schoolmarm and saloon-girl – is rigorously maintained by the movies. The dark heroine is doomed by her knowledge of the hero's sexuality, but the fair, for instance the blonde women captives in *The Searchers*, can be degraded out of their skin colour into a self-perpetuating Otherness. When the sergeant of their guard comments, 'It's hard to believe they're White', Ethan Edwards is insistent: 'They ain't White – any more. They're Comanch.' When Ethan finds that Debbie has become Scar's woman, he disowns her, making a new will declaring that he is 'without any blood kin'. The White woman 'defiled' by Indians has lost her property rights along with her property value. Elena's appearance, however, is a sign of Hollywood's capacity to represent but not to resolve contradiction. Like Debbie in *The Searchers*, Elena has become Indian, and retained her innocence: although Stone Calf treated her as his wife, there were no children. Elena is thus also figured as the Indian Princess, the representation of America as virgin soil for the settler.

There is a similar contradiction in the image of Stone Calf: the threat is intense, but easily defeated. The perception of Indian cultural weakness was at times entangled with the representation of the Indian's potency. Against the puritan myth of the Indian

'as insatiably lustful, a being of overbearing sexual power' (Richard Slotkin, *Regeneration through Violence: The Mythology of the American Frontier, 1600-1800*, Wesleyan University Press, Middletown, Connecticut, 1973, p.202) ran a counterstrain impugning his virility. The Comte de Buffon, arguing his environmentalist thesis about the American continent, blamed Indian impotence for their cultural demise:

'They have no ardour for women, and, of course, no love of mankind . . . Everything must be referred to the first cause. They are indifferent because they are weak; and this indifference to sex is the original strain which disgraces Nature, prevents her from expanding, and, by destroying the germs of life, cuts the root of society' (quoted in Robert K. Berkhofer, *The White Man's Indian: Images of the American Indian from Columbus to the Present*, Vintage Books, New York, 1978, p.43).

The anonymous author of *A Narrative of the Capture of Certain Americans at Westmoreland* (1780) observed, 'I don't remember to have heard an instance of these savages offering to violate the chastity of any of the fair sex who have fallen into their hands . . . This is principally owing to a natural inappetency in their constitution' (quoted in Winthrop D. Jordan, *White Over Black: American Attitudes towards the Negro, 1550-1812*, Penguin Books, Baltimore, Maryland, 1969, pp.162-163).

The contrasting representations of Indians are clearly incompatible, and if I were engaged in a project that sought to make *Two Rode Together* a coherent object, I would have to decide whether Stone Calf was the raping, murdering savage or not, and whether Elena is White property or Indian princess. Fortunately, however, that is not my aim. My account of the Western's generic history sees the Western as several things at once – a myth of origin, an adolescent male fantasy, an account of the individual's relation to society, and more. It is seldom only one of these things, particularly in its twentieth-century version, where the accretions of significance make it excessively meaningful. The Western is a myth written in such condensed script that its images and events are massively overdetermined with multiple significances. Its prevalence in American culture is the result of this overdetermination, and of its capacity to cross several fields of American experience, while retaining the same structure. It is written by and written in the assumptions of American culture; they are not so much its subject as its speech. The fact that American culture tells itself the Western story over and over again may even be to convince itself that its evasion of contradiction will pass as a resolution.

The twentieth-century Western is largely written in the metaphors of its eighteenth- and nineteenth-century antecedents, but the ideological currency of those metaphors has changed. The evident fact to which Brian Henderson draws attention, that the issue of Indian-White miscegenation was hardly current in 1956, makes it available as a signifier for other sets of relationships, but it is also true that the traces of its earlier significations are neither purged from it nor totally obscured by its more topical application. Thomas Jefferson would have recognised John Ford's Indians as noble or ignoble savages in conformity with Enlightenment precepts. The idea of savagism, which developed through the first half of the nineteenth century, located the Indian's place in the discourse of History as Progress. The anthropology of Edward Tyler and Lewis Henry Morgan later in the century merely compounded the existing terms of the myth of frontier conflict. In 1877, the subtitle of Morgan's book *Ancient Society* asserted that his *Researches in the Lines of Human Progress from Savagery Through Barbarism to Civilization* did indeed chart the process of History. What made it possible for Whites to incorporate the indigenous Americans as empty, malleable signifiers into their symbolic system was the White insistence, almost from first contact, that the indigenous oral culture could have no history, merely a mythology. What was pre-Columbian, pre-literate, was prehistoric. Understanding their history as an evolution according to the law of progress, Whites placed Indians in the past (see Roy Harvey Pearce, *Savagism and Civilisation: A Study of the Indian and the American Mind*, University of California Press, Berkeley, 1988, p.49). The confrontation between savagery and civilisation was seen to take place at the beginning of historical time. In *The Man Who Shot Liberty Valance*, the confrontation takes place at the moment, quite literally, of the territory's entry into the history of the United States. We can understand the Western as a myth of Origin, a story of becoming, the struggle of the frontier settlers to bring the frontier into history. Once the frontier was closed and the Indian threat had vanished, the Indian could be cast in granite or copper as a symbol in need of no further modification in line with any subsequent scientific, anthropological, or historical thought. Indians have not been significantly modified since, merely repainted.

Two Rode Together sustains an economic metaphor, in which women and Indians are regarded as property, and the characters who so regard them are disapproved of for this. When McCabe explains to Marty (Shirley Jones) what her brother would now be like (correctly, in terms of the film's representations of Indians), he goes beyond describing his appearance to tell her, 'given the chance, sister, he'd rape you . . . and when he'd finished he'd trade you off to one of the other bucks for a good knife or a bad rifle.' Quanah Parker engages in exactly such trade, of people for guns and knives, with McCabe. Elena knows that 'Stone Calf will never let me go', because she is property, but, like the other 'debased' women in the Indian camp, she believes 'I am not worth fighting for'. Like Henry J. Wringle (Willis Bouchey), McCabe finds that hunting for captives interferes with business, and he attempts to turn his errand into the wilderness into a business venture. During his exchange with Major Forsyth (John McIntire), he reveals his plans to rescue captives for money.

The Major demands, 'Just how much do you think human lives are worth, McCabe?' 'Whatever the market will bear, no more, no less', McCabe replies. Leaving the young male captive he plans to sell to Wringle with Jim Geary (Richard Widmark), he tells him, 'Keep an eye on Junior, Jim. You know he's worth a thousand bucks to me' – an uncomfortable, if ignored, double entendre. But Wringle rejects his goods: 'You couldn't pay me to take in a mad dog like that.' When McCabe protests about the boy being claimed by another family, Geary insists, 'You heard Henry J. He wouldn't take him as a gift.'

In Hollywood, Love conquers economics: Marty, like Jim, is unconcerned about the Army's low pay. Those who would make people property receive their comeuppance: Stone Calf is killed; Belle (Annelle Hayes), who tells Elena 'Everything around here belongs to me, including the livestock', loses McCabe to Elena. McCabe's desire restores Elena's knowledge of her true value as that capitalist contradiction, the property which is without price. But that contradictory process of valuation which is the containment of greed can be understood only in terms of the movie's running economic metaphor: Jim's last line to Belle, as McCabe and Elena depart for California, is 'I guess old Guth finally found something he wanted more than ten per cent of.' Having bought Elena from Quanah Parker, McCabe discovers a value outside the bourgeois processes of valuation, and invests it in the property called woman.

Women in the Western represent civilisation because they represent property values. Savages, who do not respect or acknowledge the value of property, are a threat to be exterminated. Naturally, they direct this lack of respect against civilisation's most cherished symbol of property, woman. The White woman's symbolic role as the embodiment of the civilisation that will destroy the wilderness and replace the frontier is not a position of power. As the bearer of children, civilisation, progress and history, she may represent an inevitable abstract force, but as an individual she is vulnerable to degradation – the fate worse than death from which Hatfield (John Carradine) aims to save Mrs Mallory (Louise Platt) with his last bullet in *Stagecoach*. Brian Henderson says of *The Searchers*:

'Scar's crimes – rape, murder, dismemberment, burning – eminently violate the law that dictates postponement of pleasure. His acts stand in for the terrifying libido that must be repressed and, if unrepressed, must be punished drastically. His crimes "stand in" for libido because, of course, libido cannot be represented' ('*The Searchers*: An American Dilemma' in *Movies and Methods* volume II, edited by Bill Nichols, University of California Press, Berkeley, 1985, p.436).

The Indian Other has done what may not be done, and may not be admitted to have been desired, and may not be shown. The majority of Western narratives, even in the postwar period, have retained the tradition of coy discretion in describing the fate worse than death, leaving the audience to 'fill in the blanks', to invent what, in *The Searchers*, Ethan Edwards and the movie 'thought it best to keep from you'. Henderson notes the effect this device has in requiring the viewer to project fantasies on to the film, and thus to identify with the violation and also the need to punish it. This process, which gives pleasure by exercising libido and reassurance by suppressing it, imaginatively reconstitutes the structure of the male self.

'Racist, me? My best friends are blacks: Woody Strode and my servant, who's lived with me for thirty years' (John Ford, quoted in Gallagher, 1986, p.342).

In 1960, the year before he made *Two Rode Together*, Ford made *Sergeant Rutledge*, also with Woody Strode, who plays the eponymous central character, the 'top soldier' of a Ninth Cavalry unit, accused of the murder of his commanding officer and the rape and murder of his sixteen-year-old daughter. At the climax of the courtroom drama around which the film is structured, it is revealed that the actual killer is the post's storekeeper (Fred Libby), who was driven by uncontrollable desire: 'I had to, I had to! Don't you understand? She – the way she walked, the way her body moved. She drove me crazy! I had to have her, I had to, I had to. Oh, God help me, God help me.' If Elena's account of 'the eyes on my body' sparks McCabe's desire, the beginning of *Sergeant Rutledge* inverts the pattern to repeat the threat in *The Searchers*. Fair Mary Beecher (Constance Towers) is confronted with the savage threat – first Strode, then Strode's warning of the Indians – immediately after she has been violently seized and kissed by Tom, the White officer hero (Jeffrey Hunter), on this occasion playing a 'man without a cross' in his blood). In each case, the 'provoking' of White male desire is linked to the Indian sexual threat. Ethan's psychopathic performance permits the schizophrenic/symbiotic relation between frontiersman hero and Indian villain to be rendered explicit, but the patterns described in *The Searchers* are reproduced, less emphatically, in *Stagecoach*, *My Darling Clementine*, *Two Rode Together* and *The Man Who Shot Liberty Valance*.

In *Sergeant Rutledge*, which deals overtly with White racist representations of blacks – with what Angela Davis calls 'the myth of the black rapist' – the Indians are as stereotyped as in *Stagecoach*. Strode plays Rutledge as a figure who instils into his men a belief that 'We're fighting to make us proud'; 'some day', he says, the Buffalo Soldier will have achieved sufficient dignity and pride to be accepted by Whites as 'a man' and not 'a swamprunnin' nigger'. The struggle to achieve this entry into White history (understood as progress) is a battle waged against the Indian, who in *Sergeant Rutledge* is represented entirely without sympathetic consideration. In the attack on the railroad station, Rutledge gives Mary his revolver, saying, 'You're a Western woman, you can use a gun. They'll have no mercy on you, lady, they'll have no mercy.' In the river ambush, we see the Indians blending into the land-

Still: Sergeant Rutledge – *Mary Beecher (Constance Towers) and the 'top soldier' (Woody Strode).*

scape, hiding in the tall grass by the banks, and when they attack, they seem to 'spring up out of the earth' – the words Mary used to describe her first encounter with Rutledge – 'like a nightmare'.

Rutledge's task, throughout the film, is to overcome the stereotyping of him as a raping, murdering savage, by demonstrating his difference from the raping, murdering savages who are in the movie. Rutledge's right to a place in history is asserted by his disciplined military prowess, demonstrated most spectacularly by his skill in killing Indians. The old Sergeant Skidmore (Juano Hernandez) explains to Mary Beecher (the invocation of Harriet Beecher Stowe in her name seems hardly incidental) that a 'soldier can't never think by his heart, ma'am, he's got to think by the book'. Rutledge shows that he has absorbed 'the book' of law, regulation, and the postponement of gratification, in the moment when, rather than make his escape, 'something kept telling me I had to go back'. The Black soldier demonstrates his innocence of the symbolic burden of the White man's guilt and repressed desire by his possession of that White puritan virtue, the inner voice that postpones pleasure.

In *Two Rode Together*, Strode is the raping murdering savage that he is not in *Sergeant Rutledge*: the Black actor playing the Indian playing the White man's libido is different from the Black actor playing the Black character trying to demonstrate that he is not symbolic of the White man's libido. Who is disguised as whom? Which of these is the Vanishing American with whom, according to Leslie Fiedler, the White boy first essays manhood? (Fiedler, 1968, p.182). And who, for that matter, is concealed behind a white man such as Henry Brandon (Quanah Parker in *Two Rode Together*, Chief Scar in *The Searchers*) 'playing Indian'?

There are precursors for Woody Strode's embodiment of the Child of Darkness in *Two Rode Together*. In William Gilmore Simms's *The Yemassee* (1835), one of the minor characters defies the Indians who are about to torture him: 'Ay, ye miserable red nagers, – ye don't frighten Teddy Macnamara now so aisily.' In Robert Montgomery Bird's *Nick of the Woods* (1837), Colonel Tom Bruce, commander of the station, talks of killing 'two of the red niggurs' in revenge for Major Forrester's death. Fiedler suggests that, in *Adventures of Huckleberry Finn*, Mark Twain 'turned his Negro protagonist into a Noble Savage, i.e. an Indian in blackface,' and notes Cooper's use, on the title page of *The Last of the Mohicans*, of Othello's line, 'Mislike me not for my complexion', as an instance of what he calls 'the mythological adaptation . . . of the Negro character to the myth of the Indian.' Caliban, he argues, contains within himself an anticipatory history of both Red and Black American destinies. Described as both 'a savage and [a] deformed slave', Caliban is the victim of Prospero's expropriation and his attempts to civilise him. For having tried to rape the White man's daughter, he is enslaved. With the White renegades, who introduce him to liquor, he stages an unsuccessful revolt (*see* Fiedler, 1968, and *Love and Death in the American Novel*, 1960).

The question we must ask is not so much whether or not White culture has sought to represent indigenous people accurately, as what aspect of itself it has understood them to represent. In the confrontation between savagery and civilisation which is at the heart of frontier myth, the 'Indian' has been cast as the savage. But our recognition of the function 'Indian/savage' cannot be restricted to persons of an appropriate skin colour or make-up. On the nineteenth-century stage and throughout Hollywood history, White actors and actresses have taken the speaking parts in 'speaking for the Indian'. But if the Indian is a creature of White mythology, played by Whites who disguise themselves as savages in order to behave savagely, then it is an arbitrary confirmation of a racist definition of difference to presume that the 'savage' function in the Western myth is only represented by White performers in 'Indian' costume. Savagery must be a more mobile function than such a limited prescription suggests.

The mythology of the Western adopted from the Puritans the practice of displacing forbidden desires on to people called savages, so that 'the extermination of the Indian became a cleansing of those sins from their own midst as well as the destruction of a feared enemy' (Slotkin, 1985, p.63). The purpose of the errand into the wilderness was to return unsullied. Captivity and hunter narratives alike present the encounter with the wilderness as an act of regression into a primal world where the Children of Light must combat the Children of Darkness. For if, as Robert Berkhofer explains, 'they can maintain their racial/cultural integrity in that world,

and if they can defeat the forces that seek to prevent their return to civilisation, then on their return they will be capable of renewing the moral and physical powers of the society they originally left' (Berkhofer, 1978, p.27). But the entry into the wilderness was a regression, and its danger and its temptation lay in the possibility of being mastered by the wilderness rather than mastering it. Implicit in the idea of regression was the notion that the wilderness had the power to make the civilised savage. For puritan captives, both their chastity and their souls were at issue. The hunter, 'who learns from the Indians only in order to destroy them and so make the woods safe for the white woman' (Slotkin, 1985, p.64) risks descending into savagery himself. As one character declares in *Nick of the Woods*, 'D-n me; for I'm a white Injun, and there's nothing more despisable.'

This is Leatherstocking's dilemma. With his incessant proclamation that he is 'a man without a cross', Cooper's hero, more than any other character, insists on his own racial purity. That purity also ensures his chastity, the force that motivates Western heroism, displacing sexuality into violence and guaranteeing a resolution in blood. Cooper kills his dark heroine, Cora of the tainted blood, who is desired by Uncas and Magua alike, rather than permit the forbidden act of dark seduction. Even though she is already, in her father's words, 'degraded' by her mother's ancestry, the deaths of all the novel's dark characters do not offer the possibility of compromise or integration. When, at the funeral of Cora and Uncas, Colonel Munro asks Hawkeye to tell the Lenape that 'the time shall not be distant when we may assemble around His throne without distinction of sex, or rank, or colour', the scout replies, 'To tell them this . . . would be to tell them that the snows come not in the winter, or that the sun shines fiercest when the trees are stripped of their leaves.'

But if the hero may not legitimately commune with the Other, he can easily disguise himself as one of them, as Martin does in *The Searchers* by taking off his shirt and throwing a blanket over his shoulder. The White man, and particularly the Indian Hater, may become an Indian at his convenience. In *Nick of the Woods*, 'Wrapping his blanket about his shoulders, and assuming the gait of a savage, [Nathan] stalked boldly forwards . . . relying on his disguise as all-sufficient to avert suspicion.' John Cawelti and Christine Bold have both commented on the frequency of the motif of disguise in the dime novel: in discussing the Deadwood Dick novels, Bold observes, 'It is not unusual to find Calamity Jane (the name itself a disguise) dressed up as Deadwood Dick dressed up as an old man, or to have two false Deadwood Dicks, the real one being disguised as a female fortune-teller, all in the same episode' (Bold, *Selling the Wild West: Popular Western Fiction, 1860-1960*, University of Indiana Press, 1987, p.14). Cawelti suggests that the frequency of the disguise motif in children's literature can be explained in terms of the ease with which it provides for experimenting with roles (Cawelti, 1976, p.212). There is, however, inevitably a degree of equivocation in

Still: Sergeant Rutledge – *Mary and Rutledge.*

all this cultural cross-dressing, a desire to escape the burden of one or other restricted, conventional role, most strongly the desire to escape the repressions of Whiteness. (Kenneth J.M.D. Munden's 'A Contribution to the Psychological Understanding of the Cowboy and His Myth' in *American Imago*, vol.15, no.2, Summer 1958, pp.103-148, provides a starting point for consideration of the Western as oedipal fantasy; *see also* Leslie Fiedler's argument that the true 'romance in the woods' is the ' "undisturbed and happy intercourse" of the White and Red male friends', Fiedler, 1968, p.116.) Throughout the dime novel, disguise also serves as a convenient device to cover over a central contradiction in Western narrative: the incompatibility of East and West within the conventional structures of romance. From Oliver Effingham's masquerade as Edwards in Fenimore Cooper's *The Pioneers* (1823), Western heroes have revealed themselves to be Easterners in disguise, genteel enough after all to conclude the romance by leading the heroine to the altar for the conventional wedding. In some dime novels, the same process

takes place across the sexual divide, when the Indian girl is discovered to be an upper-class White girl captured and educated by the Indians but (like Debbie in *The Searchers*) fundamentally unchanged: 'beneath the savage costume she was almost as genteel as ever' (quoted in Smith, 1950, p.112).

Examining the representation of the 'tragic mulatta' passing for White in *Imitation of Life*, *Show Boat* and other movies, Mary Ann Doane suggests that enacting the Other in order to create the self is at least potentially more problematic than Nate Salesbury found it. Using White actresses to play these parts poses 'a threat to the epistemological basis of typecasting (as well as to the very idea of racial categorization). A curious distanciation attends the knowledge that one is watching a white pretending to be a black pretending to be a white. There is one body too much.' Looking at *The Birth of a Nation* (D.W. Griffith, 1915), she suggests that it can be understood as:

'. . . a discourse on disguise as the operative mode of race relations . . . The black figures with the most important roles are actually acted by whites in blackface . . . Skin – which would seem to be the most stable guarantor of racial difference and the ground of its instant recognisability – is transformed from immediacy to sign. Blackness is a costume which is worn or removed at will by whites, while whiteness in its symbolic dimension (the white robes of the Ku Klux Klan) is also a form of masquerade which conceals an identity. This disengagement of knowledge about racial identity from skin color is consistent with the fact that the legal criterion for racial identity in the United States has historically been linked to blood rather than skin . . . Blackface could only be a hangover from vaudeville or the stage where the operation of the symbolic was not as intimately endangered by the emerging codes of photographic realism' (Doane, *Femmes Fatales: Feminism, Film Theory, Psychoanalysis*, Routledge, London, 1991, pp.227, 235).

The violent controversy generated by *The Birth of a Nation* inhibited Hollywood's use of blackface as a dramatic, rather than a comic device. In this arena of malleable signifiers, the threat of the sexual Other migrated elsewhere, among other places, to its dormant position in the Western, where it is several times disguised. Disguise permits the unification of separate identities, and separate narrative functions, within a single character. In literature, with whatever facility it is employed, it is a facile device. For the movies, disguise is more complex. The audience must see through the disguise to maintain the security of their viewing position and identification; the need for this is most obvious in films involving sexual cross-dressing, but no less legible in the idea of blackface in minstrelsy. At the same time, the transparency of disguise opens up the pretence of verisimilitude and cracks the fiction. The movie both does and does not want its audience to believe that Jeff Chandler (in *Broken Arrow*, Delmer Daves, 1950) or Burt Lancaster (in *Apache*, Robert Aldrich, 1954) is an Indian. But if the star is always himself or herself, thinly disguised as a character, the lesser luminaries of Hollywood inhabit a more incoherent space, where performances actively conflict with each other. In *Two Rode Together*, Woody Strode plays Magua to Stewart's Hawkeye and Widmark's Duncan Hayward; in *Sergeant Rutledge* he plays Uncas/Hawkeye to Jeffrey Hunter's Duncan; in *The Man Who Shot Liberty Valance*, he plays Chingachgook to Wayne's Uncas. A peripheral character in *The Man Who Shot Liberty Valance*, Strode's Pompey is nevertheless the accumulated embodiment of much racial antagonism. He presents us with all the contradictions that are the Other's lot. He is, as the Other always is, an overdetermined sign disguised as an empty signifier. None of these movies makes any significant attempt to resolve the contradictions in the representations of racism circulating around Strode, but there is in each case one Other body too much. To paraphrase Umberto Eco, the clichés begin arguing with each other (Eco, 'Casablanca: Cult Movies and Intellectual Collage" in

Travels in Hyperreality, Picador, London, 1986, p.209). It might even be argued that the cause of the most recent demise of the Western can be found in the emergence of these contradictions in the representation of racism: not so much in the collapse of a Grand Narrative as in the disguise no longer disguising.

Writing of the dime novel, Michael Denning has observed:

'If historical struggles do take place in borrowed costumes and assumed accents, if social and economic divisions appear in disguise, then the source for these disguises and the manifestation of these roles lie in the conventional characters of a society, played out in its popular narratives. The figures and characters one sees in dime novels are perhaps not the self-representation of any class, nor are they the class as represented by another; they are a body of representations that are alternately claimed, rejected, and fought over. . . . These narratives are the dream-work of the social, condensing . . . and displacing . . . the wishes, anxieties, and intractable antinomies of social life in a class society' (Denning, *Mechanic Accents: Dime Novels and Working-Class Culture in America*, Verso, London, 1987, pp.77, 81).

There are no Indians in *The Man Who Shot Liberty Valance* – that is, there are no White performers 'playing Indian'. But there is savagery in another, White guise. As Whites kill the Indian, that part of the White represented by 'the Indian' is not disposed of but left to find a new host. To perform heroic deeds, the Indian-hater needs the Indian; the lawman, similarly, needs the outlaw. The outlaw has learnt his wilderness lessons from Magua, not Chingachgook. But he knows, and is part of, the civilisation he is in rebellion against, and he is aware of a notion of law which he is outside. In *The Man Who Shot Liberty Valance*, Liberty (Lee Marvin) literally tears up the Book of Law. Later, the outlaw wants to be elected to the territorial convention. (Liberty is the agent of the ranchers who want the range kept open, but they are never seen together, and the movie makes no overt attempt to establish the relationship between large-scale business enterprise and anarchic violence.)

The Stoddards' marriage of East and West shows similar signs of discomfort to that of *The Virginian*, although it is Hallie who is the Westerner, civilised by a man who promises to show her real roses. But the return to Shinbone is motivated by Hallie's unrequited love for Doniphon, signified by the Cactus Rose on his coffin. Stoddard can only do for her what schoolmarms do for Virginians: incorporate them into history. However, Stoddard's feminine role-playing – he is teacher, dishwasher, waitress, compromiser – affords him no dignity. In their courtship, Hallie is more mother than lover, and he neither provides nor expects a sexual response. However superficially successful, his marriage and his career have been barren.

The Man Who Shot Liberty Valance is a bleak version of the Western comedy, a Fordian 'problem film'. It disapproves of its hero because it sees through his disguise and yet it cannot bring itself to believe in the survival of heroic virtue. Doniphon's ranch, like Natty's in *The Pioneers* and Ringo's in *Stagecoach*, is outside the community. But for Hallie, unlike Dallas, it is no longer possible to escape from the 'blessings of civilisation' – Doniphon burns down their future home. In following Natty's advice at the end of *The Prairie* (1827), choosing 'the clearing not the prairie', Hallie has perhaps recognised the imperatives of history, which registers progress in the transition of its heroes from 'the private man with a gun to the public man with a lawbook' (Robert B. Ray, *A Certain Tendency of the Hollywood Cinema, 1930-1980*, Princeton University Press, 1985). Doniphon's burning of his ranch-house is a recognition that, like Hannah Clegg in *Two Rode Together*, he is dead; he does not exist in the records of Shinbone. The Saint of the Woods is a martyr. *The Man Who Shot Liberty Valance* recalls Thomas Bangs Thorpe's 1854 story, 'The Big Bear of Arkansaw', in which the hunter becomes what he hunts. Written at and about a moment when the frontier appeared to have closed, it tells the tale of bear hunter Jim Doggett, who becomes so skilful that he clears all the bears out of Arkansas, and is left with nothing to kill once the last great bear, a quasi-mystical beast, surrenders himself to him:

'Doggett is left with the name of the thing he killed and of the place whose spirit the animal was – he is 'The Big Bear of Arkansaw' – but Doggett is also an anachronism, and the last view of him is indeed pathetic: a garrulous, tipsy, backwoodsman booster who vanishes from the steamboat in the night' (Slotkin, 1985, p.131).

At the territorial convention in *The Man Who Shot Liberty Valance*, we see two versions of the West's corruption: one is Doniphon, clumsy, unshaven, dirty, and, like Doggett, conspicuously in irreparable decline; the other is the rope-twirling cowboy, who would grow up to be and is descended from Roy Rogers, the Lone Ranger, Buffalo Bill – the model of Western show business. Doniphon is, somewhat improbably, in an analogous position of knowledge and comprehension to that of Willy Loman in Arthur Miller's *Death of a Salesman* (1949) and other liberal tragedians of the postwar period. Possessed of a precisely delineated degree of knowledge about his circumstances and the reasons for his condition of irrelevance, he can nevertheless do nothing to change his predicament. He tells Stoddard, 'Hallie's your girl now . . . you taught her to read and write. Now give her something to read and write about.' Significantly, this is one scene from which Hallie, the embodiment of the purity of the Western dream, is absent. The cowboy, on the other hand, represents the recuperation of contradictions, the detachment of Western skills and Western narratives from their historical context into a demonstration of pure performance skills. The contradictions which he trivialises and renders childish are resolved in the lie of the legend's triumph when Stoddard is elected, and left bitterly unresolved in Doniphon's vanishment.

The ever-moving frontier line is too unstable to be a place of resolution, and this accounts, in part, for the Western's longevity as allegory. What the Western provides is a discursive framework for the projection of unresolvable conflicts. As an 'empty' allegory for other conflicts, the Western functions as a means of understanding them according to a system of conventions which allows the allegorical expression of contradictions, and recuperates them according to a formula which does not resolve those contradictions. It is a way in which one story is disguised as another, more familiar and comfortable, one. But only so long as the Indian remained disguised as an empty signifier could the Western's narrative function in its contained generic self-consciousness. Contesting the Westerner's claim to the ascription of self, Other and national identity simply made the story of the heroic repression of savagery untellable as a Western. When the Indian as murdering, raping, ignoble savage ceased to be a marketable commodity, the function of savagery migrated to other generic fields, in the main to science fiction and horror movies, where disguise functions, in one sense, more effectively. Carol Clover has constructed a brilliantly perverse account of the generic migration of the 'settler-versus-Indian' story to rape-revenge movies such as *I Spit on Your Grave* (1977):

'. . . by making the representative of urban interests (what would normally be taken as the white male elite) a woman, and the representatives of the country (what would in the western have been Native Americans) white males, these films exactly reverse the usual system of victim sympathies. That is, with a member of the gender underclass (a woman) representing the economic overclass (the urban rich) and members of the gender overclass (males) representing the economic underclass (the rural poor), a feminist politics of rape has been deployed in the service of class and racial guilt. Raped and battered, the haves can rise to annihilate the have-nots – all in the name of feminism' (Carol J. Clover, *Men, Women and Chainsaws: Gender in the Modern Horror Film*, British Film Institute, London, 1992, p.163).

In part because indigenous cultures have to some extent succeeded in establishing autonomous identities for themselves outside the constraints of Otherness, but more because the currently dominant image of the Other is of the Noble Savage, the classical imperial narrative of heroic repression – most classically the Western – can no longer be told, as witness the radical structural revisions undertaken on the most recent cinematic version of *The Last of the Mohicans* (Michael Mann, 1992): in contemporary stories, at least, the Empire is always evil. The imperial narrative has migrated elsewhere, to a more fertile virgin soil of the imagination, where the Alien has no referent, and no-one complains about cultural distortion or argues that Aliens are peaceful hunter-gatherers leading a sustainable existence in a stable eco-system. In space, at least for the time being, no-one can hear you scream about misrepresentation.

WHY DO COWBOYS WEAR HATS IN THE BATH?
Style Politics for the Older Man
Martin Pumphrey

High Plains Drifter

You may remember the scene. The Man With No Name has just ridden into town out of the desert. He's already had a bit of bother in the barber's shop when the three heavies tried to take advantage of him. They didn't count on the gun under the apron. Now he's trying to have a bath. He's in an old tin tub and he'd be absolutely naked if it weren't for the cigar clamped between his teeth. There's some business about lighting it so we know it's there. In fact, a lot is going on. He's talking to the fat, old sheriff, and the dwarf who plays his side-kick is there too. Really, they could all be sitting round a table. The room isn't a bathroom, and the bath just seems out of place. You notice it more when the woman comes in with a gun and starts shooting. She's the one the film has already constructed as dangerous. She walks in the street instead of on the sidewalk. When she challenged the Man earlier, he raped her, and we were invited to agree that she got what she deserved. Now his defencelessness denies the justice of her desire for revenge. How will he escape? He dives under the water. The bullets ricochet harmlessly.

Levi 501s

We're in a tenement room, probably in New York. There's a young man there, blond and good-looking. A police siren wails. He looks out of the window through the Venetian blinds. Now he's putting on a pair of 501s. It's a rather elaborate ritual. The jeans fit with snug comfort as he buttons himself in. He's almost caressing himself, and as he stands half-naked, we see the sharp definition of his stomach muscles. He's obviously enjoying himself. He smooths his hair, and we see him looking at himself in the mirror. Then he turns to the dressing table. Beside his nostalgically period wristwatch is the picture of a girl. Must be *the* girl. He moves towards the bathroom. Next thing, we see him lowering himself, jeans and all, into the bath. We watch as the water creeps up over the crotch. 501s.

I want to talk about how these two bath scenes construe masculinity and examine the by now familiar

Still: Clint Eastwood wearing a cigar in High Plains Drifter, *with Billy Curtis.*

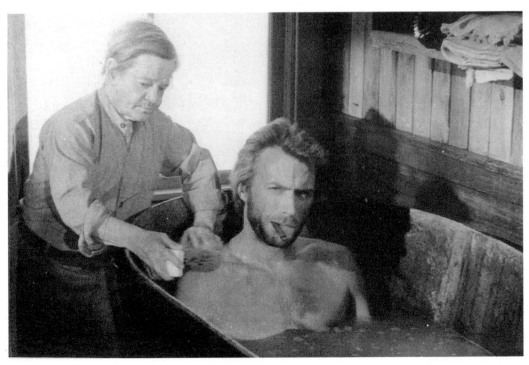

argument that in addressing men as consumers 1980s advertising fashioned a 'new man' for whom the Western is no more than a potential source of postmodern style indicators. I want to consider, that is, the question of change that has been a focus of attention in both popular and academic writing about masculinity. I want to suggest that, though there are few obvious links between the tough, violent, misogynistic masculinity associated with Clint Eastwood and the openly narcissistic, consumer-oriented masculinity of the Levi commercial, the relationship between the two is more usefully read as a dialogue than as an opposition.

The Levi commercial (not surprisingly, given the cowboy associations of earlier Levi campaigns) picks up, inflects and parodies visual codes and anxieties associated with masculinity that have been embedded in the Western almost since its beginnings. As a member of what Frank Mort ('Image Change: High Street Style and the New Man', *New Socialist*, November 1986, pp.6-8) has called 'Old Youth' – the generation of teenagers from the late 1960s/early 1970s whose lives are still structured around youth styles) – I want to consider the implications of the samenesses and differences that are the subject of that dialogue for those like myself who, in growing up, were forced to negotiate with the forms of masculinity that Westerns most emphatically endorsed.

In any discussion of the proliferation of consumer masculinities in the world around us, Westerns are of interest because, at least up to the 1970s, they occupied a prioritised position in relation to twentieth-century constructions of masculinity. Founded on the male point of view and fantasies of White, male power, they were primarily directed at male audiences, and Western heroes, whether fitted out as cowboys, marshals, cavalry officers, scouts, fur-trappers or unidentified drifters, have been regularly invoked as markers against which masculine behaviour should be judged (but see Laura Mulvey's discussion of Westerns and female spectators in 'Afterthoughts on "Visual Pleasure and Narrative Cinema" ', *Framework* 15-17, Summer 1981, pp.12-15; reprinted in Mulvey, *Visual and Other Pleasures*, Macmillan, London, 1989).

With this in mind, I want to suggest that, in quite specific ways, a comparison of these two bath scenes casts historical light on the fraught relationship between masculinity and the processes of commodity consumption in the modern world, and makes visible some of the intimate stylistic strategies that men have been expected to learn (and have been punished for failing to learn) to police the boundaries of the masculinities they inhabit. Whether these strategies have changed, can change, will change, is the question that underpins my discussion.

Over the years, washing, bathing and shaving have provided Westerns with a familiar set of narrative moments, and cleanliness (or the lack of it) has played a crucial part in their coding of character. What stands out, however, is that, while they have given a central place to codes of cleanliness, they have consistently masked the male nakedness that getting clean might be expected to involve and have

Still: Jon Voight all dressed up in Midnight Cowboy.

been evasive about the interest in male display it might be assumed to imply. Cowboys do not only wear hats in the bath. Trousers, shirts and a range of visually authentic underwear have served the same purpose. Clint Eastwood may get down to a cigar in *High Plains Drifter* (Eastwood, 1972), but in *Two Mules for Sister Sara* (Don Siegel, 1969) he is considerably more cautious. When he climbs into the bath with Shirley MacLaine at the end of the film, he takes his hat off but keeps the rest of his clothes on – guns, boots and all. Saying that this reflects the taboo on homoeroticism that has shaped mainstream cinema, though obviously true, does little to identify the complexities involved. It does not explain, for example, why only certain characters are seen naked, when, for what reasons and with what results. Women, Indians and villains in Westerns are seen decently naked and can be shown taking pleasure in dressing up; the hero cannot be, must not be, almost never is. Why, it seems reasonable to ask, in a genre so obviously obsessed with the male body – specifically with the hero's physical style – should this be so? That cowboys wear hats or anything else in the bath points to anxieties about male display that have not only shaped the Western's representations of masculinity but also, I want to argue, have profoundly influenced the processes by which individual (modern) masculinities have traditionally been learned.

It would be easy enough to pretend that my interest in all this is only academic. That is not true, however. I grew up watching Westerns. At four, I had a cowboy suit that had been bought specially in America, and 'playing cowboys' is a dominant memory from my early years. In the late 1950s, as a middle-class boy living on the northern edge of London, I followed the Lone Ranger, the Cisco Kid, Matt Dillon, Cheyenne and the other serial Western heroes on the television set my grandparents had given us. I absorbed their styles. For years, their movements shaped my own. Not surprisingly, when later, as a teenager, I saw Jon Voight in *Midnight Cowboy* (John Schlesinger, 1969) pose in front of a mirror in stetson and tasselled leather jacket, I recognised the gesture with a shock of embarrassment, recognised the strange, never-(for a man ?)-to-be-acknowledged thrill of watching myself reflected as Other, as Western hero, hand poised in readiness over an imaginary gun. This exercise, then, though hardly autobiographical, attempts to deal with more than abstractions. Beneath the discussion of texts – hidden, perhaps, but nonetheless there – lies a personal imperative to examine some of the processes through which I myself learned masculinity.

I am conscious of this directing my discussion in two ways. First, it is responsible for the fact that I have chosen to pivot my comments around the Western in the first place and have gone out of my way to challenge the commonsense belief that they give a single and unambiguous directive about what men should and should not do. In exposing contradictions in Westerns' constructions of masculinity, I want to illustrate the perhaps obvious, but, as it now seems to me, crucial point that it is precisely not the clarity or singularity of gender definitions (here, what it means to be a man) but their *confusions* and multiple possibilities that give them their power to secure the consent of individuals. The experience of not knowing exactly what masculinity involves, of choosing between masculinities on the basis of mutually contradictory imperatives, endows the process of learning masculinity with a force that certainty never could or would have. Second, it has led me, in reviewing the contrasts between the Western and recent young male fashion advertising that so obviously puts the naked male body on display, to try to consider what exactly is at stake for men in all this. What challenge is posed and to whom?

The Problem with Being Tough and Staying Clean

It has become customary to conceive of the Western as centrally concerned with the epic struggle between civilisation and savagery that historians have so often taken to have shaped American history. Film critics who have followed John Cawelti have argued that the cultural function of the genre has been, like myth, to resolve and mask conflicts between 'key American values' – conflicts, that is, between individualism and social order, freedom and law, progress and past ideals (Cawelti, 1971). From that perspective, Westerns have been read as 'foundation rituals' in which the hero's victory over the villain(s) affirms order and social structure. Indeed, Will Wright (1975) has made the question of whether the hero is assimilated into or excluded from society the determining feature of the genre's historical development.

These readings take note of the obvious fact that the relations between Western heroes and the forces that structure them are consistently ambiguous. Though their actions ultimately affirm social values, their skills and strengths – the 'toughness' that distinguishes them – are inextricably linked with the

wilderness. Laura Mulvey (in 'Afterthoughts on "Visual Pleasure and Narrative Cinema" ', *Framework* 15-17, Summer 1981) has identified this conflict in terms of the hero's choice between 'marriage' and 'not-marriage', and her formulation usefully draws attention to a point Cawelti and others have noted but whose implications have been generally ignored. Crucially, the Western has coded civilisation and wilderness in gendered terms. The town that stands for the social order that the hero must save and then settle down into or reject and leave is characterised not simply by the presence of a railway station, saloon, barber's shop and hotel, by bankers, marshals and traders, but essentially by the presence of women. The wilderness is a sphere for masculine action. Western heroes (and there are many different formulations) are thus faced not simply with bridging the divide between civilisation and savagery but with straddling the ambiguously experienced frontier between masculinity and femininity.

That ambiguity – though masked – signals conflicts embedded deep in the genre's representations of masculinity. The male toughness that distinguishes the hero from helpless females and over-feminised townsmen can generate opposing forms of behaviour (*see* Rupert Wilkinson, *American Tough*, Greenwood Press, Westport, Connecticut, 1984). Necessary as this toughness is, if the hero is to triumph in his quest, it is also potentially antisocial, destructive, anarchic – something repeatedly demonstrated by the villain(s) against whose equal toughness the hero must prove his own. In the villain, the ability to control people and situations, the 'coolness', resourcefulness, stoicism, combat and survival skills that make up that toughness are transformed into violent aggression, selfishness, deviousness and irrational obsession. While it is true that the earliest Westerns revelled in the sheer badness of desperadoes like the one who fills the opening and closing frames of Edwin S. Porter's *The Great Train Robbery* (1903), once Westerns began to take shape around star figures like G.M. 'Broncho Billy' Anderson (who figured briefly in Porter's film) and, from 1915, W.S. Hart, the attempt to mask the antisocial dimensions of male toughness became the source of the genre's most familiar moments – the refusal to draw first, the kindnesses to the weak, the glass of milk or soda pop in the bar. What those moments reveal, of course, is that the ideal of masculinity offered by Westerns in their heroes is fundamentally contradictory. Heroes must be *both* dominant and deferential, gentle and violent, self-contained and sensitive, practical and idealist, individualist and conformist, rational and intuitive, peace-loving and ready to fight without quitting at a moment's notice. Quite simply, the hero's masculine toughness must be partially feminised.

It is here that the problems begin. Westerns have always made an absolute and value-laden division between the male and female spheres, have always valued the one over the other. While they have linked masculinity with outdoor living, activity, adventure, mobility, emotional restraint and public power, they

Still: William S. Hart, clean-shaven Western hero in Tumbleweeds *(1925).*

have associated femininity with passivity, softness, Romance, and domestic containment. This goes beyond the immediate question of how characters behave. In the symbolic universe of the Western, femininity is represented as a threat to masculine independence and accorded a highly circumscribed place in the plot structure. Signalling incompleteness and inability, it either generates male action to create plot movement (and endanger men's lives) or interrupts male fun (as it does, for example, with grudging clumsiness at the close of Howard Hawks's *Red River*, 1948) to create plot endings. In existential terms, it is the negative against which masculinity is measured. Thus, incompetent men are marked as too closely linked to the feminine sphere. They are incapable of forceful action and lack combat skills; they are willing to express emotion, are idealistic or committed to Romance; they are domesticated and too willing to serve. The studious avoidance of effeminacy, of physical gestures that might imply homosexual preferences, that Westerns maintain (as gangster films do not) gives some indication of the problems involved here. In a genre that has always suggested that relationships between men are more important (or at least more interesting) than those between men and women, and has always made male friendships and conflict its focus of attention, the process of feminising the hero to distinguish his masculine toughness from that of the villain(s) has had constantly to negotiate a complexly orchestrated set of homophobic anxieties.

The problem is nowhere more acute than in relation to the code of cleanliness which has played such an important yet unremarked part in the Western's history. A host of iconographic elements have come to distinguish the genre's heroes and villains. Clothes, colours and hats have probably received the most attention. In fact, however, cleanness and neatness and a special relationship with the encoding of haircuts and facial hair provide the most consistent links between the disparate band of Western heroes – the fundamental visual indicators that distinguish them from their opponents. Crucially theirs is a particular kind of cleanliness. They are not fastidious or fussy – unlike the townsmen whose carefully manicured cleanliness and pressed clothes signal incompetence and probable dishonesty. Equally, they are not stained, grimy, or dishevelled in the style of the rough, unmannered villains. Heroes may be dusty but not dirty. Their clothes may be worn but not greasy. They seldom sweat. Above all, they have always just shaved.

Facial hair has had a complex history in the visual arts. In the Western, it has played a quite central role. Though they have changed in size and shape, voice-pitch, character and motivation, Western heroes, from the time that aggressive marketing of the safety razor shaped the face of modern masculinity, have been clean-jawed. The special qualities of Mix, Hart and the other Western heroes who emerged in the 1910s and early 1920s are confirmed in film after film by the fact that they are not afflicted by the alarming facial growths that mark their enemies. Unshavenness can signal exhaustion or illness, but until the spaghetti Westerns of the 1960s began to play with the code, habitual stubble and moustaches were unmistakable signs of villainy. At very best, beards indicate domesticated maturity and ailing old age rather than patriarchal power.

It is the coding of facial hair, for example, that identifies the evil intentions of the three men who ride through the opening credit sequence of *High Noon* (Fred Zinnemann, 1952), when narrative grammar would suggest they should be heroes. And in *The Searchers* (John Ford, 1956), it is the beard that alerts the spectator to the distinctions between the tough but domesticated masculinity of Sam the Texas Ranger/preacher (Ward Bond) and the unrelenting ('Don't believe in surrender. I still got my sabre') masculinity of John Wayne's smooth-faced Ethan.

How the hero gets clean is usually a mystery. If washing is to be shown, then outdoors is preferred and distinctly masculine gestures are obligatory – water held in cupped hands and splashed into the face, wet scarf rubbed around the neck (one remembers Randolph Scott's multi-purpose kerchief) or perhaps a rough immersing of the face in trough, basin or river. None of these require the removing of clothes. Shaving is either not explained (where did John Wayne clean up before stepping out of the desert into Ford's *Stagecoach* in 1939?) or is foregrounded in the barber's shop, a place of male camaraderie but, also, significantly, of threat. Danger hovers around these unguarded moments. On one level there is a commonsense, narrative explanation for this. Washing and shaving necessitate a certain relaxation, a dropping of defences. Covering the face, taking off guns, being wrapped in a barber's apron, are potentially lethal lapses of concentration in the fight to survive. It is not surprising in this sense that the hero is seldom seen taking a bath. Clearly, however, there is more to this. That washing, shaving and bathing are seldom made part of Western narratives (narratives devoted after all to action) is not in itself remarkable. That, when they do appear, they are activities surrounded by threat and danger suggests anxieties that require a more detailed explanation.

Though it is studiously unfussy and unobtrusive, the cleanliness that signals the moral, existential and spiritual superiority of the hero is inescapably linked with the culturally construed imperatives of femininity. It is linked, that is, not simply with modern plumbing and city life but with the concern with appearance and self-adornment that is conventionally coded as feminine. When the Western hero wears his hat in the bath, the gesture in general terms signals his estrangement from civilisation; more specifically, however, it distances him from the demands of physical display (from the imperative to be clean and dress for others, from the learned habit of looking at one's physical self through others' eyes) that have traditionally defined and constrained femininity. What is at issue here is the problematic place occupied by male display in the discourse of modern masculinity within which the Western has operated. The source of anxiety is the complexly gendered set of cultural and filmic conventions and assumptions that surround the act of looking.

Nakedness, Dandyism and the Western's Masculinities

Since the 1970s, a considerable amount of cultural studies research has been devoted to demonstrating the gendered nature of the look, and to examining how the fact that active looking, conventionally coded as masculine, organises social behaviour and, in particular, affects the production and reception of visual images. Discussion has focused on the representations of women deployed in films and advertising, on female spectatorship and on the processes of self-surveillance that are involved in learning femininity. The part played by the conventions of looking in the visual construction and learning of masculinity has been less fully attended to, although two commentaries on the subject are enlightening. Steve Neale ('*Chariots of Fire*, Images of Men', *Screen*, September/October 1982, pp.47-53; 'Masculinity as Spectacle', *Screen*, November/December 1983, pp.2-16) has pointed out that mainstream cinema, limited as it is by fears of homoeroticism, has suppressed the visual pleasures to be gained from the (erotic) contemplation of the male body just as consistently as it has offered the female body for the consumption and erotic play of the male gaze. His argument draws attention to the ways popular films have handled the look in relation to male spectacle and examines how they have directed and positioned their assumed male spectators in relation to the visual pleasures to be gained from the male body. Richard Dyer, discussing the male pin-up ('Don't Look Now', *Screen*, November/December 1984, pp.61-73), has argued that for an image to present the male body as an object to be looked at is to locate it in a feminine position and thus inevitably feminise it. In this sense, a simple reversal cannot create an equivalent of the *Playboy* centre-spread for women because normative visual codes would categorise such images of men as gay soft porn and critically undermine the model's heterosexual credibility. The term 'male model' of course is itself (still) surrounded by tabloid press assumptions about effeminacy.

Both these arguments have specific relevance to the Western. Not only are Westerns consistently constructed around the male point of view and targeted at male audiences but they constantly represent looking as an act of male control. Indeed, the demonstration of the gaze as an instrument of male power is integral to their narrative formulae, iconography and character-coding. When the hero spots the tremor of the lace curtain that identifies a hidden gunman or reads tracks for their invisible meanings, he affirms his power over his environment, a power that, through editing or camera angle, the spectator is regularly invited to share. Not surprisingly, male display causes problems. For a man to betray a desire to be looked at (to make himself a willing object of the gaze) is to transgress the natural order of the genre. Though the hero may be distinguished by style, cleanliness and appearance, he cannot be seen to invite the pleasure-seeking gaze of other characters. Equally, although he is the focus of narrative attention, he cannot be explicitly transformed into an object for the spectator's (potentially erotic) contemplation. These conflicting imperatives make the two extremes of bodily display, nakedness and dandyism, sources of confusion and anxiety.

Nakedness diminishes masculinity. In situations requiring action, simply to be without guns can be represented as 'naked', and the feminine associations of such unpreparedness are regularly made clear. The Western characters of James Stewart nicely illustrate the point – in *The Man from Laramie* (Anthony Mann, 1955) and *The Man Who Shot Liberty Valance* (John Ford, 1962) for example. In *Destry Rides Again* (George Marshall, 1939) the identification is particularly – unusually – clear. When, at one point, Stewart is challenged in a saloon and admits he does not wear a gun, he is given a mop, told to 'clean up the town' and, in a rare moment of explicit suggestiveness, overtly ridiculed as effeminate. Given this sensitivity, it is interesting to see how precisely Westerns code the showing of the physically naked, male body. Villains can be stripped and – the key issue is the removal of trousers – thus rendered powerless, but naked displays of the hero's body rarely go beyond hands and face. Combat creates the most frequent excuse for exposure. Hand-to-hand fighting not only serves to demonstrate that the hero can fight without technology but also allows him (or someone else) to remove (some of) his clothing. Beating or whipping, wounding and torture can similarly be converted into opportunities for

nakedness – usually the showing of chest and torso. Fragmenting (fetishising) close-ups of males and the male body play only a small part in the Western's traditional visual style. When used, they serve explicit narrative purposes – facial close-ups, for example, to express emotions otherwise silenced by male reserve. In spaghetti Westerns, where close-ups are relatively common, their potentially eroticising implications are obscured. In Sergio Leone's shoot-outs, for example (the argument is Steve Neale's), the spectator is not permitted to look directly at the fetishised male images on screen but is forced to experience them through the edited interaction and hostility of the combatants.

Dandyism has played an equally complex part in the Western. The dandy's city clothes are inappropriate in the hostile (masculine) environment of the hero's West. The issue is both practical and existential. To pay attention to the non-functional aspects of dress (to imply that one dresses for others) indicates weakness in a man. There are historical and sub-genre differences here. The exuberant dress and athleticism of the silent Western stars (Tom Mix, for example, but not W.S. Hart) overtly make the male body an object of visual pleasure. Dandyism is also clearly an element in sub-genres like the singing Western and in children's serials like *The Lone Ranger*. From the 1930s on, however, any significant

Still: James Stewart 'naked' in The Man Who Shot Liberty Valance, *with Lee Van Cleef, Lee Marvin and John Wayne.*

attention to bodily display in a mainstream Western, beyond neatness and characteristic individual details (Randolph Scott's multi-functional scarf again), marks a male as weak, aberrant, narcissistic. From that point on, the forms of masculinity the Western registers as most authentic are characterised by a disregard for self-exhibition.

This whole set of points is well demonstrated by *The Searchers*, a film that shows a precise sensitivity to the Western's codes of male display. From the opening song ('What makes a man to turn his back on home?') and the film's opening shot (that watches from within the enclosing frame of the homestead as Ethan, the outlaw, confederate and bank-robber, approaches across the dry Texas landscape), home and wilderness, marriage and not-marriage, masculine and feminine spheres are established as narrative polarities. Forced in conclusion to choose between the two, the film ultimately divides its allegiance between Ethan, who remains outside, and Martin, who marries into the homesteaders' community. In relation to these two and to the constellation of male characters against whom they are defined, nakedness and dandyism clearly operate as crucial signifying codes. Both Ethan and Martin are shown partially naked (shirtless) in the course of the film – Ethan once, Martin three times. Ethan's body is exposed when he is wounded. Significantly we see him then at his least attractive – dirty, unshaven, grubby, bandaged. It is the moment when the depth of the racism that feeds his desire for vengeance against the Indians he pursues is revealed. Shot out of doors, the images at that point are themselves over-exposed so that John Wayne looks uncharacteristically pale, sick, and harsh. In contrast, when Martin is shown naked, the scenes are softly and warmly lit in ways obviously designed to enhance his dark good looks and to emphasise his potential as the object of pleasurable visual attention. The distinction clearly affirms Martin's association with the feminine and domestic sphere of home; its feminising potential, however, is carefully limited by a further set of character contrasts that invoke dandyism as a sign of weakened masculinity. Thus the romantic lover Brad (Harry Carey, Jr) dresses to impress others and is soon killed (as the spectator knows he inevitably will be) in a futile attack on the Indians who have killed his fiancée. Martin is also contrasted with Charlie (Ken Curtis), the childish singing cowboy, who dresses up uncomfortably for the marriage that never takes place, and with the cavalry messenger whose too-correct clothes and manner mark him as an Eastern prig.

What my comments have not acknowledged so far, of course – and it is something that is clear in *The Searchers* – is that if, because of their associations with the spheres of femininity, both dandyism and nakedness imply weakness, then they are also signs of potential threat – they are regularly deployed, that is, as indicators of a dangerous otherness. Thus, while dandyism implies the essential weakness of the urban villain, it also gives warning of his erratic selfishness, just as in the genre's racist characterisation of Mexicans it is proof of decadence and sadism.

Frame: Charlie (Ken Curtis) serenades Laurie (Vera Miles) in The Searchers.

Most significantly, from the earliest Westerns, it has been the distinctive mark of the gunslinger or hired gun, and in him what makes it threatening becomes clear. Though its associations with the feminine sphere are masked because, as part of the gunslinger's uniform, dressing up has an apparent functionalism, it signals an ambiguous merging of categories, an overcivilised, antisocial quality, a fastidious, unrestrained murderousness. Nakedness, too, as well as being associated with potentially dangerous women (the ones who are seen taking baths) is part of Indian dress, particularly that of Indian warriors. Indian males take active pleasure in bodily display; they not only expose but paint their bodies, use make-up and wear ornate head-dresses and jewellery. Significantly, their nakedness is seldom a sign of naturalness. Rather, it warns of deviance. They fight erratically for unexplainable reasons, attack at night and in ambush, seem to have magical powers; their secret signals merge with the calls of animals and birds. Beneath the level of plot (of Indian attacks and circled wagons), their threat to the hero is an existential one. Their denial of distinctions and their transgressing of boundaries challenge and ridicule the anxiously maintained balance of opposites it is the hero's cultural mission to maintain.

I began by saying that the masculinities enacted by successive Western heroes are in fact made up of many traits that, taken in isolation, would be coded as feminine. My focus on male display identifies how that ambiguity produces a set of contradictory instructions about how men should relate to looking and makes quite clear that critiques which have talked of Westerns offering resolutions to social anxieties are deeply misleading. I think of my own shock of embarrassed recognition at Jon Voight's secret mirror-checking and realise how, for men, the anxieties surrounding looking can become enmeshed in subjectivity. While a particular visual style (grace in action, 'walking tall', and all the other key indicators of the hero's precarious stability) are constantly offered to the spectator as part of an ego ideal, Westerns categorically indicate that for a man openly to display himself (to invite others to make him the object of their gaze) is to transgress the discourse of masculinity within which those heroes are constructed. There is yet more. If the hero is required not to invite the pleasuring gaze of others, he is in turn best advised to beware of those who do – dangerous women, Indians, gunfighters and assorted deviants. Display is not only false but a mask that covers physical and existential threat. Looking, the hero's life suggests, is not a matter of pleasure but wholly of power and dominance. Looking at other men can only be legitimated in terms of defence or attack; looking at women is to invite disruption or worse. The Western hero's example condemns both non-functional self-display and the pleasuring play of the vagrant eye.

Consumer Masculinities and the Western

All this would be of only passing interest if it were not for the fact that the decline of the Western from the early 1970s was paralleled both by the sudden explosion of advertising images apparently designed, as Frank Mort (1986) argues, to encourage young men 'to look at themselves and other men . . . and to experience pleasures around the body hitherto branded as taboo or exclusively feminine' and by the emergence of a new set of adventure films that go to great lengths to display their heroes physically. There are differences between these two sets of images, but what they share is a common interest in treating the naked male body as an object of attention. In contrast, the Western, as I have suggested, places an injunction on such a manoeuvre and indeed on the whole notion of pleasurable looking that is the essence of consumer behaviour in the modern world. 'Just looking', that particular activity that distinguishes the skilled consumer, is anathema to the Western hero.

There is an important historical dimension to this in that those recent images of masculinity do seem to relate to the wider economic and cultural shift that has led contemporary marketing to encourage men (as women have traditionally been encouraged) to conceive of themselves and their bodies as sites for consumer attention. In the initial phases of its development, America's consumer economy during the late nineteenth and early twentieth centuries marked consumption – shopping – as women's work (see, for example, Stewart Ewen, *Captains of Consciousness: Advertising and the Roots of Consumer Consciousness*, McGraw Hill, New York, 1976). Only later, in the years after 1945, did the need to recruit new consumers both at home and overseas lead to a shift in this emphasis. From that point, the drive to generate and diversify consumer desires can be seen to have required a redefinition of masculinity that would encourage men to conceive of themselves – look at themselves – as consumers. Barbara Ehrenreich talks about this in *The Hearts of Men: American Dreams and the Flight from Commitment* (Pluto Press, London, 1983) in which she examines in some detail how, in the 1950s, a new consumer version of masculinity came to challenge and ultimately overthrow the dominant image of the male as breadwinner. In relation to my discussion here, Ehrenreich's argument is of interest because during the late 1940s,

1950s and 1960s, Westerns were quite clearly attempting to accommodate the shift she describes – to accommodate, that is, not only the anxieties generated by the postwar entry of women into new areas of the labour force but the legitimation of male display that was fuelling the growth of a new youth market and which, in James Dean and others, had already created a whole set of new, young, glamorous male stars.

I have cited Steve Neale's argument that the parodic recycling of familiar visual elements that characterised Sergio Leone's films made possible the covert presentation of masculinity as spectacle in the spaghetti Westerns of the 1960s and 1970s. Dandyism and the fetishisation of the male body are obvious characteristics of those films. However, attempts to transform the Western's traditional version of masculinity go back quite a bit further. The James Stewart characters mentioned earlier are conspicuous because they show no special skills with guns; similarly films from the 'fifties like William Wellman's *Yellow Sky* (1948) and Nicholas Ray's *Johnny Guitar* (1954) show a powerful, gunfighter woman dominating the central male character – at least until the demands of narrative closure take over. In terms of my argument here, what is most significant in a film like *Yellow Sky* is that the woman demonstrates her power not only with guns but by forcing Gregory Peck to get shaved and take a bath. Equally, what

Still: Anne Baxter tells Gregory Peck to take a bath in Yellow Sky.

is most significant in a film like Robert Aldrich's *Apache* (1954) is that it is clearly constructed around an attempt to explore the possibilities of the naked Western hero. Casting Burt Lancaster as an Indian – a manoeuvre usually seen as part of the liberal move to rehabilitate Native Americans in Hollywood – permitted the film to dwell openly and at length on its hero's naked torso and to show him dressing up in ways unthinkable in earlier Westerns. I have commented already on the clash of contrasting and contrastingly presented masculinities at the heart of John Ford's *The Searchers* in 1956. A similar clash is evident in a number of the major Westerns of the period – in, for example, *Red River* (Howard Hawks, 1948), *Shane* (George Stevens, 1953), and *The Big Country* (William Wyler, 1958). Quite overtly, the narratives of those films focus on the contrast between the traditionally construed and constructed masculinities of John Wayne, Van Heflin and Charlton Heston and the more glamorous masculinities of Montgomery Clift, Alan Ladd and Gregory Peck, who are overtly represented in ways that identify them as objects to be pleasurably looked at by others.

The kinds of textual conflict produced by the Western's attempts to accommodate the contemporary emergence of new consumer-oriented versions of masculinity can be nicely illustrated by *Shane,* a film that has been read conventionally as a Western concerned with the problems of violence in 'fifties America and as a selfconscious reworking of American foundation myths. What these readings ignore is the obvious visual conflict that surrounds the film's attempt to make Alan Ladd a Western hero who is both an object to be looked at with pleasure (as a pin-up) and a figure to be looked up to (as an ego ideal). Reread now in terms of how, for all its sophistication, the film essentially fails to solve the problems of male display and gendered looking, it stands as a marker of the genre's inability to respond adequately to the changing patterns of masculinity demanded by the growth of consumer economies in the postwar years.

Looking is established as a form of control in the opening shot of the film which invites the spectator to follow Shane (Alan Ladd) as he rides down into the valley where the action will take place. The point is confirmed when, in their first encounter, Shane says to the boy Joey (Brandon De Wilde): 'You were watching me. I like a man who watches things going around. Means he'll make his mark some day.' That exchange (a neat statement of the power of the phallic gaze) is preceded by a fast-edited sequence in which all three members of the Starrett family watch the stranger as he rides up. Throughout what follows, Shane remains an object of attention but, from this point on, the spectator's gaze passes solely through Mrs Starrett (Jean Arthur) and Joey. Mirroring the first-person narrative of Jack Schaefer's novel, the film seems to intend the spectator to identify primarily with the boy. Shane is consistently viewed from below, from the boy's angle of vision – looking up. The presence of Mrs Starrett, however, makes this increasingly ambiguous. At points, the spectator views Shane (with Joey) as an object of

identification, at others (with Mrs Starrett, whose emotional interest is registered in a series of looks) as an object of heterosexual, erotic desire. The two positions can become unsettlingly interchangeable. In two key scenes, Mrs Starrett and Joey are positioned together as they watch Shane – once as he stands in the rain (with hat on), framed by the window through which they and the spectator look, and once as they crouch together beneath the saloon door watching him fight.

This obvious attempt to present Ladd as a pin-up while still working within the frame of the Western creates a tension in the narrative, because ultimately the film remains committed to the older discourse of masculinity and reflects quite precisely the anxieties about male display I have been discussing. Once marked as a possible object of erotic contemplation, Shane ceases to be looked at directly by Joe Starrett despite their growing friendship – something that requires some virtuoso bashful acting and lowered eyebrows from Van Heflin. Rather, their affection for each other is expressed through fighting – first with nature in the form of the tree-trunk they uproot (a struggle in which Alan Ladd is ostentatiously stripped to the waist whilst Van Heflin remains fully clothed), then with their enemies and finally with each other. My suggestion here is *not* that the relationship between the two men is somehow covertly homosexual. I want to argue that the film's confusion about Ladd's glamorised masculinity and its attempt to render homoerotic desire unthinkable betray how fundamentally it fails to break free of the anxieties over male display and the gendered structure of looking which, throughout its history, have shaped the Western's discourse. Sadly, perhaps, it is this – the genre's own inability to change its construction of masculinity – rather than a more laudable rejection of violence that require Shane's final wounding and exclusion from the valley.

Politics, Style and Masculine Subjectivity

It has been my intention to locate the Western's discourse of masculinity in a particular historical moment – to link it with the growth of the consumer economies in America and the Western world in the first half of the twentieth century. This is not to deny that Westerns absorbed fragments of earlier historical formations of masculinity – the questing hero and the gentleman, for example – nor that it drew on nineteenth-century European and American traditions of representation that, as Margaret Walters argues in *The Male Nude* (Penguin Books, Harmondsworth, 1979), firmly established 'the nude' in the visual arts as a female figure and cast a veil over the naked male body. In other words, while there are other sources for the Western's attitudes to male display and its assertion that, for men, looking is not a matter of pleasure but power (of combat and defence), these attitudes take on *specific* meanings in relation to the initial growth of the Western

Still: Burt Lancaster as Western hero in Apache, *which dwells openly and at length on its hero's naked torso.*

consumer economies. This development set in motion a redefinition of gender that urged women to conceive of themselves as active consumers while at the same time situating the most dominant models of masculine identity, activity and relationships distinctly apart from the consumer version of modernity. Locating the Western in that historical context identifies how the twentieth century's ongoing debates about masculinity have influenced its history and clarifies the nature of its contribution to the development of twentieth-century consumer cultures.

That reading also draws attention to the fact that, for men, learning the Western's heterosexually normative discourse of masculinity involves internalising an ambiguous set of imperatives about how they should physically position themselves in relation to looking. This is a delicate issue. The gendered coding of the look has rightly been seen as the source of the most overt of the many mechanisms that empower men and disempower women in social situations. Feminist research has demonstrated in some detail the ways in which women experience the oppressive force of male looking in advertising and pornography, in public space and in the fetishising of private intimacies and has examined the act of internalising the male gaze as an intrinsic part of learning feminity. For men too, however, learning gender involves negotiating what to look at and when, where to look and with what intentions and results. Familiar as this is, it remains a largely silenced area of masculine experience. Westerns have played no small part in teaching men the pleasures

and anxieties connected with being looked at – with inviting the looks of others. Equally, they have consistently demonstrated that if looking is an assertion of power, it can also invite danger. 'You lookin' at *me?* You *lookin'* at me?' The challenge, accompanied by the familiar, vengeful stare is a prelude to the violence that marks out the boundary across which men stray at their peril.

The question of whether all this was actually changing in the 1980s is a problematic one. Certainly the Western's popularity declined radically in that decade. When I have used Westerns in undergraduate teaching, it has been clear that the university students I have been working with have had little direct experience of the genre's history and find the cowboy masculinity of Wayne (and even the less obviously dated Eastwood) as ridiculous as I once found the plastic models of the Japanese horror films of the 1950s. Though the influence is seldom acknowledged, feminism has apparently made it impossible for members of that particular youth grouping to espouse unironically the values represented by Wayne et al. Lorraine Gamman's argument that the parodic force of the *female* gaze has come to play an increasingly noticeable part in popular visual representations of gender seems to hold good here: it is clear that the current targeting of advertising at men of all ages has not only expanded the range of publicly validated masculinities that deviate from the norms enacted by Western heroes, but has actively made those norms the subject of ridicule ('Watching the Detectives' in *The Female Gaze*, edited by Lorraine Gamman and Margaret Marshment, The Women's Press, London, 1988). I have been interested, for example, by the emergence of 'the Wally' as one form of consumer masculinity (in gardening and do-it-yourself commercials structured around parody), but there are a number of others. Moreover, if only to a limited extent, involvement in the consumer world has required a wide range of men to learn domestic skills previously thought of as feminine – how to shop and take on domestic responsibilities, to discriminate over designs and home furnishings, to make choices over cuisine, to pay more than 'practical' attention to dress.

The effects of these changes are unevenly and erratically spread across generational, class, economic, professional, ethnic and regional divisions. More to the point, individual changes, being inevitably partial and (at any given moment) incomplete, produce contradictory behaviour – strange mixtures of old and new. As domestic space becomes increasingly a site of male violence, it is obvious that surface changes regularly mask a reaffirmation of older structures of power and that the disjunction between reconstructed outer behaviour and the unchanged, inner shapes of desire can generate anxieties and frustrations that erupt with lethal consequences. There are historical precedents here. In 'twenties America, for example, advertisers were remarkably successful in co-opting the deeply contentious political and social freedoms won by women in the previous two or three decades in ways that minimised their challenge to patriarchal structures and transformed them – in the narratives of the Flapper and the Modern Housewife – into triggers to generate consumption. So today, while a small range of popular images of men do indeed seem to undermine the dominant (deeply contradictory) norms of masculinity provided for the better part of this century by the Western, there are others that regularly reaffirm the white, heterosexual, middle-class assumptions, the structure of masculine identity and the same relationship with modernity that were inherent in that older (now seemingly outdated) model.

The Levi 501 commercial with which I began is an interesting text in this respect. It is all about looking at men and, on the surface, it marks a break with the Levi Strauss Company's traditional cowboy image. Given the company's drive to diversify its production and modify its image since the 1960s, the change presumably reflects some careful market research. Clearly it is not the image of the 1950s jean-wearing John Wayne but James Dean's youth-market narcissism that the commercial invokes with its nostalgia. In fact, however, it acknowledges (without ultimately dismissing) precisely those anxieties about male display that I have been discussing. The fetishing of the young man's half-naked body, the ritualistic pleasure he takes in his appearance and the invitation to the (male) viewer to share that pleasure do seem to offer something new. But what then of the closing moments of the commercial? As the young man sinks into the bath with his jeans on, is this a moment of uncharacteristic and subversive masculine behaviour (the 'baptism of a new man', as one TV pundit put it) or a recycling of the Western's hero's partially clothed bathing habits? My own feeling is that, for all its post-modern pastiche,

the commercial points backwards rather than forwards. Significantly, the young man's stance towards the modern world is one of withdrawal. Modernity intrudes into his isolation as a negative presence in the form of an ominous police siren. The photograph of the girlfriend removes any ambiguities about his sexual preferences. Without it, the commercial would have had a far more radical set of implications. And, though it appears to recode male display and positively affirm its pleasures, the young man's activities are secret. We as viewers are voyeurs. He does not pose for us. We look at him through his own eyes. He interacts with no-one, but only with images that will neither challenge nor expose him. His private mirror-checking confirms the impressions and anxieties embedded in the older (cowboy) image of Levi masculinity that the commercial superficially appears to reject (I am indebted to a discussion of this Levi commercial by Frank Mort at the annual conference of the Association for Cultural Studies at North-East London Polytechnic in March 1986).

In far more overt ways, adventure films like *Rambo* and *Commando* use potentially subversive images of masculinity to confirm familiar patterns of masculine self-conception and ways of relating to the world. To use Raymond Durgnat's words, those Stallone and Schwarzenegger vehicles offer not a new masculinity but a new militarism ('True Grit and Friendly Fire' in *Monthly Film Bulletin*, November 1987, pp.326-328; *see also* Adam Farr, 'War: Machining Male Desire', and Bob Connell, 'Masculinity, Violence and War', in *War/Masculinity*, edited by Paul Patten and Ray Poole, Intervention Publications, Sydney, Australia, 1985). On the surface, the differences between these films' representations of masculinity and the Western's are obvious. They wilfully expose the naked bodies of their heroes and openly play with images that ten years earlier were available only as gay pornography. Schwarzenegger going into battle in a body-builder's black mini-slip is an image to treasure. In one sense, that is, they do alter the Western's traditional coding of masculinity and do appear to challenge its injunctions against male display. The similarities, however, are at least as striking. Rambo and John (Schwarzenegger) Commando are as out of place in the shopping malls that they lay waste as John Wayne was in the homesteader community he rode away from in *The Searchers*. If anything, their nakedness (coded now as 'naturalness') serves only to magnify the threats and dangers they must face. Combat, wounding and violence are still needed to mask the display of their bodies. They are naked but not subversively so. Anxieties and contradictions still flow around their self-exposure. Both the traditional Western and those recent adventure films project the masculinities of their heroes as the only point of stability in a (frontier) world in which the cultural boundaries that define gender and sexuality, civilisation and anarchy, racial superiority and international order are threatened. Repressing and evading any self-conscious recognition of the *internal* contradictions their identities encompass, they construct their masculinities as defensive responses to the *external* crises of modernity

– crises that are taken as legitimation for both the violence that demonstrates their superiority and the unrelenting rejection of self-analysis that is their most fundamental characteristic. In more destructive ways, they duplicate the withdrawal into isolation that in the Levi ad makes negotiation with living others unnecessary. They enact what Klaus Theweleit in *Male Fantasies I* (Polity Press, Cambridge, 1987) describes as 'an incapacity to experience others except through fear, deceit, mistrust or domination'.

There is no single or simple conclusion to be reached here, because there are many alternative ways of responding to the re-visualising of masculinity that is happening around us. On one hand, the negative arguments (that nothing has really changed) do have an important cautionary part to play in contemporary debates about masculinity. Quite crucially, they offset the still pervasive media hype about 'the new man'. It *is* necessary to point out that new clothes (or to be exact, nostalgically recycled old styles) do not necessarily make a new masculinity and that the appearance of naked male heroes does not automatically change patriarchal power-structures (the point is well argued in Jon Savage, 'What's so New about the New Man', *Arena*, March/April 1988, pp.33-39). At the same time, if the focus of attention is (as it has been in this essay) the masculinities of those heterosexual men who learned gender when Westerns were a dominant popular form, then it must be said that this pessimism is still too often mobilised to justify familiar (self-complacent) male evasions of personal change. For men who are uncomfortable with the personal and organisational restructuring demanded by their encounters with feminism – I am thinking specifically now of those on the Left (whom Cynthia Cockburn addresses in her essay, 'Macho Men of the Left' in *Male Order: Unwrapping Masculinity*, edited by J. Rutherford and R. Chapman, Lawrence & Wishart, 1988) – it is too easy to dismiss what has emerged as a politics of style as either opportunistic or faddishly naive (*see also* Frank Mort and Nicholas Green, 'You've Never Had It So Good Again' in *Male Order*). Making style a central rather than marginal or optional issue can represent for individual men a significant shift in self-conception.

Style politics has made a series of fundamental connections between personal and public politics, and it is here that older men can learn a lot from their younger counterparts. I have argued that Westerns have played a significant role in teaching how 'a man' should or should not conceive of male display and position himself in relation to the look – in teaching that is, how 'a man' should relate to the distribution of power in social situations. In the modern world these lessons have been strictly organised around the gender distinctions dictated by the organisation of the consumer economy. The implications of such distinctions, and how deeply they have become embedded in personal behaviour, are nicely illustrated by the difficulty so many older men (myself included) had in responding to the style revolutions of the 'eighties. It is here, where refusals to change have been defended on the grounds of

'personal preference', that it becomes clear what it is that is really an issue for men in this whole debate.

I think of the nervousness with which male friends of around my own age (forty in the late 'eighties) tried to change how they looked after David Bowie went into baggy cotton suits; I think of the many who changed hardly at all; I remember the pride my father always took in the 1950s and 1960s in refusing to take notice of fashion; I remember a friend's surprised realisation that she had never actually seen her father's naked legs, and I recognise how absolutely the demands of masculinity for men of my generation and older have been registered in an aggressive indifference to dress and a silent avoidance of bodily display. When I was younger, the sports field, gym, running-track and beach were limited areas where momentarily those sanctions broke down – where the body could be rubbed, oiled, shown off. And how hard it is now for those who learned the suppressions and anxieties of heterosexual masculinity in that older school to participate in and enjoy without embarrassed self-consciousness the playful parody and deconstruction of traditional masculinities that characterise contemporary young male fashion. Because, of course, for older (and not so old) men those sanctions still apply. They dictate the doggedly characterless dark suits so familiar in the academic world, the non-frivolous, sombre fashionableness of early ageing professionals, the cautious (careful non-designer) casualness of older male fashions. What is involved here is much more than simply a choice between dark clothes or colours, tight or baggy, undemonstrative or street chic. Patriarchy has traditionally claimed its natural right to dominance on the basis of its permanence, unitary truth and resistance to change, its seriousness and no-nonsense rejection of the frivolous, superficial, ephemeral and trivial. In twentieth-century terms, that rejection has regularly been enacted by individual men as a rejection of direct personal involvement in the consumer world. For a man to play with personal styles does more than signify femininity, though that, of course, is what is assumed and ridiculed by those whom it disturbs. It projects a wholly other version of masculinity. It acknowledges, that is, identity (for men as well as women) as being fabricated and learned – contingent, historical, relational, constantly under negotiation. It accepts that masculinity, like femininity, is a thing of surfaces, not essentials. It recognises that the contradictions and differences that are encompassed by what is commonly and abstractly thought of as 'masculinity' are not simply external. On a day-to-day basis, individual men inhabit multiple and contradictory patterns of masculine behaviour – patterns that reflect both external structures and the constantly shifting inner negotiations that make up the gendered subject.

That acknowledgement is a starting point for any deconstruction of the forms of masculinity validated by the Western and can elevate style politics above the 'merely' personal. It is also what seems to distinguish the masculinities available in sub-cultural areas of the youth market from those deeply contradictory, inward-looking, un-self-critical masculinities projected by the Levi ads or the prodigiously popular Schwarzenegger films. The heterosexual norm exemplified in the Western has always been satirised and parodied within gay cultures. Drawing directly on that tradition of resistance, style politics offers heterosexual men new ways of conceptualising and acting out masculinity – not least because at the immediate level of everyday social life it ridicules the coercive homophobia that has so fundamentally shaped the processes by which masculinity has traditionally been maintained, and offers new ways in which men can relate to each other. Images of the mid 'eighties in magazines like *Arena* and *The Face* showing young men in groups (not in isolation) and inviting the (male) viewer to participate in the obvious pleasure they are taking in dressing up not only visibly feminise masculinity but decentre male subjectivity in ways that can potentially shift how individual men locate themselves within power-structures. That shift has significant implications. It makes it possible to conceive of masculinities not constructed around unselfconscious, enclosed individualisms, not wholly organised as defensive strategies against uncertainty, inner conflict, flow and change. In individual terms, such a move challenges the refusal (inability?) to negotiate, listen and compromise that still dominates so many face-to-face social interactions in which men are involved. In terms of the agenda for rethinking socialist politics in Britain (in the context of which much of this debate about changing men has been located), it may yet make possible the reimagining of political constituencies to accommodate difference and diversity and the breaking-open of the unresponsive, masculine power-structures of the Left called for by feminism (*see* Cockburn, and Mort and Green, 1988) It might even, as Richard Dyer ('Style Council', *Marxism Today*, May 1988, pp.41-43) rather optimistically suggested, brighten up the front benches of the Labour Party. Chance would be a fine thing.

An Inconclusive and Cautionary Note

Linking my discussion with ongoing debates within the Left in Britain is an appropriate way of closing – not least because it draws attention to the need to look beyond the Western for an understanding of the masculinities formed by the economic realities of international consumer capitalism in the late twentieth century. It has been customary to interpret the masculinities of those men whose desires find fullest expression in right-wing politics in terms of the model enacted by John Wayne in films like *The Searchers*. There are good historical reasons for this, but what is becoming increasingly obvious is that the operations of power in the economic era ushered in by the Big Bang have generated far more complex forms of control-oriented masculinity than those I have been discussing. In fact, in interesting and disturbing ways, men of the free-market Right have often been far more at ease with absorbing gender changes than their counterparts on the Left. Oliver Stone's modern morality play, *Wall Street* (1987), usefully charts the transformation.

As the film closes, the final decision of Bud Fox (Charlie Sheen) to turn his back on the world of high-tech finance and the limitless consumer rewards it offers aligns him reassuringly with the masculinity of his father (Martin Sheen) – with its sense of social responsibility, personal honour and integrity, the family, law, order and the community. It leaves the centre ground, however, to the charismatic presence of Gordon Gekko (Michael Douglas), the face of the future that is already amongst us. Like Ethan in *The Searchers*, Gekko floats free, not this time out into the desert, but into the airwaves in pursuit of the billion-dollar deal. Surely it is impossible to believe, as the film wants to promise, that the law will catch up with him. His is indeed a new form of masculinity. For him access to power is not (as it is for Bud's father) through social and political structures, through the family, through traditional systems of knowledge; neither is it (as it was for Wayne's characters) through physical skill, or an absolute commitment to an unchanging (even if contradictory) personal ideal and sense of self. 'I'm talking liquid', he says at one point to describe the vast wealth he is offering Bud Fox, and it is clear that his power comes precisely from his ability to accommodate high-speed change and ephemerality – to live in the flow of information and images that flash through the global networks of the international money market. His masculinity is not measured by what he produces nor even by the specific objects he owns but rather by his limitless, abstract ability to consume – indifferently, without personal involvement. Where Bud Fox ends the film naively asserting he has found himself (his own true, essential self), Gekko is 'a player' and revels in the illusions, the transience, the collapsing of categories that characterise the world (the game) he inhabits. He has no inner life, makes no division between public and private, home and office, day and night. For him personal commitments are provisional, and non-quantifiable systems of value are irrelevant except for strategic purposes. He is light-years away from what, in retrospect, look like the endearingly simple gender structures acted out by Wayne and that line of Western heroes for whom Wayne has come to stand as a symbol.

Further debates will have to consider what Gekko represents. While he subverts the masculinities I have been discussing, he is committed to conflict, control and dominance; he preaches a crude Social Darwinism and enacts a familiar abuse of femininity. Off-screen, his free-market masculinity gives support to a political project whose repressive intentions (in 1980s Britain) were signalled in the validation of homophobia enshrined in Section 28 of the Local Government Act of 1987. He doesn't wear a hat in the bath because doubtless he takes showers. His is the self-interested politics of serious hair-styles and designer suits, and I fear that his 'savage civility' will be an altogether more difficult commodity to deal with.

SOCIAL CLASS AND THE WESTERN AS MALE MELODRAMA

David Lusted

A number of the most influential approaches to the Western have viewed it as a form of mythic narrative dramatising themes of national identity. The Western hero has correspondingly been seen in mythic terms as a 'knight of the true cause' (Bazin, 1971, p.145), an idealised hero of 'romance' wielding near-magical powers (Kitses, 1969, p.15) or even as a tragic figure (Warshow, 1970). There are, however, Westerns of all periods that fit less than comfortably into this framework, among them the two from the 'fifties that I will deal with in this article, *Vera Cruz* (Robert Aldrich, 1954) and *Warlock* (Edward Dmytryk, 1959), both of which seem to be less about national identity than identity defined by social position and gender. They are films with protagonists who share in crises of identity, but whose crises are represented in ways characteristic of melodrama rather than tragedy. Perhaps because of this, the films have been critically less amenable to positioning within the canon of Westerns and therefore, understandably, less visible.

There has been very little research into relations between Western fiction and its audiences. In the absence of empirical studies, it has largely been assumed that the Western offers fantasies of male power for male and, in America, mainly rural working-class audiences (*see*, for example, Cawelti, 1971, pp.8-15). This begs questions about the fantasies audiences return to Westerns for and about the symbolic relations between the identification figure of the Western hero and the social formations of the audience.

The central conflicts in the Western are conventionally between male hero and villain, the central relationships are those of male hero and intimate (sidekick), the central group is the all-male group. Yet more than gender relations are at stake, for these relations are established in clear social hierarchies. Cowboys and miners are wage labourers; gunfighters and drifters are contract labour, often unemployed and always on the social margins. These are figures frequently antagonistic to the middle-class townsfolk, to the petit-bourgeois shopkeepers with whom relations are mostly based on trade and/or to the capitalist railroad owners and cattle barons whose offers of employment are usually refused. They are as often in non-antagonistic (indeed even protective) relation with the peasant class of the sod-busting family. Insofar as the Western can indeed be understood as male, then, it is also homo-social, i.e. implying not just gender but also social relations which inescapably imply positions in a hierarchy of social class. (The term 'homosocial' was introduced by E. Kosofsky Sedgwick in *Between Men*, Columbia University Press, 1984, to distinguish male social relations from homosexual relations. I want to preserve the descriptive value of the term and leave aside the evaluation brought in by Michael Ryan and Douglas Kellner in *Camera Politica: The Politics and Ideology of Contemporary Hollywood Film*, Indiana University Press, 1990, which refers to 'the bonding that is crucial to male power'.)

While the Western hero is temporally and spatially remote from wider male and urban working class cultures, there are at least symbolic connections. The hero as cowboy is a working man, whose involvement with the land and the seasons places him in the category of agrarian labour, but who shares with the industrialised labour of urban manufacture regimes of regulated work, discipline and routine.

The process through which the cowboy became a central figure in Western fiction has been documented by John Cawelti (1976), who focuses on the potential for romance and the dramatic opportunities in the unattached and nomadic traveller on the cattle trail. There are, however, further substantial points of audience identification. One is a shared cultural repertoire of rituals and routines that connects the social experience of particular audiences to the imaginary landscape and character relations of the Western. In particular, the male landscape of the Western speaks powerfully to the conditions of working-class labour which are overwhelmingly, if variously, of action regulated and controlled by figures of male authority. Some of these figures, such as foremen, tend visibly to come from an aspirant or deferential fragment of the working class, while others, such as managers, tend to be invisible in all but the effects of their class power (less managers than management). Antagonisms here can be unacknowledged or refused but their material effects are always felt in conditions of labour. It is in these cultural circumstances that connections between dramas in experience and in fiction can be forged.

Other heroes in the genre, like the gunfighter or the sheriff, share the situation of the cowboy, especially with regard to property and ownership. In the Western, property owners such as ranchers (e.g. *Duel in the Sun*, King Vidor, 1946, *Man without a Star*, King Vidor, 1955, *The Man from Laramie*, Anthony Mann, 1955), town elders (e.g. *Silver Lode*,

Allan Dwan, 1954, *Death of a Gunfighter*, Robert Totten and Don Siegel, 1969, *Posse*, Kirk Douglas, 1975) and other figures representing authority including Eastern lawmen (e.g. Pinkerton railroad detectives in *Butch Cassidy and the Sundance Kid*, George Roy Hill, 1969) and politicians (e.g. *Buffalo Bill*, William Wellman, 1944, *Fort Apache*, John Ford, 1948) are all conventionally minor and often negative forces. Just as conventionally, they collectively contrast with a group of greater narrative significance who are generally more positive forces: the propertyless and socially marginal cowboy and the aspirant homesteader and prospector.

The Western and Male Display

The idea of scopophilia in film – the dominant pleasure in cinema provided by the screen offering a voyeuristic look at a sexualised screen body – was introduced by Laura Mulvey ('Visual Pleasure and Narrative Cinema', first published in *Screen*, 1975, and reprinted in Mulvey, *Visual and Other Pleasures*, Routledge, London, 1989). She used Freudian psychoanalytic notions to describe how the cinema reproduces patriarchal control via a system of heterosexual male 'looks'. This works by a rhyming structure in which the heterosexual male spectator is invited to share voyeuristically in the aroused look of the male character/actor on the thereby sexualised body of the female star. The notion has attracted substantial qualification. Among investigations into the nature of the male look in relation to the figure of the Western hero, Paul Willemen argues that the look directed at the male hero in the films – especially the Westerns – of Anthony Mann is characterised by repressed homosexual voyeurism ('Anthony Mann: Looking at the Male', *Framework* 15-17, Summer 1981). Steve Neale counters by emphasising instead the auto-erotic nature of the male look on the figure of the hero – the pleasure of looking on self rather than another – and its importance in the process of identification (Neale, *Genre*, British Film Institute, 1981), and Yvonne Tasker argues that the look at the body of the modern action hero carries multiple – and not just sexual – pleasures (Tasker, *Spectacular Bodies: Gender, Genre and the Action Cinema*, Routledge, London, 1993).

More than in other male action genres, the concern of the Western with masculinity is bound up in conventions of a distinctive male display. The Western invites a look at the male hero which is unlike the scopophilic look at the body of the male pin-up in the epic film, all exposed flesh and teasing loincloths, and personified by contemporary stars such as Arnold Schwarzenegger and Sylvester Stallone. The look in the Western also differs from that look at the sexualised bodies of contemporary male style stars such as Harrison Ford or Richard Gere. In the homosocial and not just male world of the Western, it is worth asking anew how the audience is invited to look at the figure of the male and how the structure of that look relates to a wider pattern of identifications including those of social class.

The historical dimension seems important here: rather than being rigid and timeless, the look is subject to change, not least through shifts in fashion and gender relations, themselves governed by wider movements and social transformations. Westerns of the 1950s are of particular interest in this respect since there is a discernible shift over the period in the characterisation, formal presentation and consequently the identity of heroism and villainy. It is a shift that connects to changes in the representation of class and masculinity that are rooted in economic and cultural developments of the time.

A sense of these developments might begin with the postwar movement from production-led to consumption-led economics in the 1950s. This combined with changes in labour legislation to make young people into primary consumers and to allow leisure space for the emergence of youth cultures. Such changes had profound effects upon many sets of social relations, including those in which traditional notions of masculinity were tested by new forms of separation between male cultures along generational lines. The process was particularly acute in working-class male cultures where generational divisions were lived out in the stark contrast between the earlier male cultures of prewar and wartime austerity and the new consumerism of the young. In particular, the commercial fashions available to newly moneyed male youth led to unfamiliar rituals of display through dress codes and male body styles.

Many of the social-problem films of the period testify to contemporary anxieties over social change and the profound experience of conflicts arising between men in patriarchal institutions like the family and the school. In particular, there is a focus on the problem of adolescent male youth: between middle-class parents and sons (e.g. *Rebel Without a Cause*, Nicholas Ray, 1955, *The Young Stranger*, John Frankenheimer, 1957) and between middle-class professionals and male youth (e.g. *The Blackboard Jungle*, Richard Brooks, 1955, *The Young Savages*, John Frankenheimer, 1961). The pattern bears out John Hill's idea, framed around British New Wave films of the same period, that 'youth operates as a metaphor for social change' (*Sex, Class and Realism: British Cinema 1956-63*, British Film Institute, 1986, especially pp.74-82).

It is possible to discern comparable conflicts in genre films of the period, but they are dealt with less obviously, in coded, symbolic ways. These conflicts, crossed by codifications of class in the period, combine to dramatise issues of class (especially working-class) identity, but from points of view connected more with the class positions of their audiences than with the elite agendas of anxiety typical of the social dramas.

Something else that the cinema has in common with socio-economic developments of the 'fifties was an emerging 'feminisation' of male cultures through fashion and body style. A new generation of male actors, associated with the Actors' Studio, developed 'method' performance styles 'feminised' by qualities of emotionality and intensity. These qualities contrasted with the 'masculine' conventions of stoicism and restraint that characterised the performance styles of an earlier generation of genre stars such as John Wayne, Gary Cooper and Randolph Scott. In further contrast, 'method' actors like Marlon Brando, James Dean and Paul Newman starred in the new social-realist films of the period rather than in genre films. But it is worth remembering that other genre actors particularly associated with Westerns in the 1950s, including Burt Lancaster, Kirk Douglas and Richard Widmark, had performance styles and screen roles closer to their more youthful method brethren. This generation of actors problematised received notions of masculinity and masculine identity in a way that was clear in the conventions of realism that govern social dramas but less obvious in male genres like the Western. Nevertheless, these developments had significant consequences for the Western: to call masculinity into crisis in its homosocial world is to confront quite fundamental generic expectations about the Western.

The audience for films was also changing. Cinema attendances in both the American and overseas markets were in decline. As television attracted a family audience in increasing numbers, the numerically stable youth audience became a more significant market for the film industry. The greater cultural visibility of the youth audience ensured that its significance was not lost on the film industry, which began to realise the potential profit in developing product tailored to the changing demographics of its market. The conventions of the genre film may well have adapted to compete for the attention of this newly significant audience.

Melodrama, Class and Gender

Recent critical work on melodrama has placed the term again at the centre of cultural debate, not least as a reaction against quite different impulses in arguments about postmodernism. Melodrama can be understood either as a genre with inflections such as the family melodrama and the maternal melodrama or as a fictional mode equivalent to romance or mystery which can operate in any genre. It is in this second sense, as an aesthetic mode with a distinctive range of representations, forms and concerns, that melodrama is claimed by Christine Gledhill to be the central historical mode of imagining in American popular cinema ('Melodrama as Cultural Form' in Gledhill, ed., *Home Is Where the Heart Is: Studies in Melodrama and the Woman's Film*, British Film Institute, 1987, pp.28-38).

Melodrama has been continuously popular since the eighteenth century, crossing literary, theatrical and pictorial genres, and being remade in transmutations from European to American culture. Though subject to generational change, certain formal structures and sensibilities are stable. Melodrama delineates a recognisable social world of its time but dramatises contemporary political and social issues through a set of morally charged Manichean relationships. Forms of melodrama are highly codified and conventionalised, developing narratives through event rather than character psychology, with variant utopian or dystopian resolutions in which the oppressed weak overcome the oppressive strong or, where they do not, are marked as morally superior.

A central trope of melodrama is the dramatic connection between social and psychic repression, leading to an excess of misery in the central protagonist and matched by emotional tension in the audience. Indeed, excess – of drama, emotion and audience identification – is a key formal and stylistic feature of melodrama. In cinema, particularly, this is evident in forms of spectacle and in the visual excess of a stylised fictional world.

The subjects and narratives of melodrama are highly conventionalised in ways that relate to specific audiences; any particular example – for instance, a contemporary variant, soap opera – is richly textured to regular consumers but empty to the casual observer. Crucially, melodrama codes its meanings in expressive forms that signify directly for the socially marginalised groups that constitute its primary audience. As David Grimstead and Michael Booth argue, it is a mode that consistently voices the interests of majority audiences for popular cultures. (In *English Melodrama*, Herbert Jenkins, London, 1965, p.65, Michael Booth argues that melodrama was the dominant mode of working-class entertainment during the nineteenth century, that 'its basic energy was proletarian', and David Grimstead makes the political claim for 'Melodrama as Echo of the Historically Voiceless' in the title of his article in Tamara Hareven, ed., *Anonymous Americans: Explorations in Nineteenth Century Social History*, Prentice Hall, Englewood Cliffs, New Jersey, 1971, p.80.) Melodrama is associated with class cultures that traditionally place limited value on respected modes of literary expression. Combining emotional and other expressive modes of excess such as pictorial sensation and multiple narratives, melodrama is the dominant aesthetic of the common or popular culture despised by the tastes of elite groups whose social power readily sets agendas for what is considered of cultural value.

Thinking about the Western as melodrama invokes this historical dimension. Thinking about the Western as male melodrama, however, requires further argument. For good reasons, melodrama has been seen primarily as a woman's mode. In melodrama as a genre, the protagonists are frequently female, among them suffering domestics, sacrificing mothers and seduced romantic heroines. There is an obvious gender correlation between the social group represented and the composition of the audience. But as an aesthetic, the appeal of melodrama extends beyond women's fiction to incorporate socially marginalised groups more generally, including different fragments of the working classes, ethnic minorities, sub-cultures: groups whose experiences of social oppression and desires for change are the subjects imagined through melodrama.

If the classic Western of genre criticism has been seen as the site of male action, viewing the Western as male melodrama resituates it as a genre that deals with problems of homosocial identity. It is important to recognise here that masculine identity is not

Still: G.M. 'Broncho Billy' Anderson in Broncho Billy for Sheriff *(1912).*

fixed but subject to competing definitions and change. The Western can then be seen as a male action genre exploring changing expectations and notions of masculine identity through fantasy, dramatising the psychic and emotional conflicts within and between men, crediting the conventionally covert areas of male sensibility rather than the more socially acceptable terrain of male cognition, and rendering it integral to rather than separate from male action.

Dwelling on the social meanings of the Western as male melodrama also has political importance. A genre concerned with men in society as much as in myth cannot avoid the absence for many working-class men of social power, men who in the cine-psychoanalytic language of Ena Rae Hark 'symbolically if not biologically lack(ed) the signifying phallus' ('Animals or Romans: Looking at Masculinity in *Spartacus*' in Steven Cohan and Ina Rae Hark, eds, *Screening the Male: Exploring Masculinities in Hollywood Cinema*, Routledge, 1993, pp.151-172). The Western becomes a form of fantasy exploring not the objective conditions of working-class masculinity but scenarios of what that homosocial state feels like and what can be done with those feelings.

What Westerns mean to their audiences is one aspect of my interest in connections between the Western, melodrama and social class. In the tradition of genre criticism, issues of class representation and audience social formation may have been implied but I want here to make class an explicit issue by examining some relations between films and fragments of their working class male audiences in particular historical contexts (with implications for recognising points of identification for female audiences, too). My concern, then, is with the place of genre fiction in the male cultures and sub-cultures of the socially marginalised.

More personally, what lies behind this project is a long repressed impulse to bridge the realms of scholarship and biography. My working-class father has remained a passionate and loyal consumer of Western fiction throughout his life, regardless of its fluctuating commercial fortunes and unaware of critical fashions. Barely literate, he has, with a deliberation that is agonising yet inspiring to observe, read his way through library collections of pulp fiction until they, but not he, have been exhausted. He and I have watched hundreds of films, often together; the pleasures have been many but often different, the differences only recently acknowledged when the onset of blindness consigned those pleasures for him to memory alone. The pleasures as expressed and the terms of the differences often appear to relate too little to even the most celebratory strand of genre film criticism. This article is a step towards remedying certain neglects in both scholarship and biography.

The Origins of the Western in Melodrama

One rewarding path to follow in relocating the Western is to draw on recent critical interest in melodrama in ways that also take into account studies of media audiences: Jackie Stacey, *Star Gazing:*

Hollywood Cinema and Female Spectatorship (Routledge, London, 1994) reviews film theory and introduces into it an audience reception study of stars; Valerie Walkerdine, 'Video Replay: Family and Fantasy' in Victor Burgin et al, eds, *Formations of Fantasy* (Methuen, London, 1986) makes a qualitative study of a working-class family watching a Rambo video; Helen Taylor, *Scarlett's Women: Gone with the Wind and its Female Fans* (Virago, London, 1989) makes a quantitative analysis of women's memories of the film and the book; David Morley, 'Changing Paradigms in Audience Studies' in Ellen Seiter et al., eds, *Remote Control: Television, Audiences and Cultural Power* (Routledge, London, 1989) surveys the field of audience reception studies. What follows is an attempt to locate the origins of the Western film within the aesthetics of 'romance' and, in particular, melodrama. This forms the basis of an analysis of two 'fifties Westerns in relation to a distinctive period of Hollywood melodrama and to male, working-class spectators as one fragment of the total audience.

The Western emerged in the earliest days of Hollywood as a generic form of melodrama, the 'frontier melodrama', dependent on stage melodrama for its dominant narratives, themes and performance styles (Gledhill, 1987, p.23). Although some Westerns derived more than others from stage melodramas, all of them related to melodrama as a mode, implying similarities in their connection to popular audiences of the time.

In genre criticism, the origins of Western fiction are located primarily in literature, dime novels and the Wild West Show. The connections between these media and melodrama have perhaps been insufficiently noted. The novels of Fenimore Cooper and Owen Wister, like the pulp novels of Zane Grey and Louis L'Amour that followed them, are not only fictions of male action but also of romance, both in the narrow sense of stories of heterosexual (and, on occasions, homosexual) desire, and in the wider sense of narratives whose dramas are posited upon the resolution of conflict through individual direct action, decision-making and physical expression. Following Janice Radway's argument for romance as the dominant mode of popular fiction, the aesthetic would include all-male action genres such as the crime thriller and the epic as well as the Western (*Reading the Romance: Women, Patriarchy and Popular Literature*, Algonquin Books, Chapel Hill, North Carolina, 1984).

Dime novels were for many years thought of as exclusively male and centrally Western fiction, but more recent study reveals that they were generically more extensive. The readership, significantly, comprised both men and women (*see* Michael Denning, *Mechanic Accents: Dime Novels and Working Class Culture in America*, Verso, London, 1987). Again, the predominant mode was romance in Radway's sense of the term.

Yet romance and melodrama are very much related forms in popular cultures. Victorian theatrical melodrama in Britain traded off the sensational novels of the period and American stage melodrama grew from the popular cultural roots of the many different immigrant cultures. By the turn of the century, both romance and melodrama were hybrid forms, distinctive as genres of heterosexual courtship and family relations respectively but also available as modes of expression in many other contexts (*see* the works of Michael Booth, particularly *Victorian Spectacular Theatre*, Routledge, London, 1981).

There are clear connections between the Wild West Show and the circus in nineteenth-century America but the situations as well as much of the spectacle in both derive from the stage melodrama (*see* David Jamieson and Sandy Davidson, *The Love of the Circus*, Chartwell Books, Secaucus, New Jersey, 1990, pp.15-17). William F. Cody, whose Wild West Show has been taken as the model of the form, spent ten years from 1872 on theatre stages in the eastern states in melodramas featuring the exploits of Buffalo Bill, a character whose narratives he took with him when he organised his Wild West Show in 1883 (*see* William Brasner 'The Wild West Exhibition: A Fraudulent Reality' in Myron Matlaw, ed., *American Popular Entertainment*, Greenwood Press, Westport, Connecticut, 1977).

It is little surprise, therefore, to find the earliest Western film stories indebted to stage melodrama (*see* Nicholas Vardac, *Stage to Screen: Theatrical Method from Garrick to Griffith*, Cambridge University Press, 1949). Many are domestic melodramas located in frontier settings. D.W. Griffith's *The Goddess of Sagebrush Gulch* (1912) derives from his experience in theatrical melodrama and is generically typical in its combination of a romantic triangle, a betrayed and heartbroken sister, vengeful complicity in a robbery plot, a change of heart and sisters reconciled. The narrative centres on the heroine's story, a melodrama with merely incidental, possibly still emergent, characters of Western fiction – two kinds of man, Sagebrush Pete and a tenderfoot prospector, embryonic Westerner and Easterner awaiting their own drama of male romance.

An uncertain relation between melodrama and romance is evident in the series of films featuring G.M. 'Broncho Billy' Anderson, who is seen in film criticism as a founding figure for the archetypal Western hero (*see* Buscombe, 1988). Yet his origins in theatrical frontier melodramas are little acknowledged. The short narrative films variously relate male action to the family melodrama. Apart from titles like *The Claim Jumpers* (1915), in which Billy outraces the eponymous villains to file a gold claim in a simple chase structure, few are purely quest narratives like the notionally 'first' Western, *The Great Train Robbery* (1903), in which Anderson appeared.

Typical of one tendency in the Broncho Billy series is *The Outlaw and the Child* (1911), in which Billy, on the run from prison, sacrifices in turn his freedom, his water and finally his life to rescue a child who has wandered into the desert. And in *Broncho Billy's Gratefulness* (1913), the hero returns a favour by saving the life of a husband defending his wife's honour. These are essentially family melodramas resolved by the intervention of the hero.

Others in the series are more centrally melodramas and minimise Billy's role as hero. Typical of these is *Broncho Billy's Love Affair* (1912), in which a husband admits his villainy to his wife and the broken-hearted Billy years after he has falsely parted the loving couple. This is similar in plot to the structurally more complex *The Buried Letters* (1910), in which a jealous prospector pal conceals from Billy letters from Billy's wife until an Indian raid and imminent death prompt revelation. In both these examples, the dramatic emphasis lies with the melodrama of love sacrificed and reunited – in the first between heterosexual partners and, in the second, between homosocial buddies.

Most interesting of all in prefiguring an idea central to Western genre criticism – the hero as ambivalent agent of Eastern expansion into the Western frontier – is *Broncho Billy* (1909). Here, the hero falls for a city *femme fatale*, realising too late his love for the woman of the West when the woman of the East introduces Billy to her husband. Attention is centred on Billy not as man of action but as victim of betrayal, the emotional hero of melodrama.

Importantly, it appears from the dates of this film sample that generic evolution in the Western over the period of the silent film was uneven. The Broncho Billy character appeared in hundreds of short films, essentially from 1909 to 1915, and over that time the same mixed economy of melodrama and romance of male action is evident.

Later in the silent period, especially with the arrival of longer, ultimately feature-length, films, male action increasingly becomes conventional in the Western, but still grounded to some extent in melodrama. The Westerns of W.S. Hart, for instance, made mainly between 1914 and 1921, move more towards the spectacle of location and male action within it, foregrounding the role of the hero of romance who has, moreover, a moral rectitude that would become a convention of heroism in Westerns of the 1930s and 1940s. Yet the stories remain rooted in a world of theatrical melodrama – in their concern with false accusation, suffering, misunderstanding, reconciliation and redemption and in a performance style characteristic of the period. Such features of the films tend to be passed over, often with embarrassment, in Western genre criticism (Buscombe, 1988, p.30).

Melodrama, then, is a key component of Westerns of the silent period even as, over time, the genre develops more substantial romances of male action. This move is evident in Hart's films in the separation of township melodrama from epic male action in the natural landscape.

A key actor in the integration and development of the modes is Tom Mix, the last of the three major Western stars of the silent period. In a career lasting longer than those of his contemporaries (1909-28), Mix, who emerged not from theatre but from rodeo and the circus, offered a hero emphasising male display. He employed tricks, stunts and costume derived from the Wild West Shows of the period to make juvenile film dramas of heroism in male-centred action. It has been remarked that the

Stills. Below – the noble Western hero, William S. Hart, in Hell's Hinges *(1916). Opposite – the sexualised pose and dress of Tom Mix in* The Fighting Streak *(1922).*

largely functional dress of Anderson and Hart appears dowdy in contrast to Mix's show costumes with their exaggerated lines and various orders of embellishment (Buscombe, 1988, pp.31-33). But although dress and action are indeed objects of the camera's look at Mix, it is the actor's posing for the camera, separate from the nature of the look in the characteristic shot/reverse shot structure, that points to a narcissism in the figure of the hero that has no formal equivalent in the films of Anderson and Hart.

In *The Fighting Streak* (1922), for instance, Mix plays Andy, who is introduced as a 'man of peace' and exasperates his Uncle Jasper by preferring kittens to masculine horseplay. The man of action emerges later, but, even during this initial scene, the feminisation of the character is reinforced by the exemplary nature of the look at the body. Seen in mid-shot, single-plane focus and high-key lighting, Mix is coded as glamorous pin-up and clearly revels in it. The blacksmith set motivates the choice of working clothes for Mix's costume, but the style is a subtle combination of function and show, cut and worn to emphasise body shape, and dependent for its primary effect on the mid-shot and the long take on the actor's pose. The main impact derives from the sexual look at the figure of the male. The pose carries a particular shock of recognition today, for all the world a 1920s forerunner of Brando in *A Streetcar Named Desire*.

Indeed, it is the relative youth of the actor and the characters he plays that distinguishes Mix from his Western star contemporaries and governs the figure's control of the look. At this early stage of Western film production and the developing transition from theatrical melodrama to film romance, the changing structures of looking at the Western hero seem determined most strongly by his age.

Westerns of the 1950s

Phil Hardy's reference work on sound Westerns (Hardy, 1983) suggests that more Westerns were made during the 1950s than in any other decade, surprisingly even outstripping the number made in the 1930s when the list of features was augmented by the ubiquitous serials and series (a rough count is 515 Westerns made in the 'fifties, compared to 463 in the 'thirties and only 229 in the 'sixties). The sheer volume may in itself account for variation and hybridisation within the genre, but the popularity of expensive melodramas in the 'fifties may also have offered a commercial incentive for the production of forms of male melodrama (*see* Jackie Byars, *All That Hollywood Allows: Re-reading Gender in 1950s Melodramas*, Routledge, London, 1991, and Jon Halliday, *Sirk on Sirk*, Secker & Warburg, London, 1972).

Vera Cruz

Central to the idea of the Western as male melodrama are changes in the characterisation and relationships of the male protagonists. An early example of this – but suggestive of complexities to develop later – is the relationship in *Vera Cruz* between two mercenaries played by Gary Cooper and Burt Lancaster. The quest that provides the film's narrative is the rescue of gold to finance Juarista resistance campaigns in Mexico. The conflict derives from the often comic game-playing between the two gunfighters who are at odds over personal and collective gain. The hero is Cooper, the morally upright and laconic Southern gentleman with asexual, courtly manners that mark him as potential partner to the 'good woman' Mexican peasant. Lancaster is the leader of a gang of mercenaries; he is sexually active and ethnically ambiguous, and bent on personal gain in conspiracy with the 'bad woman' aristocrat. These characteristics place Lancaster's narrative function ambivalently – not the villain (a function fulfilled by Maximilian's aristocracy) but certainly villainous.

This narrative structure is disturbed by three integrated factors which collectively tend toward melodrama: Lancaster's performance style, the look at the actor/character's body and the location of the figure within vestiges of a father/son relationship between the protagonists. Together, these factors begin to mark out a new crisis of class and masculinity that increases in the Western during the 1950s.

Lancaster's performance style has an energy and intensity that contrasts with Cooper's stately demeanour and naturalistic movement. At one level, the two characters stand in the traditions of the Western hero that stem respectively from Tom Mix and W.S. Hart, but only one – Cooper – is the hero. At another level, the contrast is one of age difference between the two actors and the associated difference in generational cultures. Lancaster's character is marked by an amoral appetite for money that is of a piece with his rough sexual energy and voracious hedonism. When the gang gate-crash a regal banquet, Lancaster downs a chicken and eyes the luxury with Rabelaisian relish. At this point, looks of class disdain from the guests at the animality of Lancaster's eating habits are most apparent in Henry Brandon's sneering 'tin soldier' aristocrat. At this point,

Cooper sides with the gang and ridicules the class enemy. But this is the last time that he takes Lancaster's side so unambiguously. Thereafter, as the narrative develops, the disdainful look of social class judgement increasingly comes from Cooper.

Cooper's reaction to Lancaster's activity comes to dominate the shot/reverse shot structure with – at a third level – the look of the saddened father at the rebellious son. But point-of-view in the exchange of looks undermines generic convention and narrative expectation. The audience is not unambiguously positioned to share Cooper's judgement along with his look, because the look in *Vera Cruz* is also that of social class: of bourgeois distaste at the boorish behaviour of the mob. In Lancaster's return of the look, with an accompanying and characteristic toothy grin, there is more than the look of a son competing with the father; it registers antagonism not only between attitudes and generations but also between social classes. It is the look of one who knows but refuses his ascribed status as social inferior.

For a working-class spectator, there is a powerful recognition in exchanges like this. The Lancaster character is narratively placed as villainous, but the actor's charisma combines with an ambivalent point of view to exceed the character's narrative function. His symbolic class position troubles the drive of the narrative and, where it is shared by the spectator, may even deny it.

This is particularly evident in the otherwise conventional resolution of the stand-off. Cooper and Lancaster stare each other out in a montage of reverse shots and rhymed inserts of parts of their bodies. Neither is formally privileged: the face-off, like the look, is democratic. Continuing the rhyming

Stills: Vera Cruz. *Above – the military aristocrat (Henry Brandon) is offended by the manners of the mercenary (Burt Lancaster). Opposite – the uneasy relationship between the generation-gap protagonists (Gary Cooper and Lancaster).*

pattern, they draw their guns and fire together, but the formal pattern breaks as Lancaster falls, shot by Cooper. The narrative clearly requires resolution in favour of the moral – and, now, class – position embodied by Cooper.

But there is a sting. The result of the contest is delayed as Lancaster smiles and trick-spins his gun into its holster before his dying fall, the same gun which Cooper will finally throw away in an angry gesture of regret. The manner of the outcome and death is a performance conceit which disrupts the audience's relation to the narrative function of the scene.

The narrative is romance which speaks of the good father who must sadly but of moral necessity be the agent of the bad son's death. But the mode is melodrama which speaks of an older order tentatively maintaining control over relations questioned by an emergent underclass. The drive of romance speaks of tragedy, but the mode of melodrama speaks of politics. *Vera Cruz* can be seen as an early stage in a struggle over what kind of fiction the Western is to become during the 1950s. An earlier conception of the Western hero remains narratively powerful, but is contested by a troubling emergent alternative.

What is in effect occurring is a struggle over masculinity coded according to class identities. The contrast between competing notions of the hero arises from the different operations of romance and

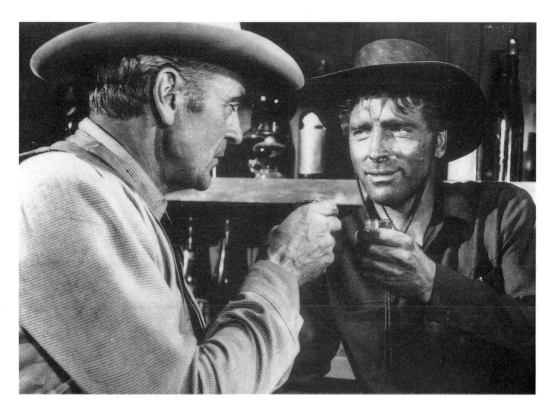

melodrama. The whole seems symbolically connected to changes in the representation of class,
generation and masculinity in the period.

In his article in this book, Martin Pumphrey
writes of the troubling effects of the politics of male
style on the Western hero of the 1950s and of challenges to notions of masculinity wrought by the
social and cultural changes of the period. The idea
is a seminal one for analysis of films like *Vera Cruz*.
It is not only in what the characters do and say but
also in the contrast between how they look (the
sensible formality of Cooper's dress and the street-
wise casuals of Lancaster, the collar and loose
trousers of the former and the open neck and figure-
hugging blacks of the latter) that conflicting notions
of male style wittily and economically express differences between generation and class, and competing
ideas of masculinity.

Lancaster shares with peers like Kirk Douglas
and Richard Widmark some of the physicality and
emotionality of performance style that characterises
the subsequent generation of middle-class actors
who graduated from the Actors' Studio, among them
Marlon Brando, Montgomery Clift and James Dean.
Even if actors like Lancaster were happier in genre
films than their 'method' contemporaries at this
time and eschewed the motivational strategies the
latter required to produce performances, their performance styles do actively express codes of open,
direct exchange and emotion.

In *Vera Cruz*, Lancaster's star persona underlines
the 'feminised' masculinity in the character's attempts at open negotiation with the older man;
Cooper's laconic responses typify a character and a
performance style based on repression of emotion:

stoicism as moral rectitude. Cooper looks at Lancaster, who plays with and rejects the gaze of suspicion and disdain, while when Cooper is the subject
of Lancaster's look, he is unable to return the gaze
and looks away. The power of this structure of looks
undermines the audience's security in identifying
the narrative positions of hero and villain and, by extension, its security in fixing notions of masculinity.

At the same time, Lancaster, like Tom Mix before him, seems to invite the look of the audience,
here partly through athletic stunts derived from his
bar-acrobatics act with Nick Cravat (performed in
films like *The Crimson Pirate*, Robert Siodmak,
1952), and partly through the taut body postures
that are characteristic of Lancaster's individual performance style and signify a state of readiness. In
cine-psychoanalysis, voyeurism, the clandestine look,
has been central to an understanding of the look at
the female body, particularly that of the female star.
Narcissism is the more appropriate term to describe
the invitation to look at this generation of actors in
the 1950s who perform as if with a realisation of new
possibilities and powers. Steve Neale's notion of the
auto-erotic look at the body of the Western hero
seems appropriate here. But the invitation to look
with pleasure at and identify with a gendered individual is also an invitation to look with pleasure at
and identify with a socially classed type.

Vera Cruz is clearly no youth culture film, but it
is evidence of how emergent male youth cultures
penetrate and disturb Westerns of the period, fuel
their fictions of male melodrama and suggest new
forms of connection, especially, with working-class
audiences. Lancaster's coded sub-cultural youth is
pitted against Cooper's older bourgeois masculinity,

Still: Warlock – *entrepreneurial capitalists and friends Henry Fonda and Anthony Quinn in one of several emotional conversations in their private interior.*

and the antagonism between two kinds of men also operates as a metaphor for social class antagonism. Competing representations of male heroism in Westerns like *Vera Cruz* reproduce in fantasy struggles over class position and class relations among its socially formed audiences.

Warlock

Warlock, made in 1959, shares with other films of the late 'fifties – *The Law and Jake Wade* (John Sturges, 1958), *The Wonderful Country* (Robert Parrish, 1959), and, perhaps finally, *The Last Sunset* (Robert Aldrich, 1961) – a characteristic division between the worlds of romance and melodrama. They are clearly melodramas, disturbed and disturbing, at times hysterical in their character relations and fevered in their crises of male identity.

Warlock is a township Western and the others have a journey structure of romance, but they all share the claustrophobic, closed world of melodrama in contrast to the open landscape of the romance Western (much assisted by the studio interiors that pass for exterior locations). In all the films, the central characters are victims of situations which test their ability to act decisively; in various ways, their central characters are torn between private, internalised emotional conflicts and public expressions of direct action. The dramas of the central characters are observed dramatically with irony and pathos. These features constitute for Thomas Elsaesser the defining characteristics of melodrama and are used here to distinguish elements of Western melodrama from qualities of direct action that characterise Western romance (Elsaesser, 'Tales of Sound and Fury' in Gledhill, 1987).

Set in a township that suffers from the villainy of a ranch-owner, who controls the town by forcefully denying it law, *Warlock* is a complex drama of troubled class identity. In the introductory scene, the ranch-owner conspires to humiliate a brave but inadequate sheriff, an act also intended to bring the township to heel. The sheriff is forced to ride a horse bareback at speed out of the town, and the film, a painfully emasculating ejection for a character in a Western. The scene is echoed but its outcome inverted in a climax in which the latest to attempt the sheriff role, a cowboy (Richard Widmark), who has changed sides and rejected the villain, organises peers and townsfolk to overcome the transgressive threat of back-shooting and thus defeat villainy. (In Westerns, back-shooting – shooting an adversary from behind – transgresses the ritual of the gunfight, which demands that an opponent is faced. Back-shooters thereby offend not just against the code of justice but against the social codes of a democratic masculinity by rejecting the public display of fair play.) The romance narrative of the film, then, repairs the earlier failure of the male and renders the Widmark character heroic, a figure of action and decisive resolution.

The film is complicated by another narrative strand, which is uneasily integrated into the first: a professional marshal/gunfighter, played by Henry Fonda, is invited by the town to replace the lost sheriff. Fonda proceeds to establish his own empire through an alternative form of capitalist control –

not property ownership like the villain, but entrepreneurialism – by taking over the gambling in the town. He is assisted by the third significant character, a disabled sidekick played by Anthony Quinn. In a familiar situation in Western fiction, the town elders turn against the pair but are too weak to eject them.

Although absolute villainy is evident in the ranch-owner, it is less clear who has the function of hero. Fonda and Widmark appear to be in narrative competition for the position, and the competition is scarcely resolved in the film's climax, a variant on the conventional face-off.

Under pressure from the town elders, Fonda is torn between choosing a life of legalised crime with Quinn and the promise of settling down with a woman of the town, a dilemma rhymed in Widmark's oscillation between the villainy of the ranch gang and settlement with another woman of the town. The dilemma serves to place Quinn antagonistically between the two men. In terms of melodrama, both Fonda and Widmark are potential victims of more powerful social forces, expressed in crises of identity which threaten to render them indecisive and unable to take action, but Fonda is trapped in them and cannot escape the melodrama, whereas Widmark escapes into a utopian resolution of romance.

Quinn is the agent of this narrative resolution of male romance and yet, as he turns up the heat on the relationships, is also the catalyst for the extravagant melodrama that counters it. Threatened by the prospect of the loss of his partner to the woman and the town (Fonda's prospective 'settling down' represents feminisation and becoming bourgeois), Quinn's attempt to confront Widmark only forces Fonda to take his place. In the ensuing gunfight, Fonda kills Quinn. Although it is not a narrative climax, the ensuing scene – in which Fonda deliriously attacks the townsfolk, burning his boats socially as he honours Quinn with a Viking funeral – certainly feels like one. The externalisation of uncontainable emotion through action expresses anger at social victimisation in a prime example of melodramatic excess.

In the climax – but, after the funeral scene, an anti-climax – Fonda, now so unstable that Grand Guignol is threatened, confronts Widmark. Instead, he throws down his guns before the injured Widmark and rides out – voluntarily, yet as conclusively as the first sheriff. The echo of the opening scene returns us to the film's discourse on masculinity. The first sheriff's loss of face ejects him unwillingly from the social order and the film. Fonda chooses the same path, rejecting the only definitions of masculinity and social position on offer to a man of his class location. If the first sheriff is the coward of romance, Fonda is the victim of melodrama.

The melodrama is played out in a number of significant locations. The external landscape is the site of male action for the figures of romance, where situations change and narratives are resolved. The internal spaces are sites of male melodrama, where characters continually talk emotionally and trawl over their traumas of identity, but resolve nothing. For Widmark, there are two spaces: the ranch, where he attempts fruitlessly to turn the loyalties of ranch-hands, and the sheriff's office, where time passes interminably in the expectation of imminent death by violence.

Fonda and Quinn move between the public space of the bar, where they live out their reputations and social power, and the private spaces of their rooms upstairs where the tensions have all the feeling of lovers' jealousies and betrayals run riot.

In the external spaces, the Widmark of romance fiction triumphs over villainy, but the performers in melodrama move into external spaces at their peril. Outside, they consistently act in ways which undermine the relationship that sustains them. Quinn shoots an informant and Fonda pursues a doomed relationship with the woman played by Dolores Michaels. In these exteriors, each man learns of the duplicity of the other. Fonda and Quinn, unlike Widmark, lack identity outside the melodrama of their rooms and hence have no place in the romance fiction. Quinn chooses death but Fonda rides out of the romance narrative, bearing his melodrama with him.

In this complex narrative movement between romance and melodrama, competing notions of class and masculinity are played out. Widmark is dress-coded as labourer with a loose, plain shirt, neutral denims and a battered hat he selfconsciously toys with. His performance style is uncharacteristically underplayed, emphasising his ordinariness, with little trace of the psychotic persona noted by Colin MacArthur in films like *Night and the City* (MacArthur, *Underworld USA*, Secker & Warburg, London, 1972, p.24). His conflict over allegiance to peers or to boss – an internal struggle over class identity – is he an ordinary Joe or a potential authority figure? – and is resolved by his own action, but an action forced upon him by circumstances. He enters the space evacuated by those socially sanctioned to take it – those of the aspirant working class represented also by Fonda. Unlike Fonda, however, Widmark secures an identity in a class location constructed by his employment as sheriff and implied heterosexual partnership.

Fonda's social position is indeed more ambiguous than this account allows, but there are grounds to locate his marshal role within the same category of working-class waged labour as Widmark. For Widmark, becoming sheriff represents upward mobility; from hired labour to the professions and from the private to the public sector. But for Fonda, the role has different connotations. Dress-coded as stylish but formal, the only one of the three who is potentially a sexualised subject of the look, he carries a social meaning that is reflected in Fonda's troubled and emotionally internalising performance style and in the character's narrative position, balanced between past and future, activity and passivity, corrupt law and loss of status, entrepreneur and criminal. In this network of meanings, Fonda embodies a working-class identity in crisis; he is the suffering hero of melodrama, never the active hero of romance.

Fonda thus emerges as a troubled hero, caught between the lowly Widmark and the excess of Quinn.

The latter's extraordinary appearance and *mise-en-scène* – peroxide blonde hair, flowered waistcoat, ornate bedroom trappings – feminises the character and points to the homosexual dimensions of the relationship with Fonda, which is the aspect of the film most remarked upon critically (Hardy, 1983, p.271). Quinn's dress works effectively as a parody of style, underlining the character's relationship to the plain Widmark and the stylish Fonda, the emotional excess of a masculine identity expressing in extreme and even grotesque form Fonda's troubled sexual and social position – Fonda has as little control over his shifting sexual identity as he has over his class location.

Warlock, then, is a parable of social identity in conditions of class mobility, exploring through melodrama the relations of social and sexual politics. The melodrama turns on the crisis of a township that is exposed as duplicitous, a crisis explored from the position of the socially marginalised. In killing Quinn, Fonda is denied the social status of an illusory authority and moves to accept the social dislocation that is confirmed in his final voluntary withdrawal. Widmark, on the other hand, exceeds his social position for the purposes of the collective. His reward is partnership rather than isolation, identity in social position (what genre critics call settlement and community) rather than the social dislocation chosen by Fonda.

Although class appears not to be an issue for much genre criticism, *Warlock* can be seen to function for male working-class audiences as a discourse on social location, exploring the trauma that arises from limitations and choices in class mobility through crises of masculine identity. The film may be seen as a metaphor for the social mobility that was coming about through education in America and Britain at the time. Its narrative deals both with the problems of class identity in the movement away from social formation (Widmark from the ranch-hands, Fonda from Quinn) towards a dislocated role in an alien and inhospitable class system (constituted by the town and its structures of authority), and with the terms in which social movement is acceptable (for Widmark) or not (to Fonda). *Warlock* deals in terms of personal and emotional crises with problems of class identity and relationship in conditions of social upheaval. This does not make *Warlock* a social drama. But it does suggest that the male melodrama of Western fantasy at least at this time had powerful social meaning for audiences whose social formation and class identity enabled them to respond to dimensions of these films that have hitherto been largely overlooked in critical writing on the Western.

Note on sources. The silent short films in this study are available from the National Film Archive catalogue of viewing prints. I have subsequently discovered that a more extensive list of titles is available in the Archive. *See also* Peter Stanfield, 'The Western 1909-14: A Cast of Villains', *Film History*, vol.1, 1987, pp.97-112.

Still: Warlock – *Richard Widmark clashes with the cowhands he must win over to survive as sheriff.*

JOHN WAYNE'S BODY

Deborah Thomas

John Wayne provides an interesting example of a star whose public image doesn't quite sit comfortably with his roles and performances in his films. This produces a tension, especially for those who respond in some way to the films while wishing to distance themselves from the political implications of the perceived star image. About John Wayne, the man, nothing much can be said, since, in Richard Dyer's words, 'To say that stars exist outside of the media texts in real life would be misleading' ('*A Star is Born* and the Construction of Authenticity', in Christine Gledhill, ed., *Stardom: Industry of Desire*, Routledge, London, 1991, p.135). One can speak meaningfully only about John Wayne the star, but this is an ambiguous term which seems sometimes to refer to the mediated 'real person' of his publicity (loving father, patriot, courageous battler against cancer) and sometimes to a sort of generalised cultural icon whose presence in a film arouses various expectations about the qualities thus guaranteed, with tenuous and uncertain reference to those of the mediated 'real person' (both are seen as brave, for example, but only Wayne as fictional amalgam is seen as a loner). So we have the real Wayne, the mediated (or constructed) 'real Wayne', the generalised fictional Wayne, and, of course, the specific fictional Wayne of specific fictional moments which, when they occur in a single film, are taken as cohering into a particular Wayne character (Ethan Edwards, Kirby Yorke, or whoever). What all these Waynes necessarily have in common is that they share the same body, and this places *some* limits on the qualities they can incorporate (or literally embody).

Although the perceived unity of all stars depends on their physical qualities in this way, John Wayne has been constructed more than most (or at least more than most White males) as a star whose meaning is profoundly corporeal. David Quinlan (*Illustrated Directory of Film Stars*, Batsford, London, 1991, p.470) describes Wayne, after *Stagecoach* (John Ford, 1939), as 'increasingly tall in the saddle, gradually becoming an American institution, as the solitary, basically friendless, almost allegorical man of action'. This has a familiar enough ring to be taken as typical. The key terms – 'tall in the saddle', 'American institution', 'solitary', 'man of action' – are as good a starting point as any. Immediately a few contrasting ideas emerge. Both 'tall in the saddle' and 'American institution' suggest the statuesque, the monumental, and to some extent the socially pertinent (more obviously in the latter phrase, but 'tall in the saddle', too, implies moral stature as well as physical height; Wayne's characters are models of rectitude for others within a shared social domain). And whereas such social attributes meet their opposites in the description of his characters as 'solitary', the frozen qualities of the statuesque/monumental are countered by the dynamism of the 'man of action'. Perhaps further analysis of Quinlan's words can resolve such apparently contrary pulls (e.g. it may be that what I've been calling the mediated real Wayne, not Wayne-as-character, is an American institution, while the characters, not Wayne, may be loners); perhaps it cannot.

One difficulty is that, even within the films themselves, Wayne's body is often seen by other characters as bearing the marks of the statuesque/monumental: tall, hard, unyielding and representative of various institutional codes. *The Sands of Iwo Jima* (Allan Dwan, 1949) provides an interesting first example. One of the men says of Stryker (Wayne) that he's 'probably got the regulations tattooed on his chest', and young Conway (John Agar) compares Stryker to his own demanding father, commenting, 'I bet they got along just fine together. Both of 'em with ramrods strapped on their backs', later adding that he's an 'extra hard product of a hard school'. Similarly, in *The Sea Chase* (John Farrow, 1955), the narrator, Jeff Napier (David Farrar), introduces the film (as well as Wayne's character, Ehrlich) as 'the story of a ship and a man who became so much a part of one another that his heart was her power, his breath her life, his stubbornness the steel of her sides'.

Wayne's characters occasionally appear to perceive themselves in such ways, although it is striking how often they inflect this with irony or distaste. Thus:

Wil Andersen (Wayne): In my regiment, Mr Nightlinger, I was known as Old Ironpants. You might keep that in mind (*The Cowboys*, Mark Rydell, 1971).

Mary McCloud (Claire Trevor): I thought they bred men of flesh and blood in Texas. I was wrong. You're made of granite.
Bob (Wayne): No, Mary. Just common clay. It bakes kinda hard in Texas (*Dark Command*, Raoul Walsh, 1940).

Michael Flynn (Barry Fitzgerald): 'Saints preserve us, what do they feed you Irishmen on . . . ?
Sean Thornton (Wayne): . . . steel and pig iron furnaces so hot a man forgets his fear o' hell. And when

you're hard enough, tough enough, other things. Other things, Michaeleen (*The Quiet Man*, Ford, 1952).

A number of issues need to be disentangled from such examples which seem to emphasise, through their imagery of metal and stone, the unyielding hardness and monumentality of Wayne's body as bearer of moral absolutes. (One can also cite such camerawork as the low-angled shot which introduces him in *Rio Bravo,* Howard Hawks, 1959, where he towers over Dean Martin with statuesque authority.) The fact remains, however, that, if other characters in the films perceive Wayne's characters as hard, indestructible bearers of institutional meanings ('the regulations tattooed on his chest'), they are usually shown to be wrong. In *The Sands of Iwo Jima*, for example, Conway is blinded by resentment of his father to the caring fatherly interest Stryker takes in him – to Stryker's softness – and his comment to Stryker before the raid on Mount Suribachi ('You're indestructible') is belied soon afterward by Stryker's death. The men who raise the flag on the mountain (in a tableau intended to suggest to viewers the famous media images of the event) provide an ironic contrast to Stryker's dead body below. What the film emphasises is Stryker's vulnerability, here physical, but clearly emotional as well (linked in this film to his loss of contact with his ten-year-old son since he split up with his wife five years earlier). This is a familiar pattern in Wayne's films, as we shall see.

So far we have looked at Wayne's perceived monumentality in terms of its physical attributes – its frozen, intractable qualities – which seem to provide

Stills. Above – Wil Andersen (John Wayne) as benevolent father figure in The Cowboys. *Opposite – a toughness compatible with the aches and pains of old age, Rooster Cogburn (John Wayne) in* True Grit.

a screen against his softer, more vulnerable traits. If we turn to the more social aspects of Wayne as statuesque/monumental – his embodiment of the law and its enforcement – we again find more than at first meets the eye. He is often cast as a representative of law and order (a cavalry officer, a marine, a marshal), yet frequently – especially in his work for Ford – he is set up in opposition to a puritanical figure whose unquestioning adherence to the letter of the law, or social convention, is seen critically – most obviously, Colonel Thursday (Henry Fonda) in *Fort Apache* (Ford, 1948), but also both Hatfield (John Carradine) and the women of the Ladies' Law and Order League in their shared disapproval of Dallas (Claire Trevor) in *Stagecoach*, Ransom Stoddard (James Stewart), whom Tom Doniphon (Wayne) repeatedly refers to as 'Pilgrim' as though to underline the point, in *The Man Who Shot Liberty Valance* (Ford, 1962), and Amelia Dedham (Elizabeth Allen) in *Donovan's Reef* (Ford, 1963), though in this last example the perception of Amelia as puritanical by the other characters, including Donovan (Wayne), is itself mistaken. Wayne's characters are much more likely to bend the law, or even to break it entirely. Thus, in *The Searchers* (Ford, 1956), Ethan (Wayne) shoots Futterman (Peter Mamakos) in the back, and, in *The Man Who Shot Liberty Valance*, Tom Doniphon kills Liberty (Lee Marvin) from a hidden position in an alley ('Cold-blooded murder', he comments later, 'but I can live with it').

Still: John Wayne and David Janssen in The Green Berets, *a film with a hawkish public image.*

Even more striking as an indication of his flexibility in the enforcement of the law is the degree of indulgence in his behaviour towards younger men or boys in his charge who don't live up to what they assume he expects of them. War films provide good examples, with his characters confessing their own fears to reassure their men ('I'm always scared', he tells a young marine in *The Sands of Iwo Jima*, and, when asked if he gets scared while on missions, in Nicholas Ray's *Flying Leathernecks*, 1951, he answers, 'Second I push that throttle forward, and any time you meet a guy who says he doesn't, avoid him. He's an idiot'). So, too, does *Cahill: United States Marshal* (Andrew V. McLaglen, 1973) in which he regretfully blames himself, rather than being roused to anger as his sons expect, for their part in a robbery in which the sheriff is killed. Although Andrew Britton has described Wayne as 'the Hollywood cinema's supreme patriarch' (in *Katharine Hepburn*, 1984, second edition Studio Vista, London/Continuum, New York, 1995, p.239), Wayne is generally not a punitive patriarchal figure, even in *The Green Berets* (Wayne and Ray Kellogg, 1968), a film which undoubtedly has a hawkish public image; he tends, rather, to be a tolerantly paternal presence (in those films where he does appear to be punitive, this can often be seen as a front or as a projection of the need to punish himself, as in, say, *The Searchers*). Indeed, one might almost suggest that he takes on a caring and protective maternal function as well, the absence or insignificance of mothers in many of the familial relationships he forges making possible his simultaneous embodiment of both roles. Of course, once its patriarchal elements are excised and the paternal is redefined in terms of such qualities as protectiveness and emotional involvement, the paternal/maternal distinction is no longer clear-cut.

The appropriation of such ambiguously paternal/maternal qualities by Wayne's characters is made more difficult when the mother is present and/or when Wayne's character is located within a domestic setting. In *Wings of Eagles* (Ford, 1957), Frank Wead (Wayne) returns to his estranged wife Min (Maureen O'Hara), and when one of their daughters is crying at night, he rushes out of bed while Min continues to sleep and immediately falls down the unfamiliar stairs of their home and breaks his back. Wayne's characters generally prefer to nudge out alternative familial spaces away from the domestic (in the cavalry, the army, on the range, and so on), even when a woman is part of the package (as we'll see in *Rio Grande*, Ford, 1950). Although Rosen (Gig Young) wrongly perceives Ralls (Wayne) as 'strange, sadistic and cold' in *Wake of the Red Witch* (Edward Ludwig, 1948), Angelique (Gail Russell) has a clearer picture: 'For one thing, you love children', she tells him. 'Oh? Afraid to admit it?' His telling reply, 'Too bad they have to grow up', applies to a far wider range of films – thus, both Debbie (Natalie Wood) in *The Searchers* and Toni (Claudia Cardinale), the young girl he has raised since her mother ran off, in *Circus World* (Henry Hathaway, 1964) unsettle the Wayne characters as soon as they become sexualised adults. There are surprisingly few actively sexual relationships between Wayne characters and women (though there are numerous past marriages broken by death or separation). Where they exist, Wayne often treats his female partners as overgrown children (displaying what seems less like sexual tenderness or passion than playful boisterousness or protectiveness: spanking them, carrying them in his arms like a child) and seems most comfortable outside the sexual fray. Perhaps this wariness of women accounts for the popular perception of his characters as loners, despite their being fairly consistently provided with close male friends and companions. So Wayne's characters resist the domestic and the sexual, but are willing paternal figures in many films (*The Sands of Iwo Jima*, *Wings of Eagles*, *Donovan's Reef*, *Circus World*, *The Cowboys*, *Cahill*: *United States Marshal* and others).

Yet if Wayne's characters often possess considerable flexibility and emotional tenderness – even if it is hidden from others beneath a less yielding facade – the toughness is real enough. However, it is neither the immovable toughness of the statuesque/monumental nor the dynamic toughness of the action hero, in whose terms he is sometimes misleadingly described. In his early (pre-*Stagecoach*) films, he *was* often shown in action (leaping on and off horses, for example, in *The Lucky Texan*, Robert N. Bradbury, 1934, in contrast to his trying to jump on a galloping horse thirty years later, in *Circus World*, when he continually misses his mark), and fistfights and shootouts occurred with reasonable frequency. But his more characteristic films, as his mature persona took shape, seem much more questioning of the violence they depict. The fistfights remain, but are seen not so much as acts of violence but as a means of integrating his characters within relationships and communities (*Red River*, Hawks, 1948, *The Quiet Man*, *Big Jake*, George Sherman, 1971) and as alternatives to the real violence of guns and sudden death; sometimes his characters' sons – actual and surrogate – inherit this function, for example, Jeff (Claude Jarman, Jr) in *Rio Grande* and Martin (Jeffrey Hunter) in *The Searchers*. But Wayne as action hero fails as often as he succeeds.

Wayne's characters are often shown as incapable of succeeding on their own, either needing others' help to stay alive (*Rio Bravo, Big Jake*) or to find and kill the villain (*The Searchers*), or even drawing back from the violence with disapproval (*Fort Apache, She Wore a Yellow Ribbon*, Ford, 1949, *The Quiet Man*), or being killed (*The Cowboys*). His failures are never failures of nerve, but of circumstance (he's outnumbered, has a misguided commanding officer, and so on). As Ehrlich (Wayne) cautions Elsa (Lana Turner) in *The Sea Chase*, 'Don't confuse sincerity of purpose with success'. His toughness is not a matter of hard muscularity (as one expects from an action hero), but of endurance, of taking punishment and of going on. Wayne's toughness is fully compatible with age, fatness, drunkenness, and physical infirmities (bad eyesight, aches and pains), as his later films make abundantly clear. Indeed, on occasion he was deliberately aged (in 'forties films like *Red River* and *She Wore a Yellow Ribbon*, for example), as though to emphasise the nature of his toughness not as the action hero's strength and speed but as a considered shouldering of responsibilities, even when he is shown to be wrong and stubbornness slides into obsession, as in *Red River* and *The Searchers*. Such 'sincerity of purpose', at its most benign, provides those in his care with a comfortable sense of protection – even though his characters don't always guarantee the safety of those they protect, they'll die trying – though at the other end of the scale the willingness to die may take a self-destructive turn.

A few examples along this continuum of ways of 'standing firm' – from protective through stubborn to obsessed – may help clarify the varied nature of Wayne's purposeful endurance. A good place to start is *Rio Lobo* (Hawks, 1970), which has a running joke about the 'comfortableness' of Cord McNally (Wayne) and his body. Thus, when he wakes to find Shasta (Jennifer O'Neill) in his arms, rather than in those of Pierre Cordona (Jorge Rivero) with whom she'll eventually end up, she explains, 'Well, he's young and I thought that . . . well, you're older, you're . . . you're comfortable', sexlessness and renunciation being built into the kind of protectiveness on offer, even in this relatively relaxed example. In *Rio Grande*, the endurance has a more negative edge and the renunciation is more problematic and erotically charged:

Yorke (Wayne) *to his son:* You've chosen my way of life. I hope you have the guts to endure it. But put out of your mind any romantic ideas that it's a way of glory. It's a life of suffering and of hardship and uncompromising devotion to your oath and your duty.

and:

Kathleen (Maureen O'Hara): You're stubborn and proud, Jeff, just like he is.
Jeff: Just like *you* are, mother.

This linking of Yorke's stubbornness to that of Kathleen is particularly interesting and is echoed in *The Searchers*, in which Martha (Dorothy Jordan), too, has elements of Ethan's tenacity – as her husband puts it, in explaining why they haven't pulled up stakes, 'Without Martha . . . she just wouldn't let a

man quit'. Similarly, Ethan explains to Martin that they will get their revenge on their Indian enemy through superior staying power: ' . . . seems like he never learns there's such a thing as a critter who'll just keep comin' on. So we'll find him in the end, I promise you. We'll find him just as sure as the turnin' of the earth.' In *Cahill: United States Marshal*, Cahill (Wayne) challenges the men who are trying to take revenge on his prisoners for supposedly killing their friend: 'I'm willin' to die tryin' to keep 'em. The question is are *you* willin' to die tryin' to take 'em? Oh, hell, get outta my way', or more simply, as his character Ehrlich puts it in *The Sea Chase*, 'I may fail but I can't quit.'

All the key elements are here and it doesn't really matter whether they derive from scriptwriters, directors or star. To quote Richard Dyer again, 'Performance is defined as what the performer does, and whether s/he, the director or some other person is authorially responsible for this is a different question altogether' (*Stars*, British Film Institute, 1979, p.165). Nevertheless, it is still worth asking whether Wayne's body is particularly well suited to carry the meanings that I have mentioned which attach themselves to his person with such regularity. I have already suggested that he lacks the body of an action hero. He has the height, but lacks the lean, hard muscularity. Characters in his films often comment on aspects of his physique – and not always flatteringly: thus, Matty (Kim Darby) in *True Grit* (Henry Hathaway, 1969) tells Rooster Cogburn (Wayne), 'You're too old and too fat to be jumping horses'. But, although Wayne's height is sometimes the subject of other characters' comments, it is more frequently used visually to convey a sense of his awkwardness in a domestic milieu, or to support other characters' perception of his rugged monumentality (even if, as argued earlier, this is later undermined). His size suggests endurance rather than speed, and its solidity is a solidity of the flesh – frequently subject to woundings by guns and arrows – rather than the impenetrable hardness of metal and stone.

Most crucial to the sense of Wayne's body as protective is the quality noted by Scar (Henry Brandon) in *The Searchers* when he names Ethan 'Big Shoulders'. The breadth of Wayne's shoulders and sheltering chest suggests the sort of comfortable protectiveness – the paternal/maternal quality noted earlier – to which Shasta responds in *Rio Lobo* when she chooses to sleep in his arms rather than in those of the man she desires. In film after film, women as well as children are lifted in his arms and sheltered against his chest (e.g. in *Wake of the Red Witch, The Searchers, Rio Bravo, True Grit*). And this is the site of his greatest vulnerability as well: for example, he gets an arrow in the chest in *Rio Grande*, an arrow in the shoulder in *The Searchers*, is shot in the shoulder and chest in *The Cowboys*, and is shot in the shoulder – and later a knife is thrown in the same spot – in *Cahill: United States Marshal*. Unlike many typical action heroes whose hard muscularity is displayed and celebrated in shots of their naked torsos – or even 'softer' heroes whose youthful sexuality is similarly put on show through bare-chested displays (e.g. Martin in *The Searchers*) – Wayne's body is seldom revealed, even when we would expect it to be (thus, he swims with his shirt on in *Donovan's Reef* and has a towel draped over his shoulders and chest when he emerges from the shower where he's waiting for some thieves to attack in *Big Jake*; when he is injured, bandages often hide his otherwise bare chest and shoulders). The main exceptions which come to mind are instructive: *The Quiet Man*, where Sean's memory of himself in the boxing ring after he has inadvertently killed his opponent fills him with horror, presented, arguably, as a horror of his masculinity itself, as well as of its consequences; *Wings of Eagles*, where Frank Wead is undergoing hydrotherapy, his naked body paralysed as a result of his fall downstairs; and *Rio Grande*, a rare example of Wayne's body eroticised, which will be looked at in more detail below.

I think enough has been said to make clear the opposing tendencies in Wayne's persona and the various ways in which his public image oversimplifies and even misrepresents – as statuesque/monumental, as patriarchal, as heroic in the action-hero mould – his actual roles and performances. I have argued that his toughness is the toughness of endurance: a literal shouldering of responsibility, a standing firm, a willingness to die. It is a paternal/maternal quality shared by some of his female counterparts but, if it involves a 'feminising' of his body (or, at least, a tendency to deny or recoil from the harder, more traditionally masculine aspects of his physicality), this is seen not as weakness, but as strength. However, correlated with such incorporation of the feminine into the self is often a renunciation of the sexual and domestic in the world outside. Yet if sexual fulfilment remains largely unattainable by most of the characters Wayne plays – but

Still: Frank Wead (John Wayne) undergoes hydrotherapy in Wings of Eagles.

his endurance an endurance of abstinence as much as of anything else – it is still hard to avoid the feeling that this is what many of his finest films are somehow about, a 'signifying absence' if ever there was one. That many of these films pose him as an enigma – 'What makes a man to wander?' (*The Searchers*), 'Who *was* Tom Doniphon?' (*The Man Who Shot Liberty Valance*), 'What kind of man *is* he, mother?' (*Rio Grande*) – suggests the erotic and his resistance to it as crucial missing pieces of the puzzle. I would like to look at two Westerns in which the erotic is an insistent and positive presence, one directed by John Ford (*Rio Grande*) and one by Howard Hawks (*Rio Bravo*), as a means both of exploring this dimension of Wayne's meaning and of comparing the use of him by the two directors most extensively associated with his finest Westerns.

Rio Grande

Rio Grande is the last of the three films that make up Ford's cavalry trilogy (with *Fort Apache* and *She Wore a Yellow Ribbon*), and it is only here that its central male character, Kirby Yorke (played by Wayne), is troubled by erotic desire, which, in the other two movies, is located and played out more simply and conventionally in the younger generation's romantic pairings off. Whereas, in *Fort Apache*, Wayne's character, Kirby York (here – is it significant? – without the 'e'), learns from Colonel Thursday's repressed and repressive example, taking on his persona and colluding in the misrepresentation of his memory at the end of the film, and whereas, in *She Wore a Yellow Ribbon*, Nathan Brittles (Wayne) is an older man long since reconciled to – and apparently comfortable with – his enduring widowhood, *Rio Grande* makes clear the emptiness of Kirby Yorke's life without his estranged wife Kathleen, and the precariousness of the suppression of his desire.

The movie begins with a series of arrivals. First, Yorke arrives back at the cavalry encampment at

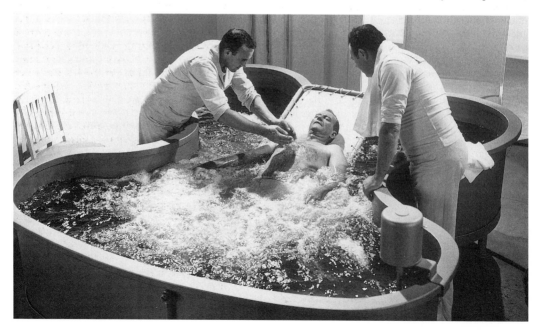

Still: Home on the Range – the frustrated relationship between Kirby (John Wayne) and Kathleen (Maureen O'Hara) in Rio Grande.

the head of his troops, some of whom are injured and on makeshift stretchers pulled by horses. A number of captive Indians, their arms bound, are in among the returning men, suggestive thematically of a barely contained disturbance in the midst of the soldiers. The families move forward to greet the troops, the women anxiously scanning the troops for their men. This is followed by the respective arrivals of Yorke's son Jeff, an under-age recruit who has volunteered after failing mathematics at West Point, and, the next evening, of Kathleen, whom Yorke hasn't seen for fifteen years, now determined to buy Jeff out of the army.

That Kathleen and Kirby still love each other is clear from the romantic music and the way their gazes meet as she arrives. Although both do their best to skirt around any acknowledgment of this immediate revival of their desires, the film leaves us in no doubt, the erotic charge between them all but surfacing from the moment of Kathleen's arrival. Kirby's restrained greeting – 'Good evening, Kathleen' – is echoed and intensified by Sergeant Quincannon (Victor McLaglen) – 'Welcome home, darlin' ' – who functions here and elsewhere to facilitate the expression and enactment of their wishes.

Above all, the erotic text is carried by the music. The movie contains at least seven separate songs (one rendered twice) which are sung by various characters or groups of characters at various times within the narrative, not to mention the music-box version of 'I'll take you home again, Kathleen' which is later sung by the regimental singers as well

as reprised on the soundtrack, and the cavalry band's version of 'Dixie' which is played at the end. This is an extraordinary amount of narratively motivated music in a non-musical film, and it is largely responsible for the way in which erotic longing and a sense of potentially wasted lives permeate so much of the movie's texture. Thus, the regimental singers act as a kind of chorus, with songs including lines like 'Hope she's gonna stay' and 'I'll take you home again, Kathleen', as well as 'I met an old woman, a-plucking young nettles', with its allusions to the cutting short of young lives by death. One of the most moving examples is the song sung by Kirby's men as they sit round a campfire and Kirby walks on his own nearby, the song's lyrics centred upon growing old with waiting, the beloved reduced to a fading shadow ('So if my longing wrings my heart and tears get in my eye, I'll hurry back again to her ere purple shadows die'). The music is inextricable from the narrative in its creation of an atmosphere which links all the film's actions to its central push towards an erotic reconciliation, before it's too late, between Kirby and Kathleen. Furthermore, and in contrast to the dry and dusty names of such Western towns as Tombstone and Shinbone (which Ford depicts in other films) or to the litany of god-forsaken stops on Colonel Thursday's itinerary en route to Fort Apache in the film of that name ('What a country, forty miles from mud-hole to mud-hole: Mule Creek, Dead Man's Squaw, Schmidt's Wells, Hangman's Flats . . . '), we have Bridesdale – Kathleen's plantation – and Fort Bliss – where the women and children are sent for safety – even if Bridesdale has been burned down on Kirby's orders during the Civil War (but later rebuilt by Kathleen), and Fort Bliss is never reached in the course of the film, as the Apaches attack the women and children first. Both exist as possible destinations in an imaginary landscape to which the narrative – and its ubiquitous musical commentary – aspire.

The Rio Grande itself provides the central image of the film, especially in the scene where, after the Indian attack on the camp, Kirby meets his Mexican counterpart in the middle of a shallow part of the river, both men being constrained by their orders not to cross, despite their being on the same side, metaphorically, in having the Apaches as a common enemy. It is an apt image of the frustrated relationship between Kirby and Kathleen, facing each other with mutual respect across a divide of fifteen years, the Indians symbolic of the obstacles in the way of an easy reconciliation.

A closer look at the first Indian attack may help to spell this out more fully. I have already mentioned the opening images of the returning troops, with captive Indians in their midst, and suggested a link with Kirby's barely suppressed desires which Kathleen's arrival so readily revives. When Kathleen says goodnight to Kirby and prepares to settle in his quarters for the night, while he leaves to sleep elsewhere ('I'm sorry to dispossess you', 'I dispossessed you more forcibly fifteen years ago'), we note Quincannon turning up at Kathleen's tent, though we don't yet know why. The display of Kirby's body as he wryly shakes his head several times and removes his shirt in readiness for bed – a simultaneous display of both his desirability and his desires, and one of the most convincingly eroticised images of John Wayne's body in all of his films – is accompanied by a gesture of frustration as he throws the shirt down and a slight stiffness in his step as he climbs into the covered wagon to sleep alone. It is a moment which beautifully balances the sensual (as in the play of the breeze in Kirby's hair) and the selfconscious (for example, in the regretful shakes of his head as he undresses and the hints of awkwardness in his movements), and the resultant combination of a powerful sexuality with both vulnerability and stoical endurance is fundamental to Wayne's appeal.

Quincannon leads Kathleen in the direction of Kirby's new quarters, but, despite the expectation this arouses that she is on her way to his bed, they continue past the wagon and over a bridge to the tent shared by Jeff and his new friends. Below the bridge, as they cross, the Indians within the camp are chanting ominously, and Quincannon orders an Indian-born trooper to tell them to be quiet and to douse their fires. Again, Kirby's sexual longings and their frustration are linked to the precariously contained threat of the Indians, both through their juxtaposition and through the earlier suggestively worded reference to his responsibility for the burning of Bridesdale fifteen years before ('I dispossessed you more forcibly . . .'). The ensuing attack on the camp – the Indians outside clearly signalled to and abetted by the Indians within – is a symbolic representation both of the destruction of Bridesdale (as the Indians set fires and pull down fences) and of the release of energies only barely contained (as the

horses, which we first see nervously milling around in the corral, leap out). Kathleen's swoon in the course of the attack is less easily attributable to simple fear (for she shows no such fear when the Indians attack the wagon train en route to Fort Bliss later on) than it is to the playing out of these other dramas.

When the General finally gives Yorke the order to cross the Rio Grande, an action which – like the Indian attack on the camp – is linked to the burning of Bridesdale fifteen years earlier (the General himself linking them in his remark to Yorke: 'I sacrificed the happiness of your home once, Kirby, to the needs of war. Now I'll probably ruin your army career'), the women and children are sent to Fort Bliss for their own protection, Kirby assigning Jeff to be part of their escort as a concession to Kathleen's wish to keep their son safe. However, since the crossing of the Rio Grande also has symbolic resonance, as I've argued earlier, as an image of the potential coming together of Kirby and Kathleen, the action serving erotic needs as well as 'the needs of war', the fact that the Indian attack on the wagon train of women and children occurs *before* the river can be crossed by the men should alert us to its function as the enactment of additional unfinished business between Kirby and Kathleen. Indeed, its end result – the capturing of the children – plays out the second major source of conflict between them: their struggle for the divided loyalties of their son, Jeff.

Whereas Kathleen deprived her husband of their son fifteen years before in retaliation for the burning of her home, Jeff's enlisting has restored him to his father, and Kathleen makes it clear that Kirby's refusal to release him from the army is the remaining obstacle to their reconciliation. Although Kirby's duty, in Kathleen's words, once made him simultaneously 'destroy two beautiful things: Bridesdale and us', the rebuilding of her home 'required just physical effort'.

Kirby: The other would require more?
Kathleen: It would be a start if you'd let Jeff go.
Kirby: And get you back?
Kathleen: If that were a condition.
Kirby: I could say yes to you very easily . . .

But Kirby's compromise, whereby Jeff can accompany his mother to Fort Bliss, backfires when the Indians attack and take the children away, and Jeff is saved while riding for help only because of the intervention of his friend Tyree (Ben Johnson), who later hand-picks Jeff – along with their friend Sandy (Harry Carey, Jr) – for his mission to get into the church where the children are being held. So the film lets Jeff prove himself in his father's eyes while depriving Kathleen of any reason to hold Kirby responsible, all blame displaced on to the Apaches.

However, this 'silencing' of Kathleen in the symbolic battle between them is not the final skirmish. For if the Indians reflect the conflicts between them, then the arrow which hits Kirby in the chest, just as the children have been rescued and the men are about to return to camp, can be seen as Kathleen's necessary – if survivable – revenge, a final cancellation of her forcible dispossession and resentments

Still: forbidden to cross the Rio Grande – Kirby Yorke with the General (J. Carroll Naish) in Rio Grande.

from the past: in effect, a face-saving. It is also, in some sense, Cupid's arrow (though it is not literally piercing Kirby through the heart – which would defeat the purpose somewhat – but near enough), restoring through his wound the relationship between him and Kathleen. But the movie doesn't end with the shot of Kathleen holding Kirby's hand as he lies on the stretcher (an image of reconciliation drained of erotic force). Rather, we are given a sunny scene of healing and recuperation. The General is the benevolent puppet-master here, the playing of 'Dixie', presumably on his orders, putting the finishing touches to his earlier directive to Kirby ('I want you to cross the Rio Grande'). It is an inspired touch on his part which, in combination with the troops parading past with the American flag, implies a postwar healing of the rift between North and South as well as of that between Kirby and Kathleen. As Kathleen twirls her parasol in triumph and delight, her girlish manner and the whiteness of her shawl and parasol present her to us as, once again, a bride, leaving us with an image of the dissolution of

lost time and of felicity restored, in place of the sense of loneliness and wasted lives that permeates so much of the rest of the film. Yet if Kathleen and Kirby are 'home' together at last, we are nonetheless left with a question which the film renders problematic but never answers: where, exactly, is home? Bridesdale? Or the United States Cavalry?

Rio Bravo

Rio Bravo is centrally concerned with the erotic education of John T. Chance (Wayne), and the 'action plot' involving the arrest and imprisonment of Joe Burdett (Claude Akins) is subsidiary – if closely linked – to this concern, as is the redemption of Dude (Dean Martin) from his state of alcoholic disgrace. What all three subplots share is a concern with the polar opposites of indulgence and denial. The film moves towards a proper balance between excess and restraint, and its triumph is that it manages to achieve this, most specifically through the creation of a central and transformative erotic relationship between Chance and Feathers (Angie Dickinson).

The plot is set in motion by Dude's thirst, leading to Joe's taunting offer of the money for a drink. He throws the coin into a spittoon, but before Dude can retrieve it, Chance kicks over the spittoon in disgust. Although he functions initially as a judgmental figure of restraint – both to Dude *and* to Joe, whom he eventually arrests for the murder of a bystander who tries, less successfully, to restrain Joe when he beats up Dude – Chance is himself excessively violent in the process, knocking Joe out with his rifle (as Dude had earlier knocked Chance out with a wooden plank) before dragging him away with Dude's help. He later hits another man in the face with his rifle in the aftermath of the murder of his friend Wheeler (Ward Bond), though Dude, in contrast, is by that point more restrained, having begun the process of self-transformation before Chance. So Chance is linked to both Dude and Joe – and they in turn to each other – by their shared potential for violence, in Dude's and Joe's cases directed against men who try to restrain them. Chance's moments of violence are more ambiguous, functioning to punish the excesses of others while nonetheless being excessive themselves. Further, if Chance is linked to Joe by such outbursts of violence, he is simultaneously a figure not merely of moral and legal restraint but of emotional and sexual restraint as well, his anger seeming to provide a partial outlet for his bottled up feelings and desires. The fact that Joe's brother Nathan (John Russell) is described by Chance as having 'got this town so bottled up that I can't get Joe out or any help in' – a remark echoed by Colorado (Ricky Nelson) when he says that the song Nathan has the musicians perform was played by the Mexicans 'for those Texas boys when they had them bottled up in the Alamo' – suggests an affinity with Nathan as well as with Joe. Nathan, too, like Chance, is excessive in his imposition of restraint (having Wheeler killed, for example, for 'talking too much'), but, unlike Chance, working indirectly (through hired killers) and outside the law.

For much of the early part of the movie, Chance is characterised by both his anger and the simultaneous bottling up of his sexual desires. If Dude's thirst sets the plot in motion, Chance's 'thirst' – after a much longer dry spell – is a great deal slower in surfacing. The anger which is an agent in his denial of his emotional and sexual needs is a response to the excesses of others ('Guess there's no sense in me telling you to cool down', Dude tells him after Wheeler's murder), but it is *also* a response to Feathers awakening his suppressed desires ('I always make you mad, don't I, John T.? Then don't make me tell you why I stayed . . . '). If Joe suggests the potential for violence in Chance, and Feathers suggests the erotic possibilities he has hitherto denied, then his efforts to get both of them out of town are logically linked. The same stagecoach that will fetch the Marshal to take Joe away is the stagecoach on which he enjoins Carlos (Pedro Gonzalez-Gonzalez) to put Feathers. If Joe is 'no good', as Chance tells Nathan, then neither is *she*, or at least that's what he convinces himself of on the basis, as it turns out, of scant evidence. Yet whereas Chance begins by asserting his authority against them both ('Joe, you're under arrest,' 'You're in trouble, lady'), the movie is at pains to align us with Feathers and

against Joe. It is not just a matter of one type of release (the sexual) being seen as preferable to another (the violent), for Joe, too, is seen on the prowl. Leaving one bar (the scene of the murder) for another, he notices a woman in the street, turns her around to see her face, and rejects her when he realises that she is Mexican. The film clearly condemns the debased nature of his sexuality, his attitude to the Mexican woman appearing little different from his attitude to the man he's murdered, and Joe's sexuality is contrasted sharply with that of Feathers.

Feathers transforms Chance by literally and metaphorically disarming him, and her playful eroticism goes hand in hand with an undermining of male authority and control, yet an undermining which, in the end, is liberating for Chance, rather than a threat. The turning point in Chance's liberation is, of course, the moment when he carries Feathers upstairs, the discreet fade being nonetheless explicit in its implications. Up to that point, whenever he moves away from the jail, Chance always either carries his rifle – often cocked and pointed before him – or has it near to hand (as in the shaving scene). When he comes downstairs to take Feathers to bed, his rifle, for the first time, is nowhere in sight, his hands finally free for other things. He easily removes the rifle she has in her lap as she sleeps and leaves it on the bar downstairs. However, the frequent scenes of arming and disarming in the film – such as Dude disarming Burdett's men, Chance deciding to let Colorado keep his guns, Stumpy prompting Chance to return Dude's guns to him, Burdett's men removing the bullets from Chance's gun before making him go to the jail to release Joe, and so on – should not be taken to imply that guns function in terms of a fairly crass sexual symbolism whereby Chance *replaces* his rifle with a phallic sexuality in whose terms he is still in charge and the relationship with Feathers is a struggle for control that was previously played out with weaponry. The ease with which he removes her gun and the fact that he then lays it aside belie any such conflict. Further, the scene where Feathers shaves Dude with a cutthroat razor and offers to do the same for Chance ('How about *you*, John T.? Shall I work on *you*?'), while straightforward in its sexual overtones, provokes Chance's smiles rather than his panic. The sexuality in which she invites him to participate is one which offers Chance a new wholeness where anger and violence are defused. But first he must be divested of the trappings of male authority and control.

This process of 'divestment' (which implies literal undressing) begins at Chance's and Feathers' first meeting when she affronts his dignity by pretending to believe that he is actually the owner of the frilly red bloomers which Carlos is holding up to him in an effort to picture them on his wife, Consuela (Estelita Rodriguez). Her remark as he leaves ('Hey, Sheriff, you forgot your pants') literally stops him in his tracks, and his combined annoyance and flustered embarrassment set her up as a disturbance to his previously secure sense of being both masculine and in control. The shared joke between the two men at the expense of the absent Consuela is now turned on

its head, as Feathers 'undresses' Chance, implying a complicity between her and Consuela (and it is surely part of the humour of the scene that Carlos – who claims to know women – has chosen such ridiculous and inappropriately over-sized bloomers for his diminutive wife: one need merely compare Feathers's outfit at the end, concocted with Consuela's help and advice, to see where Carlos has gone wrong).

At their second meeting, Chance, in contrast, refuses her suggestion that *he* search *her* for the missing aces in the card game and sees no further than her outermost clothing – the feathers – taking them wrongly to be evidence of her guilt. Following their third meeting, this process of Feathers's divesting Chance of the trappings of his authority continues when she prevents Carlos from waking him at daybreak, as he'd requested, and we see Chance hurriedly pulling on his boots and struggling to get his vest on, his physical awkwardness hinting at his growing awkwardness in the official role which these clothes represent and which Feathers undermines. At their next meeting – and their first kiss (following his acknowledgment and growing awareness that 'If I weren't in this mess it might be different . . . ') – her comment that he'd 'better run along now and do your job' further deflates him in its playfully dismissive tone: he looks at her, shrugs, makes a flustered movement with one of his hands, and is clearly at a loss for words.

Still: 'You're in trouble, lady' – Chance (John Wayne) and Feathers (Angie Dickinson) in Rio Bravo.

So the build-up to the scene in which Chance takes Feathers to bed is one of steady erosion of his self-confident façade, his anger suggesting initial resistance and his embarrassment (whereby he is metaphorically 'disarmed') suggesting uncertainty as his authority is progressively subverted and his tentative desires exposed. The morning after his night with Feathers, however, Chance is all smiles, asking Dude how he slept, playfully kissing Stumpy (Walter Brennan) on the top of his head, and joking with Colorado outside the hotel, with no trace of his earlier bad temper. For the first time, he lowers his guard and puts down his rifle, walking out of reach of the gun as several of Burdett's men approach on horseback, having apparently been disarmed by Dude, on duty at the end of the street. But Dude has, in fact, been waylaid by Burdett's men while staring at his reflected image in the water trough (an image transformed by a bath and clean clothes, though the change is, at this point, only skin-deep: as in the cases of Chance and Feathers, we should avoid confusing the outer clothes with the person inside), and one of Burdett's men is now impersonating him by wearing his hat and vest.

Chance has been literally – and not just metaphorically – disarmed by his deepening relationship with Feathers, but, although he is momentarily caught by this lowering of his defences, he is almost immediately saved by the combined efforts of Colorado and Feathers (the latter throwing a flowerpot out of the hotel window, on Colorado's instructions, to distract Burdett's men). Thus, the disarming of Chance is not presented as the dangerous and potentially fatal consequence of involvement with a woman (a 'castration', as some might put it), but as a positive step for Chance in allowing himself to trust in others, and to open himself to their care, although the movie – through Feathers's distress at the deaths of Burdett's mercenaries – doesn't let us forget that violence is still violence, however shared the responsibility. Still, the lesson for Chance is clear: he can let himself be vulnerable and still remain safe. The point is reinforced later on, when Dude and Chance are captured again and, through the combined quick thinking of Dude, Stumpy and Colorado, Chance is freed without having to fire a shot himself. There is an almost magical quality to the final hour of the film, as if Chance, by becoming sexually and emotionally vulnerable, becomes invulnerable to harm. That we see Feathers performing card tricks for Carlos, just before Dude and Chance arrive at the hotel and are captured for the second time, suggests that the magical powers are initially hers, though easy enough to learn ('It's easy, Carlos, you just weren't watching').

Chance's friends not only collectively protect him, but also collectively steer him towards Feathers. Colorado is the first to believe in her goodness and to chastise Chance for his doubts, but Dude, too, reassures him as he urges him on ('. . . I'll take care of you'). In fact, by the end of the movie, Dude and Chance have more or less changed places: Dude literally has his guns back and Chance has figuratively put his down; Dude has relinquished his thirst, pouring his drink back into the bottle without spilling a drop, and Chance has discovered his appetite, 'unbottling' his emotions and desires. Stumpy, as well, has placed himself firmly on the side of Feathers's project to eroticise Chance. Thus, he joins in the singing in the jail *not* for the song about guns and the solitary life ('My rifle, my pony and me'), but for the much more erotic song whose imagery not only links an appetite for food to the sexual, but ascribes that appetite to the woman, the man wishing, rather, to be the object of the woman's active desire ('I wish I was an apple, hanging in the tree, And every time my sweetheart passed, she'd take a bite of me'). That the song places its desires outside the confines of marriage (the line, 'I'll marry you some time', is suitably vague and dismissive) is also apposite.

What Feathers offers Chance is an unconventional ease, a steadying in an unsteady world (one has only to notice the steadying of his gaze towards her in the scenes subsequent to his carrying her upstairs, whereas his previous looks were full of uncertainty and punctuated by glances away). That she has transformed him is nowhere more apparent than in the final moments of the film, preceded by the shoot-out and final defeat of the Burdetts, with its imagery of dynamite and explosions. At an earlier stage,

Chance had told Stumpy that Dude had to 'sweat out' his desire for a drink: '. . . be nice to him and he'll fall apart in small pieces', a remark suggesting anxieties around male fragmentation. But, despite Chance's direct hit on the warehouse, Nathan and the remaining men with him emerge intact, and, with Dude's encouragement, Chance goes off to find Feathers. In final confirmation of her healing powers, she completely reverses the terms of the movie's opening. Chance's first words in the film ('Joe, you're under arrest') are now transformed into his claim – obviously scripted and provoked by her – that if she wears her overly revealing costume downstairs in the bar, he'll arrest her. Her reply coincides with his starting to put his rifle down: 'What I had to go through: put on these tights, ask a lot of questions, start to walk out. I thought you were never gonna say it.' 'Say *what*?' (laying down the gun). 'That you *loved* me.' 'I said I'd *arrest* you!' 'It means the same thing. You know that. You just won't *say* it . . .' His original authority as sheriff arresting Joe has now become eroticised and turned into a declaration of love. Chance flings Feathers's tights out of the window at the precise moment Stumpy is walking by with Dude, and Stumpy's final speculation ('You think I'll ever get to be a sheriff?') makes clear his awareness of what being a sheriff now involves.

Given the difficulties of providing a tidy conclusion to such a wide-ranging account, I will restrict myself to a few observations about both the central problem Wayne's persona seems to me to present, and the attempts to resolve it in the two films I have just examined. Because of the way the Western maps its central dichotomy of freedom and containment on to that of wilderness and home, one of its problems is how to position its central male characters with regard to the erotic. If the wilderness – in its representation as a place of unbounded space and, in Michael Wood's words, of 'invitations to loneliness' (*America in the Movies*, Secker & Warburg, London, 1975, p.49) – is generally male territory, then the pastoral (domesticated) landscape, with its imagery of fecundity and containment, is generally the woman's. These alternative topographies suggest fairly obvious corresponding alternatives for the Western hero: on the one hand, embracing loneliness and refusing eroticism's offer, and, on the other, risking diminishment within the domestic frame. Wayne's films more than most seem to emphasise the inadequacies of either route, his characters being filled with sexual longing, yet typically compelled to resist and suppress it if settling down is the price of its expression (unlike Henry Fonda's Gil Martin, for example, in *Drums Along the Mohawk*, 1939, the only pastoral Western which springs readily to mind amongst Ford's films). Nevertheless, in Wayne's case, despite the renunciation, the longing persists, and this is what sets his Westerns apart from those whose heroes can be packed off to the wilderness with little sense of loss or ongoing stoical endurance.

Rio Grande and *Rio Bravo* share a desire to sexualise Wayne's characters, but they can only do so by

Still: 'I said I'd arrest *you' – Feathers and Chance resolving their differences at the end of* Rio Bravo.

evading the problem of home, either by refusing to locate it with conviction (*Rio Grande*) or, more constructively, by opening up a non-domestic space which is neither wilderness *nor* marital home that both men and women can inhabit together (*Rio Bravo*). The conflicts leading up to *Rio Grande*'s resolution are more deep-rooted and recalcitrant than those of *Rio Bravo*, doubtless because of the more conventional basis of its relationships, and their resolution is more tenuous as a result of their much more indirect working through, which is displaced to a large extent on to the Apaches. Yet in *Rio Bravo*, too, the laying aside of Chance's gun and the eroti-

cising of his role as sheriff can only be a short-term solution, effective merely until the next bunch of bad guys rides into town. In both films, the pastoral dream is transformed into a psychic state in a landscape of the imagination, becoming, in Leo Marx's words (in *The Machine in the Garden*, Oxford University Press, 1964, p.28), 'a virtual cocoon of freedom from anxiety, guilt, and conflict – a shrine of the pleasure principle', the conflicts of a gendered world having been symbolically worked through and momentarily abandoned at the point of narrative closure. That these films are exceptional within the body of Wayne's work is evidence of the difficulties of the endeavour and of the precarious but nonetheless satisfying balance they achieve.

THE DIETRICH WESTERNS
Destry Rides Again and Rancho Notorious

Florence Jacobowitz

Marlene Dietrich was a star whose appeal was directed largely towards a female audience. She was billed in the advertisement for *Morocco* as 'Marlene Dietrich: the woman all *women* want to see'. Her onscreen persona challenged the inevitability of women's oppression, manifested in the requisite social trajectory of self-sacrifice. This was the essence of her collaborations with Josef von Sternberg. The films' support of the woman's right to satisfy her own desires first, coupled with the star's ironic detachment, contradicts the demands of resolution and narrative closure in the woman's film. The incongruity of the endings derives in part from the star's glamour. Amy Jolly tosses her heels and leaves the community to follow her lover/outcast into the deserts of Morocco; Helen Faraday, the Blonde Venus, returns to her impoverished apartment and loveless marriage and proceeds to bathe her son, dressed in an extravagant spangled sheath. Dietrich's own glamour and sophistication empowered her characters – a visual acknowledgement of self-esteem and value. The protagonists' decision to pursue what they want with whomever they desire is fortified by the persona's strength and self-confidence. Indulging in privileges customary to the male domain does not mean becoming a man. X27's gesture of fixing her lipstick before her execution at the end of *Dishonored* mocks the hypocritical male establishment who feel threatened by her ability to penetrate their world, and flaunts her gender. Dietrich's delight in adapting and glamorising male uniforms of power and privilege – top hat and tails, a Russian Army uniform, leather aviator gear – stands as a visual mockery of a system that insisted on clear gender distinctions and social separation as a means of securing a hierarchy and perpetuating injustice.

Dietrich was well aware of the significance of the offscreen image and understood the value of studio publicity in complementing her star image and generating steady interest. She orchestrated her image with care (as is attested to in great detail in Maria Riva's *Marlene Dietrich By Her Daughter*, Knopf, New York, 1992). The offscreen persona added layers to the screen image. Her sophisticated style, her European-ness, her intelligence (marked publicly by a literary coterie of lovers/friends including Erich Maria Remarque and Ernest Hemingway), the complex of suitors of both genders, and her identity as a mother and single parent (she remained married to Rudy Sieber but they lived separately) challenged American cultural notions of femininity. Dietrich's

rejection of her homeland of Nazi Germany and her commitment to the United States – she applied for American citizenship in 1937 and was sworn in around the time *Destry Rides Again* was conceived – created more tensions. She was now unequivocally American and yet a sexual mother/glamorous star whose persona retained its transgressive edge.

The decision to cast Dietrich in a Western like *Destry Rides Again* (George Marshall, 1939) at the close of a decade during which the star had built her career in the woman's film immediately creates a certain frisson. The Western is, in many ways, the genre whose concerns seem almost diametrically opposed to those suggested by the star image of Dietrich as popularised through the woman's film and melodrama. Westerns are male-centred, preoccupied with masculine identity. The genre dramatises attempts by the White frontier community to impose and establish a law-abiding settlement. The protagonist struggles to define and control the nature of his social environment and his place within it. Women are most often relegated to roles that are an adjunct to the male hero or a projection of male need – the saloon girl/prostitute versus the schoolmarm/wife.

Occasionally, though, the Western can veer towards melodrama, raising dilemmas traditionally facing female protagonists. What if the demands made of the individual to sublimate himself for the good of the frontier community are overwhelming? What if he doesn't want to, or is divided or driven by needs or a sense of justice that is inimical to the frontier community? What is the cost of establishing an oppressive White male heterosexist country? The melodramatic male Western hero surfaces, sometimes in the 'revenge' drama in which the individual (and by extension the community) suffers a trauma which he then attempts to redress.

The two Westerns conceived with Dietrich in mind, *Destry Rides Again* and *Rancho Notorious* (Fritz Lang, 1952), both dramatise the struggles that result from conflicting images of the frontier community. *Destry Rides Again* adopts a more obviously conservative position: Destry (James Stewart), in a variation on *Young Mr Lincoln* (John Ford, also released in 1939), is summoned to domesticate Bottleneck, a corrupt community in need of a strong paternal marshal. The film can accommodate comedy and the buoyant energy often associated with the musical because the hero is fundamentally solid and will accomplish his task; his unwillingness to pick up a gun does not, as is affirmed early on, mean that he is without power. *Rancho Notorious* is more subversive – it utilises the 'blinded' excessive melodramatic hero to analyse the strict regulation of gender underlying the Western's overt concerns of settlement and nationhood, and places the hero's troubled identity and actions within the demands of his social world.

The casting of Dietrich is as fundamental to the meaning of these as is the fact that they are Westerns. However different they may be, the two films

Still: Marlene Dietrich in Destry Rides Again.

both use the quintessential American genre, dedicated to exploring and mythifying America's image of itself as a nation while being heavily influenced and shaped by European emigré artistic talent. *Destry Rides Again* was produced by the Hungarian, Joe Pasternak, scripted by Felix Jackson, an ex-Berliner, with music by Frank Loesser and Frederick Holländer, also native Berliners. *Rancho Notorious* was directed by Fritz Lang, a director whose American work remained heavily influenced by his roots in the Expressionist cinema of Weimar Germany. (I have not referred directly to Lang's use of Brechtian practice in *Rancho Notorious* – *see* Robin Wood, '*Rancho Notorious, A Noir Western in Colour*', *CineAction!*, 13/14, August 1988, pp.83-93.)

Both projects were conceived and developed with Dietrich in mind for the female lead, and depend upon the audience's reading of the persona to inform the narrative with meaning. Pasternak approached Dietrich with the offer of a Western as a comeback vehicle. (Dietrich's film career was at a low, highlighted through the well-publicised exhibitors' advertisement placed in 1937 branding Dietrich, along with Katharine Hepburn and Greta Garbo, as 'box-office poison'.)

The part of Frenchy was designed to capitalise on Dietrich, who remained potentially bankable as a star commodity in spite of the hiatus in her box office popularity, which was attributable to many factors, most obvious among them the entrenchment of her image in the work of Sternberg, particularly in their two final projects. These served to validate allegations of perversion and decadence associated with her work (which were no doubt bolstered by off-screen gossip). It is in many ways miraculous that a film like *The Scarlet Empress* (1934) was made at all – it breaks almost all the rules of realist narrative film-making, beginning with the storybook collage of young Sophia's fantasies of sadomasochistic torture and ending in the heroine's bitter triumph. Sternberg's complicated use of identification invites one to identify with the woman's position and understand why she adopts strategies which are ultimately untenable: Catherine finally comes close to resembling her mad husband in her cruelty. *The Devil Is a Woman* (1935), the last Dietrich/Sternberg collaboration, incorporates a similarly complex use of identification, allowing one to empathise with Concha's delight in torturing Don Pascal to prove a point about her status as a person rather than as a possession. Both works demand that one place the protagonists' actions within a broader social frame; otherwise they are unreadable. These strategies were in place all through Sternberg's and Dietrich's collaborative career, but the final two films are particularly heightened, stylised and bitter in tone. They also go furthest in foregrounding the Dietrich persona's dependence upon irony, artifice and stasis. In many ways, Dietrich becomes visually integral to the *mise-en-scène*, to Sternberg's style and artistic vision, because the persona is used emblematically to signal transgression and resistance. This is not the place to analyse these films or the evolution of the collaboration and the tensions which intensified towards its end. One can, however, surmise that this type of extreme artifice and emphatic glamour was threatening and was not appreciated by an audience who perceived this 'exoticism' and foreignness as unnatural, not to mention increasingly unwelcome in a country on the eve of a war against Germany.

In order fully to appreciate the radical analysis of gender relations and genre in *Rancho Notorious*, one needs to look back to the more conventional *Destry Rides Again*. Pasternak's conception of Frenchy was designed to erase the worst memories of the Sternberg work while reviving the recuperable elements that could be Americanised and made acceptable. (Andrew Britton has described similar strategies used at the time to recuperate Katharine Hepburn and Greta Garbo in *Katharine Hepburn*, 1984, second edition Studio Vista, London/Continuum, New York, pp.146-149; Robin Wood, 1988, p.93, mentions other attempts, in *Desire*, Frank Borzage, 1936, and *The Garden of Allah*, Richard Boleslavsky, 1936, to separate Dietrich's persona from her work with Sternberg.) The risqué, vulgar sexuality associated with Lola-Lola, the 'showgirl' of *Der Blaue Engel* (Sternberg, 1930), is recalled and recast in a saloon

Stills: the brawl in Destry Rides Again. *Opposite – Frenchy's unladylike response to the intervention of Destry (James Stewart). Below – Destry cools off Frenchy and Lilybelle Callahan (Una Merkel).*

girl, without the ironic sophistication developed in the later Sternberg films, or the emphasis on stasis that was part of the cabaret style of sprechgesang.

As critics quickly and happily noted, Frenchy is stripped of irony, sophistication and to a large extent glamour. Steven Bach in *Marlene Dietrich: Life and Legend* (Morrow, New York, 1992, pp.251-254) delights in commending this 'new Marlene', the 'regular gal'. 'Gone were the fatalistic pauses, the fantabulous poses, the fantastic plunges into glamour that had drowned Paramount and Selznick and Korda in red ink.' He quotes a critic who wrote at the time, 'Here is a Dietrich we have long suspected existed behind that external mask of beauty and who now breaks forth with all the fury of an exploding firecracker.' Frank S. Nugent of *The New York Times* praised the 'jaunty, jocular and rowdy show which seems to have snapped Miss Dietrich out of her long von Sternberg trance.' Dietrich would not come to a set without approving and often collaborating on the conception of her characters' appearance and costume, but here was a new Dietrich who would move as well as pose, anxious to get into fist fights and roll on the ground. Maria Riva describes how Dietrich insisted on doing her own stunt work for the saloon fight: 'Una Merkel and Dietrich took their places, the cameras rolled, my mother whispered, "Una, don't hold back – kick me, hit me, tear my hair. You can punch me too – because I am going to punch you!" and with a snarl, jumped

on Merkel's back, knocking her to the floor' (Riva, 1992, p.494).

Destry Rides Again is a perfect antidote to the 'excesses' of Josef von Sternberg, and this was the intention: to salvage the star quality while removing the tarnish of 'decadence'. This means that the film would use the accoutrements of the image and defuse the more dangerous, subversive aspects of the persona that had threatened the star's career. As a bonus, a Western would affirm Dietrich's commitment to her new homeland in the United States. Dietrich is stripped of the more perverse 'European' aspects of her sexuality (retained only in her name, Frenchy) – the appropriation of male clothing and so on. Her fundamental transgressiveness is re-inflected so that her challenge no longer poses a threat. Frenchy is the heart of Bottleneck; the town adores her energy and vitality. She embodies the spirit of rebellion, the youthfulness of the still immature frontier community, but she doesn't threaten its fundamental power base. Although Frenchy is nominally 'the real boss of Bottleneck', her subservience to Kent (Brian Donlevy) is established immediately and is challenged only when it is transferred to Destry (James Stewart), who succeeds Kent in defining the town.

The film begins with a long lateral track introducing the frontier town of Bottleneck as wild and lawless, complete with shooting, brawling and bodies flying. The camera moves into the saloon and cranes up to introduce Kent's card game. As Kent is losing, he steps out of the room on to a balcony and surveys the scene from above before signalling the bartender to notify Frenchy. Dietrich's star entrance begins with her familiar voice. She is singing 'Little Joe', back to camera, and swivels around to reveal the recognisable figure that goes with the voice. After the number, Frenchy confirms the spirit of resistance invested in her star image: she hurls water over a man who slaps her, throws off another who grabs her on the dance floor and kicks a third. She then makes her way up to the card game, poses with one leg raised, evoking Lola-Lola, and proceeds to participate in a card scam by pouring hot coffee on the dupe while his cards are switched, thus cheating one of the townspeople of his gold and property. Kent's disingenuous remark about needing the luck of Frenchy's rabbit foot – the signal for her to pour the coffee – is a reminder of who really holds the power in Bottleneck.

Frenchy's challenge is drained of any of the profound significance that Dietrich's persona has in the Sternberg films. It is placed within the conventions of the Western: she is the saloon girl/entertainer set apart from the traditional women of the community. Dietrich's transgressions of gender distinctions are called forth and defused. This strategy is used throughout the film; for example, the threat of emasculation inherent in the persona is alluded to in the scene when Frenchy bets against the pants worn by Callahan (Mischa Auer) and then insists on claiming her winnings. The result is an entertaining catfight with Callahan's wife, Lilybelle (Una Merkel). The threat is thus normalised through juxtaposition with the respectable wife who also emasculates her spouse by insisting on calling him by the name of her

Still: Destry Rides Again – *Frenchy sings that she will have what the boys in the back room will have.*

dead first husband. Frenchy's claims to 'have what the boys in the backroom will have' are expressed in her willingness to indulge in a good-natured brawl, displaying the ease usually associated with masculinity. Dietrich's appropriation of masculine traits and attendant privileges is summoned forth and then negated through its placing within the comic tradition of role reversal.

Frenchy's activity and aggressive exuberance contrast with Destry's passivity, his delight in carving napkin rings and telling didactic parables. James Stewart's boyishness visually undermines his authority, as do the comic props introduced to accentuate Destry's unwillingness to contain violence through a display of prowess and more violence. Destry arrives sporting a parasol and canary belonging to Miss Tyndall (Irene Hervey) – shades of Professor Rath (Emil Jannings) in *Der Blaue Engel* – and proceeds to order milk at the bar. Frenchy awards him a mop and bucket with which to clean up the town and will eventually offer him her rabbit's foot to compensate for his unwillingness to carry a gun. Destry's 'femininity' is entertaining rather as Frenchy's 'one-of-the-boys' brashness endears her to the community. Like a Howard Hawks comedy, the film plays on gender reversals, although Destry's potency is quickly established through his ability to shoot the knobs off the wheel of a sign and Frenchy's place as Kent's girl and possession is reinforced in subtle ways – Tyndall (Jack Carson) commenting that Destry is

cutting into Kent's property through his relationship with Frenchy gets him punched, and when Destry asks Frenchy to dance, he first asks Kent for permission.

In fact, Frenchy's proclamation that she will have what the boys in the backroom are having is a little like Roland Barthes's concept of the function of inoculation in bourgeois mythologies: 'One immunizes the contents of the collective imagination by means of a small inoculation of acknowledged evil; one thus protects it against the risk of a generalized subversion' (Barthes, *Mythologies*, Hill & Wang, New York, 1972, p.150). By addressing a little contingent evil (here under cover of the generic conventions of entertainment), one can avoid a more serious threat. Destry tames Bottleneck, teaching the town the lessons of maturity by instituting law and order through a legal/judicial system. He also tames and normalises Frenchy, teaching her to find her authentic self and be a lady: 'I bet you've got kind of a lovely face under all that paint. Why don't you wipe it off someday and have a good look. Figure out how you can live up to it.' Frenchy begins to wipe off her lipstick – as she does to kiss Destry after being shot trying to save him. Artifice, excess and self-protection, the mistakes of the past, are erased. Frenchy earns her badge of femininity and her place within the community through sacrifice. It is ironic that part of Frenchy's recuperation and acceptance by the women of the community takes place when she tells them to take action and they do so by joining their 'menfolk' in the battle against Kent and his henchmen. Logic would have Frenchy lead this rebellion, but her final activity is exactly opposite – it is one of self-abnegation and self-effacement.

Although the film ultimately attempts to naturalise Dietrich, her persona is remarkably resilient and not easily harnessed. Moments like the one when she refuses to be rushed to perform, commenting 'the longer they wait the better they like it', or when she delights in 'riding' Destry following her fight with Mrs Callahan (evoking shades of the perverse aspects of Dietrich's persona which reached a pinnacle in *The Scarlet Empress*) have a life of their own beyond the parameters of the film. Frenchy overwhelms the narrative, and, as a number of critics have noted, the film acknowledges a profound sense of loss in its final moments (Britton, 1995, p.149). The re-generation of Destry's peaceful patriarchal town is embodied in his legacy – his young admirer, Claggett Jr, has adopted Destry as role model and hero. They are strolling together down Main Street when Destry's attention is caught by a young girl leading a group of children in a chorus of 'Little Joe'. The recollection of Frenchy and her vitality, appropriately revived through children, underlines the emptiness of the ideologically sanctioned couple (Destry and Miss Tyndall) and by extension of the now mature-yet-lifeless Bottleneck. The star image contradicts the demands of the film.

Rancho Notorious was conceived as a star vehicle for Dietrich and is dependent upon this star casting for its coherence. Her second (and last) Western, it recalls Frenchy in the characterisation of the former saloon-girl who is taught a moral lesson by the hero and dies in what can be read to be an act of self-sacrifice. The similarities are, in fact, superficial. Unlike *Destry Rides Again*, *Rancho Notorious* uses the fully elaborated persona established in the period of the Sternberg collaborations, and evokes it in its full glory, probing its more subversive meanings. *Rancho Notorious* raises the questions explored in the variations of the woman's film. How does an independent woman survive if she rejects the male-defined options of wife/mother or property for male pleasure? Where is her place if she demands rights denied to women? But it also goes one step further, analysing the limitations of the power achieved by the Dietrich persona through her glamour and her confident, bold sexuality. This is empowering in a society in which the valuation of a woman's beauty and glamour is inescapably defined by youth. In Altar's words, 'Every year's a threat to a woman'. The film addresses the concerns of the woman's film through an investigation of a star persona twenty years after the peak of her filmic career.

At the same time, *Rancho Notorious* is a revenge Western, which takes it close to melodrama. Although the film has been compared to the Lang *films noirs* of the period (Robin Wood, 1988, persuasively demonstrates its affinities with *The Big Heat*), it is also comparable to Lang's earlier male *noir*-melo-dramas with Edward G. Robinson and Joan Bennett (*Scarlet Street* and *Woman in the Window*) in which the man's fears of mortality and impotence, fed by the rigorous demands of a male-dominant, capitalist society, conjure up the desirable woman as a means of assuaging an unstable, insecure ego. The question of the male hero's identity (as well as that of the community) and his place within the community are subject to analysis in *Rancho Notorious*. The film establishes immediately the precariousness of the frontier settlement and its inhabitants and proceeds to question the myths of marriage, reproduction and community that uphold it. *Rancho Notorious* introduces itself as a melodramatic Western and then moves into territory traditionally explored through the woman's film. The tensions resulting from this conflict of generic concerns coalesce in Altar Keane (Dietrich). She embodies a threat at the heart of the film: it is Altar who haunts Vern (Arthur Kennedy) when the logic of a revenge Western would place Kinch (Lloyd Gough), the outlaw who unquestion-ably committed the crimes of rape and murder, as the prime object of the hero's search and the focus of the narrative.

In fact, the alter ego of the hero and the cause of the permanent deflation of his dream of settlement and community are Altar Keane and her community of Chuck-a-Luck. Altar undermines the idea of romance, the rigidity of gender roles and the picture of the homesteading community presented in the film's opening, and the characterisation of these as myths redirects Vern's passionate hate back on himself. The opening shot, after the ballad that labels the narrative as 'the old story of hate, murder and revenge', is a close-up of a young, attractive couple locked in a lengthy embrace. We learn of the couple's plans to wed shortly, to save money for eight years in order to afford a ranch, to begin a large family (despite the man's visible impatience with the young boy who briefly disturbs them). Romance is presented with exaggeration: the portrait of the kiss, the woman's desire to call their future homestead the Lost Cloud ranch (as she gazes off into the distance), the man's statement that the brooch he is giving to her was supposed to come from Paris, France, and that it is 'fine for stargazing'.

But there is a sense of unease in the town, which is oddly deserted and bathed in an eerie red after-noon light. The woman attributes the absence of the townspeople to their having all gone to visit the newly arrived triplets (another of the film's images of excess). The ease of Kinch's intrusion and sub-sequent rape and murder of Beth (Gloria Henry) attests to the reality of the community's vulnerability. Her screams are briefly heard by a child playing alone. The posse makes a perfunctory gesture of an attempt to secure the town but its members are more concerned with the reality of their vulnerability (Sioux country borders the community) and business matters (the cattle need branding). That Vern's comment, 'What if she was your wife or daughter?', is met by silence suggests that despite the claims of unity and nationhood, justice remains within the realm of every-man-for-himself.

The last words of Kinch's partner Whitey (John Doucette) – 'Chuck-a-Luck' – lead Vern to Altar Keane. The legend of Altar and by extension, Diet-rich, is generously dramatised through a series of recollections which serve to define it. The first is from a marshal who remembers Altar as the saloon girl who was the jockey who 'rode' him in a race. The star entrance of Dietrich in red and black lace saloon-girl regalia (signifying the singer/prostitute) digging her heels into her 'horse' suggests the Dietrich of *Destry Rides Again* in terms of fun and energy, but also carries overtones of sexual reversal. It places Altar at the opposite end of the spectrum of Western women from the sweet domesticated subservience of Vern's Beth. The second memory of Altar is supplied by another saloon-bar entertainer, Dolly, who remembers Altar's elegance – 'She came from the Eastern seaboard' and 'sang only in the most elegant places' – the pair of white horses pulling her carriage and the men, 'lots of men'. Although Dolly defines her as a 'glory girl' (and surmises that other women would probably 'be happy if lightning hit her'), Dolly's clear admiration speaks from a woman's point of view. Her memory of Altar is not defined by prostitution, but instead articulates the power evident in her glamour, her career and the men who would all 'uncover' (show respect by raising their hats) for Altar as she passed by. This is the Dietrich 'all women want to see', the one whose offscreen persona is as significant as her onscreen presence.

The final recollection is offered by the men who remember her working for the saloon owner, Baldy Gunder (William Frawley). This aspect of the legend

Stills: Rancho Notorious – *the legend of Altar Keane (Marlene Dietrich). Below – the 'horse race'.*
Opposite – placing her bet at the Chuck-a-Luck wheel.

tells of her resistance to male control. The story begins: 'One night, Mr Gunder didn't like the way she treated a patron or, to put first things first, Altar didn't like the way the patron treated her.' The image is of Dietrich, the languid singer smoking a cigarette, pushing away a customer who gropes at her. When Baldy accuses her of not 'smiling' enough, claiming she is paid to entertain (i.e. to be touched), she demands that Baldy, too, take his hands off her, and is fired. Altar continues to rebel by insisting on her rights to gamble at the Chuck-a-Luck wheel ('I stay here as long as I like') and it is here that she meets Frenchy Fairmont (Mel Ferrer), who is immediately attracted to Altar and is in many ways her match. He is an elegant outlaw markedly unlike the others. Frenchy's name connotes a Continental sophistication (and recalls Dietrich's Frenchy in *Destry Rides Again*). He is witty, articulate, well-mannered and also sexual – 'the fastest draw'. Frenchy, too, is aware of the Altar legend: the three men who fought a gun battle over her and died in the process, the time she rode through a hotel 'straight up the stairs . . .' on a white horse. Frenchy's stories evoke the Dietrich of *The Scarlet Empress*, the empowered woman who took most of the Russian Army as lovers. He comments on Altar's popularity in those days and implies that years have passed – 'I often wondered what had become of you' – to which Altar replies, 'Stop feeling sorry for me'. The final sequence of memories places the strength of the persona's fascination and career against the background of its most serious threat – time.

The narrative of revenge, of Vern's search for Kinch, detours around Altar past and present, and builds towards Vern's first meeting with her. Altar is legendary precisely because she is everything Beth isn't: autonomous, confrontational, never compliant and not a virgin. Her relationship with Frenchy is not defined by marriage and monogamy, and Vern resents this before he has met either of them. His final caustic comment to the man who delights in the rumour that the two are 'snug and warm' near the border is a bitter 'sounds romantic'.

When Vern finally does meet Altar he stares at her and accounts for his rudeness by explaining that it is 'unsettling' finally to see that Altar exists. Beyond the legendary Altar, the entertainer who addresses various needs and desires, he finds a refined Altar, sober and workmanlike in male attire and completely in control of her ranch and her life. The present grounds the fantasies. Altar is commanding, but she is neither a parody of masculinity nor overtly feminised. She is the star, relaxed and confident. Altar partakes of the privileges of the male world and is similarly empowered by money. She is practical and runs her community as a strict business venture. Altar makes the rules and insists on enforcing them; they equalise the status of every outlaw passing through – everyone works and contributes ten per cent of his gross take. The introduction of Altar in the present fractures any remaining identification with Vern, setting his wound-up hysteria and aggression into relief. The spectator empathises with Altar's ability, her sense of fair play.

The film has established the present in relation to its evocation of Altar's past. Chuck-a-Luck is Altar's expression of survival and independence, of her unwillingness to remain vulnerable and exploited. It exists because there is no other social place for Altar. In this sense, she is an outlaw and so aligns herself with those outside the law, offering shelter in return for the men's acceptance of her rules. The film draws on Dietrich's star image and the conventions of the woman's film which nurtured it, and Chuck-a-Luck is carefully placed within a demystified social world which is self-serving and unjust. The sanctuary of the community is a fiction, the wheel of fate and luck is rigged and controlled, towns are governed by corrupt politicians or fascist law-and-order parties, and the only governing reality is the system of capitalist exchange – safety and independence are not inherent rights but can be bought for a price. *Rancho Notorious* doesn't offer Chuck-a-Luck as an idyllic sanctuary; in fact, Altar is finally unable to keep herself and her ranch insulated from the injustices outside it. Altar's attempts to remain autonomous, the boss of her ranch, are dependent upon her ability

to charm her clientele. They become resentful and ultimately rebel against an empowered woman who has been 'riding mighty high' for a long time. As Altar knows well, her power is waning with age.

Vern avenges his pipe dream and assuages his badly shaken ego by destroying Altar and what she represents – the challenge to the Western hero. He does this through performance, staging his masculinity and seducing Altar by correctly identifying her weakness. In Altar's words, 'He's young and handsome – it's easy to take a fancy to him. He makes you remember yourself a long time back.' Vern puts his youthful masculine prowess on display by competing with Frenchy – riding a bronco (as Frenchy the 'old mustang' might have ten or twelve years back), threatening to outdraw him and becoming a bank robber. Vern's attitude towards Altar is evident in his pointed remark about the horse he is taming: 'She's a cocky filly, like a lot of women, takes a lot of breaking before she comes along nice and even.'

The concerns of the woman's film cross those of the Western in the scene in which Vern discovers

the brooch stolen from Beth. Altar agrees to entertain her guests on her birthday (after outsmarting one of them who has tried to cheat her) with a rendition of 'Get away, young man, get away'. The song shows Altar's awareness of the reasons why she is attracted to Vern and at the same time proclaims her commitment to Frenchy. She is the ageing star who still fascinates, in part because she defies the restrictions age imposes in defining glamour and power. Altar is sporting the brooch as part of her booty. The image mocks Vern's investment in this symbol of idealised romance, the means of validating the woman's objectification as a possession, whose subservience to the reproduction of the white male hegemony is needed in establishing settlement. Altar has the brooch without conditions, without male control. She uses it as a means of adornment for her own pleasure, and her open sexuality is not directed to any one man in particular.

The montage of the various men's faces after Vern notices the brooch illustrates a number of issues. On the level of plot, it indicates Vern's suspicion that any of the men had the potential to kill Beth, but it also works to identify Vern's guilt and fears. He is judged by the male community of which he is a privileged member: he has failed over the safety of his fiancée and his future, and it is incumbent upon him to rectify his failure. The faces spell out his loss – their desire is evident, and, through Altar, they continue to enjoy the pleasure Vern was denied. She serves as the monstrous incarnation of Vern's trauma.

Ironically and appropriately, Vern's strategy of vengeance and rectification is to insist that Altar recreate herself for him alone as a vision of desire, in her birthday evening dress and wearing the brooch. Altar's granting him his wish signifies her loss of control and autonomy – she is succumbing to the seduction she has resisted ('I only met one man who didn't want something behind the pretty talk') and to his demand of ownership ('You're very beautiful in the jewellery Frenchy gave you'). Altar's genuine commitment to Vern is apparent in her willingness to break a rule that will claim her life – she divulges the name of the man who brought in the brooch.

Vern's cruel outburst is framed by the film's support of its star – the audience knows she has been manipulated. The film has been careful subtly to undermine Vern's claims of Frenchy's complicity in Kinch's crime. Whitey is killed because he is unwilling to promise Kinch to 'keep his mouth shut about the girl' when they get to Chuck-a-Luck. Vern confesses his hatred for Altar, focusing on her sexuality ('What do you see? A bedroom or a morgue?') and her transgression of gender norms (the men come to Chuck-a-Luck 'to hide behind your skirts'). The ideological valuation of the good woman's purity underlines his denunciation of Altar's 'dirty life' in the past and the present ('You think a dance hall girl was a dirty life' . . . You oughta be proud of that compared to what you are now.'). The film parallels Vern's violation of Altar with Kinch's of Beth through the repeated gesture of violently tearing off the brooch.

Vern's confrontation with Altar is the revenge hero's eruption before his nemesis; getting even with Kinch is anticlimactic in comparison. Vern is also implicated in provoking the final shootout because his self-serving actions announce that Altar has broken the rules. He compromises her safety, leaving her weakened and vulnerable. Ultimately Vern contributes to the destruction of her haven of Chuck-a-Luck; he shares the outlaws' sentiments that she has been 'riding mighty high' and will some day pay for her crimes.

The tragic ending, which *Rancho Notorious* shares with many woman's films, is rooted in the female protagonist's inability to recognise the social forces that conspire against her. Altar accepts Vern's denunciations and accusations of her symbolic complicity in Beth's murder and prepares to leave; the audience judges otherwise. Vern is a man destroyed by his bitterness, and the violent rage misdirected onto Altar outweighs her crime of sheltering outlaws. Chuck-a-Luck is not viable; it ends up deserted because the men refuse to respect Altar's control of her ranch, and she is no longer able to maintain it. *Rancho Notorious* refuses to accommodate Altar's compliance with Vern within the generic strategy of moral-redemption-through-love-for-the-hero. No

Stills: Rancho Notorious – *Altar in her haven of Chuck-a-Luck. Opposite – with Vern Haskell (Arthur Kennedy). Below – dividing up the day's take, with Geary (Jack Elam, left).*

'hero' (like Tom Destry) is offered; the film has demystified the stereotype by presenting its hero as despicable. *Rancho Notorious* is also careful not to portray Altar's death dramatically, as a clear manifestation of sacrifice, even if Vern comforts Frenchy with the idea that Altar died for him and belonged to him. Vern has exploited her for his ends and can return her (no longer a threat) to her rightful owner.

The final shot, of Frenchy kneeling in mourning by Altar's body, contrasts his genuine sense of loss with Vern's calculated and heartless exploitation. The ballad informs the viewer that Vern and Frenchy ride off together but that they both died that day. This epilogue ensures that there is no possible exit, subverting the traditional mediations of the Western by refusing any semblance of community or subsequent future. The dramatised ending complies with the conventions of the woman's film; it points to Altar/Dietrich as the film's emotional centre and illustrates the impossibility of her existence in an undemocratic social world.

Lang's decision to choose the Western as a star vehicle for Dietrich was entirely different from Pasternak's in *Destry Rides Again*, a film that empties the persona of its oppositional coherence. *Rancho Notorious* demonstrates the interdependence of genres by analysing the ideological tensions underlying the conventions and determinations of the narrative. These tensions were heightened in the 'fifties with the social entrenchment of family values and traditional gender roles and an intensified mistrust of

Still: Rancho Notorious – *Altar with Frenchy Fairmont (Mel Ferrer).*

anything foreign. By focusing on Vern's animus towards Altar, *Rancho Notorious* analyses the serious threat the Dietrich persona engenders. Altar is at the heart of Chuck-a-Luck (which was the film's intended name before Howard Hughes changed it for marketing reasons). The Dietrich persona is emblematic of the radical potential of female stars to summon forth unspoken desires for protest and self-determination. Recalling the intense pleasure viewers derived from identification with the star's insolence, resistance and strength, Lang reinvents the saloon girl/prostitute stereotype as a woman who is practical, self-sufficient and nobody's property.

Lang goes beyond an investigation into the gender relations that were fundamental in establishing the nation. *Rancho Notorious* analyses the pleasure being sold through the star and her vehicle. Lang forces the audience to examine the pleasure of identification with a star by setting up a vehicle that blatantly borrows from her career and then uses the metaphor of a woman entertainer to point to the image's precarious reliance on ideological notions of glamour and beauty that depend upon youth. Although Frenchy Fairmont is ageing and is threatened by a youthful rival, he still commands respect. He doesn't identify with Altar's fear that 'every year's a threat to a woman', that age weakens her authority. Dietrich understood the power of ageing to erode the star's effectiveness and box-office appeal. Every

great female star (and most obviously Garbo) knew that age and maturity were unforgivable. Dietrich fought against this all her life and exploited every illusion that would mask and deny the effects of age. In an interview with Peter Bogdanovich (*Fritz Lang in America*, Studio Vista, London, 1967, p.77), Lang described how 'Marlene resented going gracefully into a little, tiny bit older category; she became younger and younger until finally it was hopeless'. (Steven Bach, 1992, p.355, quotes Hal Mohr, the Director of Photography who shot both *Destry Rides Again* and *Rancho Notorious*, claiming that when Dietrich asked him why she looked so much better in the former, he replied, 'I'm ten years older now'). Lang wished to portray the pathos of an ageing legend and the film does this despite the star's protests which echo Altar's 'Stop feeling sorry for me'. Both Dietrich and Altar resisted the curtailment of a woman's activity; it is this unwillingness to submit to any restriction which continued to empower Dietrich through her career as a concert performer and still informs her star appeal. *Rancho Notorious* respects this: it foregrounds the mechanics of pleasure generated by its star without destroying the meaning and resonance of her persona.

METHOD WESTERNS
The Left-Handed Gun and One-Eyed Jacks

Jonathan Bignell

Steve Vineberg has suggested that 'the Method, because of its link with realism, its affirmation of Freud, and its focus on adolescent rebellion as the core of much adult behavior, is a natural dramatic expression of the way Americans understand and define themselves' (Vineberg, *Method Actors: Three Generations of American Acting Style*, Schirmer, New York, 1991, p.xii). Americans have also expressed and understood themselves through the genre of the Western, and the convergence of Western film narrative and Method techniques is the focus of this essay. The postwar psychologisation of the hero in American cinema, though not prompted exclusively by the Method, is strikingly observable in the Method Western.

As Vineberg's remarks suggest, the hero becomes Hamlet-like, and the Western as an action-adventure genre is modified by the investigation of the hero's problems with identity. The two films I have chosen to discuss not only combine psychologised heroes, Western conventions and Method style, but also give us insights into Method's influence on directing through Arthur Penn's work in *The Left-Handed Gun* and Marlon Brando directing himself in *One-Eyed Jacks*. Penn has a very long history of involvement with the Actor's Studio, the 'home' of the Method. Brando's work on *One-Eyed Jacks* was his first attempt at directing, though he is perhaps the best known Method actor. Arthur Penn directed two more Westerns with Method stars, *Little Big Man* (1970) with Dustin Hoffman, and *The Missouri Breaks* (1976) with Brando and Jack Nicholson.

The Left-Handed Gun was produced by Fred Coe, and released by Warner Brothers in 1958. The script was based on a teleplay by Gore Vidal, *The Death of Billy The Kid*, which was broadcast as *Billy* by NBC in July 1955. The television version was also produced by Fred Coe and starred Paul Newman as Billy. *The Left-Handed Gun* was Penn's first film. It was shot in twenty-three days, with a budget of $700,000, on the Warner Brothers ranch. When the film was taken away from Penn by the studio after his rough cut, some scene lengths and the ending were changed. Bad box-office results in the United States drove the disenchanted Penn back to theatre work, but *The Left-Handed Gun* was acclaimed in Europe, especially in France, and won the Grand Prix at the Brussels Film Festival.

One-Eyed Jacks was released by Paramount in 1961. It is based on the novel *The Authentic Death of Hendry Jones* by Charles Neider, produced by Pennebaker Productions, Brando's own company and shot around Monterey, California. *One-Eyed Jacks* was originally to be directed by Stanley Kubrick, with a budget of $1.8 million, but Kubrick resigned shortly after production began. Brando threw away the script on the first day of shooting and announced that the cast would improvise. They did this for six months, four months longer than scheduled, at a cost of $42,000 per day. The film finally cost over $6 million and in its first version lasted five hours. It was cut to its present length of 141 minutes, and the downbeat ending was changed to a hopeful one. Critical reaction varied from praise for its visual beauty and setting as well as for the acting and direction, to condemnation of Brando appearing to play the same part again (himself).

Because Method actors draw on their own psychology for a part, they have often been accused of repeatedly playing themselves and thus limiting their range. This is a not dissimilar accusation to that levelled at such non-Method actors as John Wayne and Clint Eastwood who are cast in Westerns as both archetypes and mythic figures, like Newman and Brando here. Wayne and Eastwood use similarly coded gesture and speech in film after film. But the key difference from Method technique is the relative unimportance of their characters' psychological motivations and psychic histories. Newman and Brando turn these features into the central interest of their performances, and the indices of their value as star actors.

Westerns produced during the silent era set the terms for the representation of the hero, shaping the genre as one characterised by action and adventure, by grand narratives of man's struggle with nature in the heroic conquest of the West. Conflict was not within the characters, but between the hero and others, or between the hero and external forces. The performance style suited to this context owes more to melodrama than to naturalism, since heroes embodied manly virtues which were tested by the events of the narrative, and the terrain of the action was moral, not psychological. Characters functioned as emblematic types, not as complex individuals, and this dominant mode could still be observed in sound film.

The Method had a significant role in the shift of the postwar Western, which was anyway becoming increasingly psychologised, from action to introspection. The Method is based on the tenet that the actor's task is to portray a psychologically coherent character through language and gesture. Method style therefore leads to an intense psychologisation of the actor's role, and this emphasis on motivation and psychology tends to reduce the importance of the script. Lines are delivered at varying speeds and levels of volume and clarity, omitted altogether or supplemented by improvisation, as the actor tries to create the performance. Such a performance might not be recognised by the cinema audience as different from a performance that is 'true' to a script. But publicity about the Method's techniques and its disciples might well predispose the audience to respond to these actors and performances differently from non-Method ones. The director's pre-eminent creative role can also be challenged when working with actors like Newman or Brando. The director no longer just asks the actor to deliver lines and move as required, but must work with the actor's emotional feelings about his or her own part, to the possible exclusion of the apparent intention of the dramatist or of the director's overall view of the ensemble performance. Arthur Penn has said: 'I prefer to choose actors from theatre, and, what is more, from Actors' Studio, because I like to leave actors a certain freedom, and Actors' Studio people often have marvellous ideas' (quoted in Jim Hillier, 'Arthur Penn', *Screen*, vol.10, no.1, 1969, p.6).

Penn makes a virtue of the Method actor's central function, and Robin Wood has written of his work: 'Penn seems to draw exceptionally on his actors' bodies, to build up characters from characteristic movements, gestures, ways of walking' (Robin Wood, *Arthur Penn*, Studio Vista, London, 1967, p.8). Brando, too, has commented on directing *One-Eyed Jacks*, suggesting that as an actor he had been directing anyway: 'Directing by itself is hard enough. But I've found that there are no divisional lines between an actor becoming a director. Things are so subtly interlaced it is hard to know where one begins and the other ends. I have directed myself in most of the pictures I have been in' (quoted in Joe Morella & Edward Epstein, *Brando: The Unauthorized Biography*, Nelson, London, 1973, p.81).

The focus on the actor's performance, with Method's characteristic quest for authenticity and presence, might seem likely to elbow aside the generic features of the traditional Western in *The Left-Handed Gun* and *One-Eyed Jacks*. But while the effect of the Method on the representation of the hero is to subject him to serious analytical scrutiny, it does not diminish his importance, although it does continue the shift of emphasis from action to psychology. The psychologisation reshapes the myths of masculinity in the Western and brings to them a new realism of character. Both Brando and Newman play men of action whose main attributes are skill with weapons and a propensity for violence, features familiar from the iconography of outlaw heroes in Westerns. But these two heroes behave this way because they are driven by violent childlike passions over which they have little control. In both films, the heroes are determined not to compromise their sense of justice by pragmatically accepting social or legal prohibitions. Like Hamlet – or the characters

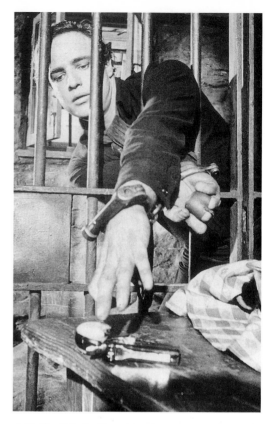

Still: Rio (Marlon Brando) in One-Eyed Jacks.

played by James Dean – they are driven by a childlike or adolescent desire to do the right thing, however destructive the consequences might be. The other side of their pre-adult emotional vigour is their difficulty in justifying their actions in rational rather than emotional terms, and in expressing themselves through conventional language and behaviour. The Method does not abandon the figure of the Western hero, but provides a psychological narrative for his actions. The Western hero has always been a fantasy of masculinity, and the Method forces an examination of what that fantasy represses and compensates for. Brando saw his approach to character as innovative. He said of his intentions in the film, referring to conventional representations of the Western hero, 'I have the obligation and the opportunity, in a recently discovered impulse, to try to communicate the things I think are important . . . to make a frontal attack on the temple of clichés. Our early day heroes were not brave one hundred percent of the time nor were they good one hundred percent of the time. My role is that of a man who is intuitive and suspicious, proud and searching. He has a touch of the vain and a childish and disproportionate sense of virtue and manly ethics. He is lonely and generally distrustful of human contacts. Properly handled, the folklore of the outdoor era contains all the vital ingredients of powerful picture-making' (quoted in Morella & Epstein, 1973, pp.79-81). We can begin to see here that Brando wanted to make a film that was conscious of the Western's role as American mythology, but his interest is centred on character. He describes his critique as an attempt at a certain kind of realism (a direction the Western was to take in the 1970s): a psychological realism, focused on his own role as a troubled outsider, that recalls another Method performance, James Dean's in *Rebel Without a Cause* (Nicholas Ray, 1955).

The Left-Handed Gun is also a film about myth, the legend of Billy the Kid. The Paul Newman character is again a disturbed outsider, and Newman plays Billy in a similarly psychologised way. Arthur Penn said that he wanted 'to find, through the Billy the Kid myth, which is very alive in the United States, the deep myths of Greek tragedy. *The Left-Handed Gun* is Oedipus in the West. There are in the Western conventions a ritual, a mythic simplicity, which make it a marvellous tragic mould' (quoted in Hillier, 1969, p.11). Penn, like Brando, is aware of the mythic role of Western stories in American culture, and of Western conventions which can be interpreted afresh. In his comparison with the Oedipus story, we can again see a focus on the psychological disturbance of the central character and a link with the best known of Sigmund Freud's psychoanalytic theories. But, once again, although the comparison between a Western story and Greek tragedy is not perhaps as incongruous as it might first appear, the recasting of Oedipus in the role of Billy runs counter to every expectation about Westerns.

The Method and the Actor

American Method acting derives from Konstantin Stanislavski, who, together with fellow Russian Vladimir Nemirovich-Danchenko, opened the Moscow Art Theatre in 1897. Stanislavski expressed through his actors his 'system' for a coherent means of ensemble acting in the theatre, with the aim of verisimilitude. Freud's investigation of psychology, which showed how the internal became manifest in speech and behaviour, was parallel to Stanislavski's focus on the psyche of the character. Americans were first exposed to a modified version of the system in 1923, when Richard Boleslavsky, a graduate of the Moscow Art Theatre school, founded the American Laboratory Theatre in New York. Three pupils from the Laboratory Theatre, Lee Strasberg, Harold Clurman and Stella Adler, founded the Group Theatre in 1931.

Strasberg went on to work at the Actors' Studio, which was founded in 1947, and took over its running from Elia Kazan in 1951. The Studio Method greatly intensified the Stanislavskian emphasis on the internal by linking the expression of character to the inner life of the actor. The Studio began as a place offering classes for actors, but under Lee Strasberg it became a laboratory for actors' exploration of character. Although the Method has become well known through the American cinema over the last forty years or so, it was designed as a training for actors working in the theatre. The links between theatre and cinema were not stressed in the training offered by the Actors' Studio, which was always premised on theatrical techniques.

Instead, the links arose both through particular actors who worked in the theatre and in film or television, among them Paul Newman, Marlon Brando and Shelley Winters, and via Elia Kazan, Arthur Penn and others who were involved in the running of the Actors' Studio but also directed for cinema or television as well as for the theatre.

Despite their differences, Adler, Clurman and Strasberg were keen to do away with the mannered style referred to as the British School. Strasberg contrasted British acting, and particularly the performances of Laurence Olivier, with the 'natural' stage or screen presence of Method-trained actors. The Studio became a magnet for actors, reaching a high point of influence in the late 'fifties. Brando attended the Studio intermittently in the late 'forties and early 'fifties, at the time when he rose to prominence as Stanley Kowalski in *A Streetcar Named Desire* directed by Elia Kazan first in the theatre and then (1951) as a film. Paul Newman became a member of the Actors' Studio in 1952, appeared in television dramas and began to get bigger stage parts before Warner offered him a five-year contract at $1,000 per week. Other Studio stars in cinema include Karl Malden (co-star of *One-Eyed Jacks*), Montgomery Clift, Steve McQueen, Robert De Niro, Robert Duvall, Anne Bancroft, and Ellen Burstyn.

'Studio work has genuinely spread out to the theatrical community – to the world', said Arthur Penn. 'It's the accepted technique of American acting' (quoted in Foster Hirsch, *A Method to their Madness: The History of the Actors' Studio*, Norton, New York, 1984, p.220). The number of people who moved into cinema as actors and directors from the Studio has ensured that a body of work has become established, and reshown on television, which demonstrates and reinforces the dominance of the Method. 'The films of Elia Kazan are the true legacy of the Actors' Studio', said Arthur Penn (quoted in Hirsch, 1984, p.330), and Kazan's *A Streetcar Named Desire*, *On the Waterfront* (1954), *East of Eden* (1955) and *Baby Doll* (1956) could be seen as showcases for the preoccupations that I shall focus on in Westerns. Arthur Penn worked as a moderator (in effect, the teacher of a masterclass) at the Actors' Studio, and also ran some playwriting sessions there. He spoke not only of the advantages of the technique, but also of its drawbacks. 'The Method gives acting a truth, an honesty, a sense of the character's inner life, all radiating from the actor's genuinely personal core; its pitfalls are self-absorption at the expense of the play and a lack of preparation of other areas of the instrument' (quoted in Hirsch, 1984, p.223). Vineberg (1991, p.6) describes what he calls 'tenets' of the Method. First, the actor aims for verisimilitude, and arrives at it through observation of actual behaviour. The psychological coherence of the character is produced by finding a 'through-line', a central disposition of the character in the piece, which is divided into 'actions', the particular playable moments realised by the actor. Genuine emotion, evoked by 'affective memory' (also known as 'emotional recall') of an emotion from the actor's life, is used as the trigger for emotion in the performance. The actor's personality is the resource from which the character's psychological truth must derive.

It is assumed that actors must be religiously devoted to their craft. Hirsch (1984, p.203) details what he calls the 'codewords' of the Method, a special language that reflects its concept of what the actor does. The actor's 'instrument' is made up of his or her body, ways of speaking and moving, and the mental approach to a part. The actor works on the 'problems' of the part, and seeks to bring out 'colours' – shifts of mood and pace. Techniques to realise the character include the 'animal exercise', where observations of zoo animals suggest movement, 'improvisation', playing 'moment to moment' as the character lives through the scene, the construction of the character's 'prior life' to explain his or her behaviour in the play, the use of 'objects' to focus and symbolise emotion, and an 'inner monologue' which runs beneath the character's consciousness as it moves through the piece.

The performance is based on the realisation of the character's psychology. The character has 'tasks' to perform, is motivated by 'wants' and a consistent 'logic' in the 'given circumstances' of the piece. If the actor is successful in Method terms, the qualities brought forth will be 'truth', 'freedom', 'aliveness', 'naturalness', 'specificity', 'spontaneity' and 'conviction'. An unsuccessful performance is characterised by being 'general', 'mental', 'memorised', 'conventional' and 'playing for results'.

From this quick sketch of the Method, some of its implications become clear. The Actors' Studio is a kind of laboratory, where actors learn a special descriptive language about what they do, and share common aims. The actor thinks of himself or herself as a professional, working hard at acquiring skills and achieving effects. The actor is self-regarding, a special person, whose work is tied intimately to the sense of self. Good Method acting comes from an intense struggle to realise the truth of character psychology through the actor's authentic self, which lies beneath the surface of his or her behaviour.

The Left-Handed Gun

Like many Western heroes, those of *The Left-Handed Gun* and *One-Eyed Jacks* are inexpressive in word and gesture, lending greater significance to the particular verbal and gestural means of signification used by the actors in these roles. The Method characteristics of Newman's and Brando's performance reinforce these thematic and character tendencies in the Western, to the extent that the resulting psychological emphasis threatens to shatter the coherence of the narrative. There are features of the Western that turn the Method towards it, but also features of the Method that undermine the Western.

In *The Left-Handed Gun*, Paul Newman plays Billy as a troubled teenager. His physical powers – strength, skill with a gun, speed of reaction – are those of an adult professional gunfighter, but emotionally and intellectually he is childlike, underdeveloped. He fixes on his employer, the rancher Mr

Tunstall (Colin Keith-Johnston), as a father figure. When Tunstall is killed, Billy uses his developed physical skills to pursue the killers in an obsessive quest for revenge which derives from feelings he can barely express, let alone understand.

The film's narrative and character premises, established by the ballad over the credit sequence, announce the main lines of Newman's performance. His 'through-line' is the quest for parental affection and guidance, which is fulfilled through Tunstall and then thwarted, so that the surplus emotional energy erupts as violence against the fragile civilisation of the West. The ballad which opens the film describes Billy as 'a left-handed boy' and as 'Death's child', 'dangerous and devilish/Gentle and wild'. The ballad invites us to 'Look on him tenderly/Speak to him gently', and Newman plays Billy as a sympathetic character, often endearingly childlike, but at the same time driven by dark forces in his own psyche, and stigmatised by the numerous grown-ups around him. Penn's description of the film as a tragedy, and of Billy as a modern Oedipus, is supported by the information given to us at the start of the film.

We are prepared for Billy's violence in the early scene when Tunstall is told that Billy, as a boy, stabbed a drunk who insulted his mother. When Tunstall, the new 'parent' is shot, Newman kneels next to his body, and rocks back and forth, alternately clamping his arms around his head and stretching them in front of him with fingers locked together. Billy is overcome with grief but cannot express it except through these exaggerated physical movements. A similar set of body movements are used after Billy's friends, Charlie (James Congdon) and Tom (James Best), are killed by Pat Garrett's posse. Newman slumps down the wall of his shack, and covers his head with his arms, racked by emotion. Newman later uses the prop of Charlie's flute, found on the shack's floor by Billy after his escape from jail, to recall this moment. Newman turns the flute over slowly in his hands, and the scene ends as he looks wistfully through a broken window.

Objects are also significant shortly after Tunstall's death when we see Billy in a gleeful mood in a saloon, fascinated by a nickelodeon, and marching vigorously back and forth to its music. Newman

Still: The Left-Handed Gun – *Billy (Paul Newman) with the body of Tunstall (Colin Keith-Johnston). Frames: below, Billy and Tunstall; opposite, Billy (top) and Moultrie (Hurd Hatfield).*

moves rapidly, jerkily, with strong body movements, a triumphantly jutting chin and a broad smile. Billy, pretending to be a soldier on parade, gets in the way and annoys the people around him. He uses a broom as a pretend rifle, but draws his real pistol on Pat Garrett (John Dehner) when surprised by him on the stairs. Newman shows Billy moving 'moment to moment' from the world of childlike imagination to adult confrontation and immediately back to childishness, as he runs up the stairs laughing and chanting Garrett's name. Newman uses body movement and rapid shifts from action to still body images to connote the intense emotions Billy feels and at the same time to establish contrasting codes of childishness and masculine proficiency. Gestural signs and symbolic objects are being used by Newman to represent Billy's 'truth' and 'aliveness', his psychological coherence, even though this coherence is based on contradictory psychological impulses.

Billy is also constructed as a character in fictionalised versions of his own life which explicitly feature in the film. Billy becomes famous in the East through the efforts of Moultrie (Hurd Hatfield), a Southerner in the 'souvenirs of the West' business, who provided the information for books called *Outlaw King* and *The Luck of Billy the Kid* which he presents to Billy on the eve of his escape from jail. Billy's shack is festooned with newspaper reports of his exploits. But Billy cannot read and attacks the parasitic Moultrie. When Moultrie discovers that Billy is 'not like the books', he sets him up to be shot by Garrett. Billy's repudiation of Moultrie's rewritings of

his life as a Western adventure is, in a sense, the cause of his death.

So there are two systems of character construction here. The mythic Billy is constructed by reputation and in various fictional representations; he is the 'Outlaw King', a latter-day Robin Hood, familiar

from pulp fiction, ballads and prewar Westerns as the morally good man forced by circumstance to live by breaking the law. This character type is non-psychological and harks back to melodrama. The film makes reference to this in order to overlay it with something else. Method performance gives Billy psychological depth and complexity, and Newman's realism of character therefore complicates inherited traditions for representing the character of the Western hero. But Penn doesn't use the 'realism' of Newman's Method performance simply to contrast 'real' and 'mythic' versions of character. Newman's gestures, in the context created by script and direction, locate Billy as the centre of several systems of signification.

The film is full of references to stories and texts, which function thematically to establish Billy as the doomed hero of a story that is already written. This begins with Tunstall reading out the biblical phrase 'through a glass darkly' and explaining it to Billy. Newman, as Billy, behaves like a clumsy child, since the adult Billy cannot read. He handles the book roughly, looks embarrassed and puzzled, and tells Tunstall that his mother used to read from the Bible. Tunstall replaces the mother in Billy's affections. Billy cannot see through darkness to this truth, though he is instinctively drawn to Tunstall. As Robin Wood points out, 'Against Billy's instinctual knowing is set the purely verbal factual knowing of the man who tells Tunstall about Billy's past . . . In Tunstall the two sorts of knowing – the conscious and the instinctual – are harmonised' (Wood, 1967,

The Left-Handed Gun. Stills: above, with four bullets, one for each of Tunstall's killers in his fist, Billy draws out the plan to ambush them; opposite, Billy and his friends in Modero, scuffling with US cavalrymen. Frames: below, Pat Garrett (John Dehner); opposite, top, Billy after the death of his friends and at his own death, and, below, having fun in Modero with Tom (James Best) and Charlie (James Congdon).

p.19). Billy's loss of his mother and his devotion to the fatherly Tunstall are linked with the biblical resonances and his childlike confusion.

Early in the film, Billy tells Tunstall that he is acquainted with a Mexican gypsy custom of burning a straw man at Easter, though he doesn't know why they do it. We are alerted here to the motif of Billy as Christlike sacrifice, which appears later with a shot of Billy and the straw man at a party in Modero. As the straw man is burned, Billy burns the newspaper

reports of his own death, saying inarticulately, 'I come awake . . . I'm a-come to life.' Newman accompanies these few words about resurrection with his outstretched hand making slow, grasping gestures – a movement that eloquently signifies his grasp on life and sense of power, and recalls the gesture of the clasped hand in which he held four bullets, one for each of Tunstall's killers. Once again the gesture belongs to two contrasting but concurrent ways of representing character. It is a psychological index, but it is used in the film as a means to link three narrative themes which revolve around Billy's

mythic status: Billy as Christ, Billy as avenging angel, and Billy as Oedipus.

The gesture is also a grasping for Celsa (Lita Milan), the woman Billy is talking to as the straw man burns. Just as the reincarnated Billy feels that he has cheated fate, so he feels able to cheat the laws of morality in following his desire for this mother figure. Celsa, who Billy seduces, is the wife of Saval (Martin Garralaga), a gunsmith and another father figure. She is both an object of Billy's desire and a surrogate mother who cared for him when he was wounded. In the last scene of the film, Billy sacrifices himself, offering himself to be shot by Garrett in the doorway of a house. Newman uses another slow gesture, raising his open gun-hand to Garrett, signalling a desire for help and also a willing participation in his expected death. Like the initial grasping gesture (which it recalls), this one has a multiple psychological meaning, and is again thematic, belonging to both psychological and mythic systems of character presentation. The open hand is an acceptance of Billy's fate, a Christ-like benediction of his killer, Garrett, and the abandonment of the gun that turned Billy into Billy the Kid, the mythic hero.

One of the problems of discussing Newman's

performance (or Brando's in *One-Eyed Jacks*) is that the Method is a process for achieving a result, not the result itself. It is difficult to separate the contributions of the actors from those of the directors, especially in cases like these, where the directors are themselves Method devotees, and the scripts, too, are significant. Method techniques are effective for an actor delivering Billy's final line to Saval, 'I come here not to kill, not to kill him. I lost Tom, I lost Charlie, I can't read, I got myself all killed.' This is the moment preceding Billy's death and the significant gesture Newman uses at that point. The line is ambiguous, contains apparent non-sequiturs, and is motivated by inner turmoil. The words represent a stream of consciousness, and could be explained only by reference to a Freudian analysis of the relationship of expression (linguistic or gestural) to the inner psyche of the character.

Billy's disruption of Saval and Celsa's relationship obviously has oedipal overtones, particularly as Billy rejects all other women in the film, and stays closely tied to his young male friends, Charlie and Tom, with whom he indulges in various pranks and horseplay. Billy's passionate identifications and his inability to control his desires, together with his aptitude for violence, necessarily result in his expulsion from social networks as well as familial ones. Billy cannot grow up, and his feelings threaten another adult couple, Garrett and his wife, when Billy shoots the last of Tunstall's killers at Garrett's wedding. Garrett, a reluctant sheriff, also declares himself 'married' to the town, and Billy destroys not only family but also community. He is a rebel with several causes, the pursuit of which alienates him from potential parental figures and gets his young friends killed.

Penn's reference to the tragic dimensions of Billy's character points to the appropriateness of Newman's use of often static and rather exaggerated bodily movement and gesture. These moments arrest the narrative flow to show psychic and emotional forces over which Billy has little control, and simultaneously point out the character's emblematic and mythic status in the narrative. As Robin Wood has written, 'What immediately strikes one in the films of Arthur Penn . . . [is] an intense awareness of, and emphasis on, physical expression' (Wood, 1967, p.6). The mythic dimension should have been reinforced at the end of the film in a social context. Penn wanted to show a village procession carrying Billy's body, a 'little ritual to close the cycle of the legend' (Penn quoted in Hillier, 1969, p.11).

Billy's plan to revenge Tunstall's death is based on crude retributive violence, and leads to his own death; his sense of natural Old Testament justice runs counter to rational 'civilised' law. Robin Wood has commented, 'throughout the film we have the sense of instinctual urges and perceptions reaching only partial conscious definition and never subjected to the test of rationality' (Wood, 1967, p.19). Billy is at the same time an innocent child and an obsessive killer, and Newman's Method techniques offer a means to hold these contradictory characteristics together. The linking of gesture to themes in the narrative also pulls together the film's psychologisation and its investigation of the mythic hero, which would otherwise be quite distinct registers. *The Left-Handed Gun* self-consciously plays on the character of Billy the Kid as a textual construct in the tradition of the Western, and modifies the model of the hero that this presupposes by supercharging it with Newman's Method performance and its inherent psychologisation.

One-Eyed Jacks

Brando enrolled at the Dramatic Workshop of the New School for Social Research in New York in 1943, then studied with Stella Adler, who taught, with Strasberg and other Stanislavskians, at the Workshop. Adler said 'His style is the perfect marriage of intuition and intelligence' (quoted in Morella & Epstein, 1973, p.15). While Adler's techniques were not as focused on the actor's psychology as those of Strasberg, 'intuition' and inner talent were similarly valued. Brando said of her:

'She is a teacher not only of acting but of life itself. I wouldn't want to say that it's psychotherapy, but it has very clear psychotherapeutic results. People learn about the mechanism of feeling' (quoted in Lawrence Grobel, *Conversations with Marlon Brando*, Bloomsbury, London, 1991, p.124).

For Adler, as for Lee Strasberg, the text of the play, not the character, was the starting-point for the actor. 'You have to work in the style of the piece', Adler said (quoted in Hirsch, 1984, p.215). But Brando's remarks about her show that, for him, acting was a process of learning about reality, and that the mechanism for this was learning about himself. The emphasis on personal authenticity and depth of emotional experience parallels the emphases of the Actors' Studio Method, and Brando went on to join the Studio, studying acting there for several years.

In *One-Eyed Jacks*, Brando stars as a bank robber, Rio, deserted by his friend Dad Longworth (Karl Malden), captured and imprisoned. The majority of the film is occupied by the story of Rio's revenge on Dad, who has gone straight and become sheriff of Monterey. Amory (Ben Johnson), another bandit, recruits Rio to rob the Monterey bank. Like *The Left-Handed Gun*, the film contains plot elements and characters derived from traditional Western stories. The central character is an outlaw, who commits crimes with the help of a gang of gunmen. The outlaw and his gang are perceived as a threat by the citizens of the developing town of Monterey, and are in conflict with its sheriff and his deputy. Rio gets his revenge, killing Dad and shooting the deputy Lon (Slim Pickens), and rides off into the distance after a romantic parting from his sweetheart. These are the familiar ingredients of a revenge narrative, in which an outlaw hero uses his status as an outsider and his aptitude for physical action to purge the emergent civilisation, represented by the town, of the corrupt individuals who undermine it. But this outline of the narrative structure describes only

Still: One-Eyed Jacks – *Sheriff Dad Longworth (Karl Malden) joins in the fun at Monterey's town festival.*

part of the plot framework of *One-Eyed Jacks* and misrepresents the dynamics of character interaction in the film – issues of morality and identity, represented by emblematic characters, are not the only focus of the film.

The centre of the film is the relationship between Rio and Dad, and more precisely the effect each has on the psychology of the other. While the rivalry between Rio and Dad is motivated by particular events and actions, it becomes the occasion for the film to explore the obsessive and excessive emotions which it generates. This emphasis on the inner life of the central characters, and in particular the psychology of the hero, derives from Brando's Method preoccupations as both actor and director. The generic plot framework and narrative structure of the Western are overlaid by a psycho-sexual investigation of the central characters.

The film draws on the oedipal issues that were evident in *The Left-Handed Gun* most obviously in Rio's rivalry with the aptly named Dad. The generational conflict between them is visually marked by Rio's clean-shaven and lithe outdoor appearance as against Dad's moustache, suit and placing in interior domestic settings. Dad is a figure of apparent authority, with a public role as sheriff, for example at Monterey's town festival. Although he appears friendly and capable, a leader of the community, the fundamental untrustworthiness that led to Rio's capture is signalled early on by his irresponsible

drunkenness at the festival. He is also a family man, apparently solicitous towards his wife Maria (Katy Jurado) and indulgent towards his stepdaughter Louisa (Pina Pellicer), but his fear that Rio has seduced Louisa leads to an eruption of violent anger. Rio struggles to expose Dad's public role as a fiction which conceals an inner truth of opportunism, selfishness and vindictiveness. Both the revenge plot and the generational conflict are articulated through the emphasis on character. Character, in turn, is represented in Method terms as a pseudo-Freudian quest for a truth that is internal and not immediately legible in either speech or action.

Brando plays Rio as a passionate and driven young man, whose chief characteristics are his impassive face end quiet control of his desire for vengeance. He speaks slowly and quietly, stares slowly and even closes his eyes during dialogue scenes. The technique represents Rio as a man with a hatred so intense as to block normal expression. As in *The Left-Handed Gun*, language is both inadequate to reveal depths of character and manipulated in social exchanges where the potential eruption of purgative but chaotic violence is signalled by gesture and facial expression, not by words. Brando deploys the soft, rather slurred speech and flat facial expression that were already his trademarks. He was already known as the paragon of the Method, and his brooding screen presence here depends on our awareness of a continuity with his other film parts. When Rio encounters Dad at his ranch in Monterey, the camera narrows visible space down to a two-shot of Brando's and Malden's faces. Malden allows

Dad's fear – and his determination to stick by the story of his innocence in Rio's capture – to be revealed by nervous eye and face movement. By contrast, Brando uses his face as a blank mask and languidly speaks the line, 'A man can't stay angry for five years. [Pause] Can he?' The audience is aware that Rio is still very angry, but Brando's blank face allows Dad to take his words at face value, despite the knowledge that he is capable of lying. Here, language is ambiguous. Dad chooses to understand the line as a declaration by Rio that he is not seeking revenge, taking language to mirror intention transparently. But, by contrast, the audience receives the line as evidence of Rio's control of his hatred and of his strategic deferral of revenge. We are asked to read Rio's character as determined by emotions below the surface and not revealed by facial expression or by speech. This decoding of Brando's performance is reinforced not only by earlier events in the narrative, but also by our knowledge of Brando as a Method actor and the expectations this sets up. Having already been alerted by the narrative to Rio's desire for vengeance, the spectator takes the blank face as a mask. It tells of Rio's iron determination to deceive and destroy Dad, and opens up a fascinating distance between Rio's surface control and the submerged violence it conceals. Christine Gledhill has remarked that the 'ideology of the camera as observer and the face as window to the soul opened up new significatory possibilities in terms of the inwardness and personality of the performer . . . Method is the contemporary performance mode most able to deliver 'presence' . . . (Christine Gledhill, 'Signs of Melodrama' in Gledhill, ed., *Stardom: Industry of Desire*, Routledge, London, 1991, p.224).

Still: One-Eyed Jacks – *Dad whips Rio in the main street of Monterey, a public spectacle of violence.*

The exchange between Rio and Dad here uses the potential of the close-up to deliver psychological complexity. We are shown actors playing characters who are each concealing something from the other: Dad's fear of Rio, and Rio's hatred of Dad. We see the actors signifying both a surface deception and a submerged emotion that is recognised but pushed aside by the other character. This requires particular skill, and we see Brando and Malden fulfilling our expectations of Method stars by creating a powerful sense of presence and psychological reality. Story becomes relatively unimportant here, since it is displaced by the achievement of three interrelating layers of signification: the surface reality of character, the deeper reality of character and the presence of the actor. The two central characters are performers – as Rio and Dad attempt to deceive, they are performing for each other – and Brando and Malden are performing their performances. *One-Eyed Jacks* problematises the hero (and also his antagonist) by focusing on these multiple levels of identity.

Probably the most arresting scene in the film is another performance, when Dad Longworth flogs Rio in Monterey's main street in front of an audience of townspeople. Sheriff Longworth declares to his audience that he is cleaning up the town by ejecting a bandit. But on another, personal level, Dad is demonstrating his continuing dominance over Rio and his power to frustrate and tyrannise him. He is exerting his power as a father as well as a sheriff, since he is afraid that Rio has seduced his stepdaughter. The scene is not just arresting because of its extreme violence, but literally arresting because it holds up the film's narrative in favour of a concentration on Brando's display of emotion, a performance solely for the camera. A single wide shot is held for most of the scene. The camera is positioned to see Rio's face in close-up and, behind him, Dad's sadistic glee as he wields the whip. There is no clear shot of Rio's exposed back.

Clearly, the scene is set up by Brando to reveal the violence of the action through Brando's (and Malden's) facial expression, posture and movement. At the beginning of the scene, Brando clenches his facial muscles; he kneels, but remains silent. Brando's face is again a mask. As the blows fall, Brando's body remains rigid, but appears forced to sink lower by the pain. His face dips forward and his mouth opens. Brando's non-verbal expressiveness conveys the emotions of his character and solicits the audience's identification. Once again, this expressiveness is based on a denial of expression, a rigidity and blankness which refer us from the external surface to the boiling emotions within.

Part of the effectiveness of the scene comes from the use of extras in the key wide-shot and other inserted shots of the surrounding townspeople. Brando offered a cash bonus for the extra with the most horrified expression in the scene. The horror and fascination of the townspeople provides a conduit for the spectator's expected reaction, and somewhat defuses the excess and concentration of Brando's performance. The scene ends with Dad crushing Rio's gun hand, symbolically castrating him, with the butt of a shotgun. The camera doesn't show the gun's impact on Rio's hand, but a gasp from the unseen townspeople identifies the brutality of the action and stands in the place of the cinema audience's reaction to it. The 'truth' and 'aliveness' of Brando's and Malden's performances are authenticated by the response of the crowd and the worked-for response of the cinema audience.

It is the shocking truth of Brando's performance, more than its role in the story or its demonstration of Rio's moral superiority to Dad, that is central to the significance of the scene. In story terms, the whipping is a further deferral of Rio's revenge, but the brutality and length of the scene override its function in this respect. Dad is shown to be sadistic, and Rio's self-control shows his strength of character. But the characters are not only to be measured in moral terms. They are unique individuals who are motivated by exaggerated, even neurotic, fixations resulting from their psycho-sexual roles in relation to each other. The whipping scene is not like a set piece in a more conventional Western, it is an occasion for bravura performance and the spectacle of psychological realism.

The Method focus on psychic disturbance is united in the film with a pseudo-Freudian subtext and the use of symbolic objects, as exemplified in the action following the whipping scene. Rio retreats to the seashore and sits by the sea wrapping a necklace round his hand; we cut to a shot of him binding up his healed fingers to shoot again. Rio had bought the necklace and given it to Dad's step-daughter

Louisa, saying it was his mother's, as part of a successful effort to seduce her and thus shame Dad. Rio is 'wrapped up in' Louisa and has fallen in love with her. The plan to shoot Dad and to dishonour his step-child is bound up with a phallic struggle between the two men, which seems to have been won by Dad as he crushes Rio's hand. But Rio has conceived a child by Louisa, thus emasculating Dad and usurping his position by becoming a dad himself (Dad has no children of his own). Brando's use of objects (necklace, binding-straps, gun, Rio's hand) ties these strands together and links the surface of the revenge story to a deeper level of obsessive sexual rivalry.

The inner intensity masked by surface appearance parallels the film's thematic rejection of speech and appearance as the access to truth. Lies and stories push the action forward, but they cover an inner truth that is virtually inarticulable. Early in the film, Rio tells lies to a Mexican girl to whom he gives a jewel to purchase sexual favours, and he tells a similar lie to Louisa when he gives her the necklace. Dad's deputy spies on Rio and reports to Dad. Rio tells a lie to Dad about his capture, and Dad has told a partial lie about his past to enable him to become sheriff. Louisa conceals her pregnancy from, and then reveals it to, both Rio and Dad (though Maria has already informed Dad). Rio tells his 'sad tale' to Louisa, saying 'I can't [forget]. I gotta die to forget that.' Before his final escape, Rio says to Dad, 'You're a one-eyed Jack around here, Dad, but I seen the other side of your face.' There are very many of these occasions where words are spoken or withheld, and where the truth is located in inner experience and problematically related to language and action. As in *The Left-Handed Gun*. Brando's film proposes that there are instinctual truths and a deep level of psychological truth. These either conflict with surface and language, or cannot easily be reconciled to them.

The Method's preoccupations, then, add a specifically psychological realism to the conventionalised and symbolic world of the Western, a psychologisation that is in some ways alien to mythic characters like Billy the Kid, or to the protagonists of Brando's film. The new note that the Method introduces to the Western is particularly evident in the versions of masculinity provided by the performances, which run against the grain of the genre's conventions for representing the male hero. The effect is to diminish (but not remove) the importance of action, adventure, and morality, in favour of psychological realism, psycho-sexual themes and a narrative arrested in the interests of introspection, which become the distinguishing features of the films.

Method technique leads to the revealing of contradictory emotions moment by moment in order to show that the hero's character is determined by a psychic core that is evident at the surface only momentarily and ambiguously. But characters that fit with this treatment tend towards psychological instability, like the outlaws of *The Left-Handed Gun* and *One-Eyed Jacks*. In more recent Westerns, these problematic models of masculinity can be found in

the work of, for instance, Sergio Leone and Sam Peckinpah, in which Method-trained actors are rarely much in evidence.

Masculinity becomes a fragile construction, in which the individual subject's performance moves further away from being the 'natural' expression of a coherent identity, though the 'naturalness' of masculinity in the Western was already open to question. The Method version of masculinity is realised through the difficult process of articulating a problematic interior self. Action in the external world is still an index of the Western hero's character, but

Still: One-Eyed Jacks – *Louisa (Pina Pellicer) tells Rio that she is carrying his child.*

character becomes only the tantalising image of the enigmatic truth of the psyche, which is represented as existing before and beneath character. The versions of masculine identity proposed in the Western genre are thus supplemented and complicated by the Method, and bring the films into line with one of the dominant themes in postwar American cinema: the problematic quest for the authentic self.

GENRE AND HISTORY
Fort Apache and
The Man Who Shot Liberty Valance
Douglas Pye

By the end of the nineteenth century, the popular Western had achieved a form in which evocation of the historic West served as springboard for extravagant and fantastic tales of adventure, as far removed from 'history' as from representation of the contemporary world. Central to the dime novel in particular were nostalgia and sentimental social primitivism, through which, however, potentially antisocial values (of anarchic individualism, for instance) could be harmlessly expressed. Some of the ideological processes through which these values are neutralised are obvious enough. The Westerner is made, 'naturally', as it were, a gentleman and vulnerable to the charms and virtue of the Eastern lady, a development epitomised in Owen Wister's *The Virginian* (1902), the climax of what Leslie Fiedler calls the 'Sir Walter Scottification' of the West. This partial fusion of anarchic Western and acceptable Eastern values is one means by which the genre manages to have it both ways: it can simultaneously endorse nostalgically valued primitivism and mime the inevitable eclipse of these values by social forms. The West and the Westerner are ideological constructions guaranteeing, as it were, their own demise. More important here, though, are the methods of masking the inevitable emergence of the present which the genre implies. The generic West is essentially timeless, constantly re-enacting the same actions and processes. The primitivism and utopianism maintain their power through the suppression of any awareness of the present in relation to which they can be critically viewed. The form remains vital by being unreflective – the condition of its viability is not to know the present. The result is that these fictions exist in a sense outside time, creating a world that announces itself as the past, even 'history', yet operates ideologically to suppress knowledge of both the past and the present.

John Ford's value system was determined, at least in part, by the fictional forms that he inherited. In reactivating the potential of the Western to reflect imaginatively on American history, the terms Ford reinvents are essentially those of the nineteenth century. Even outside the Western, the terms Ford seems able to bring to even a contemporary setting – in *The Last Hurrah* (1958), say – are those of an imagined past. Part of Ford's remarkable achievement is to invest these terms with a new and often intensely moving life. But his values – with their centre in the family and the small agrarian community and their distrust of any larger institutional

framework – are, in the mid-twentieth century, primitive and anachronistic. As Michael Wilmington and Joseph McBride suggest, 'it . . . seems unfitting to call him a modern artist at all' (*John Ford*, Secker & Warburg London, 1974).

Putting this negatively, one might identify some of Ford's weaknesses with those of the genre. His treatment of Indians, for instance, and particularly his inability to create more than stereotypes even in *Cheyenne Autumn* (1964), has as much to do with the given roles and traditions of representing Indians within the Western as it does with a failure in Ford. Andrew Sarris comments accurately, in *The John Ford Movie Mystery* (Indiana University Press, 1976), that 'ideology comes wrapped up in the genre so that racism can never be dissociated from the romance'. By and large, Indians are condemned to a role as primitives, doomed to defeat in what is at root a triumphalist white genre. It is, however, difficult to think of many directors who have created Indian characters any more successfully than Ford.

More positively, though, much of what is of major interest in Ford's films, as well as many of the deepest contradictions, come from his recurrent, empirical encounter with generic material and traditional images. I am thinking particularly of the development (which is neither simple nor continuous) in the ways community and society are represented in his Westerns, away from structures in which social groups are threatened from outside, or in which society can be escaped from, towards a more inclusive view which internalises generic conflicts and refuses characters any simple 'escape'. The results are films which rest firmly on the formula Western but which come as close to any in the genre to the ambivalence and complexity of James Fenimore Cooper's Leatherstocking series.

In *Stagecoach* (1939), the view of developing America is implicitly critical, but remains largely unfocused. The two towns in the film are equally unpleasant, but in different ways: the first is dominated by the excessive refinement and rigid morality of the Ladies' Law and Order League, while Lordsburg is presented as a night town of saloons and brothels. The journey between the towns enacts the tensions between a disparate group of Americans who achieve a fragile unity with the birth of a baby at the mid-point of the film, as the group is at its greatest distance from 'civilisation' and thus in the greatest danger. The scene following the birth is clearly presented as an image of ideal harmony,

Still: Stagecoach – *the Ladies' Law and Order League.*

with the baby as the tangible sign of the American future. Yet it is a unity achieved under special conditions, and even then the group around the baby excludes the mother, the strait-laced Lucy (Louise Platt), and the absconding banker, Gatewood (Berton Churchill). The brief unity achieved in that scene is finally dissipated after the arrival in Lordsburg – Lucy is received back into the arms of her refined friends, while Dallas (Claire Trevor) and Ringo (John Wayne) revert to their positions as social outcasts. The 'natural' morality associated with Dallas, Ringo and Doc Boone (Thomas Mitchell) seems doomed by the development of 'civilisation'. The final movement of the film, however, in conforming to generic expectation, on the one hand maintains the implicit criticism of society and on the other evades the implications of the inevitable victory of social forms and values. Thus, Ringo's killing of the Plummers implies the inadequacy of institutionalised law, and Dallas's and Ringo's need to escape west (over the border into Mexico, in fact) indicates the sterile exclusiveness of social values; but the existence of the West offers an asocial space and time where the social conflicts presented by the film will not apply. The West exists as a 'safety valve' (to misuse a nineteenth-century term), when thematic and narrative pressures get too high.

The escape west is central to the traditions Henry Nash Smith describes in *Virgin Land* (1950) – land beyond the frontier feeding the dream of perfected life – and became a staple ingredient of the formula Western, as one of a number of more or less mechanical narrative possibilities, with little or no meaning of the thematic or moral force it carries in, say, Fenimore Cooper. Ford's use of the motif in *Stagecoach* and later films owes less to Fenimore Cooper than to this tradition of naive and unreflective Western fiction in which narrative patterns long outlived whatever original meanings they might have had. In other words, as Ford's career continues, his films might be seen as animating a degree of meaning in the motif, which had remained frozen, as it were, in the mindless repetitions of the genre. This meaning depends in the first instance on the West retaining naively positive associations within the genre. In the literature of the previous two decades, it is worth remembering, these associations had been virtually reversed. In Scott Fitzgerald's 'The Diamond as Big as the Ritz', or *The Great Gatsby*, the Dream has become bloated and debased, focused on the accumulation of massive wealth, and in 'The Diamond as Big as the Ritz', the sunset, the traditional, if ambiguous, image of the West, hope and future, becomes the centre of corruption, described as a gigantic bruise spreading its poisoned blood across the sky.

Of the other Ford films that employ the motif of escape west in one form or another, *Wagon Master* (1950) and *Two Rode Together* (1961) seem closest to *Stagecoach* in their use of the West as a way of escaping a society that is seen as constricting or corrupt. *Wagon Master*, with its explicit Promised Land imagery is the clearest of all in creating the fertile valley as an earthly paradise, beyond society. Part of the problem with the film is its placing in Ford's career. It seems the least complex and perhaps the most formally perfect of all Ford's Westerns, but as a more or less unequivocal affirmation of community values and pioneer enterprise, it seems out of chronology, coming, as it does, after *Fort Apache* (1948) and *She Wore a Yellow Ribbon* (1949). McBride and Wilmington (1972) argue that it is a more problematic film than it has generally been taken for, but their argument seems to me to run counter to the film's strategy, which is to reduce internal conflict to manageable proportions. Given this, it is probably best to see the film as a quite conscious homage or reverie, deliberately reduced in scale, evoking the dream of the pioneers in its simplest form. As a homage, it uses the escape west in a touching and harmless way, but, as in *Stagecoach*, the movement is away from the conflicts inherent in advancing American society (the town at the beginning of the film) which threaten the values of community – finally an evasion.

A second generic motif that recurs in Ford's films is that of the external threat. I am thinking less of Indians here (although the threat of Indians can be looked at similarly) than of characters like the Plummers in *Stagecoach*, the Clantons in *My Darling Clementine* (1946), the Cleggs in *Wagon Master* and to a lesser extent Liberty Valance. The Clantons and Cleggs most clearly suggest the characteristics they all share: they are unredeemable grotesques who seem at their most extreme to verge

Still: Wagon Master.

on the psychotic – essentially, perhaps, morality play figures. They are also seen as threats from outside the community, and this is vital, for it means that they can finally be killed with little sense of loss or of moral conflict, leaving the emergent community intact. The use of this motif is damaging because it suggests that community is distinct from society, even that the Cleggs and Clantons are essentially non-social – threats that come from nowhere (certainly, in Ford's value system, it is difficult to see how they could have been born of woman).

It is less damaging to *Wagon Master*, perhaps, than to *My Darling Clementine*, which implicitly dramatises a view of society within Tombstone itself that in its variety goes beyond the later film. Tombstone is heterogeneous, containing a variety of social types, settings and implied ways of life that cannot readily merge into an image of harmonious community. Yet a central part of the film's project, embodying an optimism that is very much of its immediately postwar moment, is of course to imply such a movement towards the development of community. The dance sequence is a beautiful, affirmative image of new American civilisation emerging in the desert, its mythic evocation of community completed as Clementine (Cathy Downs) and Wyatt (Henry Fonda), the embodiments of the best of East and West, are welcomed onto the floor of the half-built church on which the dance is taking place. But the harmony of the sequence depends on its exclusion of those characters incapable of integration into community, just as the scene following the birth of the

Still: My Darling Clementine – '. . . *our new marshal and his lady fair), Wyatt Earp (Henry Fonda) and Clementine Carter (Cathy Downs) join the dance.*

baby in *Stagecoach* must exclude Lucy and Gatewood. In *My Darling Clementine*, this must clearly involve the villainous Clantons who, like the Cleggs in *Wagon Master*, have to be killed to clear the way for the emergent community. But it also involves Doc Holliday (Victor Mature) and Chihuahua (Linda Darnell). As gambler and bar girl, familiar generic figures, Doc and Chihuahua, unlike the Clantons, belong to the town, although primarily to its night-time rather than its daytime identity. A further aspect of the town's development under the influence of Wyatt's civilising mission is precisely to move from the 'Wide awake, wide open town' shown in the night scenes when the Earps arrive, to its tamed, daytime identity at the end which allows Wyatt to leave and Clementine, the Boston lady, to become the new schoolmarm. The future, in other words, is that imaged in the dance, and in order to achieve it, Doc and Chihuahua will finally not simply be excluded but killed off. Generically, their deaths are perfectly appropriate: the bar girl is frequently killed and the flawed Doc Holliday has numerous close relatives in the doctors and gamblers of the genre. In this film, though, their deaths allow Ford to evade the tensions inherent in the social world he has created – the division of the town into night and day, church and saloon. It is striking, too, that the problems solved by killing Doc and Chihuahua include not only those of uncontrolled violence and overt sexuality, but that of Chihuahua's ethnic identity. Coded in some ways as Mexican, she is referred

to as Indian (Wyatt, in one of the film's most uncomfortable moments, threatens to send her back to the reservation). The community so beautifully imaged in the dance sequence is implicitly built on repression and is entirely White.

Equally significant in this context is the treatment of the hero in *Clementine*. Henry Fonda's Wyatt Earp is a figure of supreme authority and perfected moral identity whose slight social embarrassments do nothing to undermine the way in which a Western identity and a commitment to civilisation are integrated in his character without significant strain. The potentially problematic dimensions of this division between the values of the West and of the East are dramatised not through Wyatt but through Doc, whose consumptive cough can be understood as the physical manifestation of a corrosive psychic split. It is also particularly telling that the familiar conflict between the bar girl and the lady for the affections of the hero (a conflict that is regularly used to dramatise the hero's divided identity) is similarly displaced on to Doc.

These strategies offer Ford ways of keeping at bay the tensions that the film has created but cannot resolve. Perhaps more than any other film, *My Darling Clementine* dramatises the displacement of generic motifs by Ford's intervention: the displacement of the two opposed women from the hero to a secondary figure; the displacement of the revenge theme by a celebration of community, with a consequent lack of definition in the revenge and law-and-order impulses in Wyatt Earp. The image of emergent community, with all the resonance it could have in 1946, collides with the implied image of a more inclusive and complex social organisation produced by the traditional generic elements.

The evasions inherent in Ford's use of the two motifs I have mentioned are part of the wider problem of how society is conceived in his films: they enable the dream of ideal community to be preserved, free from internal conflicts. *Stagecoach* contains a view of civilisation which logically must crush community, but Dallas and Ringo are allowed to escape; *My Darling Clementine* preserves community by refusing to weld the generic world into an inclusive view of civilisation.

Inherent in the conflicts and contortions of these films is the problem of history. The reality that they are unable to confront (in fact seem desperate to suppress) is that of the contemporary world, a heterogeneous, modern society which is inimical to the 'traditional' values of family and community. There seems no way available to Ford in these films of reconciling a view of emergent civilisation, and its implications, with the image of community.

However, after *My Darling Clementine*, Ford's Westerns begin to find quite new solutions to this problem. The process begins with *Fort Apache* (1948), and the cavalry movies, in their military inflection of the Western, play a major role in the direction Ford increasingly takes. Certainly each of his richest films, by which I mean *Fort Apache, The Searchers* (1956) and *The Man Who Shot Liberty Valance* (1962), contains an affirmation of home, family, community, but simultaneously an implicit recognition that what sustained these 'traditional' value centres is dead. In effect, these films present a fusion of the familiar generic world of the West and implicit images of contemporary America. This gradually involves a remarkable historicising of Ford's sense of the West and the development, beginning in *Fort Apache* and fully realised in *The Man Who Liberty Valance*, of a dual perspective on the processes presented, although to achieve this, Ford is involved in strategies as contorted as anything in the genre at large.

The question which in some ways seems to underpin *Fort Apache* and (more clearly) *The Man Who Shot Liberty Valance* is 'How did that past become this present?' Not that the question is explicitly posed; if it were, it could easily be exposed as a non-question – that past and this present have little directly to do with one another. What the films present as the past (as fact) is of course an image – its reality is imaginative not actual. It exists, as it were, on a different ontological plane to the present. That past did not become this present. Yet I think the implicit question is structurally central to both films.

The cavalry films can be seen at one level as an attempt to deal with the tensions and difficulties raised for Ford in the Western proper (or perhaps, from another point of view, to continue to evade them). At any rate, the cavalry films substitute for the dangerous dynamism of the generic world the static order of the US Cavalry in which 'Sun and moon change, but the army's always the same'. The army shares with communities in other Ford films social diversity within a unity given by devotion to a common cause, but here military discipline and the hierarchy of rank implies a unity quite different from the feeling in, say, the *My Darling Clementine* dance, of a community unified in celebration and aspiration – a rigid framework rather than an organic unity. The tension between images of community and the containing military framework becomes central to the trilogy.

In narrowing his focus to the cavalry, Ford also limits the problem of social development, as dramatised in *Stagecoach* and *My Darling Clementine*. Although the purpose of the cavalry is explicitly seen as keeping the West safe for American westward expansion, it is striking how few civilians appear in the trilogy. Apart from army families (who are a special case), in *Fort Apache* only the Indian Agent appears between the opening scenes and the film's coda. Effectively, this excludes the kinds of external threat represented by the Clantons in *My Darling Clementine* and enables the army to function as an almost inclusive image of society within which, subject to military order, community must find its place. The logic of this situation, together with the role of Washington, reintroduces the issue of social development, but in a quite different form.

Although the historical events in the foreground of the cavalry trilogy are the Indian wars, the determining experience remains that of the Civil War, which is central to the immediate past of the main characters in all three films. For Ford, it is clear, the Civil War remained the great trauma of American history – the war that broke the Union and threatened the dream of extending nationally the values of harmony and reconciliation that characterise Ford's ideal communities. In *Fort Apache*, the war and its aftermath have exerted a determining influence on many of the characters: loss of wartime rank, changes of allegiance, undemanding or unwanted postings. Lt Col Thursday (Henry Fonda) was a wartime general; Sgt Major O'Rourke (Ward Bond), a Major; Sgt Beaufort (Pedro Armendariz), a Confederate officer. All the cavalry films have ex-Confederate soldiers serving in the US Cavalry with loss of rank. The trilogy is permeated throughout by a sense of disrupted careers and disturbed lives. Particularly in *Fort Apache*, though, the shuffling of rank and postings carries a sense that goes beyond military necessity to suggest decisions taken almost whimsically by a distant War Department out of touch with military realities and individual worth. The films opens, for instance, with Thursday's outburst about the injustice of his posting ('Blast an ungrateful War Department . . .') to the wilderness ('End of the rainbow, Fort Apache!'), a command he doesn't want and for which his recent diplomatic service in Europe has hardly fitted him. The appointment is capricious and, in the event, disastrous.

Not only does individual will seem powerless in this situation but characters' attempts to influence the course of their careers rebound with harsh and disproportionate irony. Repeated requests by Captain Collingwood (George O'Brien) for a transfer to an instructor's post at West Point are finally answered as he rides out to his death with the regiment; Thursday's attempts to make his name and achieve glory destroy the command but bring him posthumously the glory he craved.

These elements begin to provide a dimension that extends Ford's treatment of community and society very significantly: the containing order of cavalry life is itself subject to a wider order which is neither benign nor caring. *Fort Apache* can perhaps be seen as dramatising a process of breakdown in traditional order following the Civil War, which has consequences for any kind of harmonious life in America. Within this context, 'traditional sanctity and loveliness' cannot survive, *have not* survived, and the context is explicitly historical, setting a date on the process and providing an initial cause.

The theme of arbitrary and even mischievous control is treated in other ways, too. In particular, the scenes which it has been common to write off as 'comic relief' relate to the more weighty drama rather as A.P. Rossiter argues (in *Angel with Horns*, Longman Green, London, 1961) the low-life scenes in *Henry IV* do to the drama of state, by parody and ironic parallel. For Rossiter, Shakespeare's vision in these plays produces apparently incompatible but equally valid views of the historical process: 'The doubleness of implicit values in those situations which are ambivalent; those which can be seen as serious and farcical; as pathetic and absurd; as abominable and laughable . . .' In *Fort Apache*, the element of parody or comic parallel is present from an early

point in the drill scenes with the new recruits. In the first, the words of Sergeant Mulcahy (Victor McLaglen) almost repeat those of Colonel Thursday to his officers in an earlier scene. Thursday intends to 'Make this the finest regiment on the frontier', Mulcahy 'to make this squad the finest body of men in the American Army'. Both recruit scenes treat (but in a quite different key) the theme of arbitrary changes of rank – recruits are promoted to acting corporal on the basis of being Irish or of having had 'the honour to fight for the Confederacy in the late hostilities'. Later in the film, the sergeants themselves are the victims of lightning demotions after their mammoth drinking session at the Indian Agency, reduced to privates and made to shovel manure for a day. The gargantuan thirst that characterises sergeants in all Ford's cavalry films also becomes part of the thematic web of the film, paralleling the heavy drinking that accompanies Captain Collingwood's unspecified disgrace. In the comic scenes, human consequences are, to a degree, suspended, but the sense of relative wellbeing in itself contributes to the irony – the officers' demotions and postings have more serious consequences. Potential tragedy in the central drama is underpinned by a comic world which both parodies the military virtues and, by more specific parallels, suggests the absurdity that is another side of the disorder affecting army (and, by extension, American) life.

Within this context, Thursday appears an archaic figure, unable to adjust to a world in which the absolute authority of rank and the symmetry of rank and class have been qualified. He is almost incredulous, for instance, when he learns first that Sgt Major O'Rourke is a former major and then that he holds the Medal of Honour, yet later Thursday still talks of 'the gulf separating your class and mine'.

Stills: Fort Apache. *Above – the Grand March at the non-commissioned officers' dance. Opposite – Sergeants Mulcahy (Victor McLaglen), Beaufort (Pedro Armendariz), Quincannon (Dick Foran) and Shattuck (Jack Pennick).*

He is created as the victim of changes in what remains for him an unchanging world. Army regulations and ritual remain the unifying framework of the film, but Thursday's misfortune is to be placed in a situation which demands adjustments in the way the framework is seen and, paralleling these, adjustments to new fighting conditions. Another quotation from Rossiter is relevant: 'The Tudor myth system of Order, Degree etc., was too rigid, too black and white, too doctrinaire and narrowly moral for Shakespeare's mind; it falsified his fuller experience of man; consequently, while employing it as Frame, he had to undermine it, to qualify it with equivocations . . .' Military tradition is Ford's system of order and degree, endorsed, but hedged about by doubts and qualifications, and seen ambivalently.

Opposed to Thursday, and representing an order related to but qualitatively different from his inflexible code, is the life of Fort Apache. It isn't necessary to argue at any length the value the film attaches to the community of the fort – it is imaged perfectly and unambiguously in the dance sequences and the scenes of family life. The fort is represented as a nexus of human values: proper respect is extended to rank and protocol, but this co-exists with a sense of human worth that expresses itself in attitudes of co-operation and thoughtfulness. Fort Apache is one of Ford's most beautiful and richly created communities, but its values are given particular force by the context within which they are expressed. The turbulence of post-Civil War conditions and the

nature of the West make flexibility essential: where a sergeant may be an ex-major, or a trooper an ex-general, even military life cannot be based exclusively on rank. This means, rather remarkably, that the Fort Apache community is a progressive response to the historical situation defined by the film – not a sentimental dream but, in the circumstances prevailing, a social (and military?) necessity.

At the same time, though, the controlling framework of rank and the long arm of Washington make the community infinitely vulnerable and insecure. It is threatened not simply by the Indians, who provide the overt threat, but by the very principles of military life which provide its unifying frame. The most vivid image of this vulnerability is the interrupted dance – so often a highly charged moment in Ford's films. Here two dances are interrupted, not by external figures like the Cleggs in *Wagon Master*, but by the commanding officer of the fort. The first, a dance to celebrate George Washington's birthday, is interrupted as Thursday arrives unexpectedly at the fort; the second as Thursday orders the regiment to prepare to march. Finally, when Thursday's command is destroyed as a result of his folly, so is the community which is identified with it.

The development from *My Darling Clementine* to *Fort Apache* is, I think, very remarkable. Ford historicises his West and unites it, through the use of the army as metaphor of social order, to a total view of society shaken by the Civil War and its aftermath. The film presents an ambivalent, poised view of the containing military and social order, registering the necessity of the framework but seeing it as tragic and, in a sense, absurd. Most remarkable, perhaps, is the way the film finds a historical place for community and in doing so makes it subject to a greater determining social order.

This account of the film helps, I think, to clarify some aspects of the famous crux of the ending – the centre of extensive debate and disagreement among Ford critics (*see* note at the end of this article). York (John Wayne), now a Colonel and Commanding Officer at the fort, receives a party of Eastern journalists in his (previously Thursday's) office. As the sequence goes on, it becomes clear that in certain details of his dress, speech and bearing, York, who was previously associated with the flexible mores of the Fort Apache community and who opposed Thursday's military actions, has adopted aspects of Thursday's identity. A portrait of Thursday hangs on his wall; in his responses to the visitors' comments he endorses the glorious image of Thursday that has been created in the East and declares the wildly inaccurate painting of Thursday's charge described by one journalist 'correct in every detail'. Because Ford offers no representation of the time (at least three years?) between the battle and the film's coda we can only interpret the change in York in terms of the presentation of the scene and our knowledge of the previous context. The rigidity and studied control of York as he responds to the visitors suggests, after his earlier incarnation, a role deliberately taken on and enforced by will. Wayne's performance, indeed, communicates clearly (to us though not to the journalists) a sense of knowledge suppressed and sympathies stifled.

As important as his endorsement of the myth of Thursday, however, is the way in which York rebukes the visitor who suggests that, while Thursday's name lives on, the names of the men who died with him are forgotten. 'They're not forgotten', he asserts, 'because they haven't died. They're living – right out there' (he gestures through the window towards the desert). 'They'll keep on living as long as the regiment lives . . . the faces may change, the names, but they're there, they're the regiment, the regular army.' York turns back from the window to his visitors and continues: 'Now and fifty years from now. They're better men than they used to be. Thursday did that. Made it a command to be proud of.' Thursday's legacy and those who died under his command are integrated, in other words, into the idea of institutional immortality .

Interpreting the apparent changes in York is inevitably difficult. What it seems to imply is an overriding need, after the destruction of the fort's community, to affirm some form of continuity – in this case the continuity of the regiment – partly, certainly, in the wider interests of the army and the nation but, at the personal level, as a way of coping with the loss of friends and colleagues in an action York knows to have been incompetently led. It is, in this reading, an act of stoical self-denial, given its meaning by the experience of disaster and loss, and finding expression in the sinking of self into the impersonality of regimental tradition. Such a view of York would be consistent with the deeply pessimistic perception of history which I take to be at the heart of the film.

Less easy to account for, though, is the *film's* relationship to York's rhetoric of regimental continuity and to his changed manner and appearance. The slightly comic rigidity of some of York's actions here might imply at one level a continuation of the sense of absurdity that is so central to the bulk of the film. There is also something of that in the names of York's godson, offspring of the Sergeant-Major's son and the Colonel's daughter – Michael Thursday York O'Rourke. This slight edge of absurdity is quite compatible with the film's tragic view of events, underlined in much of the detail of the ending, including the stoical family group in the outer office and the final images of the women and child watching the regiment ride out. More difficult to integrate are the ghostly images of Thursday at the head of his troops which appear under York's reflection in the window as he asserts the immortality of the fallen soldiers. These cannot reasonably be understood as York's images; their superimposition is a piece of filmic rhetoric which together with the Battle Hymn of the Republic that rises to accompany the ghostly images as York speaks, is difficult to take as anything other than the film's endorsement of York's stirring speech. Here the film's viewpoint seems to fuse uncritically with York's in an affirmation of the abstract unity of the regiment and its role in putting down the Apaches that seems incompatible with the complex of values – human and military – celebrated earlier.

It seems to me difficult not to see the rhetorical intensification of this moment as out of character with the traditional dramatic impersonality that is predominant in the film. Clashes in Hollywood films between the bulk of a movie and its conclusion are not unusual, of course; the institutional pressure to produce an upbeat conclusion often produces abrupt or seemingly tacked-on 'happy endings' – a situation which some directors could manipulate to their own purposes. I am much less convinced than some writers that Ford is in firm control of what happens

at the end of *Fort Apache*, but what underpins the rhetoric of the coda is nevertheless significant. In one respect at least, the effect is reminiscent of Ford's film of *The Grapes of Wrath* (1940). That celebrates the idea of family ('at least we're together') even as it charts the disintegration of the Joads, until Tom (Henry Fonda) is finally about to leave Ma (Jane Darwell). At this point of final destruction of the family, the characters and the film reach, as in *Fort Apache*, for a new and much more abstract level of rhetoric – for something other than family to affirm. About to leave in order to avoid the police, Tom invokes the idea advanced by his dead friend Casey (John Carradine) of 'one big soul' of which individuals are a part. Just as York asserts that Collingwood and the others are not dead, but live on in the idea of the regiment, so Tom, comforting his mother, suggests that although he is leaving, he will still be present – in fact that he will be everywhere: 'I'll be all round in the dark . . . Wherever there's a cop beating up a guy, I'll be there . . .' We can see that Tom is both reaching for a new level of understanding of the relationships between people and trying to find and give comfort as the family disintegrates. Not surprisingly, Ma cannot understand what he means. But as the film ends, Ma's final speech also contains a crucial change of terms. She affirms not the *family*, the existence of which has been the focus of her life and which has now been shattered – but the *people*: 'Looked like we was beat . . . but we keep a-coming. We're the people that live. We'll go on forever. We're the people.' It is in its way wonderfully moving, but what is being affirmed now is the resilience not of individuals but of the mass; as in *Fort Apache*, the abstract replaces the concrete. In both cases, what seems to motivate the shift in rhetorical level is loss of family and community – the centres of value to which the films give their most whole-hearted commitment – and the emergence of a bleak and comfortless modern world dominated by impersonal social and economic forces. For the most part, the films see and represent this process very clearly. But for the characters and for the film-maker, it is as though the extent of the loss cannot be fully admitted or its implications sustained, the reversion to what Rossiter refers to as a 'one-eyed' view of things stridently attempting to deny the pain.

In other words, if the myth-making in the coda of *Fort Apache* seems too openly endorsed after what has gone before, it may be that Ford could not sustain the ambiguities inherent in the rest of the film, or finally confront the destruction of community. Like York, Ford, in effect, reaches for the dehumanised unity of the regiment *because* of the extinction of the community that sustained real values.

Almost however one reads the ending, though, there are further implications in the film's account of what has happened since Thursday's last stand. The painting of Thursday's charge whose accuracy York endorses hangs in Washington, the source of the orders that sent Thursday to the West in the first place and the centre of the disorder affecting army life in the film. But Washington is now also shown as the focus, even the source, of the myth-making that surrounds the events which we have earlier witnessed. Effectively, the *legend* of Thursday and his regiment de-historicises the event, it removes the determining social context which the film has presented and creates a static, timeless image of an individual hero, frozen forever in a heroic pose. Through the creation of this transcendent figure, the legend denudes the event of its historical meaning and suppresses both human loss and potential blame. The new significance which Thursday takes on rein-forces national unity and simultaneously precludes inquiry into the system or the man. This deeply re-actionary process has its corollary at a personal level in the repression to which York subjects himself.

This break between 'fact' and 'legend', between the bulk of the film and its coda, opens up a method of dramatising the break between 'that past' and 'this present' by juxtaposing two perspectives on events, which in turn embody and represent a his-torical shift. The presentation in the bulk of the narrative is identified as reality – as history – and a gap is opened between this history and the mythic reworking identified with the East – the view of events that will be perpetuated. Ford embeds his dream of community within a narrative that purports to show the facts, so conferring on it historical reality and simultaneously denying its ideological status, while the East/Washington is seen as the source of a radically misleading rhetoric based on the creation of transcendent heroes who stand apart from history in a timeless frieze. In effect, the remaking of history for ideological ends which is central to the Western genre (and to Ford's project here) is transferred to the East and there exposed as myth making. Thurs-day has become a hero for children's adventure stories – as the newspaper man says, 'the idol of every schoolboy in America'. He has become, in fact, a fitting hero for the Western.

These are not meanings one can confidently as-cribe to Ford or to the film's overall project; they can be constructed from the conflicting 'voices' that underlie the assertive rhetoric of the coda. But what is perhaps only a possibility in *Fort Apache* achieves much fuller and more integrated expression in *The Man Who Shot Liberty Valance*.

The Man Who Shot Liberty Valance draws on the central traditions of the genre in a way that *Fort Apache*, as a Cavalry film, does not and so raises again the potential collision of emergent social forms and community that posed such a problem in *Stage-coach* and *My Darling Clementine*. In those films, the generic world was too diverse to be accepted in-clusively, and community was variously hived off. It is one indication of how much Ford had developed that *The Man Who Shot Liberty Valance* is much more inclusive in its acceptance of the generic world. One possible reason for this is that the old West in *The Man Who Shot Liberty Valance* is pre-sented within the structure of the film as dead: we see it only in a flashback. In fact, the flashback struc-ture provides the solution to the problem of social development. By using flashback, in itself compar-atively rare in the Western, the film can juxtapose

the past and the present that has emerged from it. In other words, the film's structure offers a base for the dual perspective implied by the end of *Fort Apache*: a 'factual' view of the past and another view associated with, in this case, a lifeless present. The flashback also preordains the outcome of the story and the movement of history – the past has given way to the present; Ransom Stoddard (James Stewart) has survived and become a senator, while Tom Doni-phon (John Wayne) has died forgotten. The emphasis of the film therefore shifts from 'What happened?' towards 'How did it happen? How did that past become this present?' The question takes on con-siderable intensity because within the flashback, there seems no way in which the forces of 'civilis-ation' can emerge triumphant – the given historical outcome seems dramatised as an impossibility.

The recognition of the past as dead colours (if that is not an inappropriate word for a film made, significantly, in black and white) the whole presen-tation of old Shinbone in the film. What is striking, as a number of Ford critics have pointed out, is how many of the elements that one expects of a Ford Western are missing here. Landscape is hardly a visual presence at all, although the desert is a central *term* in the film. There are none of the social rituals, dances particularly, that one associates with Fordian community. Although the film is centrally concerned with a funeral, we do not see the cere-mony – in fact, Ranse and Hallie Stoddard (Vera Miles) leave before it takes place. Unlike funerals in other Ford films, Tom's is a socially marginal event, an image of breakdown, discontinuity and loss. In old Shinbone, too, there is an overall sense of reconstruction rather than the apparently sponta-neous life of, say, the dance in *My Darling Clemen-tine*. Community as something alive, to be believed in, now seems firmly a thing of the past, both within the drama and in Ford's imagination. It is partly this, I think, that gives the film its particular clarity – there are none of the emotional confusions of earlier films.

Consonant with this is the schematic nature of the film both in the prominence of thematic structure (the garden/desert opposition) and in the particular configuration of central characters. In this latter re-spect the film seems, perhaps surprisingly, to relate to earlier and more primitive forms of the genre. This is most obvious in Liberty Valance (Lee Marvin), whose name itself is almost allegorical and who seems a kind of throwback to the villainous and two-dimensional Clantons in *My Darling Clementine* and Cleggs in *Wagon Master*. But just as Liberty is a version of an old generic figure, the bad Westerner, so Ranse (the Easterner) and Tom (the good West-erner) relate very clearly to generic stereotypes; all three types in combination invoke generic expecta-tions that are crucial to the film's meanings.

The Easterner who arrives in a Western town un-tutored in Western mores and values is present in the earliest film Westerns. In films like *The Great Train Robbery* (1903) and *Life of an American Cowboy* (1903), he is a marginal figure, a butt for the cow-boys who shoot at the saloon floor around his feet

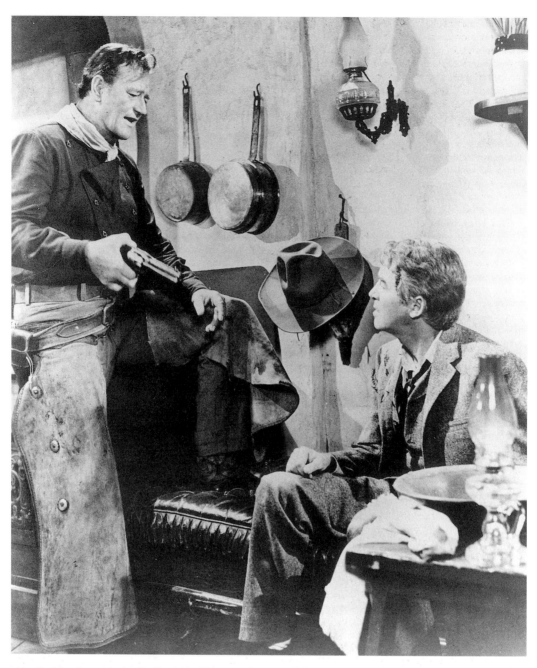

to make him dance. As he develops, the Easterner is characteristically weak, misguided and powerless – a figure of symbolic impotence. But by 1912, and perhaps earlier, there were films (*The Making of Broncho Billy*, 1913, for instance) in which the Easterner, initially humiliated, deliberately takes on Western characteristics – clothes, manner, and finally skilled gunplay – to revenge himself for his earlier humiliation. He becomes, quite unproblematically, a Westerner. Both possibilities, frequently intertwined, retain a strong presence in the genre in endless films of which *Cowboy* (Delmer Daves, 1958) and *The Big Country* (William Wyler, 1958) could stand as examples from the period just before *The Man Who Shot Liberty Valance*.

The good and bad Westerners also go back to the beginning of the film Western and into the literary Westerns of the nineteenth century. Characteristically, their antagonism (however it is dramatised, and the variations are endless) climaxes in a fight to the death, most familiarly but by no means invariably, a face-off. The locus classicus of the postwar Western in this respect is probably *Shane* (George Stevens, 1953), but variations would include a number of Anthony Mann's films (*Bend of the River*, 1952, for example) and of Budd Boetticher's. Most familiarly, the hero's victory makes the future safe for community – the townspeople, homesteaders, and so on – and he is frequently poised at the end of the film to enter the community himself.

At the heart of the Western, too, is the figure of the transcendent hero – most common in juvenile Westerns and dime novels, but a significant presence throughout the genre, often a point of reference even where he is absent. At his simplest he is something like The Lone Ranger: invulnerable, endowed with almost superhuman skill, unencumbered by most human limitations – a fantastic, impossible figure. The line of descent of this figure, as of so much in the genre, is from Fenimore Cooper's Leatherstocking, who transcends the limitations of both White and Red civilisations, pointing towards an ideal, though historically impossible, American society.

In its handling of the two Westerners, *The Man Who Shot Liberty Valance* demonstrates what is implicit in many Westerns though frequently denied by the endings: that they are bound in a relationship of reciprocal implication – as relative terms in the generic pattern, they can have no independent life. Thus Tom Doniphon can remain central to Shinbone only while Liberty Valance lives; this in turn suggests that the vitality of old Shinbone depends on a social situation in which the balance between anarchy and control is precariously maintained. Unlike the Clantons, who are external to the community in *My Darling Clementine*, Liberty Valance, however

Stills: The Man Who Shot Liberty Valance. *Opposite – Westerner (John Wayne) and Easterner (James Stewart). Below – Ranse seems to kill Liberty (Lee Marvin).*

much he threatens the town and its chosen future, is integral to its life. The film refuses what remains generically possible, that Tom could shoot Liberty and continue to lead community into the beckoning future. When Tom shoots Liberty from the shadows and cedes, as Peter Wollen says, his charismatic authority to Ranse, he condemns himself to a socially marginal existence. This represents a radical break with generic pattern – hero and villain do not confront each other at all. Equally important, it is a definitive break with the ideological operation inherent in the pattern, in which the good Westerner remains centre stage, poised to enter community or to ride on. This pattern and its ideological implications are capable of varied and complex emphasis, of course: in some of Anthony Mann's films, for instance, the hero wins after a struggle of tremendous intensity and violence; he seems totally drained, as if part of himself has been killed (*see* 'The Collapse of Fantasy' in this book). The entry into community there is less than triumphant. But Ford refuses even that kind of alternative. The old West and the present are incompatible: the old West dies immediately the tensions on which it is centred are resolved. This change of world is mimed in one of the most obviously expressive pieces of editing in Ford, from Tom's burning house to the raucous but spurious animation of the political convention.

In its treatment of the Easterner, too, the film breaks a generic pattern. Although Ranse eventually

takes up the gun, he doesn't learn to use it – he does not become a Westerner. In fact, iconographically and in other ways, he remains emphatically of the East. For much of the film, too, he wears an apron and waits at table – a job explicitly seen in Western terms as unmanly: he is, as Liberty says, 'the new waitress'. Physically he is contrasted with both Tom and Liberty, and it is useful to compare James Stewart here and as the hero of Anthony Mann Westerns to get a sense of the performance decisions involved. Here he is gangling, somewhat uncoordinated, limp. He is physically humiliated by both Tom and Liberty – treatment entirely consistent with the generic stereotype. Though he obtains a gun, it is tiny – almost a toy in Tom's hand — and he remains incompetent with it.

I mention these very obvious facts because of the role they play in the gunfight, in which Ranse's physical awkwardness, his unease with a gun, and the apron he is wearing, are prominent. Iconographically, he is presented as a figure of no power, even as one of symbolic impotence. This is not to take away from the dramatic context, which emphasises Ranse's determination and courage but to indicate the nature of the decisions taken out of the very large range of possible alternatives. We know, of course, from the opening section of the film, that Ranse survived, but generically the only outcome is that he will be killed. What we see in the first presentation of the gunfight is in fact generically the impossible, an outcome which completely overturns the generic pattern. Although the gunfight could have been staged very differently, it is initially shown in such a way that the knowledge which Ranse, as narrator of the flashback, and the film possess – that Tom killed Liberty – is withheld from us. We see Ranse kill Liberty and, together with the audience within the drama, accept an impossibility.

Crucially, it is this 'knowledge', that Ranse is the man who shot Liberty Valance, on which the future's view of the event will be based. The legend that will continue to be printed has the effect of implicitly denying the vitality and strength of the old West. Fusing in a single individual the Easterner and the man with the gun while retaining the dominant Eastern persona is, from the point of view of the emerging civilisation, an ideological triumph. Like the myth of manifest destiny, the legend validates the destruction of one world in the cause of a new one which is seen as inherently superior. But for Ford, the 'fact' (*Tom* killed Liberty) *explains* the death of the old West, the otherwise unaccountable (impossible) triumph of an inferior civilisation. The gunfight *as it is seen* and passed down to the future results in the creation of a transcendent figure, 'the man who shot Liberty Valance', who unites book and gun, East and West – like Leatherstocking, a figure capable of resolving contradictions, of binding together the antinomies. The *film*, however, denies the possibility of transcendence – it demonstrates that in fact, no-one can unite the opposites. In *appearing* to do so, though, Ranse ('the man who shot Liberty Valance') validates the movement of history. He becomes the potently emblematic but inherently insubstantial transitional figure.

The Man Who Shot Liberty Valance, then, brings into focus the historical transition which is simultaneously enacted and denied by the operations of the Western as a whole. The film fulfils the promise of *Fort Apache* in providing a structure by means of which the valued past can be set against a lifeless present and the transition process exposed. By identifying as misrepresentations ideological operations which are fundamental to the genre itself, and identifying them as hostile to the Old West, the image of the West is removed from ideology and re-presented as 'history'. The result, in a splendid paradox, is that Ford's West is destroyed by processes identical to those which brought the genre itself into existence.

Note: In combining parts of two articles published in *Movie* 22 (Spring 1976) and 25 (Winter 1977/78) for publication here, I have tried to clarify certain obscurities in the original pieces, without significantly revising the central argument, which I believe still holds. I should acknowledge, however, Leland Poague's critique of my account of *Fort Apache* (*Cinema Journal*, vol.27, no. 2 Winter 1988). Much of what Poague argues rests, I think, on taking one section of the article out of the context of a broader argument about representations of social development in Ford's Westerns, but I accept that my original account of the ending of *Fort Apache* offered assertion where some more detailed argument was needed. The slightly longer section in this version of the article is intended to make my argument and its basis clearer. About his reading of some of the detail of the film's ending I have no disagreement with Poague but our interpretations of the significance of Ford's strategies remain rather different.

Frames: The Man Who Shot Liberty Valance – *as Ranse shoots and misses, Tom fires from the shadows.*

THE WESTERNS OF DELMER DAVES

Michael Walker

Between 1950 and 1958, Delmer Daves directed (and in some cases scripted or co-scripted} a series of Westerns which usually receive favourable comment in books on the genre, but which have not to my knowledge been extensively examined as a body of work, at least in English. This article looks at all the films, apart from the modern Western *Return of the Texan* (1952), but including *White Feather* (Robert D. Webb, 1955), which Daves co-wrote and which, I shall argue, is recognisably a Daves movie.

The nine films may be divided into two groups: those in which Indians play a significant role – *Broken Arrow* (1950), *Drum Beat* (1954), *White Feather*, and *The Last Wagon* (1956) – and those in which they do not: *Jubal* (1956), *3:10 to Yuma* (1957), *Cowboy* (1958), *The Badlanders* (1958) and *The Hanging Tree* (1958). The first three of the Indian films are based on real-life events and deal with Government-inspired attempts by the Whites to neutralise the Native American threat. *The Last Wagon* is structurally rather different – it is primarily concerned with a wagon drive through hostile Apache territory – but across all four films character types (e.g. the White racist), themes (e.g. miscegenation) and settings (e.g. the river) recur. Four of the remaining films may be grouped in pairs. In *3:10 to Yuma* and *Cowboy*, the focus is on the relationship between two men, one of whom (played by Glenn Ford in both films) is the leader of an all-male group; the other is struggling to perform a task of which he has no experience. *Jubal* and *The Hanging Tree* show the hero entering an already established community (ranching and mining respectively) and being rather uneasily integrated; both films possess powerful villains whose sway over the community leads to a climactic sequence in which the hero is almost lynched. *The Badlanders*, a Western remake of *The Asphalt Jungle* (John Huston, 1950), is the outsider: it is set in 1898, significantly later than the other films – all of which are set between 1870 and 1880 – and is the least marked by Daves's authorship.

Daves thus covers a variety of different areas of the Western genre. The early movies all deal with the 'Indian question' during the crucial decade when the Whites' imperialist drive to the West had usurped so much Native American territory that the tribes were fighting their last battles before surrender and, ultimately, exile to reservations. But, whereas in John Ford's films such as *Fort Apache* (1948), *She Wore a Yellow Ribbon* (1949), *Rio Grande* (1950)

and *The Searchers* (1956), the conflict is dramatised from a predominantly White point of view, Daves is much more divided in his loyalties. *Broken Arrow* was hailed at the time as a breakthrough in the sympathetic treatment of the Native American. Although, across the four movies, the representations of Native Americans are not all equally positive, Daves arguably went further in this direction than any other director of the period, in itself a fair achievement. And in *The Last Wagon*, working at a different angle to the issue from in the three 'historical' Indian movies, he was able to fashion a distinctly progressive anti-White narrative.

3:10 to Yuma and *Cowboy* centre on the homesteader and the cowboy respectively. But although they are structurally similar, their narratives are quite different. That of *Cowboy* is relatively loose and episodic: it may be summarised as the initiation of the young hero into the life of a cowboy. *3:10 to Yuma*, by contrast, is a beautifully plotted morality tale, in which its hero is taken out of the harsh but mundane world of homesteading and confronted with the sort of challenge with which heroes have grappled since the earliest narratives. Nevertheless, these two films are perhaps the Daves Westerns most typical of the genre. In them, rather than carve out his own distinctive trail through the territory, he treads relatively well-worn paths: in *Cowboy*, the cattle drive; in *3:10 to Yuma*, the *Shane* (George Stevens, 1953) story of the struggling homesteader plus the *High Noon* (Fred Zinnemann, 1952) story of the strong hero and the weak town.

Jubal and *The Hanging Tree* are different again: as well as being Westerns, they are also 'fifties melodramas. Each deals with a hero, in flight from his past, who enters a community bringing his demons with him and triggers an eruption of desire and violence. Immediately after *The Hanging Tree*, Daves would move on to 'specialise' in family/teenage melodramas – beginning with *A Summer Place* (1959) – and here he signals his intuitive grasp of the genre's essentials: the nature of the hero's past trauma and its relationship to his present; the complex of tensions that can be generated in a small-scale society; the violence of the community.

In an interview with Christopher Wicking, Daves stressed both his roots and his own experiences as contributing to his wish to portray the West 'honestly'. His maternal grandfather crossed the plains twice with the Mormons in a covered wagon and later became a Pony Express rider; his paternal grandmother was born in California two months after her mother had made a covered-wagon crossing. When he himself graduated from university in 1926 he went to live for three months in the Arizona desert with Hopis and Navajos. He comments: 'Out of respect for these people, you can't tell stories of the west and have it fake' (*Screen*, July/October 1969, p.59). His Western career parallels that of Anthony Mann: both directed their first Westerns in 1949 on a pro-Indian theme (*Broken Arrow* and Mann's *Devil's Doorway*, 1950); both directed James Stewart at the beginning of his Western career (*Broken Arrow* and Mann's *Winchester 73*, 1950) and Gary Cooper at the end of his (Mann's *Man of the West*, 1958, and *The Hanging Tree*). Daves's Westerns overall lack the coherence and intensity of Mann's – it was not until *The Last Wagon* that he achieved a comparable stylistic force – but at their best they are no less complex. Like Mann, Daves makes excellent use of landscape, both visually and symbolically. And, like Mann's, his Westerns are distinguished by highly personal themes and preoccupations which mark him, in this genre at least, as a distinctive *auteur*.

The Indian Films

Broken Arrow was adapted from Elliott Arnold's 1947 novel *Blood Brother*. Although the script is credited to Michael Blankfort, recent research by Larry Ceplair (*Cineaste*, vol.18, no.2, 1991) has established that it was in fact the work of Albert Maltz, one of the Hollywood Ten – who had written *The Pride of the Marines* (1945) for Daves – and that Blankfort acted as Maltz's front when the latter was blacklisted, taking no payment for this. It was producer Julian Blaustein who approached Maltz and who subsequently sold the package (script, James Stewart as star, himself as producer) with Blankfort's name on it to Darryl F. Zanuck at 20th Century-Fox, where Daves was under contract. Blankfort won a Screen Writers Guild award for the script, and Ceplair reports (*Cineaste*, vol.18, no.4, 1991) having now managed to get the Guild to correct its records, but adds that there is no legal or contractual mechanism to oblige 20th Century-Fox to alter the credits on its prints or videos.

In his foreword to the novel, Arnold states that the parts of the story dealing with the Apache leader Cochise, his relationship with army scout Tom Jeffords and the subsequent peacemaking mission of General Howard were based on fact and that, where possible, he used the records left by Jeffords and Howard for details of what was actually said on different occasions. The character of the Indian heroine Sonseeahray was invented. Beginning in 1855 with Cochise returning from a successful raid into Mexico and continuing until his death in 1874, the novel extends over a much longer time period than the film, which begins in 1870 with Jeffords. The novel is in the third person, but the film is narrated in voice-over by Jeffords (James Stewart), which, particularly as there is no sense of its being in flashback, makes it seem to be in the first person. The focus, then, is different in the film: Jeffords is to

be our guide into the world of the Chiricahua Apaches: we see and interpret events through his eyes.

There is little doubt that Maltz adopted this technique as a tactic to prepare the (White) 1950 audience for a rather different view of the Indian to that promulgated by most previous Westerns. At the beginning of the film, Jeffords's voice-over mentions the ten-year war with the Apaches: 'a bloody no-give, no-take war'. But, from his early encounters – with an injured Apache boy whom he nurses and with the Apache warriors who subsequently spare his life because he cared for the boy – Jeffords 'learns' about the Indians: that 'Apache mothers cried about their sons, that Apache men had a sense of fair play'. These discoveries are set against his earlier statement: 'Apaches are wild animals, we all said.' The 'we' clearly refers to White Americans in 1950 just as much as those in the narrative.

Although *Broken Arrow* was not the first pro-Indian Western, William Everson considers that it went further than earlier films: 'no film had been really unreservedly pro-Indian' (*A Pictorial History of the Western Film*, Citadel, Secaucus, New Jersey, 1971, p.201). Moreover, the famous earlier pro-Indian films had tended to deal with the issue in terms of injustice to Native Americans who had thus far behaved, on the Whites' terms, honourably. *Ramona*, filmed four times – the first version by D.W. Griffith in 1910, the last by Henry King in 1936 – is about the victimisation of Indians who have become both farmers and Christians. *The Vanishing American* (George B. Seitz, 1925) is about the exploitation and dispossession of reservation Navajos who fought in World War I. *Devil's Doorway* is similar in that its Shoshone chief fought with the Union Army before returning home to be confronted with dispossession from his homelands.

I would not wish to deny the force of these films, all of them melodramas of protest in which the Indian hero is killed, but *Broken Arrow* is different. Although it softens the bitter anti-American sentiments of Arnold's novel, it still deals with Indians who have not attempted to co-operate with the Whites, and it respects the Apache culture, which it takes some pains to present accurately. The film has been criticised more recently by Native American activists for its use of White actors in the key roles of Cochise (Jeff Chandler) and Sonseeahray (Debra Paget), and for the subtle racism whereby the 'bad' Indian, Geronimo is, by contrast, played by a Native American, Jay Silverheels (*see*, for example, articles in *The Pretend Indians: Images of Native Americans in the Movies*, edited by Gretchen M. Bataille and Charles L.P. Silet, Iowa State University Press, 1980). The latter critique is, indeed, unanswerable, but the former is more problematic. In *The War, the West and the Wilderness* (Secker & Warburg, London, 1979), Kevin Brownlow quotes Iron Eyes Cody, a Native American actor in many Westerns of the era, including *Broken Arrow*: 'Indians have no tradition of acting or plays. Our culture consists more of ceremonial. There were very few Indian actors because we weren't conditioned to it. In any case, the studios only put forward those names which the banks would put money up for' (p.348). The last point is crucial: one simply cannot imagine Zanuck seeing the value of casting Native Americans in starring roles when he would have to do battle with the Front Office over the issue. It would be forty years before this particular 'convention' was broken – still against the wishes of the financiers – in *Dances with Wolves* (Kevin Costner, 1990).

When the Apache warriors first confront Jeffords, the issue of scalping comes up. It is established that Whites are prepared to pay 'many dollars' for an Apache scalp, whereas the Apaches themselves do not scalp. This complete reversal of the traditional position that scalping was a barbaric Indian practice is an early sign of the film's iconoclasm. Even so, the ruthlessness of the Apaches in war is not glossed over. Although the men spare Jeffords's life, they promptly tie him up and ambush a group of White prospectors who, like Jeffords, have entered the Apache lands to seek gold. With Jeffords forced to watch, the Apaches then kill the three survivors in a brutal manner: two are hanged (one upside down), the third is buried in the ground up to his neck, his eyes rubbed with mescal juice to attract ants. Filmed in silhouette against the sky at dusk, the scene is unusually violent for its time, and it is consistent with the film's later position that the leader of this Apache band should be Gokliya, the future Geronimo. Even so, the brutality here is motivated: the buried man had in his possession three Apache scalps.

At his boarding house in Tucson, Jeffords is approached by Colonel Bernall (Raymond Bramley), who is confident that he can defeat Cochise in six months and wants Jeffords's assistance as scout. Citing Cochise's brilliance as a military tactician, Jeffords scorns Bernall's ambitions and declines his request. A number of other people are present, including Terry (Joyce MacKenzie), a major character in the novel (she loves Jeffords throughout and he turns to her after the death of Sonseeahray) but here restricted to this one appearance, although Will Wright in *Six Guns and Society* (1975) comments that she seems 'an apparent girlfriend' (p 82). (That she is in the film at all suggests that her part was originally larger, but was pruned to focus more strongly on the main romance.)

Also present is a prospector who escaped the ambush and has inflated the number of Apaches involved from five to fifty. On hearing Jeffords's version of the story, Ben Slade (Will Geer), the film's most vociferous Indian hater, demands to know why he didn't kill the wounded Apache boy. In the heated exchange that follows, Jeffords says that it wasn't Cochise who started this war, but 'a snooty lieutenant, fresh out of the East', who hanged Cochise's brother and five others after inviting them to talks under a flag of truce. Again, the film provides a powerful justification for the Apaches' war-like behaviour. In response, John Lowrie (Robert Griffin), a trader, concedes that the Whites have not always 'done right', but adds, 'we're bringing civilisation here, ain't we? Clothes, carpets, hats, boots, medicine . . . I got a wagonload of first class whisky

waiting for me in the East. I could sell that at a dollar a bottle if it wasn't for Cochise.' The last point underlines the irony with which the speech is presented: the equation of civilisation with the availability of Western consumer goods.

It is apparent that each of the men contributing to the argument thinks in purely personal terms: Bernall seeks glory as the tamer of Cochise, Slade hates the Apache because they slaughtered his family, Lowrie resents the loss of trade. And, since each is committed to the ideology of the Whites as 'bringing civilisation', each is adamant that Cochise must be fought and defeated. (Later, Lowrie is more explicit: 'We'll have peace when every Apache is hung from a tree!') It is Jeffords's revulsion at the killing that causes him to try and seek another way. He asks Juan (Bill Wilkerson), an Apache living in town, to teach him the Apache language and customs. Cochise has succeeded in closing down both the Butterfield stage and the mail into Tucson: Jeffords plans to visit him and ask him to permit the mail riders to pass in safety. Jeffords says to Juan that he wants to learn Apache ways 'in here', gesturing towards his heart. The expression and gesture mark Jeffords's intuitive empathy with the Apaches: they are later used to signal authenticity of feeling by both Sonseeahray and Cochise. By the same token, in the Apache camp Jeffords always wears the amulet given him by the Apache boy at the beginning.

When Jeffords arrives at Cochise's camp, the latter makes his position clear: 'We fight for our land against Americans who try to take it.' Jeffords's argument is, nevertheless, a strong one: that the Whites will always outnumber the Apaches and peace may be the only way the latter can survive. He argues that allowing the mail to pass safely will show the Whites that Cochise is a man of honour. As the men talk, a rapport is established; by evening, Cochise has changed into dark green clothes which subtly match Jeffords's grey. The rapport leads Cochise to introduce Jeffords to the poetically named Sonseeahray ('Morning Star'), who is in a sacred state during her ceremonial transition to womanhood. Accordingly, Jeffords meets the Indian heroine when she is 'white painted lady, mother of life', a goddess-like image. The scene comes from the novel but, as their relationship develops into a budding love affair, the nature of this first encounter raises an important question: what sort of idealised image of womanhood is Jeffords falling in love with?

Cochise agrees to Jeffords's request, but he does not call off the war. When Colonel Bernall leads out a wagon train with a cavalry escort as a lure to trap Cochise, the latter outwits him, orchestrating a preplanned attack in which the cavalry are routed and the wagons captured. Among the Apache losses is the boy befriended by Jeffords, an indication of the harshness of the Apaches' world: he was only fourteen, but considered to be a man. Bernall is also killed, but General Howard (Basil Ruysdael), accompanying him, survives. Another survivor, a driver (John Doucette), convinced that Cochise must have had inside knowledge about Bernall's tactics (which included soldiers hidden in the wagons), tells his

story to the suspicious Tucson residents in such a way that the men turn on Jeffords and are about to lynch him when Howard intervenes. Howard, it turns out, has been sent by President Grant to make a 'fair peace' with the Apaches. Bringing with him a Bible rather than a sword, he wants Jeffords to take him to Cochise. Before this happens, however, Jeffords pursues his courtship of Sonseeahray.

Will Wright relates *Broken Arrow* to the 'classical plot' of the Western (the hero rides into town and cleans it up) by noting that, here, 'the hero joins and protects the enemies of society (the Apaches) and society itself takes the role of the villain' (p.83). However, in one respect, the film registers uncertainty around its project: the representation of Tucson society includes vivid scenes and characters, whereas that of Apache society is focused on very few characters and a few representative rituals. There is little feeling of a community: Cochise's wife Nalikadeya (Argentina Brunetti) is kept strictly in the background; his sons (who appear in *Taza, Son of Cochise*, Douglas Sirk, 1953) are not even mentioned; Sonseeahray's parents are mentioned but never seen. A consequence of this pruning of significant Apache characters is that Cochise becomes, in effect, a father figure to Sonseeahray. It is he who points out that Sonseeahray has been asked for by another man, Nahilzay (John War Eagle), but who supports the interracial relationship when it becomes clear that Sonseeahray genuinely prefers Jeffords and they want to marry. Equally, it is he who warns them of the consequences of marrying – they will be fully accepted in neither Apache nor White

Stills: Broken Arrow. *Above – Ben Slade (Will Geer) and other Tucson residents about to threaten Tom Jeffords (James Stewart) with lynching. Opposite – Cochise (Jeff Chandler) and his wife Nalikadeya (Argentina Brunetti) look on as Jeffords and Sonseeahray (Debra Paget) are married.*

society – and so draws attention to the problem of racism which is at the core of the film. And, when Nahilzay tries to kill Jeffords, it is Cochise who tells him that he has betrayed the promise of safety given to Jeffords and summarily executes him.

When Jeffords brings General Howard to Cochise's camp, and the peace talks begin, it is apparent that the film is weaving together the two stories – the love affair and the search for peace – so that both reach fruition at the same time. Again, however, Cochise must first deal with a threat within the tribe. Although Howard's peace treaty gives the Apaches a specified territory, Gokliya resents the loss of warrior status. To Cochise's assurance that 'The American government will give us cattle – we will raise them and trade them . . .', he responds scornfully: 'It is not the Apache way to be grandmothers to cattle. Cochise has lost his taste for battle and so he is ready to surrender.' Cochise, thinking of the long term, argues for change: 'The Americans keep cattle, but they are not soft or weak. Why should not the Apache learn new ways . . . The Americans are growing stronger, while we are growing weaker.' He breaks the arrow to signal that he will try the path of peace and says that those who do not agree should walk away. This leads to a split amongst the

Chiricahuas. Assuming the name of Geronimo – 'the name Mexican enemies have given me' – Gokliya takes the chiefs who agree with him and leaves.

The conflict between those who want to fight and those who want peace is one which has never lost its relevance or urgency. Writing on Daves in *Positif* 50-52 (March 1963), Bertrand Tavernier stressed how modern the film seemed. Daves, clearly, is on the side of peace, but pacifism is by no means the preferred option in most Westerns. There is also the question of whose interests the peace serves. In *Seeing Is Believing* (Pluto Press, London, 1984), Peter Biskind rereads selected 'fifties Hollywood movies in terms of the politics of the period. He argues that *Broken Arrow* shows American cunning: dividing the Apaches, making peace with the liberal Cochise and ostracising the extremist Geronimo so that he may be hunted down. Of Cochise's stand, Biskind says: 'He's fallen for the foreign aid carrot; he's already on line for the Marshall Plan, a suppliant asking for handouts rather than an equal demanding his rights' (p.236). Unfortunately, if the events in the film are related to subsequent real-life history, Biskind's cynical interpretation is valid: the Americans broke the treaty agreed with Cochise (in 1876, two years after his death). But, in the terms established by the film, Cochise is thinking rationally about the best way of providing a future for his people on the assumption that the Americans would, like Jeffords, be men of honour.

It became a convention, in Westerns where 'preserving the peace' was a dominant issue, that hotheads or warmongers on one or both sides would recklessly or deliberately threaten this: *Cheyenne Autumn* (John Ford, 1964) shows this almost diagrammatically in the battles precipitated first by Red Shirt (Sal Mineo), then by Lieutenant Scott (Patrick Wayne). In *Broken Arrow*, no sooner has Cochise declared that he will try peace, than the Butterfield Stage, which has started running again into Tucson, is attacked by Geronimo (at the river, always a crucial threshold in Daves's Westerns). However, since Jeffords is conveniently present at this moment, he is able to send a smoke signal to Cochise's men to come and drive the 'renegades' away. Biskind scathingly relates this ploy to the policy of Vietnamisation in the late 'sixties (p.238). But, in the film's terms, Geronimo is being expelled into the outer reaches – Mexico – in order to neutralise him as a threat. He would, of course, return: historically, as the most notoriously hostile and intransigent of the Native American leaders resisting White oppression, and cinematically, in a whole series of subsequent Westerns, right up to the present. Indeed, Geronimo has captured the imagination of film-makers over the years far more effectively than Cochise, a comment on the dominant view in Westerns of the Native American: the title of the latest film about him – *Geronimo: An American Legend* (Walter Hill, 1994) – emphasising the potency of his image.

But, so far as *Broken Arrow* is concerned, Geronimo's presence disturbs the pacifist project. It is part of the film's strategy that all the Apache warmongers are despatched before the wedding ceremony, so that it can proceed in an Apache camp unthreatened by internal tensions. The ceremony is simple and poetic; after it, the couple ride white horses across the river to their honeymoon wickiup. Although the film is here going against Production Code disapproval of miscegenation – which continued until 1956 – this was 'acceptable' because, as in the novel, Sonseeahray is subsequently killed, the usual fate for the non-White partner in films made

under the Code. However, the death of such figures is not necessarily reactionary. When Broken Lance (Robert Taylor) dies of his wounds at the end of *Devil's Doorway*, his death represents the fate of thousands of Native Americans who tried to retain their homelands against the Whites' ruthless drive to possess them. In this case, the hero's death fuels the film's protest at the Whites' treatment of the indigenous peoples.

In *Broken Arrow*, Sonseeahray is killed in an ambush by Whites, led by Ben Slade, which mirrors Geronimo's attack on the stagecoach. Again, the setting is a river's edge; again, when the ambush goes wrong – the intended target, Cochise, escapes, killing Slade and his son – it is to Mexico that the ambushers try to flee. Moreover, as Jeffords cradles Sonseeahray's body and swears vengeance, Cochise seeks to prevent this by drawing the parallel: 'Geronimo broke the peace no less than these Whites.

Still: Broken Arrow – *Jeffords cradles Sonseeahray's body and swears vengeance; Cochise argues against this.*

As I bear the murder of my people, so you will bear the murder of your wife . . . No-one on my territory will open war again, not even you.'

In that Cochise's words have their desired effect, the film is once more departing decisively from Western formula. Dozens of Westerns – particularly in the 'fifties – are motivated by the hero seeking revenge for the death of a loved one. Although there is a coda in which we learn that the remaining Whites who mounted the ambush have been rounded up, the film nonetheless remains true to its pacifist project. General Howard even tells Jeffords: 'Your very loss has brought our people together and the will to peace.' The film ends with Jeffords riding off alone into the wilderness, but with his voice-over concurring with Howard's judgement: 'As time passed, I came to know that the death of Sonseeahray put a seal upon the peace.' However, this seems to me like a rationalisation: I feel that Sonseeahray died because she presented too much of a problem for the film. At the end of her penultimate scene, she says to Jeffords: 'In time to come

we will see our children ride white horses, maybe.' Poignant though this comment is in retrospect, it also draws attention to an issue even trickier than miscegenation: mixed race children. Quite simply, the film could not handle it.

Although *Broken Arrow* is for the most part an honourable Western, it is not a very dynamic one. Particularly in the Apache camp, many scenes have a static quality, with two or three people simply talking. Compared with the passionate love scenes which grace later Daves movies, the love affair here is relatively bland, as if Daves was a little uneasy about his material and chose to present it discreetly rather than intensely. He certainly seems more at home with the relationship between Jeffords and Cochise, which begins with a shared understanding and develops into a closeness that bonds the two men together. But this relationship, in turn, is emphasised at the expense of Cochise's role as warrior chief. In part, this arises out of the mode of narration adopted by the film to preserve the sense that Jeffords is telling the story: he is in almost every scene, and those he does not witness are narrated with his voice-over in words which indicate that they have been described to him. There is only one sequence which breaks this narrative pattern: Cochise's attack on Colonel Bernall's wagon train. Here alone we see Cochise's skill as a military tactician, with such details as arrows being fired at strategic points to trigger off separate waves of the Apaches' attack (a detail reused in *The Last Wagon*). Chandler imbues Cochise with great presence – it is, in fact, a fine performance and strong justification for the casting – but this is the only scene, save the climax, when he is allowed the space to be active. This, together with the circumspection in the treatment of the love affair, limits the force of the film.

In *The Return of the Vanishing American* (1968), Leslie Fiedler examines the mythical nature of the Western genre. Of the four archetypal narratives that he discusses, two are invoked in *Broken Arrow*: 'The Myth of Love in the Woods' (White man/Indian woman, archetypally Captain John Smith and Pocahontas) and 'The Myth of Good Companions in the Wilderness' (White man/Indian man, archetypally, Natty Bumppo and Chingachook). Supporting Fiedler's thesis that the latter is the most potent of the myths, it is the one that here carries the greater charge. As in the title of the novel, the relationship between Jeffords and Cochise is characterised as that of 'blood brothers', and Sonseeahray is introduced into the narrative primarily, it seems, so that Jeffords's empathy with the Apaches can find an acceptable heterosexual outlet. Nevertheless, this relationship, too, is expressed in mythical terms: after the marriage, Jeffords compares them to Adam and Eve, and hence, by association, the Apache world to the Garden of Eden. But the implicit triangle of Indian blood brother, White man and Indian wife is inherently unstable, and the serpent is introduced in the form of White racism, which kills Sonseeahray and destroys Jeffords's idyll. At the end, he is condemned to wander for ever between the two worlds.

Whatever the limitations of *Broken Arrow*, it has its place as a film that genuinely attempts to view sympathetically the predicament of Native Americans. *Drum Beat*, Daves's next significant Western, seems a serious betrayal of that position. Here the racism of the Western returns with a vengeance: the hero, Johnny MacKay (Alan Ladd) is an ex-Indian fighter and proud of it, the Indian Modoc leader, Captain Jack (Charles Bronson) is a savage murderer, and the one White man to speak up for the Indians, a clergyman, Dr Thomas (Richard Gaines), is mocked and belittled. Like *Broken Arrow*, the film has a White racist extremist, Bill Scatterwhite (Robert Keith). But, where Ben Slade had some justification for his hatred of the Apaches in the massacre of his family, Scatterwhite snarls racist abuse at the Modocs from the beginning and strikes one of them with his pistol. When the man, Modoc Jim (Frank de Kova), takes revenge by murdering Scatterwhite's girl, Lily (Isabel Jewell), Scatterwhite pursues him to Captain Jack's lodge and shoots him. This provokes a bloody uprising by the Modocs, in which a number of White settlers are killed. Although Scatterwhite expresses a certain regret at these deaths, it is Captain Jack's Modocs whom the film really blames, and Scatterwhite and MacKay become allies in the attempts to deal with them. The film does sustain a certain difference in their attitudes, but the hero and the White racist are nevertheless of a very similar mind about the Indians. The contrast with *Broken Arrow* is blatant.

However, it could be argued that the association between the hero and the White racist undermines the hero rather than compromises the film. The more closely one examines the film, the more one senses another voice, speaking against its dominant discourse. The film was made for Alan Ladd's production company Jaguar, which may have imposed certain restrictions on Daves, but it was scripted (from his own research) as well as directed by him, making it a highly personal project. In a letter dated August 1960 published in *Positif* 50-52 (p.117), he says that the film is 'almost a documentary about the wars conducted by the Modoc Indians, made in a manner which conforms totally to the truth, as if one had done a course in history as honestly as possible'. But this seems to be a history from which the point of view of the Native American has been expunged. Dee Brown's account of the actual events (in Chapter 10 of *Bury my Heart at Wounded Knee*, Pan, London, 1972) is very different. However, although the film is undoubtedly racist in its dominant discourse, there are details and inconsistencies which disturb its anti-Indian project, moving it closer to Brown's account. It's as if Daves's sympathy for the Native American was not so much expelled as suppressed, and it emerges in a subtext which suggests a rather different view of events from that recounted on the surface.

The film begins in 1872 with MacKay being summoned to the White House by President Grant (Hayden Rorke) and asked if he would be prepared to act as Peace Commissioner for the Modoc country (on the California/ Oregon border). To bring peace,

Stills: Drum Beat. *Above – Johnny MacKay in the White House, addressing Nancy (Audrey Dalton); Dr Thomas (Richard Gaines) on the left, President Grant (Hayden Rorke) standing right. Opposite – Nancy and MacKay discover her uncle's farm a smoking ruin.*

it will be necessary to get Captain Jack and his men back on the reservation. The President is presented as a fair man: his request will require MacKay to give up his Indian fighter role, and he wants peace to be achieved without guns, if possible. Twice, later, the film cuts back to him in the White House in the wake of Captain Jack's killings, and each time he acts as the voice of reason against those who seek violent revenge. But the dominant discourse in this first White House scene is nevertheless anti-Indian. Dr Thomas's condemnation of Indian fighters is answered by MacKay's account of the Indian massacre of his family, which includes the detail that his sisters, aged twelve and fourteen, were captured rather than killed, but 'they didn't last long: Indian women got jealous and stoned them to death'. This unpleasant little story neatly combines Indian savagery – both male and female – with the superior sexual desirability of White girls. As Philip French (1973, p.79) succinctly points out, 'Unlike other racial minorities or foreigners, the Indian was unprotected by the Hays Office Code, box-office caution, or political influence'.

In this scene, miscegenation is initially referred to in terms that suggest procurement. MacKay says that the reason why some White settlers have praised Captain Jack is because he supplied them with Indian wives. Immediately interested, Nancy Meek (Audrey Dalton), a friend of the President's daughter, asks if MacKay had also been offered an Indian wife; he had, but had declined. However, he admits that the practice was common out West: 'There aren't enough White women to go around.' Later, Nancy – who travels west with MacKay – looks on as Toby (Marisa Pavan), a young Modoc who loves MacKay, offers herself to him. Immediately after

this, Nancy says that she's made up her mind to stay out West. Although it would not have been possible for Nancy to hear what Toby was saying, the structure of the film makes it clear that Nancy is staying to save MacKay from the dangers of miscegenation. If we can take it that Terry in *Broken Arrow* represents the possibility of romance for Jeffords, then in all three 'historical' Indian films the hero has a choice between a White and an Indian woman. In *Broken Arrow* and *White Feather*, he chooses the Indian woman, but in *Drum Beat*, given the film's project, such a choice is unthinkable.

Nancy travels West in order to join her uncle and aunt on their farm and 'become a Westerner'. Towards the end of the journey, she and MacKay are with Lily in the stagecoach driven by Scatterwhite. Lily is looking forward to riding up top. MacKay comments, 'used to be my job, riding with Bill' – when he was an Indian fighter, Nancy explains. Lily suggests that her absence from the carriage will enable MacKay and Nancy to 'have some fun'. And so, when the stagecoach stops at a river crossing – the site of Geronimo's attack on the stage in *Broken Arrow* – and Lily is killed by Modoc Jim as soon as she climbs up top, it's as if the Indian is acting as the agent of MacKay's unconscious. First, Lily is 'usurping' the position that MacKay occupied before he was made into a peace commissioner. Second, her sexual suggestiveness (she repeats her flirtatious encouragement to them the second before she's shot) disturbs him – Ladd's boyish screen persona was rarely comfortable in physically romantic situations. Here we have the beginnings of an alternative reading of the film. Since Lily's murder triggers the sequence of events that results in the Modoc uprising, it's as if the film is saying that MacKay may speak for peace, but unconsciously he wants war, so that he can return to his Indian fighter role. We note that, for all his famed prowess in the role, MacKay is able only to wound the fleeing Modoc Jim, even though he shoots four times. Symbolically, he cannot kill his alter ego. Moreover, Daves cuts from MacKay's first shot to Lily falling from the stagecoach, as if MacKay himself had shot her.

At Lily's funeral, Scatterwhite swears revenge. He tells Blaine Crackel (Elisha Cook Jr) that he's taking over MacKay's role as Indian fighter. (Crackel is a familiar Western villain, the local Indian agent/store-owner, who here demonstrates his renegade persona by consorting with Captain Jack.) For his part, MacKay does his best to control Scatterwhite's vengefulness: 'Don't go running off half-wild killing Modocs – only one got Lily'. Scatterwhite's response is characteristic: 'You think she was only worth one of them devils?' When he leaves, MacKay says to Nancy, 'For every Modoc he kills, they'll kill three Whites. The land will be piled high with hate. Peace – it'll just be a joke.' This is the first of a number of speeches MacKay makes in his capacity as peace commissioner. But each time something happens to undermine his affirmed position.

In this instance, MacKay and Nancy drive up to her uncle's farm to discover it still smoking from an Indian attack and both her relatives killed. But the way this is filmed is very odd: we see the arrival of the buggy in long shot; the couple get out and walk towards the camera. Only then, as the camera pans and tracks back with the couple, are the smoking ruins revealed. The whole scene, including the discovery of the bodies, is filmed in one take, but the absence of any reaction shots reduces the impact of the attack: contrast the equivalent scene in *The Searchers* (John Ford, 1956). One can only assume that Daves was so anxious not to arouse anger against the Modocs in the hero and heroine at this stage that he pointedly played down their emotional shock. Even Nancy's mourning is elided: we do not see a funeral.

On the surface, the film says that Captain Jack carried out these killings because he took a fancy to the medals Colonel Meek (Richard Cutting) was wearing. But Jack also felt threatened by Meek – a farmer now suddenly appearing in cavalry uniform. The film presents Jack's fear of 'brass buttons' (i.e. the cavalry) as paranoid, and his compulsive appropriation of cavalry jackets and insignia as an affectation rather than an attempt to gain power over the enemy by seizing his signifiers of status. Nevertheless, the subtext allows one to see – albeit in a distorted form – something of Jack's own point of view: as in Dee Brown's account, the cavalry are indeed a threat, however much the film tries to absolve them.

Toby and her brother Manok (Anthony Caruso) are the children of the 'old chief' and are committed to peace, which means being good Indians and staying on the reservation. They show their commitment by accompanying MacKay when he rides to visit Captain Jack in his lodge. Their journey is one of the film's most effective sequences. In *The Return of the Vanishing American*, Fiedler links 'going west' into Indian territory with 'going mad' (p.185). Several times before they make the journey, Manok and Toby speak of it as 'crazy', and the journey itself is punctuated with a series of encounters with Modoc warriors which – in CinemaScope, at least – have a ritualistic, mythical feel. Circling round the three riders and then sweeping past them, the warriors' movements symbolically evoke the whirlpool and the cataract to disturb and unsettle them. Mythically, the journey is like a descent into the underworld: its final stage – emphasised by a crane down – shows MacKay climb down the ladder into Captain

131

Inside the lodge are Captain Jack and around fifty Modoc warriors. MacKay goes in alone to confront them, and still speaks as the voice of reason: 'More killing means war . . . In war, only one side wins. In peace, both sides win.' Backed by the militancy of his warriors, Jack resists the peace overtures. Then, as MacKay climbs out of the lodge – echoing Lily climbing 'up top' – Modoc Jim shoots at him. Jack deflects the shot, but then signals to Jim to follow MacKay. This reworks the material of Lily's murder. Unlike Lily, MacKay successfully makes it up top, and when Jim emerges from the lodge and takes aim at him, Scatterwhite rides up out of nowhere and shoots him. Again, it is as if another character is acting for MacKay, the link in this instance strengthened by Scatterwhite's declaration that he was taking over MacKay's old role. In its dominant discourse, the film is of course simply keeping MacKay free from the taint of killing. But the more aggressive characters who carry out the killings which lead to war can be seen as projections of MacKay's unconscious.

After the murders of the settlers, Jack and his men occupy a stronghold on top of the Lava Beds (volcanic rock formations riddled with caves), repulsing the cavalry sent to dislodge them. It is here that Crackel is revealed, predictably, also to be a gun runner, a crime for which the film contrives a prompt death. After the cavalry's defeat, a peace delegation is assembled, including MacKay, General Canby (Warner Anderson), Dr Thomas and Mr Dyar (Frank Ferguson), another Indian agent. As they gather, two of the film's ideological positions are restated: Jack is again linked with 'the underworld'

Still: Drum Beat – *MacKay confronts Captain Jack (Charles Bronson) and his warriors in Jack's semi-subterranean lodge.*

(Mr Dyar: 'Even the Indians believe them caves lead straight to hell'), and the pacifist impulses of Dr Thomas are again scorned, this time by women who have lost husbands and sons in the Modoc uprising. Mr Dyar explains: 'You see, Doc, out this way the Bible and brotherly love gets all mixed up with Indian hate.' What we have just witnessed, however, is White hate. The film seems unaware of the irony, but it is another example of the ways in which the position of the Whites is, however unconsciously, undermined.

The night before the peace council, there is a love scene between MacKay and Nancy which foreshadows the wonderfully sensuous seduction scenes of *The Last Wagon* and *3:10 to Yuma*: as Nancy and MacKay embrace, she punctuates the kisses with erotic murmurings: 'he'll have to know how to plough' (kiss) 'plant seeds' (kiss) 'harvest' (kiss). Clearly, this was all too much for Alan Ladd; he's rescued by someone calling him to headquarters.

Toby and Manok have come to warn the White delegates that Jack and his men intend to use the peace council to kill them. As Toby speaks, the most warlike of the Modocs, Scarface Charlie (Rodolpho Acosta), who has followed them, listens outside. It was he who pressured Jack into agreeing to the murder of the peace delegates: he threw a woman's shawl over Jack's shoulders and taunted him: 'You kill general or you chickenhearted woman.' Positioned behind Manok inside the room so that he looks like his shadow, Scarface Charlie here represents the archetypal Indian lurking in the darkness – what is repressed behind the front of those seeking to be 'civilised'. Given that Scarface is not shown to use the information he gleans, this implication seems to be the only point of his being there – another sign of the film's negative view of the Indians.

Despite Toby's warning, General Canby and Dr Thomas attend the peace council unarmed, the latter even saying, 'If it is God's will that I give my life to achieve a peace, I am willing to do so.' Here he is not ridiculed, but given the dignity of a man who is prepared to die for his beliefs. MacKay, too, was going to attend unarmed: it takes the intervention of both women to provide him with a gun. When a Western reaches the point where it is the women who insist on the hero being armed, the ideological project is evidently under some strain: the contradiction between MacKay's official role as peace commissioner and the role dictated by the logic of the situation is almost at breaking point.

Daves directs the scene of council itself with genuine tension, as all six of those who want peace (including Toby and Manok) seek to manage the situation so that it does not erupt into violence. They fail: Jack refuses to moderate his demands, loses his temper, pulls out his hidden gun and starts firing. This precipitates a sudden shoot-out in which Canby, Thomas and MacKay are all hit, the first two fatally. As a Modoc goes to scalp MacKay, Toby rushes forward to stop him and is herself brutally murdered, a virtual replay of the death of Sonseeahray in *Broken Arrow*, as Toby finally rolls towards the unconscious MacKay. Her intervention saves his life: the cavalry, who were overseeing the council from a distance, react to the violence with cannon fire which drives the Modocs away.

After these killings, President Grant finally accedes to MacKay's request to take a volunteer force to track down the Modocs. MacKay had been chafing under the restrictions of his peace commissioner role for some time; now he is released, once more, as an Indian fighter. Scatterwhite accompanies him, as does Manok, seeking revenge for Toby's murder. Suddenly, however, the film becomes much more clumsy and cliché-ridden: in particular, there is a scene in a log cabin where a succession of people – Scatterwhite, a cavalry officer, Scarface and a party of Modocs – burst in one after the other, as in a very bad stage melodrama.

When MacKay finally catches up with Jack, they fight hand to hand in one of Daves's favourite settings, a section of river where the water is funnelled down a narrow gap between rocks. A similar setting was used to dramatise Ben Slade's body being swept away in *Broken Arrow*; the setting reappears in *The Last Wagon*. Here, however, it leads to a striking association: as the two men emerge into the calmer waters on the other side of the rapids, MacKay knocks Jack out and hauls him ashore. In doing this, he duplicates what he did to save Toby from the river as a young girl, the moment, she tells him, when she fell in love with him. The implication is unmistakable: Jack is, in some sense, replacing Toby.

This suggests that *Drum Beat*, too, should be examined in terms of Fiedler's mythical Western narratives. When MacKay and Jack first meet – in the latter's lodge – they greet each other as old enemies, but in a manner which implies more. Jack is holding a rifle between his legs, and, as the tension rises, his aggression towards MacKay manifests itself in some highly phallic gestures with the weapon. Later, Jack expresses his disgust that MacKay, once a fighter, should become 'peace man'. In effect, we have here a different sort of blood brotherhood: that of worthy opponents. But, because the peace process dictates the trajectory of the movie, they can only briefly have such a relationship. The homoerotic overtones do not really surface until the final confrontation between the men, when Jack shouts 'You come get gun, Johnny: you come get me', and they soon get down to some vigorous wrestling.

Then, in their final scene together – set in jail, as Jack is about to hang – the overtones become all but explicit. Jack and MacKay imagine remeeting in the Indian equivalent of heaven, into which Jack will ask for MacKay to be admitted because he's a good fighter. Although, as in *Broken Arrow*, the Indian heroine is sacrificed, here it is for the mundane purpose of freeing the hero for the white heroine, with whom he goes off at the end. But the final conversation is between MacKay and Jack, and it is there that the mythical material of the film lies.

Although the subtext in *Drum Beat* makes it a much more intriguing film – not least in undermining the Alan Ladd persona of the idealised golden-haired Western hero – ultimately it cannot satisfactorily compensate for the overt anti-Indian ideology. In the jail scene, MacKay comments: 'We could have saved a lot of lives, Jack, if you hadn't grabbed country that wasn't yours.' The unconscious hypocrisy is breathtaking: history is rewritten so that it was the Indians, not the Whites, who took the land that wasn't theirs.

One explanation for the ideological difference between *Broken Arrow* and *Drum Beat* could be McCarthyism. In 1950, the political climate was more amenable to a liberal film like *Broken Arrow*. By 1954, after four years of Joseph McCarthy's attacks on the Left, even liberalism could seem politically suspect. *Drum Beat*, with its depiction of the failure of liberalism (the peace council) and the necessity for direct military action against the Indian (read communist) enemy, registers the shift to the right only too clearly. One of the films Daves had directed during the intervening years was the very silly cold war melodrama *Never Let Me Go* (1953). On the other hand, it is a measure of Daves's deeper integrity that *Drum Beat* should contain so many disturbances to its official project.

In a two-part article on Daves in *Films & Filming* (April & May 1963), Richard Whitehall says that *White Feather*, which Daves co-scripted (with Leo Townsend), was also to have been directed by him, but was taken over by Robert D. Webb when Daves left 20th Century-Fox. Although generally ignored in discussions of Daves's films (an exception is Mike Wallington's useful but highly compressed piece on Daves's Westerns in *Cinema* 4, October 1969), the film is patently a Daves project. It was adapted from John Prebble's short story, 'My Great-Aunt Appearing Day' (published in *Spanish Stirrup and other stories*, Penguin, 1975), and repeatedly reworks the original along lines that conform to other Daves Westerns. It begins in Wyoming in 1877, with the voice-over of Josh Tanner (Robert Wagner) echoing Jeffords's introduction to *Broken Arrow*: 'What you are about to see actually happened. The only difference will be that the Indians . . . speak in our language so that you can understand them.' Its narrative then reprises the earlier film's pro-Indian stance, with an interracial romance in which Debra Paget again plays the Indian heroine.

After a near-brush with a band of Cheyenne warriors led by Little Dog (Jeffrey Hunter) and American Horse (Hugh O'Brian), Tanner arrives in Fort Laramie. He is a surveyor, hired by St Louis businessmen to lay out the town of the future – an indication of the point which the West has reached: the Indians are about to be displaced from their traditional lands and marched off to the reservation. Five tribes are involved, but only four (the Crows, Sioux, Blackfeet and Arapahos) have agreed to sign the 'peace treaty': the Cheyennes, under Chief Broken Hand (Eduard Franz), Little Dog's father, are still holding out. Colonel Lindsay (John Lund), in charge of the fort, is responsible for keeping the peace. He is under no illusions about the future, referring to 'the prospectors, thieves and gamblers waiting to crawl all over (Cheyenne) territory the moment the treaty is signed'. Chief amongst the riff-raff is the sutler Magruder (Emile Meyer), who stirs up the Whites with stories of gold lying about on the ground in the Indian territory across the river. This film's racist extremist, he completes Daves's trio of unpleasant traders/storekeepers. It is Magruder's daughter Ann (Virginia Leith), an entirely sympathetic figure, who represents the White 'choice of partner' for the hero in this movie, but his friendship with her is cut short when he meets the Indian heroine, Appearing Day (Debra Paget).

A significant difference from *Broken Arrow* is that the reservations here are not located within the tribes' traditional lands, which is, of course, much closer to the actual historical experience of the vast majority of Native Americans (and, according to Dee Brown, was part of the reason behind Captain Jack's uprising). The film recognises not simply the misery of such resettlements, but their precariousness. When, late in the film, Colonel Lindsay and Tanner see the start of the exodus of the tribes to the reservations, Tanner's deeply ironic comment is: 'Heading for the Promised Land: I wonder how long they'll be able to live on promises.' And so, as the film moves inexorably towards the point at which the Cheyennes, too, submit to White authority and leave for the reservation, it charts what is in effect a defeat for the tribe. The terms under which this defeat occurs forms the dramatic focus of the movie.

Cheyenne resistance to signing the treaty is led by Little Dog and American Horse who, like Geronimo, resent their loss of warrior status. But, whereas Geronimo's hostility towards the Whites was criticised, Little Dog and American Horse become friends with Tanner, which gives their point of view a much more sympathetic airing. This is seen when Broken Hand announces that, in the interests of his people, he has decided to sign the treaty. (A crucial factor behind his decision is the absence of buffalo: if they do stay and fight the Whites, they will have no food – a succinct reference to the successful White ploy of starving the Native Americans into submission.) As Little Dog walks off in defiance, Broken Hand asks Tanner to go and speak to him. This scene, set in the lodge (tipi) of the medicine man, is the equivalent of the scenes when Jeffords talks to Cochise in his wickiup and when MacKay confronts Captain Jack in his lodge. In each case, the White man seeks to find words that will convince the Indian of the desirability of peace. Cochise responds as a wise leader, with an intelligent appraisal of Jeffords's arguments. Surrounded by his warriors, Jack responds as a war lord, with calculated defiance. Little Dog is the most divided: on the one hand, he respects his father; on the other, he cannot accept that the Cheyennes should simply give in to the Whites' demands, abandon their traditional way of living and go meekly to the reservation.

But these scenes in *Broken Arrow* and *Drum Beat* also have a homoerotic dimension: they are crucial to the Fiedler notion of bonding between the White man and the Indian. In *White Feather*, this is less clear; although Little Dog is armed with the knife Tanner gave him, his use of it suggests aggression rather than displaced sexuality. However, at the end of the film, when Little Dog is killed on the battlefield by the cavalry, Tanner goes to tend his body, and the care with which he does this carries an unmistakable erotic charge.

It is perhaps also significant that Appearing Day – with whom Tanner has already begun a romance – is Little Dog's sister. And, as Tanner leaves the medicine man's lodge, as if to emphasise the switch from a forbidden relationship to an acceptable one, Appearing Day meets him. Tentatively, she raises the possibility of going herself into the 'White man's world'. This scene between them – in which she clearly shows her feelings for Tanner – is witnessed by American Horse and, after Tanner has ridden off, he slaps Appearing Day around. The violence is clearly meant to signal an assumed proprietorship, although thus far American Horse has shown no interest whatsoever in Appearing Day. He has spent his time with Little Dog and the other Cheyenne warriors showing off his manly prowess, with lots of whooping and posturing. His treatment of Appearing Day here indicts the adolescence of the warrior's world. That she should be attracted to the 'White man's world' is not surprising: in her first love scene with Tanner, it was established that White men, unlike Indians, kiss women.

Although this would seem to be swinging the film away from a sympathetic view of the Cheyenne, it is partly determined by a need to set up a sexual rivalry between Tanner and American Horse which can be exploited at the film's climax. Nevertheless, there is still a failure in all three of these Indian films to deal with sexual relationships between Native American men and women. The omission is most serious in *Broken Arrow*, where Cochise is not simply a 'warrior male' (Klaus Theweleit's useful term from

Male Fantasies I, Polity Press, Cambridge, 1987), prone to taunt other males with being 'like women', but a more mature figure. The problem does, nevertheless, seem linked to the Indian 'warrior male' ideology. The one Indian couple with a close, loving relationship are Toby and Manok in *Drum Beat*, who are referred to as 'the peace Modocs'. However, they are brother and sister.

The resistance of Little Dog and American Horse to the signing of the treaty is eventually resolved when the two of them declare their own war on the cavalry. As soon as the treaty is signed, a Cheyenne rides in and casts down a white feather. Broken Hand interprets: 'It is a challenge. My son and American Horse are not bound by your paper. They have chosen to fight and wait for you in the hills.'

Although it is common for Westerns which deal with Native Americans to signal this in their titles, those of Daves's three 'historical' Indian Westerns also refer to the war and peace antinomy at the heart of each film. 'Broken arrow' signifies Cochise's gesture of peace; 'Drum beat', Jack's declaration of war (the drums are beaten – to much warlike display from Jack's warriors – immediately after Scatterwhite has shot Modoc Jim); 'White feather', Little Dog and American Horse's challenge. Each title focuses with some precision on a metaphor for the film.

In *White Feather*, the challenge leads to a superb set piece, in which, in front of the whole Cheyenne village, the two warriors confront the massed ranks of the cavalry. For Broken Hand, it is a question of ensuring that the men, as Cheyennes, die honourably. For Lindsay, it is a matter of controlling the cavalry so that the Indians shoot first. Many of the Cheyenne spectators are young warriors, just itching for an excuse to attack the troops themselves. The first round of the confrontation is won by the two Indians: when Lindsay sends a rank of cavalry to

Still: White Feather – *Josh Tanner (Robert Wagner) finds Appearing Day (Debra Paget) in his bed; Ann (Virginia Leith) looks on dispprovingly.*

bring them in, they ride round it, shouting taunts and causing the horses to panic and buck. As the young Cheyenne men roar their approval, the confrontation suddenly seems like a spectator sport in which spectators threaten to spill over into the arena.

Accounts of the film in reference works – beginning with the *Monthly Film Bulletin* synopsis in May 1955 – generally state that Tanner fights with and/ or kills one or both of the Cheyenne warriors in this scene. Not so: in order to break the deadlock with the cavalry, he taunts American Horse into shooting at him, but it is Broken Hand who then shoots American Horse. He does this because Tanner was unarmed when American Horse fired: 'American Horse has shamed us before the White man. Little Dog will not do so.' As Broken Hand himself carries out the killing, this helps contain the tension between the restless Cheyenne spectators and the cavalry. He kills to keep the peace, which, of course, is his overall aim, too. But there is also an ideological ploy: American Horse, like Nahilzay in *Broken Arrow*, is a frustrated suitor of the Indian heroine; in killing this figure, the Chief in effect clears the way for the interracial marriage. Although one could argue that the Indian heroine's preference for the White hero belittles the Indian suitor, it is of course Hollywood convention that the heroine will prefer the film's hero, played by the main star, to the 'other man', played by an actor of lesser status. And it is certainly progressive, by the standards of the time, that the films should champion an interracial relationship.

Little Dog, who is like a young amalgam of Cochise and Geronimo, is handled quite differently. Although he declares that he will fight with Tanner,

Appearing Day rides forward to act as mediator, obliging him to acknowledge Tanner's friendship. This ensures that Little Dog will indeed then do as his father wishes and act out the role of the 'last Cheyenne warrior', dying in a suicidal attack on the cavalry. The final sequence of the film again emphasises the switch from the forbidden to the acceptable relationship. The scene in which Tanner tends Little Dog's body lasts a full three minutes, during which Appearing Day waits patiently in the background and then goes to fetch her brother's horse. Beside the body, Tanner finds the comb he earlier gave Little Dog and, lovingly, places it in Little Dog's hand. Then he announces that he and Appearing Day are going to be married. As they ride off into the sunset, his voice-over records that Broken Hand lived to see his grandson enter West Point. There are two distinct ironies in this: the son will join the ranks of those who oppressed his mother's people but, at the same time, he will continue the warrior tradition within the acceptable framework of American imperialism.

Set in the sort of pastoral locations not often associated with the Western, and beautifully photographed in cool pastels – and CinemaScope – by Lucien Ballard, *White Feather* is a surprisingly effective Western. It is rare to find a film as early as 1955 permitting a 'happy ending' between a White man and an Indian woman, although it is notable that Debra Paget's makeup here is not as dark as in *Broken Arrow*: she is already made to appear almost White. Equally, whereas in the two earlier movies it was the Indian heroine who was sacrificed, here it is the young Indian hero. The deaths of Little Dog and American Horse purge the Cheyennes of their warlike men, thus pacifying them for the reservation. It is under those conditions that Appearing Day is 'freed' to enter the White man's world for a happy ending.

Although these three 'historical' Indian films by no means represent Daves's best work in the genre, they are significant achievements. In each, the pacifist project undoubtedly works against the interests

Still: White Feather – *Appearing Day and Tanner beside the body of Little Dog (Jeffrey Hunter).*

of the Native Americans, but that, after all, is part of North American history, and in the early 'fifties one could only go so far in indicting White imperialism. At the same time, Daves's focus in the first two movies on the relatively enlightened attitude of the Eastern establishment (here embodied in President Grant and his emissaries) has the support of a least one more recent historian. In *The New Country: A Social History of the American Frontier 1776-1890* (Oxford University Press, New York, 1974), Richard A. Bartlett writes: 'For in essence, the federal government assumed the position of moral agent, trying to defend the Indians from the acquisitiveness and blind hatred of the frontiersmen' (pp.24-25). Bartlett goes on to note the contradictions in this position, and it is to Daves's credit that both the position and some of the contradictions should be apparent in the movies.

Having made *Jubal* for Columbia, Daves returned to 20th Century-Fox to direct *The Last Wagon*, which was produced by William B. Hawks, Howard's brother, and scripted by Daves, James Edward Grant and Gwen Bagni Gielgud (from Gielgud's original story). It begins with a striking inversion of the opening of *White Feather*. The earlier movie begins with Tanner solicitously fishing the body of a man killed by the Cheyennes out of a river and putting it on a horse, but *The Last Wagon* begins with a pre-credit sequence in which Comanche Todd (Richard Widmark) ruthlessly shoots a man off his horse into a river: the hero is introduced as the killer.

Immediately after the credits, it becomes apparent that Todd is on the run; three more men on horseback spot him on foot in the valley below and open fire. He returns their fire and manages to kill one of them before running out of bullets. Fleeing into Apache territory, he still contrives to ambush and kill another pursuer before being captured by the last, Sheriff Bull Harper (George Mathews). Harper manacles Todd and attaches him by a rope to his own horse. When Todd can't keep on his feet behind the horse, he's dragged along the ground.

The film has begun in the middle of a story, and it is a long time before these opening scenes are explained. The implicit positioning of Todd as 'like' the Indians in *White Feather* introduces one element. Although he is White, Todd was adopted as a boy by the Comanches and raised by them – hence his name – and, as the film continues, it is apparent that he is still, in all but birth, a Comanche. But his motive for these early killings is not explained until the end of the movie, when we learn that the four Harper brothers raped and murdered Todd's Comanche wife and savagely killed his two sons. Although we assume that the three men we see Todd kill in these opening scenes must be the other three brothers, certain subsequent details simply don't make sense unless there is a substantial time lapse between the first killing and the second: Todd being hunted for a reward and, later, the military interest in capturing him. In auteurist terms, the film can also be seen as beginning at the point where *Broken Arrow* ends, with Todd carrying out the revenge that was denied Jeffords. Nevertheless, although Todd's revenge is structurally significant, the lack of concern with its details suggests it was not of great import to Daves.

Harper and Todd encounter a wagon train of emigrants heading west to Tucson. There are links, here, with the wagon train of Rawhiders in *Jubal*, not least in the presence on the wagon train of the heroine, again played by Felicia Farr. Led by Colonel Normand (Douglas Kennedy), the emigrants, like the Rawhiders, consider themselves Christians, and they are appalled at the sadistic way Harper

treats his prisoner, roping him savagely to a wagon wheel and denying him food. When Billy (Tommy Rettig), the young brother of Jenny (Farr), takes Todd some food, Harper shoots it away. This leads to Normand insisting that Todd has one hand free so that he can eat. But when Clint (Ray Stricklyn), a youth travelling with his mother and sister, then offers Todd a smoke, Harper beats him up. In the confusion caused by the emigrants running to help Clint, one of them drops an axe close to Todd. Todd seizes it with his free hand and throws it at Harper, killing him.

When Jenny and Normand first objected to the way Harper was treating Todd, Harper snarled out his justification: that Todd had killed three of his brothers and that 'any Indian-lovin' White who chooses Comanches against his own kind is no rotten good . . . he's what they scrape off the bottom of the barrel.' The speech identifies Harper as a vicious racist: despite Todd's early ruthlessness, there is no question that it is Harper who is really the villain. (In Daves's Westerns, the few lawmen who do appear are almost all villains, signalling the corruptness of white frontier society.) Accordingly, there is poetic justice in the manner of Harper's death: he is killed by a traditional Indian weapon, a hatchet, thrown with typical Indian skill. Although the emigrants are shocked by the killing, and Normand declines to listen to Todd's side of the story, the film suggests that their outrage may be camouflage. Not only is the axe dropped in a very convenient place, but the

Still: The Last Wagon – *Bull Harper (George Mathews) drags Comanche Todd (Richard Widmark) into the emigrants' camp; Colonel Normand (Douglas Kennedy), on horseback, protests.*

emigrants back Harper towards Todd, so that the man ends up close enough for Todd to attack him. It looks very like a collective Freudian slip; after all, Harper was a singularly unpleasant piece of work.

The emigrants have come from 'beyond the Mississippi' – they are Easterners – and are ill protected for a journey through hostile Indian territory. (The year is 1873, but it's as if the elaborate peace-making of *Broken Arrow* had never taken place: the trails into Tucson are still as dangerous as ever for the Whites.) Half an hour into the film, most of them are killed in a night-time Apache attack, and it is up to Todd, the only adult male survivor, to lead the others to safety.

The other survivors are a group of young people who were absent from camp at the time of the raid. Ridge (Nick Adams), Billy, and Normand's two daughters, Jolie (Susan Kohner) and Valinda (Stephanie Griffin), had slipped off for a moonlight swim whilst the adults slept; Jenny and Clint had gone looking for them. In retrospect, what is particularly remarkable about this sequence is its inversion of the formula of the modern slasher movie, in which the teenagers are killed by the monster when they go off for 'illicit' sex. Within the conventions of 1956, skinny-dipping clearly stands in for sex (and the way the episode is discussed by the young people emphasises this), but here it is their families who are killed. Now, this could be seen as punishment for their transgression. In the woman's film, in particular, the heroine can be punished for 'illicit' sex by the death of a loved one, as in *Woman of Affairs* (Clarence Brown, 1928) and *Mildred Pierce* (Michael Curtiz, 1945). But, if the Apaches are seen, rather,

as an embodiment of the young people's collective id – just as the Comanches are an expression of the hero's id in *The Searchers* – then the emigrants' deaths point to an unconscious wish on the part of the young people to be free from the fetters of White civilisation. Since the narrative here remains with the young people, we do not see the Apache attack, but Todd's survival is clearly miraculous: the wagon he was tied to was pushed off the cliff. This, too, supports such a reading: the only survivor is (in effect) Indian and thus not implicated in the unconscious hostility. Moreover, since Todd's expertise now provides their only way of getting out of the territory alive, the young people have to learn from him 'the ways of the Indian' in order to survive.

Such a reading is certainly not in the film's dominant discourse. The young people are extremely upset at the deaths of their families and, although Todd educates them in Indian ways, this is not achieved without resistance, at least from Valinda and Ridge. But the project of their education is central. Here their youthfulness is doubly significant, since it relates the film to other mid-'fifties films about youth, as the skinny-dipping episode emphasises. In essence, the young people have to learn to trust Todd, just as in *Blackboard Jungle* (Richard Brooks, 1955) they have to learn to trust Glenn Ford's schoolteacher and in *Rebel Without a Cause* (Nicholas Ray, 1955) Edward Platt's juvenile officer. Their education needs be such that, when Todd is finally brought before a court to answer charges of murder,

Still: The Last Wagon – *Todd and Jenny (Felicia Farr).*

they will all stand up for him. In the 'fifties movies with a contemporary setting, these authority figures, however liberal-minded they may be, are, in Biskind's phrase, 'agents of social control'. Todd, however, is a very different figure. In *The Western* by George N. Fenin and William K. Everson (Penguin, Harmondsworth, 1977, p.337), he is described, astonishingly, as a Nazi-stereotype leader. In fact, he is a White man who, in effect, has 'gone native'. He believes in Indian justice, displays Indian skills and accepts an Indian belief system. He tells Jenny that he lost his Christian faith when he was eight and his father, a circuit preacher, died in his arms, despite his fervent prayers. It was then that he was adopted by a Comanche chief who raised him as his own son.

Although the Apaches who attack the wagon train are shadowy, threatening figures who massacre women and children – in other words, standard Hollywood Indians – Daves still provides them with a strong motive for their attack. Todd reconnoitres their camp, and discovers that they are seeking revenge for the slaughter by Whites of over a hundred Apache women and children. But it is the use the film makes of the character of Todd that enables *The Last Wagon* to be viewed in a relatively positive light from a Native American point of view. With the deaths of those who stood for 'White civilisation', including Christianity, Todd takes over. This duplicates the events of his childhood: Normand's death echoes his father's; the orphaned youngsters himself as a boy; he himself assumes the role of the Comanche rescuer. The ideological switch from Christianity is reinforced by the imagery. Daves's films are haunted by threatened or actual hangings, and it is characteristic that, when the young people return to discover the massacre, the bodies of the men, including Normand, are hanging from trees. But these images of death are here answered by the spectacular shot of Todd, still attached to the wagon wheel, hauled back up the cliff. Given the miraculous nature of his survival, and the overtones of crucifixion in the way he is fastened to the wheel, this is like a resurrection. Literally and symbolically, the Christian Normand is replaced by the pagan Todd, an interpretation which gains strength from the fact that it was Todd who was expected to hang. Todd immediately takes command, sweeping aside the young people's Christian wish to bury their dead (it will reveal to the Apaches that there were survivors) and citing, instead, Indian beliefs: that someone dies well if he gives his life for his loved ones; that Indians don't suffer when someone is killed because they believe the dead go to a better life in the 'high ground'. The extent to which this assists the young people is uncertain, but it is striking that Christian beliefs are not even mentioned. During the hazardous journey that lies ahead – that of the eponymous last wagon – Todd knows that their survival depends upon them 'thinking Indian'.

The film's implicit privileging of the Indian over the Christian is stated first through Billy. When Todd kills Harper, Billy reacts excitedly: 'Gosh, I guess Comanches are about the best battle-axe throwers there are.' Jenny tries to recast the event along more acceptable lines ('Mr Todd's not a Comanche; he was trying to help Clint'), but we know that helping Clint was strictly secondary; Billy's enthusiasm for the kill is much closer to Todd's own response. Shortly afterwards, having confirmed that Todd really did kill the men as the sheriff claimed, Billy tells him that he'd like it if Todd went to Heaven when he was hanged, so that he, Billy, could join him there later: 'We can go scouting – things like that.' This reworking of the final conversation between MacKay and Jack in *Drum Beat* is quite remarkable. It is because Todd is such a good killer, just as it was because MacKay was such a good fighter, that Billy and Jack respectively would like to share eternity with them – a notion highly subversive of Christian ideology. (It is also somewhat subversive that Normand should conduct a public prayer, thanking the Lord for guiding the wagon train through hostile territory, only hours before most of its members are massacred. Hollywood films are normally very careful not to link a prayer with its negation.) Billy's trust of Todd never wavers, and their relationship is later presented explicitly in father and son terms.

Whereas Clint is sensible and soon follows Jenny and Billy in trusting Todd, Ridge is extremely hostile to any point of view other than his own. Aggressive, suspicious and generally uncooperative, he relates closely to other 'fifties movie juvenile delinquents (and Nick Adams played just this role in other films, including *Rebel Without a Cause*). Like the 'rebels' in these movies, Ridge challenges as a matter of course everything that the adult authority-figure says. However, the film suggests strongly that he reacts in this way because he fears Todd: he is the one who insists that Todd's manacles stay on. His conversion to an acceptance of Todd is the most simplistic: he merely has to learn that Todd is an honourable man who would not go back on his word or betray them.

The sisters may likewise be related to contemporary social concerns in that they raise – very directly – the issue of racism. Their mothers were different: Jolie's was a Navajo; Valinda's was White. And, from their first scene together, Valinda expresses disgust at having a half-sister who is part Indian. But the film relates her racism to her sexual fears and fantasies: she comments to Jolie on Jenny's behaviour with Todd (still roped to the wagon wheel): 'She's washing his face . . . imagine being so man-hungry that you'd throw yourself at an Indian-loving murderer.' The lasciviousness in her voice tells us that she is projecting her own desires on to Jenny; similarly, when she describes Jolie's conception in equally prurient terms, we sense her repressed attraction to that which she, as a 'good girl', feels obliged to condemn. Jolie recognises her sister's emotional dishonesty ('You're the one who's shameless'), but she nevertheless seems to accept the racist attacks: she even says to her father 'She has reason to be hurt – she's ashamed of me before the others.'

If one substitutes Black for Native American, one can again sense the contemporary resonances in the film's representations. As one of the rare mixed-race characters in Daves's work, Jolie carries a great

deal of ideological weight, and it is crucial to the film's project that, during the journey, she should be like Clint, practical and reliable. Valinda, by contrast, is like Ridge, hostile and uncooperative. Late in the journey, she is bitten by a rattlesnake, and the venom pumping round her veins may be seen as a concrete expression of her racism. Just as Jolie learns from Todd to have pride in her Native American ancestry, so Valinda needs to learn racial tolerance: to purge the venom from her veins.

Although Todd is freed from the wheel, he remains manacled. Since he is in this state because of the combined efforts of the Whites who are most openly hostile and/or racist (including Valinda, who we learn later has the keys), his plight symbolises the Whites' treatment of the Indian. And, given the significance of chains as a symbol of Black slavery, again it is not only the Indian who is invoked. In the scene when he talks to Jenny about his childhood, Todd severs the manacle chain. It breaks on the words 'That's how I became a Comanche', linking becoming a Comanche with the breaking of (White man's) chains.

As Todd files through the chain, Jenny carves each of their names on a separate metal cup; a strategy for rationing water. When Valinda is feverish after the rattlesnake bite, she discovers – from the names on the cups – that the others have been giving her their water rations. Her experience here is like an inversion of the Christian communion: in place of one cup passed from person to person, she receives a series of cups which give her life. Up to this

Still: The Last Wagon – '. . . *imagine being so man-hungry that you'd throw yourself at an Indian-loving murderer'. Valinda (Stephanie Griffin) talks about Jenny and Todd to Jolie (Susan Kohner).*

point, Valinda has maintained her racist hostility – which she has applied to Todd as much as to Jolie. Now, relenting, she reveals just how much she has hated Todd: all along she has been carrying the key to his manacles. Again the reworking of a Christian feature is used to underline a moment of transformation – when Valinda recognises her own racism and changes. Thanks to Todd's expertise and the others' care, Valinda survives. When she speaks up for Todd during the trial, it sounds corny – 'He made me grow up' – but it accurately expresses the film's overall project regarding the young people.

Jenny is en route to a prospective husband in Tucson. Her falling for the hero during the journey is entirely conventional, but the manner in which this is articulated is not. First, there are intriguing overtones in the manner in which she is first attracted to Todd: the savage way Harper treats him calls forth her nurturing impulses, but the way he is trussed up, helpless, could also be said to eroticise his body. We note that the scene which so arouses Valinda is not shown, as if the film were afraid to visualise such a tenderly erotic moment. Second, sex is introduced openly into the conversation between Jenny and Todd: using an Indian metaphor, Todd speaks of a girl being 'broken in' and asks Jenny if she's been broken in yet. (As with other Indian male-female relationships in Daves, male sexism is apparent: 'Girls and ponies both, the younger you break 'em in, the better.') Third, Jenny's sexual surrender to Todd is unusually explicit for a mid-'fifties movie. It is preceded by one of Daves's wonderful seduction scenes, with tight close-ups and Todd murmuring in Jenny's ear about the beauties of the outdoor life he leads. In effect, she is being seduced into the world of the Indian. Jenny has followed Todd to his lookout, high on a hill, which takes her away from the hidden wagon and towards the Apache threat. This threat – of imminent attack – enables her to rationalise what she is about to do: 'If this is to be our last night, I'd like to spend it with you, and discover what sort of roof the stars might have made.'

When Todd broke the chain earlier, he recognised its value – still attached to the manacles – as a weapon. At that point, he was released as a warrior, as his subsequent fights with an eagle and with two Apaches showed. But now he has been completely freed from his fetters: Valinda has given him the key. This releases both his familial and his romantic side. First, he asks Billy to unlock the manacles, commenting that, if his sons had lived, he'd have liked them to have grown up to be like Billy. Again through the metaphor of 'breaking the chains', Todd here is adopting Billy as he himself was adopted by the Comanche chief. Second, he sleeps with Jenny. The next morning, when he and Jenny return to the wagon to be met by a cavalry patrol to whom Todd had signalled, Billy claims to be his son, Jenny his wife. This inserts Todd into a family structure and, even though his expertise is then called upon to save the patrol as well as his own party from the Apaches, he carries out no more killings.

The young people are not, however, Todd's most remarkable converts. His trial at the end of the movie is run by General Howard (Carl Benton Reid), the same 'Bible-reading Howard' who sought peace with Cochise in Broken Arrow. But, as Todd first uses the Civil War to illustrate the inconsistency in the Whites' distinction between war and murder and then argues that his killing of the Harper brothers was no more than a Comanche version of the sentence – hanging – which would have been passed by the Whites, he significantly shakes Howard's hitherto secure sense of right and wrong. (During this, Daves makes a point of positioning a group of Indians at the back of the court behind Todd.) But Todd doesn't stop there. His basic argument is that laws may differ, but 'Justice don't change – even in places where they give medals for killing Indians; medals like that one you're wearing.' Such a direct attack on a figure who, in Broken Arrow, was a significant peacemaker, is a measure of the film's underlying radicalism. Jenny, however, realises that Todd is damaging his case with such a personal attack, and introduces another argument: yes, Todd took four lives, but he also gave six lives back; more, if those in the cavalry patrol are counted. It is then that the young people speak up for Todd. Admitting that he is moved by this argument, Howard sentences Todd by asking Jenny and Billy, 'Do you take him into custody for as long as you both shall live?'

In effect, the sentence is marriage, and Jenny (who has put on a white dress for the occasion) responds in kind, 'Yes, I do', Billy adding 'Me, too'.

Todd is back in manacles when he is brought before Howard, and here they are set in opposition to Howard's Bible (which is to hand on his desk). But, as Todd argues his case, he invokes the Bible to support his point about justice. At the last moment, Christianity makes a comeback: Todd wins his argument and is released. However, if one sees the film as a reworking of the material of Broken Arrow with the hero able to overcome the death of his Indian wife and accept a White woman as partner, its ending still reaffirms a commitment to the lifestyle of the Indian. At the end of Broken Arrow, in contrast to the novel, Jeffords was not destined to return to Tucson and settle down with Terry. Similarly, in The Last Wagon, Todd diverts Jenny from her prospective husband in Tucson, and takes her and Billy with him back into the Native American territory of the wilderness.

The weave of ideological threads in the trial sequence is remarkable. The trial is of Todd as Indian and is necessary in order to achieve closure in terms acceptable to Hollywood in 1956. Todd, in effect, passes through the White man's law in order to be liberated, once more, as Indian. Here Jenny's intervention is clearly crucial: she is speaking on behalf of White society. But, from another point of view – and here the presence of General Howard is inspired – the trial is the equivalent of the peacemaking scenes in the other three Indian movies: it is the scene in which Whites and Indians negotiate the terms under which, their past differences set aside, they can live together peacefully. And, by effecting this agreement in a coded form, the film can propose a more radical solution: Todd is certainly not headed for a reservation at the end.

Filmed almost entirely on location by Wilfrid Cline, The Last Wagon is one of the most beautiful of Daves's Westerns. Thematically it is a journey Western, in which the physical journey is also a spiritual one, leading to a moral change in the travellers. But, whereas in the journey Westerns of both Anthony Mann and Budd Boetticher the change is normally restricted to the hero, here all those making the journey are morally transformed. However, it is the terms under which the changes occur that makes the film so remarkable for its time. Whether dealing with the killing of enemies, the learning of survival skills, the seduction of the heroine or a critique of racism, it is the way of the Indian that is consistently validated.

3:10 to Yuma and Cowboy

3:10 to Yuma is Daves's only black-and-white Western and, from the opening credits sequence, he makes vivid use of the textures and contrasts of monochrome photography. From a close-up of parched, cracked earth, the camera tilts and cranes up, and a stagecoach, black against the grey of the surrounding mudflats, appears along the horizon and turns and heads towards the camera. As it

Still: 3:10 to Yuma - *Emmy (Felicia Farr) and Wade (Glenn Ford) in the seduction scene.*

passes, Daves cuts to a travelling shot with the camera on the front of the coach. At this point, the last remaining credit – Daves's name as director – is superimposed, first on the black shadows of the horses travelling over the earth then, as the camera pans, on the horses themselves, carrying the coach, and the narrative, forward. This association of Daves's name with both the dramatic shadows and the driving force of the horses themselves is a highly self-conscious gesture. Throughout the 'fifties, Daves became more and more assured technically, and here he flamboyantly signals his expertise. Visually, *3:10 to Yuma* is undoubtedly one of his most stylish films, with shot after shot strikingly composed.

Further along its journey, the stagecoach's path is blocked by a herd of cattle. The driver pulls to a halt, but swirling dust conceals the nature of the blockage. When the dust clears, we see that the coach is surrounded by men on horseback with their guns drawn. The driver raises his hands.

Both the baked earth and the dust are elements in the film's thematic design, concrete expressions of the drought that has driven homesteader Dan Evans (Van Heflin) to the point where he is desperate for water for his cattle. It is these cattle that the gunmen, led by Ben Wade (Glenn Ford), have used to halt the coach, and Dan and his two young sons arrive on the scene as the robbery is being carried out. When the coach driver seizes the opportunity to pull a gun and use a gang member as a shield, Wade promptly shoots his own man and then the driver. He takes all the horses – including those of Dan and his boys – and rides off with his men to the town of

Bisbee. Dan assures Mr Butterfield (Robert Emhardt), the owner of the stage line who is on the now stranded coach, that he will return with a horse as soon as he has rounded up his cattle.

It was on this movie that Daves began to use the crane more overtly, another contribution to the film's stylishness. When Dan and the boys return to the ranch, his wife Alice (Leora Dana) comes running out to greet them. As she does this, the camera – accompanied by George Duning's wistful theme – sweeps lyrically down to meet her, a prelude to the depiction of an usually strong husband and wife relationship. Although the drought has made both partners nervous and anxious about the future – which shows in their edgy conversation as Dan prepares to return to the stranded coach – by the end of this short scene they have re-established a harmonious, hopeful accord. Dan has agreed to Alice's plan to go to Bisbee and try to borrow the $200 necessary to rent six months' water rights, and he is now much more optimistic – it's bound to rain in six months: 'All this'll be green . . . maybe you and me won't be so tired all the time: in six months we'll be happy, won't we?' Reassuringly, Alice smiles back: 'Sure, we'll be happy.' Then, as Dan rides off, the camera in high shot shows Alice and the boys in the middle-ground watching him depart into the distance: here the crane down, again linked to the music, brings the scene visually to a graceful conclusion.

In *Shane*, the opening scene shows Alan Ladd's eponymous hero arriving at the ranch of Van Heflin's homesteader and being offered a drink of water. The extended emphasis on water in this first ranch scene in *3:10 to Yuma* – while talking to Alice, Dan drinks some, then washes, then both of them fill canteens – seems like a deliberate reference to the earlier movie, as does the presence of the two young sons. It's as if the narrative springs in part from a conscious reworking of *Shane*: here Van Heflin will assume the mantle of 'Western hero' that was denied him in the earlier movie. But the links go further. When a captured Ben Wade later shares an evening meal with Dan's family, the combination of the charmed response of Alice and the excited reaction of the boys evokes the first meal scene in *Shane*, with Wade as the equivalent of Shane – the romantic figure. The glamorous gunfighter has been replaced by the glamorous killer, a shift that points the way towards the development of the Western hero in the 'sixties and beyond.

But, whereas *Shane* – through such devices as the repeated reaction shots of Joey (Brandon De Wilde) – keeps insisting on a 'child's eye view' of events, *3:10 to Yuma* promotes a much more adult narrative. Of course, the boys want their father to be a hero, and, of course, he finally enacts the role, but here it is done without the inexorable movement towards conventional Western gunplay that can be seen in *Shane* and a thousand other Westerns. Daves shows little interest, in any of his Westerns, in who is 'the fastest gun west of the Pecos', an issue that one suspects appeals primarily to adolescent males. At the climax of Elmore Leonard's short story (published in *The Killers*, ed. Peter Dawson, Bantam, New York, 1955), Dan's prototype – who is a deputy marshal – does exactly what Western heroes are supposed to do and blasts his way through the gang members who are blocking his route to the train. Eschewing such conventional heroics, Daves's film proposes a rather more radical solution.

Wade's sexual charisma is first evident in a sequence in Bisbee, after he has sent the marshal (Ford Rainey) and posse back to the stranded coach so that he and his men can make a safe getaway across the border to Mexico. But Wade himself, attracted by the barmaid Emmy (Felicia Farr), stays behind. He discovers that he's seen her before, singing in a dance hall in Dodge City. As she tells him why she should subsequently have come to a place like Bisbee ('I got to coughing too much. Doctors said I should breathe dry air'), he gently reaches and touches one of her curls. The unexpected gesture, and the way Wade goes on to reminisce about the dance hall and the money he spent there, clearly arouse Emmy, and the look she gives him as she re-enters the saloon makes him follow her inside. As he approaches her, Daves tracks in to a tight two-shot of their faces. There is no question that Emmy is inviting the seduction: as Wade wonders about the colour of her eyes, Daves cuts to another, even tighter, angle to emphasise the impact of the devastating look she gives him as she answers. Their kiss is followed by a discreet Production Code dissolve to Dan and Butterfield, en route to Bisbee, as they pass the grave of the gang member who was shot by Wade. After a short scene in which they meet up with the posse, Daves dissolves back to Emmy and Wade coming out of the bedroom. Again Daves moves into a tight two-shot of their faces. Emmy

knows that Wade won't be coming back to Bisbee, but says she's got something to remember: 'Funny, some men you can see every day for ten years and never notice; some men you see once and they're with you the rest of your life.' This post-coital scene is full of tenderness; the return of gang member Charlie Prince (Richard Jaeckel), concerned about Wade's failure to follow him, is a rude interruption.

Like the seduction scene in *The Last Wagon*, these brief scenes between Emmy and Wade demonstrate Daves's remarkable talent for an eroticism discreet enough to get by the normally highly censorious Production Code. It is also striking in a Western of this period that such a sexually attractive figure as Wade should also be a cold-blooded killer. Indeed, Daves emphasises this by providing, in place of the sex between Emmy and Wade, a reminder of the latter's ruthlessness. After Wade has been captured, there is a further reminder when the stagecoach is retrieved and brought into Bisbee: on it is the body of the driver, Bill Moons. The film is making it clear that, for all his undoubted charm, Wade is still a killer, who shows not a flicker of guilt at the two deaths he causes. Later, he will tell Dan that Bill Moons drew first, but that's a rationalisation: in effect, he murdered both men.

Although Wade is captured, Prince escapes and rides off. Knowing that he will be back with the rest of the gang to rescue Wade, Butterfield offers $200 to those who will volunteer to help get Wade to Yuma and jail. Having failed in his attempt to borrow money, Dan volunteers. He and Alex Potter (Henry Jones), the other volunteer, ride back to his ranch, whilst Wade himself is placed on the now retrieved stagecoach and driven after them. As Emmy stands in the road and watches the stagecoach depart, Daves echoes the earlier shot of Alice and the boys: a high shot with Emmy in the middle ground and the coach travelling away into the distance. It is part of the formal strength of the film that we could see the two matching high shots as not simply linking the feelings of the two women left behind, but as bringing to a close the film's first and second acts.

By now all the main characters have been introduced and the situation expertly laid out. This is entirely the work of Halsted Welles's script: Leonard's short story does not begin until the two men arrive at the Contention Hotel and it has nothing of this background. The film's third act comprises the journey to Contention, with a stopover at Dan's ranch, where Wade shares the evening meal cooked by Alice and, while Dan is out of the room, exercises his charm on her. Alice is captivated and Dan, observing them, is immediately jealous. The two male protagonists may be seen as husband figure and lover figure, character types familiar in melodrama and the woman's film, but usually reinflected in Westerns. Although there are certainly plenty of Westerns in which a wife is attracted to a more romantic figure than her husband – e.g. *Shane*, *Jubal* and *The Searchers* – none of the heroes in these films has the seductive skills that Wade so effortlessly displays. One can entirely understand Dan's jealousy.

Riding through the night, Dan, Alex and Wade arrive in Contention at dawn to be met by Butterfield. Dan and Wade are ensconced in the hotel's bridal suite to wait for the 3.10 to Yuma. Although there are brief scenes with Butterfield (in the lobby) and Alex (on the outskirts of town), most of the rest of the film – a long fourth act – is set in this room as the hours grind by. Early on, Wade tries jumping Dan to test him, and discovers that he doesn't shoot. Dan says 'You know I will next time', but Wade's sceptical 'Do I?' suggests his perceptiveness: Dan utters subsequent warnings, but he never shoots. Wade begins to try bribing Dan to let him go free. When Dan points out the contradiction – Wade is supposedly sure that his men will rescue him – Wade agrees: 'They're coming, only . . . I like to do things . . . real peaceful.' In fact, Dan is unaware of one possible motive for Wade's seeking to bribe him. As he left the Evans ranch, Wade said to Alice (of Dan), 'I hope I can send him back to you all right'. The words seemed sincerely meant, and Wade – foreseeing the way that, by 3 p.m., Dan would be left alone to take him to the train – could well be trying to fulfil them.

However, Wade's assertion that he likes to do things 'peaceful' is promptly ironised by Bill Moons's funeral procession passing the hotel. (On the coffin is a dog, which is a little too close to Stevens's embarrassing use of the dog during the funeral in *Shane*.) This causes Dan to become pointedly sarcastic and Wade to claim self-defence. Later, the Moons family return from the funeral, and enter the lobby

Still: 3:10 to Yuma – *in the hotel room, Butterfield (Robert Emhardt, centre) about to chicken out; with Wade and Dan Evans (Van Heflin).*

for a drink. We learn that they buried Bill without waiting for a preacher, a small detail that nevertheless reinforces the fundamentally secular nature of Daves's West, from which men of the cloth are almost entirely absent. Butterfield is also at the bar, and Bill's brother, Bob (Sheridan Comerate), demanding to know why Butterfield didn't attend the funeral, learns that Wade is upstairs. Bob forces his way past Dan into the hotel room and threatens to kill Wade. Dan outfaces him, but in the struggle a shot is fired and this alerts Charlie Prince – in Contention to look for Wade – to Wade's whereabouts. Again he rides off for the rest of the gang. Realising that help will now be needed to get Wade to the train, Butterfield goes to round up some men.

It's at this point that the film comes to seem rather too obviously like *High Noon*, an unfortunate model. A whole sequence of events arises out of the comparison: the emphasis on the steadily diminishing time before the fateful moment when the train arrives; the fact that all the men enlisted to help, including Butterfield himself, chicken out, leaving Dan to get Wade to the station on his own; the way that Dan makes it, even though he would have been killed by the gang but for a sudden volte-face by Wade, who saves his life – the equivalent of the pacifist Amy (Grace Kelly) shooting one of the *High Noon* badmen in the back in order to help her beleaguered husband.

Nevertheless, the links with *High Noon* are a minor irritant; one still continues to feel the presence of Daves's intelligence. The bridal-suite setting; Wade spending most of the time lying back on the bed; the agitation he induces in Dan manifesting itself in the latter's restless manipulation of the sawn-off shotgun – all these would suggest a homoeroticised

subtext to the temptations offered by Wade. But, although there is an element of this, I feel that the confrontation is more accurately viewed as one between an expert lover and an uneasy husband. Wade displays himself as lover – hence the significance of the bridal bed – as part of his armoury of temptation: he is both taunting Dan and offering him the material means to become like himself. Referring to these scenes, Daves has spoken of 'the story of Faust and Mephistopheles transposed to the Far West' (*Positif* 50-52, p.118). And Wade's steadily increasing offer – eventually reaching $10,000, which is sufficient to make Dan very uneasy – does indeed have an element of Mephistopheles's temptations: he argues that wealth, by removing the need for such hard labour, can rejuvenate. Describing how he would have treated a wife like Alice ('I'd feed her better, I'd get her pretty dresses . . . I wouldn't make her work so hard'), he ends with a direct taunt: 'I'll bet she was a real beautiful girl before she met you.' Dan is so close to shooting Wade on this occasion that the latter has to calm him down, sending him to the window to see if the gang has arrived yet. The sequence of shots that then occurs is very suggestive: a deep focus shot of Dan sitting tensely at the window in the foreground, with Wade lying on the bed in the background; dissolve to a pan across the dusty road into town, empty of life; cut back to a medium shot of Dan; cut to the road from a different angle, with the gang members in the distance, riding in. It's as if they have been conjured up by the tensions between the two men, both as a censor – echoing Prince's return to the Bisbee saloon twenty-four hours earlier, when he arrived to break up the love scene between Wade and Emmy – and as a way of redirecting Dan's urge towards violence. When Dan does finally fire a shot, it is out of the window at one of the gang.

In *Movie* 20 (Spring 1975, p.43), Douglas Pye argues that *3:10 to Yuma* may be seen as an allegory in which 'the drought (is an) expression of and punishment for the spiritual state of the people. Their atrophy of will and resigned selfishness stand in a necessary relationship to the blight on the land in a way that clearly evokes the Waste Land of Grail legends'. He goes on to argue that the rain which falls at the end – heralded by thunder, which has been heard a number of times during the film – arises symbolically out of Dan's act of selfless heroism. Dan insists on going through with his task of taking Wade to the train not because of money (Butterfield has told him he'll pay him anyway), but because Alex has been ruthlessly murdered by Wade's gang: 'The town drunk gave his life so that people should be able to live in decency and peace together.'

The argument is a compelling one, identifying a thematic core around which the film is organised, and there are other details that support it. When Wade arrives in Bisbee, he discovers that everyone except Emmy is having a siesta, a very un-American activity: in *Man of Conquest* (George Nichols, Jr, 1939), Sam Houston (Richard Dix) defeats Santa Ana's Mexican army by the sneaky device of attacking them during their siesta. This expression of the people's lack of energy in *3:10 to Yuma* is complemented by the way that Wade himself immobilises everyday life: he strands the stage line owner in one of his coaches; he deprives a homesteader of the horses necessary for his work. As the film's villain, he contributes to the 'atrophy'; Daves is careful to keep track, in the early scenes, of the choreography of horses necessary to redeem the situation and get things moving again. Indeed, one of the motifs woven through the film is the elaborate use of stage-coaches and horses necessary to 'correct' Wade's initial disruption of transport, which is given far more stress than his theft of gold. The final shot of the train – which 'answers' the opening shot of the stage-coach – expresses the success of the operation.

Although I would certainly support Douglas Pye's basic argument here, I feel that the film goes further: it is not just Dan's act as hero that symbolically produces the rain; Alice, too, is implicated. After Prince has ridden off to round up the other gang members, Wade looks out of the window and comments that the street is emptying of people: 'Guess they figure a storm is blowing up.' On this, Daves dissolves to Alice, riding a buggy into Bisbee. From a brief conversation with other women, we gather that she's going to drive to Contention to stop Dan risking his life. And, at the moment when she finally arrives – shortly before 3 p.m. – thunder is heard. It's as if, symbolically, her concern for Dan is bringing the thunder, and with it the desperately needed rain.

However, by the time Alice arrives, Alex has been brutally murdered. Seeing a man on a roof opposite the hotel, he shouts Dan a warning, and when Dan shoots the man, Prince shoots Alex in the back at point-blank range. Gang members then drag him into the hotel and hang him, and when Alice arrives at the hotel, she is confronted by the sight of Alex hanging from the chandelier. Clearly, this is meant as a warning – and it has already served to scare Butterfield off – but, when Alice finds Dan and begs him not to go through with taking Wade to the train, he says that Alex's death means that he has to. Although the film is verging here on the 'a man's gotta do . . .' cliché, this scene between and Dan and Alice is nevertheless strangely touching. Alice answers the substance of Wade's earlier taunt in her moving testament, 'If I ever said anything that made you think I was complaining . . . it just isn't true . . . I love everything, every minute, all the worry, the work.' At the same time, her arrival and concern have renewed Dan's self-confidence: he isn't just reassuring her when he says he'll make it. Linked, through Dan's reference to the pearls he hasn't been able to give Alice, to the farewell scene between Wade and Emmy (Wade said he would send Emmy some pearls), the scene ends with Alice both recognising Dan's moral position and accepting his new-found self-assurance. When, in the lobby, he tells her he'll soon be back from Yuma, she says she'll be waiting.

In Britain, any visual suggestion that Alex has been hanged was clumsily censored from the film in 1957, and censored prints are still being shown on

television. Three complete scenes are missing: Butterfield seeing the body; Alice's tentative movement through the hotel, calling for Dan – in which the body is shown hanging above her; and, most importantly, the scene in which Dan, Wade and Butterfield leave the hotel room and go down into the lobby, ending with Dan's farewell to Alice. Throughout the second and third scenes, Daves repeatedly emphasises the presence of the hanging body – either through shots of the body itself, or its expressionistic shadow on the wall – which presumably accounts for the extent of the cutting. Like most censorship of the period, the cuts are artistically damaging, not simply in removing the specific focus on Alex's sacrifice and Dan's courage, but also because these scenes contain the most impressive deep focus shots in the entire film. One, in particular, includes the three men leaving the room in the foreground, the body visible through the banisters in the middle ground, Alice descending the stairs – also seen through the banisters – in the background, and the shadow of the body on the wall behind her.

It is the fifth act, in which Dan successfully guides Wade through the town to the depot despite the attempts of the gang to shoot him, that really pushes the film into the heavily clichéd territory of *High Noon*. By contrast, Daves's and Welles's reworking of Leonard's final confrontation with the gang – Wade's sudden decision at the last moment to save Dan's life by jumping on the train with him – has a certain logic. He is repaying Dan for saving him from

Still: 3:10 to Yuma – *the hotel lobby. Watched by Wade, Dan says farewell to Alice (Leora Dana); in the background, the shadow cast by the body of Alex Potter.*

Bob Moons and is philosophical about prison: 'I've broken out of Yuma before.' As the two men reach the train, the swirling dust of the opening scenes is replaced by steam from the engine, a neat visual parallel which leads into the rain that falls at the very end of the film. Again this is associated not simply with Dan's success, but also with Alice: she and Butterfield are waiting to watch the train pass and, as Dan waves to her, the rain starts to fall.

3:10 to Yuma is undoubtedly one of Daves's finest films. Although perhaps less original than most of his Westerns, it is beautifully realised: script, performances and imagery all work together to create a very complete work. And behind this is his concern for a 'realism' of the West: showing the harsh conditions under which men and women lived and worked.

A concern for realism is at the heart of Daves's next film, *Cowboy*. In the *Screen* interview, he says: 'In *Cowboy* . . . I wanted very much to say "This is how the cowboy lived and what he did". It was really a documentary of the life of a cowboy, based . . . on Frank Harris's book, but we took liberties with it, because I think Harris lied about fifty per cent of the time . . .' Scripted by the reliable Edmund H. North, beautifully shot by Charles Lawton, Jr, in a deep-hued Technicolor which even today looks highly

146

distinctive, *Cowboy* is nevertheless one of Daves's least satisfactory Westerns, as the impulse towards 'documentary' pulls the narrative away from the complexly elaborated form of his better movies. The basic story of Frank Harris (Jack Lemmon) joining up with Tom Reece (Glenn Ford) and his men and learning 'the ways of the cowboy' is simply too thin to sustain a ninety-minute movie. Moreover, the portrait of the cowboy which emerges is fundamentally unpleasant: sexist, racist, selfish, bullying. When Daves seeks to reverse this in the last third of the movie, it stands out as a glaring contradiction.

The film begins in Chicago in 1872, with desk clerk Harris enamoured of the beautiful Mexican Maria Vidal (Anna Kashfi), who is staying with her father in the hotel. Señor Vidal (Donald Randolph) soon puts a stop to the romance by taking Maria back to Mexico. His departure coincides with the arrival of Reece and his men, who sweep into the hotel at the end of their two-month cattle drive north. Witnessed by Harris, the two men greet each other, and Reece agrees to come to Guadalupe to buy Señor Vidal's cattle. Harris has already declared his wish to 'get into the cattle business': joining Reece will thus enable him to fulfil both his ambitions.

When Reece and his men arrive in the hotel, they are treated like royalty: given their regular suite of rooms and prompt, lavish service. Here, far from showing the 'gritty realism' of the life of the cowboy, the film actively promotes him as a larger-than-life personality. Striding around a hotel room filled with stiff Chicago businessmen, Reece simultaneously helps himself to a luxurious buffet, expertly negotiates a price for his cattle and discusses going to the opera. He then takes a bath, a familiar post-trail ritual, here gingered up by Reece firing bullets at cockroaches he sees or imagines he sees on the wall. His audience is Harris, trying to argue his case for becoming a cowboy, which Reece has little difficulty in satirising: 'You mean lyin' there under the stars, listenin' to the boys singin' around the campfire and your faithful old horse standin' there grazin' at the grass by your side.' He launches into a diatribe against the horse: 'A horse has a brain just about the size of a walnut; they're mean, they're treacherous and they're stupid.' Funny though this is, it is later revealed to be mere rhetoric: when Reece accepts a challenge at a fiesta in Mexico to ring a bull's horn, he makes a point of doing it on foot, rather than risking his horse being cut by the cattle horns, as the Mexican challenger had done.

In other words, it is difficult to know how to take Reece's behaviour here: is it all just a performance for the city folk? Does he really care about the opera, or is it just an excuse to display himself with glamorous women? Certainly opera and women are quickly forgotten when, back at the hotel, the question of poker comes up. It's as if Reece behaves in a flamboyant manner in town because it's expected: he manages to keep it up for only one night before he's back on the trail.

Harris helps Reece out when he runs short of gambling money; this obliges Reece, against his better judgement, to take Harris along as a partner. Once on the trail, the film becomes a series of sketches, loosely linked, of Harris's initiation into the rigours of cowboy life. In an early scene, Curtis (Richard Jaeckel) casts a rattlesnake among the men as a joke and, after it has been bandied around, an unsuspecting cowboy (Strother Martin) is fatally bitten. As he lies there dying, the men continue to crack jokes – there is a running gag about Joe Capper (King Donovan) having once eaten the haunch of an Indian – and, as soon as he dies, Curtis starts to remove his boots. This provokes Harris into going for Curtis, but Reece hurls him to the ground: 'Just because somebody does something stupid, there's no reason to cause more trouble.' As the man is buried, Reece makes a funeral speech which is profoundly matter-of-fact: 'In the long run I don't think it would have made any difference' – if it hadn't been a snake, one of the other perils of trail life would probably have killed the unfortunate (and nameless) cowboy.

In *The Last Wagon*, Daves used the incident of Valinda being bitten by a rattlesnake to weave together a number of thematic threads. In *Cowboy*, the scene is skilfully directed – the movement from horseplay to stupid 'accident' is well caught – but otherwise it merely serves to emphasise the men's collective callousness. This is what life is like on the trail, and Harris must learn to live with it.

When they arrive in Guadalupe, Harris discovers that Maria has been married. This abrupt thwarting of his romantic aspirations changes him, gradually making him as hard and cynical as the other cowboys. He is further disillusioned when he tries to rally support for Charlie (Dick York), the camp Lothario, whose attentions to a Mexican woman in a cantina threaten to provoke violence. Although, as Reece implies, Harris's eagerness to help Charlie – which will involve a confrontation with Mexican men – stems partly from personal motives, the indifference of the other cowboys to Charlie's fate emphasises their selfishness. When Harris starts back to the cantina, Reece violently stops him, hurling a crowbar to knock him down and then roasting him over a campfire until he submits. The nature of the assault suggests branding – the crowbar was next to the fire and even looks like a branding iron – an intimation of the sadism of Reece's attack. That the hurled crowbar also echoes the hurled rattlesnake should, one would have thought, further indict Reece.

This is not, however, the point of view adopted by the film. The next day, Charlie is shown to have only minor injuries: implicitly, Reece was right to stop Harris stirring up trouble. There is a brief conversation between Reece and Paco Mendoza (Victor Manuel Mendoza), the most level-headed of the cowboys, in which Mendoza likens Reece's hard treatment of Harris to the way he himself was treated by his father. The moral is clear: it is tough treatment that makes tough men. However, having established this suitably macho ideology, the film promptly starts to backtrack. Only at this stage – over an hour into the movie – does the actual cattle drive start, and as it heads north it encounters one of the familiar dangers of the trail: Indians. (The gag is still running: 'Must make you feel kinda hungry, eh, Joe?') Going after some strays, Harris becomes isolated from the rest of the men, presenting the Comanches with an easy target. Against the advice of the others and against the grain of his behaviour until now, Reece decides to save Harris by stampeding the main herd towards him. Although this does save Harris, he is distinctly ungrateful: he is a part owner of the herd and Reece's action has scattered it across the territory.

Reece is wounded in the action, which prompts the now embittered Harris to take over as trail boss. In rounding up the scattered herd, he drives the men to the point where they start fighting with one another. Another moral: cowboys may be tough, but an inexperienced boss can push them too hard. As they approach Wichita – where the cattle are to be transferred to a stock train – Doc Bender (Brian Donlevy), a cowhand who was once town marshal, decides he will try settling down there. He gave up being marshal because his reputation with a gun meant that he was forever killing young tearaways, but he now feels that, in retirement, things should be peaceful. However, as the cattle are being loaded, news comes that he has once more been forced to shoot someone and, as this was an old friend, he has hanged himself. All the men except Harris are suitably shocked and, when Reece confronts him over his lack of concern, Harris quotes Reece's own words back at him: 'In the long run it doesn't make any difference – that's what you said.' But the film is now insisting on a more humane ideology: once again, Harris's attitude is criticised. The blatant contradiction is emphasised by Reece's words: 'If you had anything inside you that was worth saving, I'd beat you till you couldn't stand up . . .'

The hanging of Doc Bender anticipates the fate which threatens Frail at the end of The Hanging Tree. These two are the only figures in Daves's Westerns with the reputation of being fast with a gun and, as soon as each proves it – Frail when he shoots Frenchy – he surrenders to the death drive. It is a fascinating comment on Daves's (perhaps unconscious) feelings about what it means to be 'the fastest gun'.

Reece and Harris are finally reconciled on the train journey to Chicago, when Harris goes to rescue some cattle from being trampled to death in the freight wagons and Reece goes to help him. Their newfound comradeship is then celebrated in a re-run of the cowboys-in-Chicago scenes at the beginning, except that now Harris is behaving just as extravagantly as Reece. The final scene shows them both taking a bath, and Harris shooting a cockroach on the wall. They roar with laughter.

One can understand why Daves would want to make a film like Cowboy: it was an early attempt to portray the West 'as it was', without the traditional mythicising. And visually the film is indeed very impressive, with the deep reds and greens of the Chicago hotel set against the dusty yellows of the trail and the compositions again being consistently

vivid. In particular, the night scenes around the camp fire are filmed more convincingly 'night for night' than in any other Daves movie except Broken Arrow: the surrounding darkness really is black, rather than the conventional 'day for night' of the vast majority of Westerns. However, this stylishness cannot really compensate for a narrative that is both lightweight and self-contradictory. Daves's best movies – The Hanging Tree, 3:10 to Yuma, The Last Wagon – seem much more impressive on repeated viewings. With Cowboy, the opposite is the case.

In Camera Obscura 3/4, Raymond Bellour says: 'If you take Westerns as different as those of John Ford or Anthony Mann, Samuel Fuller or Delmer Daves, you notice that the problematic of the formation of the (heterosexual) couple is absolutely central in all of them' (p.88). Of Daves's Westerns, the only two which do not fit this pattern are 3:10 to Yuma and Cowboy, although one could argue that, in the former movie, the marriage of Dan and Alice is implicitly strengthened by the narrative events. Nevertheless, both movies propose an alternative scenario: the formation of a relationship between two men, one the structural hero (Dan, Harris), the other played by Glenn Ford as a charismatic leader of men and the film's star. Whether charming and dangerous (3:10 to Yuma) or tough and uncompromising (Cowboy), Ford is the focal point of the hero's ordeal, and the heterosexual romance is replaced by a test for the hero in which Ford is both taskmaster and referee. Since the hero is rewarded for successfully completing the task with an intimate relationship with Ford, there is a sense in which the films are about sublimated homosexuality. At the end of Cowboy, the two are even bathing together and celebrating by firing off pistol shots. This suggests a splendidly Freudian interpretation of the rain at the end of 3:10 to Yuma as the celebration of male fertilising power. Certainly it falls on Alice as well, but she's left behind with the sexually unexciting Butterfield; the two men go off together. It is also notable that as Dan and Wade leave the gang behind, Dan shoots Prince, whose over-protective concern for Wade has carried a definite charge. Indeed, when Prince interrupted Wade and Emmy with a peremptory 'What happened to you?', one sensed his jealous resentment. Then, when Prince questions the barman (George Mitchell) in the Contention hotel, he says that it's his wife he's looking for: 'She ran off with a travelling man – I figured he'd bring her here.' The fact that the person he's looking for is upstairs in the bridal suite with another man seems distinctly intriguing.

The White Settlement Films

Adapted by Daves and Russell Hughes from Paul Wellman's 'epic historical novel', Jubal Troop (1939), Jubal uses material only from the first few chapters of the novel and even then extensively reworks this: for example, the film's villain, Pinky (Rod Steiger), does not appear in the novel. In auteurist terms, this is a crucial change. Like Frenchy (Karl Malden) and Grubb (George C. Scott) in The Hanging Tree, Pinky is no ordinary villain. As with the archvillains of nineteenth-century stage melodrama, the villainy of these figures acts like a curse on the hero and almost succeeds in destroying him. Through these men and their influence over the other members of their respective communities, Daves extends his critique of the White settlements which was apparent in the negative view of the citizens of Tucson in *Broken Arrow*. In the Indian communities in Daves's films, there may be warmongers, but they are nothing like the corrupt and evil figures we have here. In Daves's West, it is White society that gives birth to monsters.

Set in Wyoming in 1880, *Jubal* begins with its hero, Jubal Troop (Glenn Ford) emerging on foot out of the mountains in a state of collapse. Rancher Shep Horgan (Ernest Borgnine) finds him and takes him home to recover. Pinky, one of Shep's cowhands, takes an instant dislike to Jubal. By contrast, Shep, jovial and easy-going, offers Jubal a job, telling him not to worry about Pinky: 'He was born with a great fat burr in his britches.' Shep is unaware that his young and attractive wife Mae (Valerie French), frustrated by the emptiness of ranch life and by her husband's insensitivity to her needs, has had an affair with Pinky. But Mae now spurns Pinky and sets her sights on Jubal.

The plot suggests a cross between *Shane* and a James M. Cain novel such as *The Postman Always Rings Twice* (1934). The *noir* overtones are enhanced by Jubal's pessimism – he admits to Shep that he's never been able to settle and says that he carries bad luck around with him – but a more crucial generic influence is melodrama. The film possesses the Freudian features of many 'fifties Hollywood melodramas, both in its concern with the eruption of desire within an already established community and in locating a source for the hero's neurosis in a childhood 'traumatic event'. It is to Naomi (Felicia Farr), the film's 'good woman', that Jubal tells his story. When he was seven years old, living with his (unmarried) parents on a barge, he fell into the river. Witnessing this, his mother refused to rescue him; his father leapt in and saved him, but was himself killed – another boat came out of the darkness and its propeller tore him to pieces. Afterwards, Jubal's mother accused him: 'Why couldn't it have been you?' Jubal fled from home: 'I ain't stopped running since: till Shep gave me this job.'

The childhood incident is invented for the film, an example of Daves's intuitive feeling for melodramatic material. It may be read as an oedipal narrative in which the 'true' oedipal meaning is repressed: the young Jubal denying his attraction to his mother; the oncoming boat as 'the return of the repressed', enacting the murder of the father which Jubal unconsciously desired. It is not surprising that his reaction was to flee.

From the moment he rescues Jubal – echoing the childhood trauma – Shep becomes a replacement father-figure. When Jubal proves his worth as a cowboy, Shep offers him the job of foreman. Jubal comments, 'Since my father died, you're the only man who went out of his way to help me.' As he says this, he is seated, and Shep and Mae are standing together in front of him: Daves's camera angles emphasise that Jubal is looking up, like a child before adults. Although the surrogate father/son relationship is made somewhat problematic by Glenn Ford's being too old for the role – in the novel, Jubal is only eighteen at this point – the film nevertheless insists on it. But this reintroduces the repressed oedipal material which lay behind Jubal's childhood trauma and from which he fled: Mae sets out to seduce him.

Jubal is strongly attracted to Mae, but resists her advances. In the words of a sympathetic cowhand, Sam (Noah Beery, Jr): 'There weren't a man on this outfit that didn't pop his eyes when he first seen Mae . . . but he gets over it . . . 'cos Shep is such a nice feller he feels like he's doing him dirt.' A good son-figure submits to the sexual authority of the father-figure. However, Pinky, a bad son-figure, responds jealously to the change in Mae. As Jubal and Mae dance to the pianola, Daves dissolves from them to Pinky shooting a mountain lion: symbolically, they are Pinky's target. Pinky's resentment of Jubal is increased when he learns that Jubal rather than he will become foreman.

Naomi is the daughter of Shem (Basil Ruysdael), the leader of a religious group of nomads called the Rawhiders (so-called, we are informed in the novel, for 'their habit of using rawhide for every conceivable purpose') who are travelling hopefully across the continent in search of 'the promised land'. The Rawhiders in the film are cleaned up from their rather negative representation in the novel, in which they are like wayfaring hillbillies, inbred and dirty. They stop on Shep's land to enable some of their group to recover from sickness. Pinky and men from a neighbouring ranch start to drive them off; Jubal intervenes and, accepting Shem's word that they're Christian and law-abiding, says that they can stay. In deciding in their favour, he is aided by the testimony of Reb (Charles Bronson), a cowboy who has been riding with them.

During this scene, Naomi has been standing beside her father. This first meeting between her and Jubal is badly handled: the close-up of her designed to indicate her attraction to him is taken from a later scene (when she is wearing a completely different dress) and Jubal registers no real interest in her at all; it is Pinky, recounting the scene to Shep later, who suggests that Jubal favoured the Rawhiders because a girl gave him the eye and 'his guts got mushy inside'. However, this directorial clumsiness is followed, some five minutes later, by an example of Hollywood film-making at its most audacious. Reb accompanies Jubal back to the ranch, and Shep agrees to give him a job. By now, it is night. In the ranchhouse, Shep goes up to bed, leaving Mae downstairs; in the bunkhouse, Jubal and Reb prepare for bed. Jubal and Mae look across at each other from their respective windows, she raising the net curtains by way of invitation, he rolling a cigarette. Daves cuts rhythmically between the two, using both point-of-view shots and close-ups to suggest the currents between them. At this point, Reb casually comments: 'Tried to roll them cigarettes once, but I couldn't learn to keep my finger out.' Wordlessly,

Jubal shows Reb that he's managed to keep his finger out.

There is no doubt that the sexual double entendre is intentional. Apart from the context and timing, Reb is presented as a pretty sharp character – he and Jubal quickly become partners – and he had seen how Mae found an excuse to speak to Jubal at the end of the preceding scene with Shep. But for such an outrageous comment to be in a Production Code movie is almost unthinkable, especially as it is inserted into a sequence of genuine erotic tension: Mae displays herself at the window so effectively that Jubal is lured outside to meet her. They meet in the barn, and although Jubal manages to keep his distance, we learn of Mae's frustrations as Shep's wife: 'I'm no more than his pet filly, his heifer . . . to men maybe he's great; to a woman, he's an animal.' Earlier, Shep spoke of sex in terms of riding: 'The liveliest little filly I ever rode was the redheaded daughter of a fire-eating preacher'. This speech – again couched in language that is remarkably explicit for its time – supports Mae's complaint. The film is not unsympathetic to Mae's predicament, as a woman, on a ranch with 'Ten thousand acres of lonesomeness' and an 'animal' for a husband.

Although Jubal does start making trips to the Rawhider camp to see Naomi, their meetings are

Stills: Jubal. *Above – Naomi (Felicia Farr) and Jubal (Glenn Ford). Opposite – Mae (Valerie French) visits the men during the round-up, with, to her right, Jubal, Reb (Charles Bronson), Shep (Ernest Borgnine) and Pinky (Rod Steiger).*

circumscribed. According to Rawhider custom, she has been promised to one of their own group, Jake (Robert Knapp), even though she doesn't like him. Then, during round-up, she comes to say goodbye: they're leaving tomorrow. With Jubal's romance seemingly at an end, Mae arrives, visiting the camp that night on a pretext. The looks she gives Jubal, jealously observed by Pinky, signal her intentions plainly enough. And so, when an innocently unaware Shep asks Jubal to escort her back to the ranch – 'We've been having mountain lion trouble' – the irony is that Mae is the predator. Jubal once more resists her advances, but when he doesn't return to the camp – and Reb sets off to look for him – Pinky wakes Shep and raises his suspicions about this turn of events. Uneasily, Shep starts back to the ranch to confront Mae.

He finds her asleep on her own, but his arrival wakes her, and it is Jubal's name that she utters. Here, again, the film comes across as melodrama: a moment of carelessness reveals the true feelings of a character. When Shep angrily asks her if Jubal was with her, she hesitates and then – out of resentment at both men – says that he was, and that she hates Shep. Taking a rifle, Shep sets off to kill Jubal.

This leads to a showdown in the local bar, where Jubal has retreated to feel sorry for himself and Reb has joined him. When Shep arrives, he refuses to listen to Jubal's story, and starts shooting. But Jubal is unarmed, which prompts Reb to come to his defence: he hurls a table to distract Shep and throws Jubal a gun. Jubal returns Shep's fire and kills him.

As critics have noted, Pinky's manipulation of Shep's suspicions evokes Iago. But his villainy goes further. Not only was he guilty of the crime he accuses Jubal of committing but, when he learns that Shep is dead, he tries to move in with Mae and, when she rejects him, he violently attacks her. In the absence of any lawmen, he then mobilises a posse against Jubal, saying that Shep was legitimately defending his honour as husband and that the trick of Reb throwing Jubal a gun – which we earlier saw the men rehearse – was all part of the plot to kill Shep. During this scene, Pinky is carrying Shep's rifle, which he displays to the gathered men like an ensign to orchestrate their feelings against Jubal. This also signals that he, Pinky, now possesses the phallus. He promotes himself as the new father-figure, seeking retribution on the transgressive son.

In effect, the oedipal triangle has been played out with Mae, the mother-figure, as the seducer, and Jubal, the son-figure, as the unwilling killer of the father-figure. This is like an enactment of the repressed oedipal trauma from which Jubal fled as a child – a narrative return of the repressed – and its outcome, unsurprisingly, has a similar traumatic effect on him (rendered by the film as a physical wound occasioned by the gunfight). Jeb takes him to hide out with the Rawhiders, who are already on the move. This brings Naomi back into the story; like Jenny in *The Last Wagon*, she now becomes a nurturing figure, tending Jubal's wound and restoring him to health.

In the meantime, the posse hunt for Jubal. They are finally led to his hideout by Jake, who is seeking revenge on the man who he believes has displaced him in Naomi's affections. This act of betrayal conveniently gets rid of Jake: Shem (the new benevolent father-figure) expels him from the community, thereby freeing Naomi for a happy ending with Jubal. But, before this can happen, the question of Jubal's guilt needs to be resolved. Pursued by the posse, he rides back to the ranch to seek the truth from Mae. He finds her in the barn, dying as a result of Pinky's attack, which evidently included rape. But Mae lives long enough to inform the posse of Pinky's guilt, and Jubal – catching him as he tries to escape – ensures that he will face his punishment. As Jubal and Reb ride away to join Naomi, a swinging pulley hints to us that Pinky will be the subject of the lynching that he has been demanding for Jubal.

The site of sex and violence, the barn also features in an aspect of the film which is tantalisingly underdeveloped: the sense of Pinky as representing the drives of Jubal's id. It is in the barn that Mae makes her first advances to Jubal – and the smoke from the forge he is using, to say nothing of the heated branding iron, indicate his arousal. His rejection of her is immediately followed by the arrival of Pinky, demanding 'A little of what I'm missing'. Jubal later goes to the barn for his night-time rendezvous with Mae – a scene which suggests that he was close to succumbing to her desires. Jubal seems not to know about Pinky's relationship with Mae: like the repressed, it is outside his conscious awareness. Even Pinky's savage attack on Mae occurs at a point where Jubal, suspecting her of helping to set Shep against him, would certainly have blamed her for causing Shep's death. Although this reading of the film is tentative, it is highly suggestive: one can see how close the film comes to indicting the hero. In effect, the hero's oedipal guilt has been displaced on to Pinky, but the film – through its incisive analysis of the hero's neuroses – still makes it clear that, in fantasy, he is nevertheless implicated.

Still: Jubal – *Pinky tries to rouse the men against Jubal, but Sam (Noah Beery, Jr) and Carson (John Dierkes) are unmoved.*

More difficult to read are the parallels between the two sets of relationships in which Jubal finds himself: the Shep/Shem name link, Pinky's and Jake's similar resentment that the women they want should prefer Jubal; their seeking revenge; Jubal entering both communities as an outsider. However, if the events with Mae and Shep are indeed like a delayed oedipal trauma, then the film is in effect taking Jubal through them so that he can achieve 'normative manhood'. Since the film ends with Naomi leading Jubal and Reb as they ride away from the ranch, we assume that they are heading back to the Rawhiders' wagon train. And, with the Rawhiders, Jubal can be reinserted as a 'good' son-figure who, with the new father-figure's blessing, can marry Naomi and grow up himself to be a father-figure. In the way his role echoes Pinky's, Jake is then like a residue of the past which is explicitly shown to be no longer a problem: Shem enacts the expulsion which Shep failed to realise was necessary.

Nevertheless, there is still an unresolved quality to the ending. Earlier, Naomi told Jubal how much she longed for a roof over her head, one of the three things that Shep had said were worth fighting for. Although doubly emphasised, this aspiration is forgotten by the end. Similarly, the film shows a hero who is convinced that 'bad luck' is forever causing him to move on and who, at the end, is once again obliged to move on, having caused, albeit unintentionally, the death of the man who was like a father to him. However, in one respect the ending is typical of Daves: Naomi, Jubal and Reb are heading away from the White settlement.

Filmed on location by Charles Lawton, Jr in the area of Wyoming where it was set – Grand Teton country, around Jackson Hole, near the setting of *Shane* – *Jubal* makes superb use of the landscape, but is otherwise one of Daves's more uneven films. At its best, in its depiction of the complex and contradictory triangle of relationships between Jubal, Shep and Mae, it is as good as anything he has done.

But there are clear problems: the clumsiness evident in Naomi's first scene is symptomatic of the underdevelopment of her role, and Daves himself has said that Steiger's Method-style performance was inappropriate for a Western (*Positif* 50-52, p.118). Nevertheless, it remains an intriguing film, its uncertainties a reflection of Daves's increasing ambivalence about the settlement of the West.

The Badlanders, a loose remake of *The Asphalt Jungle*, is the Western Daves was least happy with: in *Positif* he says that he only did it as a favour to Alan Ladd, and that Richard Collins's script was a mess. Stylistically the film shows the strides that Daves made during the 'fifties: the action is frequently taut and exciting, with a dynamically involved camera worthy of Anthony Mann. But the script is indeed unsatisfactory, mainly in its failure to weave together the separate strands of the narrative. It is intriguing to see how the characters from Huston's film have been reworked, but the heist plot itself is entirely conventional. However, the film possesses a feature which is potentially much more interesting: an exploration of the Mexican community as an oppressed group within the town of Prescott, Arizona, at the turn of the century. Although a minor work in Daves's Western oeuvre, the film may thus be included with the other White settlement films.

Richard Collins was one of the original nineteen men summoned to appear before the House Un-American Activities Committee in 1947. Although, later, he would rescue himself from being blacklisted by naming names, *The Badlanders* is sufficiently critical of American exploitation of the disadvantaged to suggest that he did not entirely sell out on his left-wing sympathies. Prescott is a gold-mining town which imports cheap Mexican labour. The Mexicans live in one part of town, the Whites in the other, the two parts separated by a dry gulch bridge. Although the town is gold-rich, the Mexicans are poor, whilst the Whites who run it are wealthy, powerful and corrupt.

Lounsberry (Kent Smith), the equivalent of the Louis Calhern figure from *The Asphalt Jungle*, is much richer and more crooked than his predecessor: he married the owner of the Lisbon goldmine for her millions and has been involved in rustling cattle from Mexico. (I suspect that this reference is in the film to suggest that the Mexican workers are illegal immigrants, smuggled, like the cattle, across the border.) The criminal entrepreneur, Sample (Robert Emhardt), structurally the Marc Lawrence figure, is here also the most powerful political figure in town. The town's lawmen, like Sheriff Harper in *The Last Wagon*, are both corrupt. The marshal (Karl Swenson) is like the Barry Kelley figure (a corrupt cop) in Huston's film: in the past, he has framed the Dutchman (Ladd) for robbery; now he gives him until sundown the next day to get out of town. The deputy marshal, Leslie (Adam Williams), assumes the Brad Dexter role (a hired gun) in the attempted double-cross after the robbery. The only significant White female character, Ada (Claire Kelly), the Marilyn Monroe figure, is even more exploited than her predecessor: when the Dutchman first meets her, she has been locked in her hotel room by possessive sugar daddy Lounsberry. The only betrayal of this implicit critique of the Whites is that the leader of the town's thugs is Comanche (Anthony Caruso), a 'half-breed', a betrayal that is underlined by Caruso's role as one of the gang members in *The Asphalt Jungle*.

The film begins in Yuma Penitentiary in 1898. After some powerful scenes suggesting the savagery of the penal system, the Dutchman and John McBain (Ernest Borgnine) are both released on the same day. Respectively the equivalents of the Sam Jaffe and Sterling Hayden characters in *The Asphalt Jungle*, both are past victims of the greed and corruption that, in Hollywood movies at least, are invariably associated with gold mining and gold towns. Once a rancher, McBain has served ten years for killing Bascom, then the owner of the Lisbon mine, who cheated McBain out of his land in the pursuit of gold. The Dutchman, a mining engineer, has served two years after being cheated out of his commission by a manager of the same mine and, with the assistance of the marshal, railroaded into jail. He intends to obtain compensation by robbing the mine and, knowing McBain's interest, sets out to recruit him to help.

McBain becomes friendly with Anita (Katy Jurado) – the Jean Hagen figure – a Mexican whom he rescues from a mauling by Comanche and some other thugs. Through her he learns of the poverty of the Mexicans' world: a young woman forced to have a baby without a doctor; her own baby that died. Only when McBain and Anita spend the night together does he learn that she is a prostitute. But he refuses to view her in such terms: 'I see inside – what I see is good.' At the end of the film, the two of them are heading for Durango, Mexico, escaping

Still: The Badlanders – McBain (Ernest Borgnine), Anita (Katy Jurado) and the Dutchman (Alan Ladd) celebrate the Mexican victory over the White oppressors.

the corrupt and exploitative American society. The Dutchman is also given an embryonic romance with Ada, but it is bland by comparison; again it is the interracial relationship in which Daves shows most interest.

The third member of the heist team is another Mexican, the 'powder monkey' Vincente (Nehemiah Persoff), the equivalent of Anthony Caruso in Huston's film. (Although we also see White miners, it seems that the Mexicans have the most dangerous jobs.) Like his predecessor in the earlier film, he is injured during the robbery, but the others get him home safely to his wife and child, and McBain's final words to him are 'Join me in Mexico, huh?' Together with the Dutchman's parting comment to McBain, 'I'll meet you in Durango in June. We might even punch cattle together', this clearly goes against the dominant ideological view that, in Robin Wood's words 'America [is] the land where everyone actually is/can be happy' ('Ideology, Genre, Auteur' in *Film Comment* January/February 1977). With the rarest of exceptions – and it is highly relevant that one of them should be another Daves movie, *Dark Passage* (1947) – Hollywood films of the studio era simply did not envisage happy endings in which fugitive heroes and heroines escape from the United States to another country. Here, it is Huston's film that is by far the more conventional (and, indeed, reactionary): all the characters involved in the robbery either die or are caught. In *The Badlanders*, despite leaving a dead deputy in Lounsberry's library, they not only escape, but also make off with the gold, which McBain and Anita are taking across the border and which the Dutchman says they'll split three ways. Fourteen years before *The Getaway* (Sam Peckinpah, 1972), the ending of which seemed so ground-breaking, Daves and Collins had supplied exactly the same happy ending: the robbers escaping to Mexico with the loot.

After the failed double-cross, Lounsberry and Sample set out to track down the gold, using the thugs to terrorise Vincente and his wife into talking (the Mexicans, again, as victims of violence). This leads to a climax in which the Dutchman is cornered with the wagonload of gold in the Mexican quarter and McBain races to his aid. The two seem to be trapped, but Anita promptly mobilises the Mexicans to come to their rescue. The Mexicans are already in costume for their annual fiesta, which includes a staged version of the Battle of the Alamo. And so, when Anita starts the 'battle' early in order to get rid of the white villains, the Mexicans are symbolically refighting the Alamo. It is a profoundly satisfying scene: the White oppressors are roundly defeated and driven back over the dry gulch bridge.

Made for Gary Cooper's own production company, Baroda, *The Hanging Tree* was adapted by Wendell Mayes and Halsted Welles from Dorothy M. Johnson's novella. All three were talented writers: Mayes went on to write three superb scripts for Otto Preminger (*Anatomy of a Murder*, 1959, *Advise and Consent*, 1962, and *In Harm's Way*, 1964); Welles had already scripted the brilliant *3:10 to Yuma*; Johnson won the annual 'best short story of the West'

award for *The Hanging Tree* in 1957 and was also the author of the short stories 'The Man Who Shot Liberty Valance' (1949) and 'A Man Called Horse' (1953), later made into significant Westerns. With both a strong source story and skilful scriptwriters, Daves was provided here with excellent material; unsurprisingly, *The Hanging Tree* is a very fine movie indeed.

Like most Westerns, including Daves's, the film begins with the hero arriving at a new place: in this instance, the mining camp of Skull Creek, Montana, in 1873. Designed by art director Daniel B. Cathcart and built in the mountains forty miles from Yakima, Washington, the camp is a superb example of Hollywood art design. It is displayed in a slow pan, as Dr Joe Frail (Cooper) rides along a cliff overlooking the camp: in one direction, the ribbon of miners' tents go along the river into the distance; in another, a few scattered wooden buildings are surrounded by a messy construction site and a further collection of tents, mostly occupied by prostitutes. The sense of a settlement being chaotically assembled is vividly conveyed. In many respects, the camp anticipates that in *Ride the High Country* (Sam Peckinpah, 1962), particularly in its foregrounding of the presence of prostitutes. Indeed, as Frail arrives on the hill, a wagonload of prostitutes is noisily welcomed into the township below.

Frail buys a cabin on the hill, looking down on the settlement; clearly the geography is symbolically significant. In fact, if the Hanging Tree itself is also included, we can see the elements of a suggestive Freudian design. Frail passes the Hanging Tree as he first rides into Skull Creek. A man arriving with his family comments: 'Every new mining town's got to have its hanging tree: makes folks feel respectable.' These, the first spoken words in the film, encapsulate its social theme. Through the law of the lynch mob, the gold-hungry citizens protect their sense of right and wrong. In effect, the Hanging Tree – which is at the top of the hill, above Frail's cabin – symbolises the town's collective superego. By contrast, the settlement in the valley, founded on greed, the site of prostitution, gambling and violence, symbolises the id. Frail, positioned between the two, is the fragile (frail) ego, sometimes looking down moralistically on the seething id below (aligning himself with the superego) but sometimes tempted down into it. In the early scenes, he remains aloof from the township during the day (patients come to him), but nevertheless goes down at night to gamble in the saloon.

Other Westerns have of course drawn attention to the readiness of pioneer communities to resort to the law of the lynch mob. At the beginning of *The Tall Men* (Raoul Walsh, 1955), Ben Allison (Clark Gable), noticing a man hanging from a tree, comments 'Looks like we're getting close to civilisation.' The second scene in *Bend of the River* (Anthony Mann, 1952) shows Glyn McLintock (James Stewart) save Emerson Cole (Arthur Kennedy) from lynching for a crime (stealing a horse) he claims he did not commit. But *The Hanging Tree*, like *Broken Arrow* and, especially, *The Ox-Bow Incident* (William Wellman, 1943), goes further in its indictment by identifying the lynch mob mentality with the thinking of ordinary citizens, who think themselves civilised.

The readiness of the citizens to form themselves into a lynch mob is shown early. Frenchy, the first of the film's remarkable villains, is introduced as he guards some mining works. Spotting a young man, Rune (Ben Piazza), trying to steal from a sluice, he shoots at him, and the miners set out in pursuit. Immediately they become a lynch mob: Rune knows that, if they catch him, he'll hang. Although he has been wounded by Frenchy's bullet, he climbs the cliff up to Frail who has been watching the pursuit below. Exhausted by the time he reaches the top, he is saved by Frail when the latter responds to his need for medical assistance.

In that Frail subsequently takes Rune on as his servant, the situation is similar to the opening of *Jubal*, in which Shep rescues and then employs Jubal. But the conditions are crucially different. Shep employs Jubal for wages; Frail insists that, since he's saved Rune's life, the latter will become his bondservant. He'll ensure that Rune sticks by this arrangement by keeping the bullet he dug out: 'Even if they didn't see your face, this could be your mark for the Hanging Tree'. Frail's invocation of the Hanging Tree to support his threat is significant. In his dealings with others – particularly Rune – Frail is only too ready to adopt the role of a severe superego. At the same time, as an Ego-figure, he is also subject to conflicting, contradictory impulses. For example, we see Frail discard the incriminating bullet, but Rune does not know this, and his relationship with Frail – to whom he is structurally a son-figure – is contaminated by the resentment he feels at being held hostage and treated as little more than a slave.

There are, nevertheless, clear links with *Jubal*: again the film is basically a melodrama in a Western setting and features a hero in flight from his past. But the nature of the past – again invented for the film – is reinflected: Jubal's past traumatic event was that of a son; Frail's is that of a mature man. We are not told precise details, but deduce from the accounts given that his wife committed suicide after he had killed her lover – his own brother – whereupon he burned down the marital home. Insofar as there are oedipal overtones here, they are both displaced – brother instead of son – and taken to a violent extreme: Frail acts like an enraged patriarch, punishing the transgressive couple. Psychologically, the formal black that he wears connotes his tense, repressed self, but iconographically it also suggests he is in mourning for his past, like Robert Ryan's marshal in *The Proud Ones* (Robert D. Webb, 1956), who also wears black throughout the film.

When Rune, under Frail's orders, goes down into the township to announce the presence of a 'doctor on the hill', the prostitutes laugh: 'What do we want with a doctor?' Later, we see the consequence of this cavalier attitude: the one prostitute who does come to Frail is dying. Ahead of its time in stressing the prostitutes' presence in the camp, the film also refers to the dangers of their work: when Frenchy says to Frail 'You ain't doing the redhead any good, are you?' he replies, 'No, I guess nobody ever has'.

As Rune completes his tour of the township, the second of the film's villains makes an entrance. Grubb is a mad preacher, whose extraordinary rhetoric – 'If you bring your sick to the butcher doctor, they will die: his instruments are foul with sin' – suggests nothing so much as a throwback to the medieval. In the film's Freudian design, where Frenchy is ultimately revealed to be an id-villain, so Grubb is essentially a superego-villain, wishing to seek out and punish what he considers to be 'sin'. (At the film's climax he frenziedly torches the prostitutes' tents.) Exemplifying the 'corruption' commonly associated with mining towns, which I mentioned in relation to *The Badlanders*, Grubb may be seen as a mining-camp perversion of a pastor. Exposing Grubb as a whisky drinker, Frail drives him away, firing at his feet as he flees in order to scare him. This aggression indicates unease, as though Grubb, for all his apparent lunacy, is nevertheless a genuine threat to Frail – a threat that is later chillingly fulfilled.

About twenty minutes into the film, Daves shows a stagecoach being held up. In a rapid series of shots – six in ten seconds – we see a highly impressionistic staging of the hold-up: the robber drawing his gun and shooting, the coach horses rearing frantically, a man falling forward as he's shot, a woman behind him screaming as the horses panic and race away. The woman is Elizabeth Mahler (Maria Schell) and the man her father. Daves stages the hold-up in this elliptical manner to suggest her subjective experience: the incident – in which her father is killed – becomes her traumatic event, which she relives in feverish nightmares for some time afterwards. The panicking horses catapult the coach down a hillside, and it is three days before the alarm is raised and even longer before Elizabeth is found (by an excited Frenchy). By this stage, she is suffering from severe sunburn and is temporarily blind. As she will require a long period of recuperation, Frail and Rune move her into a cabin adjacent to theirs.

As Elizabeth is being brought by wagon into the town, Grubb accosts Rune: 'I hear tell she's a foreigner. Is she loose-virtued?' The accusation, and Rune's irate response – 'What does that mean? She's foreign, she's blind and she's burnt bad' – occur as they pass under the Hanging Tree, associating Grubb's thinking with the symbolism of the tree. Elizabeth's arrival also excites another element of the settlement community: the 'respectable ladies', led by Edna Flaunce (Virginia Gregg), the wife of store-owner Tom Flaunce (Karl Swenson). They take it upon themselves to visit in order to find out whether Elizabeth is, in Edna's words, 'decent'. Frail denies them this satisfaction, but their division of women into the decent and the fallen is but a bourgeois version of Grubb's warped fundamentalism. Both ideologies would support the view that a hanging tree could act as a guarantee of respectability.

Elizabeth slowly recovers, but remains blindfolded whilst her eyes heal. During this, Daves uses an eloquent metaphor: Frail calling for Rune to bring the lamp so that he can see Elizabeth more clearly. Three times he does this, each time marking a step in

her recovery and culminating in the scene in which the bandages on her eyes are removed and she sees the lamplight indistinctly, as in a fog. The feeling created by these moments is of a protective concern: just as Frail is causing a physical light to be brought to her, so he is overseeing the restoration of her sight, her own light.

As a doctor, Frail – as here – is shown to be both expert and caring. But, as a man, he is hard and uncompromising. Chafing under his harsh regime, Rune begins to agree with Grubb: 'If you ain't the Devil, he's sure sitting on your shoulder.' On this, Daves cuts to a close-up of Frail, tensely lighting a cigar, in which he looks remarkably demonic. But the film makes it clear that Frail's displays of toughness are bound up with a combination of guilt and defensiveness at his violent past. When Society Red (John Dierkes), resentful at having lost his gold claim to Frail in a poker game, refers to this past, Frail knocks him to the ground. Mike Wallington (1969, pp.6-7) points out that many of Daves's heroes 'have a past they are trying to come to terms with': Cochise, Johnny MacKay, Comanche Todd, Jubal. But Frail is the only figure who is himself responsible for the violence of that past, and his difficulties in coming to terms with it are thus correspondingly more acute.

During Elizabeth's period of recuperation, Frail seeks to discourage her from wanting to stay in Skull Creek by telling her what she will see when she recovers her sight: 'A crawling ant hill that can blow away with the first wind from the next strike; and

you'll see some of the scum of the world.' The anthill metaphor is a description of the way the camp looks from Frail's vantage point on the hill: it is an image generated by his own self-imposed detachment from the community. But his assessment is to an extent supported by the film, as the opening pursuit of Rune makes clear. Frail also feels that he belongs in such a community: when Elizabeth asks 'Why are you here, then – and Rune?' he replies 'Maybe we belong here.' Living in a mining camp, with 'some of the scum of the world', is a kind of penance. But, at the same time, Frail's own aloofness from the community causes resentment: the hostility with which he is viewed is partly a product of his own attitude.

This is illustrated by an incident in which Frail is gambling in the saloon, and Frenchy, refused by a prostitute on the grounds that she does not give credit, goes to Elizabeth's cabin and voyeuristically spies on her. Alone inside, still blindfolded, she is feeling her way around cautiously; she lights the lamp – a re-use of the motif that almost painfully stresses her vulnerability. Cutting the cord to her signal bell – so that she cannot summon Rune – Frenchy persuades her to open the door. At first, seeking a grub-stake to enable him to dig for gold, he is ingratiating. But, when he discovers that she hasn't any money, he becomes openly lecherous, and Elizabeth is saved only by the timely return of Frail.

But Frail is not content simply to scare Frenchy off: again, assuming the role of a punitive superego figure, he pursues Frenchy back down to the saloon and beats him up. He tells Frenchy that he'll kill him if he finds him on the hill again. As he rides off, Grubb steps into the shot to repeat his warning: 'That butcher doctor is the Devil, and you must cast him out!' Society Red then expresses the point of view of the community: 'Looks like the Doc's gonna keep the little lady all to himself.' The sequence ends with Grubb, Frenchy and Society Red, their faces one behind the other in a tight close-up, watching Frail ride away. As Frenchy declares that one day Frail will 'get kicked back', he and Grubb exchange a look of mutual understanding. Clearly we are not meant to share the hostility towards Frail of these three, but we can see how his aggressiveness – which has now been directed at each of them – creates such an attitude.

Although Grubb's mad preacher is basically a stereotype, making much the same dark pronouncements on each appearance, Frenchy, superbly played by Karl Malden, is a far more interesting character. We have become accustomed, in Western villains, to predictability: they're mean, lecherous, vicious; they cheat, steal, murder (Liberty Valance may be taken as an archetypal example). Frenchy is more like a product of his environment: crude, dirty, uneducated, cunning, greedy, with the sort of 'base' sexual appetite that became commonplace in Westerns made after the end of the Production Code. When he finds the semi-conscious Elizabeth, he comments to the others: 'Ain't much left from the neck up, but she sure is all woman from there down.' Seeing, from their reaction, that he's said something inappropriate, he quickly responds: 'I was only trying to pay her a compliment – nothing wrong in that.' His crudeness is balanced by his naivety – he also takes a childlike delight in the way Elizabeth stubbornly clings to the canteen of water he has given her to drink. For all his baseness, Frenchy is a member of the mining community in a way that Frail is not. In the men's confrontation in the saloon, it is Frenchy – characterising Frail as possessive about Elizabeth – who gets the more sympathetic response from the customers.

When Frail arrives back on the hill, Rune accuses him of over-reacting to Frenchy's behaviour: 'She said he didn't do nothing to her.' Frail retorts 'I don't care. I don't want any of them near her.' Rune then draws a connection with Frail's past: 'You don't own her, Doc. Is that how it was before? You tried to own somebody until they hated you?' Frail's reaction – he almost strikes Rune – indicates that Rune is right. In effect, Frail is re-enacting in the present the tensions of his past: violence at any threat to a woman he considers is under his care; a need to control people by having power over them. There is no logical reason for his failure to treat Rune decently and, although Elizabeth does need protecting from men like Frenchy, what seems really to gall Frail is Frenchy's cutting the bell cord: a symbolic castration. Whereas, in *Jubal*, the events in the present which echo Jubal's past happen outside

the hero's control, Frail himself is here to a large extent the cause of the equivalent events.

When Frail removes Elizabeth's blindfold bandages, he cups her face in a gesture of tenderness. Responding, she says, 'I cannot see you yet, but I love you for everything.' It is the response of a grateful child to a protective father and, of course, Frail is like a father-figure to Elizabeth, directly replacing her own father. The parallels with Jubal, in which Shep saves Jubal and becomes his father-figure, apply to Elizabeth as well as to Rune. This helps clarify Frail's behaviour. In effect, the three of them form an embryonic family, which structurally replaces Frail's dead family, but in more explicitly oedipal terms. It's as if Frail dominates Rune in order to 'castrate' him (to repress his sexuality), the punishment he would have liked to inflict on his brother, and he is indeed successful in that Rune shows no sexual interest whatsoever in Elizabeth. But Frail's relationship with Elizabeth thus becomes overdetermined: she is a patient, a daughter-figure and a potential replacement for his dead wife. This mix is so potent that, as soon as Elizabeth really does recover her sight and makes advances to him, he pushes her away, trying to insist that she leave Skull Creek and return to Europe.

Elizabeth, however, refuses to be put off. She begins by defying Frail, saying that he will no longer tell her what to do, and that she's staying. Frail rationalises: 'In six weeks, this could be a ghost town, with no one here.' Elizabeth's response is almost epic: 'I'll be here. I'll plant ghost wheat and raise ghost cattle, and right here I'll build a ghost house.' Her declaration of independence is promptly followed by another from Rune, who is both confused and annoyed to find that Frail has not kept the incriminating bullet – his period of servitude was, strictly speaking, unnecessary. However, there has been a positive side to Frail's treatment of Rune. The tough older hero educating the callow youth is a familiar Western situation, but Rune has not been taught how to shoot (as he is in Johnson's story) but how to care for others, and one of the things he has learned is social responsibility. In effect, Frail has rehabilitated a surly outcast and given him an accepted place in the community.

Released from Frail, Elizabeth and Rune go to Tom Flaunce to raise money for a grub-stake. Although the jewellery Elizabeth produces as collateral is worthless, Frail tells Tom in private that he'll pay for whatever they need. This gesture could be seen as generous – it is not long before their bill exceeds $1,000 – but it is yet another of example of Frail seeking, however indirectly, to control the people he feels responsible for, like an overprotective father. Elizabeth and Rune then become partners with Frenchy, who has already picked out a likely spot to prospect. This unexpected teaming re-emphasises that Frenchy is not at all a conventional villain: in a montage sequence showing them building the mining works – the sluice and the box for the earth – Frenchy works just as hard as the others. The exuberance with which the three of them celebrate the first rush of water down the sluice also contrasts sharply with the tension and restraint of Rune's and Elizabeth's scenes with Frail.

But Frail is still an extremely potent figure in their lives, as is shown when, one day, he calls by. Although he stays only a minute and does not dismount, Elizabeth and Rune are so obviously pleased to see him ('We both miss you, doctor') that he passes through like a beloved father, a charismatic figure whose mixture of warmth and detached self-sufficiency tantalises those who love him. As he rides off, Daves cuts to a long shot looking down on the mine, showing the other three characters – Elizabeth bottom right, Rune up the hill top left, and Frenchy on the sluice-box between them – simply watching him, their lives strangely touched by his unexpected visit. Seeing his effect on Elizabeth and Rune, Frenchy becomes jealous and resentful, and is provoked into making a lecherous lunge at Elizabeth. She fends him off, but then, in a rare lapse from the characteristic toughness of Daves's pioneer women, she goes into her tent to cry. Frenchy thinks it's on his account ('I'm poison, eh?'), but it's clearly primarily a response to Frail's fleeting visit.

Shortly afterwards, Elizabeth is told by Mrs Flaunce that Frail has been providing for them all along: 'You've been kept, like any harlot.' This provokes Elizabeth to accuse Frail: 'It's very cruel the way you draw [people] to you and then turn them away if they get too close. Do you like to torture?' Her attack leads him to refer to his past, but only cryptically. He admits that the story told about him is true and says that the two people were his wife and his brother 'and I have no right to forget.' This is the first time he has said anything about his past, and Elizabeth asks, 'You want to tell me why?' It is a moment which offers the chance of genuine communication, but Frail refuses it. He is still emotionally frozen.

Throughout the 'fifties, Cooper often played men who were aloof and inflexible. It was *Man of the West* (Anthony Mann, 1958) which introduced psychological depth to this, relating it to a past in which Link (Cooper) had been a badman. *The Hanging Tree* and *They Came to Cordura* (Robert Rossen, 1959) followed suit: in all three films, Cooper's hero is given a past (cowardice in *They Came to Cordura*) which he must deal with in order to achieve release from his demons, the violence of this experience being a measure of the grip of the past.

In *The Hanging Tree*, the relevant sequence of events begins with Elizabeth, Rune and Frenchy striking gold: a large tree blows down in a storm and its roots are filled with nuggets. This introduction of a second tree extends the film's symbolic system. Located in the valley, this tree releases the gold which in turn releases the forces of chaos/the id. Back at Skull Creek, Frenchy treats the miners to whisky and, whilst he cleans himself up, encourages them to start a bonfire to celebrate. With the men becoming increasingly drunk, it is only a matter of time before the fire spreads, and the sober citizens, led by the Flaunces, are obliged to form a 'bucket brigade' to try to put it out.

Learning that Frail is out of town, the newly groomed Frenchy seizes his chance. Whilst Society Red and other men hold Rune down, Frenchy goes to Elizabeth's cabin. As she tries desperately to fight him off, Daves cuts to the township below, where Grubb is wildly setting fire to the prostitutes' tents crying 'Put a torch to the butcher doctor's house!' At this point, with each villain melodramatically acting out his Freudian role in the film's schema, Frail returns to town. With the raging fires below and the threatened rape above, he is confronted with a displaced version of his past traumatic event, in which Grubb is like a superego return of the repressed, re-enacting Frail's virulent impulse to burn down his own home.

Frail enters Elizabeth's cabin just as Frenchy is about to rape her and hurls him down the stairs. Frenchy then fires at Frail, provoking the latter into a merciless killing, firing shot after shot into Frenchy, who stumbles out of the cabin and down to the cliff edge. Frail kicks the lifeless body on to the rocks below, symbolically returning Frenchy to the depths. This scene has been witnessed by the drunks who followed Frenchy and Grubb up the hill and, under Grubb's orders, they turn instantly into a lynch mob, dragging Frail up to the Hanging Tree and placing him on the back of a wagon with the noose around his neck. There is no discussion as to the legitimacy of this action; the men are simply out for blood. Throughout this, Frail is entirely passive, and we can see that he submits to his punishment not through guilt at killing Frenchy, but through guilt at his past.

The tree in the valley was uprooted immediately after Frenchy's gloomy comment that the nuggets they had so far found were 'probably left by that flood in the Bible'. Since the invocation of the Old Testament seemed to trigger the tree's fall, it is as if God were responsible for releasing the gold and hence the forces of chaos. And now, as Frail is about to be hanged, the Old Testament is again invoked. Just before he releases the horses to pull away the wagon, Grubb quotes Genesis: 'Whoso sheddeth man's blood, by man shall his blood be shed'. Again – as in *The Last Wagon* – one senses a strong anti-Christian bias.

Frail is saved by the arrival of Elizabeth and Rune who, with increasing desperation, offer first all their gold and then their claim for Frail's release. Just as rapidly, the crowd swings in a new direction, grabbing for the gold pouring from the sacks, frenziedly grasping after the claim paper as it blows in the wind. Rune releases the rope from Frail's neck; Elizabeth joins him at the wagon. The camera cranes back on a tableau of the three of them, Rune slumped in the wagon, Frail bending down and embracing Elizabeth.

From one point of view, this climax produces a profoundly cathartic ending. The lynch mob recalls the one from which Frail saved Rune at the beginning, but here it acts as an embodiment of the self-destructive forces within Frail himself, gaining power from his internalised guilt. The crowd itself – that dangerously volatile formation brilliantly analysed by Elias Canetti in *Crowds and Power* (Penguin, Harmondsworth, 1973) – expresses, too, the collective

Still: The Hanging Tree – *Rune and Elizabeth offer their gold to save Frail from hanging.*

thinking of the whole community, as it switches, almost without pause, from blood lust to gold lust. Once again, Daves presents a deeply pessimistic portrait of White pioneer society.

From another point of view, the ending is uneasy. As so often in Daves's Westerns, it celebrates the union of a hero and heroine who have no future in the film's community. But crucially, we do not see them leave. The posed look of the tableau – to say nothing of the unfortunate use of Marty Robbins's ballad – suggests an attempt to freeze the action in an imposition of closure. But the Hanging Tree still stands (contrast the ending of *Ride Lonesome*, Budd Boetticher, 1959), Rune looks out of place, and the embrace of hero and heroine is awkward: Frail, like Rune, is still on the wagon: Elizabeth is standing beside it. Both are now wearing black, as if Elizabeth has joined Frail in his mourning, and the noose hangs ominously over all three of them. Visually the shot is superb, but it contains significant unresolved tensions.

The Hanging Tree is, nevertheless, the most complex and moving of Daves's Westerns, its resonances and beauties becoming more apparent on each viewing. The crane shots which became intrusive in Daves's 'sixties melodramas are here integrated into a supple, flowing *mise-en-scène*: the camera is constantly mobile, constantly seeking fresh perspectives. At the same time, whether in the mountain landscapes or the cluttered interiors, the film's imagery is invariably governed by Daves's strong sense of composition. His final Western, *The Hanging Tree*, stands as a superb summation of his work in the genre.

A point often made about Daves's Westerns is that, unlike Anthony Mann's or Budd Boetticher's, they are all so different that they are difficult to talk about collectively. But the fact that they may be grouped together points to the presence of common themes, and it is not difficult to isolate a fairly coherent set of positions. All the Indian movies deal to a greater or lesser extent with the issue of racism, and their shifting perspectives may be seen as a reflection of political currents of the 'fifties.

The first three Indian movies blend carefully researched historical events in the pacification of the Native American tribes with mythical material relating to Fiedler's notion of the bonding of the White man and the Indian in the wilderness. This dialectical play between history and myth is, of course, a feature of many Westerns, but Daves's comments on his films tend to emphasise single strands of intention, particularly historical authenticity and 'realism'. The effect is to underplay the mythic power of the Western tradition and the complexities that characterise his work. At times, these can be identified only as sub-texts which underly the films' more explicit concerns and which develop perspectives on generic themes such as those discussed by Leslie Fiedler. But, more consistently, the view of White settlement that Daves's Westerns imply is a bleak one.

Jubal and *The Hanging Tree* are the films that are centrally about Western communities, and it is striking how critically Daves views them. Lacking representatives of law and order, the communities become volatile and prone to violence, which is shown in particular in the transformation of solid

citizens into a lynch mob, a motif seen as early as *Broken Arrow*. (Actual or potential hangings occur in every Daves Western except *White Feather* and *The Badlanders*.) The traditional one-street Western town, with its familiar parade of buildings, made only one appearance in Daves's Westerns, when the set from *The Ox-Bow Incident* was recast as Tucson in *Broken Arrow*. After that, Daves evidently ensured that his settlements conformed to a less stereotyped format, and his townships are notable for the absence of those familiar icons of civilisation, church and school. The absence is symptomatic. Whatever hope for the central characters may attach to the films' endings is set against the background of a society that offers no positive basis for communal life.

Still: The Hanging Tree – *the final embrace.*

A TIME AND A PLACE
Budd Boetticher and the Western

Mike Dibb

My encounter with Budd Boetticher's films involves two times and two places, separated by more than thirty years. The first time was 1960 and the place was Trinity College, Dublin; the second was 1992 and the place was Lone Pine, California. In the meantime, I have learnt how to pronounce his name correctly – Be-ti-ker – and have met and talked with the man himself at his home near San Diego. These personal details are important. Too often we like to discuss movies, or for that matter books and paintings, as if they exist out there with a value and a meaning that can be disentangled from all the connecting tissue of thoughts, feelings and personal circumstance that surround our engagement with them.

1960 was the year in which I discovered American cinema, or rather discovered that I could take it seriously as well as enjoy it. This was just before television took over, when Dublin allegedly had the highest per-capita rate of cinema-going in Western Europe. Every cinema had a double bill that changed three times a week. I was introduced to *Cahiers du Cinéma*, which was heavily into *auteur* theory and American movies. 'King Arthur' was the emphatic title of Jean-Luc Godard's revue of Arthur Penn's *The Left-Handed Gun* – heady stuff and a lot more interesting than my academic studies. My most important acquisition, however, was a copy of *Vingt Ans du Cinéma Américain*, edited by Bertrand Tavernier. It was brought over from Paris by a friend and, as we scanned the Dublin evening papers together, it seemed that almost every Hollywood movie mentioned was in continuous circulation.

I had been seeing Hollywood movies every week of my life since the age of eight. As a family we went to the cinema regularly and my father, being a systematic man, kept a little book with a list of films to look out for, based on the reviews of *The Observer* film critic, C.A. Lejeune. She was, I seem to remember, rather patronising about Westerns unless they were obviously presented as 'significant', which often turned out to mean portentous; the rest went into the category of 'horse operas', a term which now, when separated from C.A. Le J.'s dismissive connotations, I rather like. It emphasises the horse as the lyrical centre of the Western; it also underlines the importance and pleasure of encountering again and again the Western's particular mythology and stylised forms of presentation: of action, character, speech, violence and, not least, music, so often neglected but always so potent. And this is where Budd Boetticher comes in. I cannot think of another director whose films take the simplest and most archetypal conventions of the genre and rearrange them in such a playful, intelligent and unpatronising way.

The first two films I saw were *Comanche Station* (1960) and *Ride Lonesome* (1959), two of the four films (*Seven Men from Now*, 1956, and *The Tall T*, 1957, were the others), that Boetticher made in collaboration with the writer Burt Kennedy, actor Randolph Scott, producer Harry Joe Brown and, as I now realise, the landscape of Lone Pine. Together these films form a unique quartet, a set of themes and variations on roughly the same story and with roughly the same number of characters, made within a four-year period from 1956 to 1960, and all of them shot in the same place. This quartet has a unity that sets it apart from Boetticher's other work, and these are the only films of his to which I want to refer.

Of course, when I see them again today I see them differently. I first watched them on a wide screen in a big cinema; indeed I was introduced to Boetticher's films by Charles Barr, who at that time was preparing a postgraduate thesis on CinemaScope. Nowadays, apart from very occasional outings at specialist cinemas and festivals, the films turn up at odd times on television, which is where I have had to catch up with them, unsatisfactorily scanned and visually diminished to fit the small rectangular format.

I have now visited the location where all four films were made, and I realise how important it was. Lone Pine is a small, two-motel town in northern California, a three- to four-hour drive from Los Angeles. Nearby, in the few square miles between Lone Pine and the road up to Mount Whitney, is an unusual outcrop of boulders and canyons called the Alabama Hills. For over seventy years, it has been one of Hollywood's favourite locations, and several hundred films have been made there. From time to time, this landscape has stood in for India, Texas, Mexico, Peru and Argentina. But ever since the first silent film crews went there in the 1920s, it has been used as a location for Westerns, from small-scale series like *The Lone Ranger* to the massive *How the West Was Won*. Tom Mix, William Boyd, Gene Autry, Roy Rogers, Tim Holt, John Wayne and Clint Eastwood are a few of the many male heroes who have galloped to the rescue around the same rocks.

Lone Pine is a magical place, at once both intimate and epic. Significantly, the only way to traverse it is on foot or by horse. In the daytime, under a hot sun, it seems to present itself as a natural location in

which to tell a story, and what better story than a Western. In the evening, it takes on another kind of mystery. You can walk across the rocks by moonlight without the aid of a torch and, as you do so, feel yourself part of a day-for-night sequence.

It is also a wonderfully economical location, the perfect place for tight schedules and small budgets. You can put a tripod almost anywhere and, spinning the camera through 360 degrees, pick up a variety of different shots, each beautifully lit, particularly in the early morning or late afternoon. No wonder so many people came. But, for me, no-one before or since has exploited the dramatic potential of this place more lyrically and effectively than Budd Boetticher and his various cameramen. His are the quintessential films about being in Lone Pine. The fact that so many people had been there before was in a sense a help. The place is alive with the sounds and memories of drifting cowboys, laconic dialogue, galloping posses, gunshots, campfires, stagecoaches and hold-ups. There is an early exchange in *Ride Lonesome* which seems to me to speak both for the characters and the filmmakers: 'A man needs a reason to ride this country – You gotta reason? – Seemed like a good idea.'

Because Lone Pine is a place where so many of the stereotypical images of the Western have been located, it became for Boetticher and his writing collaborator Burt Kennedy the perfect place in which to rework the conventions of the genre in a playful and imaginative way. Randolph Scott's expressively inexpressive face echoed the stones. He and his horse could emerge out of this landscape at the start of the film and return back into it at the end. In *Comanche Station*, the last of the cycle and I think formally the

Stills. Above – Jefferson Cody (Randolph Scott) in Comanche Station. *Opposite –* Ride Lonesome: *top, Ben Brigade (Scott) and Billy John (James Best); bottom, the hanging tree.*

best, this happens within exactly the same frame of the Alabama Hills against a backdrop of Mount Whitney. Scott enters right to left at the beginning and exits left to right at the end – at once both economical and elegant. As Budd himself confirmed when I met him: 'The great thing about Lone Pine is that you don't need to go anywhere else . . . we had sand, desert, a river, mountains, all the volcanic structures, it's amazing – it looks like it was built there for movies . . . Burt Kennedy and I just went from one place to another rewriting scenes to fit the rocks which is what you should do.'

The beginning of *Comanche Station* is also a very good reminder of how much happens visually within these films. Nothing is said for several minutes and when the dialogue comes, it is sparse, even a little familiar: 'Alright, Lady, What's your name? – Nancy Lowe – I should'a known – Why d'ya come? – Seemed like a good idea.' Seeing any one of these films reminds you of the others. For instance, some scenes seem almost interchangeable, odd lines of dialogue get repeated; what looks like the hanging tree from *Ride Lonesome* turns up in the middle of the river in *Comanche Station*. But, in the case of these four films familiarity elicits pleasure rather than contempt – indeed it is often one of the mainsprings of the humour. Burt Kennedy obviously enjoys the use of conversational patterns, in which certain words and phrases are repeated almost like rhyme: 'Like you, for instance? – Like me, in particular . . . Sure

hope I amount to something. – Yeah, sure was a shame. – Shame? – Shame that my pa didn't amount to anything.' He also likes the familiar archaisms of Western speech, so of course all the women – there is only one in each film – are referred to as 'Ma'am', people are always 'obliged' to each other, and everything that Scott plans he 'full intends to do'.

The films consist of alternating scenes of action and dialogue, movement and repose. Boetticher loves horses, and much of the lyricism of the films comes from his pleasure in the rhythms of riding through varieties of landscape. Almost everything happens in the open air. An isolated swing station or a cave in the rocks is the closest we get to a social space; elsewhere it is the campfire and the coffee pot (indeed it confirms the general truth that in the Western the cup of coffee is as important a focus of social interaction as the cup of tea in British cinema). Boetticher also loves the rhythms of speech and elicits vivid performances from his actors. The lines

163

Still, above: Brigade and Carrie (Karen Steele) in
Ride Lonesome. *Photograph, opposite: John Wayne
visits Scott and Boetticher during the shooting of* Seven
Men from Now.

are as well choreographed as the action, to bring out
every nuance of irony and humour.' The villains
were the stars in my films', said Budd. 'They stole
every film they were in.' In fact, having found so
many good new actors is one of the things of which
he is most proud. Lee Marvin, Richard Boone,
Henry Silva, Craig Stevens, Richard Rust, James
Best, Claude Akins and James Coburn all cut their
teeth in his films, and were often given their opportunity to shine through the generosity of Randolph
Scott. He was the still centre around which the may-
hem revolved. 'Every picture he would let the villain
upstage him!' Boetticher told me, adding that when
James Coburn made his first appearance in *Ride
Lonesome*, Scott was so impressed that he insisted
on more scenes being written for him, and these
became some of the best and funniest in the film.

'Young . . . mostly' is the characteristic reply of
one Young Gun when asked his age. There is always
a pair of Young-mostly Guns in each film, social
orphans with 'no folks, no schoolin' ', who dream
of amounting to something and are often surprised
by emotion: 'One day I'm going to get me some
land, and I'm going to have pigs, cattle and chickens,
and I'm going to be a farmer . . . and do all the
things I've ever wanted to do and you know something? We're going to be partners right down the
middle – We are? – Yeah . . . Jim, how long have
you and I been riding together? – Four years maybe?
– More like seven . . . don't you know that I like

you? – No, I never knew that!' They are also surprised by each other's achievements: 'I didn't know
you could read, Dobie – Well, Frank, I ain't much
with books and newspapers but plain words, y'know,
like signs, wrappers and such I do pretty good!' Always, they are attached to and dependent on a no-
good but charming father figure, who they begin to
mistrust, rightly as it turns out, as they always die.
Death is the risk that everyone takes in a world where
cowardice and shooting someone in the back are
the worst crimes; but death is always quick, and there
is rarely much blood.

Boetticher is clearly not much interested in history
or communities. His world is a long way from John
Ford's and closer to but less rugged and complex
than that of Anthony Mann. For Boetticher, the
Western is perfect as a terrain for fables, preferably
set in a landscape that is everywhere and nowhere,
'Once upon a time there was a man . . .' He shows
no moral or sociological concern for the historical
roots of the conflicts between the indigenous Indians
and the White settlers. Indians are not individualised,
rather seen as an abstract threat, just another problem to be overcome or another way to lose your life.
In this cycle of films, everyone is a loner, and the
Randolph Scott character is the loneliest of all. The
difference is that his loneliness is chosen; he is a man
with a mission, albeit a private one, morally ambiguous and often wrongly bent on vengeance; he
is driven 'to do what a man has to do', but is pretty
pessimistic about the outcome. He is opposed by a
man of the same age who is is alone because he has
stepped outside the law. The two always seem to
know each other from the past and know more about
the other than each would like. This can become

the pivot for simple moral dialogues on the ironies of fate and also the trigger for much of the action as each tries to out-manoeuvre the other.

The other trigger for the action is, of course, the fate of the woman. In these very male films, and in common with most Westerns, there is absolutely no risk of political correctness, and stereotypes abound. Whereas, 'A man does one thing in his life he can be proud . . . a woman should cook good.' Women are the objects of unconsummated desire, but beyond that a bit of a mystery: 'The way I look at it a woman's a woman, ain't that right Frank? – If you say so!' Boetticher's interest in Spanish/Mexican culture expresses itself throughout his films, not least in the way women are seen. His values grow out of the cultural tradition in which the male code of honour is a driving force and from which Don Juan was born. As he said of himself: 'I was the worst macho in the world but I hate the word.' His films are directed with the puritanism of the hellraiser; a cleavage, a torn blouse, a discreet wash in a river and a rare kiss are the nearest one gets to explicit sex. On the surface, women may appear to have a central importance: they are dreamed about, desired, even fought over but . . . they are never seen for themselves. They are really just tokens in what are always struggles between men.

Another key Hispanic influence is the bullfight, an activity whose meaning is also defined, like the Western, by shared rituals and codes of behaviour. As a young man, Boetticher was also a boxer and athlete. In all these activities, professionalism is essential to a sense of self worth, any visible hint of cowardice is unacceptable, everything must be accomplished with dignity and grace. These are the virile attitudes and moral values which pass seamlessly and effectively from the closed world of Budd's sporting arenas to the closed world of his Westerns. They are the attitudes that still sustain his lifestyle.

When I went to see him, we met in the stables of his small ranch near San Diego. On the wall were stills from some of his films alongside photographs of his bullfighting friends. Together with his wife, he rears a rare breed of Portuguese horses, which are powerful and beautiful. Nearby he has a small arena with a half-moon, colonnaded stand of seating forming a miniature bull ring in which he can train and ride his horses. Despite his age, Boetticher is still a strong man, which obviously matters to him. As I watched him interacting with his horses, I could feel the existential pleasure which this kind of activity gives him. I was also very much reminded of the horse-roping and bull-riding scene in *The Tall T* in which Randolph Scott's ageing virility is put to the test. Like all physical and sporting rituals, the contest can seem at one level pointless, even faintly ridiculous. On the other hand, at its best, it can be significant and thrilling.

I can never recover the excitement of first seeing these Boetticher Westerns. Watching them again, I find them thinner than they seemed then, and some of the stereotypes are not entirely redeemed by irony and humour. But, having now encountered the generous energy of the man and visited Lone Pine, I

feel I understand the source of their vitality. In a very particular way, the films are a direct expression of the strengths and limitations of the men who made them. The camaraderie and humour involved in their making still comes through in the playing. And throughout all four films, there is always the landscape around Lone Pine, effortlessly photogenic, skilfully deployed without a hint of self-conscious artifice.

It also seems to me that the time when this quartet was made is important. In the late 'fifties, it was still possible to make this kind of small-scale independent film. Very soon, television was going to change the landscape of cinema, and very soon the Western itself was going to be in trouble, torn between the twin stools of too great a naivety and an over-aware sophistication. Budd Boetticher and his team arrived just in time to manage this balancing act pretty well . . . or pretty well, mostly.

In 1957, having just seen *Seven Men from Now,* the great French critic André Bazin wrote the first and still possibly the best piece about Budd Boetticher and, as he had the first word, it is perhaps appropriate for him to have the last: 'The fundamental problem of the contemporary Western springs without doubt from the dilemma of intelligence and innocence . . . [In *Seven Men from Now*] there are no symbols, no philosophical implications, not a shadow

Still: Seven Men from Now – *Ben Stride (Randolph Scott) with Annie (Gail Russell) and John Greer (Walter Reed) in the Alabama Hills.*

of psychology, nothing but ultra conventional characters engaged in exceedingly familiar acts, but placed in their setting in an extraordinarily ingenious way, with a use of detail which renders every scene interesting . . . even more than the inventiveness which thought up the twists in the plot, I admire the humour with which everything is treated . . . the irony does not diminish the characters, but it allows their naivety and the director's intelligence to co-exist without tension. For it is indeed the most intelligent Western I know while being the least intellectual, the most subtle and the least aestheticising.'

It is very perceptive, an exemplary piece of film writing. What Bazin wrote about *Seven Men from Now* applies to the other three films that followed it. Bazin also understood how, in a genre of filmmaking that is as full of conventional stereotypes and narrative devices as the Western, freshness and originality often come from imaginative reworking and respect for the familiar. He also understood, in a way that some of his fellow writers at the time did not, that authorship is a collective enterprise. Boetticher's Ranown cycle owes a great deal of its success to the fact that it was one of those rare moments when the right group of people managed to come together at the right time and place. The ground rules were set but, exploiting rather than resisting the limitations, Budd and Co found an unusual degree of harmony and freedom. And in Lone Pine's Alabama Hills they found the perfect setting in which to invent and improvise their short series of four memorable chamber Westerns.

THE COLLAPSE OF FANTASY
Masculinity in the Westerns of Anthony Mann

Douglas Pye

Anthony Mann's last great Western, *Man of the West* (1958), opens with a credit sequence which almost archetypally invokes one of the central images of the tradition, the lone horseman in a Western landscape. The credits announce 'Gary Cooper', 'Man of the West', and successive shots bring the rider closer: a man clearly in repose, at ease in the saddle, solitary and self-contained. It seems effortlessly to conjure up the whole tradition in which the fantasy of such a figure is pivotal.

In immediate contrast, the first post-credit sequence presents a bustling Western town into which Cooper rides and here Mann draws on other aspects of Cooper's persona: he is affable, helpful, hesitant, but apparently slightly ill at ease, out of place, in town. As he prepares for a train journey, he changes his clothes and packs his guns into a carpet bag. He is comically terrified of the train and fits with great difficulty into the cramped seats. We learn that he

has been sent by the people of his settlement to hire a schoolteacher. Within a short time, the train has been attacked and Cooper is left by the trackside with two companions as the train disappears. Now a third persona gradually appears. Approaching the apparently abandoned farm where they will seek shelter, he takes off his coat and tie, returning to the more familiar appearance of the Westerner, and we soon learn that he was once a member of the murderous Tobin gang.

This juxtaposition of images of the hero is unusually extreme and implicitly poses one of the film's central questions – what is the relationship between these versions of the same man? How are the archetypal Westerner, the hick and the ex-outlaw

Still: Man of the West – *Link Jones (Gary Cooper), Sam Beasley (Arthur O'Connell) and Billie Ellis (Julie London) left by the train.*

connected? This is perhaps the most schematic representation of a concern with the nature and identity of the Western hero that runs right through Mann's Westerns and particularly, in addition to *Man of the West*, the five extraordinary films starring James Stewart, a collaboration between director and star comparable in achievement to Stewart's films with Hitchcock during the same period. In fact, to borrow something Andrew Britton has suggested about Hitchcock, we need to see these films both as popular narratives and as being about the conventions of such narratives. Like Hitchcock, in exploring the identity of the familiar action hero, Mann also analyses and problematises assumptions about masculinity which are inherent in popular genres, developing, as he does so, a substantial critique of central aspects of the traditional Western.

It is striking how little the Western has been discussed in these terms. This may be a symptom of the wider phenomenon of the genre having been consigned to the critical back-burner in recent years after being central to genre studies from, roughly, the mid 'sixties to the mid 'seventies. Other genres – notably melodrama and *film noir* – have become the focus of study in terms of gender and representation – work that has changed the face of film theory and criticism. Even the continuing strand of work on the Western has had little to say about gender, with the exception of one or two writers including Steve Neale and more recently, Martin Pumphrey, whose splendidly titled article, 'Why Do Cowboys Wear Hats in the Bath?' (reprinted in this book), provided the impetus for my own rescanning of the field. One effect has been that the Western seems like another country in genre criticism, barely integrated into wider discussions of representation in 'forties and 'fifties Hollywood. To give one symptomatic example: Joan Mellen's feminist survey of masculinity in American film, *Big Bad Wolves* (Elm Tree Books, London, 1978), refers to a few high-profile Westerns of the 1950s but contains not a single reference to Anthony Mann.

In studies of the Western itself, Mann has long been seen as central to the new inflections of the genre that characterised the post-war period – the 'superwestern', 'adult' or 'psychological' Western which was variously celebrated or criticised for bringing new social and psychological aspects to the old formula. These were often films with more problematic heroes and more critical attitudes to American civilisation than had been common. It was a period which John Cawelti (1976, p.247) describes as shifting the genre from the myth of foundation to a concern with social transition, the passing of the Old West into modern society and the Western hero's increasingly complex and ambiguous relationship to that process.

These are very much Mann's concerns. There is a familiar and, to an extent, justified tendency to characterise his handling of the Western as 'mythic' and 'archetypal' and to see the heroes as over-reachers, finally 'brought low', as Jim Kitses suggests (Kitses, 1969, p.35 – Kitses's account of Mann's films remains indispensable but appeared before

issues of gender and representation had become central to genre study). But recurrently those tendencies and that motif are mapped on to a narrative in which social change is taking place rapidly and the old frontier days are passing or have passed. Particularly clear in the films entirely scripted by Borden Chase, *Bend of the River* (1952) and *The Far Country* (1955), but also elsewhere, as in *Man of the West*, is a sense of 'stages of society' (from the most primitive to the much more advanced) rapidly succeeding each other. These are aspects of the films that Kitses associates with the writer Borden Chase and plays down his reading of Mann's central concerns (Kitses, 1969, p.52). They seem to me to have a much greater significance than Kitses allows them. Indeed, the films take on the implications of social change for the Western hero to a much greater extent than most others of the period.

The Far Country is in some ways the clearest, most schematic, treatment of these issues. The film begins in Seattle in 1896 – on the north-western seaboard and at the very end of the familiar historical period of the Western. The action moves with Jeff (James Stewart) north to the gold fields and out of the United States. Jeff is constantly reminded by his partner, Ben (Walter Brennan), of the farm in Utah they have agreed to buy together but he is determined to push on from the disappearing frontier of westward expansion, to look for new frontiers, even beyond the United States.

Jeff's movement is in line with the traditional motif of the hero's escape West at the end of Western narratives, but the film develops that movement to

Still: The Far Country – *Ben (Walter Brennan) and Jeff (James Stewart) in the gold fields.*

its logical conclusion. Dawson, the location of the gold camp, is geographically a cul-de-sac, with only one way in and out – Two Mile Pass, where gold miners are ambushed and murdered as the forces of corruption follow the discovery of gold. Jeff stands by while the gold camp is taken over and his unshakeable refusal to acknowledge any human responsibility becomes increasingly disturbing, its perversity underlined by his commitment to Ben. Characteristically, he searches for another way out of Dawson to avoid the pass – continuing to look for ways of evading both social obligation and confrontation. But as he and Ben launch the raft that Jeff believes will enable him to escape by river, they are attacked. Jeff is wounded and Ben killed.

In its context, the implications of the shooting in relation to Jeff's insistence on not getting involved seem paradoxical. On the one hand, the attack seems to confirm Jeff's aspiration to isolation and emotional invulnerability: if it hadn't been for Ben, who inadvertently gave away their escape plan, Jeff would have got away. On the other hand, with Jeff's commitment to Ben having been made so clear in the film, the shooting emphasises the perversity and destructiveness – finally the sheer impossibility – of his denial of human contact. The hero has reached a dead end at several levels. The geography dramatises both the cul-de-sac in which the character finds himself and Mann's analysis of the situation of the Western hero. The social/historical dimensions of the film give the drama of the hero a significant context in the end of the traditional frontier and the remorseless social process in which the cooperative individual enterprise of the original Dawson community is overrun by corrupt exploitation of the law and ruthless entrepreneurial capitalism. 'The blessings of civilisation' from which Doc Boone (Thomas Mitchell) helps to save Dallas (Claire Trevor) and Ringo (John Wayne) at the end of John Ford's *Stagecoach* (1939) will inevitably eradicate the positive but defenceless values of pioneer communities. The hero's dead-end is personal and historical: the possibilities of the unexplored West are no longer imaginatively available.

The end of the film, when Jeff has acted against the villains, seems to have saved the 'nice people' and be poised to settle, stands in apparent tension with that gloomy scenario, but it has its own complexities and I will return to it in relation to other endings. For the moment, I want to stress the film's analysis of the essentially untenable position of its hero. Jeff repeatedly asserts a kind of transcendence, but the transcendence available for heroes in earlier forms of the genre, of confident action and perfected moral identity, is precisely what Mann denies.

We might briefly juxtapose what Mann is doing here with John Ford's *My Darling Clementine* (1946), in which Ford is still able (just!) to dramatise both a serene hero who internalises the wilderness/civilisation opposition without apparent strain *and* an affirmative vision of a new, lovely American civilisation growing in the West, made possible by the hero's action. But with characteristic complexity (*see* 'Genre and History' in this book), Ford achieves

these affirmative elements with some strain in the film as a whole, by, for instance, killing off the threats to the emergent community and, more significantly for this context, by displacing the more problematic divisions between wilderness and civilisation from Wyatt (Henry Fonda) on to Doc Holliday (Victor Mature), who is also among the characters finally killed. Tellingly, Doc also becomes the focus for the attention of the two traditional and opposed women, the bar girl, Chihuahua (Linda Darnell), and Eastern lady, Clementine Carter (Cathy Downs), who has come from the East to reclaim Doc.

In Mann's films, the contradictions that Ford displaces on to Doc Holliday are focused on the hero himself and become dramatised very intensely as a psychic split that is impossible to resolve. The terms of that division are essentially traditional. They are presented as competing images of masculinity: on one hand, the claims of settlement, civilisation and social responsibility, and on the other of wandering, wilderness and independence. These are of course obsessive oppositions that are endlessly recycled in American culture and have produced familiar conventions of character and situation. In an account of how genre films negotiate such contradictions, Robin Wood wittily sums up the familiar types and the dilemmas they implicitly dramatise:

'The ideal male: the virile adventurer, the potent, untrammelled man of action.

The ideal female: wife and mother, perfect companion, the endlessly dependable mainstay of heart and home.

Since these combine into a couple of quite staggering incompatibility, each has his or her shadow.

The settled husband/father, dependable but dull.

The erotic woman/adventuress, gambling lady, saloon "entertainer"/fascinating but dangerous, liable to betray the hero or turn into a black panther' ('Ideology, Genre, Auteur', *Film Comment*, vol.13, no.3, January/February 1977, reprinted in *Film Genre Reader*, ed. Barry K. Grant, University of Texas Press, 1977).

In terms of masculinity, the implicit debate is clear: can a man be a man *and* settled? Or, as Martin Pumphrey puts it, 'How far can masculinity survive contact with the feminine sphere?' (entry on Masculinity in Buscombe, 1988). Ford's Doc Holliday points to one inflection of the dilemma – the self-destructive, corrosive impact of the division if it is internalised. The impossibility of resolution is rooted in a fantasy of male independence which seeks to deny the fear of impotence that haunts the hero threatened by marriage. Mann's films are still gripped by the power of that fantasy but its implications are exposed with remarkable clarity and intensity.

In principle, the situation of the hero would suggest that a choice is available: for instance, as in *Bend of the River*, to settle and become a farmer, or, as in *The Far Country*, to refuse that option. In many versions of the Western, the hero makes such a choice, and either rides on as the film ends, or is poised to become settled. The contradictions inherent in the hero's position are in effect papered over. But in Mann, not only does choice hardly seem an appropriate word to use, but each of the apparent options is presented in ways that undercut any residual positive connotations the genre might allow.

Life outside settlement is presented recurrently as negative in the extreme. Jeff's drive for independence in *The Far Country* is self-destructive and perverse; Howie Kemp (James Stewart) in *The Naked Spur* (1953) has become a bounty hunter; Glyn McLyntock (Stewart) in *Bend of the River* was a raider on the Kansas/Missouri border; Link Jones (Gary Cooper) in *Man of the West* was a murderous outlaw. The traditional life of male independence is characterised as savage, neurotic, regressive. Robin Wood's 'ideal man', a fantasy figure of supreme completeness, is transformed into a nightmare of psychological trauma, violence and hysteria. The fantasy of preserving male independence by moving on is not only no longer available – it has become almost psychotic.

The analysis of the hero in these terms is intensified by the use of the motif of the double, one of the most familiar dramatic structures in male-centred movies, but one capable of inflections with very different ideological implications. In its simplest forms, the relationship between the two figures is one of opposition: hero and villain. The hero can vanquish the villain, whether in the Western or the story of investigation, and restore moral order. The relationship becomes increasingly complex as it is dramatised not just by opposition but by similarity: the hero and villain constructed as versions of each other or as bound in a mutually defining relationship: two sides of the same coin. This can take many forms. *The Man Who Shot Liberty Valance* demonstrates particularly clearly that the Western hero cannot retain his power and authority after the villain has been killed: in shooting Liberty Valance (Lee Marvin), Tom Doniphon (John Wayne) writes himself out of the future. Equally, in the film's symbolic structure, the villain can become a projection of forces within but repressed by the hero. Central relationships in Mann's films seem recurrently of this kind, a second man created as a more or less clear version of the hero, linked by blood and/or background (*Winchester 73*, 1950, *Bend of the River*, *Man of the West*) and sometimes given parallels in personality – the relaxed and humorous as well as ruthless and violent aspects of the hero's character (*Bend of the River*, *The Far Country*, *The Man from Laramie*, 1955).

The link between the literal narrative and these less tangible levels is perhaps clearest in *Bend of the River* and *Man of the West*. In *Bend of the River*, Glyn McLyntock, searching for a way around the mountains for the wagon train he is guiding, comes across Emerson Cole (Arthur Kennedy), who is just about to be hanged for horse-stealing. The link between them is made visually in a zip pan and in Glyn's fingering of his own neck (it later transpires that he, too, once narrowly escaped hanging). The men have identical backgrounds as raiders on the Kansas/Missouri border. It is as though, in seeking to evade not only the mountain but his own past, Glyn conjures up the image of that past. Early in *Man of the West*, it is implied that outlaw gangs are things of the past. But as Link Jones leaves the town on the train, his old gang re-emerges. The sense of them as ghosts called up by Link losing his precarious place in civilisation is almost tangible when they appear out of the darkness in the shack to which Link takes Billie (Julie London) and Sam Beasley (Arthur O'Connell) after the train robbery. In both cases, the hero has to confront and destroy these figures from his past, a process of both disavowal and, I think, self destruction. He has, in other words, to deny and disavow his kinship with the double by killing him, in order to assert his own difference, but in killing, the hero is forced to use his innate violence against a figure who is a version of himself.

The end of *Man of the West* is particularly rich: the figure whom Link has to kill has been a 'father' to him, and the final sections have a much more explicit sexual dimension than the other films. When Link returns from Lassoo after killing the remaining gang members, he finds that Doc Tobin (Lee J. Cobb) has raped Billie. The Tobin gang has something in common with other monstrous male families in the postwar Western, such as the Clantons in *My Darling Clementine*, the Cleggs in *Wagon Master* (John Ford, 1950) and the Hammonds in Sam Peckinpah's *Ride the High Country* (1962). Each is presented as irredeemably evil, with strong elements of grotesqueness, bordering on madness, but also of clan loyalty, in the characters. Each embodies one extreme of Western wilderness – a savagery inimical to 'community' – but in the symbolic economy of the films, each is held in more or less complex relationship to the more positively presented characters. Most simply, the Cleggs are the 'snakes' which must be killed before the promised land can be entered, but even in the relatively simple, almost allegorical world of *Wagon Master*, they represent one temptation in the wilderness – the absence of moral restraint – that must be exorcised from the perfected community. The Clantons have a similar function, while also paralleling the Earps – the good and bad Westerners who meet in the desert in the first moments of the film. In *Ride the High Country*, the eruption of the Hammonds at the Knudsen farm suggests one of their functions in the film – to embody the forces denied by the repressive regime of Knudsen (R.G. Armstrong), and perhaps by the moral rectitude of Steve (Joel McCrea). The sense of these male clans as embodiments of unconstrained appetite is forcefully demonstrated in their essentially predatory and violent relationships with women, dramatised most intensely in the act or threat of rape. By contrast, the Western hero's treatment of women is traditionally courteous and restrained – 'gentlemanly' in fact.

Particularly disturbing in *Man of the West* is the hero's past as a member of the monstrous Tobin gang, a fact which focuses the questions implicit in the conflicting personae presented in the film's

Still: the savage side of the Mann hero – James Stewart and Jack Lambert in Bend of the River.

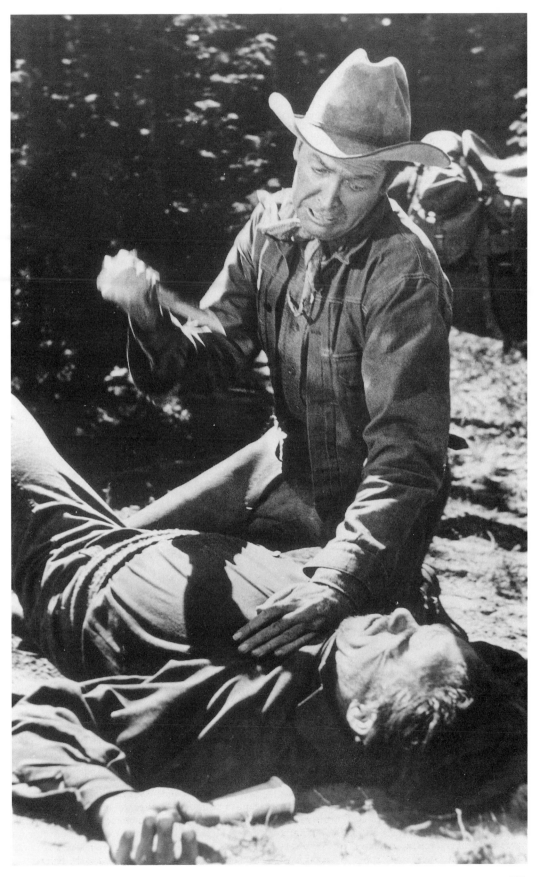

opening sequences. The fantasy icon of the serene horseman resolves itself into the two incompatible but (in the film's logic) intimately related images – that of the almost comic Western 'hick' on his errand to confirm his place in settlement and the psychotic outlaw. The first cannot be chosen without confronting and disavowing the second.

Doc's rape of Billie is his final attempt to act out his patriarchal authority over his 'son', and it defines an essential component of the savage masculinity he embodies. Link has to kill his 'father', not for moral reasons alone, but also, in the logic of the relationship, both to reject and replace him. But in order to assert his independence of his past and his right to enter civilisation, he has to kill, using skills which identify him with the man he kills, rather than with the society he wants to enter. The paradox is a familiar one, but is given particular intensity in the 'son'/'father' relationship in *Man of the West*. Jim Kitses suggests that the film requires us finally to see that Doc Tobin was the 'Man of the West'. Yet if we follow the logic of the film's symbolic structure, perhaps this is not an alternative identification of the title figure; rather, the implication may be that what is inherent in that serene and solitary figure in the credits is this crazed old man, the embodiment of a murderous patriarchal masculinity.

Clearly these representations of the hero cannot simply be reduced to issues of character or of symbolic structure. A major determinant is the historical setting. The fantasy has soured because the period of the frontier is passing. With male independence a nightmare and the safety valve of the West no longer available, settlement cannot be evaded.

Indeed, Mann's heroes invariably end the films framed with a woman and apparently poised to settle. But in a variety of ways the films also place question marks over this resolution. There is no alternative to settlement, but the fantasy that these figures can, like Owen Wister's Virginian, keep their identity and strength as Westerners while contentedly and successfully settling is strongly undercut.

The strategies at work here are differently articulated in each film. *Bend of the River* has perhaps the most apparently affirmative ending, with the wagons containing winter supplies finally reaching the fertile Oregon valley and being greeted by 'nice people'. But here the rhetoric of the happy ending, linked as it has been throughout to the sententious moralising and 'happy valley' imagery used by the Jay C. Flippen character, in itself gives the last scenes a somewhat illusory feel. As in *The Far Country*, the movement of exploitation and violence into the area as gold is discovered implies a relentless social process from which the settlers cannot remain detached. In *The Far Country* and *Winchester 73*, James Stewart is left respectively with the characters played by Corinne Calvet and Shelley Winters. In neither case has a relationship developed that seems a likely basis for the marriage that the end seems to indicate. Renée (Corinne Calvet) in *The Far Country* is created as a largely sexless adolescent whose crush on Jeff is not matched by any corresponding romantic or sexual interest in her on Jeff's

part: the incongruity of their coupling could not be clearer. In *The Naked Spur*, in which the casting of Janet Leigh and the development of the character give Lina rather greater force and presence, Mann uses an ending in which the *couple* are seen moving further West, in this case towards California. But any positive connotations are qualified by an extraordinarily bleak final image – the couple riding away through a landscape of blighted and dead trees.

Man of the West is a further variant. In Billie, the film has perhaps the strongest female figure in Mann's Westerns, but the possibility of a relationship developing between Link and Billie is blocked from the outset by Link already being married. The ending, as they drive back towards the settlements, is very moving. Billie makes quite explicit the impossibility of the lovely fantasy that they might become a couple. It is significant that we never see the small settlement (referred to by Link at different points as Good Hope and Sawmill – 'five days ride West of here') where Link has married and settled. Good Hope, which is evoked but never seen, comes to seem as illusory as Lassoo, the gold-rich settlement of which Doc Tobin dreams but which is revealed as a ghost town. It is as though the film's action is given its significance by being played out between two illusions, two fantasies – that of perfect community and that of the wide-open, Wild West of the outlaw.

There is a third but less common ending in the Western – the death of the hero – which offers a further way of resolving (or evading) the tensions of the narrative, but Mann uses it, as far as I am aware, only in *Devil's Doorway* (1950), his first Western. The exception seems significant. The hero of the film is an Indian who has served in the US Cavalry but who dies fighting the cavalry in defence of land Indians cannot now own under the Homestead Act. Jim Kitses notes: 'As in *El Cid* ten years later, the film ends on a strange note of dark exaltation – victory through death' (Kitses, 1969, p.44). The link with *El Cid* is revealing, too, in that in both endings, exaltation is mingled with an elegiac quality. It is this possibility that Sam Peckinpah repeatedly exploits in his Westerns, but whereas to Peckinpah's world the affirmation of doomed romantic individualism is central, it has no place in Mann's – his major Westerns have very little of the elegiac about them.

The sense that we get of Mann's protagonists is of men trapped within and struggling to escape a narrow, stifling, traditional definition of masculinity, in which the male images evoked in the quotation from Robin Wood are constantly in tension. Whether they wish to pull free of human contact or reject their anti-social past in order to settle, they are forced to exist in a destructive force field, pushed and pulled between magnetic poles which simultaneously attract and repel. Neither path is viable because each is a fantasy dependent on the opposite that it attempts to reject: the fear of settlement, linked to past betrayal by women, fuels the obsessive independence of Howie Kemp and Jeff Webster; the attempt to reject a murderous past underpins the settlement dreams of Glyn McLyntock and Link Jones.

Still: the hero and his 'double' – Arthur Kennedy and James Stewart in Bend of the River.

In recent years the genre that has been the focus of discussions of gender representation and ideological entrapment in destructive social roles has been domestic melodrama. Although these debates have centred on feminist readings and on representations of women, the great male-centred melodramas of the 'fifties (films directed by Douglas Sirk, Nicholas Ray and Vincente Minnelli among others) have also received significant attention. Laura Mulvey comments on Sirk's *The Tarnished Angels* (1957) and *Written on the Wind* (1956): 'Roger Schumann . . . and Kyle Hadley . . . (both played by Robert Stack) are tortured and torn by the mystique of masculinity, haunted by phallic obsessions and fear of impotence. In these two films Sirk provides an extremely rare epitaph, an insight into *men* as victims of patriarchal society. He shows castration anxiety, not (as is common) personified by a vengeful woman but presented *dreadfully* and without mediation' ('Notes on Sirk and Melodrama', *Movie* 25, 1978, p.17).

This is the terrain of what Michael Walker calls 'the melodrama of passion', as opposed to the 'melodrama of action' represented by the Hollywood action genres. Melodramas of passion are concerned 'not with the external dynamic of action but with the internal traumas of passion (the emotions)' ('Melodrama and the American Cinema', *Movie* 29/30, 1982, p.17). The categories, as Walker recognises, are not entirely clear-cut, and it seems to me that Mann's Westerns, in their focus on the unstable and tortured masculinity of their heroes, demand to be seen alongside – indeed as part of – the 'fifties cycle of male melodramas. Like the protagonists of melodrama, Mann's heroes are in a sense victims, lacking the self-knowledge either of the traditional Westerner or of the tragic hero and enacting a drama of intractable situations. They also share with so many of the *women* of melodrama – and some men, for instance, Dave (Frank Sinatra) in *Some Came Running* (Minnelli, 1958) – an apparent choice of two paths, in which each seems equally unsatisfactory but synthesis is impossible. The dilemma seems insistent: must choose, must lose. Like their contemporaries in melodrama, Mann's protagonists are prisoners of a masculinity coded in hopelessly contradictory ways.

The question that remains at the end of these extraordinary movies is often what state the hero is in. After the climactic conflicts Mann's heroes often seem drained, 'brought low', as Kitses puts it. As he says, 'we must ask what kind of success it is that accounts for the destruction of a father or a brother, and how this equips the character for a role in the community' (Kitses, 1969, p.43). If the violence is a kind of exorcism, it also leaves the question of what is left for settlement. The exhaustion and even despair of the heroes at the end of some of the movies cannot simply be read, in the context of the films as a whole, as a temporary state. *The Naked Spur* is particularly explicit about the hero's state. Almost to the end, Howie Kemp keeps hysterically trying to pull the body of Ben Vandergroat (Robert Ryan) out of the river for the bounty before finally collapsing with a desperate cry into the arms of Lina. The pull of nihilistic isolation and the fear of commitment remain powerfully present as the film ends.

But if the hero seems almost destroyed, it is important to ask whether the 'destruction' carries only negative connotations. It is clear that much of the intensity of these films, as of contemporary male melodrama, springs from a critical engagement with versions of masculinity that are deeply rooted in the culture – and that the tensions inherent in this field do not readily admit of resolution. Mann's films, however, are particularly clear-sighted in their demolition of the two fantasies that are central to Western resolutions: the fantasy of the 'ideal man' and the fantasy of such a figure contentedly settled. At the end of the films the heroes often seem deflated and drained, and the endings less than uplifting (even at times bleak). This may, however, connote not the end of the Western hero in a negative, regretful, elegiac sense, but – positively and remarkably – the collapse of fantasy.

DRUMS ALONG THE MOHAWK

Robin Wood

Drums Along the Mohawk, generally the least valued of the three films that John Ford made in 1939 (the others are *Stagecoach* and *Young Mr Lincoln*), is perhaps the finest. It also offers one of the most complete elaborations in the classical Hollywood cinema of a positively conceived ideology of America – an ideology artistically validated within the workings of the film by the intensity of Ford's commitment to it, whatever we may think of it politically. (*Outside* the film, one doesn't have to look far to find its ideological position qualified within Ford's own work: its juxtaposition with *Stagecoach* in itself raises ideological contradictions that Ford never really resolved.)

The film is based on a novel which in its turn is based on historical events; the novel distorts history, the film distorts the novel; the only 'historical' figure to survive the transitions is General Herkimer. The film must be read as dramatic poem rather than as historical reconstruction: its thematic-ideological concerns take precedence at all points over historical accuracy. It is perfectly conceived for (or a perfectly

logical product of) its contemporary historical moment – America just emerging from the Depression; the world on the brink of a war to defend Democracy against Fascism. The film shows the American people (in microcosm) struggling against hardship and disaster, overcoming them and preparing for new effort (the last line of dialogue is Henry Fonda's 'We'd better get back to work – there's goin' to be a heap of things to do from now on').

Structuring the film are two ideological assumptions that are never overtly questioned (if they are felt to be implicitly questioned, this is from the sense – doubtless much stronger in 1995 than in 1939 – of the suppressions and distortions that the film's affirmation necessitates): the rightness of white democratic-capitalist civilisation, hence of 'settling' (a homely, personalised version of imperialism), hence of subjugating or exterminating the Indians; the

Still: Drums Along the Mohawk – *Lana (Claudette Colbert) tends to the traumatised Gil (Henry Fonda).*

goodness of monogamy/family as the repository of virtue and civilisation's basic unit and foundation. We can trace in some detail the way the film develops and continuously connects these two projects.

Its essential progress can be seen in terms of widening circles, of a process whereby smaller units become incorporated in larger units without losing their identity (rather, having their identity more clearly defined and strengthened). Before the film begins, the *individual*, Gil Martin (Henry Fonda), has gone into the wilderness and built a log cabin. The first scene shows his wedding to Lana Borst (Claudette Colbert) and their departure for the wilderness. In the course of the film, the *couple* becomes a *family*, and we see the family become integrated in the *community*. The final sequence, centred on the carrying in of the new American flag, shows the community recognising itself as part of a newly founded *nation*.

The linearity of this process is offset by the repeated establishing of links between the units: the film wants to assert that each – individual, family, community – retains its own integrity, its own character, even when it is assimilated into a larger structure, while the larger structure depends upon the dedication and loyalty of its units. Lana's first (unsuccessful) pregnancy is announced during the couple's introduction to the fort community. When her second child is born, it is greeted as a *communal* child ('We've got a baby boy'). The Hallowe'en dance (the film's central, and quintessentially Fordian, celebration of community) also celebrates a new wedding; Gil leaves the dance to watch his sleeping son, Lana leaves to watch him watching ('Please God, let this go on forever'). The last scene, triumphantly extending the idea of community to multi-racial democracy, links Lana with the new flag ('It's a pretty flag, isn't it?'). In the course of the film, her clothing subtly acquires red, white and blue, but only in the last scene are the three colours united in her dress and bonnet; in one shot, Lana (left of screen) is compositionally balanced with the flag (right of screen).

The centrality of Woman – of a certain concept of Woman – to Ford's view of civilisation is epitomised by this moment. Woman for Ford is at once the pretext for civilisation (the cabin is built for her) and (as wife and mother) the guarantee of its continuity. And he characteristically endows his women with the finest attributes: strength, fortitude, integrity, nobility. The price of this is of course that their role remains at bottom firmly 'traditional', whatever apparent deviations the films produce. A central concern of *Drums Along the Mohawk* is the education of Lana as frontierswoman (rather as a central concern of *She Wore a Yellow Ribbon* ten years later will be the education of Olivia Dandridge – Joanne Dru – as cavalry wife). In the course of this, Lana must learn to be able to do man's work (stacking corn with Gil) and take on certain 'masculine' attributes, culminating in her donning of a uniform and shooting an Indian with a rifle. Yet the overlay of 'manliness' serves mainly to emphasise Lana's 'natural' femininity: the corn-stacking scene stresses Gil's concern

over the blisters on her pretty hands, a point taken up later in the beautiful moment when Mrs McClennan (Edna May Oliver), inspecting Lana's hands to see if she's suitable as hired help, nods and smiles with approval – the approval being, clearly, for *both* the hands' natural delicacy *and* the callouses. When Howard Hawks's women (already possessing 'masculine' attributes of aggressiveness, dominance, etc.) put on men's clothes, there is always a strong suggestion of potential androgyny; Lana is never more feminine than when wearing uniform (a point stressed by her very un-Hawksian faint at the foot of the ladder when Gil leaves to get reinforcements: when she shoots the Indian at close quarters, she inflicts no more than a light wound).

Lana is one of Ford's 'girls from the East', a figure variously inflected in the Lucy Mallory (Louise Platt) of *Stagecoach,* the Clementine Carter (Cathy Downs) of *My Darling Clementine* (1946), the Olivia Dandridge of *She Wore a Yellow Ribbon* (1949). The figure is always viewed with a degree of ambivalence; on the one hand, she is seen as bringing to the West a superior refinement, a cultivated sensibility; on the other, she is admired according to her ability to transcend all that. Even Clementine Carter (whose refinement, expressed through her manners and her clothes, seems unambiguously valued throughout the film) is valued even more when she discards the fine clothes and Boston bonnet of the Easterner for the simple print dress and loose hair of the Western schoolteacher. One might argue that it is merely the external accoutrements of refinement that are discarded – that the 'cultivated sensibility' survives the changes of clothes. Yet it is not clear that Ford sees the source of the qualities he admires as deriving from 'civilisation': rather, he appears to regard them as natural, overlaid rather than created by 'culture'. The foil for Lana throughout *Drums Along the Mohawk* is the snobbish and affected Mrs Demooth (Kay Linaker), who is castigated by the film for her failure to cast off the manners and attitudes of the East. The problem – uncertainty as to exactly what value is being placed on 'superior refinement' – is quite central to Ford's work, to its paradoxes and contradictions.

As 'girl from the East' who becomes frontierswoman, Lana is at the centre of the interplay throughout the film between the 'natural' and the 'civilised'. She is connected (through her established family and Dutch ancestry) not only to the developed civilisation of New England but to the Old World; thus her integration into the growing community/new nation epitomises the movie's aspirations to 'creating' an America that is inclusive, assimilating the finest from all the available sources. The opening scene stresses the formality and order of an advanced civilisation: its first image is a close-up of Lana's tightly packed, intricately composed bridal bouquet; during the ceremony, bride and groom are neatly and symmetrically framed by the arched windows behind them; a similar arched window frames Lana as she throws the bouquet from the staircase. The first shots outside the house reveal the honeymoon vehicle: a covered wagon with a cow tied on behind. The movement from culture into nature is beautifully expressed in a single composition: in the mid foreground, square to the camera, two low walls defining the bounds of the estate, on either side of the gateway to the wilderness; beyond them, the covered wagon moving off between the ranks of trees; beyond that, virgin forest. The same movement is marked by the progression of fertility images: the tight, formal bridal bouquet; the loose bunch of flowers tied round the neck of the cow behind the wagon; subsequently, the corn that Gil and Lana stack together.

The opening sequence is an exemplary instance of the masking of ideology beneath the personalisation of realist fiction. What we see – economically and touchingly presented – is a young couple bravely venturing into the wilderness to build civilisation; the political reality this conceals is no less than American imperialism, the seizing of land as private property, the extermination of the Indians. All this is sanctioned and dignified by nature (the cycle of the generations) and religion ('It's the way it's been since Bible days', says the clergyman, comforting Lana's weeping mother – the American wilderness becomes the Promised Land, the subjugation of the Indians is validated not only by Manifest Destiny but by Divine Ordinance).

The film's attitude to civilisation and its relationship to the 'natural' are further defined in the scene in which Lana shows her home to the women from the fort – specifically, through two emblems, the pheasant's feather and the white china teapot. Part of the significance of the former is its uselessness – its value is purely as object-of-beauty, it is *pure* emblem. Crucially, both are linked to the idea of transmission: of the feather, Lana remarks that her mother told her that there are times when such things are more important than bread; the teapot belonged to her grandmother. Both carry connotations beyond the aesthetic: the feather, though removed from its natural context, is a product of nature rather than art, the teapot is as much for use as ornament. Mrs Demooth's reactions are used to define the significance of both: of the feather she remarks that they had a lot of them at home and threw them out because they gathered dust; the teapot elicits the reaction, 'We always ate off Wedgwood.' Against the use of artefacts to establish prestige and superiority is set Lana's quiet pride in her possessions as links with home and the past: the scene embodies those notions of tradition and continuity so dear to Ford and linked again to the notion of woman as transmitter.

The interplay between nature and civilisation is inherent in Ford's visual style, centred on 'composition', the one artistic ability on which he prided himself ('. . . the only thing I always had was an eye for composition – I don't know where I got it – and that's all I *did* have', Peter Bogdanovich, *John Ford*, Studio Vista, London, 1967). Ford 'got it' from the whole tradition of 'realist' painting since the Renaissance (but especially from nineteenth-century Romanticism and its extension into photography): one of the main functions of 'composition' in *Drums Along the Mohawk* is the conversion of nature into works of art. Especially, of course, man-in-nature: Ford almost never uses landscapes *solely* for their pictorial beauty, but rather for the dignity they confer upon the meticulously placed human beings. One might contrast the compositions of Anthony Mann, which habitually present man at odds with nature.

Still: Drums Along the Mohawk – *Gil's departure with the militia.*

Ford's allegiance to the past, his rootedness in a tradition that by 1939 was already obsolete, are expressed above all in his compositional sense, perhaps the last distinguished manifestation of the Romantic vision of a possible harmony between nature and humanity (as against what one might loosely call the Existentialist vision, variously inflected in the work of Budd Boetticher and Mann, of nature as apathetic or hostile). Nature, in the landscapes of *Drums Along the Mohawk*, becomes the ultimate validation of settling, of home, of monogamy/family: the couple, the cabin, the corn-stacks, surrounded by virgin forest, in compositions whose every component has its precise, harmonious place.

The point must not, however, be allowed to stand without qualification: the sense of harmony and wholeness is everywhere counterpointed with a sense of transience (the cabin and crops are destroyed, the white china teapot smashed; Lana's 'Please God, let this go on forever' is immediately followed, in terms of screen time, by the next Indian uprising) and loss (actual or potential). This in itself scarcely threatens the film's ideological position (the Romantic view of man-in-nature has never precluded a sense of the tragic); rather, it adds depth and complexity to it. The scene of Gil's departure with the militia (one of the film's great set pieces) is a fine example. Mrs McClennan's farewell links Gil to her dead husband Barney (she gives him Barney's whiskey flask and kisses him before Lana does, so that 'you won't go off with the taste of a widow in your mouth'). As Lana runs across the stream and over the hillside to watch the men march away, the compositions (with their characteristic depth-of-field), besides ennobling the scene with a traditional beauty, have the function of showing, within the same frame, the ever-widening distance between the woman and the men. Crucial to the scene's poignancy and sense of the precarious is Gil's failure to see Lana – he keeps looking back to the house, she is running across the hill, and her desperate efforts to remain in sight as long as possible go unnoticed.

This continual counterpointing of affirmation and loss makes it less paradoxical that the film should use Mrs McClennan, a childless widow, to uphold its monogamy/family ideology. What is stressed repeatedly is her fidelity to Barney: 'When Barney kissed you, you *stayed* kissed', as she tells Adam Hartmann (Ward Bond) at the Hallowe'en party, denying the potency of the film's one really erotic embrace. The fidelity extends, obsessively, to the marital bed, whose preservation becomes her main concern when three Indians infiltrate her home. Her cry to Barney as she dies is ambiguous – either she believes she is nearing him, or, frightened, she feels the need for his (and only his) protection: either reading underlines the film's sense of the naturalness and grandeur of the marriage union. Implicitly, she 'adopts' Gil and Lana as her children, seeing in them a replica of Barney and herself: she presents Gil with Barney's flask, and later with the crib that one of Barney's soldiers made for the child she never had. The film holds up for our admiration her strength, stoicism and resilience (the character is

among Ford's most vivid and endearing creations), but all these are related to her fidelity to her dead husband and non-existent family. One feels, indeed, that, with her aggressive 'manliness' and ready acceptance of the man's work on the farm, she has kept Barney alive by *becoming* him.

According to Freud, a society built on monogamy and family is inherently repressive: there will be a great amount of surplus (basic sexual) energy for which an outlet will have to be found. In Ford's work, the commitment to traditional values goes with a continual preoccupation with the ways in which surplus energy can be safely contained: work, communal celebrations, harmless (if often very violent) horseplay. The Independence Day celebration sequences of *Young Mr Lincoln* exemplify this, and also the accompanying sense of the precariousness of the containment: the parade, with the 'comic' violence when a boy catapults a horse, the tug-o'-war and log-splitting, the bonfire; but also the fight and the murder outside the circle of the community.

The sense of coherence and wholeness which *Drums Along the Mohawk* communicates (despite its emphasis on horror, hardship, struggle and loss) can be partly accounted for in terms of its success in suggesting the possibility of such containment within the community, and the projection of that-which-cannot-be-contained on to forces regarded as purely external. The film is rich in scenes of purposeful communal activity – scenes whose vividness and vitality testify to the strength of Ford's response: the drilling of the militia, the land-clearing, the Hallowe'en dance. The traditional account of Ford's development – a progress from affirmation to disillusionment – is highly questionable: beside *Drums Along the Mohawk* one has to set other films from the same period (*Stagecoach*, *The Long Voyage Home*, 1940, *Tobacco Road*, 1941) whose tone is very different. In fact, the central Fordian paradox is already implicit in *Drums Along the Mohawk*: his dedication to the development of a civilisation that will inevitably render obsolete the very values he celebrates. The ideal Fordian community (the concept embodied very precisely in the communal dances of *Drums Along the Mohawk*, *My Darling Clementine* and *Wagon Master*, 1950) is by definition transient because it can exist only at an early stage of the development which gives it its motivation: the church must perpetually remain unroofed, the pioneers must be forever moving towards the Promised Land, there must always be 'a heap of things to do from now on'. That the affirmation of *Drums Along the Mohawk* is as convincing and moving as it is certainly has something to do with the period in which it was made (even by the time of *Wagon Master* similar attempts at affirmation have become forced and artificial, without any convincing social context). It has more to do, however, with the period in which it is *set*: of all Ford's films about America, it is the earliest in history, crucially before the Civil War was even a remote threat.

It will have been noticed that this account of the film has so far scrupulously avoided all of its problems – all those aspects that seriously qualify (without

Still: Drums Along the Mohawk – *the civilians are moved into the fort.*

completely destroying) its 'affirmation' and 'coherence', elements that threaten and disturb the secure functioning of its ideology. The problems can be located in three minor characters, though their ultimate source is the Indians. Of the three, the parson (Arthur Shields) is the most nearly assimilable into the film's coherence and the least necessary to its narrative: he contributes nothing essential to the plot development and is clearly in the film to lend colour to the life of the fort and to add the support of religion to the notion of community solidarity. The disturbance arises from the character's excessiveness – what makes him 'colourful' also makes him monstrous.

The church service is treated primarily as comedy (Ford's view of religion is strongly rooted in his sense of the desirability of social cohesion; it has little of the transcendental or metaphysical; when his material forces this upon him – as in *The Fugitive*, 1947 – he becomes rhetorical and pretentious). Yet it bears serious consideration, linking in the space of seconds sexual repressiveness, social prejudice, capitalism and militarism within the sanction of the Christian church. The parson calls for the congregation's prayers on three counts: a) for a girl who is keeping company with a Massachusetts man ('. . . and Thou knowest no good can come of that'); b) for a storekeeper with 'the flux', this leading directly into a commercial for his newly arrived goods; c) for the wrath of God to fall upon the enemy (the British, but more specifically the insurgent Indians). The fundamental contradiction inherent in the Judaeo-Christian religious tradition is dramatised in

the parson, who vigorously invokes 'Jehovah, God of battles' against the 'sons of Belial', then collapses after the siege in a state of shock because 'I killed a man'. The man, however, is presumably old Joe (Francis Ford), whom the parson shot as an act of mercy when the 'sons of Belial' were about to burn him alive; we have also seen him shoot numerous Indians. The film never fully confronts the implications of this, and its attitude to the parson remains equivocal: by making him comic and quaint, it manages neither to endorse nor reject him.

This leads conveniently to a consideration of the role of the Indians in the film, and of its other two problematic characters Caldwell (John Carradine) and Blueback (Chief Big Tree). If 'nature' is settling, monogamy, family, home, farming the land, it is also, in a more obvious sense, the Indians: see, for example, their beautiful and ominous first appearance when they emerge out of the hazily sunlit woods as if a direct emanation from nature. In its treatment of the Indians (as in, for example, its definition of the role of women) the film can always claim for itself the alibi of historical accuracy: we are after all, in 1776, and the view of the Indians as 'sons of Belial', 'painted heathen devils', etc., closely reproduces the opinion of the founding fathers of modern, White America. Yet the plea of 'historical accuracy' is at best threadbare – the film is accurate only at its own convenience and mythologises history at every point.

The Puritan view of the Indians (as historically

documented) has two aspects that are directly relevant here. First, they were *literally* devils, or, at least children of the Devil; second, they were sexually unrestrained and promiscuous. The two, of course, go inseparably together: the close association (almost identity) of Indians/devils/free sexuality is central to the meaning of the Hallowe'en dance, with its 'demon' lanterns made out of pumpkins (one of them teasingly juxtaposed with the grinning head of Francis Ford, whose younger brother's ambivalence seems encapsulated in that single image). The dance is the supreme expression in the film of the socialised and sanctioned release of energy – which is to say, the *containment* of energy; it juxtaposes the new monogamous union and the Gil/Lana/baby family with the sense that 'devils' can be contained, made harmless and humorous, even while their presence is acknowledged. Yet the 'devils' of the Hallowe'en dance return as the Indians. The puritan view can of course be easily interpreted in the light of Freud's theory of projection: as something that is projected on to some 'other' in order to be effectively disowned and condemned. The Indians had to be destroyed because (for the Puritans) they embodied precisely those drives that were forbidden – that must not even be allowed access to consciousness. The point is acknowledged in one of the film's 'comic' moments: awaiting the Indian attack, on the fort's parapet, the parson forces Christian Reall (Eddie Collins) to throw away his jar of liquor (his excuse for drinking it is to keep it from the Indians) telling him to 'Beware the heathen within thine own breast': the threat the Indians represent is not merely external.

The association of the Indians with the return of repressed sexual energies is fairly consistent in Ford's work (and not only in his); it reaches its fullest elaboration in *The Searchers* (1956). The simplest, most explicit form it takes is the dread of miscegenation. The fear that women will be killed by the Indians seems to be surpassed by the fear that they will be sexually defiled by them: thus Hatfield (John Carradine) in *Stagecoach* saves his last bullet for the head of Lucy Mallory. But the unconscious of *Drums Along the Mohawk* (for the unconscious thinks, too, in its own way) is haunted by more subtle linkages.

What makes Caldwell problematic is his mysteriousness. Without any basis in historical fact, he is given only the vaguest political explanation, which the potency of his 'image' in the film completely transcends. The film needs him to make plausible one of its contradictory myths about the Indians – that they were helpless, misguided children who would have done no harm had it not been for the use made of them by unscrupulous Tories. He is linked to the Indians throughout as the force that organises and directs them; his potency is suggested by the strength and suggestive beauty of certain compositions, notably the shot following the drilling of the newly recruited militia: a sudden cut to long-shot, the men reduced to distant midgets, the foreground dominated by Caldwell watching from the darkness of the trees, hand on hip so that his black cape is spread out as if to swallow up the marching figures who are suddenly vulnerably tiny. Caldwell derives, in fact, less from history than from fiction and other movies: from romantic melodrama (with his eye patch and cape, he immediately evokes the highwayman); from the horror film (the figure emerging from the darkness, connected on his first appearance with flames, the cape giving him in this context connotations of the vampire) – both source-figures carry strong associations of sexual threat.

Caldwell is introduced on the word 'Honeymooners' – the landlord of the inn is pointing out to him the virginal Gil and Lana. He crosses to their table and immediately starts talking about the possibility of an Indian uprising in the Mohawk valley. He then precedes the young couple up the stairs to the bedchambers, and the landlord, speculating about his eye patch, suggests that he lost an eye looking into things he had no business looking into. Lana looks uneasy; Gil asks her if the talk of Indians scared her. As they mount the stairs towards their bedroom she replies, 'I wasn't thinking about the Indians.'

Blueback is linked to Caldwell through the structure of the images: Gil and Lana arrive at the inn, Caldwell emerges out of the darkness as threat; they arrive at the cabin, Blueback emerges out of the darkness (and, now, the storm) as threat. The horror film connotations are much stronger here: the log cabin, approached through dark woods to the accompaniment of rain, thunder and lightning, becomes the Old Dark House. Blueback, appearing as if supernaturally in a flash of lightning, photographed from a low angle, is almost the Frankenstein monster. Lana collapses into hysteria, flees across the room, and cowers on the bed as Blueback advances: the notion of the Indian as a specifically *sexual* threat is very clear.

Yet the film insists, of course, that Blueback is not a *real* threat: he is the safe, friendly, well-intentioned, Christianised Indian who has come to deliver half a deer. He is the film's desperate attempt to solve the Indian problem – its uneasy acknowledgment that the 'sons of Belial' may perhaps be human beings after all and therefore deserving of a solution other than total extermination. The film tries to give Blueback dignity (significantly, in the salute of the flag in the final sequence), but the ignominy of his situation (belonging to neither the White nor the Indian culture – though the latter is not really permitted an existence) keeps manifesting itself. He *has* to be a comic character – the film could not sustain a serious consideration of his position. In the interests of authenticity, Ford cast a Native American in the role – with results quite beyond the film's control. The actor's painful, laborious delivery of every line and gesture imposed on him becomes expressive in a way scarcely containable within the fiction: one is uncomfortably aware at every point of the forcing on him of White man's language and the whole White notion of 'performance', a tradition apparently quite alien to Indian culture. (The ignominy extends entirely beyond the diegesis: in the final cast-list Chief Big Tree's name appears below those of numerous White bit-part

179

players with roles far smaller than his.) The film cannot conceal the awkwardness of Blueback's position in White civilisation: in it without being of it. Significantly, though the dialogue suggests that he is experienced with women, the film can allow him no sex life, no home. With the single exception of the drinking bout in an outhouse during the childbirth sequence, he appears completely isolated; even in church, he remains an anomaly and a disturbance, retaining vestiges of independence (the insistence on wearing a hat), hopefully calling out 'Hallejuyah!' at inappropriate moments. One of the film's most embarrassing moments is his warning cry that interrupts the communal land-clearing, 'Indians on the warpath' – as if he himself wasn't one. The film can't explain how one of the 'heathen devils' became Blueback – he has to be kept totally isolated from them, an anomaly everywhere, hence no more than the merest token 'answer' to the Indian problem.

Again, the film can hide behind the alibi of historical accuracy: his dress, style of hair, etc., identify Blueback as belonging to a different tribe (the distinction corresponds to the traditional Cheyenne/ Apache opposition common in Hollywood films – see, for example, *Stagecoach*, which produces its Blueback figure in the first few minutes as a contrast to Geronimo). Such a distinction, whatever claims it may have to 'authenticity', can scarcely be free from its own brand of mythologising; in the present instance, it seems to me completely over-ridden by the film's evident desire to reinforce a dual 'myth' of the Indian, of whom it can offer but two images: the screaming devil and the incongruous, comic, Christianised, castrated servant. The two images correspond precisely to the two ways in which, according to Barthes (*Mythologies*, Paladin, London, 1973, p.151), bourgeois society deals with 'the other': it can either deny it or convert it into a harmless replica of itself.

Blueback apart, the Indians of *Drums Along the Mohawk* are never individualised, and scarcely conceived as human beings at all: they have no wives, no families (only once is an Indian woman visible in the film – in long-shot in the closing scene), and only a corporate identity as an emanation of 'natural' savagery. Their eruption (under Caldwell's direction) threatens White civilisation generally, but is linked specifically to White monogamy, family, home. The first uprising provokes Lana's miscarriage; the second is signalled by the abrupt appearance of three Indians in Mrs McClennan's bedroom, as she lies asleep on the bed she shared with Barney, as if they are the manifestation of her dreams. Later, on the parapet of the fort, she invokes Barney; as if in response, an Indian rises up and shoots her. The film repeatedly stresses the horror of the war, which can be taken to signify the terrible price of repression, on both political and psychological levels.

The final sequences of the film are worth considering in detail – especially, the detail of their significant juxtapositions. Gil's search for Lana within the devastated fort is counterpointed with the soldiers' search for Caldwell: at one point, they mistake Gil for him. The destruction of Caldwell (the Indians'

potency) is necessary for the final reconstitution of the family. Gil is led to Lana eventually by the child's cries; at the moment husband and wife are reunited, the cries stop. There follows the film's single most extraordinary moment: Blueback rises up in the pulpit and pulls down Caldwell's eye patch over his own eye. The moment fuses in a single image the film's three 'problem' characters in a drastic effort of resolution, Caldwell destroyed by the safe, castrated Indian who then wordlessly usurps the parson's position, making himself into a visual sermon about the repression on which our civilisation is built.

The film can then proceed to its final affirmation: the war ended, the new flag carried in and raised to the chapel belfry, 'My country 'tis of thee' on the soundtrack, Blueback saluting and Daisy (Beulah Hall Jones), Mrs McClennan's Black servant, gazing in admiration, the two ennobled by separate low-angle close shots (as precise a cinematic equivalent for Barthes's Black soldier on the cover of *Paris-Match* as one could ask for). The myth of America as true multi-racial democracy seems (in retrospect from the 'nineties) at once enforced and exposed, the claim to the realisation of the ideals of freedom and equality now appearing almost derisory. Yet the ending remains, even today, very moving, partly because of its Fordian fervour and commitment, partly because it is magnificently sustained by the structure of the whole film, of which it is the absolutely logical culmination; partly, perhaps, because the idealism now appears so much more vulnerable than Ford could have intended.

Still: Drums Along the Mohawk – *Lana in uniform in the climactic assault.*

DODGE CITY

Charles Barr

From a scene in a newspaper office, a quick dissolve gives us the image of a gunbelt in close-up, with a sheriff's star fixed to it. It is hanging on a coat stand next to a window. We at once infer that the sheriff is nearby, and that he will be unarmed. After a moment, a hostile face peers in at the window (on the right of the frame), and we infer that this man is likely to be looking for the sheriff. These inferences are confirmed when the man moves from window to door, enters the room – a barbershop – and draws a gun on the sheriff, who is seated inside, getting a shave. To show this, the camera has moved right and panned left, in order to follow the incomer's entry while keeping the gunbelt in shot: as he advances, we can see the sheriff's gun hanging unattainably from its belt in the foreground. While emphasising his vulnerability to the armed intruder, the camera movement at the same time endows the gunbelt with a (literally) disembodied authority of its own: it seems to keep the man under surveillance. And, sure enough, the sheriff's power is at once seen to operate even when he is separated from its physical symbol and support: feeling for an improvised weapon (a razor strop), he rapidly disarms and ejects his attacker, who is then led off to jail by a passing deputy.

The sheriff meanwhile starts to strap on his gunbelt, but this is done casually within a long shot, and there is no suggestion that he was at fault in not wearing it in the barber's chair. Had he done so, the scene would have lost half its resonance.

There is a lot more to it than the basic narrative as described above. Back to the opening image: sheriff's star on gunbelt, hanging on coat stand, window at the right. Through this window, before the face appears, we can see movement. Out of focus in the background, this functions as a conventional aid to realism by giving a sense of a world outside the barbershop, confirming that we are on the main street of the town. There is not enough visual detail to distract from the narrative, but we register a female passer-by in a hat and a long dress – always, in generic iconography, a sign of the civilising of the wild West. Simultaneously, we hear a voice, from the interior space, which has the same dual role: functional, in helping to orient us and in providing another layer of realistic detail – barbers are talkative – and also thematically meaningful. The monologue begins off-camera before the intruder appears, is linked to its speaker as the camera moves to reveal the shop interior, and ends at the precise moment when the gun is pointed at the sheriff:

'Of course I ain't a man who believes in taxes. But I can see they're a necessary evil. Somebody's got to pay for schools and churches and such things – especially now that the town's getting so durn big. Yes sir, they do say there's nothing certain except taxes and – death.'

This initial shot runs for 17 seconds (and the whole scene for no more than 50). Even taken out of their story context, the visual and aural elements I have described combine to create a remarkable density of meaning. The elegant woman walking unafraid in the streets is, like the barbershop itself, part of a civilising process which is represented by schools and churches and thus requires a tax system; which is incompatible with the rule of the gun; which has to be underpinned by a strong, legitimate authority. The sheriff's gunbelt stands metonymically for this

Frames, appearing on this and subsequent pages: the barbershop sequence in Dodge City.

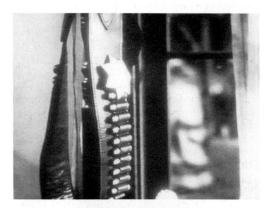

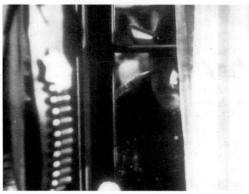

(editor), and Max Steiner (composer), plus others on both sides of the camera. Without being rude, one can term it a 'production line' film. Needing another Errol Flynn vehicle, Warner turns, for variation, to the Western, a genre that has been out of favour for high-status features throughout most of the decade. And Curtiz and his team discover, or in some cases rediscover, the sheer richness of the genre's vocabulary, and take advantage of the way in which, to quote Jim Kitses in *Horizons West* (1969):

' . . . over the years, a highly sophisticated sub-language of the cinema has been created that is intuitively understood by the audience, a firm basis for art. It is not just that in approaching the Western a director has a structure that is saturated with conceptual significance: the core of meanings is in the imagery itself . . .'

It is precisely its production-line status that makes

authority, which has all the more force when the gun can be wielded symbolically rather than physically, as at the barber's. In this little vignette of a scene, legitimate authority confronts and defeats the law of the gun, and records another victory in the long struggle to make the streets safe for women in long dresses and to establish a civilised dispensation of homes, churches, and unwelcome but 'necessary' taxes.

Not only the film, *Dodge City* (1939), but the genre, the Western, is here in miniature.

I called the density of meaning remarkable, and it is, but the scene is at the same time quite unremarkable, in that it's an unobtrusive building block in the narrative of a popular genre film, made for a major studio (Warner) by a team of unpretentious contracted professionals who had worked together several times already in rapid succession and would do so again: Michael Curtiz (director), Errol Flynn (star), Sol Polito (cinematographer), George Amy

and rephrasing . . . [it constitutes] a kind of cinematic source book of the West . . . Moreover, it is to *Dodge City* rather than *Stagecoach* that we must look for the source of the thematic ideas worked out by Ford himself from *My Darling Clementine* to *The Man Who Shot Liberty Valance*.'

Morse's admirable essay seems to have had little influence on critical writing in the two decades since it appeared in *Monogram 6* (1975), though it is reprinted in the Curtiz section of *Passport to Hollywood* (McGraw Hill, New York, 1976), an anthology on film immigrants edited by Don Whittemore and Philip Cecchettini. *Dodge City*, Curtiz and Flynn continue to attract little attention compared with *Stagecoach*, Ford and Wayne; James Robertson's book on Curtiz, *The Casablanca Man* (1993), is critically more lightweight than one would have thought it possible for an author study from a reputable publisher (Routledge) to get away with in the 1990s.

The centrality of *Dodge City* to the Western and its development, argued at the commercial level by Buscombe and at the thematic one by Morse, can be demonstrated equally at the most detailed level of narrative and formal organisation, as the barbershop scene suggests. In the context of the film as a whole, that scene relates to a formidable network of imagery to do with guns, authority, taxes, churches, women, and the safety of the streets – in short, the process of civilising the West.

'The Civil War has ended.
Armies disband –
the nation turns to the building of the west.'

This opening title is followed by a close-up of the funnel of a speeding train, belching black smoke. The train overtakes a stage coach, triumphantly. Inside are the capitalist developers – of, respectively, the railroad and of the settlements that it will promote – heading towards the celebration of a new railhead. On the train, a Black servant causes amusement by his nervousness at the speed of the journey (nearly 20 mph): 'I don't like this zizzing along.' At the railhead, an Indian holds the spike which is ceremonially driven in before the speeches start. Unless I have missed a fleeting appearance in the corner of the frame somewhere, we will see no more Blacks and no more Indians for the rest of the film. Where *Drums Along the Mohawk*, in the same year, manipulates them as willing subordinates in its vision of White nation-building (*see* Robin Wood's essay in this book), *Dodge City* simply alludes to them, and then, with breathtaking insouciance, excludes them from the terms of the narrative. Frontier savagery will not, in this film, be represented by Indians.

Colonel Dodge (Henry O'Neill) marks the ceremony with the oration of a true Western entrepreneur:

'Ladies and gentlemen. Today a great chapter of history has been written. And we take justifiable pride in bringing this railroad to the terminal furthest West in this country. Some day, and I believe it will be in the near future, a great city will spring from this very spot upon which we now stand: a city which

Dodge City such a good illustration of this. Kitses himself chooses, as his first reference point, the Sunday morning sequence in *My Darling Clementine* (John Ford, 1946), a celebrated and 'poetic' high point in the work of a Western specialist. He could equally have reached for an unspecial narrative scene by a director with no great personal stake in the Western, like Curtiz's scene in the barbershop.

In his monograph on *Stagecoach* (British Film Institute, 1992), Edward Buscombe points out that, among 1939 Westerns, considerably greater resources, in production and promotion alike, went into *Dodge City* (which is in Technicolor) than into Ford's far more celebrated film, and suggests that it was *Dodge City*'s commercial success, along with that of *Jesse James* (Henry King, 1939), that was decisive in restoring the high-budget Western to favour after the dip of the mid-1930s. David Morse has developed the same *Dodge City/Stagecoach* opposition in thematic terms, seeing the former as a 'seminal' influence because of the sheer wealth of incident and imagery it deploys to tell its exemplary story of town-taming:

'It is no derogation of *Stagecoach* but rather a recognition of the film's outstanding quality to point out that precisely because of its classic simplicity, clarity of outline and economy of structure it represented a formula that could not easily be varied or have changes rung upon it in the traditional Hollywood manner . . . On the other hand, it is the very openness of *Dodge City*, the sheer multiplicity, verging on redundancy, of its thematic and iconographical material, that leaves open the possibility of rearticulation

will represent all that the West stands for – honesty, courage, morality, and culture, for all the noble virtues of civilisation. I can see a great metropolis of homes, churches, schools, a fine decent city which will become the flower of the prairie . . .'

The exuberant gunfire that applauds this vision merges seamlessly into the anarchic gunfire of the near future: by 1872, the place has become, as more written titles tell us, 'the wide-open Babylon of the frontier . . . a town that knew no ethics but cash and killing'. Typically, the written message is at once duplicated in images, a montage of violence; much of the pleasure of the film comes from its energetic overdetermination of meaning. The montage contains a brief shot of a CLOSED sign going up outside the sheriff's office. As if this weren't eloquent enough in itself, the frame is extravagantly tilted, the letter S in the word Closed is written the wrong way round, and Steiner's music emphasises the disharmony.

Civilisation versus wildness: the film is as explicit, as graphic, as knowing, in its articulation of these antinomies as Ford is in *The Man Who Shot Liberty Valance*, or as Kitses in *Horizons West*, and it continues in the same vein.

Montage gives way to narrative, and a decent cattleman is cold-bloodedly shot dead in the saloon, leaving a wife and young son. Legitimate authority is exposed as powerless. Cut to the film's first domestic interior, a drawing room, where the local doctor (played by familiar character actor Henry Travers, whose fussy, cuddly persona goes with the elaborate

Still: Dodge City – *dignitaries and cattlemen celebrate the arrival of the railroad. Top centre: Colonel Dodge (Henry O'Neill). Below, left to right: Rusty (Alan Hale), Wade Hatton (Errol Flynn) and Tex (Guinn 'Big Boy' Williams).*

furniture and the pastel shades) laments that all the respectable settlers are going to rival towns: 'We're the public disgrace of America.' His wife responds with the first significant line that the film grants to a woman (other than a song in the saloon): 'It's becoming unsafe for women to walk on the streets of this town. And as for children . . .'

We already know very well who is destined to clean up the town and make its streets safe for women and children: the star of the film, Errol Flynn. He was in Dodge City on the day of the railhead ceremony, but there is no sign of him six years later. His Wade Hatton is loosely based on Wyatt Earp. Like Henry Fonda's Earp in *My Darling Clementine*, who trailed associations from his three Ford/Fox heroes of quietly charismatic integrity – *The Young Mr Lincoln* (1939), Gil Martin in *Drums Along the Mohawk* (1939) and Tom Joad in *The Grapes of Wrath* (1940) – Flynn brings to his role a strong star image built up through a series of films made for a single studio and a single director. These two town-taming Westerns, linked by David Morse at the end of the passage quoted earlier, offer a suggestive comparison at various levels: one of the key variables, along with director and moment of production (immediately before, and after, World War II) is the star persona.

Before *Dodge City*, Curtiz and Flynn had made six films together, none of them Westerns. Three of Flynn's roles made an especially strong impact: the pirate of *Captain Blood* (1935); the army officer who led *The Charge of the Light Brigade* (1936); and the title role in *The Adventures of Robin Hood* (1938). Crucial to the appeal of all three characters is their outlaw status. Even Major Geoffrey Vickers, a loyal soldier, has altered the Light Brigade's orders by an act of mutinous forgery, so that the eventual charge carries the same combination of physical exhilaration with outlaw defiance as the rope-swinging exploits of Flynn's pirate and forestman. All three characters, of course, have rebelled against authorities who are unjust or incompetent, and they have higher loyalties: to the principles of Justice, and to the (rightful) English crown. So the films, and their audiences, can have it both ways in the classic manner, enjoying subversive behaviour which is not ideologically threatening – particularly not to American audiences. This is not far from the tensions that are central to the appeal of the Western, but the transplanting of the Flynn persona to the West is quite a complex process.

The Hollywood version of England and its overseas empire, the setting for Flynn's earlier successes, offered a rich supply of effete and corrupt establishment figures, redolent of centuries of stuffy tradition, for him to campaign against: on the frontier of republican America, no equivalent is available, except on the much smaller scale of a figure like Gatewood (Berton Churchill), the crooked banker of *Stagecoach*. John Wayne's Ringo Kid in fact has the 'good outlaw' status of Flynn's earlier roles, but it's hard to imagine Flynn in that part: his causes are always public ones, or at least have a public dimension, and the figure of Hatton in *Dodge City* – the leader of men who gives up his itinerant cowboy life to establish a just society – makes sense as his first big American role (Irish-American, in fact, when he remembers the accent), and as his entry into the Western.

The danger that he and the film have to avoid is that of Hatton being too conformist a figure. At the start, he and his two sidekicks, Rusty (Alan Hale) and Tex (Guinn 'Big Boy' Williams), are presented as being firmly at the service of the capitalists engaged in the development of the West. At the ceremony that celebrates the new railhead, it's Hatton who publicly suggests that the settlement be named after Colonel Dodge. One way in which the film negotiates this problem is by the conventional generic strategy of setting Hatton up as an individualist and a wanderer. Immediately after his naming of the new town, the Colonel tries to persuade him to settle there and help give it stability. He won't consider it, and Rusty explains his refusal by telling the Colonel of Hatton's record as a freelance adventurer in a series of wars and jobs and countries: 'He's the most movin'-on man you ever saw.' When, after the six-year break, they pass through Dodge City again, to deliver and sell a big herd of cattle, Hatton reacts so forthrightly to the heavies who run the place that he is implored to take the job of

sheriff. Again, he insists that he will be moving on, until a major outrage changes his mind.

Hatton is thus set on a trajectory from individualism to social responsibility, from wandering to settling, that has become thoroughly familiar within the genre, although I know of no earlier film that had used it with quite the same clarity of emphasis. But in itself, this is a bit tame for Flynn. The film's additional strategy is to split him, in effect, into three, giving him two alter egos which express the nonconformist outlaw spirit more vigorously than it is safe to do through Hatton himself.

The scene everyone remembers from *Dodge City* is the protracted and exhilarating brawl in the saloon in which the Civil War is refought and the furniture comprehensively broken up. This happens after Hatton has brought the cattle in, during the brief period of rest and recreation that precedes moving on. The brawl is the sort of acrobatic action set-piece with which Flynn had become identified, yet he is absent from it; and he has to be, else he would not have the gravitas to become sheriff in due course. The film has to contrive his absence without making him seem a tame spoil-sport, and it provides a shamelessly mechanical line for him to say to Rusty, outside the saloon: 'I've got a call to make down here, so you're on your own.' We learn nothing about this call and there is no cross-cutting between him and the brawl; it's purely a device to keep him away. Tex and Rusty will participate, as it were, on his behalf.

But Rusty too has a call to make that initially keeps him from the saloon. When Tex and friends press him to come in with them for the standard ritual of celebrating the end of a long trail and the payment of wages, he refuses because he has taken the pledge of abstinence. The comic incongruity of this (in terms both of what we have seen of Rusty hitherto, and of the actor, Alan Hale, in previous roles such as Little John to Flynn's Robin Hood) is multiplied when he voluntarily enters the meeting of the ladies' section of the Pure Prairie League. Hymn-singing, tea-drinking, pots of jam on a side-table, and bonneted ladies – the imagery of refinement is laid on very thick. Asked whether he is married, he reacts with a nervous spasm that audibly shakes his teacup in its saucer.

Meanwhile, in the saloon next door, Tex and friends drink whiskey, respond eagerly to provocation, and soon get caught up in escalating violence, with Tex taking the lead at every stage.

Once again, the core antinomy of the Western couldn't be more knowingly, more diagrammatically constructed than in this famously entertaining set-piece. On one side of the wall, unrestrained all-male wildness, on the other side, the female space of refinement and civilisation and settling and the question of marriage. In the short term, it is no contest: the brawl crashes through the dividing wall, and the troubled Rusty joins in with a loud yippee. In the longer term, things will be different.

Dodge City hardly fits the category of the psychological Western, and there are few stars who convey less psychological inwardness than Errol Flynn; instead, psychic conflicts are externalised, played out in action. While Hatton's ego is occupied somewhere offstage, Rusty, incongruously and temporarily, represents the superego, Tex the id. The forces of the id are stronger: in Flynn's physical absence, they can be cathartically indulged, and played out, as in dream, *for* him, as for the spectator.

Lying exhausted as the brawl ends, Rusty is detained by Jeff Surrett (Bruce Cabot), owner of the devastated saloon, terroriser of the town, enemy of the law. He takes Rusty off to be hanged. Hatton, with gun, intervenes successfully, and marches Surrett off to the sheriff's office, which is still closed. Too bad. Saving Rusty is the main thing. At a meeting convened in the female-dominated space of the doctor's house, Hatton courteously but very firmly turns down the plea to become sheriff himself. With Tex and Rusty, he'll be moving on the next day.

It's a politer version of the reply given to a similar request, in Ford's Tombstone. Fonda's Wyatt Earp is 'not interested' in the job of Marshal: what causes him to take it is the discovery, when he rides back to camp, that his own brother has been killed and his cattle taken. In contrast, the turning-point for Hatton has nothing to do with violence either against his own property or against the quasi-family of Tex and Rusty. Preparing to leave town, he watches a group of women and children leave by horse and cart on a church outing. A sudden gunfight on the main street causes the horse to panic, and even Hatton's athletic dash to the rescue – at last, a moment of real action for Flynn – cannot prevent a young boy being dragged to his death.

This is the same boy whose father we saw murdered early in the film by Surrett and his cronies: told that he is now the man of the family, he has taken to wearing a mock sheriff's badge as a token of this precocious authority. Now, as he lies dead on the street, the camera moves from Hatton's face to the childish badge; quick dissolve to a real sheriff's badge on a gunbelt; pull back to frame Hatton, as he buckles on the belt, looking grim; then move left and down, following his glance, to a newspaper headline announcing 'HATTON BECOMES SHERIFF'. Reinforced by portentous music, it's another emphatic, even oppressive, 'overdetermination' of meaning and leads into a montage of cleaning up the town as Hatton enforces a gun law and throws offenders into jail.

The menace to women and children, then, is what decides him. Flynn's persona is essentially chivalric,

as in his pirate films (both *Captain Blood* and its 1940 successor *The Sea Hawk*), and in *Robin Hood*, and in *The Charge of the Light Brigade*, where his mutinous actions were motivated by the burning desire to avenge a tribal leader's massacre of army wives and children (none of them his own). Atrocities will be avenged.

It's a truism to say that Westerns tell us at least as much about the time they are made as about the time in which they are set. David Morse's essay is convincing in its reading of *Dodge City* as a Western version of a 1930s gangster film, with Surrett and cronies as public enemies who must be eliminated, and a crusading press which helps to stir up public awareness through banner headlines (sometimes in montage form). This helps to explain the absence of Indians: the film is about the threat to civilisation posed by the savage Other from within the city, not from outside. Morse also discusses the political significance of the figure of the 'reluctant hero', but without, curiously, relating it to 1939. *Dodge City*, in its heavily coded form, surely contributes to the debate about American policy towards the crisis in Europe, its sympathies being, like Roosevelt's, anti-isolationist. We don't want to get involved, to play sheriff, but Nazi-style atrocities may force us to, even if they don't threaten our personal interests directly. In contrast, *My Darling Clementine* can be seen (though other political readings are possible – *see* Peter Biskind's *Seeing Is Believing*, Random House, New York, 1983) as a retrospect on the war from a slightly different angle, that of the Irish Ford and the pro-Republican Fox as opposed to Curtiz (a European Jew) and the pro-Roosevelt Warner: their America was 'not interested' in intervening, until (with Pearl Harbor) its own family and property were directly attacked.

So: Hatton takes the job and cleans up Dodge City, with a combination of single-mindedness, humour and efficiency, through a narrative that still has some way to go but does not need to be chronicled in detail. Even from a selective account of the film to this point, it can be seen how much extra meaning the brief barbershop scene, described at the start, accumulates from its context. Once Hatton takes power, Surrett and his gang are doomed, and they all die in a final action sequence. But, like *My Darling Clementine* after the elimination of the Clantons, *Dodge City* has a significant epilogue.

The wildness of the saloon (id) may have triumphed over the refinement of the Pure Prairie League (superego) in the central brawl scene, but the triangle of Hatton-Tex-Rusty now has a very different balance. Tex makes a bid for freedom, but Hatton is too clever for him, and he stays part of the law-enforcement team. The epilogue finds the three men in the upstairs drawing-room of Doc

Stills: Dodge City. *Left – Wade and Rusty confront Jeff Surrett (Bruce Cabot). Opposite – the newspaper office, with Mrs Cole (Gloria Holden), who has lost her son and husband to Dodge City violence, editor Joe Clemens (Frank McHugh), soon to become another victim, and Abbie Irvine (Olivia De Havilland).*

Irvine's house, with its elegant curtains and wallpaper and chairs. It's as if all of them have joined the Pure Prairie League after all. The first image of the sequence is of a peaceful main street busy with people (women in long dresses prominent among them); we hear church music, and Rusty comments on the scene as the camera pulls back inside the room:

'Now listen to that – singing hymns, and it ain't even Sunday. No-one in sight even friendly drunk. Doggone if this place ain't getting so pure and noble it ain't fit to live in.'

And Tex announces that he is 'sure enough going back to Texas now'.

Enter Colonel Dodge. It turns out that, since giving his name to the place, he has gone to develop Virginia City in Nevada, and is building a railway to link it with San Francisco. It's a rich town, but also 'a wild, murderous town. Worse than Dodge City ever was, before you cleaned it up, and that's saying a good deal. I want you to come back there with me.'

This splits Hatton's psyche apart again. Tex and Rusty jump at the prospect of regressing from civilised West to wild West; Hatton admits it would be 'a great trip', but it's out of the question since he is getting married next week.

Hatton's progress up to this point has been comparable with that of Cole Hardin (Gary Cooper) in

The Westerner, made by William Wyler in the following year, 1940. Interviewed in the American magazine *Camera Obscura* ('A Journal of Feminism and Film Theory', issue 3/4, 1979), Raymond Bellour cites *The Westerner* as an exemplary instance of the 'classic' Western, and specifically of Anthony Mann's principle that 'without women the Western wouldn't work'. To paraphrase drastically: Hardin is the archetypal Western wanderer who is drawn into befriending a homesteading family and fighting their battles against marauding cattlemen and the crude frontier justice of their ally, 'Judge' Roy Bean (Walter Brennan); at the end, with the two main father-figures dead, he takes the place of the good (homesteading) one by marrying his daughter. Central to the Western genre, in Bellour's reading, is the giving of a territorial dimension to this standard oedipal narrative. The film opens on a map of Texas; the epilogue starts with a similar map, then pulls out to locate it on the wall of the newlyweds' home. The couple look complacently out of the window at the trail of incoming homesteaders. The man possesses both the woman and the land; the woman has tamed and domesticated both the man and the land; the personal and territorial dimensions reinforce, and are symbolic of, one another.

My account of *Dodge City* has so far contrived not to mention the romance between Hatton and the doctor's niece, Abbie – the story makes sense without

it, and yet without it the film 'wouldn't work'. Abbie is played by Olivia De Havilland, who has been Flynn's regular love interest from *Captain Blood* onward, and the shape of the role, as she moves from hostility to love, is as predictable as the casting; so is the structure of opposition between Abbie and Ann Sheridan's saloon girl, Ruby – akin to, though less intense than, that between (My Darling) Clementine (Cathy Downs) and Chihuahua (Linda Darnell). Throughout the narrative, Abbie acts both as incentive to, and as reward for, Hatton's acts of public responsibility. At the meeting in her uncle's house, she was scathing about his rejection of public office; in the runaway cart setting out on the church outing, it was she from whom the doomed boy took over the reins. Every visual and verbal reference to women and children and homes and churches finds its specific meaning and embodiment in Abbie. Hatton's engagement to her represents, in line with Bellour's model, both his territorial conquest – the town is now successfully tamed – and his domestication. The bandage on his finger, acquired, we infer, in the final struggle with the heavies on a burning train, operates as an unobtrusive marker of symbolic castration (compare the much more obtrusive one on the forcibly settled wanderer L.B. Jeffries of *Rear Window*, Alfred Hitchcock, 1954).

But with one bound, Hatton can still be free, a roamer and an adventurer. Unlike Jeffries and Hardin, and their audiences, he can go back to having the best of both worlds. Refusing Dodge's offer, he tells him, not without wistfulness, of the impending honeymoon in the East and of the decision to 'settle down'. Unknown to him, Abbie, pausing at the door with a tray of lemonade, has overheard the conversation. After handing round the glasses, she goes up to the Colonel and sweetly asks him: 'When do we start for Virginia City?'

Hatton is too polite to do more than look gratified. But Rusty and Tex at once enter the shot at his shoulders, making a culminating triangle image that echoes the way we first saw them, and they holler the wild delight that he can't express on his own account.

Where does this leave Abbie, and the woman spectator? Evidently marginalised: subordinated to male desire, and conniving in their own subordination. But this seems too simplistic a reading; at least, others are available.

As in other respects, the film is more sophisticated, more knowing, in its treatment of gender issues than might at first appear, even foregrounding them in a mid-film discussion. Hatton is startled to find Abbie working as a journalist on the town's newspaper. Challenged by him, she explains that 'the paper needed to have someone who could write the things that would interest its women readers': things like gossip and babies and clothes. Women will constitute, as the town develops, a significant share of the paper's potential readership, just as they do of the cinema audience, and the scene functions as a displaced discussion of why women might like to watch Westerns; if studios are now committing big budgets to them, women will need to be attracted.

In his *Stagecoach* monograph, Buscombe describes how the female audience was targeted in that film's marketing, through an emphasis on the women characters and their wardrobe, and on the incident of the baby's birth during the journey. I have not researched the marketing of *Dodge City*, but it would be no surprise to find a comparable targeting of women through, for instance, an emphasis on costume design in Technicolor. At the same time, the tone of Abbie's speech about women's readership is at least half ironic, teasing Hatton about his stereotyped assumptions about what women are interested in and fit for. Abbie herself, in this scene, wears pink, opposite Hatton's blue-for-a-boy shirt, but we find her, soon after, in blue herself, as she turns serious investigative journalist in order to help build up a court case against Surrett.

Where Hatton's main movement is from wanderer to settler, Abbie moves, if anything, in the opposite direction. She is first seen on the journey to join her aunt and uncle in Dodge City, hating the life of the cattle trail; in town, she moves from the purely domestic sphere to a job; she ends on the trail again, this time cheerfully so, whatever her underlying motives. Giving up the Dodge City home and the Eastern honeymoon may not simply be an act of sacrifice for her man; married life may be more fulfilling for her on the trail, and on the frontier, than in the genteel home – why can't she, like the boys, be allowed to feel on her own account a certain dissatisfaction with the tame middle-America of the civilised settlement?

The point is not that such a reading is correct, but that both are possible: Abbie as conventionally subservient, Abbie as a progressive underminer of feminine stereotypes. This is a dimension of the 'openness' that David Morse drew attention to, which is not just a quantitative inclusiveness ('a cinematic source book of the West') but a thematic one. *Dodge City* holds in a peculiarly satisfying tension the key antinomies of the genre: wandering/settling, wildness/civilisation, male/female. The final quick transition from interior to exterior has the same compressed eloquence as the barbershop scene. From the elegant drawing room, to horse-drawn wagons on the trail, silhouetted against a glowing orange sunset, a wonderfully over-the-top image, with matching music; then the happy couple holding the reins, then back to the sunset.

Among other things, it is an image of generic renewal. Genre cinema brings one film to a resolution while encouraging the audience to come back for another. The final knowing device of *Dodge City* is to build this aspect, too, into the narrative itself, making the coda into a trailer. The work of this film, this place, has been finished, brought to equilibrium, and the team turn their attention to the next job and prepare themselves for the renewed attractions of the wide open spaces and of violent frontier conflict. Hatton and Dodge and company set out for Virginia City; and Flynn and Curtiz and company look ahead to their next Western assignment for Warner, which will indeed be entitled *Virginia City*. And that is, in every sense, another story.

DUEL IN THE SUN
The Destruction of an Ideological System

Robin Wood

Whether you can make sense of *Duel in the Sun* (1946) has always been at issue; many, indeed, question whether the film merits the attempt. Initial responses mainly vacillated between ridicule and disgust: the feeling that the film is both absurd and degrading is epitomised in its familiar popular re-christening as 'Lust in the Dust'. There was a general satisfaction in the sense that David O. Selznick, after the universal acclaim of *Gone With the Wind* (Victor Fleming, 1939) and *Rebecca* (Alfred Hitchcock, 1940), had not only overreached but made himself ridiculous, and deserved humiliation for his hubris. A parallel, recent reaction is the almost universal ridicule that greeted *Heaven's Gate* (1980) after the young upstart Michael Cimino's multi-Oscared *The Deer Hunter* (1978). The awe and idolatry that spectacular success in Hollywood inspires inevitably has as its corollary a profound resentment and readiness to pounce on the first 'lapse'.

Still, today, it is virtually impossible to convince the majority of film students that *Duel in the Sun* is even a good movie, let alone a great one. I use it frequently on courses as a provocation and a challenge, with the modest hope of convincing students that it is at least interesting, and screenings are invariably disrupted by the recurrent and contagious laughter of those who wish to express (and inflict on everyone else) their sophisticated superiority to such obvious trash. Melodrama as a genre, and the 'melodramatic' as a stylistic choice, are now widely accepted by intellectuals as legitimate modes of artistic expression within the classical Hollywood cinema, but general viewers persist in finding them embarrassing and ridiculous. The ridicule is, of course, a defence against the embarrassment, and it is the embarrassment, above all, that makes melodrama so interesting.

I have argued elsewhere, in an article on Vincente Minnelli's 1949 *Madame Bovary* (*CineAction!* 7), that the excesses of the melodramatic style are the expression of hysteria (always an embarrassing phenomenon), and that the source of hysteria is the feeling of powerlessness – which explains why Freud, in the context of late nineteenth-century Viennese bourgeois culture, associated it primarily with women, a perfectly legitimate perception that today provokes a deal of unjustified feminist anger. I also suggested, in the same article, that the star image of Jennifer Jones is centred on hysteria, whether she is playing Ruby Gentry or Saint Bernadette (which is why her mere presence has such a disruptive effect within the otherwise thoroughly conservative and conformist *Since You Went Away*, John Cromwell, 1944). Jones is clearly crucial to *Duel in the Sun*: one can imagine other stars as Pearl (Gene Tierney, for example), but none would have brought to the role quite such a hysterical edge, from her opening dance to her bloody demise. Hysteria must be seen as a form of active, if impotent, protest; if it lacks revolutionary *effect*, it has revolutionary *meaning*.

Duel in the Sun, however, is not simply a film about a hysterical protagonist: by virtue of its melodramatic excess it must be considered one of Hollywood's hysterical texts. Looked at superficially, Pearl (like Ruby Gentry after her) is a fairly typical representative of the 'bad girl' stereotype, the girl from 'the wrong side of the tracks', who – from a combination of ignorance, unrepressed energy, and a 'bad' environment – must, whatever her intentions, wreak havoc on bourgeois security and be punished for it, leaving the hero and the entirely boring 'good girl' to their supposedly contented but uneventful future of domesticity. But the film is emphatically and demonstrably on Pearl's side: her hysteria – its disruptive influence, its revolutionary implications – pervades every aspect of the film, determines its style, produces its storms, its lurid sunsets, the intolerable heat of its sun, and finally precludes any possibility of that satisfying and pacifying sense of resolution that is supposed to be a permanent and necessary feature of traditional narrative. If she had survived the final duel, she might well have declared, amid the ruins of ideological coherence, like Medea in Pier Paolo Pasolini's great work, that 'Nothing is possible any more'.

Although it is not of primary importance, one may ask what is the probable source (aside from Pearl and Jones) of the film's melodramatic excess – consider, in other words, that difficult question of authorship. Very much 'A David O. Selznick Production', the film is attributed to King Vidor as director, but it is common knowledge that numerous other directors (not even counting 'second units', and including, for a few days, Josef von Sternberg) came and went. It seems also to be documented that Selznick shot parts of it himself, besides playing a dominant role in the overall conception (as he had previously done on *Gone with the Wind* and on 'Hitchcock's' *Rebecca*). I am not going to attempt the task (both impossible and pointless) of speculating as to who was responsible for this or that. What does seem interesting is how the film relates to the careers of both Selznick and Vidor. Selznick, as one of Hollywood's 'creative'

Stills: Duel in the Sun. *Animal magnetism – Pearl (Jennifer Jones) and Lewt (Gregory Peck).*

producers (he played a very active role in his own productions and clearly saw himself as much more than a businessman), showed a consistent interest in the woman-centred melodrama; he was also married to Jennifer Jones and conceived *Duel in the Sun* partly as a vehicle for her which would at once redefine and extend her persona. *Gone With the Wind, Rebecca,* and *Since You Went Away* (arguably his three most ambitious films, at least in terms of the 'prestige production') are all concerned, in very different ways, with the struggles of a woman to survive and establish herself in a world where men make the rules; the first two also exhibit a fascination with the transgressive woman (Scarlett, Rebecca) who refuses to be contained by them. Vidor was previously associated with films on 'important' social issues, before women's oppression was generally recognised as one of them: *The Big Parade, The Crowd, Our Daily Bread.* These films all show a tendency toward the 'melodramatic' (for audiences today, with their

much more acute awareness of racism, and of the insidious positions into which Hollywood films about all-Black communities are forced to contort themselves, melodrama is the only aspect of *Hallelujah!* that makes the film endurable), but they are consistently male-centred. For Vidor, *Duel in the Sun* can be seen as a turning-point, the first film in an extraordinary (and still monstrously underrated) trilogy continued in *Ruby Gentry* and completed in *Beyond the Forest*: films uncompromisingly committed to their female protagonists' hysterical and 'excessive' responses to their entrapment within the male order. *Duel in the Sun* can be seen as at once the culmination of Selznick's fascination with female transgression and the beginning of Vidor's.

The introduction to Jim Kitses's *Horizons West* (1969), with its grid of structural antinomies, is one of the seminal texts in the study of the Western, and indeed of genre in general. It still retains its usefulness provided it is seen (as Kitses explicitly intended) as a starting point for the exploration of individual films, rather than a straitjacket into which every Western must be squeezed. For many great

Westerns, it provides no more than a means of defining their divergence, their specificity: the 'master antinomy', wilderness/civilisation, won't get you very far in understanding *Rio Bravo* or *Rancho Notorious*, which relate more to the respective authorial systems of Howard Hawks and Fritz Lang than to the generic system of the Western. But it has proved indispensable for an understanding of John Ford, and when you apply it to *Duel in the Sun*, an apparently diffuse, sprawling, anomalous work suddenly makes perfect sense, so long as 'sense' is not equated with ideological coherence.

Indeed, the first point to be made about the specifically American ideology (an idiosyncratic variation on or inflection of the patriarchal capitalist ideology of western civilisation) is that it is not coherent: it is riddled with contradictions, which it must work continuously to conceal or appear to reconcile. The point to be made about the wilderness/civilisation antinomy, and its close relative and derivative wandering/settling, is that both sides of the opposition are simultaneously valued and deplored. The 'safer' Westerns attempt the work of concealment/recon-

ciliation. Take *Shane* (George Stevens, 1953), for example. Shane, the wanderer from the wilderness, retains (or is meant to – Alan Ladd's insuperable blandness works against it) the charisma that the settled family man has forfeited, but his function is to sacrifice himself for family and settlement, the film contemplating his final, famous ride away into the mountains with a kind of pleasant regret and nostalgia that goes easily with a sense of satisfaction: the resolution is classically perfect. The film comes as close as is possible to reconciling ideological contradiction: compare Ethan (John Wayne) riding away at the end of *The Searchers* (John Ford, 1956), leaving behind him the total wreckage of ideological (not to mention narrative) coherence.

It is the achievement of *Duel in the Sun* to leave the ideology a heap of irreparable debris while maintaining perfect coherence in the narrative. Nowhere in it will we find any equivalent to Laurie's abrupt and unprepared sentiment in *The Searchers* that Ethan *ought* to kill Debbie because her mother would have wanted it, an utterance that manages to be at once totally out of character and obviously untrue;

or Debbie's abrupt but convenient reconversion from a passionate Comanche squaw to a sweet little puritan White girl (considered as motivation, Ethan's repetition of his early gesture of lifting her in his arms is ludicrously insufficient). Or, above all, the hopelessly vacillating and unthinking presentation of the Indians, the attitude towards whom lurches about from scene to scene (the treatment of 'Look' is especially problematic and distasteful). *Duel in the Sun* should rightly occupy the place of *The Searchers* as the Hollywood cinema's most challenging and subversive statement about American civilisation, as this is achieved without the necessity of disintegrating before our eyes. I'm afraid that the reason why the film does not occupy that position may be that its central figure, around whom everything revolves, is not a man but a woman, not John Wayne but Jennifer Jones.

No one is likely to question that Pearl is the centre of the narrative. What may be slightly less obvious is that she is the centre of its dramatisation of ideological contradiction. A chart may be useful to demonstrate this, without by any means exhausting its implications:

FATHERS:
McCanles   Chavez

MOTHERS:
Indian Woman ——— PEARL ——— Laurabelle

LOVERS:
Lewt   Jesse

The forces that tear Pearl apart are not merely allegiances to alternative characters, but contradictions in the ideology, which are recognised uncompromisingly as irreconcilable. Roughly, the left side of the chart corresponds to 'wilderness', the right to 'civilisation', though in this film nothing is that simple: the crippled land-baron, Senator McCanles (Lionel Barrymore), is scarcely a 'wanderer', the decadent gambler Chavez (Herbert Marshall) a highly untypical representative of the 'settler', the opposition complicated further by the obvious North/South antinomy. But the essential point is that the film consistently undercuts any possibility of the spectator finding one side 'good', the other 'bad': *Duel in the Sun* offers no easy options. The ideological choices by which Pearl is torn are exposed as equally unacceptable, unfulfilling, incomplete, along with the characters who embody them.

1) *The Fathers.* If McCanles – who lives in a great mansion, has built himself an empire, is symbolically crippled and cannot control his horse – scarcely appears a figure of the wilderness, he represents a primitive phase in the evolution of capitalism that retains clear vestiges of it. He is the brutal patriarch of barbarism, adamantly opposed to the 'progress' that threatens his way of life (in the tangible shape of the railroad), tyrannical, insensitive, virulently

192

racist and wholeheartedly committed to the most debased forms of 'masculinity', which he encourages in his son Lewt (Gregory Peck). The inappropriateness of his marriage to the ultra-refined Southern lady Laurabelle (Lillian Gish) is precisely balanced (as a kind of mirror-inversion) by the pairing of the Southern gentleman Chavez with a Native American woman (Tilly Losch). Chavez, despite his degradation in the eyes of society, clings on to his self-image of genteel refinement and respectability, ultimately murdering the woman whose energies he cannot control or circumscribe. McCanles doesn't murder Laurabelle, yet her death is felt to parallel that of Pearl's biological mother: she dies because Mc-Canles has deprived her of anything to live for.

2) *The Mothers.* Pearl's Native American mother is succinctly characterised by a dance (her death during the film's first few minutes scarcely allowing for detailed character development); her adoptive mother Laurabelle is characterised by a song. The dance, in the drinking and gambling saloon of the film's opening, is public, exhibitionist, expressive of a violent and uncontrollable energy and vividly marked by 'possession of the phallus': Losch (the character is not identified by name), as she circles the platform, is juxtaposed with a cannon, and the dance culminates in her firing of a pistol. The film links this immediately to sexual freedom, as she joyfully offers herself to members of her all-male audience. Although she is at the opposite end of the social scale, she has to die for precisely the same reason that Rebecca died in Selznick's earlier work. The character of course embodies a racist stereotype, an entire mythology of 'Indianicity' encompassing all Puritanism's fears of 'the return of the repressed'. In the context of the film, however, these traits are no more condemned than their opposites. Traditionally, in the Western, untrammelled energy (a 'natural' value of the wilderness, which civilisation inhibits) has been the preserve of the male (the 'savage redskin', Liberty Valance himself). It is crucial to the particularity of *Duel in the Sun* that it is here associated with the unrepressed female, and the unbreakable bond between mother and daughter is established at the outset, the mother's dance inside the saloon imitated by Pearl's outside it. The typical Western heroine has traditionally been the bearer of civilisation, the motivation for clearing the land, building the cabin, exterminating the 'savage' both within and without, her role being that of wife, mother, nurturer; and women who fail to meet these requirements (typically, the 'saloon entertainer') can hope for no happier fate than a redemptive death,

Still: Duel in the Sun – *the puritanical and lascivious sin-killer (Walter Huston) verbally assaults Pearl under the anxious gaze of Laurabelle.*

taking a bullet intended for the hero. *Duel in the Sun*, more perhaps than any other Western, concerns itself *positively* with the problem of female energy within the terms of the genre (which are roughly the terms of ideology).

Losch's opposite is Laurabelle the 'beautiful dreamer': the song, an archetypal expression of repression/sublimation, is associated with her throughout on the soundtrack, and she briefly plays and sings it. Against the active, 'phallic' woman is set the passive, symbolically castrated woman of patriarchal culture, the film's supreme embodiment of the 'civilised', whose life is reduced to a 'dream' within which she is powerless to act. Laurabelle is a character who seems to live only for her death scene, fragile, chronically sickly and impotent. Her attempts to civilise Pearl, to transform her into the traditional 'good girl', are never endorsed by the film: if it shows uncontrolled energy to be essentially destructive, it presents its repression as equally so. Hence the appropriateness of the two mothers' respective deaths, Losch shot down with a lover by her husband, Laurabelle gradually worn down by hers and literally wasting away. Her death inspires one of the most complex and stunning of the film's many melodramatic images: her empty rocking-chair, on the bedroom balcony, rocking violently in the storm, the traditional emblem of resignation and passive consolation juxtaposed with the forces of nature that she has spent her life denying.

Her death acquires another complex resonance in retrospect from the film's ending: her crawl from her deathbed towards her husband (unnoticed by him until it is too late) foreshadows Pearl's famous death-crawl through the desert dust to the dying Lewt. Both characters, destroyed by conflicts that are as much ideological as personal, can find no reconciliation in life.

Finally, one may note in passing the subtle use the film makes of Vashti (Butterfly McQueen) in relation to Laurabelle. Today's audiences, quite understandably, find Vashti an embarrassment: in many ways a repeat performance of McQueen's Prissy in *Gone With the Wind*, Vashti appears to be merely the stereotype of the 'stupid nigger', a sort of female version of Stepin Fetchit, and I would agree that the film gets too much mileage out of her stupidity. Yet she also provides it with one of its most poignant moments: unable to answer Lewt's question as to where everyone has gone, she reveals that the training she has received from gentle Laurabelle (whose own training has clearly given her as clear an idea of the 'correct' social position of Blacks as it has of that of women) has included the instruction that she is never to ask questions but is merely to 'go about her business'. Suddenly the stupidity receives an explanation, and as abruptly it ceases to be comic: Vashti has been *taught* to be stupid, and by the film's apparently faultless embodiment of the finest feminine virtues. Laurabelle's moral perfection is not without its weaknesses, another of which is her inability (as a woman and a good Christian) to see through Walter Huston's simultaneously puritanical and lascivious 'sin-killer'.

3) *The Lovers*. The function of Jesse (Joseph Cotten) and Lewt within the film's system of ideological contraries is succinctly defined by the parents' use of the same two words to describe them. Senator McCanles refers to Lewt proudly as 'My son, Ma'am'; Laurabelle counters this subsequently by asserting of Jesse, 'My son, Senator'. Lewt is characterised by wildness, energy, brutalism and a total egocentricity, Jesse by gentleness, consideration for others, a commitment to the progress of civilisation, and (although he is capable of standing by his principles) by a general ineffectuality. Lewt is associated with horses and the values of the Old West, Jesse with the railroad and the future (it is one of the film's nicer ironies that, outlawed, Lewt amuses himself by provoking train crashes). In keeping with the film's fundamental principle of construction, neither brother receives its endorsement. Like the two mothers and the two fathers, each is lacking – rendered incomplete, one might say, by an ideological system built upon irreconcilable and mutually exclusive oppositions.

In the most valuable article I have read on *Duel in the Sun* (*Framework* 15/16/17, 1981), Laura Mulvey compares it with *The Man Who Shot Liberty Valance* (John Ford, 1962), drawing parallels between the ideological functions of the leading characters. What must be stressed is that Lewt is not Tom Doniphon (he entirely lacks Doniphon's moral stature) and Jesse is not Ransom Stoddard (he lacks Stoddard's charismatic legal authority). The elegiac quality of Ford's film (which no-one would characterise as a 'hysterical text') has no place in Vidor's. *Duel in the Sun* expresses not the slightest nostalgia for the Old West: it cannot do so precisely because its leading character, our only possible identification-figure, is a woman. The choice (if that is what it can be called) it offers is between the brutalised and the ineffectual – it calls to mind Oscar Wilde's celebrated dictum that America is the only country that has passed directly from barbarism to decadence without any intervening period of civilisation. Despite the similarities in their use of the archetypal antinomies, the quandaries the two films dramatise are really quite different: that of Ford's film is that both sides of the wilderness/civilisation opposition are highly valued but cannot coexist; that of *Duel in the Sun* is that neither is, and if one wishes to find 'positive value', one must begin to search elsewhere. That is why *Duel in the Sun*, rightly understood, must strike us now as by far the more 'modern' of the two (which does not necessarily make it the better): its quandary is essentially ours today, as we struggle to find meaning amid the ideological wreckage it so vividly anticipates.

4) *Pearl*. Pearl, then, is not only the film's main character but the centre of its system of oppositions, continually torn apart by the contrary pulls of ideological conflict. Inheriting from her mother a 'natural' energy and activeness, taught by her father to be ashamed of the legacy, taught by McCanles to be ashamed of her colour, initiated by Laurabelle (whom her father idolised) into the mysteries of femininity and female castration, attracted at once

Still: Duel in the Sun – *Jesse facilitates the 'progress' of civilisation by cutting the wire to make way for the railroad; with Otto Kruger and Harry Carey.*

to Jesse's kindness and respect and to Lewt's wildness and sexual charisma, she is led inevitably into an unresolvable quandary that can end only in death. And death *is* merely an end, not a resolution, which the film cannot possibly offer. Neither is it the death of the 'bad girl' of Western tradition: unlike Chihuahua in *My Darling Clementine*, Pearl can neither be treated with contempt while she lives nor be sentimentalised when she dies. By killing Lewt, she chooses Jesse (though not by that time as a potential mate, a possibility earlier foreclosed by his own feeble indecision and subsequently by his finding the appropriate 'good girl'); yet, having mortally wounded Lewt, she must 'choose' him also, and die with him in a notably harsh, messy and unromantic *Liebestod*.

Like all the other major characters, Pearl has her opposite: the eminently civilised (read insipid and colourless) White woman who represents, in her union with Jesse, the civilised future, and in whom

the film shows no interest whatever. 'Colourless' indeed: the scene on the staircase between the two women, before Pearl rides off on her fatal mission, is striking in its visual contrast between Pearl's rich brown skin and the pasty pallor of Helen (Joan Tetzel), whose father, the future's corporation capitalist, is played by Otto Kruger, an actor consistently cast as a villain through most of his career. Civilisation triumphs, more or less, but the film conspicuously fails to celebrate it. And we all know that the spirit of the wilderness – of Lewt, whose charisma the film steadfastly refuses to glamorise – lives on today, in ever more debased forms, in the streets of all our 'civilised' cities. *Duel in the Sun* dramatises an ideological system that was rotten at its very foundations, and leaves it a heap of rubble.

NOTES ON PURSUED

Andrew Britton

The main concern and emphasis in *Pursued* (Raoul Walsh, 1947) might be described as the social determination of neurosis. The film belongs to a key area of Hollywood cinema that embraces films in many genres, from the musical (*The Pirate*, Vincente Minnelli, 1948) to the Western (*The Searchers*, John Ford, 1956) to the thriller (*Shadow of a Doubt*, Alfred Hitchcock, 1943), and deals in the form of symbolic drama with sexual repression in the bourgeois American family.

The film establishes that, with the exception of Jake Dingle (Alan Hale), all the characters – Jeb Rand (Robert Mitchum), Thorley Callum (Teresa Wright), Adam Callum (John Rodney), Ma Callum (Judith Anderson), Grant Callum (Dean Jagger), Prentice McComber (Harry Carey, Jr) – are clearly being 'pursued', either literally or metaphorically or both, and are 'in pursuit'. Hence the pervasive use, as a background, of the vast, precipitous walls of rock, dwarfing the riders below, which become associated symbolically with the repression of which Grant is the source and, finally, the victim. The flashback that makes up the bulk of the film begins and ends with the mountains: Ma, and then Grant, emerge from their shadow in its opening scene, and the chase in which it culminates is dominated by them. They recur, too, with the death of Adam, Jeb's departure for the war (he rides away towards them), and the colt-incident, in which the young Jeb, standing over and accusing Adam, is framed from a low angle against them. The mountains suggest, strikingly and simply, the inescapable repressiveness of which the characters are simultaneously embodiments and victims.

Jeb might be described as the 'subject' of the flashback to the extent that we are invited to believe that he is giving an account of his experience. In fact, the strict subjective authenticity of the flashback is violated constantly throughout the film, and once it has been established that the action is occurring 'in the past', there is no attempt whatever to restrict us to Jeb's consciousness, on the (correct) assumption that the audience won't notice what is, in 'realist' terms, a fundamental discrepancy. Thus, the flashback does not constitute, in any consistent sense, a 'first-person narration' – a claim one might make for, say, Edward Dmytryk's *Murder My Sweet* (1944). *Pursued* works in a way more closely comparable to a Hitchcock film, encouraging us to identify with the emotional predicament of the central character. There are eight key scenes in the film in which

Jeb does not appear and which he could not know about:

1) the conversation between Ma and Grant in the hotel
2) Grant's temptation of Adam at the homecoming celebrations
3) Adam's conversation with Thorley after his fight with Jeb
4) the consultation of the jury at the inquest
5) Grant's temptation of Prentice
6) Ma's conversation with Thorley after Jeb's proposal
7) the gathering of the Callums after the wedding
8) Thorley's rejection of Ma in the denouement.

Even in the scenes in which Jeb does appear, we are constantly allowed to become aware of things of which he is not – the song sequence is the clearest example of this. Thus Jeb can be described as the 'subject' of the flashback only in the dramatic sense – he is the protagonist of a narrative which is centrally concerned with the nature of his experience. He is not in any sense the narrator of the film; he is merely the figure with whom the audience identifies.

In the sequence which precedes the opening of the flashback, as Jeb struggles to remember, the phantom figure of Grant appears to him, framed in the barren landscape by the ruined uprights of the doorway, with splintered wooden spars jutting into the image from above. The image establishes, first, the *diffuseness* of the threat that Grant embodies. It is a threat which crosses time (a generation), and is here associated with the arid desolation of the surrounding country, thus confirming a symbolism already implicit in the first shot of the film – the great block of mountains looming over Thorley as she rides to meet Jeb at the burnt-out ranch at Bear Paw Butte, where the killing of his family took place. Subsequently, Grant acts *through* Adam, Prentice, Ma, Thorley and the war. He is both an individual and an all-pervading force. Second, the phantom is a) an intruder from outside who b) suddenly appears. These elements, in juxtaposition, suggest an ambivalence that will be central to the film: Grant acts consistently in the name of the family and its purity – that is, in the name of the basic institution of bourgeois democracy – and is here associated with the disruption of families, with death, sterility and the past.

Nothing in the film encourages us to believe that the child Jeb is not remembering the killing of his

Still: Pursued. *Jeb (Robert Mitchum) rides through a landscape of repressio .*

family as it 'really' happened. The superimpositions of the ghostly images of spurs vividly suggest that already, a few moments after it has occurred, the event has become nightmare and, in the way in which the spurred boots appear to be trampling on the child, redefine the motif of subjection, vulnerability, persecution, that is stated in the first shot of the distant rider – here, Jeb 'crushed' by his neurosis.

The cry of 'Daddy! Daddy!' by the child in the flashback is followed by the narrated remark 'But my father wasn't there', which is perfectly true – his father has been killed and the body dragged out, as we see at the end. The narration merely attempts to explain why the child's cry was unanswered. The significant point here is that on the cry 'Daddy! Daddy!', Walsh cuts to a shot of Ma Callum, prostrate, and dragging herself towards the trap-door: what is being stressed is 'Ma-as-father', a status which the film quickly confirms – Ma is fearless, aggressive, independent; owner of the ranch, head of the family; associated, both here and at the end, with a phallic rifle. She is associated not with the word 'mother', but with the phrase '*your* mother' (Jeb is

speaking to Thorley). Part of the significance of the very striking birth imagery in the opening scene, and its echoes (Jeb lifted out of the dark hole into the light; Ma's wagon emerging out of the black shadows of the mountain into the moonlight; Ma letting light into the dark cabin, first by opening the door, and then by lighting a lamp) is its irony: the birth is preceded by massacre and the stages of the emergence into light and safety (hole, clearing, cabin, flight) are steps towards collapse and disintegration.

Ma's first action on bringing the young Jeb into her house is to light the lantern on the table. During her conversation with him after she has seen Grant at the hotel, they are framed with a lamp between them – one on a low table, the other in a bracket on the wall. The same configuration is used for their farewell as Jeb leaves for the war (a lamp on a table between them, and beyond it a fire in the grate; another lamp on the wall as they part at the door) and in the scene following Jeb's visit to Bear Paw

Butte, which ends with a very 'posed' low-angle medium shot of Jeb, the globe of a lamp filling the right of the frame, and another 'balancing' it in the background. In the following scene, Jeb's break with Adam and Thorley's failure to reconcile them, all three characters are framed with lamps beside and/or behind them, and during the song sequence, lamps separate Jeb and Thorley, and Thorley and Adam. Towards the end of the film, this motif comes nearest to explicit presentation: consider, for example, the extraordinary moment in which Thorley carries a lamp into Ma's bedroom after her drive with Jeb, the scene lit in such a way that Thorley's face is in complete darkness, all the light concentrated on her white blouse, which glows with luminous brilliance. Later in the same scene, when she is telling Ma that she intends to kill Jeb, Thorley is framed behind the bars at the foot of the bedstead, an unlit lamp on a table beside her; and the wedding-night sequence exploits similar compositions.

The film begins with the 'flashes' of the massacre (the destruction of a home) and proceeds through a narrative in which exterior scenes involving gunfire (or lightning in the visit to Bear Paw Butte) are interspersed with interior scenes in which all the characters are separated, dominated, surrounded by lamps and fires. The Bear Paw Butte scene, for example, is preceded by one in which Thorley rejects Jeb's plan of elopement, and followed, via a wipe from Jeb fleeing home in long shot while the storm rages around him, by a shot of Thorley throwing wood on the fire. Thorley's name is habitually abbreviated to Thor, the name of the Norse god of thunder and lightning – and of the home. The lamp motif reaches its climax in the attempted murder of

Still: Pursued. *Below – the nightmare begins for the young Jeb. Above – Grant Callum (Dean Jagger) and Ma Callum (Judith Anderson) with the body of her lover, Jeb's father.*

Jeb on the honeymoon night, when Thorley shoots at him and hits a lamp instead. The imagery has suggested throughout that the household is a circuit of repressed tensions which are released in the gunfire, and the images of lamp and gun are linked in the figures of the women – Ma, whose 'crime' is responsible for the interior shooting of the traumatic scene, and who lights the first lamp; and Thorley, who *becomes* the radiance of the lamp she carries, and then, in her white bridal negligée, becomes the bearer of the gun. The home and its representatives, the women – the keepers of the flame – become the 'keepers' of the hero's neurosis.

In this respect, *Pursued* strikingly resembles Hitchcock's *Spellbound* (1945), in which the sexual pathology of the hero (Gregory Peck) is also associated with the threat of a dominating woman. In both cases, too, the woman is associated in her turn with a malevolent, dangerous, possessive male figure – here Grant Callum, in *Spellbound* Dr Murchison (Leo G. Carroll) – who is, implicitly, impotent. While *Spellbound* seems to me to invite an oedipal reading, the emphasis in *Pursued* is somewhat different.

Let us now consider the nature of the original traumatic event. Ma Callum, married to Grant's brother, commits adultery with Jeb Rand's father. In revenge, Grant wipes out the Rands; Jeb's parents, sister and brothers are killed, as is Grant's brother (the deceived husband), and Grant himself loses his arm. There are two basic issues here:

1) Ma has broken a social/sexual taboo. She has had an erotic relationship outside marriage, and has thus violated the concept of the family.

2) Grant sets himself up as a figure of (ideological) retribution in the name of family honour – that is, in the name of the family as an inviolable social/moral absolute.

The relationships of the original event are repeated and elaborated in the main narrative, with Jeb in the role of his father, Thorley in Ma's, and Adam in Grant's. Grant and Ma survive from the previous generation – Grant attempting to complete his revenge on the Rands and on Ma (thus explicitly, as before, on the side of retribution), and Ma attempting to cancel the guilt she feels for Jeb's losing his family by adopting him into her own (thus, ostensibly, on the side of conciliation).

The main narrative thread of *Pursued* is therefore the feud between two tight, nuclear families, which is associated quite explicitly with the perversion, morbidity and repression of sexual impulses and the disruption of a love affair. It may be compared with the feud in Mark Twain's *Adventures of Huckleberry Finn* (1884), a novel that represents the classic statement in American art of disgust with and rejection of the family: everything in the book proceeds from complex variations on this dominant theme. For Grant, Ma's crime is that 'she forgot she was married to a Callum'; and, at the end of the film, his coercion of the remnants of the clan to finish the feud after Jeb's marriage to Thorley is rooted in the idea of family solidarity: 'Seeing as we're all Callums, I don't have to tell you what we're going to do about it.' His obsession with family purity is directly linked to his symbolic impotence through the wounded shooting arm, which he loses in the act of vengeance, and the final eruption of the Callums evokes strong parallels with the vicious, perverse all-male families which recur so significantly in John Ford's

Still: Pursued – *desert, dead wood and the eruption of the Callums.*

films – *My Darling Clementine* was made in 1946, the year before *Pursued*. The incest theme, which is fundamental to the film, develops around the Callums, in Grant's revulsion at Ma's adultery and Adam's attachment to Thorley. It is inseparable, that is, from the associations of 'family purity' and 'impotence' which accrue to Grant and the surrogates whom the lost arm compels him to use (Adam, Prentice, his relatives).

Grant is continually linked with the defence of the basic institutions of American ideology – the family: 'correct' sexual morality ('thou shalt not commit adultery'), patriotism (he appears as the recruitment officer for the Union army, leading the volunteers in the oath of allegiance, and a portrait of Lincoln presides over his office), hard work and application (he incites Adam's resentment of Jeb by pointing out that dedicated labour goes unrewarded while praise is heaped on the glamorous war-hero – 'Too bad they don't have a brass-band for a good cattle-tally!') and the law (he appears as the county prosecutor at the inquest).

These associations permit a series of disturbing and subversive ironies. Thus the War (first mentioned by a figure identical to the poster Uncle Sam as 'a real *shooting* war') becomes perverse, the defence of the great, clean American family, a magnification of the destructive sexual pathology embodied in Grant, with guns replacing the lost phallus. (An interesting cross-reference here is Edward Dmytryk's *Crossfire* – made, like *Pursued*, in 1947 – in which a similar link is implied between war and unresolved erotic tensions, and in which the psychosis of the Robert Ryan character is connected with an obsession with the inviolability of country and family – 'He don't respect the service, he don't respect his mother').

Such implications are a key strategy in *film noir*, in which, again and again, the villain is there to suggest that American ideology gives birth to monsters.

199

Other elements in the film, of course, are there to place such implications safely. Thus, while Grant's association with American law and order is inherently subversive, his villainy can be used to suggest also that he is a corrupted individual, and that the institution itself is basically sound. Hence the importance of the coroner at the inquest, whose sound commonsense can intuit Jeb's innocence and Grant's malicious hypocrisy, and triumph over the indifference of the jury ('Don't stand to reason that a man that shot down a dozen fellas in battle'ld shoot down his own brother without givin' him a chance'). The reaffirmation of the benign, homely, incorruptible rightness of American justice does not cancel the more disquieting inference, although it is clearly meant to do so.

Ma attempts to resolve her 'crime' and her responsibility to Jeb by adopting him into her family, and the film's central irony derives from the fact that Grant's impulse to vengeance and Ma's to reconciliation both involve the repression of Jeb's true identity. Killing him and adopting him both become efforts to destroy him as a Rand (as his father's son). The key scenes here are those which follow the colt incident. Ma infers at once that Grant is responsible, and seeks him out to tell him that she 'won't let [him] start it up all over again', and that 'that night ended it for him' (Jeb). The dialogue continues:

Grant: A night like that don't have an end! What happened then'll make him do things just like spirits were whispering in his ears, saying 'Kill! Kill! Kill!'
Ma: The spirits may speak to you, but not to him. I don't believe in your spirits.

When Ma insists that she loves Jeb 'like my own son', Grant replies, 'What makes you think that boy loves you?' and threatens that he will 'leave that Rand alone – let him grow up – just to see what happens to you when he's big enough to start asking questions', assuring her that 'someday you'll wish I hadn't missed my shot'.

Ma emphatically denies this ('That's one day that'll never come! He's a good boy'), but on her return to the ranch, takes Jeb aside at once, and when she is certain that he remembers nothing, insists that 'what you don't remember don't matter. You belong here with us now . . . Don't ask questions of the past – it has no answers for you. Grow up strong in the love that's here for you. As long as you love in return nothing can happen.' When she adds 'You *do* love us, don't you, Jeb?' he makes no reply.

In the next scene, Ma, in the presence of her children, Adam and Thorley, adopts Jeb into the family – officially, i.e. in terms of property. 'Everything we have or ever will belongs to you three from this day on', and, embracing them all within her arms, tells them: 'You three yourselves are the finest thing there is – a family.' The adoption is ratified by Ma's once more taking Jeb aside and asking him if he would 'like to use our name today'. Jeb declines this: 'If you don't mind, I'd like to use my own name – Jeb Rand.' Ma hesitates, then smiles and embraces him; and at once Jeb backs away from her in horror as the memory intrudes into consciousness.

Ma's action turns on her need to deny Jeb the knowledge of his past because of her role in the death of his family; the tensions result from the imposition

Still: Pursued – Jeb *(Robert Mitchum) by the graves of his family at Bear Paw Butte.*

of a family relationship where none exists. The law which has been offended is the ideological proscription of adultery, so that Jeb becomes a 'signifier' of guilt. Thus the first real threat to her relationship with Jeb follows his discovery of Bear Paw Butte, and the renewal of his demands about his identity and his past ('I want to understand'), which she bitterly rejects. The relationship is one, not of repressed love, but of repressed fear and resentment.

In his book *Soul Murder: Persecution in the Family* (Allen Lane, London, 1973), the American psychiatrist Morton Schatzman offers a critique of Freud's analysis of the Schreber case, in which Freud arrived at his theory of the nature of paranoia. Schatzman suggests that Freud disregarded the particularities (social, familial, ideological) of the context in which Schreber's 'paranoid' symptoms were produced.

Schatzman suggests that the social/ideological context which Freud discounts in his analysis of Schreber is that of 'the authoritarian, patriarchal, nineteenth-century family', a structure which, '(like many today) was a *factory* for authoritarian ideologies'. He concludes that psychoanalysis has, to some extent, 'protected and acquiesced in' those ideologies, with their assumptions about 'the position of women and children' and their 'cosmological' connotations – 'a male God atop a hierarchy of accomplices, deputies and servants' (consider Grant Callum in *Pursued*). Considering this repressive, totalitarian ideological context, of which 'threatened and actual castration' was a part (both as a punishment for masturbation and as a 'cure' for 'mental illness'), he suggests that Freud's proposed explanation of 'castration fears' in terms of phylogenetic memory, hallucinated (unreal) persecution by the father, and 'the discovery of the female genitals', are 'gratuitous', and that Freud's choice of data (Schatzman re-names them 'capta' – the taken) and the actual methods of his analysis embody unquestioned ideological assumptions.

Schatzman distinguishes between repression as defined by psychoanalysis ('an *intra*personal defence built to ward off real, imagined, or phantasied harm') and what he calls '*trans*personal' repression: 'A person (often a parent) orders another person (often a child) to forget thoughts, feelings, or acts that the first person cannot or will not allow in the other . . . If the first person's aim is to protect himself from experience of which he fears the other may remind him, if the other experiences too much, the order serves as a transpersonal *defence*.' This is exactly analogous to Ma's attitude to Jeb, and her defence becomes 'an *attack* on the other person's experience'. Schatzman suggests that both the symptoms of the person who is called 'paranoid' and the behaviour of the 'paranoidogenic person' (his term for one who 'generates paranoid states in others) can be explained in terms of an identical 'sequence of operations' on repressed or forbidden desire – 'denial, reversal and projection'; these operations can be described as reversals in syntax and are socially determined. It is interesting to bear in mind, too, Schatzman's contention that 'paranoidogenicity . . . may be 'inherited' . . . by each generation teaching the next one to fear certain possibilities of mind' – a contention suggested in the whole procedure of Jeb's adoption, and the development of the Ma/Thorley relationship in the second half of the film.

By killing Grant, Ma is symbolically ratifying a relationship analogous to the one for which she was punished. Just as the birth imagery of the traumatic scene was undermined by the prevailing intimations of death, as Ma brought Jeb simultaneously into light and safety, and into the family and repression, so Grant's death becomes Jeb's birth: Jeb tells Ma, 'You've given me back my life.' The final image of the film – the couple, on horseback, riding away from the camera, the ruined house and Ma – clearly celebrates a (romantic) release from the constrictions of the family, which is seen as essentially death-oriented. Ma is thus rejecting the perversion of the law of the father (in retributive, sexual morality) embodied in her brother-in-law, and by which she, too, has been contaminated. The two generations are reconciled when the older generation destroys its own, exteriorised, perversity. The suggestion is that the forces which Grant represents, and which are shown insistently throughout the film to be interior to *all* the characters, can be absolutely exorcised (*Spellbound* again provides an interesting parallel), through the death of the 'villain.'

Thorley's role here is to emphasise the essential difference between herself and Ma: 'You lost the man you loved. He died here. *My* man won't – unless they kill me too!' Thorley's rejection of Ma here is crucial. In their conversation just before the marriage, Thorley has agreed to a temporary separation from Ma until Jeb has been killed – 'We'll be together again soon.' The intention at this stage is to regress to the sterility of the family relationship once the outsider has been killed. At the climax of the film, this intention is reversed. Thorley accuses her mother of having 'failed' Jeb's father and herself, and of having withheld the truth from Jeb through shame, the charges representing, in effect, an indictment of the ideology of the family which dictates that Ma's love is a 'crime', imposes guilt for it and demands that consciousness of it be repressed. The film's inability to contain its own subversion of the family is very clear. The ending can work only because there is no equivalent of the taboo of Ma's marriage vows to be broken: bourgeois ideology can easily accommodate the 'non-social' romantic couple. Thus, despite the ostensible reconciliation, Jeb and Thorley ride away from family and civilisation at the end, like Huck Finn lighting out for the Territory.

The incest theme in *Pursued* comes nearest to explicitness in Adam's attachment to Thorley. Adam is clearly presented in parallel to Grant: he occupies Grant's 'place' in the younger generation (brother, instead of brother-in-law, to the offending woman, so that his 'perversity' becomes correspondingly more pronounced), and there are again suggestions of impotence:

a) the obsession with his sister (as a part of the ranch that he inherits by right),

Still: Pursued – *Thorley (Teresa Wright), Ma, Adam (John Rodney) and Jeb.*

b) his general ineffectuality,

c) the abbreviation of his name to 'Ad' (this relates, too, to his constant association with the account books – Add – his potency is not in his sexuality, but in his control of the ledgers, and Jeb threatens not only his possession of Thorley but his sole right to the accumulating capital of the ranch),

d) the implication that he is not properly virile (Thorley calls him a 'back-fence gossip').

In the scenes preceding the ambush, he and Grant are deliberately blurred together, so that both become embodiments of one force: we see, first, Adam resolving to ride into town in pursuit of Jeb ('Looks as if we're gonna have to set things right'); then, at the end of the sequence at Dingle's place, as Jeb is beginning his ride back to the ranch, Grant appears, suddenly and inexplicably, out of the darkness and vanishes again. Finally, Adam ambushes Jeb in the ravine. The blurring is appropriate, since Grant has, symbolically, 'possessed' Adam, their conversation in the saloon on the day of Jeb's homecoming being treated both as temptation by the devil and temptation by repressed desire. Grant emerges out of Adam's disquiet at Jeb's safe and glorious return.

In Adam's confrontation with Thorley after his fight with Jeb, we are presented very economically with two facets of sexual repression. Thorley 'solves' the problem of her desire for Jeb by admitting him into the family – that is, by desexualising her desire and trying to perpetuate the relationship which *makes* the desire a problem in the first place. Thus, when

Adam asks her in horror if she hates him, she replies that she loves him, and that 'I always thought the three of us would never be apart'. Adam's response is practically a declaration of love: 'Three! Three! You're always saying that! Why does *he* count? It's you and me!'

Thorley's 'solution' is an aggravation for Adam: her need to de-sexualise her desire for Jeb and adopt him as brother actually inflames the erotic tension for Adam. Thorley accuses him of thinking of her as his property: the ranch 'has been a wife to you . . . because you don't *have* a wife! Well, I don't belong to it! You can take me off that dog-eared tally-book you carry around!' Capitalist possessiveness and incestuous possessiveness are linked, the enclosed family unit being seen as the breeding ground for both.

The Adam/Jeb relationship is complex and important. Consider the scene at the beginning of the film, when the three children meet for the first time. Lying in bed, his head towards the door, is a boy (Adam) clad in a white nightshirt, his hands behind his head compulsively gripping the ironwork of the bedstead, as though in pain or distress. As his figure is too distant to be distinguished clearly, our first impression might be of a woman in childbirth – or, at least, in intense pain and anguish. The camera pans left, and Jeb climbs on to the other end of the bed. We become aware of a girl (Thorley), her head at the other end of the bed from Adam's. When Jeb and Thorley look at each other for the first time, this is shown in the one image, without cutting. By contrast, Walsh cuts between close-ups of Adam and Jeb staring at one another, conveying at once an opposition, on which the subsequent narrative will enlarge, and a symbolic likeness – Jeb's face left of frame, Adam's right of frame, suddenly become, across the cut, reflections of each other. Adam's initial strange movements increase this suggestiveness, as if he, like Jeb, were possessed by a nightmare.

The symbolic significance of the parallel is clinched in the song sequence, part of the 'thanksgiving', as Ma calls it, for Jeb's safe return from the war. The scene is based almost entirely on an exchange of surreptitious glances between the characters (it is analogous to the dance scene): the celebration of family togetherness is characterised by silent, private communications from which at least one person is always excluded.

The scene begins with a medium shot of a table in the sitting-room with the three 'children' gathered round it: Jeb in uniform, standing, left of frame, Thorley standing next to him, and Adam sitting, resigned and despondent, his body hunched up, his eyes fixed on the floor. Ma comes in from the background, carrying a bottle of wine and glasses on a tray. She proposes a toast – 'Welcome to my son Jeb' – and Thorley, unseen by the others, prods Adam and gives him an admonishing look to make him join in. She says to Jeb, 'To you, Jeb – and *you* must drink to *me*', putting her arm around him. As the camera pans round the table from left to right (Jeb-Thorley-Adam-Ma), we see Adam noticing Thorley's gesture, and looking away again bitterly.

The climax of the scene is the singing of the 'Londonderry Air' by Adam and Jeb to the tune of the music-box, as they used to do as children. The camera pans up from a close-up of the box to frame Jeb and Thorley in low-angle medium-shot, and Jeb begins to sing on his own:

'. . . once more I waken
The sweetness of thy slumb'ring strain;
In tears, alas, farewell was taken,'

Thorley moves out of frame right at the end of the second line, leaving Jeb alone. At the beginning of the next line – 'And now in tears we meet again', Walsh cuts to a medium-shot of all four characters from roughly behind Jeb, and we see Ma, noticing that Adam is looking down sadly, put her hand on his shoulder and smile at him. On the next line, Adam joins in:

'Yet even then our peace was singing
Her halcyon song o'er land and sea;'

Beyond the table, Ma and Thorley exchange smiles, and then Thorley glances between Adam and Jeb, neither of whom are looking at the women, both being totally absorbed in the song. For the last two lines, Walsh cuts to a medium close shot of Adam and Jeb, Jeb left of frame looking down, his head above Adam's, Adam right of frame, looking off left – a composition that seems to 'contain' the opposing close-ups of the two boys on the bed:

'Though joy and hope to others bringing,
She only brought you tears to weep.'

As the song ends, Jeb nods slightly in Adam's direction, and they exchange a brief glance. There is a sudden, sharp cry of pain from beyond the frame, which turns out to come from the dog, but is clearly

intended to evoke, at first, a human voice. Everybody laughs merrily, their unity apparently confirmed. The next scene is the communal meal which breaks up with the beginning of Adam's jibing, resentful provocation of Jeb, the insistence that Jeb is an intruder ('I call it the *Rand* share').

The scene is remarkable for the polarisation of the male and female characters on each side of the table, both pairs united, the men oblivious of the women, and for the fact that Adam and Jeb are brought together, for the only time in the film, by a song which implies betrayal by a woman. This is emphasised by the final cut, which leaves only their faces in frame for the last two lines of the song. At the same time, they actually look at each other only for an instant – Walsh enforces their separateness even within the bond established by the song's theme. In both song and narrative, peace, reconciliation, reunion across time are allegorised as a woman (Ma bring Jeb into the family; Thorley acts as mediator between Jeb and Adam; Ma brings in the communion wine; both women coerce Adam into the celebration by touching him); and, in the treatment of the last lines, the men are seen as victims of the woman as peace-maker, who is transformed into the woman as destroyer. One thinks immediately of Ma's rejection of Jeb after the inquest into Adam's death: 'For me, you're walking up the gallow steps! I built that gallows. I tied the noose. All the love I had for you is dead.' She has been building the gallows all the way through the film, from the moment when she rescues Jeb from his hiding-place. The birth imagery, then, is significant here, the inference being that, both as an agent of disruption (Ma's adultery) and as an agent of reconciliation (Ma's, then Thorley's, adoption of Jeb), the woman is lethal. Two families disintegrate because of Ma's 'crime'; a third disintegrates through her attempt to absolve it. In both cases, the destructiveness is seen as ideologically determined – Ma cannot love Jeb's father because adultery is forbidden; Thorley cannot love Jeb because Ma has made him her brother.

Let us compare the song sequence with the dance sequence. The dance is the scene of the first meeting between Jeb and Thorley after Adam's death – like the song, it shows us a reunion after a long passage of time. Jeb arrives with Dingle, who, in the second half of the film, becomes Jeb's business partner.

The dance begins with Jeb's 'appropriation' of Thorley, who acquiesces against her will and her expressed intentions ('I'd rather have people look at me than dance with someone I hate!'). Walsh cuts from the couple to

1) Ma in close-up. She sees what Jeb is doing, and is obviously furious and desperate. She turns right. Cut to
2) Grant in close-up. He also looks right. Cut to
3) Jeb and Thorley dancing. Cut to
4) Grant looking right. Cut to
5) Thorley's suitor, Prentice, coming into the room in medium long-shot, carrying some glasses of punch for Thorley and himself.

Still: Pursued. *The wedding night – Jeb and Thorley.*

The cutting sequence suggests a telepathic transference of intent. Ma silently evokes Grant's intervention: he, in turn, and in a repetition of her movements, silently evokes Prentice as his instrument. The whole movement is initiated by Thorley's repressed rage at Jeb's approach, which is an expression of desire for her, and which, of course, takes advantage of the fact that etiquette requires her compliance. The exchanged looks in the song sequence convey the two women's desire to achieve unity. Here, the family tensions have already exploded, and the looks convey the desire, once more silent, private, and inexplicit, to force a dissolution. It is now Prentice who brings the communion drinks; and he is made to relinquish them for a gun.

Walsh cuts back a wide shot of the room full of dancers (6) and then to Jeb and Thorley (7). Cut to

8) Ma in close-up, looking as though searching for someone. Cut to
9) Dingle in medium shot, looking off right, then left. Cut to
10) Grant going over to the orchestra in medium long-shot, to get them to finish the dance.

In this sequence, a) Grant initiates his move against Jeb; b) the shot of Dingle 'intervenes' between those of Ma and Grant, prefiguring his decisive intervention in the duel between Jeb and Prentice.

Jeb has now adopted Dingle's style of dress – an immaculate black suit – which is also the costume worn by Grant Callum throughout the film (except in the traumatic scene). Dingle is benevolent, Grant is malign; both are 'tricky'. Grant operates through deceit and hypocrisy, under the cover of law, and is distinguished by a certain diabolism in his ability to possess and manipulate other characters, in his 'dispersed presence'. Dingle owns a gambling den called 'The Honest Wheel', and refers to himself as 'Honest

Jake Dingle'. He also runs a crooked game, and we see him instructing one of his croupiers, through a loaded glance, to see that Jeb wins at roulette, deliberately in order to counteract Jeb's previous 'bad luck' with Adam – 'Maybe you played into a cold deck.' He also provides and deals the cards with which Jeb wins at poker. An explicit antithesis with Callum is established in the dialogue, Dingle telling Jeb before the card-game that 'Luck's sure riding on your shoulder tonight', and Jeb telling Thorley at the end of the film, before the shoot-out, that 'There was a black dog riding my back, and yours, too'. Dingle's last act in the film, before his abrupt disappearance from the action, is to disarm Grant – the camera tracks back from a close-up of the gun in Grant's hand as he hides in a dark alley to ambush Jeb and reveals Dingle behind him, covering him with another gun.

Thus while Grant suggests malignant trickery (ambushes, facades, hiding up the back way), Dingle's trickery is attentively, kindly providential, operating the wheel of fortune on Jeb's behalf. Most important, Dingle is presented in opposition to any idea of family, so that the offer of a partnership at the Honest Wheel ('We'd make a great combination, you and myself') counterbalances the threat of enforced adoption at the ranch. Both Adam and Thorley explicitly disapprove of gambling, the former, when he throws Jeb out, associating it with laziness, as opposed to work and earning your money, which are part and parcel of the family ethos – 'You've been drawin' that money for lyin' in the shade. Lucky if I didn't have six of my riders stretched out beside you playin' pitch.' The opposition of male companionship/'irresponsibility'/rejection of family on one hand, and marriage/'responsibility'/family life on the other, is central to American culture, and Jeb is a victim of this tension, his black suit emphasising a link with both Grant and Dingle. This also helps to explain the love-duet aspect of the song with Adam, both men finding a momentary unity as the victims of a woman.

Similarly, we note an important sexual opposition. Jeb's persecutors are either aggressive, potent women (the woman with the phallus) or men who are shown as impotent and 'unmanned.' Prentice succumbs to Grant's temptation precisely because Grant works on his doubts about his 'virility'. Grant insinuates that unless he avenges Jeb's 'insult' to Thorley at the dance, 'You're not the man I took you for', to which Prentice replies, lowering his head in shame so that it is obscured by shadows, I'll do what's right.' He adds a moment later that he is 'not much good with a gun'. We have seen him earlier, during the recruiting sequence, behind the counter in his father's store, resentful that 'Dad won't let me' join up, this father/son pair forming a contrast to Grant and Jeb through the former's evident determination, as one of the soldiers remarks, 'to get [Jeb] into this war'. It is one of the film's main strategies to imply that the parent, whether protective or aggressive, generates anxiety in the children, the anxiety being traced back to its roots in ideology – here the relation between war and 'manhood': impotent father-figure tries to send youth off to war; protective father keeps son away from war, thus creating fear of impotence.

Dingle, as opposed to all these, is individually potent (the wheel, the disarming of Grant) and/because he lacks a family. The problem of the film is to reconcile Jeb's 'potency' with an ideologically approved relationship (marriage) that will not be sexually repressive. This is achieved through the symbolism of the wedding-night sequence. Jeb surrenders his gun to Thorley so that she can kill him with it, and at the very moment at which she possesses the weapon, Thorley discovers that she is unable to use it ('Your hand shook – but not because you hate me'). The battle of opposing wills – imaged as opposing stares – is resolved by her surrender. Thus the defeat of the forces of sexual repression is simultaneous with the woman's perception and admission that she has loved the potent male all the time. It is by means of this procedure that *Pursued* can present the family as 'a factory for authoritarian ideologies' (Schatzman) and yet move towards the affirmation of the basic unit of the bourgeois family – the couple, rendered as reborn (fully virile) male, and reborn (fully devoted) female. The conclusiveness of the denouement is an insistence that 'it will be different from now on'.

We are now in a position to describe the series of breakdowns which Jeb suffers during the action, and which represent a complex network of tensions:

1) *The traumatic event,* which establishes Grant Callum as the agent of persecution (in Schatzman's terms, 'the paranoidogenic person') and identifies him with socially determined sexual repression, in the name of the family.

2) *Jeb embraced by Ma,* which associates Jeb's neurosis with an attempt to absorb him into the Callum family, and thus with a threat to the identity to which he clings. The correlation between Ma and Grant at this point has already been discussed.

3) *The War.* The breakdown here is associated both with Grant's persecution (he is the recruiting agent), and with the impediment of Jeb's union with Thorley. In their final conversation before Jeb leaves for the war, each confesses to the overwhelming repression of desire which has been forced on them by the imposition of the family relationship ('I had to go on every day pretending. Watching you all day, letting you touch me, at night going in my room, lying there thinking about it'), and which is now perpetuated by the intervention of the war.

4) *The discovery of the ranch at Bear Paw Butte,* which follows Thorley's rejection of Jeb's proposal to elope and her insistence on the decorum and propriety of courtship, the desire here to 'pretend we didn't grow up together' ironically balancing her previous protest against having to 'pretend' to think of him as a brother. Thus the emergence of the trauma (accompanied by a sense of suffocation – 'Suddenly I couldn't breathe') is prompted, not by a kiss, but by the repression of it: Jeb's anxiety is a response to Thorley's ridiculing of his premonitions and her barring of his desire to escape from the family, a denial which takes the form of subjecting him to the etiquette through which alone sex can be naturalised in bourgeois society. Thorley's proposition has a double function from her point of view. It secures Jeb as a potential husband, while at the same time distancing indefinitely the physical consummation of marriage – even the most innocuous physical contact is forbidden 'till you've bought the ring'. By the same token, it keeps Jeb 'in the family', it keeps 'the three of us together', it preserves the non-sexual communion of childhood. After the death of Adam, Thorley uses the courtship proprieties as a weapon: they become her means of humiliating Jeb and of masking her plan to destroy him: on the wedding night, 'That moment he thinks he has me, he'll lose everything.' The courtship scene exactly reproduces the images of it conjured up earlier by Thorley: and the references, through the wine ('just for Christmas and holidays') and the music-box ('An old-fashioned tune. Some people don't care for it'), to the song sequence, underline the fragility and illusoriness of that apparent reunion. Here, bourgeois good manners become, literally, masks for murder, and Jeb, in his humiliation, denounces them: 'It's worse than fighting and yelling in the streets!'

5) *Prentice's burial.* Prentice, as we have seen, is Grant's surrogate, and the attack by the two 'paranoidogenic' agents releases the memory of the original persecution – 'He was one more part of the mystery of people hating me. I had that feeling of some lost and awful thing come over me again' – Jeb's narration at this point is juxtaposed with the spurred, trampling feet of the pall-bearers, in an echo of the traumatic scene.

WESTWARD THE WOMEN
Feminising the Wilderness

Peter William Evans

Westward the Women (William Wellman, 1951) is one of several wagon-train Westerns of the early 'fifties; others include *Wagon Master* (John Ford, 1950), *Bend of the River* (Anthony Mann, 1952) and *Passage West* (Lewis Foster, 1952). It demands critical attention, if only because of its uncharacteristic focus on women, and, unlike *Rancho Notorious* (Fritz Lang, 1952), *Johnny Guitar* (Nicholas Ray, 1954) and *Forty Guns* (Samuel Fuller, 1957), on a group of women rather than one or two female protagonists. Ultimately, the film is contradictory, defining women in terms of conventional notions of marriage and domesticity while also finding space for alternative definitions of femininity, affirming as well as undermining difference.

Its narrative is about the transport of women to the West (something given much lighter treatment in the Gene Autry film, *Valley of Fire*, John English, 1951). The women's mission is to marry into a community of eager, female-starved pioneers and thereby convert the wilderness into a garden, reflecting a dominant pattern in a genre in which civilisation is often identified with the female. As the old man addressing the newly arrived young woman puts it in another Wellman film set in the wilderness, *Track of the Cat* (1954), 'You have no idea of the pleasure it is to have you under this roof', as if the very presence of a woman gives meaning and purpose to the civilising process to which he and other men in the wilderness are committed. It also, of course, reaffirms 'fifties American attitudes towards sex and gender. Its recourse to stereotypes of female characterisation – a cavalcade of virgins, whores, tomboys, matrons, good/bad and bad/good girls abandoning city comforts for the parched ravines and scowling slopes of the wilderness – confirms the ideological drives of the narrative. Nevertheless, the film also succeeds, in a genre traditionally concerned with male desire, in representing the more heroic, less 'feminine' forms of female desire. It also allows room for interrogation of its own conformist tendencies, questioning to some extent its various endorsements of conventional forms of subjectivity: through the ordeals of their migration, the women eventually break free of imprisoning stereotypes, even if only temporarily; the Westerner is eventually forced to investigate the roots of prejudice. However, like many other Hollywood films – including non-Westerns –

Westward the Women is guilty of compromising its good intentions towards the representation of women's experience because it appears to liberate its female characters only through male initiative. A seasoned misogynist, not a woman, resurrects the women's dormant strength, courage, endurance and other sterling qualities often primarily identified with masculinity. The transformation of the women into honorary males reflects at one level the Westerner's dread of a sex whose otherness he must either contain through traditional strategies (domesticity, confinement, sexual demonisation, etc.), or else reconstruct in a crucible of normative male subjectivity, where women become intelligible only if they can somehow be taught to be more like men.

As *Westward the Women* is a film made at one of many crossroads in recent American history, its allegiances to the traditional ideals of masculinity that were exemplified by the no-nonsense heroics of 'forties Westerners like John Wayne and Gary Cooper are partially offset by hesitations that would later be more unambiguously expressed by Marlon Brando, Paul Newman, Montgomery Clift and others. At the very least, though, the film addresses in this most virile of genres women-related issues, raising questions en route about the ways in which female subjectivity and desire are constructed.

Robert Taylor

The casting of Robert Taylor in *Westward the Women* as the wagon-train leader coming to terms with his own ambivalent attitudes to women opens up discussion of late 'forties and early 'fifties ideals of masculinity. Here, Taylor's persona still retains some of the overwhelmingly romantic aura from his 'thirties musicals and melodramas (e.g. *Broadway Melody of 1938*, Roy Del Ruth, 1937, and *Camille*, George Cukor, 1937). However, he is beginning here to develop more austere, inflexible and dour Cold War tendencies that are well suited to his Law-of-the-Father roles in historical swashbucklers like Richard Thorpe's *Ivanhoe* (1952) and *Quentin Durward* (1956) before finally lapsing into the self-conscious cynicism of his performances in, for example, *Party Girl* (Nicholas Ray, 1958) and *A House Is not a Home* (Russell Rouse, 1964). In advancing middle age, he preserves much of his box-office appeal from

Still: Westward the Woman – *an inhospitable setting reflects the violence of the unreconstructed patriarch, Buck (Robert Taylor) as he seeks to 'tame' Danon (Denise Darcel).*

earlier films ('You're rather romantic, aren't you?' Vivien Leigh commented in *Waterloo Bridge*, Mervyn LeRoy, 1940). Robert Taylor as Buck, not an arrant dandy like such Western contemporaries as Roy Rogers, Gene Autry or Lash LaRue, takes the compliment about his beautiful face from Danon (Denise Darcel) like a man who has been no stranger to matinée idolatry:

Danon: Hey! Get ready!
Buck: For what?
Danon: I'm going to tell you how much I love you.
Buck: Yeah?
Danon: Yeah, from the first time I saw your beautiful face . . . It's beautiful to me. It's a nice rugged face. Beard and all. I love it. Did you like to hear that? Well, I like to hear it too.
Buck: All right. You've got a nice rugged face.

The significant word in these exchanges is 'beautiful'. As the film is more than usually sensitive to questions of language, the choice of the word 'beautiful', as distinct from the perhaps more typical 'handsome', invites scrutiny. Taylor's looks, especially in his 'thirties and 'forties roles (e.g. *Billy the Kid*, David Miller, 1941), admit more feminine nuances than those of such icons of unadulterated masculinity as Clark Gable and Spencer Tracy. His ruggedness is not beyond suspicion, as even the *New York Times* reviewer notes: '. . . Mr Taylor himself is suspicious as the hard-boiled boss-man of the wagon train . . . Mr Taylor's toughness is as clear and brittle as a pane of glass' (Bosley Crowther, *New York Times*, 1952, reprinted in *The New York Times Film*

Reviews, vol.4, Arno Press, New York, 1970, p.2579). Under threat from various processes of feminisation, the 'fifties male mounts a rearguard action, helped by a text that surrounds his unconvincing virility with visual and verbal assurances about it.

His shadowy stubble gives the once clean-shaven profile of the early Taylor a rougher edge, earning Danon's disapproval early on in the film: 'Don't you ever shave? You look so dirty.' And Taylor's masculinity is asserted through a variety of strategies, most significantly name (Buck – a virile handle for a masterful hero), speech (autocratic), action (peremptory and decisive) and physical appearance. Whereas, later, Danon has occasion to comment on Buck's gruff speech and behaviour, here, early on, as the wagon train begins its slow progress across the inhospitable landscape, the film provides a woman with the opportunity for ironising the Westerner's characteristically rugged looks. Whereas, say, Gary Cooper needed no such protection, Taylor's facial hair is – like Samson's flowing locks – his safeguard against the threat of feminisation, something against which, by the end of the film, there appears to be no complete defence.

Danon's two references to Taylor's good looks – at first objecting to and then admiring his unattended beard – make several points simultaneously. The formulation by a female of remarks

Still: Westward the Women – *the batttle of the sexes played out between Buck and Danon on the road to redefinition of gender.*

about male appearance is related to the film's less conservative drives acknowledging women's pleasure in the spectacle of male objects of desire. It also reaffirms the status of women as the civilisers and tamers of male wildness and independence. While the film's early moments see the Westerner resisting female designs on his traditional masculinity, its ending shows him clean-shaven, capitulating to the female, preparing to join the queue of fellow Westerners obediently sacrificing independence for domesticity. The film is by no means alone in the genre in preferring the garden to the wilderness, in the process associating women, again characteristically, with entrapment.

Taylor's appeal as Buck is defined as both conventional and unconventional, and the film is at pains to show that although it approves of less inflexible forms of masculinity – a more feminised ideal of male 'beauty' (not handsomeness) – it nevertheless still holds on to tradition in other ways. So, Danon comments on Buck's beautiful face, while simultaneously remarking on the attractiveness of his ruggedness. Although the film seems unable to make up its mind about Taylor's unreconstructed or feminised looks, it does at least problematise the issue, seemingly never remaining sanguine over the durability of traditional norms. And yet, although Taylor's ruggedness is ultimately questionable, there is a disturbing side to his persona, designed to appeal to the more conservative drives of female – as well as of male – desire.

A friendly witness at the hearings of the House UnAmerican Activities Committee, Taylor seems very much a role model for conformist times.

His HUAC contributions were hardly edifying: publicly regretting his involvement in *Song of Russia* (Gregory Ratoff, 1943, a film described by Ayn Rand as pro-Soviet propaganda because it showed so many cheerful Russian children), he sought to atone by remarking: '. . . I can name a few who seem to sort of disrupt things once in a while. Whether or not they are Communists I don't know . . . One chap we have currently, I think, is Mr Howard Da Silva. He always seems to have something to say at the wrong time . . . they should all be sent back to Russia or some other unpleasant place' (Victor S. Navasky, *Naming Names*, John Calder, London, 1982, p.79). From the early 'fifties onwards, Taylor's feminised good looks – thick, wavy, raven hair, big blue eyes – become increasingly solemn. David Thomson (*A Biographical Dictionary of the Cinema*, Secker & Warburg, London, 1975, pp.555-556) compares his fate to Tyrone Power's, of 'hollow, gorgeous youth, dwindling into anxiety'. Perhaps, though, there is more depth to Taylor's misanthropy. Public identification with the McCarthyists (not in itself unusual for the times) seems to inform his various Arthurian or swashbuckling roles, and so, too, does the cancer from which he was by now suffering. He is the champion of chivalry and justice, defending, in *Ivanhoe*, the monarchy (Richard the Lionheart), the enslaved (Wamba), and ethnic minorities (the Jews, represented by Rebecca and her father Isaac of York). His manliness is tested in *Knights of the Round Table* (Richard Thorpe, 1953) in duels first with Mordred's henchmen and then with Arthur himself. In *Quentin Durward*, his virtues are referred to indirectly when the evil King Louis remarks to his barber: 'I find I am developing considerable affection for men of daring, acuteness and imagination, qualities I seldom find around me.'

Taylor's invariably heroic persona in these films exudes safeness, reliability and resoluteness, all – as the medieval Scottish ambassador warns Durward – somewhat quixotic attributes, though they also represent the rhetoric of an American postwar ideology that is nervous about the erosion of beliefs that were once less directly challenged: 'You are a handsome, proud, gallant, honourable (*pause*) and slightly obsolete figure. I say it in admiration and all nostalgia. The lances are being put away. Gunpowder sits where the judges were. History is creating a new sort of world: cruel, political, thoughtful, violent. Louis is its symbol. If you're to match him, my Scottish cavalier, you may have to restrain your more glorious impulses.'

In all these films, though they are sometimes – especially in *Quentin Durward* – punctuated by humour, Taylor has his characteristic look of sober misanthropy, his tortured eyebrows expressing the resolve and anger of the supremacist male clinging to tradition in uncertain times. It is as though the feminine strains, the 'beauty' remarked on by Danon, or the unconvincing manliness noted by Thomson are straitjacketed by an unnatural masculinity, giving the impression of a man carrying a burden of repression, too conventionalised by ideology, too austere for desire. Instinct has here turned in on itself, nurturing a sadistic streak well suited to the demands of his role as Buck, the man's man of the West, who makes physical prowess, not love, the arbiter of identity. Both here and in *Quo Vadis* (Mervyn LeRoy), also made in 1951, Taylor's sadism can best be explained through analysis of the negative implications of conventional attitudes towards women.

Women characters expose the tyrannies of patriarchal attitudes in *Westward the Women*; in *Quo Vadis*, too, a woman confronts the Taylor character with his own repression: 'What a way for a conqueror to win a woman, to buy her like an unresisting beast. What false security you must have in your heart and soul, in your manhood, Marcus Vinicius. What hidden scorn you must have for yourself.' In *Westward the Women*, the Taylor character's hostility towards women, reaching a climax in the scene in which he uses his whip on Danon before striking her jaw, is ultimately rooted in oedipal anger and in the desire to keep women in their place. The urge to batter a woman finally overwhelms Buck when, with the excuse that he is preparing Danon for the rifle's kickback, he knocks her shoulder hard during extempore shooting practice. Later, not content with lashing her with his bull whip, he smacks her face twice: first, he claims, for riding her horse to death; second, 'for me'. The film touches on extremely problematic territory here, making its point about the seductiveness of male aggression partly through the entirely questionable strategy of having a woman say that a blow to her head has succeeded in bringing her to her senses:

Buck: Did I knock some sense into you?
Danon: Yes, I'll be alright now.

As regards the representation of women the moment is, to say the least, disturbing. As a reflection on male violence, the scene has its own gruesome justification, prompted as it is by an acknowledgement of the reality of male aggression. As Adam Jukes puts it vis-à-vis a general discussion of male violence, '. . . whenever a man's authority . . . is challenged by his female partner he will feel threatened by impotence and helplessness if he fails to exercise his dominance' (*Why Men Hate Women*, Free Association Press, London, 1993, p.259).

Buck's violence is a sign, then, not of the disintegration of conventional values, but of a perceived need for their reaffirmation, for exercising control over another, a reminder to a woman of her weakness and subordination to male authority. Jukes makes the further point that individual instances of male violence do not exist in a vacuum. They are made possible because of a culture of female submissiveness, in which insubordination, or acting out of role, are rewarded with various forms of punishment. The violence committed against Danon by Buck bears out these views: his simmering hostility towards women in general and Danon in particular finally explodes at a point in this scene when he no longer seems prepared to tolerate Danon's defiance and, by extension, her representation of women as trouble. Her assertiveness, constant answering back and persistent use of a foreign language all help create a composite image of female recalcitrance and transgression against the Law of the Father. Yet, for all his hostility, Buck is also drawn to Danon. What he sees are the foreignness, easy virtue and buxom, almost maternally defined sexuality, all of which attract the repressed, self-loathing male alarmed by his own susceptibility and weakness. As he is caught in the crossfire of warring passions, the film explores the causes of the conventional male's neurosis.

In part, this is done through the Japanese cook Ito (Henry Nakamura), who becomes a sort of confidant and alter ego, the ethnic cowboy sidekick, a half-man (his size is regularly scoffed at by the Caucasian tough guys on the wagon train), and 'allowed fool' ironising Buck, exposing as far as possible the shortcomings of the Westerner, yet acting towards his heroic partner, as Roy Rogers once said of George 'Gabby' Hayes, as father, buddy, brother all wrapped up in one (David Rothel, *Those Great Cowboy Sidekicks*, Scarecrow Press, Metuchen, New Jersey, 1984). Ito belongs to the film's patterns of complex questions related to ethnicity. Indians, French and Italian women, as well as a Japanese male, all contribute to the film's characteristic confusions created by a melting-pot ideology that is at once celebrating and troubled by otherness. Ito's Japaneseness clearly also gestures towards American initiatives, for strategic, economic and other reasons, for reconciliation with a former enemy. While the Westerner is contemptuous of Denise Darcel's Frenchness, he remains grudgingly tolerant of Ito's regular preference for expressing his most private, usually critical, thoughts in Japanese rather than English. The film allows the Japanese male, however ultimately ridiculous he seems by comparison with his Anglo-Saxon counterpart,

Still: Westward the Women – *Buck's machismo is undermined by Ito (Henry Nakamura).*

to speak his mind: 'I say you wrong Big Boss. You drive too hard. No man do what these ladies do. And this Danon, she does two, three times more.' Buck's masculinity, symbolised by his expertise with the bull-whip, is ridiculed by Ito, half his size, but bigger than Buck in common human decency, when he parodies Buck's lashing of the mules into order. Ito's irreverential attitude towards Buck and through him towards supremacist masculinity is consistently expressed through speech and gesture in strategies that are designed to explore the ambiguities of codes regulating gender as well as verbal discourse.

Linguistically, Ito is always an irritation to Buck, who is often heard irascibly asking, 'What did you say?' whenever Ito resorts to his own vernacular. While Buck is more tolerant of Japanese than of French, the use of a foreign language to place in question the cruder values of the American way contributes towards a gradual dismantling of the Westerner's insular fear of otherness. Ito's comically subversive behaviour also helps soften rigidly defined codes of gender. The most interesting examples of this occur when, first, the camera alternately shows Buck and Ito in two-shot, followed by another two-shot of Danon and Laurie (Julie Bishop), preparing to sleep in their respective wagons, and second, when Ito narrates a strange, comic story in which he acts out the roles of landlord, penniless female tenant and heroic male lover. Both occasions highlight what has been termed the 'difficulty of difference'.

The Women

A second source of criticism of the Westerner and the values he represents is provided by the Westward women themselves. As Henry Nash Smith (1950) remarks, women made an impact early on in Western Dime novels like *Wild Edna, the Girl Brigand* (1878), and *Denver Doll, the Detective Queen* (1882). Although, as Smith and others argue, the film Western ultimately owes its origins to the Leatherstocking novels, James Fenimore Cooper's heroines are genteel, invariably passive and eroticised, eventually becoming more active – initially through cross-dressing – in revenge narratives. But in the dime novels, Calamity Jane soon began to rival the heroics of Deadwood Dick. In films, as George N. Fenin and William K. Everson point out in *The Western: From the Silents to the Seventies* (Grossman, New York, 1973), women are portrayed at first as the companions of the pioneers, although as time passed they would constantly find themselves caught between two contradictory tendencies, 'between the sentimental and mythological conception of the pure but weak and defenceless female, without any personality of her own, essentially dependent on the hero, and the titillatingly aggressive heroine'. In the late 'thirties, Western heroines (e.g. Barbara Stanwyck in *Annie*

Still: Westward the Women – *Danon demands respect.*

Oakley, George Stevens, 1935), like those of many other genres – notably screwball comedy – often reflect significant advances in women's emancipation. In contrast, late 'forties and 'fifties heroines (like Marilyn Monroe in *River of No Return*, Otto Preminger, 1954), restore women to more traditional roles: even in films that nominally respect the demands of historical accuracy, they are condemned to obey traditional, sex-dominated box-office imperatives. So, for instance, in *Calamity Jane and Sam Bass* (George Sherman, 1949), Yvonne de Carlo's eligibility for the role of the notorious Amazon had little to do with sharpshooting and almost everything to do with her provocative sexuality. As Jenni Calder notes, the real Calamity Jane was a repulsive character, though someone who in her coarseness, promiscuity and inebriation reflected the harsh realities of frontier life (Calder, 1974, p.160).

The iconic Western woman as either decent and long-suffering matron (like Jean Arthur in *Shane*), or sexually aggressive adventuress (e.g. Jane Russell in *The Outlaw*, Howard Hughes, 1943), is only rarely avoided in favour of someone who has 'the courage, determination, independence and incredible capacity for endurance' (Calder, 1974, p.158). *Westward the Women* is in this sense a film that, however momentarily, allows women to overthrow stereotype. This satifies the audience's confused desires for the representation of women as freedom-seeking heroines availing themselves of the wide open spaces of the frontier while simultaneously remaining true to an ideal of domesticity – an ideal which is ultimately seen as a destructive influence on the Western hero and which the truly independent man like Tom Dunson (John Wayne) in *Red River* (Howard Hawks, 1948) will have to resist:

'Put your arms around me, Tom. Hold me. Feel me in your arms. Do I feel weak, Tom? I don't, do I? OK, you'll need me. You'll need a woman. You'll need what a woman can give you to do what you have to do. Oh, listen to me Tom, listen with your head and your heart too. The sun only shines half the time Tom. The other half is night.'

However, *Westward the Women*'s heavy concentration on the liberation offered by the wilderness all but subdues the conservative force of the film's closure. The more traditional drives of the narrative seek to categorise the prairie heroines as 'ladies', the more radical ones – highlighted in the title – offer them the more dignified, ideologically innocent status of 'women'. When the women finally reach Roy's valley, the sign that greets them is 'Welcome Ladies'. It has, of course, been written by men who have neither accompanied them on the wagon train from Chicago, nor witnessed their mail-order brides' transformation along the way from ladies into women. The Californians prepare to treat their future spouses in ways familiar to them from tradition, but whether the women resist these measures, maintaining their newly acquired identities, or whether they slip back into their more familiar socialised roles remains a question unanswered in the film's final moments of restored order and matrimonial euphoria. Like the real women of postwar America, who had violated male preserves during the war years, the Westward women seem set for battles that in a sense have only just begun.

As a mainstream Hollywood film, *Westward the Women* is hedged in by most of the usual constraints. When the women are shown taking their first bath on their journey across the desert, the camera catches their hitched-up skirts revealing bare thighs in medium shot, with some of the voyeuristic aura that surrounds Silvana Mangano labouring in the rice fields of *Riso Amaro* (Giuseppe de Santis, 1949). Equally, the wilderness is portrayed not only as a testing ground for the Westerner's virility, but also as a place actually owned by men, here the old patriarch Roy, whose authority will be passed on to the young pioneers who will be populating the virgin land through marriage to the Westward women. In a self-conscious reference to *Red River*, in which John Wayne urges Montgomery Clift to 'Take 'em to Missouri, Matt', John McIntire instructs Robert Taylor to 'Take 'em to my valley, Buck'. As Annette Kolodny remarks in a discussion of the colonisation of the West by the earliest pioneers ('Honing a Habitable Languagescape. Women's Images for the New World's Frontiers' in Sally McConnell-Giner, Ruth Borker and Nelly Furman, ed., *Women and Language in Literature and Society*, Praeger, Westport, Connecticut, p.189), the landscape had already been masculinised before the arrival of significant numbers of women, the wilderness invested with a heavy symbolism already identifying the territory with a femininity ripe for exploitation:

'To avoid the heart of that particular darkness, ever since Columbus, male adventurers to the New World have projected upon it a metaphorical complex which represented for them all forms of comfort, protection, nurture, and, at the same time, guaranteed them both possession and mastery: almost inevitably, then, exploiting a gender predilection already available in most Indo-European languages, the landscape became an experiential analogue of the human feminine.'

Yet, as Kolodny notes, women did go on to break free of these constructions, imposing on the wilderness their own perceptions and experiences, as may be judged by the testimony of early American women writers like Cornelia Greene, Eliza Lucas, Ann Bradstreet and others. *Westward the Women* is a film that catches this tension between rival gender-specific perceptions, offsetting traditional strategies with more radical ones, in a narrative in which the act of representation is itself problematised.

The women here are not wholly controlled by monolithic stereotypes of representation. Although the narrative prioritises its French star. Denise Darcel (and the sex-related issues provoked by her presence), other women are regularly brought into focus to raise widely different concerns. Many of them do, admittedly, belong to familiar categories: the pregnant woman leaving home to avoid scandal, the Italian immigrant looking for a place to raise her fatherless son, and so on. Others, though, in their hoydenish manners, playfully satirise the Westerner while registering their own suspicion of difference. One of these brides-to-be is a sharpshooter, another, after every utterance she makes, spits like a saloon-bar lizard, and yet another, a male-friendly virago significantly named Patience (Hope Emerson) seems more manly than the wagon-train scout. This woman's quirky use of nautical language, which gives her a distinguishing colourful individuality, is also part of the strategy to problematise the discourse, both verbal and visual, through which women are often represented.

Patience's patois recalls the nineteenth-century description in Francis Parkman's *The Oregon Trail* of the prairie as a swelling ocean: 'The prairie was like a turbulent ocean, suddenly congealed when its waves were at the highest . . . ' (reprinted Oxford University Press, 1940, p.136). But her imagery works in at least two further ways, to identify the speaker both with a traditionally male calling (seafaring), and with otherness, a challenge to hegemonic speech patterns associated with Buck. Patience's characteristic vocabulary, composed of words like 'starboard', 'portside', 'landlubber' and 'running aground', has its comic rationale. But, more seriously, it also serves to challenge what feminist linguists have defined as submissive patterns of discourse learnt by women ready to accept their inferior status in conventional social systems. Never a propitious environment for the development of a filmic '*écriture feminine*', the Hollywood cinema produced in films like *Westward the Women* moments in which its own premises have been exposed. In usurping male discourse, Patience becomes the character who, above all, in Hélène Cixous's words, is 'not afraid to recognise in . . . herself the presence of both sexes, not afraid to open . . . herself up to the presence of the other, to the circulation of multiple drives and desires', undermining through language the power of the dominant group (quoted in Susan Rubin Suleiman, *The Female Body in Western Culture. Contemporary Perspectives*, Harvard University Press, 1986, p.16).

The questioning of male discourse is paralleled in the visual representation of the women. Even here, of course, the issues are not only deliberately problematised but in themselves essentially problematic, most obviously so in the treatment of the film's female star, Denise Darcel. For the greater part of her rather limited Hollywood career Denise Darcel played sex objects. *Battleground* (William Wellman, 1950), *Tarzan and the Slave-Girl* (Lee Sholem, 1950) and *Dangerous when Wet* (Charles Walters, 1953), for instance, are all films that exploit her then fashionably bosomy figure. Yet she was no dumb blonde. She brought to these films not only a ready-made – 'different' – European sexiness, but also a volatile temper, impatient with many of the assumptions of the American male. So, for instance, though stereotypically christened 'Lola' in *Tarzan and the Slave-Girl*, she is fearless enough to inform a local chieftain that she is 'not afraid of any man'. Her masochistic surrender to Robert Taylor's sadistic courtship seems, therefore, all the more contentious.

This is perhaps the film's crudest moment, through the example of Danon cruelly submitting all assertive women to the authority of the patriarchal law. The more the film shows women capable of energy, independence and assertiveness, the more it feels compelled to punish them. What the film gives with one hand – the spectacle of women's beauty, togetherness and strength – it takes with the other. But, as Jeanine Basinger has noted, *Westward the Women* is 'one of the few films to present overt, positive sisterhood' (*A Woman's View. How Hollywood Spoke to Women, 1930-1960*, Chatto & Windus, London, 1993, p.470). The women are often seen colonising their space in the frame, working supportively together, both in typically female-related scenes – e.g. when one of the women gives birth – or in conventionally male-orientated ones, like the defence of the wagon train against Indians. They are also shown working together to guide the heavy wagons inch by inch down the stony slopes. They resist the more questionable behaviour of the men, especially Buck, on their journey. In all this, the film offers pleasures that reach beyond those said to be available exclusively through the perspectives of patriarchal prejudice (*see* Judith Mayne, *The Woman at the Keyhole*, Feminism and Women's Cinema, Indiana University Press, 1990).

At its closure, the film refuses to abandon its interest in Denise Darcel as an icon of French beauty, but nevertheless remains aware of some of the issues involved in the representation of men and women, reminding the audience that men are not the sole bearers of the look. Patience, the character constantly posing the greatest challenge to patriarchy, informs the men: 'You can look us over, but don't think you're going to do the choosing.' While the women accept a traditional role as objects of the male gaze, they also

Still: Westward the Women.

insist on reversing the process. Just as Denise Darcel had earlier felt no inhibitions about complimenting Taylor on his 'beautiful' face, so now at the end we are given not only Denise Darcel in a pose – cleaned up, wearing a deeply cut dress, curled hair arranged in such a way as to draw attention to her breasts – designed to arouse heterosexual males in the audience, but also a glimpse of her returning Buck's stare. First, she sees him through the wooden frame of the platform where the brides are searching for their grooms. Then she is intercut with him in medium shot conversing across the back of a horse, approving of his now clean-shaven profile: 'You're nice and smooth. It's a beautiful face and I love it.' While the frame draws attention to the constraints of Buck's unreconstructed masculinity, the echo of the word 'beautiful' and the pair's commitment to each other across the horse – which here signifies shared ordeals, energy and virility – suggest that a lesson has been learnt, difference reduced, identity enhanced and otherness demystified.

Yet the memory of Buck's sadism and Danon's masochistic surrender remains. Too many questions are left unanswered. While Freud defines female masochism as being inspired by hostile feelings towards the mother, Gilles Deleuze (*Masochism: An Interpretation of Coldness and Cruelty*, Braziller, New York, 1971) describes it as a perversion that reacts against the symbolic order, a reactivation of pre-oedipal desires. There is an element of both tendencies in Danon's surrender to Buck. From one point of view, her ultimate submission is an embrace of the father – as represented by the initially unreconstructed patriarch Buck – a desire for the father's penis, and a usurpation of the place in his affections of the mother, who has earned her daughter's hatred for failing to provide her with a penis. If one follows Jessica Benjamin's argument that the female submits to the male to gain access 'to a world that is otherwise closed to her' (*The Bonds of Love. Psychoanalysis, Feminism and the Problem of Domination*, Virago, London, 1990, p.116), Freud's account, based on the workings of the unconscious, can be given an additional, socially inflected set of determinants.

What is undeniably true of Danon, as of the millions of women in 'fifties America whom at many levels she represents, is that her masochism is a crucial element of her constructed femininity chosen, as Jukes (1992, p.241) remarks, 'at the expense of . . . sadistic, aggressive drives which will always be a source of anxiety'. Jukes adds that once it can be proved that 'women are innately passive, this provides a perfect rationale for their [men's] power base' (p.243). In its failure to deliver a radical agenda for the understanding of the psycho-social constructedness of subjectivity, *Westward the Women* is inevitably a film of its time, but it is also a film which, in finding repeated opportunities for at least airing some of these tangled issues, can also be said to be truly ahead of it.

SHANE THROUGH FIVE DECADES

Bob Baker

1953: Joe

The first few hundred feet of the picture state the agenda for the remaining several thousand: the convergence of opposites and complementaries. The opening images present a rider descending from the hills and crossing a plain; a farmhouse at the foot of a mountain range whose peaks emerge from banks of cloud; an adjacent stream running out from marshland, mist rising off the water, a deer drinking in the shallows. The film-makers have not neglected to include a drift of smoke from the farmhouse chimney. Inserted into this 'Once upon a time . . .' imagery is the farmer himself, sweaty and unshaven in his cluttered yard, chopping at an ugly old stump.

The rider – Shane (Alan Ladd), the hero – comes alongside the farmer, Joe Starrett (Van Heflin), who is dressed in worn, stained work clothes, while Shane wears smooth, butter-coloured buckskins and rides a well-groomed chestnut horse. This is the intro, finishing with the camera panning from ground level to encompass Shane and his horse as they wheel towards Starrett who stands offering a ladle of water. Shane dismounts to accept it, entering Starrett's world. Thus the framework is laid for a juxtaposition of the enchanted and the prosaic, romance and documentary, the truth and the legend.

In briefest outline, the narrative to which this is pegged runs thus: Joe and Marian Starrett (Jean Arthur) with their son Joey (Brandon De Wilde) are among a number of families homesteading on the Wyoming range in defiance of the local cattle ranchers, the Ryker brothers, Rufus (Emile Meyer) and Morgan (John Dierkes). Shane, whose past is enigmatic but clearly much to do with violence, agrees to work as the Starretts' hired hand. The growing, awkward affection between Shane and both Marian and Joey is paralleled by the escalating brutality of the farmer/cattleman conflict. Eventually Shane forsakes

Still: Shane. Below – Marian (Jean Arthur) and Joe (Van Heflin) invite passing stranger Shane (Alan Ladd) to supper. Opposite – Joe and Shane do battle with the stump.

his attempt to settle down, reassumes his gunfighter persona, kills the opposition, and rides away from problems solved and unresolved.

'There is no varnish or glamour on the settlers' life; one can believe that in Wyoming sixty years ago, there were just such homesteads, such stores and bar-rooms, and that the battle for the rights of rough farmers was fought in just this unheroic way . . .' Dilys Powell's notice (*The Sunday Times*, 6th September 1953) is typical, in that the aspect which most impressed contemporary reviewers was the realism, the part of the film which seeks to retrieve a historical reality from the genre's tangle of myth, wish-fantasy and show business. The farm, initially portrayed in story-book images, nevertheless looks the sort of place a family could live off. The town is an isolated, ramshackle huddle of buildings, not even deemed worthy of a name, as authentic, probably, as research in photographic archives could make it. A visit to the general store finds Joe contemplating the homburgs and corsets of a Sears, Roebuck catalogue, while Marian has her first encounter with a glass jar.

Karel Reisz in *Monthly Film Bulletin* (September 1953) also emphasised the 'unromantic and entirely convincing evocation of the period . . . a kind of dramatic documentary . . . a killing, for instance, is shown as a sordid and brutal affair and the dead man is mourned'. This refers to the murder of the homesteader Torrey (Elisha Cook, Jr), a sequence in which the character of an autumn day is carefully rendered – the mist, the rain-sodden ground, thunder rolling in the distance, clouds crossing the sun – not for the purposes of melodrama, but rather to reinforce the feeling of actuality about what is taking place. The bulk of the movie was shot around Jackson, Wyoming, and the freshness, the unCalifornianess of it all impinges on almost every sequence.

Not so, however, in the first of several passages in which the director attempts to synthesise the 'documentary' aspect – loosely speaking, Joe's side of the picture, the literal side – with the allusive, 'poetic' aspect, Shane's side, where images are meant to suggest meanings beyond the plain literal. This is a scene in which the two men combine to uproot that obtrusive stump. We lurch back to Hollywood for a studio mock-up of the farmyard in late evening, lit for maximum visibility. The scene is thus back in the 'Once upon a time' mode – stump removal by twilight – except that the director also communicates the exertion, the back-aching physicality of the chore. As Shane and Starrett heave against the stump, the camera pushes steadily in towards them, so that subjectively we seem to be shoving against the men, while imaginatively we are shoving with them – strange but effective. The composer, Victor Young, further elevates the passage with surging strings and brass, conveying triumph, rejoicing. In the result, we watch the tedious, muscle-aching process of bringing the Starretts' property to order, but also a microcosm of pioneer toil, of every wilderness tamed and domesticated, and, incidentally, a demonstration of what was not yet known as male bonding.

A similar synthesis is achieved in the scene of

Torrey's funeral, where what we are shown evokes the touching awkwardness of the farmers in this quasi-formal situation; the camera pans slowly away from the graveside, registering the bored, not quite comprehending children, the patient animals: the reality, creatively imagined, of a funeral on the Wyoming range, circa 1890. At the same time, the bleak setting – a bare hill on a bare prairie – the low-angle shots of the mourners silhouetted against a cold blue sky, the shifting, darkening quality of the light, blown tumbleweed, a startled horse – all serve to communicate the desolateness of the occasion, the sense of the precariousness of life at this place and time, and beyond that the precariousness of life anywhere.

Characterisation, too, has this dual-level quality. Joe can take a relaxed view of Shane's relationship with Marian because, like King Arthur with his Guinevere until it was too late, an emotion as unworthy as jealousy could not impinge on his innate nobleness; and also because he is so unimaginative, so ingenuous that he only dimly sees what a dull figure he now cuts alongside the glamorous Shane. The resolution of Joe's story is, like the film's other resolutions, agreeably equivocal. He has, thanks to Shane, survived the reign of the Rykers; but, again thanks to Shane, he has been denied his chance to act out the role of hero.

Certainly one expects any work which isn't, in Jean Renoir's phrase 'merely an ingenious reporting of events' to function in a binary, ternary, etc., way; a funeral sequence is bound to evoke feelings of mortality of both a general and a particular sort. The problem with *Shane* is the systematic, self-conscious way that George Stevens sets about it – a self-consciousness that, in the climate of the times, a decade on, contrived to diminish the movie and its director.

1963: Joey

It's a reliable principle that any film, even the most superficial, will metamorphose about every ten years, or seem to turn itself to a different angle, as it is affected by a revised set of contexts. So it was that by circa 1963 there emerged an awareness, at least on the part of anyone following or shaping the practice of auteurism, of George Stevens as a director whose earlier work was still deemed respectworthy, but who latterly, and via such movies as *Shane*, had become – in '63-speak – Establishment. Now he tackled only 'important' subjects, and success was measured in Oscar nominations. To V.F. Perkins (*Movie* 4, November 1962), he was a 'member of the Wyler-Zinnemann clan [who] victimises his audience as unscrupulously as anyone'. To Andrew Sarris (*Film Culture*, Spring 1963), his 'technique . . . seems laboured . . . overelaborated . . . ponderously old fashioned'.

Justification for such disapproval might have been sought in the redundancy of the simile which superimposes images of a burning farmhouse over the faces of the Starretts as catastrophe looms; in the naive swank of such shots as the one which, in the first scene, frames Shane neatly between the deer's antlers; in the misjudgement of the attempt to rack the audience's nerves by having Joey rocket around the homestead yelling, 'Bang! Bang!' when we want to concentrate on the Starretts' conversation; in the absence of a sense of the ridiculous about the over-busy soundtrack, with its litany of barnyard noises; in the meaningless cross-cutting with which Stevens tries to inflate the scene of Shane's ride to the showdown.

As to the larger public, their reactions are unrecorded, save via what may be inferred from box-office returns. Clearly, a substantial audience still existed for the film: at a time when any movie not in current release tended to be hard to find, the renters ensured that *Shane* was on the whole reasonably accessible. Still, it is difficult to conceive of a work running more crosswise to what has come to be perceived, in the generalised, simplified way of

Still: Shane – *Joe presides over the funeral of Torrey, Joey (Brandon De Wilde) with Shane behind him.*

these things, as the spirit of the times, than *Shane* in 1963. *Private Eye*, the style of cool insouciance as variously manifested by Jean-Luc Godard, by Julie Christie in *Billy Liar*, by the emergent Beatles . . . How would *Shane*, with its contending directorial levels of complexity and pomposity, play against such background noise? How would, say, the funeral scene appear, incorporating as it does such elements, edited out in the description above, as a grating insert of villainous laughter, an eminently parodiable address by Starrett to the homesteaders ('We can have a regular settlement . . . a church and a school . . . '), the sucker shot of Torrey's dog pawing his coffin? Not cool, man. Richard Whitehall linked *Shane* with *High Noon* calling them 'Westerns for people who despise Westerns' (*Motion* 6, Spring 1963). Most films go through a difficult age, and that of *Shane* can be identified quite precisely.

It was around the figure of Joey that much of the awkwardness seemed to accumulate. The novel by Jack Schaefer on which the film is based adopts a first-person narrative – Joey as an adult recalling a childhood adventure. This first-person plan persists vestigially in the movie: Joey is around in most of the scenes; the film is full of reaction shots, as he watches Shane arrive, fight, ride away. Indeed, it has been asserted that the film presents a 'child's-eye view', that Shane is a little boy's fantasy, imagined off a glimpsed passing stranger who didn't stop for a drink of water (*see* Robert Warshow, 1954). This predicates another, separate two-tier movie: a realistically presented setting, a plausible set of subsidiary characters and a dreamy, fabulous figure at the centre of it all. The problem, technically, is that this movie, in which Shane is only a chimera, has to co-exist with the other movie in which he must be taken sufficiently seriously for his relationship with Marian to concern and move us. Characteristically, in a work so concerned to do two things at once, Stevens elects to make both these films: the presentation of Shane as a man who handles everything perfectly – fighting, farming, dancing, even eating a meal – is apposite to various aspects of either scenario. A more disenchanted, 1963-ish reading of Joey's presence is that he represents an alibi. The director, conscious of the idealised, inadequately complicated nature of his hero, arranges matters so as to seem to be saying, 'This is not how I, George Stevens, artist, see the character, it's merely how a ten-year-old mind has construed him.' After all, though, one would like to propose a version of the film without Joey, or at least one that pushes him much further into the background; or alternatively to imagine a substitute character, Josephine, for the interesting violence that it would visit on a number of stereotypes.

1973: Marian

But in 1953, in 1963, expectations of a scene in which Shane helped Little Jo Starrett to polish up her fast-draw technique could have been fulfilled only in the context of farce (as in *Cat Ballou*, Eliot Silverstein, 1965). Another ten years on, however, and a shift in conventions can be seen to have taken place, whereby the unthinkable has graduated to the feasible and then escalated to the unavoidable. For instance: no reason for a 1973 Starrett to meet the Rykers on their own terms. A dark night, a clump of bushes and a shotgun would meet the case, with no forfeit involved as regards audience sympathy. Thus did Shane become redundant, he and the film beginning their slippage towards the status of period piece. A meticulous sifter of mid-'sixties Westerns would probably end up identifying late 1966, when the two-year-old *A Fistful of Dollars* reached the USA, to late 1967, when the William Graham/Blake Edwards *Waterhole #3* was released, as the timespan during which the tone of the genre shifted decisively. In any case, if cinematic developments had subverted the Shane/Starrett sector of the picture, then the swell of feminist ideals in society at large (and in film criticism: Molly Haskell's *From Reverence to Rape*, Holt, Rinehart & Winston, New York, appeared in 1974) ensured that a subsidiary narrative – that of Marian – came to seem somewhat more piquant and engrossing than it had hitherto.

When we first glimpse her, we are outside looking in, catching her singing to herself as she moves around the homestead: a signal that the cheerless side of farming life will not impinge greatly on Marian's movie. Her costumes – mostly an accumulation of battered cast-offs – and a related, lonely passage in which she picks among her few belongings for something stylish to wear, before pulling out her old wedding dress – these serve to represent whatever degree of drudgery and deprivation the viewer feels appropriate.

As the film proceeds, Marian finds herself, like numerous heroines past and still to come, contemplating this choice: to remain faithful to a doggedly kind, unimaginative husband, honest Joe, comfortable endomorph, or to succumb to the temptations presented by the romantic, dangerous Shane, glamorous ectomorph. A further duality thus emerges:

as well as supplying, with Shane, an identification figure congenial to what may be caricatured as the male imagination, the film also offers an alternative fantasy which those so inclined can tune into. In the narrative, the working out of this drama of affections must of necessity be given precedence over the film's impulses towards realism. If Marian's life were presented with the bleakness that is historically appropriate, with Joey (perhaps multiplied by ten) presented as a whining, unaesthetic nuisance, then her predicament would be uninteresting. Of course, she would have to choose Shane, just as Shane would be obliged to liberate her. By omitting any degree of hardship in Marian's circumstances, though, a satisfying conflict can be placed before the audience.

Two lines of dialogue key the two men's attitudes to Marian. From Joe: 'You heard what my little woman said . . .' (she has just invited Shane to supper), the phrase defining her status succinctly – loved, protected, subordinated. From Shane, in response to a fairly mild insinuation by Ryker, 'Pretty wife Starrett's got . . .', a roar of, 'Why, you dirty, stinking old man!' In a George Stevens movie, where voice levels seldom rise higher than the conversational, this constitutes a denunciatory rage of Old Testament proportions. Two things, as usual, are going on here. Shane is fulfilling the conditions of a traditional Western hero, courtly as regards women, obliged to react violently when they are spoken of disrespectfully. But he is also behaving in character, over-reacting because Ryker's words imply nothing less than the truth. Thus Shane discloses the pivot of his relationship with Marian – an attraction that, so long as Joe is on the scene, may not even be verbalised, let alone acted upon.

If the question, 'romance or realism?' answered itself in this context, a further decision, to do with genre, must have seemed to the film-makers much less clear-cut: whether the requirements of the love story or those of the Western should be allowed to prevail. When Starrett and Shane come to blows over which of them is to turn up for the showdown, the film's dynamic is equally at stake. If Starrett wins, the film will be steering directly towards a conclusion whereby he will die heroically (Shane can polish off any surviving Rykers), thus offering the availability of a final image in which Shane and Marian share the frame together, the moral codes of all concerned having been fully observed; the film will then have been about how the farmer's wife experienced tragedy and romance. Instead Stevens elects to make a film primarily about a Westerner acting out his heroic, lonesome destiny, with a sad sub-plot in which Marian has a near miss with a tempting stranger. But the tension between these two alternatives, these two fantasies, and the game of tag they play with each other is always fruitful.

The climax of the Marian narrative is positioned as curtain-raiser to the shoot-out with the Rykers five minutes later, a reminder that her part of the film indeed represents only secondary business. It begins with the men fighting it out, partly for the privilege of risking death on her behalf. Shane clubs Starrett with his gun butt (end of the Joe narrative) and prepares to ride off to meet the Rykers. 'Please, Shane . . . please,' says Marian, laying down a pause as tension-filled as any in the gunfight scene, before adding 'Take care of yourself', then defining and concluding their relationship with a firm handshake. Shane rides away and we with him, and The End might as well appear for this layer of the movie which, along with, say, Frank Borzage's *Lazybones* (1925) and the Noël Coward/David Lean *Brief Encounter* (1945), completes a triptych of variations on the theme of the poignancy of non-consummation.

1983: Ryker

A 1983 perception of the film could hardly fail to be influenced by Michael Cimino's *Heaven's Gate* of three years before, which realigned similar data to that drawn on by Stevens (the Johnson County, Wyoming 'cattle war') so as to present the director's view of the political and moral implications. The comparisons are perfectly clear-cut since in almost every aspect but subject the two films go in separate directions. The matter of scale, for instance: Cimino, with a running time of (originally) nearly four hours, avails himself of the widest possible canvas, congested with a diversity of characters, situations and settings. Stevens, on the other hand, distils his material to the concentrated minimum. His main characters number only half a dozen, with Shane himself denied a background or even a full name; and the entire film is played out in the

environs of the Starrett homestead, in those of the town's general store/saloon, or on the trail between, a journey we make enough times (with stop-offs at two neighbouring farms) to become familiar with the landmarks: the stream, the short cut over Cemetery Hill, the broken 'N' of three silver birches on the outskirts of town. But it is the didacticism espoused by Cimino and avoided by Stevens that most separates the films. In *Heaven's Gate*, the director emphasises the cattlemen's background of wealth and privilege, their sheer upperclassness – as opposed to the victimised squatters, the 'mudfuckers', immigrant peasants who seem to have come trudging on to the scene from a Dovzhenko movie. Stevens, however, has found it advisable to muffle any sense of class distinction, by removing all outward indications thereof. The Rykers' ranch, for instance, like Detective Columbo's wife or the front of Snoopy's kennel, is never shown, the brothers seemingly operating out of a back room in the general store. Thus, when the farmers hold a Fourth of July dance, although the Rykers are naturally not invited, there seems no social reason why they shouldn't be.

In *Shane*, the audience is to some extent headed off from arbitrating the semi-legalistic conflict of

Stills: Shane. Above – Joe prepares to shoot it out with the Rykers despite Marian's objections. Opposite – Torrey (Elisha Cook, Jr) is shot down by hired gunman Wilson (Jack Palance), while the Rykers, Rufus (Emile Meyer, behind the swing doors) and Morgan (John Dierkes, seated right) watch.

settlers *versus* ranchers or the rights and wrongs of the Homestead Act and instead corralled into the easy ethical framework of peaceful settlers *versus* terrorising ranchers. Nevertheless, the Rykers are allowed their say. 'Right! You in the right!' explodes Rufe Ryker indignantly. In big close-up against a night sky, the wind tossing his grey hair to moderately heroic-looking effect, he first tries to end the conflict, albeit on his own terms, then, having failed, passionately denounces the Starretts for taking advantage of the sacrifices made by others, for having no moral right to the land they are occupying. Starrett's response is, 'He only wants to grow his beef, and what we want to grow up is families.' And it's true that if the Rykers do have parents, wives, children then, as with their ranch, it is by inference only – no sign of them ever reaches the screen. In this respect the Rykers are exceptional: the figure of the cattleman's invariably regrettable offspring was already, in 1953, on its way to becoming a stereotype. But the fecund farmers/castrated cattlemen insinuation helps steer audience sympathies in the required direction, and, more importantly, the way is open for a clear-cut resolution of the story: a clutch of dependent Rykers would certainly make for an anomalous ending.

For Cimino, precise equivalents of the Rykers are impermissible; his ideology could not accommodate them. He presents a world of absentee landowners, guys in suits, dividend-drawers who fly into a class-driven rage when their interests are threatened. This refutes the stereotype found in the bulk of conventional Western fiction (B-Westerns, television Westerns) where the cattleman or woman is favourably portrayed – for example, the Hopalong Cassidy series where the Bar-20 ranch is the centre of stability in a world of rustlers, flash floods, stampedes and similar paraphernalia, a 'safe zone', the equivalent of 221B Baker Street. The issue 'Who owns the land?', if it appears at all, is usually plot-orientated (oil is discovered, the railroad is coming through) and is mediated by some third party – crooked lawyer or banker – who can be abolished in the last reel, thus restoring harmony. In less routine works, one finds in the giving of names a declension of acceptability, starting with 'rancher' (= benevolent, e.g. the nurturing father-figure in *The Left-Handed Gun*, Arthur Penn, 1958), descending to 'cattle baron' (= ambivalent, e.g. the stern, hard-bitten patriarchs of *The Sea of Grass*, Elia Kazan, 1946, *The Big Country*, William Wyler, 1958) and finishing with 'land pirate' (= malevolent, e.g. the parasitic Chicago speculator in *Wild Bill Hickok Rides*, Ray Enright, a 1941 stupidisation of the Johnson County skirmishes). But usually – as in *Shane* – the cattle raisers are at least part of the immediate environment, they are seen as themselves contributors, not part of a system that depends on exploitation.

In the circumstances, the gulf between Cimino and Stevens could scarcely be wider. The climax of *Heaven's Gate* has the settlers banding together in a mirror image of their oppressors' Cattlemen's Association and venturing out to do battle: class warfare in the most literal sense. In *Shane*, the audience is being invited to admire heroism in the individual, and the director is therefore obliged to calumniate villainy in the individual also. The Rykers, he implies, have no intrinsic connection with society as a whole. For Cimino, the cattle and land owners are the very epitome of society as a whole.

1993: Shane

Shane continues to accumulate fresh resonances, different perspectives. Falling immediately under the heading 'related material', the 1985 television-based *D-Day to Berlin* is a posthumous assembly of footage shot by Stevens while commanding a 'special coverage unit' attached to the American forces as they advanced into Europe. One had always assumed in a casual sort of way that Stevens's army service accounted for the more sombre tone of his postwar work and for the disappearance of the streak of frivolity which ran through many of his 1930s films, notably *Gunga Din* (1939), with its swathes of extras tumbling picturesquely before the Gatling gun. The assumption receives distressing corroboration in these rediscovered images of death and devastation, which culminate in the nightmare Stevens found and recorded at Dachau. One understands a little more sharply the outflow of tenderness in *I Remember Mama* (1948) and, in *Shane*, the decision to stage the killing of Torrey amid a sea of mud.

The 1980s also delivered a late crop of movies that can be seen as deriving directly from *Shane* (and indirectly from whatever distant prototype one cares to identify). The narrative premise – stranger protecting vulnerable family unit from brutes and bullies – is a useful basis for a star vehicle. Its advantage is that the stranger, being merely transitory, can develop to audience-gratifying effect from a state of disinterest to one of passionate involvement and partake of the associated stratagem whereby a hero has extraordinary powers, invariably to do with violence, if only he will release them. As attractive a proposition for Burt Reynolds (*Malone*, Harley Cokliss, 1987) or Jean-Claude Van Damme (*Nowhere to Run*, Robert Harmon, 1992) as it had been for Alan Ladd in 1953. Clint Eastwood's *Pale Rider* (1985) refers to *Shane* in a manner which may euphemistically be described as homage or dysphemistically as outright plagiarism, but has the distinction of carrying the super-toughness of its hero to the ultimate extreme: as in Eastwood's *High Plains Drifter* (1972), he is a ghost, ergo already dead, ergo invulnerable.

A fogeyish view of the matter would be that there we have a measure of the times: the only acceptable manifestation of such qualities as restraint and self-sacrifice is via the association of them with a supernatural character. Even in 1953, however, Shane seemed a slightly unreal, mythical figure – the Joey perception. More precisely, he can be seen as expressing, again and most centrally, two opposite/complementary ideas. First there is the programme, systematically worked through, to render Shane as the embodiment of all the social qualities of the traditional Western hero – gentle and imaginative when dealing with children, courtly and respectful in his relationships with women, dignified and plain-dealing with his peers, courageous when righting wrongs: everything the audience would care to be, if only life wasn't life. But it is the anti-social aspect of the Western hero – his 'moving on' ethos, his solitariness – which the film most hauntingly evokes.

'There's no living with a killing . . . Right or wrong, it's a brand and the brand sticks. There's no going back.' Thus, in the last scene of the film, does Shane console Joey, and the film-makers placate the audience with a not-very-convincing explanation for the hero's resumption of his wanderings – and the fuse on the tiny device, planted an hour earlier, establishing that the territory stands in need of a strong law enforcer finally sputters and dies. Clearly, a different imperative is involved, whereby settling down is not an option.

When Shane rides away, he leaves behind him – renounces – not only the Starrett family but also Chris (Ben Johnson), a Ryker hand who has changed sides and could have become Shane's sidekick, his pard. But Shane's aloneness is finally inviolate, and his film emerges as a rather subversive affirmation of the allure of solitariness. Indeed the film-makers are so anxious to hurry their hero on his way that they have him leave town with an untreated bullet wound. The movie's final image is of self-sufficient Shane, awkward in the saddle but evidently still surviving, riding by the same landscape he passed in the opening shot: just his rifle, his pony and him.

A couple of cinematic cross-references make interesting distinctions. The theme of solitariness as something positively sought was pushed to its furthest limits in Alain Jessua's *La Vie à l'envers* (1964), in which the hero withdraws not because he finds other people particularly troubling but because he enjoys his own company so much; society handles this by finding him insane. In John Ford's *The Searchers* (1956), another film framed by a rhymed arrival and departure, the central character, Edwards (John Wayne), is – like Shane – unable finally to manage the business of becoming part of something. But Edwards is presented as too violent, too abrasive, useful only in times of crisis; he rejects but is also rejected. He is Shane stripped of glamour and generally dirtied up, and when he walks away at the end of his movie there is no equivalent to the echoing cry of 'Come back, Shane'.

Shane never did come back, of course – no *Shane II et seq.* – although in one sense he never really went away. This has always been one of the most high-profile of movies, conventionally referred to as a 'classic', imitated, parodied (as late as 1993 in *Sodbusters*, Eugene Levy) and available in one manifestation or another, theatrical, televisual, on cassette – to an extent which, one may assume, can only be true of stories which so stimulate or comfort that audiences wish to be told them again and again. Among that part of the population – whether in Britain or the United States – now as senescent as the film itself, there can only be a minority who have not found *Shane* crossing their fields of vision at least once in their lives.

'What a pity such a character as Shane should be seen in one film and then forgotten!' wrote Miss G. Clarke of Birmingham to the magazine *Picturegoer* (20th February 1954), being awarded the sum of two guineas for her sentiment. Whoever she was and wherever she is, Miss Clarke saw, in the long run, the mitigation of at least one part of her complaint. Shane never has been forgotten.

JOHNNY GUITAR

V.F. Perkins

'Play it again, Johnny Guitar.' These words do not occur in Nicholas Ray's film, and they echo those which notoriously do not quite occur in *Casablanca* (Michael Curtiz, 1942). Still, the echo is not all that distant. The words are heard in Peggy Lee's lyrics for the title song that she sang on a record whose popularity did much to promote *Johnny Guitar* (Nicholas Ray, 1954). She recorded them for use in the film (behind the opening titles, presumably) but they were dropped at some stage in the editing so that her vocal version of Victor Young's romantic theme is heard only for one verse over the finale.

'Play it again . . .' in the lyric refers to the scene in which Johnny (Sterling Hayden) answers a request from his employer, saloon keeper Vienna (Joan Crawford), to play a tune with a lot of love in it. His choice brings the soundtrack's romance theme for the first time into the world of the characters and turns out, as time has gone by, to stir fine and painful memories for Vienna. When she tells Johnny to play something else, it is not just the tune she is rejecting but also his invitation to revisit an undefined scene of shared ecstasy and anguish. The status of the longed-for and forbidden melody in *Johnny Guitar*, and its relationship to 'As Time Goes By', are one element of the film's negotiation with popular culture and what was possible in the Western in Hollywood in 1953/54. A barefaced lift from a successful model, it is as much a contemplation and a subversion as it is a theft.

The most immediate precedent for the Western title song was the Ned Washington/Dmitri Tiomkin Oscar-winner from *High Noon* (Fred Zinnemann, 1952). 'Do not forsake me, oh my darling' gestures towards romance ('on this our wedding day') but is preoccupied with the shoot-out and the chivalric test of courage. It sold hugely in two competing versions featuring the manly voices of Tex Ritter and Frankie Laine. The hard and massive male sound was successful again, in the year of *Johnny Guitar*, when Tennessee Ernie Ford sang the title number for *River of No Return* (Otto Preminger, 1954). By contrast, Peggy Lee did not make a big noise, and her voice was anything but hard-edged. She was renowned for the subtlety of her musicianship rather than her force; her way with a song was soft, warm and delicate. 'Johnny Guitar' refuses the familiar Yeehaw! dimension of the Western anthem, its celebration of strenuous and rugged action. The refrain of 'Johnny Guitar' could be the slogan for a Western poster: 'There was never a man like . . .

the one they call Johnny Guitar.' Indeed, it recalls Paramount's claim in 1953 that 'there never was a picture like *Shane*'. Yet the mention of the guitar is the ballad's nearest approach to generic definition. Above all, it is a reproachful song of adoration, addressed by a woman to a man, and focused on the anxiety and pain of her attachment.

The choice of Peggy Lee as *Johnny Guitar*'s vocalist amounted to an advertisement of the film's claim to offer something new, a difference focused on the matter of gender. It confirmed what was plain to the filmgoers of the day. The title was *Johnny Guitar*, but the name above it was Joan Crawford's. As one of the tiny number of Westerns where the crucial casting was that of the leading woman, *Johnny Guitar* set itself problems about the kind of Western drama that could be centred on a female character. But the range of answers that it could explore was crucially conditioned by its construction as a vehicle for Joan Crawford. The casting links the three terms Western, Woman and Star to another that has marked the picture ever since its first release: Weird.

By 1953, Crawford's stardom was peculiar and desperate. No other star was comparably menaced by the shade of Norma Desmond in *Sunset Boulevard* (Billy Wilder, 1950). Battling to hold her audience while the cinema business itself was in crisis, Crawford was making, from film to film, the changes that she had relied on to renew her image and her career once a decade since her start in 1925. Switches of genre from thriller (*Sudden Fear*, David Miller, 1952) to musical (*Torch Song*, Charles Walters, 1953) and now to Western gave each movie the air of a comeback. *Torch Song*'s trailer had splashed 'Crawford as you've always remembered her. Crawford as you'll never forget her . . . The New Joan Crawford in her first Technicolor triumph.' The Republic Pictures press book for *Johnny Guitar* followed with 'a new Joan Crawford in the most startling role of her colorful screen history'. These were uncomfortable efforts to exploit familiarity without quite evoking age. (Another *Torch Song* slogan proclaimed Crawford the Eternal Female!) Through a play on expectation, they promoted the old as the new – reliably the same yet surprisingly different. The Crawford brand identified a movie sub-genre now suffering the same strains of generic renewal as the Western itself at a time when the singing cowboys, a recent staple of Republic's output, had already moved into series television. In both instances, expanding the scale of proven effects to render them newly spectacular carried the risk of broadening them to the point of grotesquerie.

In one respect, the threat to Crawford was greater than that to the Western. She had more to lose from the move into colour. There was no other star so identified with a make-up. In black and white, the Crawford image used the planes of the face as the ground for an elegant and expressive design with poised exaggerations uniting the wilful with the stylish. The bold lines given to the mouth and eyebrows were gestures of confidence, bringing them up to scale with her large eyes, but the matching depended on monochrome to unify these features as closely related shades of grey. In colour, the different elements of the design threatened to riot as the red gash of the lips became less convincingly a complement to the blackened arches of eyebrow. This threat had been fully realised in *Torch Song*, where the problem of hair colour, too, had been variously approached but at no point pleasingly resolved. Loaded with colour stock, the camera, for so long Crawford's adoring ally, was beginning to see her face differently; it became less enchanted by the magnificence of the bones, less dazzled by the play of light across the contours, and disrespectfully inquisitive about the tone and texture of the skin. In black and white, the face was an achieved product of the will; translation into colour, with the foundation displayed, upset its balance and turned the Crawford make-up into a mask – more a covering

than a projection of identity. In any case, make-up it brazenly was, a product of the Max Factor era and a glaring anachronism in any depiction of the West that aspired to realism. There was no question of developing the story as a representative exploration of women's lives on the frontier. A Crawford Western in colour had to accommodate the movie star as a distinctly perceptible presence alongside that of her fictional character. *Torch Song* had skirted some of the difficulties through its theatrical setting and its all-studio shooting. Somehow *Johnny Guitar* had to make the whiff of the studio compatible with the outdoor action of an oater.

These difficulties arose from the requirement of glamour for a figure late in her forties. Crawford lacked the range and flexibility of technique to support a transition to character roles. Glamour demanded her presentation as the focus of desire, which in turn depended on her being seen to be desired by the desirable. But she faced a co-star crisis. She had maintained her stardom beyond that of most of her contemporaries, and the remaining male stars of her generation were being paired with

Still: Johnny Guitar. *Below – 'Could you spare that smoke, friend?' Armed with a coffee cup, Johnny (Sterling Hayden) intervenes between the Dancing Kid (Scott Brady) and the posse; Corey (Royal Dano) looks on. Opposite – Vienna (Joan Crawford) stands outside her private quarters to receive the posse led by Emma (Mercedes McCambridge, back to camera).*

much younger women. In the years around 1953 Clark Gable (b.1901) appeared with Ava Gardner, Grace Kelly, Gene Tierney and Lana Turner – the oldest of whom was twenty years his junior. Most often now Crawford's name stood alone above the title. That tribute to her eminence was also a sign of her predicament. It was 1962 when Crawford next shared the screen with a star whose celebrity matched her own, and that was in the special circumstances of Robert Aldrich's *What Ever Happened to Baby Jane? Johnny Guitar* provided her with two leading men, dramatising her allure by having them compete for her affections, but neither Sterling Hayden in the name part nor Scott Brady as his rival, the Dancing Kid, was a major star.

Crawford's isolation had unavoidably entered into the dramatic fabric of her movies. Her character was regularly brought to crisis by the emotional costs of keeping others in awe – in admiration and terror – of her force. *Johnny Guitar* addresses the problem of integrating this figure into a Western by combining two of the genre's three most isolated roles: the gunman hero and the saloon woman. More precisely, it gives Crawford the role of the saloon woman while fitting her out with some of the gunman's iconography and fitting her into the gunman's place in the narrative structure. She receives the initial unresolved challenge, and she faces her antagonist in the climactic duel.

Making the saloon woman the hero was almost as big a twist as making the gunfighter female. The saloon woman's regular role was to offer a sexual option not based on community and family, one that could sustain the hero in his unattached and nomadic state by holding out the hotel – the place where beds are paid for – as a thinkable erotic alternative to the home. Removing the saloon woman from her marginal, oppositional place in the structure – the place that typically she would at last vacate and all but renounce in stopping a bullet for the hero – could not be only a structural change. It entailed an upheaval in the system of values which was furthered, in a move that accommodated Crawford's gifts of command as well as her age, by promoting her to be the owner rather than an employee of the saloon. We are first shown Vienna's place as an isolated building remote from any community. Its interior is large, amply furnished and staffed. Everything is in place to service a boom in drinking and gambling, but it is echoingly empty of patrons. Organised for a prosperity that has yet to arrive, it is unwelcoming to a lone stranger. No cordiality informs the barman's rasped demand, 'What's your pleasure?' It turns out that Vienna has erected her place on land that she knows (she has come by the knowledge corruptly) to be the site of a railroad development. She is doubly a speculator since she aims to get rich on a multiplication of land values as well as an influx of spenders. Her pioneering has a mercenary end. Her property stands in contradiction to the traditional icons of benign development: the home, the school, the church.

Vienna's capital has been built on the sale of her virtue and is now invested in an enterprise that lacks the moral prestige of farming or indeed of villain-targeted gun slinging. She is unapologetic about her greed. The film neither announces nor ultimately constructs a scheme to dramatise her moral education or reform. (None of her supporters is shown to deplore her venality.) But with neither her goals nor her methods offered for admiration, and given a troubling vehemence in her pursuit of them, the protagonist is an anti-heroine whose hold on our sympathy results first from the glamour of stardom and then from the character's fortitude in opposing more numerous and more disreputable foes.

When it assigns the hero's position to the saloon woman – and through ownership makes her presence in the saloon a form of settlement rather than an accessory to the wanderer's life – the film sets up an ideological turmoil that affects the genre's other woman. That figure of chastity, dedicated to the puritan values of toil, thrift and endurance, is called into question at the same time as she is propelled into prominence. If Vienna is the hero and not, in the received terms, virtuous, her counterpart becomes the female villain, with the attributes of the good woman damagingly inflected. In Emma Small (Mercedes McCambridge), maidenhood and decorous sexual reticence become appetite unacknowledged and distorted by denial; temperance and rectitude become killjoy bigotry, a persecuting fervour directed with hypocrisy at the sinfulness of others. In dress and manner, she is a close relation of the hellfire Bible-basher; McCambridge herself has referred to her costume as a 'slightly modified nun's habit'.

Constructing the villain in this way is partly a matter of creating an interesting and worthily formidable antagonist for the star. The film's narrative pattern is that of the siege; the objectives of staying put and surviving – ordinarily undramatic – gain force in face of the threat from an enemy set on penetrating and destroying the citadel.

A gambling house is an odd kind of citadel, but the design of Vienna's place is eloquent. It brings together aspects of a shack, a mansion and a fortress. In its fortress dimension, it is made to endure and to withstand attack. Though formed of wood, its sides are sunk into the cliff-face behind so that the rear wall is solid stone, rough and earth-coloured. The resulting image embodies Vienna's boast that she has built her house upon the rock. The red glow of the exposed stone is so pronounced whenever the back wall is in shot that we are kept aware of Vienna's defiant assertion that she is here to stay. The dust storm that blows outside during the opening sequences characterises Vienna's as a place of refuge but also stresses its stability; the gusts enter its rooms only as noise and have not the power to make its fabric shake or creak. While the rock secures the rear of the building, the window of Vienna's private quarters surmounts the front entrance like a castle lookout. It is the product and a token of her concern never to be taken by surprise, the architectural expression of wariness. So the building declares what it cannot satisfy, its owner's hunger for security.

By constructing Vienna as a woman desperate to defend the position she has won, and by constructing the plot so that she is under virulent attack, the film draws on the reality of Joan Crawford's situation, exploits the resonances of her screen persona and works with the actress's peculiar powers. A Crawford role had glamorously to combine authority and pathos, a difficult trick. To establish her strength of will and her command was not the hard part; she had learned to stand her ground with conviction, and she could use her eyes and voice masterfully to govern the tone of any exchange. The price for her command was stiffness, the steel that informed her assumptions of graciousness, the control of manner – most evident in her careful speech and the deliberate pace of her movements and responses – that could block the suggestion of spontaneous (tender) feeling and betray the calculation in her projections of vulnerability and need.

One of the film's strategies for dealing with these problems is to frame Crawford's performance as a spectacle and almost never to seem to seek intimacy. It causes Vienna herself to do a lot of acting, and it stresses the masking of her private self in the interests of her performed authority. The movie's famous love scene plays on her control. Johnny's 'Tell me something nice . . . Lie to me' is a demeaning request for a performance: 'Anything nice you might say to me would be a lie'. Vienna counters first by demanding that Johnny give her the lines – 'What do you want to hear?' – and then by reading them back flatly so as to seem to accept rather than to contest Johnny's accusations. She turns the tables by demonstrating that Johnny's lack of trust, his protection of his right to feel betrayed, means that it makes little difference what she says or how she says it. When she recites 'All these years I've waited', her tone says 'I am doing what you asked, telling you a lie.' She throws back to Johnny the task of deciding whether he will hear the lie in the words or in the tone. At the same time, her caustic performance accuses Johnny of handing her a rotten script, one that raises false issues and can as a result only be rendered badly, without energy or conviction.

The risk in the film's fascination with the spectacle of performance is of ending up with a flatly posturing figure devoid of interior life. The obvious way to counter that danger might be to create moments where Vienna's control is broken and to require the actress to relax her command so as to let herself and the character be found off guard. That may have been outside the range of Crawford's abilities and certainly it is not Nicholas Ray's method here. He stresses and exaggerates Vienna/Crawford's command, but frames it precariously (as in the construction of the decor) so that it emerges not as the authority of confidence or vanity – in which case the exterior and the interior would be without tension – but as an insistence born of terror. Command is what Vienna clings to.

The film is able to use the undertow of panic in Crawford's self assertion, producing a character that the star can inhabit as well as perform by making Vienna carry with her an ineradicable conviction

and fear of the world's contempt. She is trying to reach a height from which she will be unassailable, but she is afflicted with a doubt as to whether eminence secures her from censure or creates a larger exposure to it. The character is driven by knowledge of the ugliness from which she has come, and Crawford has only to play the exterior – the effortful poise and authority, the investment in the perfected mask – for it to be palpable how violent is her process of concealment and denial, how deep her sense of taint. The relevant contrast is with Barbara Stanwyck who retains and cherishes her capacity for coarseness in no matter what sphere of prosperity or elegance. For Stanwyck, a wretched past can be a source of useful knowledge rather than of shame, to be drawn on rather than erased; her *Stella Dallas* (King Vidor, 1937) is made to pay for her inability wholly to regret or despise the life she has left behind. With Crawford, the sense of herself as victim, and the feeling that the position won has continuously and strenuously to be held, persist through any degree of achievement. They produce the ferocity for which the later Crawford was noted. That collision of authority with panic meant that her intensity was always at the edge of the grotesque and needed only an element of play to become parodic.

Johnny Guitar builds its style on an understanding of Crawford's stardom by combining a precisely graded exaggeration of effects with an unusual overtness of construction. Victor Young's music is masterly in its comprehension of and contribution to the film's peculiar idiom. A grandly symphonic score employing a large orchestra, it is very high-toned in its deployment of leitmotif, its melodic use of percussion and drums, and its provision of concertino

Still: Johnny Guitar – *resisting the mob, Vienna turns a domestic light into a Molotov cocktail. Emma will shortly do the same to greater effect.*

opportunities for piano and guitar. But in the scenes of action and confrontation, it regularly goes to the limit of seemingly naive pictorialism by duplicating the image or mickey-mousing its movement. Characters struggle uphill to a background of effortfully stepped rising chords. Falls to earth are marked with tumbling or crashing descents into the bass. Qualities of movement are closely described and thus boldly displayed by an accompaniment that exerts itself to turn action into choreography. But it is not just events in the film's world that Young seeks to annotate. He can seem to be counting off the shot changes, as if on the fingers of one hand, with jabbing chimes to greet the arrival of each new image. The music often repeats and at times takes over from diegetic sound effects, submerging the noise of a waterfall with harp glissandi or ousting the hiss and crackle of spreading flame with wavering wind figures that also evoke the crazy glee of an arsonist. In a literal spirit, too, it takes upon itself to echo processes of thought with stinging shifts in the musical line to signal each fresh realisation: there is a lovely one when a floored and cornered Vienna spots a possibly handy gun lying nearby. There are moments when the music declares its humour and invites us to share a joke with figures on screen. For the most part, however, an ironic attitude informs but does not undermine the construction of effects.

The star is drawn into complicity with the film's musical devices, exposing them within the world of the fiction, when the vigilantes invade Vienna's for the second time, now to denounce her as an accomplice to the bank robbery committed by the Kid's gang. They are not aware that she has seconds ago made herself an accessory to the crime by hiding one of the robbers on her premises. They enter the saloon to find her alone, playing the piano; the tune she has just started is, of course, 'Johnny Guitar'. Her assumption of calm and her attempt to demean the posse by seeming untroubled in its presence are conveyed by having her continue to play the melody as she started, in the reflective vein of a nocturne: Vienna declares that the posse is intruding on a private space (the saloon has now become her home). She plays, softly and slowly, a rather naive arrangement with small elaborations that she treats with more care than finesse. She is musing over this intimate melody in what could be a ruminative improvisation or an effort to recall how it used to go. A lack of evenness in her touch carries a hint of distraction but confirms that this is a personal communion, not offered for the benefit or to the judgment of others. When spoken to, Vienna speaks over the notes with a controlled show of indifference so that the music becomes a supportive counterpoint to her mood. (The sense that this is background music as well as Vienna's music is constructed by a sound balance that never lets the piano compromise the audibility of speech, and heightened by camera angles that mask Crawford's hands so that we never see them touch the keyboard.) Her playing develops through the interrogation as an emotional commentary. Its hesitations and resumptions, its changes of key and dynamic, inflect what is said and articulate what is unspoken. Vienna's second playing of the refrain reflects a point of deadlock in the negotiation. When she rises from the piano, abandoning the tune in the middle of a bar, a final discord with both hands slammed into the keys results from but also announces, rhetorically, the exhaustion of her patience.

The use of the piano here can stand as an emblem of the movie's way with music. The hyperbolic quality of Young's score is appreciated even as it contributes to the urgency of conflict and the vividness of emotional depiction. Intensification is calculated to arrive at, but not to pass, the edge of absurdity. The daring in this process constructs an aesthetic suspense that defines the film's special thrill.

In this regard, the musical strategy is in harmony with visual design that uses blocks of colour, strong line and a bold separation of foreground from background – aided by costumes made up from one-fabric, one-colour elements – to evoke a comic-book approach to composition. That inspiration inflects but does not contradict the film's quest for eloquence and beauty.

More evidently bizarre is a use of the camera to construct characters' remarks as soliloquies and their private gestures as asides. The most glaring instance occurs at the start of the film, just after Vienna's introduction, and it sets a frame of reference for later, more sober uses of the device. Vienna has overridden the reasoned objections of one of her staff, Sam (Robert Osterloh), and ordered him to fetch a lamp to hang outside. Osterloh walks straight towards the camera smirking, then says, as if confiding in us, 'I never saw a woman who was more a man. She thinks like one, acts like one and sometimes makes me feel like I'm not.' After 'acts like one', a cut to a fresh set-up rescues his action, reinserting it into the fictional world by showing that the character is speaking through a hatchway to the kitchen-hand, Tom (John Carradine). The shock of the effect could have been muted if the viewpoint had been prepared as Tom's eyeline. But such a marking is not merely withheld, it is contradicted. To have the actor head for and speak into the camera is to compromise the integrity of the fictional world and to unsettle our confidence in the identity of performer and role. Since there is no camera in the world of the characters, the actor (who can be aware of the camera) is distinguished from his character (who cannot). The camera's interception of the moment produces this effect by exploiting the modes of presence and absence specific to cinema. But it does so without having the actor step out of his role or break his performance.

To address remarks or gestures to the camera is a device used more in comedy than in melodrama and most frequent in a special sub-genre of comedy, the spoof. Bob Hope, for instance, celebrated a spectacularly implausible twist in events by turning to the audience with the challenge 'Let's see them top this on television'. That was at the end of *Son of Paleface* (Frank Tashlin, 1952), one of a pair of pictures that had burlesqued the genre by taking the familiar Hope figure of the cowardly and incompetent braggart out West and having him gulled and outgunned by a cross-dressed Jane Russell, whose friends call her Mike. (Oddly enough, Roy Rogers appeared as an undercover gunman with the alias of 'The Guitar Player'. It is pleasantly credible that the Paleface movies may have been at the back of Roy Chanslor's mind when he plotted the original novel of *Johnny Guitar* and that the figure of Jane Russell in gunfighter garb may have influenced the look designed for Joan Crawford.)

Where the spoof performs a relatively straightforward reversal of Western formulas, particularly by making jokes out of the lead male's failures of courage, integrity and competence, *Johnny Guitar*'s play with the genre involves a more intricate and challenging pattern in which established expectations are in some respects maintained, in some varied or reversed and in some exposed through over-fulfilment.

Ray's movie was made at a time when A-feature Westerns were aspiring to treat serious themes and to stress their solemnity by means of a weighty style; George Stevens pronounced his concern to 'aggrandise the Western legend' in *Shane* (1953). With its contemporary reference, its themes of persecution and demagoguery, and its insistence on obscurities of psychological motivation, *Johnny Guitar* was part of the general trend. But it was wildly aberrant in obliging these elements to coexist with Z-feature and serial-movie plot devices that point up its attachment to the most extravagant traditions of blood-and-thunder melodrama.

Still: Johnny Guitar. *Emma and town boss McIvers (Ward Bond) react to the Marshal's attempt (offscreen) to safeguard Vienna.*

There is a proliferation of aliases: the pacific Johnny Guitar is in reality the gunfighter Johnny Logan, while Vienna (no surname) and the Dancing Kid are evidently assumed identities. Correspondingly, we have an underground escape by hidden mineshaft and a secret lair reached through a cave whose entrance is screened by a curtain of water. At crucial points, outlandish coincidence propels the plot. When Emma leads the posse to Vienna's to carry her off for lynching, two obstacles stand in her way – the marshal (Frank Ferguson), who demands an orderly trial, and Vienna's old retainer, Tom, who pulls a gun to drive the posse out. Emma shoots Tom, and his falling spasm sets off his pistol to fire a bullet that fells the marshal.

The lynching follows the familiar pattern of the serials in which the apparently final catastrophe at the end of one episode would be amazingly averted at the start of the next. Vienna's hands are tied. She is mounted on a horse that stands in a gully. The noose round her neck is slung from a beam of the bridge overhead. Emma takes a whip to strike the horse whose bolting will plunge Vienna to her death. But at just that moment, Johnny, concealed on top of the bridge, cuts the rope; the horse carries Vienna off, giving her a start on the confounded lynchers. A fresh chapter opens. Such brazen moments are

not safely hived off into special sectors of the film. Vienna's remarkable escape comes only seconds after the hanging of the adolescent Turkey (Ben Cooper), when terror and pitiless brutality were strongly conveyed.

In *Son of Paleface*, Bob Hope is on his way to an assignation with Jane Russell when he receives an old sidekick's advice: 'Don't forget, this is the West where men are men.' 'That's what she likes about me', he replies, 'I'm a novelty.' The spoof's way with Western manhood is to turn it on its head. But *Johnny Guitar* acts on the perception that, so long as it stays within the genre, a Western cannot lose its preoccupation with masculinity even when it has women in its leading roles. It tells us this at the moment that it first presents Vienna. Old Tom has been constructed as the housemaid; he has emerged from his place in the kitchen to fetch a broom from the bar, and he welcomes Johnny with these words: 'That's a lot of man you're carrying in those boots, stranger. You know, there's something about a tall man that makes people sit up and take notice.' Although addressed to Johnny, and intriguingly so, the words play over the image of Vienna alone, seen from below as the camera looks up to her position of advantage on the landing above the saloon. It is Joan Crawford in trousers and riding boots with a tie at the neck of her dark shirt. Though she is not (yet) wearing a gunbelt, she stands erect, silent and challenging, as if poised for the draw. Her figure is not entirely masculinised. The trousers are closely

Frames: Johnny Guitar. *Top to bottom: the display of manhood by Turkey (Ben Cooper); Johnny's response, with Old Tom (John Carradine) in the background; Turkey worries over the state of his weapon.*

tailored – shaped more like tights than denims – and belted to show off her waist. But the image is definite enough for Tom's words to adhere as a first description of this woman: 'That's a lot of man . . .'

Johnny Guitar makes its closest approaches to overt parody in its overfulfilment of the expectation that a Western will dramatise myths of masculinity. When the adolescent Turkey sets out to prove his manhood to Vienna by showing off with his gun, Johnny blazes into action and shoots the pistol out of Turkey's hand. In the aftermath, Turkey's crisis of self-doubt is shown in his abashed and speechless withdrawal. His attention is divided between contemplation of the man who bested him and

anxiety over the abused weapon, which is returned to its holster and then taken out again for further unhappy inspection. The symbolic function of the gun and of gunplay is glaringly at issue here. (For Johnny, too, since his need to assert his prowess has been shown as psychotic.)

The articulation of desires and worries around the phallic value of weaponry extends to Emma. 'That's big talk for a little gun', she says when Vienna tries to expel the posse on its first visit. It is through its presentation of Emma that the film insists most on the inspection of subtext and the exposure of unacknowledged motives. Vienna makes a number of notably anachronistic attempts at reading Emma's subconscious in order to explain her enmity. They all centre on Emma's feeling for the Dancing Kid, as in 'You want the Kid and you're so ashamed of it you want him dead.' What this ignores or represses is that Emma allows no distinction between the Kid and Vienna: 'I say they are [the same]. They both cast the same shadow.' Emma's words repeatedly couple Vienna and the Kid, but since we have been so strongly directed to ponder her hidden motives, we can hardly fail to see that the goal of her actions is the annihilation of Vienna and that the Kid is a relatively insignificant accessory to that desire.

Emma is fascinated by Vienna and the *filth* that she represents. The bond between the two women is such that each can claim, with justice, to see through the other. The challenges that pass between them are exploratory and teasing:

Emma: You don't have the nerve.
Vienna: Try me!

and

Emma: I'm coming up, Vienna.
Vienna: I'm waiting.

Their words balance and mesh, sounding their entanglement. At the dissolution of their first public confrontation, Emma approaches Vienna to speak to her in intimacy. Vienna steps down the stairs towards her and stops to hear what she has to say. Excitement chokes Emma's speech at first, until she is able to get out, 'I'm going to kill you.' The words emerge with a coaxing softness that makes them as much inviting as threatening, and her eyes hold Vienna with a kind of awe. Vienna's return – 'I know. If I don't kill you first' – accepts the fatality of their mutual involvement but refuses the intimacy. She cuts off further exchange by striding away from Emma; she is not going to any particular spot, and her gaze is rigidly fixed ahead to deny contact.

A vital constituent of the film's weirdness is its flaunting of the erotic dimension of hatred. The embittered exchanges between Johnny and Vienna are germane here. But it is in the conflict of the women that the theme achieves its freest expression. Since these women are in evident ways performing the roles usually taken by men, the effect is to bring erotic subtexts of the Western so near the surface as to display them in their intensity and their confusion.

DOUBLE VISION
Miscegenation and Point of View in The Searchers

Douglas Pye

The history of the Western is littered with movies that attempt to develop liberal perspectives on the historical treatment of Native Americans. However, the racism that is inherent in the traditions of the genre makes almost any attempt to produce an anti-racist Western a paradoxical, even contradictory, enterprise. It is, in effect, impossible to escape the genre's informing White supremacist terms.

The Searchers (John Ford, 1956) is no exception. But it is different in a number of ways from most other Westerns which attempt to look critically at racism. Although it offers critical perspectives, it is not a liberal movie in any significant sense: its representation of a deeply racist and obsessive Western hero and of the vicious attitudes to miscegenation located at the heart of White civilisation is disturbing in ways that go far beyond the liberalism of, say, *Broken Arrow* (Delmer Daves, 1950) or even the much later *Little Big Man* (Arthur Penn, 1970). *The Searchers* allows no comfortable identification with or disengagement from its hero (who is both monstrous *and* John Wayne) or easy detachment from other expressions by White characters of racial fear and hatred. The film probably goes further than any other Western in dramatising and implicating us in the neurosis of racism. But in wrestling as a Western with the ideological and psycho-sexual complex that underlies attitudes to race, it is working *within* almost intractable traditions of representation. Much of what is fascinating about *The Searchers* lies in the resulting struggle to control point of view – in fact, in its multiple forms of incoherence.

This is not intended as a revisionist account of *The Searchers*, an attempt to challenge its critical standing. I share the widely held view that the film is one of the great Westerns. Rather, I want to look at aspects of the film which have been noted by some writers as troubling or in some way problematical but which have tended (with one or two exceptions) to be marginalised within wider analyses. In particular, I want to consider them not as failures of realisation or artistic control but as problems rooted in the film's engagement with generic tradition.

As many critics have noted, there are several important ways in which the film develops clear and critical perspectives on racism in White society. Almost from the outset, when Ethan (John Wayne) greets Martin Pawley (Jeffrey Hunter)- 'Fella could mistake you for a half breed' – Ethan's obsessive hatred of Indians and of the idea of mixed blood are presented in ways designed to distance us from him.

The film develops this aspect of Ethan while simultaneously implying the ways in which at times Ethan demonstrates a kinship with the objects of his hatred. Increasingly, and in ways that seem entirely controlled, the film detaches us from Ethan so that we are required to perceive the neurotic and irrational nature of his attitudes and actions. Martin's letter to Laurie (Vera Miles), which functions as a kind of embedded narrative in the middle of the film, acts partly in this way by framing in voice-over Ethan's shooting of the buffalo to deny winter food to the Comanches. (In other ways, the containing framework of the letter is less clear in its implications for point of view, as I will argue later.)

The interruption of Ethan's slaughter of the buffalo by the cavalry bugle and the cavalry's entrance – straight, as it turns out from the massacre of a Comanche village – also marks eloquently the way in which Ethan's racial hatred is repeated at the institutional level in the genocidal actions of the US Cavalry. Later, as it becomes clear that Ethan intends to kill, not rescue, Debby once she has been taken as a squaw, the film's distance from Ethan is again unambiguous. The final and in some ways most extraordinary moment of this strand of the film's treatment of racial hatred comes in Laurie's appalling outburst to Martin, just before the last movement of the film, in which she describes Debby as 'the leavings a Comanche buck has sold time and time again to the highest bidder' and declares that Martha, Debby's dead mother, would want Ethan to put a bullet in her brain. The speech is particularly shocking coming from Laurie, apparently one of the film's sanest and most sympathetic characters. But that is clearly the film's point:

Frame: The Searchers – *the arrival of the US Cavalry.*

Laurie's hideous outburst locates the disgust and loathing of miscegenation not simply in Ethan but at the heart of the White community. Ethan is, in this respect at least, not an aberrant but a representative figure.

These perspectives are in themselves coherent and remarkable. The film traces a network of racist loathing from Ethan, into White society and out to the implementation of government policy by the cavalry. Particularly extraordinary in the film's context are the creation of a hero obsessed by racial hatred and the perception that such attitudes, rooted deep in society and in the psyche, are found not only in the villainous, ignorant or aberrant but in people like Laurie who are in other respects sympathetic and caring.

Other aspects of the film are consistent with its critical distance from Ethan's attitudes. In part, both Martin and Debby seem to offer much more positive and rational perspectives on relationships between the races. In the early parts of the film, Martin's identity is created very strikingly in relation to his Cherokee ancestry ('an eighth Cherokee, the rest's Welsh and English') – bare-back riding, moccasins, skin and hair colour, the ability to read a trail. He embodies the possibility of integration, of harmonious mixing of the races. In Natalie Wood's early appearances as the grown-up Debby, too, cross-cultural assimilation, living contentedly with another race, is raised as a real possibility. The Comanches are not monstrous but a people with whom Debby identifies: 'These are my people – go, Martin, go.'

But in many other ways, as I have suggested, the film's point of view on this material is far less clear.

Still: The Searchers. *Above – the first appearance of the grown-up Debby (Natalie Wood) as Ethan (John Wayne) and Martin (Jeffrey Hunter) meet Scar (Henry Brandon). Opposite – after Martin has kicked her down the hill, Ethan tries to get information from Look (Beulah Archuletta).*

Take two pivotal episodes, both contained within the narrative of Martin's letter to Laurie: that involving 'Look' (Beulah Archuletta), the young Indian woman whom Martin inadvertently 'marries' as he trades with her tribe, and the slightly later scene involving the White women recaptured from the Comanches. The fact that each is contained in Martin's letter invites the thought that Martin's sceptical and questioning attitude to Ethan might govern the ways in which we are invited to respond to the two scenes. Certainly, there are parts of the letter narrative in which Martin's voice signals a cognitive and evaluative distance from Ethan, as in his introduction to the shooting of the Buffalo as 'Something . . . I ain't got straight in my own mind yet'. But the episodes of Look and the captives are much less obviously framed. Point of view proves much more fugitive in each case.

The only words of Martin's that we hear in the Look section give little away. The initial lines that Laurie reads about Look come *after* we have been shown the scene in which Ethan tells Martin that he has inadvertently bought a wife and are in fact quite misleading: Martin proposes to tell her 'how I got myself a wife . . .' Nothing in his language here or later corresponds to his response to Look in the dramatised, as opposed to narrated version of events.

When we witness the events with Look, there is nothing in the treatment which suggests a mediated or partial view; the episodes are presented in ways consistent with other episodes in the film, including those outside Martin's letter. The next voice-over, which comes after Ethan and Martin discover the next morning that Look has gone, leaving the sign of an arrow made of small stones, acts as a bridge to the shooting of the buffalo. Here Martin's voice begins, with 'Maybe she left other signs for us to follow but . . .' There is a cut to Laurie, who continues, '. . . we'll never know, 'cause it snowed that day and all the next week.' Another cut introduces the two men approaching the buffalo herd in a snowy landscape. The only other voice-over about Look comes after they have found her dead in the Comanche village. As Martin leaves the tepee containing Look's body, his voice picks up the narration and concludes: 'What Look was doing there – whether she'd come to warn them or maybe to find Debby for me – there's no way of knowing.' Look and her actions, in other words, remain enigmas to Martin; his words in the letter convey little in the way of attitude.

In the wider structure of the film, one determinant on the presentation of Look is that she has the function of paralleling Charlie McCorry (Ken Curtis), each being constructed as a comically (even grotesquely) inappropriate potential partner for Martin and Laurie respectively. To cement that link, Ford dresses each in a bowler hat (Charlie as part of the outfit he wears to marry Laurie), one of a network of linking details between characters that permeates the film. One function of the grotesquerie, at any rate in Charlie's case, is as part of a wider vision of marriage and its possibilities that is central to the film's critical perspective on civilisation. The implication is of women becoming tired of waiting for the desirable men who refuse to settle and marrying the available Charlie – in the way, perhaps, that Martha married Ethan's dull and worthy brother Aaron. For the parallel to work, both Charlie and Look have therefore to be created in ways that invite us to laugh at them, although this cannot fully account for the way in which Look is represented and treated.

She is from the outset a figure of fun – fat, comically modest and, in conventional terms, sexually unattractive. Martin's dismay at the fact that he has unwittingly bought her and his frustration at being unable to make her understand what he is saying are also comically treated, his discomfort underlined by Ethan's laughter at Martin's embarrassment. If the terms of Look's representation are in themselves problematical (though in line with the structural role assigned to the character), the episode creates more intense difficulties when Martin literally kicks Look down the hill as she settles down to sleep beside him. What are we to make of the film's point of view? Ethan's laughter and the conventionally funny image of Look rolling down the hill might suggest that we are intended to share Ethan's response.

But it is difficult (now, at any rate) not to experience the treatment of Look as brutal and painful. If it is intended as comic (even grotesquely comic), the effect seems ill-calculated, the humour unpleasant and misogynistic. If, on the other hand, we are being invited to be critical of Ethan's response, or indeed of Martin's action, it is difficult to account for the decisions that have gone into the construction of Look as a character. In terms of the way the episode is organised – narratively, within Martin's

Frames: The Searchers. *Left – Laurie (Vera Miles) reads Martin's letter to her parents (John Qualen and Olive Carey). Above – Martin and the White captives.*

letter, as well as visually and dramatically – it is hard to mount an argument that will convincingly show how point of view is being *controlled* here. We may want to suggest that the episode is intended to be suffused by Ethan's distorted way of seeing, but evidence for such a view is, as Peter Lehman argues in his article on the Look episodes ('Looking at Look's Missing Reverse Shot, *Wide Angle*, vol.4, no.4, 1981), hard to find. It becomes difficult not to suspect that Ford can treat Look in this way because in terms of the traditions within which he is working, sex between a White man and a Native American woman is unthreatening and so capable of treatment as comedy, while sexual contact between a White woman and a non-White man is an entirely different matter. This is of course Ethan's view, and in this respect as in the whole presentation of Look, the film seems uncomfortably close to attitudes of which elsewhere it is critical.

In almost the next sequence, Look is found dead in a tepee, killed in the cavalry's attack on the Comanche village. We might consider that in this chilling moment there is an implicit rebuke to our previous attitude to Look – as well as Ethan and Martin's. It certainly confirms a presentation of the US Cavalry (now killers of innocent women) very different from that in Ford's earlier films. But the sentimentalisation of Look's death can also seem a conventional way of evading the problems of her continued presence in the narrative.

Peter Lehman accounts for the uneasy treatment of Look in psychoanalytical terms: 'Ford has "let too much" into the film – . . . there is too much dangerous, repressed, sensitive material being dealt with', material, that is, about inter-racial sexuality. 'The almost unbearable tensions raised by *The Searchers* need an outlet . . . Ford needs to be able to behave like a high-school kid. *He* needs to kick Look down the hill – *he* needs to laugh at it' (p.68). This argument perhaps makes the matter too individual. If it is plausible to speak of 'repressed material' here, it is the nature of representation within the tradition that needs addressing rather than (or at least as well as) the psychology of John Ford. In Ford's films, after all, sex is frequently deflected into horseplay. What makes this scene different is its focus on a Native American woman, a character who can be constructed and treated as she is – a way few other women are treated in Ford, though aspects of the treatment of Chihuahua (Linda Darnell) in *My*

Darling Clementine offer uncomfortable parallels – because the tradition allows it. In other words, the film *is* complicit with Ethan here, because, in terms of the genre, it doesn't matter that Look is presented in this way; and it is highly unlikely that the film-makers in 1956 would have considered their decisions in any way problematic.

In this sense the Look episode may be a moment 'profoundly and symptomatically out of control', as Peter Lehman suggests (p.68), but it is a moment representative of rather than out of line with the film's negotiation of its material. It is certainly not, as Lehman argues, the sole exception to the film's otherwise mature and complex handling of its sexual and racial themes.

Comparable but even more extreme problems of interpretation surround the White captive sequence. Ethan and Martin ask at the army camp to see the White women recaptured in the raid on the Comanche village. Martin produces Debby's doll in the hope that one of the women or girls will recognise it. Although the episode is still within Martin's letter, narrative voice is suspended throughout this section so that no perspective is offered through voice-over. Two women are seen initially, one seated on a bench against the wall, a wide-brimmed hat masking her face, a dark blanket round her shoulder. She is never shown in close-up, does not speak and acts only by leaning forward to pat the more obviously distressed woman seated at her feet. This second woman seems not only upset but, as we see her and hear her cries in the course of the scene, appears to have been mentally unhinged by her experiences. In the way she cradles something in her arms and later snatches the doll from Martin, there might be an implication that she has lost her baby. The other two women are much younger – one perhaps in her mid teens, the other younger still. The younger clings to her companion and stares fearfully up at Martin as he holds out the doll. The older girl smiles almost manically, and her equally direct look at Martin carries strong sexual overtones. The representation of the women carries powerful connotations of *at least* traumatic shock; in two cases – the woman on the floor and the older girl – of experiences that have driven them mad.

The scene is presented simply, in six shots. The first frames the door at the rear left of the frame and the first pair of women. The woman on the floor croons softly to herself or to something she is holding in her arms. She turns towards the door and screams as the men enter, until a soldier (Jack Pennick) gives her what seems to be a child's rattle on a piece of leather or cloth, and she quietens, comforted by the other seated woman. Martin walks forward, looks down at the women, and turns frame right; the camera adjusts right to reveal the backs of the two girls, wrapped in a red blanket. As they begin to stand, helped to their feet by two soldiers, there is a cut to almost a reverse angle, showing the two girls from the front and from Martin's left (his shoulder is just in shot). Martin produces Debby's doll, but the girls make no response. Cut back to the first set up; Martin turns to leave and the camera moves left with him, excluding the two girls and reframing the woman on the floor, who snatches the doll and screams. At the rear of the shot, the army officer says, 'It's difficult to believe they're White.' Ethan takes a step or two towards the camera and the woman and replies 'They ain't White anymore – they're Comanche.' As he moves back towards the door, there is a cut to a shot of the doorway, Ethan walks into frame from the left, turns and looks back out of frame towards the woman on the floor. The camera dollies into medium close-up. Shot 5 is Ethan's point of view of the woman on the ground, holding and crooning at the doll. Shot six returns to Ethan and he turns towards the door.

This is to say that Ethan's point of view (in the limited, visual sense of the term) is given in one shot (shot 5), and the scene ends by stressing the effect on him of seeing the captives. The other shots, however, are spatially quite independent of Ethan – in fact, he is a significant visual presence in only one – shot 3 – and then at some distance from the camera.

What does Ethan think he sees when he looks back and how does it relate to what we are shown? His dialogue is clear and brutal: 'They ain't White anymore – they're Comanche.' For Ethan, the horror of miscegenation is so great that he perceives it as producing a racial change – a change in *nature*. It seems clear from its context within the film that Ethan's appalling belief is intended to distance us even further from him. He takes what has happened to the women as vindication of his hatred of Indians and of his attitude to miscegenation. Following the dialogue as they do, the last three shots seem to underline this, but also, in the shots of Ethan's face, make graphically clear that Ethan himself is on the verge of madness caused by his obsessive hatred. In other words, the detached and critical point of view on Ethan developed in the scene is consistent with what the film has been doing in its representation of Ethan since Martin's first appearance.

Yet the presentation of the women themselves is much more puzzling. If Ethan's response to them is to be rejected, their trauma and madness nevertheless seem to be given to us objectively, independent of any informing and potentially distorting view.

They *have* been traumatised and driven mad. If the implication is that captivity inevitably produces such effects, this again seems rather too close to Ethan's view for comfort. Even if we stand back from the distressing, even horrific, effect of the scene and try to ask whether any explanations of the women's states are possible other than their sexual experiences, the scene offers us no significant help. Details may imply fear of the soldiers (with the possibility that it is the attack on the village has traumatised them) or loss of a child, but there is no real support for a view markedly different from what Ethan thinks he sees. This seems a different case from the wider pattern of what Peter Lehman (in William Luhr and Peter Lehman, *Authorship and Narrative in the Cinema*, Putnam, New York, 1977, p.134) calls the film's epistemological theme – the network of moments in which actions or their consequences are not shown, or questions of perception or knowledge are posed. We may be distanced here from Ethan, but there seems little or no ambiguity in the presentation of the women.

These sequences create perhaps the most obvious questions for interpretation in a film which is full of such questions. The representations of Look and the White captives sit very uncomfortably, in their apparent complicity with Ethan's attitudes, with the film's analysis of racism in White society.

There is a further apparent contradiction between the implication of the captive scene and the very different outcome of Debby's captivity and her experiences as one of Scar's wives. How has Debby escaped the fate of the other White female captives? There is no convincing explanation. There is no evidence, for instance, that she was captured younger than the others (a frequent suggestion by students in class discussion) and therefore has been able to assimilate more easily, or that her experience has been qualitatively different. The film is silent on these matters. It is finally as difficult here as it is in the other problem moments that I have mentioned to square this contradiction with the sense of the film's viewpoint being complex but also under control. This is what Joseph McBride and Michael Wilmington (*John Ford*, Secker and Warburg, 1974, p.162) attempt in proposing that the representation of Debby enables us to *place* the White captive scene: 'The scene in which Ethan finds the mad White women is so disturbing that the spectator may momentarily wonder whether Ford is not succumbing to the same fear of miscegenation . . . But our first glimpse of Debby as a woman makes it clear that the fear has a purely neurotic base . . . Miscegenation has not destroyed her identity, but deepened it.' The problem with this, I think, is that the way Debby is represented can extend our sense of the different impulses at work in the film's treatment of miscegenation but it cannot change the way in which the captive sequence is realised or the problem of viewpoint it contains. If the fear *is* neurotic, then the neurosis is not wholly confined to the film's characters.

Each of these problems points to a highly fraught negotiation of issues that cannot be resolved, in the film's context, into a coherent set of perspectives.

At the heart of this troubled and troubling process of negotiation is miscegenation itself, the sexual act which is the focus of Ethan's and Laurie's fear and hatred but which the film, in its commitment to dramatising its material, has itself to confront imaginatively. It is much to the film's credit that it refuses to take refuge in easy liberal attitudes but tries to engage with the horror that the act or the thought of it generates in the society Ford is representing. The consequence of doing this, however, is to produce these fundamental inconsistencies. In the material we have looked at here, two attitudes are present: in one, inter-racial marriage can produce the well-balanced Martin and apparently well-integrated Debby; in the other, miscegenation can be imagined only as rape and its results as madness, violence and death. The film might wish at one level of intention to embrace the first and distance us from the second, but the imaginative power of the latter in the traditions of the captivity narrative on which the film draws is such that it blurs the more rational discriminations at which the film seems to aim.

The two attitudes are in themselves intimately linked to the dual vision of the Indians which is central to the genre as a whole: they are historically wronged peoples with legitimate grievances against the Whites (for instance, Scar's two sons have been killed by White men), but they are also the 'Other', the monstrous eruption of forces feared and denied in White civilisation. The first offers a historical perspective, represented perhaps marginally in *The Searchers*, with the Comanches as a community, like the White settlers. In the second, they have only a symbolic function; they are not an autonomous people but, in effect, terms in the generic equation. It is at this second level that the frequently discussed idea of Scar and Ethan as 'alter egos' makes sense in the symbolic economy of the film. Its divided vision of miscegenation is rooted in the severe constraints of the Western's ways of seeing.

How deeply the film is informed even by the details of traditional representation in these areas can be seen in the striking difference in appearance between Debby and the other captive women. Debby is the only White woman in the film with black hair and dark colouring. All the White captives we see are blonde; Debby's sister, Lucy, has fair hair and pale colouring. Once perceived, the pattern seems emphatic. In realist terms, it would of course be absurd to suggest that Debby comes through unscathed because of her hair colour, or that the other women go mad because they are blonde. Yet at another, less literal, level and in the context of the traditions on which the film draws, these decisions have a different order of significance.

The division between dark and fair women is deeply rooted in the Western. As in so many other aspects of the genre, James Fenimore Cooper provides an early and telling example. Much of the action in *The Last of the Mohicans* (1826) centres on Colonel Munro's two daughters: Alice, of the 'dazzling complexion, fair golden hair, and bright blue eyes' and Cora, whose 'tresses . . . were shining and black. Her complexion was not brown, but it rather appeared charged with the colour of rich blood, that seemed ready to burst its bounds'. They are half-sisters, and Cora's 'rich blood' signifies mixed race. Character traits are developed in a corresponding way: Alice is delicate and fearful, characteristically 'veiling her eyes in horror', and Cora stronger and, crucially, more sensual. She can respond, for instance, to the beauty of the Mohican, Uncas: 'Who that looks at this creature of nature, remembers the shade of his skin', a remark which produces from her White companions 'a short, and apparently embarrassed silence'! The archetypes are very clear, and Alice and Cora have thousands of descendants in the genre, among them Ford's women in *The Searchers*.

The association of sensuality with the dark woman remains very powerful, although the link with mixed race that is made in *The Last of the Mohicans* is not consistently maintained in the genre – Debby, for instance is as 'White' racially as the other women in *The Searchers*. Something of its force and meaning remain, however, as though some explanation is required to account for the phenomenon of the sexual White woman. The fair woman is the essence of White womanhood, unable to withstand contact with the alien other. As Richard Maltby writes in 'A Better Sense of History' in this book, 'The dark heroine is doomed by her knowledge of the hero's sexuality, but the fair, for instance the blonde women captives in *The Searchers*, can be degraded out of their skin colour . . .' Maltby also offers a broader perspective on Ford's use of this system: 'The female survivors of Ford's captivity narratives are dark women, physically unmarked by their ordeal, unlike their fair counterparts. To survive as a woman in the wilderness, to be degraded and yet unblemished, is to embody a contradiction in patriarchy's construction of true womanhood, to indicate, perhaps, a forbidden desire'.

It is in relation to this tradition of representation and its cultural implications that Ford's treatment of Debby and the other captives 'makes sense', although it is not a sense that can be integrated into the film's powerful but partial analysis of racial hatred. It is impossible to know what the film-makers intended by the decisions they took in creating these women, how consciously or unconsciously they drew on the tradition, but the resulting contradictions suggest that in this fraught area of representation the material is in a sense out of control, and that the tradition, powerfully internalised by generations of film-makers and writers, 'speaks through' the film in spite of the presence of other, conflicting intentions.

The kinds of tension that the film has generated are highlighted starkly by its final movements. Here, in a number of ways, contradictions inherent in the film's conflicting relationships to tradition are exposed in the evasions that come with the push towards resolution. In two key ways these relate to the dual vision of the Comanches and of miscegenation. The need to close down ambiguity in these areas can account, for instance, for the treatment of the final battle. In the overall pattern of the film, the attack on the Edwards's ranch is paralleled by the cavalry's massacre of the Comanche village, and logically the final attack on Scar's camp could become the third in a series of massacre and counter massacre that embodies one aspect of the film's view of the destructive relationship between the races. In fact, the treatment of the attack is partly but crucially deflected into comedy by the inept young lieutenant (Patrick Wayne), his sabre, and the undignified wound suffered by Sam Clayton (Ward Bond). Although we have no choice but to *understand* what is happening as a massacre, very little that we *see* offers us this view. Strongly related to this is Debby's sudden willingness to go with Martin when he enters Scar's tent. Earlier she had refused; the Comanches were her people. When she responds 'Yes, Marty, yes' to his waking her with the prospect of rescue, her conversion seems to relate less to psychologically motivated change than to the need to switch the Comanches into their 'Other' mode prior to the final attack on their camp, in order to move the film towards its resolution. Unlike our view of the aftermath of the cavalry attack in which Look was killed, it is clearly important that in this final battle we should be left with no sense of outrage or of human loss.

Equally, it is vital in terms of the need to achieve some kind of affirmative ending to the search that Debby should be returned safely to White society. Her wholly unmotivated change is the more or less desperate strategy that will enable her to go willingly. The film simply has to drop its earlier suggestion of her contented assimilation. Along the way, it is important to note, the signifiers of Martin's Indian ancestry have also been dropped; when he wraps himself in a blanket to enter Scar's camp, it is simply a disguise – there are no implications about his cultural identity.

This simplifies the complex connotations of the last section of the film. There are, for instance, very uncomfortable undercurrents, after Laurie's outburst, to Debby's return, although the film chooses not to foreground these in the way that, several years later, *Two Rode Together* (1961) does. And whatever

Still: The Searchers – *Sam Clayton (Ward Bond) and Lt Greenhill (Patrick Wayne) before the attack.*

the contortions of the last movement, the ending, as it refocuses on Ethan, remains remarkably moving. The film sustains complexity around Ethan but finds it impossible to sustain other complexities that it has generated.

It is tempting to refer these various aspects of incoherence in *The Searchers* to Ford himself – there is after all plenty of biographical evidence to suggest that he was as contradictory as any of us. But as I have written elsewhere, much of what is of major interest in Ford's films, as well as many of the deepest contradictions, come from his recurrent encounter with generic material and traditional images (*Movie* 22, 1976). Ford's personality as a film-maker was formed in considerable part by the forms and meanings of the tradition, and, in turn, his films have become part of what we understand the Western to be. This is not quite to say, as Richard Maltby does that 'Every Western is a palimpsest, a manuscript written on the pages of an earlier, partially erased book, carrying traces of its previous inscriptions'. Although the metaphor is extremely evocative, it implies too inert a model of the relationship between individual film, film-maker and the tradition. Perhaps it would be more accurate, though equally metaphorical, to say that Ford internalised the 'language' of the Western and, however unconsciously, its accumulated resonances.

The tradition remained an active presence, not an underlying, partly suppressed layer, in his films, which might be seen, as his career develops, as a dialogue both in and with the 'language' he inherited. The films make clear – none more so than *The Searchers* – that some parts of the 'language' became more visible to him than others, more amenable to engagement and inflection. He could respond 'to a problem he had found in tradition', the words used by E.H. Gombrich to describe Raphael engaging with inherited ways of painting the Virgin and Child (*Norm and Form*, Phaidon, London, 1966, p.69). Some problems, however, are less tractable than others and in 1950s America, tackling miscegenation in popular cinema and particularly in the Western was probably as intractable a problem as one could find. It is hardly surprising that the film contains both material that has been critically worked on and given forceful dramatic form and material that seems barely to have been engaged with imaginatively at all. The aspects of the film I have discussed can be seen as offering available solutions from the repertoire of the genre to problems the film cannot solve or even fully articulate. The particular contradictions of the film are testimony to the intensity with which Ford and his collaborators wrestled with the ideological complex of racism and sexuality within a genre the basic terms of which exist to incorporate rather than to criticise racist fears and phobias. It is an attempt which is as perverse as it is admirable – in fact admirable partly because it is perverse.

There is perhaps a further perversity in claiming that the film's incoherence is an essential aspect of its greatness. But this is actually to say that the greatness of *The Searchers* lies in what it achieves within its context and its traditions.

HELLER IN PINK TIGHTS

Richard Lippe

In 'Afterthoughts on "Visual Pleasure and Narrative Cinema" Inspired by *Duel in the Sun*' (*Framework* 15-17, Summer 1981, pp.12-15) Laura Mulvey extends the scope of her seminal psychoanalytic article (*Screen*, Autumn, 1975) by addressing the question of a possible relationship between the female viewer's identification and pleasure, and classic American cinema. According to the initial argument, identification and pleasure are constructed by and for a male point of view which, according to Freud, is based on the principle of activity. Hence, women in the audience are barred from sharing this experience because their identity has been based on passivity which is accomplished during the oedipal stage by the repression of their desire to be 'active'.

Mulvey, by returning to Freud, suggests that in the pre-oedipal phase the female shared with the male a desire to be active (just as the male also expressed a desire to be passive) and, although this is abandoned, it isn't ever completely repressed. The female retains this desire to express her active self and assert her sexual identity as a complex of both the active and the passive, but, given the structures of expression available to women, this can only be done in half-measure. For Mulvey, this dilemma is seen in *Duel in the Sun* (King Vidor, 1946): the woman either accepts her femininity (passivity), which, given her desires, will be a form of destruction, or is destroyed in the attempt to express both needs, which is what happens to Pearl (Jennifer Jones).

While *Duel in the Sun* is traditionally classified as a Western, Mulvey suggests that the film is actually a melodrama since the female occupies the centre of the narrative. The film is structured on the division in Pearl rather than on the split between the two male characters – Lewt (Gregory Peck), corresponding to regressive 'masculinity', which is destructive because it is pre-oedipal in its disregard for the law, and Jesse (Joseph Cotten), corresponding to acceptance into the symbolic order which would place Pearl as feminine. In melodrama, the female can be the central character, and her sexual function can be other than that of simply offering her identity to the hero in the form of 'marriage' so that both can be placed in their assigned societal roles within the established order. As Mulvey points out, melodrama offers the possibility of direct confrontation with the issues of sexuality and sexual identity.

Mulvey's view of the tension between 'passive' femininity and regressive 'masculinity' in the presentation of the female provides the context in which

I want to discuss *Heller in Pink Tights* (George Cukor, 1960), a film that explores the same conflict as *Duel in the Sun* but manages to produce a narrative that functions to offer a more positive image of the woman's ability to deal with the situation. It affords the viewer an identification and pleasure that, while circumscribed, isn't negated by an unresolvable tension culminating in death.

Like *Duel in the Sun*, *Heller in Pink Tights* is a Western in that it contains basic elements and conventions associated with the genre. The film, which is based on 'Heller With a Gun', a story by the Western pulp writer Louis L'Amour, was co-scripted by Dudley Nichols, who worked on a number of important Westerns including *Stagecoach* (John Ford, 1939) and *The Big Sky* (Howard Hawks, 1952). The title change to *Heller in Pink Tights* acknowledges the central importance of Sophia Loren's presence – Carlo Ponti produced the film as a vehicle for his wife, just as David O. Selznick had produced *Duel in the Sun* for Jennifer Jones. Angie (Sophia Loren) is at the centre of a narrative which George Cukor defines (in Gavin Lambert, *On Cukor*, Putnam, New York, 1972) as a romantic comedy as much as a Western. As in Mulvey's view of *Duel in the Sun*, it shifts the dramatic interest from the traditional emphasis on the hero defining himself by action to an investigation of Angie's attempt to explore her identity. Like *Duel in the Sun*, it asks Freud's infamous question 'What does *she* want?'.

In *Heller in Pink Tights*, Angie, like Pearl, is situated in a narrative that splits the 'hero' function between two men who are given meaning through Angie's responses, which express conflicting needs and desires. Mabry (Steve Forrest) is the charismatic gunman/outlaw who corresponds to Lewt, while Tom (Anthony Quinn) is the manager/director of the theatrical troupe and somewhat akin to Jesse in having a similar sense of business and culture. Although both films employ the same structure, there are a number of crucial differences in its use and the presentation of the characters' functions. For instance, although Tom is associated with business and culture, his profession, the theatre, puts him outside the symbolic system which places Jesse as an upholder of the law in *Duel in the Sun*. More importantly, Angie, as a travelling-show actress, she can confront her erotic desires through indulgence in her own, and Mabry's, physicality because her professional status means that she does not have to be a respectable 'lady'.

Still: Heller in Pink Tights – Angie (Sophia Loren), as Mazeppa, is the 'heller in pink tights.

In the opening scenes of the film, the troupe is fleeing the law because Angie has gone on a dress-buying spree and can't afford to pay for her purchases. While Angie, the main 'attraction' of the troupe, which stages productions such as *La Belle Hélène*, is fully aware of the visual impact of her physicality and knows how to make the most of it, the emphasis on her interest in extravagant finery also acknowledges an innate sensuality. Sexual desire surfaces when she encounters Mabry, who embodies virility, in part by his status as a gunman – a man of physical action who defies the law. While part of Mabry's appeal may be his defiance, the next scene in the saloon, in which Angie objectifies Mabry by watching him through hidden viewing windows, indicates that her primary interest in him is as a sex object. Cukor accents this role reversal in several ways: the interior of the saloon, a 'male' space, is an intense orange-red colour, but it is Angie's physical presence that dominates. With her silvery blond hair and dress of dark greyish blues and purples, she makes the space a lavish articulation of sensuously elegant colours; in the objectifying scene, Angie opens up viewing panels which, when closed, are disguised as an oil painting – a typical nineteenth-century reclining female nude designed for the appreciation of a male clientele.

Angie's attraction to Mabry is tempered when she witnesses his potential for violence, as he roughs up another man who is threatening him. This makes her retreat to Tom, who doesn't intimidate in this way. Rather, Tom's mode of intimidation is the desire for stability and, in particular, marriage. When Tom broaches the subject, Angie counters the proposal by stating that what she wants is to star in *Mazeppa*, which would make her a celebrity. Angie's

wish is granted, and on stage as Mazeppa she becomes a 'heller in pink tights'. Off-stage, in the saloon, the pink tights are exchanged for a stunning white dress which later takes on symbolic significance as Angie must divest herself of it and other finery to save her life; but here she bewitches with illusion (tricks with coloured silk scarves) and sells photographic images of her 'magical' charms. Femininity is the tool she uses to get into a poker game, which takes on the character of a sexual challenge as she and Mabry call each other's bluff until Angie bets herself as a stake.

Angie flees before Mabry is able to collect, not because, at this point, she isn't willing to pay the 'debt', but because he is again associated with an eruption of violence. The appeal of regressive 'masculinity' is once more signalled as a destructive force. In the journey sequence, Angie has to confront this element in Mabry and herself. In fact, the journey is centred on different aspects of the sensual/erotic and violence. Although not the most significant, a striking manifestation of this is the Indian raid on the abandoned wagons which contain the troupe's costumes and include Angie's fancy dresses. The film depicts the Indians as 'primitives' – not in the conventional manner by signifying their otherness in terms of dress and language, but, rather, by their response of wonderment and aggression to the costumes and props they find in the wagons. As the raid progresses, more and more of the intensely coloured costumes are thrown from the wagons, with bits and pieces donned by the Indians and other articles thrown into the air. Cukor builds the scene's exhilaration

Still: Heller in Pink Tights – *Mabry (Steve Forrest) about to collect his winnings in the shape of Angie.*

until a sensuous riot of colours fills the screen, culminating in the orgasmic release of the costumes and wagons being set on fire by the Indians.

Against generic expectations, Mabry functions as a positive force by saving the troupe from his counterparts, the murderous Indians, but his presence on the journey becomes a disruptive influence, gradually making Angie question both her desire for Mabry and her attitude towards Tom, who is forced to acknowledge the Angie/Mabry relationship. It is Mabry's insistence on collecting the 'debt', knowing that, under the circumstances, Angie will have to hurt Tom emotionally to fulfil the payment, that makes her aware of the potential self-destructiveness of her pursuit of the erotic. Again, Cukor focuses these scenes on an interplay of the sensual and the violent. The landscape itself provides a sensual/violent backdrop, with the cove, the river and its rapids as locations for the action. Appropriately, Angie is wearing a simple muslin dress coloured a muted olive green contrasting with the fabrics and colours that she wore earlier and will wear later when she reclaims her sensuality. Here, the sensual gives way to the dark aspects of violence, first in the scene between Mabry and Angie in the cove and, immediately following, in the juxtaposition of Mabry beating a gunman who has been sent to kill him with Angie's recognition of the emotional pain she has inflicted on Tom.

The responses of Mabry and Angie in this sequence are important in the narrative's resolution. Mabry, although he has the chance, doesn't kill the gunman (this is a Western in which no killings are depicted) thereby countering the generic expectations that would make him a 'villain' and, in a conventional narrative resolution, necessitate his death.

In *Duel in the Sun*, Lewt is shown to be a killer when he shoots dead the defenceless Sam (Charles Bickford) and, later, wounds the equally defenceless Jesse. Angie's subsequent actions release her from becoming a doomed heroine, just as Mabry's release him from becoming a doomed villain. She is able to extricate herself from the destructive aspect of the situation – violence – by negotiating her relations with not only Mabry and Tom but also De Leon (Ramon Novarro), a shady businessman who is the real villain of the narrative.

Although Mabry's potential for violence is seen to be tempered, the result of the cove scene is that Angie abandons her erotic bond with him. Instead, *she* transforms their relationship into a business arrangement by agreeing to work for Mabry as a courier who, carrying a note instead of a gun, is to collect the money De Leon owes him. Angie, in her encounter with De Leon, exploits her femininity both in her dress and by letting him think that he can use her to get Mabry. After taking De Leon's money, instead of giving it to Mabry, she buys the town hall in Bonanza and converts it into a theatre. She then uses her charm on Tom to convince him that *she* can't direct the production of *Mazeppa*, but needs him and the troupe. Given the structure of the narrative, Angie is the initiator of action, producing the *mise-en-scène* throughout the film: her need for him to direct is largely a gesture of affection.

Angie, by using her intelligence and, when necessary, her 'femininity', manages to get a permanent theatre for the troupe, repay Mabry by getting a loan at the local bank, and produce a situation in which Mabry and Tom are temporarily aligned as Tom conspires to help save Mabry's life. These developments, especially the connection between Tom and Mabry, are contrary to genre expectations and, also, to a degree, to the narrative pattern outlined by Mulvey which maintains that the woman must fail in asserting 'masculinisation'.

Mulvey contrasts *Duel in the Sun* with *The Man Who Shot Liberty Valance* (John Ford, 1962), which also splits the hero figure (John Wayne/James Stewart), but in which she sees the two men rather than the woman as personifying the split at the heart of the narrative. In *The Man Who Shot Liberty Valance*, the woman's function is 'marriage' as a means of containing the erotic, in different ways, for both the male and the female. While it can be argued that the ending of *Heller in Pink Tights* effects the same function by having Angie marry Tom, I feel that the presentation of both Angie and Tom throughout the film undermines an easy reading of Angie as becoming passive and accepting a correct femininity (e.g. marriage). For instance, she is consistently responsible for initiating her adventures. This even includes her marriage, in that Angie, without knowing whether Tom still wants to marry her, illegally takes his name as a means to get the money she needs to pay Mabry, and later confronts him with a proposal of marriage, which is very much bound up with their partnership in the theatre she has bought. (Bourgeois marriage as a 'sacred' institution is twice held up to ridicule in the film: in the shock and outrage expressed by the Cheyenne theatre owner concerning *La Belle Hélène* and in Angie's comments on the family portraits in De Leon's office.)

Significantly, although she chooses Tom, the resolution of the narrative doesn't completely deny the potential for Angie to pursue erotic needs. Mabry, who represented sexual passion, has survived, in part, through Tom's help, implying that the erotic hasn't been destroyed or totally rejected. And, as I have mentioned, Tom's function in the narrative doesn't correspond to the symbolic male who, as Mulvey puts it, represents 'impotence rewarded by political and financial power'. Rather, Tom, who shares Angie's identification with the theatre, relates to a profession that, while not free on the public/personal level from societal dictates, offers, to an extent, the possibility of creatively expanding personal needs. Off and on stage, the theatre is an environment in which masculine and feminine identification is less rigidly defined and coded, allowing Angie a space to continue expressing an active/sexual self. It can also accommodate Tom's non-violent (but not asexual) identity, which Angie has come to value. Appropriately, the film's intimate final scene is played on stage in a darkened theatre. It is unfortunate that Gavin Lambert is allowed by Cukor in their interview book to dismiss the film's sensitive and intelligent treatment of the resolution with the remark: 'It's a pity the script disintegrates completely at the end, which is just ordinary melodrama.'

While *Heller in Pink Tights* isn't radical in the sense of consciously breaking with the ideological position of Hollywood cinema, it nevertheless demonstrates that narrative patterns allow more scope for inflection than is often assumed; like genres, they are products of social, cultural and historical determination. In particular, the film presents Angie as a woman who is neither destroyed because of asserting a considerable degree of regressive masculinity nor completely assimilated into correct femininity, which would limit her function to marriage, barring participation in the male-oriented world of expressive action. Rather, the film leaves her in a position that allows her to continue to test the parameters of the social order regulating the concepts of male and female identity; it also suggests that she has gained some insight into both the negative and positive aspects of those parameters.

The inflections that affect the narrative pattern, like the shift in emphasis from Western to both melodrama and comedy, can be attributed to Cukor. Of course, as a Hollywood director, Cukor functioned in relation to a vast complex of inputs into a film, but his interests and sensibility are crucial to *Heller in Pink Tights*. In Lambert's book, after acknowledging that the project was set up by Ponti/Loren at Paramount, Cukor indicates what appealed to him: 'Truth to tell, there was never a story, but the *subject* attracted me. I'd always wanted to do a picture about a troupe of travelling actors and their adventures in the pioneer days. It always struck me as romantic and scary and authentically real.' The 'subject' is the actors and their experiences, not the symbolic West, as it would be for a Western director like John Ford. Incidentally, it is interesting to compare Cukor's film to Ford's *Wagon Master* (1950), which centres on a troupe of travelling actors. In *Wagon Master*, the actors are also outsiders, but their function in the film is to move towards acceptance of and integration into the broader structures that represent, through Travis Blue (Ben Johnson) and the Mormons, social order and the establishment of community. The actors in *Heller in Pink Tights*, on the other hand, remain outsiders. They find no positive values in Bonanza and Cheyenne but, instead, a pretence of respectability which masks the corruption of social order by physical and financial power.

In fact, the spirit of community found in the film exists within the troupe, despite their individual conflicts. While Angie is juxtaposed with Lorna (Eileen Heckart) and Della (Margaret O'Brien) as a sexual antagonist on various levels, she ultimately shares with them a bond of friendship and professionalism that is stronger than the rivalry for Tom's attentions. When Angie manages to acquire the theatre, they are the first to acknowledge her achievement and, unlike Tom who must be coaxed, work willingly with Angie. Although the mother/daughter tensions between Lorna and Della, which mount in parallel to the Angie/Tom conflict, continue to exist, there is no suggestion that either woman would consider leaving the troupe to resolve the issues. If there is another communal group in the film, it is the prostitutes who help Angie get the work clothes she needs – again, women who are outside the social order.

Unlike *Duel in the Sun*, in which Pearl is contrasted to a very proper lady who fulfils Jesse's ideal

Still: Heller in Pink Tights – Tom (Anthony Quinn),
the actor, and Mabry, the gunman, join forces.

image of femininity, *Heller in Pink Tights* does not
provide the conventional counterpoint to the transgressing heroine. Instead, Angie is paralleled with
Della, who also has to rebel in order to establish her
identity. Lorna attempts to contain Della's sexuality
by insisting that she is still an ingénue when it is
clear that Della wants to be recognised as a woman
and an adult actress. While it would appear that
Lorna's motive is merely vanity, the personal and
professional aspects of the situation indicate an exploitation of sexuality and a simultaneous attempt to
deny its existence. On one hand, Lorna tells Della
she is too young to understand about women like
Angie while, on the other, she is willing to hawk
photographs of her daughter using a pitch which implies that she is selling child pornography. During
the course of the film, Della becomes more assertive
about her needs and, although Lorna continues to
protest, she, like Angie, is shown to be capable of
independence. In a sense, Della and Angie function
as complementary rather than contrasting identities,
as both are defying social structures that can be used
to contain them.

Many of Cukor's films are centred on show
people. Loren, in *Heller in Pink Tights*, responds well
to Cukor's guidance, giving a very accomplished performance, playing comedy and drama with grace

and intelligence. In the saloon scenes, she is de-
lightful as the consummate professional, performing
magic, selling photographs of herself and pretending that she is naive about poker; on the other hand,
she subtly informs a dramatic encounter with Quinn
in which she confesses having a difficulty, at times,
in telling the truth with the suggestion that, as a
woman, she hasn't been expected to be other than
duplicitous. (Contrary to the opinions expressed in
Lambert's book, I think Quinn's performance serves
the film well. His character isn't meant to convey
much surface charm or humour.) This was a point
in Loren's Hollywood career when she was attempting to establish herself as a serious actress rather than
a sex symbol. And while her elegant form-fitting
costumes contribute to a sensual presence, Cukor
relies on her acting to produce a sexual appeal composed of physical, emotional and intellectual responses. He doesn't exploit Loren's physicality by
photographing her in postures meant to titillate the
audience – *Heller in Pink Tights* has no nude bathing
scene, no bathtub scene, no occasion for Loren to
undress for the camera. Throughout the film Loren
wears a blond wig, calling our attention both to her
identity on and off the screen as an actor, and to the
artifice involved in both the theatre and film. Cukor,
like Angie, delights in such artifice, creating beauty
by his extravagant and stylish use of colour, celebrating what is termed a feminine sensibility in a genre
that has been dedicated to glorifying the male.

NOT WITH A BANG
The End of the West in
Lonely Are the Brave, The Misfits and Hud

Edward Gallafent

It has seemed self-evident that John Huston's *The Misfits* (1961), David Miller's *Lonely are the Brave* (1962) and Martin Ritt's *Hud* (1963) belong to the same group of Westerns – in his foreword to *The BFI Companion to the Western* (1988), Richard Schickel calls it the 'End-of-the-West Westerns of the 1960s'. Of course, there are questions – What West? What end? – to be asked, and we may begin by looking again at the fact commonly quoted to explain the appearance of the subject at this time: the advancing age of a group of Western stars. These figures, all born in the first decade of the century, were substantial presences on screen in the 'forties and 'fifties: Gary Cooper and Clark Gable (both born in 1901), Randolph Scott (b.1903), Joel McCrea and Ward Bond (b.1905), John Wayne (b.1907) and James Stewart (b.1908). Thus the youngest of these was in his early fifties at the beginning of the 1960s; Cooper and Gable were approaching sixty. Melvyn Douglas, whose character's old age and death are subjects in *Hud,* shares the year of his birth with Gable and Cooper.

The early 'sixties were marked by a significant cluster of deaths, both of actors who had worked substantially in Westerns and of old-timers in Western movies. Perhaps by coincidence, the groups hardly overlap. The period could be said to begin with the depletion of those associated with John Ford's world, by the deaths of Victor McLaglen and Russell Simpson in 1959, and Ward Bond and Dudley Nichols in 1960. In the summer of 1960, John Huston was shooting *The Misfits*, in which Gable's role is not that of an old man and in which his character does not die, but Gable died shortly after the film was completed, in November 1960, and Gary Cooper died in 1961.

That the subject of the deaths of old-timers is addressed in Westerns of this period is part of the common knowledge of the genre. In Sam Peckinpah's *Ride the High Country* (1962), the character played by Joel McCrea dies, and the film also provided Randolph Scott's final role, although he lived for another quarter of a century. Ford's *The Man who Shot Liberty Valance* (1962) concentrates on youth and age: we do not see the passing of the arid decades of middle age in the lives of the characters played by its veteran stars, James Stewart and John Wayne. Wayne appears only as a young man in the film's central flashback but, in Ford's words, he is 'the motivation for the whole thing'. The framing sequences make it clear that the meaning of the film turns on our consideration of its subjects in the light of the death of a figure whom we do not see, the old man that the Wayne character had become; perhaps the suggestion is that in the changed world of the developed West this figure can be the subject of such meditations only when he is in his coffin.

It is difficult to establish how far films like these two made use of their audience's sense that some of the crucial figures embodying the screened myths of the West were now near the end of their lives. This is a complex issue, with a reach beyond the literal fact of an obituary notice or a death on screen. An audience's sense of the end of a life – or of an era – can have a relation to the accumulated experience of an actor in a way that is not unconnected with his or her age, but which is not identical to it; I am thinking of the measure of time contained in the years over which individuals form part of an audience's experience of film. Thus, we know that an actor whom we remember from films that we saw twenty or thirty years ago is older now, and this is a time-scheme that need have no relation to whether the parts played (then or now) are younger or older. This awareness deepens our acknowledgement of mortality: our understanding that the likelihood of an actor's death or retirement can mean that any screen role may now be a last appearance. (That it is possible for some actors to have a succession of roles in their sixth or seventh decade may extend this acknowledgement, but it does not contradict it.)

The sense of loss or contraction, of a generation passing in the early 'sixties, is also marked in the demise of two major writers, both born in the late nineteenth century, both massively celebrated in the 'fifties, and both associated with elements of American traditions of the outdoors. Ernest Hemingway's death in 1961 followed sharply on that of his long-standing friend Gary Cooper, who, learning that they were both ill, had told him 'I bet I beat you to the barn.' William Faulkner died almost exactly a year later, in July 1962.

One footnote seems appropriate. It would be perverse in this context not to notice the premature death of Marilyn Monroe in August 1962; any viewing of *The Misfits* after this point cannot escape the knowledge that in a movie which is uncharacteristic of Huston's previous work in that nobody is killed in the narrative, the principals were both dead within two years of the completion of filming.

The three films that I will discuss can be distinguished from the larger group of end-of-the-West movies by their striking of one other note. They are all set in the contemporary West, addressing the American civilisation of the early 'sixties audience, and in so doing they raise the 'question of another kind of ending. They are asking about an America in which, although the process of settlement has long been concluded, it had historically been possible to become, or remain, some kind of Westerner by an act of choice, a deliberate embrace. These films are part of an interrogation of whether this choice is becoming an impossible one in contemporary America – that is to say, whether the penalties imposed on those who try to make it are becoming so great that they cannot be endured, or entail sacrifices that seem not to be worthwhile. This question is not confined to film – a version of it is addressed in Jack Kerouac's *On The Road* (1957) in the presentation of the doomed Dean Moriarty, 'a sideburned hero of the snowy west'.

Lonely Are the Brave takes a very American figure, one not unlike Moriarty, a man whose fantasy is that the world is different from the one we know. *The Misfits,* the only one of the films to include a successful sexual relationship, asks a question familiar in the Western: what changes in behaviour such a relationship might require, and what losses might be acknowledged. *Hud* frames its questions around a family refusing change, inflecting it differently in the case of each principal actor – virginity, marriage and death are the points of resistance.

Lonely Are the Brave

The pre-credits sequence of *Lonely Are the Brave* plays a simple game with our expectations. The film opens with a shot of empty country, a subdued growling tone on the soundtrack. The camera moves to reveal a Westerner in repose, enjoying a smoke by the embers of his campfire. He raises his eyes to the big sky – and we see the source of the film's initial sound effect, the jets that are slicing the heavens into neat ribbons with their vapour trails. This surprise indicator of modernity is also the first use of a

metaphor that will appear through the whole film, the modern world experienced as something not always tangible, but seen in the image of a dividing line that breaks up or interrupts a world of infinitely extensive space. This line is variously represented as a wire fence, as a highway, as the border between Mexico and the United States, as the bars of a jail.

The screenplay of the film is by Dalton Trumbo, a figure of the older generation who had experienced perhaps the most famous 'invisible' barrier in Hollywood history, that of the blacklist. Trumbo's plot, based on an Edward Abbey novel, contrasts two childhood friends, the Westerner Jake Burns (Kirk Douglas) and the writer Paul Bondi (Michael Kane). Paul has been arrested and sentenced to a jail term for political activism: helping others who have crossed a border – illegal immigrants – to find food and employment. On hearing news of this, Jake sets out with the explicit intention of springing his friend from jail.

Jake picks fights in order to land in jail and then breaks out again with the aid of hacksaws concealed in his boots. In the sequences of sawing through one of the bars and subsequently of bending down its cut end, the film uses action and song to celebrate the collective efforts of Jake, Paul and the other prisoners in the cell. But despite this collective involvement, Jake is unable to persuade Paul to break jail with him. Jake offers him an image of space, of escape to a place free of government, where Paul's son can become a 'natural man', but Trumbo gives Paul, the film's representative intellectual, the insight that escape is no longer a matter of cutting through iron bars, and that the act of placing yourself on the other side of such a barrier does not offer freedom but a more permanent form of persecution, with him and his family 'running for the rest of our lives'. The final conversation between the two men takes place after Jake has wriggled though the opening and is on the outside – but it is photographed in a series of shots that associates the bars equally with the images of both figures.

Jake seems to make the assumption that the world of the jail is untouched by time, as if it were in some frontier town in a Western. He regards his escapade of 'breaking into' jail as a piece of old-fashioned adventure and various details sustain a mood of comedy – once arrested, Jake finds that he now has to pick yet another fight, this time with the cops who, thinking to be kind to him, are preparing to let him go. And on the inside, we see a piece of stage business that might easily be lifted from a classical Western, an interlude with a stock character, a 'preacher' who gives a rhetorical account of his downfall – 'my temptation was women'.

Complementing this comedy is material very different in tone but not in point, involving the prison guard, Gutierrez (George Kennedy). We might notice that Jake is talking to Paul about being hungry

Stills: Lonely Are the Brave. *Left – technology and the cowboy. Opposite – pausing at barriers. Jake Burns (Kirk Douglas) breaks out of jail, while Paul Bondi (Michael Kane) looks on.*

when he first encounters Gutierrez, and the hostility between the two men is focused in a quip by Jake about bad temper and death. It turns out that what Gutierrez is hungry for is the opportunity to give Jake a surreptitious beating, an act which Jake perceives not as a horror, but more as a guarantee that here violence and the appetite for it still operate in the traditional way. The keynote is familiarity, as if something similar has taken place many times before. As Gutierrez comes to collect him for his beating, we see Jake quickly tearing material from his shirt and packing his nostrils and gums with rags, saying, '. . . if a man gives me fair notice.' After he returns, he holds in his hand the tooth that Gutierrez has knocked out, with rueful awareness that such moments are part of a series: 'Sure hate to lose the big ones . . .' In these roles, as later in their roles of pursued and pursuer, Jake and Gutierrez are linked, and distinguished from the intellectual – both of them call Paul 'College Boy'.

So here is the familiar gusto with which the Westerner approaches drinking and fist-fighting. Jake lays direct claim to this – his description of a drinking session at the beginning of the film is that it 'rinses your insides out, sweetens your breath, tones up your skin', in other words it is an extension of the bath and the good meal that we have just seen him enjoying – another appetite satisfied. But the film observes a distance between how Jake understands violence, and what we see it to be. The initial fight, in which Jake carries out his plan of going to a little bar and deliberately picking a scrap, offers as its figure of violence a man associated with the grimness of warfare, an amputee called Lapatten (Bill Raisch), who tells Jake that he lost his arm at Okinawa. This man is later described by the cops as 'loco' – the motive of his quarrelling with Jake is a hysterical insistence on his crippled state, seen in the way he uses the stump of his arm and his shirtsleeve, in the fighting. For the audience, the presentation of the fight is negative until its final moments, when the general mêlée dissolves as the cops arrive, to the accompaniment of energetically upbeat music on the soundtrack.

Do Jake's attitudes to the violence of Lapatten and Gutierrez constitute a critique of the character? The two can hardly be said to represent a modernity to which he is blind. Neither man has qualities that are specific to the times – wars have always produced bitter veterans and jails sadistic guards. So while we may be uneasy at the brio with which the film allows Jake to accept their violence – and his own – it is part of the seductiveness of this character and the charm that is given to the role by Kirk Douglas that we do not question it very deeply. We understand it as part of the tradition with which he identifies himself, where he finds his humour and courage, and it is not seriously challenged.

There is another obvious candidate to be the image of modernity that will crush the cowboy: twentieth-century technology, notably the means of transport and surveillance involved in the pursuit of Jake. The rider on horseback is chased by cops in cars, a sheriff and deputy in a Jeep, a spotter plane

and two tyro pilots flying a helicopter from the local army base. The film raises the subject of technology in its opening minutes, with a sequence in which Jake crosses a busy highway on his skittish horse, making cars swerve dangerously to avoid him. The subsequent action is punctuated by a series of moments in which a lorry carrying a heavy load is glimpsed travelling across America. It is this lorry that, in the dark and the rain, collides with Jake and his horse as he crosses the highway again at the end of the film.

This raises a number of questions. What point is being made by identifying this precise lorry? Is the device of making the horse skittish, and especially frightened by traffic, simply a way of finding a plausible explanation for the accident that ends the movie? And given that we have earlier seen Jake's reaction to the threat of machines to be a cunning one (successfully shooting at the tail rotor of a helicopter), isn't it odd that this experienced rider cannot wait for an adequate lull in the traffic before attempting to cross, particularly given the bad weather? Is there a point here about not learning from your past mistakes, or about the impenetrability of Jake's view of the world?

We might take the message to be a fairly simple one, about the power of technology, a nostalgia for an America innocent of it, and possibly something about inevitability. The charting of the progress of the lorry looks as if it wants to suggest this, as if nothing short of a juggernaut appearing from the darkness is able to destroy the Western hero, or is felt to be an appropriate way of representing this ending. Perhaps our seduction by Douglas's charm is to be countered by the knowledge that his nemesis is hurling towards him, but the insistence on this seems a crude way of representing the threat of the modern.

The contemporary order is differently presented in the man who leads the hunt for the fugitive Jake, the sheriff Maury Johnson (Walter Matthau), who is introduced to us in a sequence interpolated into the scenes of Jake's arrival in jail. We see two cluttered rooms which exemplify the distance from a Western interior – a female secretary, a bank of electronic communications equipment. Even the wall of 'wanted' posters are detailed mugshots, not the playbill-like announcements of the Western. We see the sheriff looking out of the barred window of the office. He is fascinated by a form of behaviour, watching a dog that takes the same route from post to post in the street below every day, and he places this for us with a joke about performance: 'You'd think he was under contract.' Inside the room, a point is made about language and repetition. Harry, the radio operator, answers everything addressed to him by turning the words into a query – when Johnson tells Harry that this gets on his nerves the reply is 'Nerves?'

Both gags are reprised in the sequence in the same set with Johnson after Jake's jailbreak. Johnson understands that Jake's violence can be connected with the energy of the Westerner – as Harry reads out Jake's war record, the sheriff connects the date of each occasion with a national celebration. He moves to the window, and for the first time we see the view, the mountains into which Jake is riding.

The critique of Johnson's world is offered as a comedy, through his baffled amazement at a milieu governed by habit or routine. The film presents the idea that such lives might be unsatisfying through the subject of appetite. The exchanges between Johnson and his men are sprinkled with references to eating, as if this at least is a reliable pleasure. Johnson himself is shown as a man who obsessively consumes chewing gum, which seems to be an emblem in the film of frustration – having something to chew on which doesn't exactly offer nourishment.

In the pursuit sequences, Johnson's attitude is of resignation at the inevitability of the escalation of violence, in which he himself takes no direct part, but also of admiration for Jake's prowess. Although he leads the hunt, he never comes close to Jake, seeing him only through binoculars, and in the final scene, confronted with the badly injured man lying on the highway, he will say that he does not know if this is his quarry, 'I can't tell – man I'm looking for, I never saw him this close.' At one point, looking up at the vast mesa, he describes Jake as a ghost.

Perhaps what is meant here is not quite literal, not a matter of his physical distance from Jake, (which, after all, he chooses not to disturb; he could have come up closer if he had wanted to) but of Johnson's sense of Jake's remoteness, of the rider's separation from the modern world: such figures are to be thought of as ghosts even when they are literally somewhere up there in front of you.

Finally, we can consider Jake's relation to the world through his relation to a woman, Gerry (Gena Rowlands), Paul's wife but implicitly Jake's childhood sweetheart. Some of what she has to do is very familiar – to represent wife and mother and homemaker, in other words, what this civilisation thinks of itself as being for. Of course, she also has to represent an acknowledgement of Jake's sexual attractiveness and, when she sends him off after the jailbreak, of the absolute loss represented by his departing glamour. But there is a trace of reserve. For Paul and Gerry are not farmers and settlers as they might have been in an earlier Western, but artists, a writer and a painter. As Jake is about to leave Gerry for the last time, he tries a conventional compliment about her paintings: Gerry snaps back, 'They're lousy.' Is this part of a deeper impatience with such a man?

The terms around which *Lonely Are the Brave* works, the settled and wandering males, literal and metaphorical sons, are part of what is familiar to us when Jake lectures Gerry. He talks about her being an Easterner, about fences and borders, about himself being selfish, a 'born cripple', as opposed to Paul whom he honours as the plain man given dimension by commitment to his family. But one central quality of modernity here is fragmentation, the isolation of these figures from each other. If we think, say, of the farm in *Shane*, it at least contains settler, wife, son and gunslinger together, under the same roof and variously photographed in the same frame. Here we see a world so fragmented, so composed

of impassable borders, that we never see the settler figure out prison, or the wife outside the setting of her house, or the son awake. Only Jake can move between the members of this family – we never see any one of its three members in the same shot as any other. Add to this the remoteness of Jake for Johnson and we have a world in which no-one achieves sustained contact with anyone else. Not its violence but its disseverance defines it.

The Misfits

The Misfits demands that we bring our knowledge of the background of one of its stars to any viewing of it. This is partly a matter external to the film, our awareness that Arthur Miller's script was written – or, rather, rewritten with a major role designed around Marilyn Monroe, Miller's wife at the time – from his earlier *Esquire* story about cowboys rounding up wild ponies and selling them to be killed and turned into dog food. Complementary detail inside the film points to the Monroe character's status as a performer – her opening sequence, in which we see her dressing and making up, invokes the image of an actor's dressing room, and the narrative shows a character learning her lines. Later in the film, others try to coax a 'performance' out of her or are delighted or nonplussed by the sudden unexpected delivery of one. Her past role is as a dancer, a creative artist whose sense of her talent has been confused by the seaminess that others have claimed to find in it – the visual evidence of this, a collection of photographs pasted up inside a wardrobe door, is recognisably a group of stills from the star's past work.

Elements not self-evident in the film are the terms in which John Huston conceived and elicited the

performances, and how the film-making was experienced by actors and crew. Among these are the decision, contrary to common practice, to shoot the film sequentially, in the order of Miller's script, and the choice of genuine wild horses for the final sequences. The decision as to how the film would end was apparently left very late into the shooting, and despite the use of stunt doubles, the dangers of using wild animals were evidently real. It is difficult to define the kind of authenticity aimed at here, but such strategies appear to be part of Huston's interest in investing the project with qualities of indeterminacy and risk. In the background, too, is the nagging presence of the anecdotes about the making of the film. These deal primarily with the disintegrating marriage of Monroe and Miller and give accounts which confirm star myth: the talent wrecked by indiscipline, by drug-taking and by illness (Monroe); the calm, patient veteran actor, waiting on set for the other to turn up (Gable). The deaths of both stars produced attempts by participants and onlookers to draw morals or write epitaphs. But all this should not obscure the independent use of Monroe's star persona made by *The Misfits*. We cannot forget the other details, but they are not the most important elements of the background – these are provided by Monroe's and Gable's screen careers previous to 1960.

The film was described on its release by *Variety* as an 'adventure drama' – is it necessary to state that it is a romance? This is not surprising given the elements of its two major stars that were perceived as marketable – Monroe had just made *Let's Make Love* (George Cukor, 1960) with Yves Montand, and Gable *It Started in Naples* (Melville Shavelson, 1960) with Sophia Loren. In *The Misfits*, the pattern of romance begins with a princess in a tower – Roslyn Taber (Monroe), first photographed looking down from the window of a Reno rooming house. She frees herself by divorce from an undesirable partner, crosses a bridge over a river, is talked into escaping from the city into the 'green world' of comedic/romance myth. (This might be thought to be a little difficult in Nevada, but a conversation about the smell of sage – 'like green perfume' – establishes the point exactly. Roslyn and her suitors, Guido (Eli Wallach) and Gay Langland (Clark Gable), arrive at a cabin in the country, where she finds herself having to choose between the two men. She responds by getting drunk, and confounds her companions by dancing alone in the darkening countryside. This seems to be taken as a signal by Guido that she has chosen Gay – Guido leaves, and after a sequence which is nominally a drive in a car, Gay takes her back to the cabin, where they spend the night together. (At this point, we are about thirty minutes into the running time of the film.)

There are elements here – particularly the movement from city to country and the choice of a lover after an interlude of drinking which is presented as having an effect of enchantment – which connect back to a tradition in film comedy and thence to earlier strains of comedy and romance. (*Bringing up Baby*, Howard Hawks, 1938, and *The Philadelphia Story*, George Cukor, 1940, form the essential context here: *see* Stanley Cavell's discussion of these films in his *Pursuits of Happiness: The Hollywood Comedy of Remarriage*, Harvard University Press, 1981.)

The film has begun with Guido as a mechanic fixing Roslyn's car. Her friend and landlady Isabel Steer (Thelma Ritter) explains that this new, expensive car was a gift, a 'divorce present from her husband'. When Guido expresses surprise – 'They're giving presents for divorces now?' – Isabel counters with the image of the 'single yellow rose' that her husband sends her annually on the anniversary of their divorce. 'Of course he never did pay me the alimony. But then, I wouldn't want to put a man out, you know?' It also emerges here that Roslyn's Cadillac is damaged because men keep on crashing into it to strike up a conversation with her. When Guido tells Roslyn that the car is fixed, she replies with some asperity, 'I'll never drive that car again.'

An opposition is set up between a world in which sexual relations are expressed through a gift associated with nature and explicitly not with money, and one where desire is linked to consumption and payment and invokes aggression and danger (Isabel has a broken arm; Guido asks her if she broke it in the car). Isabel's story of Roslyn and the car introduces an important subject: modern transport as a form of oppression. This is mainly raised, not through pursuit or accident, as in *Lonely Are the Brave*, but in images of containment, of figures framed or confined by the interiors of cars and trucks.

The film offers Gay Langland as cowboy – opposed to 'business' and 'wages' and, like Jake Burns, unattached to any one place, committed to an ideal expressed in a speech beginning with the words 'just live'. Against this it poses Guido, who is associated with the mechanisms of modernity, with his truck and later with his 'plane. When Guido walks Roslyn around his cabin in the country, the stress is on the corruption of his role as settler into that of consumer, showing off its luxuries: 'Gas refrigerator . . . here's the bathroom – ceramic tile.' The negative association with machines is expressed in the two stories of his past, that 'his wife is dead because he didn't have a spare tyre' (these are Roslyn's words) and his association with warfare – his aviation skills were learned as a bomber pilot.

Guido's sexual desire for Roslyn is linked to his role as consumer. When he and Gay meet her after her divorce, Guido insists that he will be the one who pays for the group's drinks. In the subsequent party at the cabin, we see Gay and Roslyn dancing together. When Isabel mentions that Roslyn used to teach dancing, Guido asks, 'In a dance hall?' and he now moves in on her, ousting Gay with the words 'How about the landlord?'. These are muted hints, but the implication is that Guido's sexual interest in Roslyn sharpens when he understands that she was a hired dance 'teacher', that at least this relation to her body could once be bought. And the dancing skills that we now see him exhibit suggest how some of his time in the forces was spent – commenting on his footwork here, Gay twice calls him 'pilot'.

Dancing gives us a measure of the distance between Guido and Gay. After his brief waltz with Roslyn, we do not see Gay dance with her again, but when she dances alone, barefoot in the dusk, he seems to recognise the intensity of her abandonment to it, the necessity of it for her, and is not threatened by it. When they become lovers, he does not wish to repress her past as an 'interpretational' dancer, but to recognise it as something that has been part of her life. In the background of both lives lurks the subject of prostitution – the murkiness of Roslyn's past in the clubs is matched by Gay's role as an escort to the rich Reno divorcees.

The connection between Roslyn's past and the activities of the Westerner becomes clearer in the Dayton rodeo sequence, which presents two forms of show. The first, in which Roslyn 'performs' in the rodeo's bar, playing a game with a child's bat and ball, centres on her body. The second, horse and bull riding, focuses on physical force acting on another beautiful body, that of a young rodeo performer, Perce Howland (Montgomery Clift).

At the rodeo Huston shows energies only barely in control. Roslyn's performance just avoids causing a brawl when one of the onlookers touches her, and the sequences in which we see men mounted on horses and bulls are brief explosions of violence that stress danger and potential damage rather than skill. Nobody has an attitude to this violence that we are asked to admire – Perce's bravado slides into groggy, alcohol-fuelled masochism, Guido is substantially indifferent, Roslyn in a state of hysterical

Still: The Misfits – *'Just live.'* Gay Langland *(Clark Gable) with Isabel (Thelma Ritter) and Roslyn (Marilyn Monroe).*

terror at the threat of permanent injury or death. It is a demonic world in which the insignificance of potential death turns on the isolation of these people from each other, rendering as irony their close physical proximity. Only Isabel is offered as representing a denser world of feeling in her chance meeting with her ex-husband and his wife. Significantly, they figure in the rodeo sequence for only a moment and then exclude themselves from it.

The quality of this isolation is expressed in the scenes leading up to and away from the rodeo, in which the principals try to communicate with each other, or with their loved ones, starting with the introduction of Perse and the wrenching quality of his telephone call to his mother. Here Huston's use of the imagery of physical confinement is finely articulated, with Perse in the telephone booth, opening and closing its door as the tone of the conversation changes, and the group of listeners a few yards away remaining seated inside their car. The point is extended later in the ride home from the rodeo, which foregrounds a line introduced in Perse's phone call: 'Say Hello.' This time, Guido, driving the car, is speaking to Roslyn seated in the back of it, asking her at least to say hello to him. As in a telephone call, he cannot look at her, but the point is also the deadliness of the situation, the threat that this guilty bomber pilot will crash the car. Between the two scenes this isolation is further annotated and lost contacts are mourned in Perse's account of the break-up of his family and Gay's despair at the indifference of his children.

These sequences lead directly into the final movement of the movie, the 'mustanging' expedition that has been canvassed almost from its opening. This rounding up of the wild horses that still live in the mountains above Reno offers an escape to open high country and a chance to exercise a traditional Westerner's skill of dominating and taming a truly wild animal, not in the context of a degraded performance, but with a respectable relation to money, something which produces cash and yet is not 'wages'. It is obliquely related to the image of the cattle drive, rounding up animals and moving them across the American landscape which is seen as a tradition of the West.

One way in which the mustanging differs from the rodeo is that the latter was not staged for Roslyn's benefit, and her reaction to its violence was seen as an anomaly or misunderstanding. At the end of the previous sequence, Gay's last words to Roslyn were a promise and a cri de coeur, wondering about settling down to farming, claiming that he's a good man – somehow the mustanging is to make all this clear. By this point in the film, the mustanging has acquired a function beyond its economic purpose, for part of what is at stake is the issue of justifying the hunting to Roslyn, who is neither a Westerner nor part of an older generation, and whose past speaks of other worlds and traditions.

The process begins with a conversation with Gay in which Roslyn is asked to accept that the captured horses are no longer tamed, but killed for petfood. This is an accusation of disingenuousness, or thoughtlessness, about modern convenience: 'What did you think was in those cans?' Then there is the fact of modernity, represented as ever in changed transport technology: 'Kids ride motor scooters now'. It is followed by the reference to history, the claim that the act is given dimension through its connection with the past, 'mustang blood pulling all the ploughs in the West' (this last piety supported by suitably reverential music on the soundtrack).

Finally, there is an appeal to Roslyn's biography, to the idea that all histories are histories of compromise, that the forces that have brought Gay to this place are not so very unlike those that measure the distance between Roslyn's first dancing, and what that dancing became, or what was made of it. What he says to her is, 'This is how I dance.' We should be careful to take this not as Miller or Huston crudely pointing up a reading of the material for us but as a part of the romance – it is not so much a convincing analogy as a way for Gay to remind Roslyn that he loves her, or 'take my hat off to you', as he puts it. In this scene, she recognises at least this element of the speech for what it is.

The sequence on the following morning announces what none of the men has admitted, that this is not just a chamber version of the great roundups of the past, but an American ending – the last hunt. We see Guido climbing into his plane, wearing the flying jacket that has seen him through his wartime combat missions. As he loads his shotgun – to scare the horses – he tells Roslyn that she should fly with him, for she will 'never see this again in history'. The configuration in which the horses finally appear confirms this – there are only six of them, but more significantly, as one stallion, four mares and a colt they represent a minimal breeding unit, a kind of equine Edenic family, poised between growth and extinction. The meaning of this is dramatised in the breathless questions Roslyn asks Perce from her position inside the cab of the lorry, and it is after this that she realises the absoluteness of the killing and tries to fight the men roping down the stallion.

The appearance of only six horses means the abandonment of the fiction that the business of the roundup is to convert Roslyn to a vision of its essential rightness. It becomes, rather, a question of how you give something up, or what it is exactly that you acknowledge that you are giving up. After a speech which expresses the changed times, Gay asks the other men, 'Why don't we give her these horses?' But there is a problem – we may take him to understand that freeing the horses will then be her doing, not something to which he will have to admit. This may be seen as an evasion, and gifts to this woman have a bad history, if we remember the Cadillac with which the film opened. It is no better to buy something – Roslyn, behind the men, responds with 'How much do you want for them?' –

Still: The Misfits – *the end of an era. Perce (Montgomery Clift), Gay, Roslyn and Guido (Eli Wallach) contemplate the roped horse.*

an offer seen as a way of purchasing some part of Gay, and again it is rejected.

The situation seems like an impasse – Gay grimly continues tying up the horses, Perce refuses the guilt of the business by refusing the money and Roslyn takes refuge in a version of her response to the rodeo, screaming hysterically at the men. The way Huston places her in longshot here seems to make a point about the diminished authority of such behaviour. Finally Perce releases the horses – he can do so because no dense relation to any of the others complicates this act for him.

But how can Gay accept this release, and renounce the image of himself as hunter that is bound up in the way he has lived? It is achieved by a ritual, a return to a past world. We have seen the horses captured with plane and gun, chased by the lorry, worn down by roping them to heavy tyres which they dragged along until they tired themselves out. Now, in a move which has famous precedents in American culture, we see all this modernity and technology fall away. Gay, on foot, launches himself at the stallion, and Huston shows him alone, wrestling the beast to the ground.

Of course a lot of the footage here is stunt-work, a familiar combination of close-ups of the actors and long shots of the stuntmen performing the dangerous acts. But this sequence includes a crucial shot that insists on its authenticity, a shot of Gay being dragged along the ground by the horse. Doc Erikson, Huston's production designer, describes the organisation of the shot as relatively routine, involving Gable being padded and dragged on a leather mat behind a truck. But the image seems to have been invoked in comment about Gable's subsequent death, the blame variously attributed to Huston and Gable himself for insisting on it. The fascination with this, the construction of it as some final, wrongheaded but touching and fatal moment of insistence on authenticity, is an example of the difficulty of extracting the film from the myths circulating around its players and their relationships to ideas of age, death, and the Westerner's insistence on authenticity.

Gay ties the captured stallion to the truck. Now he can symbolically separate the worlds of nature and modern technologies by severing the rope that binds them – he does not untie the rope again, but cuts it with a knife. To send the horses back to the mountains is to reposition this last breeding group as a possible promise of a new Eden, a foundation of a herd of the future. Huston has Roslyn echo the image of separating the beast from the machine a moment later, when she frees their dog, which is tied next to Guido's plane. (The oddness of the continuity here, given that our last sight of the plane was of Guido preparing to take off just before the release of the horses and then aborting the flight, may confirm that this visual pun is not casual.) Reunited by this, the couple drive off together, the final dialogue speaking of their hopes of fertility and recovered sense of direction. Guido, shouting at the retreating truck, threatens them with the image of the mechanised, urbanised world of contemporary America.

Hud

Even the titles of *The Misfits* and *Lonely Are the Brave* hint at something that we might expect of their cowboys, the adoption of the role as a form of retreat or withdrawal. Such misfits and loners can preserve their image of themselves unaltered – Jake Burns – or try to find a way of reinserting themselves into a changed America – Gay Langland – but both start from the premise of being marginal figures, aware of the possibility of their irrelevance to the modern world.

Being a cowboy may not be an adopted role, but a situation in which you find yourself as a result of birth, within a system of property and inheritance. This is the West of the ranch, the 'spread', the world of ownership, money and their relation to family role. It appears in the strain of the Western closely related to family melodrama, dealing with patriarchal power, its transmission to sons and daughters and different understandings of legitimate and illegitimate claims to such power.

In *Hud*, Homer Bannon (Melvyn Douglas) owns a spread outside a small Texas town, which he works with his son Hud (Paul Newman), his grandson – Hud's nephew – Lon (Brandon De Wilde) and a few hired hands. There are no Bannon women; the house is kept by a hired cook, Alma (Patricia Neal). Homer is becoming an old man, but his world holds together until one of his cows dies of suspected foot-and-mouth disease, the initiating event of the film. The herd is quarantined; there are scenes of violent antagonism between father and son, and Hud attempts to rape Alma. Foot-and-mouth disease is confirmed, and the herd is destroyed on government orders. Alma leaves, Homer dies, Lon leaves, and Hud is left alone in the farmhouse.

Indisputably, there are trajectories of decline here, and the meaning of *Hud* depends on how we read them. The destruction of the herd feels like an essay on modernity, on the investigation and identification of disease by scientific method, and on contemporary methods of control. The sequence of the herd being driven into a pit, killed by gunfire, covered in lime and buried in a mass grave seems obviously to echo the imagery of the holocaust and the atrocities of the century's warfare, and it appears that this connection was clear when the film was made.

Alongside this is the interpretation of the family melodrama, the reading of Homer as a morally upright figure who rejects Hud's proposal of selling off the infected herd, and accuses Hud of being 'an unprincipled man' in more than one way. Does Hud also represent modernity, seen as an abandonment of the principle and law embodied in Homer in favour of behaving 'in a lenient manner' in matters moral and sexual? Is the film committed to a view of the contemporary as a state of decline, Hud's cynical sneer replacing the pieties of the old West that are embodied by his father?

Critical reaction to *Hud* seems mainly to have been to read it in this way, as a sober, scathing attack on modernity and materialism, a lament for the lost

Still: Hud – *principle and law. Homer Bannon (Melvyn Douglas) as the Western patriarch.*

Western past, a piece of American self-laceration appropriate to the year of the presidential assassination. This view is adequately summarised in one contemporary interpretation of *Hud* that takes issue with it, Pauline Kael's 'Hud, Deep in the Divided Heart of Hollywood' (1964, reprinted in *I Lost it at the Movies*, Little, Brown, Boston, 1965). Kael sees the film as expressing a contradiction, between 'the cant of the makers' liberal serious intentions' and the 'celebration and glorification of materialism' that she argues is unintentionally presented through the figure of Hud, and crucially through the casting of Paul Newman in the role. Such a reading has its problems. Kael writes of 'the surprise of the slightly perverse ending', and the claim that Hud/Newman is the figure with whom the audience identifies involves a remarkable passage in which she attempts to justify his attack on Alma. Kael's account of the film essentially takes it as an example of the industry's cynical self-serving tendencies – 'shallow' and 'such a mess', it is nonetheless taken to be 'an archetypal Hollywood movie'. Her piece has the same mood of disgust with contemporary America as the writings of the critics whom she attacks, at one point even touching directly on the subject of the presidential assassination.

Both readings of the film depend on the promotion of qualities associated with the Western. Kael responds to the energy, honesty, vigour and glamour of the Westerner felt in the Paul Newman role, and others to the probity, gravity, sense of tradition and respect for law assigned to the Melvyn Douglas role. Both accounts see these qualities as very crudely in conflict and take the role of the critic to be the identification of the one that the film asks us to

prefer. I want to argue for a different reading of the film, which takes these qualities to be assigned to the characters roughly as I have described them, but which sees them as complementary, as varieties of narcissism, of grasping for power. We can see the figures of Homer and Hud as essentially alike, locked together in a relation that neither can avoid. The issue becomes not one of the promotion of a particular set of values, but the fragility of the world represented by the whole Bannon household in the face of passing time. (Almost the first thing the film does is to remind us of the times in an image of the changing West, a horse riding patiently in the trailer of the truck, and in an annotation of time and cultural change, the announcer on Lon's transistor radio giving an exact timecheck.)

These issues may become clearer if we try to describe how the principals see them, how they understand themselves and their actions. Part of the problem of reading *Hud* has arisen from a failure to ask what inner lives these characters have, what they understand about their own motivations and those of others.

Homer knows that he is an old man – he knows that what keeps him alive is his absolute authority. We see this in the two sequences that Ritt sets around the body of the dead cow. In the first, Homer announces that he is calling in the government vet, and in the second he agrees that the herd will have to be destroyed if foot-and-mouth disease is confirmed. We should notice that Hud and Lon are present on both occasions; in the first case, Homer has sent Lon to fetch Hud from town. Why? The apparent explanation, that he needs Hud's advice, looks thin – nothing supports the case that Hud has specialist knowledge, or that Homer might be influenced by his opinion. The reason is rather that Homer's power is expressed by his denying the suggestions that Hud makes, and it is equally clear that Hud makes them in the knowledge that they will be denied. What we understand about Homer, even by this point, is that his authority is unchallengeable, his will inflexible – it is not possible that his son and grandson are unaware of this.

The whole narrative of the testing, diagnosis and final destruction of the herd is an expression of Homer's power – not simply in his assent to the process, but in his implicit acceptance of these events as appropriate, as if it were right that, as his life nears its end, the images of the West that he associates with the past should be eclipsed. This is most clear in the case of the representative Edenic animal couple of this film, the pair of longhorned cattle. Their role as standing in for the old West can be identified through the speech that Homer makes over them, comparable to the moment in *The Misfits* in which Gay speaks of the analogous role of the ponies. Here, however, the longhorns are shot, an act that Homer insists on performing himself. His last act of authority in the film is to order Hud and Lon to bury them.

Thus an old man's feeling that the world is running down is apparently confirmed, and Hud and Lon will inherit a world from which the cattle have at least temporarily disappeared. But the cattle disease is an accident. Its origin is never definitely established in the film, and the government vet compares it to a 'bolt of lightning'. While the methods of control may be modern, the disease itself is not. The point is not its actual modernity, but the desire of both Homer and Hud to see it in this way, as a metaphor for the end of an era from which they are unable to detach themselves. It corresponds to a view of the West as something properly understood as in the past, something to which the younger generation are not entitled, or which they cannot embody.

Arguing that Hud feels this depends on our view of his attitude to Homer. Is he cold-heartedly waiting to inherit the spread, and sell off the oil leases? Does he simply stand for a world of technology replacing that of nature, as we have seen in Guido in *The Misfits*? Consider the possible meaning of his resentment of Homer, and specifically of Homer's old age, suggested when, early in the film, after Hud has been 'rousted' out of bed with a woman, he and Lon drive back to the ranch to inspect the dead cow for the first time.

Hud: . . . he [Homer] hasn't asked me about anything in fifteen years. I just work out there from the shoulders down, myself.

Still: Hud – *catastrophe. Hud (Paul Newman), Homer and Lon (Brandon De Wilde) look on as the government vets inspect the dead animal.*

Lon: You going to be able to make it all day, after a night like you put in?
Hud: I ain't a hundred years old like him, I don't need a week's sleep to be fresh.
Lon: He can't help being an old man, Hud.

Hud does not reply to these last words – Ritt offers a shot of him looking at Lon, and he starts to drive his Cadillac faster than before.

Hud's behaviour here, and in the rest of the film, can be read not as cold-bloodedness, but as a performance of sarcasm and energy, covering – ineffectively – an obsessive love of his father. (The casting of Paul Newman is suggestive, if we recall his role in *The Left-Handed Gun*, Arthur Penn, 1958.) Notice the number of instances when Hud directly expresses care for Homer: his concern when his father is sitting exhausted after the cattle roundup, and at the scene of the old man's collapse in the diner after the cinema visit that evening, followed by the offer to help Homer upstairs when they arrive back at the house. That these gestures of care are rejected by the old man – Hud knows in advance that they will be rejected – only serves to stress the strength of the feeling that underlies them. Later, Hud's defence of his father's honesty to the government vets over the question of shooting the longhorns is strikingly positioned. It takes place when relations between father and son are nominally at their worst, and in a context – dealing with government men – in which Hud has been condemned for his lack of principle.

The case against this, that father and son represent opposite worlds, seems to focus on the reading of one crucial scene – Hud's proposal to sell off the herd before the quarantine is imposed – and one plot development, Hud's claim that he is initiating legal process to have Homer declared incompetent and so take control of the ranch.

I have already made the point that Hud knows perfectly well that there is no chance that Homer will accept his proposal; it functions not as a practical alternative, but as a cry of rage and frustration at Hud's lack of any access to power as catastrophe approaches. The speech itself, which begins with the cry, 'Why, this whole country's run on epidemics – where've you been?' is not an endorsement of modernity but a polemic against it: 'Big business, price-fixing, crooked TV shows, income tax finagling, souped-up expense accounts.' It expresses not Hud's embrace of the modern but the deep mistrust of it that he shares with Homer.

The matter of the legal process is not unrelated. It offers Hud not as wishing to replace Homer's authority with something different in kind, but to reproduce it, to transfer his father's absolute power to himself – we may say that he wishes to become his father. My argument that Hud is deeply committed to his father and to the world he represents or holds together – that this commitment is what his anger and rebellion expresses – provides a way of reading Hud's choice of sexual partners. The attractiveness to Hud of married women like Mrs Truman Peters (Yvette Vickers) is that they hold no future, no possibility of movement forward into marriage and family, and thus no acknowledgement of the passing of the old generation – as long as Hud sticks to them, he can stop time. This feeling is differently inflected in the behaviour of Lon, whose evident unwillingness to take up with girls at all, to lose his virginity, indicates a related impulse.

The opposite possibility, embodied in the woman who could become Hud's partner and thus offer a future, is of course presented through Alma. The film makes this clear in the evening sequence that takes place on the Bannon porch, where talk about the girls in Lon's future goes along with flirtation between Alma and Hud. The idea is reinforced a little later in a sequence in which Hud charms Alma in a visit to her cabin – even after the attempted rape, the trace of this lost possibility remains in the film in the sequence of Alma's departure, when she tells Hud that 'it would have happened eventually without the roughhouse'.

The forces that Ritt shows destroying this possibility relate to the connections between masculinity, love and violence. The approach to these issues is through the subject of male camaraderie, idealised in the account of the relation of Hud and his dead brother Norman. After a pig-wrestling sequence has offered a form of physical fun, Hud introduces Lon to drinking and partners him in a brawl. The tone of this has some of the comedy of related material in *Lonely Are the Brave*, but it gives way, as both men sober up, to a moment that includes an identification and a confession. Hud effectively argues that

Lon has now replaced Norman, recreating the lost bond of the brothers, but he also confesses the story of Norman's death, when Hud crashed their car.

This leads into two closely related sequences in which Hud and Homer confront each other. In the first, Hud is condemned by his father not – as he supposes, or hopes – for Norman's death but for his selfishness, his failure to love. Hud cannot make a direct reply to this, cannot tell his father that he loves him, but the film has already supplied us with that knowledge in other ways. Newman's performance in this scene is sufficient indication of his pain to confute the accusation of emotional deadness. What he says in reply – it is the only direct mention of this figure in the entire film – is 'My mother loved me, but she died'.

The second sequence, on the following night, takes up these hints. Hud is drunk and at his most aggressive and vicious. When Homer delivers a line that effectively wishes to reject his paternity of Hud ('How'd a man like you come to be a son to me'), Hud's speech in reply, introduced with a cry of rage that cannot be reproduced in print, is:

'That's easy, I wasn't no bundle left on your doorstep, wasn't found in no bulrushes. *[Homer slams the door in the face of these words.]* You had the same feelings below your belt as any other man. That's how you got stuck with me as a son. Whether you like it or not.'

Hud goes downstairs, apparently to sober up, but sees Alma outside her cabin. Apparently on an impulse, he attempts violently to rape her.

These scenes give rise to questions. Who was Hud's mother, and how did she die? Why does Hud associate his birth with feelings in his father that he seems to identify with his own attitudes to women? What exactly is he trying to express, or being compelled to repeat, in the attack on Alma? That there is to be no answer to these questions distinguishes *Hud* from the strain of melodrama, exemplified by *East of Eden* (Elia Kazan, 1955) or *Home from the Hill* (Vincente Minnelli, 1960), to which it relates. The point is not the exposure of the gothic past, with the possibility of a kind of resolution, but the gesture to a truth which Hud and Homer both know and of which they cannot speak: that the quality of their relationships to women are not what divides them but what they share, inextricable from the impulse to power and control that built and sustained the ranch. The literal details of family history, like the death of Hud's brother, finally function only as indications of shared emotional ruthlessness, the preparedness of both Homer and Hud to bury anything that stands in their way. (The subject of burial recurs at crucial points in the film, around the herd, the longhorns, Norman, Homer himself.)

The final way in which I wish to discuss the meaning of *Hud* is through the subject of food. This is persistently an issue in the film, a way in which the characters communicate meaning to themselves and to us. Consider how extensively it figures – the direct references include Lon's visit to the diner which opens the film, and the three sequences of

meals in the kitchen at the ranch, plus Alma eating food in Hud's car, the diner scene after Homer and Lon have been to the cinema, and Hud's attempt to seduce Alma while she is cooking.

In *Lonely Are the Brave* and *The Misfits*, the cooking and eating of food expresses feelings about those appetites that the characters can satisfy, or know how to satisfy. Food in *Hud* is a form of definition, both of self and others – in the opening minutes we have references to Hud and steak, to Lon and doughnuts, and Hud's annotation of Homer's age: 'You're pouring coffee in your saucer as usual.' The Bannon family meals are evidently celebrative, as are the occasions of eating while discussing other appetites, such as Alma's lift home in Hud's car, in which she feeds herself on groceries and gossip about his love life, and the scene on the family porch with the ice-cream that Hud describes punningly as 'peachy'. Alongside this there is the image of the herd itself, a representation of the fertility of the West, of the idea of cornucopia, a massively extensive source of food. The destruction of the herd then becomes the negation of this – the dead beasts buried, not even food for buzzards. (This could be compared with the degradation of the idea of food in *The Misfits*, horses turned from source of Western energy to food for dogs.) The end of the herd is closely associated in the film with the loss of Alma, the provider of nourishment.

Alma's departure at the end of *Hud* is arguably the key to understanding the disintegration to which the film points. It is the first of the three events – the others are Homer's death and Lon's departure – that dissolve the group and express the fragility of the family. Its survival up to this point turns out to have depended not on the shifting of these roles into the more conventional ones – Alma becoming Hud's

Stills: Hud. Above – male camaraderie. Hud takes Lon to a bar. Below – the compulsion to repeat? Hud's attempted rape of Alma (Patricia Neal).

wife and effectively Lon's mother – but on making no change, on not disturbing a world in which these characters appear in facsimiles of family roles.

Such an illusion, seen in the sequence on the Bannon porch at the end of the evening meal and in the two scenes in Lon's bedroom, in which Alma can play the role of his mother, may be the more touching because this fragility is sensed. The second scene in Lon's room, in which Alma cares for the injured boy, is a finely articulated expression of the feeling that exists in this provisional family. As usual, its detail is worked out around food, or at least what you have in your mouth – Alma has given Lon a drink of lemonade, and he is embarrassed at how to dispose of the pips. Seeing this, she holds out her hand – her line is 'Come on, they're only lemon seeds.' For a moment, disgust, the act of spitting something out, is transformed into an image of

tenderness. We may notice, if we like, that this is allied, in a way about which the film is tactful, to the imagery of sexual impregnation – but the delicacy here enriches the image rather than coarsening it.

Trying to make out what notion of the end of the West these three films have in common, we may be struck by how much of this is an image of the progressive depopulation of a world – the hush that falls as actors leave the stage or set. These are not narratives of dynamic change – the very American subject of one world being swept away by another, by a new kind of technology or social order. Notice how small a part is played by guns in the films; violence with guns has been, and remains, a subject in the Western but it is not the one in front of us here.

There is little trace in the films of references to the contemporary world – cities, weaponry, newspapers, media technology, the race question in early-'sixties America. Only Lon in *Hud*, with his pocket transistor set and liking for the radio in the Cadillac, wants contact with the outside – significantly Homer and Hud are both given occasions to object to this intrusion. Certainly, changed transport technology figures, but although this is used to provide metaphors for the characters' experience of their situation, it is not usually offered as directly responsible for it. (Guido chases the wild ponies by plane, but the plane is not responsible for there being only a few animals.) Perhaps only money has this role. In both *The Misfits* and *Hud*, the cement that binds working groups together is shifting from blood kinship to wages. Perce's woeful comment that his stepfather 'offered me wages . . . on my father's place' is echoed at the end of *Hud* when Hud offers Lon employment.

The West that the films show us is a natural world that is strangely diminished and unable to sustain itself – the half-dozen ponies in *The Misfits*, the diseased herd in *Hud*. Accompanying this is a sense of confusion over what settlement in such a world might mean, how a life out here could be sustained. Perhaps it is from this anxiety about sustenance that the insistent interest in food emerges, as if the act of cooking or eating food becomes a way in which these figures can assert that they know how to nourish themselves.

Related to this is the meaning of a threshold, of the ability to move between the world inside the home and that outside it. In *Hud*, it is briefly possible to take food out on to the porch and imagine a future – the comparable moment in *The Misfits* is the business of supplying the cabin with what it significantly lacks, a doorstep, and Roslyn's triumphal repetition of the act of going in and out of the door. But even here, the suppressed anxiety conveyed in Monroe's performance suggests the strain of a world in which a gesture as simple as this has to be reinvented, or insisted upon. Both films show the frailty of attempts to extend the domestic impulse a little beyond the doorway – garden flowers trampled underfoot (*The Misfits*) or crushed under the wheels of a car (*Hud*).

Both *The Misfits* and *Lonely Are the Brave* offer ways of leaving the West, the escape routes of love or death. In *The Misfits*, the ending can be cautiously positive, the figure of Gable offered as able both to celebrate the past of the West and to turn his back on it – part of the subject of the film has been Gay and Roslyn learning to accept their pasts and not be trapped by them. The anxiety as to exactly what alternative world is possible for the lovers is not solved.

In *Lonely Are the Brave*, the comparable question does not need an answer. The film offers with, I think, only partial success, the Westerner as a man who finds that he ceases to be real in the eyes of the world, who becomes a ghost. But does the world also cease to be real for him? One reading of Jake's accident would be that he is knocked down because he no longer recognises the dangers of the highway as actual ones. But the use of the 'spooky' horse complicates this, offering the more literal reading of bad luck or poor calculation.

Of the three films, only *Hud* acknowledges that the energies which constructed the West might in themselves be flawed and finally unable to sustain a humane world for more than a brief period. Lon's act of self-imposed exile which ends *Hud* invokes the terms of the classical Western, in which the exiling of figures such as the gunslinger from the community was – however regretfully – undertaken in the name of the progress of civilisation. Compare the situation at the end of *Shane* (George Stevens, 1953) – the obvious context given the casting of Brandon De Wilde in both films. In *Shane*, the figure of violence and eroticism must exile himself to ensure the stability of the family and the continuity of settlement, and the child played by De Wilde mourns his passing. In *Hud*, it is Lon – Brandon De Wilde still in the role of the virginal child – who leaves. Hud's doom is that of stasis, his glamour useless, denied even the release implicit in the act of sacrifice, of exile from a family that no longer exists. His final cry to Lon – 'This world is so full of crap, a man's going to get into it sooner or later, whether he's careful or not' – is his cynical telescoping of the ethical basis that sustained the Western, that distinguished the Liberty Valances from the Tom Doniphons, a distinction that Hud must now deny if his life is to be bearable.

In the last moments of *Hud*, Ritt takes us into the Bannon house. There is no nostalgia for this space, no sense of contemplation of the values it once embodied, only an undistinguished couple of rooms. There is no music: we have had that, a plaintive guitar melody, for the shots of the empty corrals a little earlier. In place of nourishment, Hud opens a beer, makes a vague gesture of dismissal in the direction of Lon's retreat, slams the door. The end title rolls. What the Bannons once represented has disappeared – not overcome by a new order, but obliterated as the figures who sustained it have died or withdrawn. The keynote is emptiness or silence, an idea of civilisation that nobody will remember. Looking forward into the 'seventies, the connection is not with the explicit violence of a strain of later Westerns, but with the consideration that the act of settlement is not a first stage of civilisation but an experiment doomed to failure and obscurity.

HOW THE WEST WAS WON
History, Spectacle and the American Mountains

Sheldon Hall

'The story of the peopling of America has not yet been written. We do not understand ourselves' (Frederick Jackson Turner, 'The Significance of History', 1891, reprinted in *Frontier and Section*, Prentice Hall, Englewood Cliffs, New Jersey, 1961).

'The name "Cinerama" is an anagram of "American" ' (Greg Kimble, '*How the West Was Won* – in Cinerama', *American Cinematographer*, October 1983).

Although it might be thought that the genre is inherently 'epic' in its relation to history and myth, Westerns of authentically epic scale and ambition are relatively few in number and have generally been confined to certain distinct periods in the genre's history. There were, for example, brief cycles in the late silent and early sound periods *(The Covered Wagon*, James Cruze, 1923; *The Iron Horse*, John Ford, 1924; *Tumbleweeds*, King Baggott, 1925; *The Big Trail*, Raoul Walsh, 1930; *Cimarron*, Wesley Ruggles, 1931), in the late 'thirties and early 'forties *(The Plainsman*, Cecil B. De Mille, 1936; *Union Pacific*, De Mille, 1939; *They Died With Their Boots On*, Walsh, 1941), and throughout the 'roadshow' era of the late 'fifties and 'sixties (from *The Big Country*, William Wyler, 1958 and *The Alamo*, John Wayne, 1960 to *The Wild Bunch*, Sam Peckinpah, 1969 and *Little Big Man*, Arthur Penn, 1970).

A consistent feature of the epic sub-genre is the attention paid to history as a substantive issue, a process to be dramatised or pictured. Epic Westerns are generally the most conscious of the genre's basis in an actual, as opposed to mythic, past, although they are no more scrupulous than most in their fidelity to documented fact. I want to consider *How the West Was Won* (Henry Hathaway, John Ford and George Marshall, 1962) as a representative instance of the epic Western, focusing in particular on its enactment of a version of American history that owes a great deal to Frederick Jackson Turner's frontier thesis, and on the implications for this project of the film's basis in generic convention and reliance on visual spectacle.

Genre as Circus

'Imagine every stock – classic, if you like – Western situation, and then picture it at least twice as large as you've ever seen it on the screen previously, and you begin to get the right idea of the movie' (F. Maurice Speed, *What's On In London*, 2nd November 1962).

For the opening ceremony of the 1984 Los Angeles Olympic Games, the film and television producer David L. Wolper was commissioned to stage a lavish musical production number celebrating American history and showbusiness traditions. The resulting entertainment, loud, brash and flamboyant, was entitled 'How the West Was Won' and featured scores of dancers, in 'frontier' period dress, high-kicking to a selection of popular folk songs together with the main theme from Alfred Newman's score for the MGM film (which also incorporates traditional folk songs and features them separately as overture, intermission and exit music in the full roadshow version). The performance was widely cited as proof of the coarseness and vulgarity of American popular culture (rather than its vitality), and contrasted with the disciplined grace and refinement of the gymnastic display which had opened the 1980 Moscow games. No-one, however, could have been surprised by which cultural traditions (musical, Western) had been chosen to represent Americanness to the world. It's revealing also that a motion-picture producer, rather than a theatrical impresario, should have been selected to take charge of the task.

Wolper's Olympic revue was itself part of another longstanding American tradition: the historical pageant, the other manifestations of which have included Buffalo Bill's Wild West Shows, Independence Day parades, certain features of Disneyland theme parks, the Western in film and literature, and those re-enactments by stuntmen of shoot-outs and other episodes that continue to attract tourists to back-lot studio sets long after the clapboard towns stopped being used for actual movies. The function of such phenomena is not to interrogate history, but to offer a fanciful, consensual representation of the past as a spectacle for the entertainment (and patriotic edification) of the present (pageantry is not, of course, a uniquely American mode). For Frederick Jackson Turner, pageantry exists 'for the purpose of satisfying our curiosity' ('The Significance of History', in *Frontier and Section*, p.11; subsequent page numbers refer to this collection of Turner's essays), an essentially romantic pursuit closer to the writing of fiction than to history proper. It is a mode that Turner does not condemn in itself 'providing that truthfulness of substance rather than vivacity of style be the end sought' (p.12).

The title *How the West Was Won* was derived from a series of pictorial articles published in *Life* magazine in 1959, and presumably refers to Theodore

Roosevelt's book *The Winning of the West* (1889-96), with its triumphalist overtones of imperial conquest. The rights to the title were bought by Bing Crosby, who used it for an album of period songs, and subsequently sold the rights on to MGM. It is shared by a later television series, *The MacAhans: How the West Was Won* (1976), which also duplicates the film's narrative strategy: an account of the fortunes, through several generations, of a single (White, Anglo-Saxon) fictional family chosen as representative of pioneer stock, taking in as many facets as possible both of nineteenth-century American history and of the Western genre. (Comparable also are the 1979 mini-series *Centennial*, based on James A. Michener's best-selling novel, and *Roots*, 1977-78, based on Alex Haley's book, which traces an African-American family from the eighteenth to the twentieth century, and the 1931 and 1960 film versions of Edna Ferber's family saga *Cimarron*.) The title was also used for a 1968 exhibition of paintings by such artists as Frederick Remington and Charles B. Russell, whose work is evoked by the background designs to the opening credits of the 1962 film.

The intent in *How the West Was Won* was clearly not just to make a Western, but to produce a definitive Western, one that could embrace all or most of the genre's historical time-frame and repertoire of narrative situations. As Kim Newman points out in his *Wild West Movies* (Bloomsbury, London, 1990), this is one of a number of films to have attempted this kind of generic composite, with varying degrees of success (others include *Dodge City*, Michael Curtiz, 1939, and *Silverado*, Lawrence Kasdan, 1985; *Little Big Man* is a satirical variation on the pattern). *How the West Was Won* also signals its ambitions by assembling an all-star cast, giving star billing to more

than a dozen players, many either associated particularly with the genre (John Wayne, James Stewart, Henry Fonda) or with previous celebrated Westerns (Gregory Peck, Robert Preston, Eli Wallach). Most notably, it employs not one but three directors, all best known for their work in the Western, each assigned to one or more distinct episodes: Henry Hathaway, John Ford, George Marshall.

The object of James R. Webb's screenplay, then, is partly to be a survey and sampler of the genre to which it pays tribute: to tell not merely a Western story but also the story of the Western. What concerns the film is not just the pastness, the historicity, of its mainly fictional events, but their Westernness (it was originally announced as *The Great Western Story*, e.g. in *Kine Weekly*, 30th June 1960). The film operates very successfully as a compendium of generic pleasures. In using narrative essentially as a framework within which these pleasures can be contained, it testifies both to their inherent appeal and to its own decadence as a generic text. In a period when the genre was moving increasingly towards revisionist self-consciousness and the meaning and ideological function of the West and the Western were being examined critically by Ford (in another, more personal and intimate – though no less Turneresque – context: that of *The Man Who Shot Liberty Valance*, 1962), Peckinpah and others, Webb and Hathaway/ Ford/Marshall attempted to fix the Western purely in terms of its repertoire of external signs and conventions, its iconography, rather than through a dramatic analysis of its historical significance.

(I have chosen not to dwell on Ford's contribution, or on the question of authorship as such, as these are issues that invariably preoccupy other writers on the film; my emphasis is on the generic, formal and historical factors that affect all three directors. For the record, Hathaway later claimed that the original, five-episode concept of the film was his, and that he had to 'do over' Marshall's contribution; Ford's he considered 'lousy'. For the interview with him, and other useful background information, *see* Kimble, 1993.)

Still: How the West Was Won. *Linus Rawlings (James Stewart) and Eve Prescott (Carroll Baker), with Eve Prescott (Debbie Reynolds) in the background. Although the aspect ratio of this still (2:1) is by no means as great as the 2.76:1 of Cinerama, it suggests some of the process's extreme depth of focus.*

Photograph: Henry Hathaway lining up a shot with the Cinerama camera for 'The River' in How the West Was Won, *with Debbie Reynolds, Carroll Baker and Karl Malden.*

How the West Was Won also exists to celebrate its own manner of production and presentation. As the first narrative feature to be made and shown in three-strip Cinerama, the film functions partly as a show-case for its technology. The choice of a Western for the first Cinerama dramatic picture is a reflection of the role that spectacle has always played in the genre, however modestly budgeted the movie. It seems also to have been an attempt to render as narrative the patriotic montage ('America the Beautiful') that concluded the original Cinerama programme, *This is Cinerama* (1952), and reputedly delighted a tearful President Eisenhower. The celebration and promotion of Americanness had always been a component of Cinerama documentaries (John Belton discusses this in his *Widescreen Cinema*, University of California Press, 1992), but its continuation as narrative in *How the West Was Won* entailed a greater effort of ideological will and exposed it to a number of contradictions and conflicting impulses.

The film is now virtually impossible to see in its original, three-strip format, which was quickly rendered obsolete by the various single-camera 70mm formats (Todd-AO, Super and Ultra Panavision, Super Technirama) developed in the 1950s to rival the three-camera system, as these soon proved to be more flexible and cost-efficient. But as no simultaneous single-camera version of *How the West Was Won* was shot, all the single-strip 70mm and 35mm anamorphic prints used for reissue and subsequent-run engagements were struck from the Cinerama negative, preserving the vertical lines that divided the three strips. It is thus possible to gauge the visual effect of the Cinerama format even when the film is seen 'flat'. (The full-length roadshow version is available on laserdisc and as a 'letterboxed' VHS video from MGM/UA.) One striking consequence of the use in the process of extreme wide-angle lenses is the peculiar sense of excessive depth to the image: actors have only to move even slightly forward or backwards and the effect given is of abruptly altered proximity, as the character looms into close-up or recedes into long-shot in a single step. This sense of exaggerated perspective is accompanied by one of distended horizontal space: the slight differences of angle between the three cameras ensure that whenever some object (a log, say) crosses the screen from one panel to another, it bends in the middle (a distraction that was compensated for by the extreme curve of the Cinerama screen). In addition, each Cinerama image has three vanishing points (*see* Kimble, 1983, for further details on the technical difficulties raised by shooting in the process).

While each director finds his own method of composing in the 2.76:1 aspect ratio, the intrinsic properties of Cinerama arguably overcome any attempt to assimilate them to a traditional visual aesthetic (the mythical 'transparency' of classical Hollywood cinema). The process itself was as central an attraction in the film's publicity as its cast or theme: patrons complained when the film was generally released in standard 70mm or CinemaScope after its long-running premiere roadshow engagements. Cinerama itself is the only 'star' to get above-the-title billing, and each of the five distinct narrative episodes (with the partial exception of Ford's) is built around a sequence of action or spectacle that is designed to focus attention on the format and its capacity to evoke empathetic sensation in the spectator: a raft coursing down a wild river, a wagon train chased by Indians, a buffalo stampede, a runaway train. (Two later Westerns released under the Cinerama banner but filmed in single-lens 70mm, employ similar set pieces: *The Hallelujah Trail*, John Sturges, 1965, and *Custer of the West*, Robert Siodmak, 1968.) The Civil War battle scenes, in the only episode praised by the film's reviewers as an instance of a clear directorial identity imposing itself on the spectacle, were shot neither by Ford, as was universally assumed, nor by anyone connected with the film: they are lifted entire from Edward Dmytryk's *Raintree County* (1957). These brief scenes *are* exceptional, if only because, having been filmed in MGM Camera 65, later renamed Ultra Panavision (which was also used to film the second-unit material for *How the West Was Won*, including all sequences involving back projection), they lack the striking visual characteristics that I have attributed to the three-strip process.

This emphasis on widescreen spectacle was derided by critics at the time as a symptom of the film's inflated pretensions and top-heavy production values: 'Is this the ultimate in Hollywood elephantiasis?' asked John Gillett in *Sight and Sound* (Winter 1962-63, p.1). In a period marked by the proliferation of high-cost blockbusters, *How the West Was Won* could be seen to represent the genre expanding under commercial pressure. The terms in which the film was criticised were remarkably consistent: again and again, it was described as a fairground sideshow, a carnival, a circus or a pageant. The metaphors are intended to connote spectacle without substance, existing for its own sake, and thus the marginalising of narrative and drama. Critical tastes have always preferred economy to excess, story to spectacle, and its inversion of these criteria seems to have placed *How the West Was Won* outside cinematic categories altogether, propelling it towards varieties of popular theatre. It is the peculiar distinction of Cinerama to be both exaggeratedly cinematic, in drawing attention to the surface of the screen and its distortion of space, and somehow less than cinematic, for its displacement of narrative in favour of spectacle.

What it might indicate instead is the possibility of an *alternative* set of cinematic criteria, for which we need to look beyond the primacy given to narrative in classical cinema. Tom Gunning has advanced the proposition (in *Wide Angle*, Fall 1986, reprinted in *Early Cinema: Space, Frame, Narrative*, ed. Thomas Elsaesser, British Film Institute, 1990 – page references are from the latter) that pre-classical cinema might constitute a 'cinema of attractions', a term derived from Sergei Eisenstein, who saw the 'montage of attractions' as a response to, and rejection of, the dominance of classicism. This mode, which characterised cinema until about 1906-07, is described by Gunning as possessing the following characteristics:

1) Film scenarios may essentially be *pretexts* for tricks and theatrical/cinematic effects (as in the films of Georges Méliès), or loosely structured re-enactments of familiar scenes (from popular novels, plays, folklore or news events) set free from a self-contained, self-explanatory narrative context.
2) Cinema is conceived as a means of presenting *views* to an audience: a way of *showing*, rather than of narrating. This stresses the centrality of *spectacle* as a source of pleasure and allows the possibility of addressing the audience directly, acknowledging and returning its gaze.
3) The form of cinema itself is a chief attraction: the window and its frame, as well as the view, provide pleasure. Close-ups, camera movements, and so on, thus exert their own fascination, independent of their dramatic or narrative function.
4) The experience of watching the film may be accompanied by extra-filmic attractions ('offscreen supplements') in the theatre or viewing space: the film itself is only one component of the total entertainment environment. One might note here the additional attractions offered by blockbuster roadshows such as *How the West Was Won* which distinguish them from 'ordinary', casual movie presentation: live orchestral overtures, drinks at intermission, lavish theatrical surroundings, souvenir brochures, the formality of booked seats and separate performances.

Seen in these terms, *How the West Was Won* is a Western of attractions, a spectacle in which generic conventions are successively introduced rather like speciality acts in a circus or vaudeville show, where the providers of spectacle are not just the various stunt sequences but also the properties of the medium (Cinerama) itself. For Mark Shivas, the film is 'a spectacle in which the ingredients are standard, known and loved', and in which the action set-pieces 'cease to be real but become instead demonstrations of staggering showmanship' (*Movie* 6, January 1963, p.29).

Gunning acknowledges that current Hollywood cinema – which the blockbuster cycle of the 'fifties and 'sixties directly anticipated – has gravitated towards the fragmentation of narrative in favour of spectacle characteristic of a cinema of attractions: 'Clearly in some sense recent spectacle cinema has reaffirmed its roots in stimulus and carnival rides, in what might be called the Spielberg-Lucas-Coppola cinema of effects' (p.61). Such films have constantly invited, and received, a comparison to 'carnival rides', especially that of the rollercoaster, the descriptive metaphor that every reviewer of *Star Wars*, *Raiders of the Lost Ark*, *Die Hard* or *Speed* automatically reaches for. It is worth remembering here the potency of the rollercoaster image in early wide-screen productions: rollercoaster sequences were used to demonstrate the spectacular potentialities of a larger, wider or stereoscopic image (most famously in the opening sequence of *This is Cinerama*, but also in test films for both CinemaScope

The rollercoaster, its associations with the fairground and amusement park and its function as pure thrill-provider, stand as the herald and symbol of modern Hollywood, and also provide a link with the cinema's origins in popular entertainment and with its early formal development. 'For Eisenstein and his friend Yutkevich,' Gunning remarks, their notion of an anti-narrative spectacle was 'primarily represented [by] their favourite fairground attraction, the roller coaster, or as it was known then in Russia, the American Mountains' (p.59).

History as Spectacle

'Our American literature is not a single thing. It is a choral song of many sections' (Frederick Jackson Turner, 'Sections and Nation', 1922).

Although the narrative of *How the West Was Won* is fragmented and episodic, more pretext than determinant, it is neither irrelevant nor lacking in substance: as an epic Western, the film is also an attempt to represent American history. The version of history on which James R. Webb's screenplay draws most heavily is Frederick Jackson Turner's proposition that 'the existence of an area of free land, its continuous recession, and the advance of American settlement of American settlement westward, explain American development'. This seminal thesis, which has been taken to underpin virtually the entire Western genre and the conception of American history on which it depends – the essay in which it appears is described by Edward Countryman as 'the single most important piece of writing ever produced about the American past' (Buscombe, 1988, p.124) – is borne out literally by the film's narrative structure. For all that it ignores Turner's strictures against the romanticising of history for the sake of a lively style, Webb's screenplay does try, at least partly, to reproduce his conception of American history in terms of 'social, rather than heroic-individualistic concerns' (*Frontier and Section*, p.125).

Turner develops his argument (in 'The Significance of the Frontier in American History', which was first delivered as a lecture in 1893) by comparing the continual movement of the frontier to that of a glacier, each successive shift in its boundaries being marked by traces left behind in the moraine-like form of frontier characteristics: qualities of 'coarseness and strength combined with acuteness and inquisitiveness; that practical, inventive turn of mind, quick to find expedients; that masterful grasp of material things, lacking in the artistic but powerful to effect great ends; that restless, nervous energy; that dominant individualism, working for good and for evil, and withal that buoyancy and exuberance that comes with freedom . . .' (*Frontier and Section*, p.61). With each shift, each movement westward, the growing Western civilisation was returned to the conditions of the frontier: 'a recurrence of the process of evolution [was] reached in the process of expansion . . . American social development has been continually beginning again on the frontier' (p.38). According to Turner, then, the 'winning of the West' proceeded in a series of phases, each of

which necessitated a partial return to primitivism, to year zero, with the prospect of renewed growth at each stage. (The veracity or otherwise of this as an accurate historical account has been frequently challenged by historians, but that does not affect my own argument, which is concerned with its significance as the dominant, most widely disseminated conceptualisation of America's past. *See* Countryman, in Buscombe, 1988, pp.124-125, for a useful summary of the flaws and limitations of Turner's work and brief discussion of other films marked by its influence, including *Shane*, George Stevens, 1953, and *Monte Walsh*, William Fraker, 1970.)

The structure of Webb's screenplay directly echoes Turner's thesis, with its series of self-contained but successively evolving episodes, each incorporating a new Western landscape, a new set of narrative variants. Each episode is founded on a pattern of westward travel and movement, and in each a mode of transport figures as a defining motif: raft, canoe, riverboat, covered wagon, railway train, horse, buckboard. Each miniature narrative concludes with the protagonist(s) moving on, anticipating some new future. (Cinerama seems a particularly apt format in which to present this: John Belton has drawn attention to the fascination that films in the process have with moving vehicles, travel and transport, from the tourist journeys of travelogues like *Cinerama Holiday*, 1955, *South Seas Adventure*, 1958, and *Search for Paradise*, 1957, to the narratives of features such as *It's a Mad, Mad, Mad, Mad World*, Stanley Kramer, 1963, *Grand Prix*, John Frankenheimer, 1966, and *2001: A Space Odyssey*, Stanley Kubrick, 1968.)

The adventures of the Prescott/Rawlings family are thus fused and identified with the development of Western (American) civilisation as it passes through the successive phases of growth, movement and renewal. The episodes, chronologically listed as they appear in the film, are as follows:

1) The Rivers (Hathaway)
2) The Plains (Hathaway)
- Intermission -
3) The Civil War (Ford)
4) The Railroad (Marshall)
5) The Outlaws (Hathaway)

The first two episodes centre on the courtship and marriage of the two Prescott sisters, Eve (Carroll Baker) and Lilith (Debbie Reynolds); the second half's main protagonist is Eve's son, Zeb Rawlings (George Peppard), though Eve and Lilith also make brief appearances in episodes three and five respectively. Doug McLelland, in *The Unkindest Cut* (Tantivy/Barnes, 1975) has speculated on the existence of a sixth episode, possibly to have been inserted between 'The Railroad' and 'The Outlaws' – or, more likely in the light of Hathaway's comments (Kimble, 1983, pp.91-92), incorporated into the former – but removed before the film's release. One major character, played by Hope Lange, the wife of the Pony Express rider, Jethro Stuart (Henry Fonda), was eliminated in last-minute editing. (Lange's credit still appeared in trade publicity published after the film's London première in November 1962, before its American opening the following year.) This would account for Carolyn Jones's otherwise inexplicably belated and aged appearance as Zeb's wife in episode five. Noting the darkness of Jones's make-up, McLelland ventures that the subject of this missing material might have been racism ('The Prejudice').

Certainly, this would have helped compensate for one of the film's more glaring dramatic omissions, but there are several respects in which the film verges on incoherence. Webb's narrative concentrates to the point of embarrassment on White characters. (The choice of the quintessentially English 'Greensleeves' as the tune for the theme song 'A Home in the Meadow' suggests what kind of Promised Land the protagonists might be looking forward to.) There are no Black characters, speaking or otherwise, even in the Civil War episode. Other racial minorities are similarly excluded, or pushed to the margins: two Chinese gold prospectors are glimpsed by the riverside when Lilith visits her worthless claim, and a poster by her caravan later in the same episode advertises 'Ling Wong – iron and washing'. But there are no Orientals to be seen helping build the railroad in episode four. Even Mexicans are given short shrift: despite the iconic presence of Rodolfo Acosta among his gang, and contrary to reasonable audience expectations, Eli Wallach's swarthy, sombrero-wearing bandit is identified as Charlie Gant.

It is in the treatment of Native Americans that the film's ideological evasions become most apparent. Indians figure three times in the narrative. In the first episode, they are briefly seen as friends and peaceful trading partners of Linus Rawlings, the mountain man played by James Stewart. In the second, they are unmotivated hostiles attacking the wagon train carrying Lilith and Cleve Van Valen (Gregory Peck). In the fourth episode, they are the victims of technological progress and corporate capitalist expansion in the form of the railroad, responding to the Whites' breaking of treaties by stampeding a herd of buffalo through the railway workers' encampment. (Richard Widmark's cynical railroad operator comments that the cries of wounded and dying are 'the sound of new life going on'.) These three images of Native Americans against the background of the westward expansion of White civilisation are so disparate that some more explicit comment or analysis would seem to be called for. But Webb gives his Indians (described in Spencer Tracy's opening narration as 'primitive man') no dialogue, no scene in which to dramatise their own point of view – though Zeb is at least shown to be a sympathiser.

These evasions could be blamed on the film's status as a 'blockbuster' Western, rather than a small-scale 'psychological', 'message' or 'problem' picture (generic variants which proliferated during the 1950s). At a cost of $14 million, How the West Was Won was the most expensive Western yet made, the average budget for a Hollywood picture in 1961-62 being some $2 million. (See Joel Finler, The Hollywood Story, Octopus, London, 1988, pp.125-126, for comparative budgets and box-office figures.)

Given the need to attract as large an audience as possible, the desire not to offend conservative White groups might well have exercised an overriding pressure to avoid raising controversy: how can one, in all conscience, celebrate the winning of the West if one is made too conscious of those who lost it? John Ford's subsequent epic Western Cheyenne Autumn (1964), also produced, like How the West Was Won, by Bernard Smith, was a relative box-office disappointment when it attempted a large-scale, pro-Indian treatment of the 'Indian problem'.

Another explanation is the film's heritage-industry conception of history as essentially a chronological diary of past events, which, as they are past, can no longer be questioned, but simply re-enacted. The Native American population may have been conquered, exploited and genocidally reduced, but that is all water under the bridge now. Mark Shivas touched on this:

'In dialogue and in visual form it celebrates an American contradiction – a longing for the simple life, idealising the man of the soil, and at the same time the headlong rush of Progress . . . We see the buffalo hunters arrive in trainloads, the railroad cut the Indians' land in two. It is all regretted, but the railroad must be built. Nobody really questions that; nothing must stand in the way of progress whatever the cost' (Shivas, 1963, p.28).

It must be admitted that this 'failure to confront the historic agony of American race relations' was shared by Turner, for whom 'the Indians' only function was to get out of the way, and the presence of a black minority was a huge sideshow' (Countryman, in Buscombe, 1988, p.125).

The film's complacency, or confusion, is repeated elsewhere: in, for example, its curiously unsettled sexual politics. The first-half narrative is unusual among Westerns in being centred upon the desires and actions of two young women, Eve and Lilith Prescott. In 'The Rivers', Eve successfully woos and wins the reluctant mountain man, Linus Rawlings, persuading him to settle down with her and build a farm. Admitting her stubbornness, Linus reckons that he has 'seen that varmint for the last time' (meaning, doubly, the bear which he claims to have killed in the manner of Davy Crockett, and the fictitious beast with which he was nearly lured to his doom by a female river pirate). We are subsequently told, in 'The Civil War', that Linus deserted his farm and family 'when the first bugle blew', and has died on an operating table at Shiloh; Eve dies of grief when Zeb follows his father into uniform.

In 'The Plains', Lilith is first pursued and then abandoned by a roguish gambler, Cleve Van Valen, whose interest in her is sparked by her inheritance of a gold mine. When he leaves her, she becomes a saloon entertainer and music-hall singer and dancer (thus allowing the film to include several energetic production numbers, surely calculated to appeal to women in the audience). Cleve eventually returns and marries her, but the couple remain childless. We later learn, in 'The Outlaws', that they have investments in the railroad – they are thus implicated

Still: How the West Was Won – Linus about to 'see the varmint', with Dora Hawkins (Brigid Bazlen) and Captain Hawkins (Walter Brennan).

in the betrayal of the Indians in episode four (in which they do not appear). Lilith reappears in the final episode, after Cleve's death, to assure Julie Rawlings that her husband Zeb is justified in facing up, in the spirit of *High Noon*, to a gang of train-robbing outlaws, and to lead the family in a final reprise of 'A Home in the Meadow' as they ride in a buggy through Monument Valley.

The familiar tension between settlement and wandering, for so long admitted to be at the heart of the Western's gender politics, is thus played out among the male characters, while the Prescott women (suffering or enduring) are effectively presented as matriarchs to the nation. Linus and Cleve are allowed to disappear into domesticity (literally, for once they have agreed to marry, they are dead to the narrative and cease to play a part in it), while for Zeb horizons are left open: he crosses one at the end of each of the film's second-half episodes. Very little of this subtextual material is developed thematically by Webb's screenplay, but Zeb's role is crucial for what he represents about Americanness. He articulates it himself in the script's most telling line: 'That's what I like about this country – there's

always greener grass on the other side of the hill . . . Maybe I'll just have to climb a higher hill to find it.' While this chimes beautifully with Turner's frontier thesis, it also provides the rationale for the film's ideological incoherence.

The episodic, fragmentary structure of the narrative allows it to incorporate an extensive cross-section of the Western's generic patterns at the expense of being unable to reconcile their often contradictory meanings. The separate episodes pull in different directions: one using the Indians as action-movie cannon fodder, another expressing regret for their betrayal by the Whites whose earlier killing of them we had been expected to cheer. In a final attempt to describe the film's historical project, we might invoke another of Turner's theses and note the relevance here of his conception of America as comprising as many as five distinct sections, each with its own character, concerns and identity, sometimes in conflict, but pledging allegiance to a common flag.

How the West Was Won evinces 'migratory sectionalism' (Turner's phrase) just as much as the nation whose history it attempts to represent. Like America, it displays a peculiar kind of unity in diversity. Constantly in flux, it is held together only by its appeal to generic and technological spectacle, to the American Mountains of Cinerama and the Western.

ULZANA'S RAID

Douglas Pye

The crisis that affected the traditional American action genres in the late 'sixties and early 'seventies has been to some extent obscured by the ideological retrenchment and stylistic conservatism characteristic of so much recent Hollywood cinema. But the crisis was real, dramatised most intelligently and passionately in the work of directors like Sam Peckinpah, Arthur Penn and Robert Altman, but equally vividly in other ways in Hollywood production as a whole, and continuing as a deep vein through the 'seventies, even when generic (or at any rate formulaic) structures appeared to be newly buoyant. The determinants of the crisis, which clearly relate both to changes in the industry and its audience(s) and to wider political, economic and social factors, are beyond the scope of this article, but its formal manifestations are reasonably clear and familiar.

Its clearest and in some ways most symptomatic feature is self-consciousness – a foregrounding of generic conventions, sometimes affectionate, frequently parodic, but communicating a familiarity with and simultaneous distance from generic traditions, which is far removed from the inwardness with genre of a John Ford or a Howard Hawks – even when they are at their most self-conscious (*The Man Who Shot Liberty Valance*, Ford, 1962) or parodic (*Rio Bravo*, Hawks, 1959). In terms of the construction of the films, however, narrative organisation may well be the central factor, particularly as this is focused by the moral and emotional identity of the protagonist and his range of power and control. Peckinpah's Westerns display the issues very sharply, for instance, in their representations of worlds his heroes cannot control – increasingly, anonymous and corporate societies unresponsive to individual will and action, which reduce the protagonists' range of decision-making finally to a choice of how to die. Peckinpah also frequently presents heroes who are conventionally morally dubious and/or whose values achieve positive force, sometimes paradoxically, against a social background of grotesque institutionalised violence and corruption. Many of the central narrative functions, the actions which move the story forward, are removed from the hero at the same time as his moral identity is questioned, so that the traditional symmetry of moral rightness and control over significant action is broken. Sergio Leone's Westerns provide another reference point from a different tradition of film-making. In *The Good, the Bad, and the Ugly* (1966), for instance, the plot is furthered often not by individual action (think

of the occasions on which Clint Eastwood is saved from Lee Van Cleef) but by arbitrary and unpredictable intrusions from the wider world (the Civil War), to create a sense of national or, more properly, cosmic disorder, which is presented by Leone as grotesque comedy.

These characteristics are not absolutely new to the 'sixties; what is new, I think, is their dominance, their infiltration at many levels of genre production. It is possible to trace the moral questioning of the hero and of his control back through the 'fifties and 'forties into, for instance, *film noir*, although here *film noir* needs to be placed in the context of all Hollywood production, most of which had a very different and more conventional orientation. Similarly in the Western, the increasing complexity of the hero's psychology, which has long been held to be characteristic of postwar Westerns, applies only, for most of the period, to a small part of Western production – Anthony Mann is not that representative. *The Searchers* (John Ford, 1956) and *Rio Bravo* provide useful reference points in the mid to late 'fifties – *The Searchers* in this context also being significant for the ways in which it seems to be drawn on in *Ulzana's Raid* (Robert Aldrich, 1972). Ford and Hawks make very different but parallel uses of John Wayne's persona: Ford inflects it towards psychic division; Hawks treats Wayne's asserted autonomy in a way that carries a clear but contained edge of parody. In both films, while Wayne's character dominates, he does not control the narrative development: in *Rio Bravo* other characters repeatedly perform crucial actions, while in *The Searchers* Ethan Edwards not only fails to find Debbie (other characters do that), but climactic actions that would traditionally be reserved for the hero (rescuing Debbie, killing Scar) are displaced on to Martin Pawley (Jeffrey Hunter), a character who (again significantly for *Ulzana's Raid*) is part-Indian, although, after the opening section of the film, Ford chooses largely to forget that fact.

But these films, and their counterparts in other genres, are exceptional in the 'fifties, and they achieve their frequently complex articulations of viewpoint by reference to sets of viable conventions validated by a moral consensus of a quite traditional kind.

If the narrative displacement of the hero is a central factor in the crisis of genre, it carries with it, as I have suggested, implications for the moral universe of the films and their articulation of point of view (which belongs as much to narrative organisation as to performance and *mise-en-scène*); in turn, point of view is crucially linked to stylistic developments involving, among other things, the widespread use of zoom and telephoto lenses. The total effect, particularly in many Westerns, is of destabilisation, a break with the symmetry (even decorum) that traditionally held narrative, character, values, style and viewpoint in functional and reciprocal relationship. The increasing difficulty dramatised in these films of endorsing any kind of traditional social values posed particular problems for the Western, whose equilibrium traditionally depended on the tensions between the more or less stable terms of hero, villain and community. But in one strand of the Western, erosion of moral reference points and the consequent reversal of values came into a brief but significant relationship with the late 'sixties celebration of Indians – 'the return of the vanishing American' – to produce the 'Vietnam Western' of the early 'seventies. Paradoxically, in a sense, the genre found perhaps the most immediate link in its history with contemporary American life at the very point when it seemed to be losing its traditional viability for film-makers.

The Western, and particularly the Western involving Indians, has always been in some sense 'about' imperialism, with the American continent itself the conquered land, and the conquest of land and original inhabitants the manifest destiny of White Americans. From its origins, although the dominant tendency was celebration (in the popular Western frequently quite unproblematic celebration) of westward expansion, more ambivalent responses remained common, but critical representations of American civilisation were generally held in check by endorsement of individuals and/or, as in Ford, family and primitive community. With the almost complete reversal of moral poles in a number of Westerns in the late 'sixties and early 'seventies, conquest of the Indian is seen unambiguously as the triumph of a corrupt and morally bankrupt civilisation, a perception only too easily applicable to the Vietnam War.

Little Big Man (Arthur Penn, 1970) is perhaps the locus classicus of the Vietnam Western, not only because of its scale and ambition, but because it very clearly exemplifies the reversal of values and some of its attendant dangers (it also makes obvious the link between its representation of Indians and 'sixties counter-cultures). In addition, it presents just about the most extreme case of the displaced Western hero. The range of significant action available to Jack Crabb (Dustin Hoffman) is not simply limited – despite all the various roles he plays, it is more or less non-existent. He is constantly at the mercy of circumstances over which he can exercise no control. He is essentially a function not simply of the narrative but of the film's thematic structure, its thesis, and his multiple roles and adventures are the occasion for the exposure of the worthlessness of White civilisation and its juxtaposition with the idealised world of the Cheyennes. White civilisation is alienated from nature, its representatives by turn

foolish, intolerant, mad, narcissistic, hypocritical, vicious and repressed. At the same time, the conventions of the Western are parodied and exposed – we are encouraged to feel knowing about and superior to both the conventions and Penn's characters. By contrast the Cheyennes are 'human beings', in harmony with nature, wise, tolerant, honourable and unrepressed. The Indians, that is, take their meanings not from their representation as an autonomous culture but, in spite of Arthur Penn's reversals, from their thematic opposition to Whites, as is entirely normal in the genre. The specific terms of their representation as an ideal community derive from the commune dreams and alternative life styles of the 'sixties – Penn's 'human beings' (as has often been noted) are in fact hippies.

The attack on White American civilisation and the critique of America's involvement in Vietnam implied by the virtual extinction of the Cheyennes are clearly not opportunistic responses in Penn; they seem to spring from a despair about individual and political solutions that is itself a product of the apparent failure of liberalism as a political and social stance (one can trace the development in Penn's earlier films). But however deeply motivated the impulse, *Little Big Man*'s terms are crucially limiting. In creating the Cheyennes as he does, Penn effectively excludes any kind of specific social or political reference: the hippy dream, whatever its own social determinants, asserted itself as ahistorical and natural; in the film, it represents a retreat into sentimental fantasy, not, one feels, animated by conviction but essentially set up to be destroyed. The effect of dream becoming nightmare with the massacre is then both obvious and, for all the power of Penn's realisation, easy. The representation of the White world is, given its reciprocal thematic relationship to the Indians, no less crude and, although the moral terms are reversed, no less sentimental.

These objections are at one level social and political – Penn's film does not adequately represent either its historical events or the contemporary reality it aspires to evoke – but his methods also have aesthetic consequences. Perhaps the most important of these, given the complexity and intelligence of Penn's best films, is the way in which the despair that permeates the film destroys the possibility of meaningful discrimination in point of view. Where the film aspires to such complexity (in some of the Custer scenes, more problematically in the Washita River massacre), it seems to me in detail almost unreadable; more generally, the massive assertion of its simple moral oppositions allows a very narrow range of effect – for all its almost prodigal variety of incident, the pay-off in terms of meaning is remarkably thin. In a film directed by someone else, these things might be of only passing interest; it is the fact that *Little Big Man* is directed by Penn that makes it, if not representative, then certainly profoundly symptomatic.

Within these contexts, of genre and of allusion to Vietnam, *Ulzana's Raid* seems an exemplary Western, perhaps the most intelligent and rigorous of the 'seventies. It exemplifies the characteristics I have attempted to outline, but responds precisely and clear-sightedly to the challenges, most notably in its awareness of the history and conventions of the Western (it is conscious without excesses of self-consciousness and distanced without parody) and in its representations of Native Americans and the conflict of opposing value systems.

Although I don't want to develop an authorial analysis it is, I think, important to note that a good deal of the film's success in negotiating the difficulties inherent in its project must be attributed to Alan Sharp's script. Sharp's work as a scriptwriter, notably in *Ulzana's Raid* and *Night Moves* (Penn, 1975) but also in other films – the Westerns *The Hired Hand* (Peter Fonda, 1971) and *Billy Two Hats* (Ted Kotcheff, 1974), for instance – is consistently fine and has received less comment than it merits. The films are themselves eloquent of Sharp's fondness for and knowledge of generic traditions, but as a morsel of external evidence, his *A Green Tree in Gedde* (Michael Joseph, London, 1965) must be the only novel ever written to contain a reference to Hugo Fregonese's *Apache Drums* (1951).

Ulzana's Raid is set in Arizona, apparently in the mid 1880s (the Sergeant talks of a previous patrol, clearly some time before, as having happened in 1881). Little is made of the date, but it means that the action takes place at a time when the major Indian campaigns were all but over: Geronimo's break from the reservation, to which the film's story may indirectly refer, was in 1885 and his surrender in 1886; the massacre at Wounded Knee was in 1890. The film centres, then, not on a major military operation like that in Ford's *Fort Apache* (1948), which, as an earlier cavalry Western, is in several respects a useful reference point, but on the break from a reservation of a very small number of Apaches – a raid. Whatever critical perspectives are developed on the cavalry and White society are given particular force, then, by the raid exposing the incapacity of the cavalry in a way that the whole of Cochise's army cannot in *Fort Apache*, and this at almost the moment of final White ascendancy in the West.

The cavalry's situation, however, is defined initially through its relationship to landscape. The opening sequence (in the British release print, that is – in North America and in prints shown on British television, there was a pre-credits sequence of Ulzana escaping from the reservation) presents Fort Lowell not as a fort in the normal sense but as an adobe command building and a collection of tents perched insecurely in a barren landscape that stretches away beyond the fort, apparently offering no natural advantages. The sense of incongruity and impermanence, the lack of any meaningful relationship to the land, is reinforced by the visual organisation of the opening sequence, in which shots from a variety of angles and positions, some quite unexpected, are juxtaposed in a way that fragments space – conveying a sense of unease, even incoherence, rather than an orderly introduction to setting.

Further incongruity is introduced by the baseball game taking place on the edge of the camp, with the plain stretching away endlessly beyond the makeshift playing area. Like the fort itself, it is an intrusion, out of place, slightly ridiculous. But, as significantly, it introduces a set of images and ideas that will run through and partly structure the film.

Still: Ulzana's Raid – *Ke-Ni-Tay (Jorge Luke) and McIntosh (Burt Lancaster) trailing Ulzana.*

The game, obviously enough, is governed by rules which precisely define its nature and range of possibilities, with the umpire as the final source of authority, his decisions supposedly resting on the bedrock of rules. In the baseball sequence, these issues are etched in lightly, as comedy; the attention of Lieutenant DeBuin (Bruce Davison) is only half on the game as a rider comes in shouting the news of Ulzana's break, but his decisions are final, even when they are wrong and provoke a minor mutiny among the players. The relationship between the arbitrariness of command (DeBuin knows even less about Apaches than he does about baseball) and the consequences of not playing by the rules is extended later, much more seriously, to the patrol. Tracking Ulzana becomes like an elaborate game (of chess perhaps rather than baseball) and is seen explicitly as that by the scout, McIntosh (Burt Lancaster) – 'Remember the rules, Lieutenant: first one to make a mistake gets to bury some people.' But no-one in the cavalry knows the rules – without McIntosh and more importantly Ke-Ni-Tay (Jorge Luke) they would be playing blind, hopelessly out of the game.

Intersecting with the image of the game in the opening sequence are the hierarchy of the cavalry (DeBuin's authority rests ultimately on his rank rather than on his expertise) and the regulations that govern the army's conduct in any given situation. The commanding officer, Major Cartwright (Douglas Watson), introduced in the second sequence, can be identified generically with the figure of the rigid cavalry commander (Colonel Thursday in *Fort Apache* is a convenient example) who insists on acting exclusively, and often disastrously, by the book. But here the figure is significantly inflected. The book makes an actual appearance, brandished by Major Cartwright as he gives his orders, but it is clear in Douglas Watson's performance (the acting in the film is uniformly splendid) that he invokes regulations not out of conviction but with a kind of tired resignation: they may not be appropriate, but, since he does not understand Apaches, they are all he has. The Major is a man who knows that he is out of his depth and who calculatedly refuses to take individual responsibility by doing only what is prescribed. He (and it is an attitude taken up in a somewhat different way by McIntosh) is going through a set of more or less meaningless but given moves.

The early sequences, then, make clear both how out of place the cavalry is here and the failure of conviction that lies behind the mechanical application of regulations, the lack of any system of belief that will support and justify the historical situation of the army. This failure of conviction is central to the film and provides the context for the incongruity of White civilisation in Arizona. We come to see that what supports the army's role is not a coherent set of beliefs but (the Vietnam allusion is clear) the residual and morally empty assertion of White supremacy.

The idea of rules extends finally, therefore, to the value systems and specifically the religious beliefs of the two cultures. Christianity is introduced in the early discussion between Major Cartwright and De-Buin, who has inherited from his clergyman father a set of idealistic beliefs that emerge and are tested as the film progresses. This first scene turns on the question of whether it is possible to be both a soldier and a Christian, the Major's scepticism crystallised in his use of General Sheridan's epigram (in which he substitutes Arizona for Texas): 'If I owned Hell and Arizona, I'd live in Hell and rent out Arizona'. The implication, that Arizona is inimical to Christian values, is essentially Other, is deflected here by De-Buin's own amused and sceptical response, but the challenge of the land and the Apaches to the Christianity that should support American civilisation is at the heart of the film. It is dramatised most repeatedly but not exclusively in DeBuin's development from naive idealism, through incoherent hatred to what might be (although the end of the film is not without ambiguity) a tentative new attitude bordering, perhaps, as with the Major and McIntosh, on resignation.

Central to this development are the sequences involving the attack on the farm run by Rukeyser (Karl Swenson) and its aftermath, in which the two value systems are first explicitly juxtaposed. The sequence of the attack is organised in such a way that we are increasingly restricted to Rukeyser's viewpoint, or at least largely to inside the house, so that we are compelled to interpret as he does the withdrawal of the Apaches and the sound of the bugle. It is entirely possible that the cavalry has arrived – we know that they were heading for the farm – and the familiarity of the last-minute rescue as a generic motif reinforces the likelihood that we will accept (or at least want to accept) what seems to be happening. But generic rhetoric and restriction of viewpoint are used here to invert expectation and to criticise the values inherent in the generic motif. Specifically, perhaps, the sequence draws on the most famous of all last-minute cavalry rescues, that in *Stagecoach* (John Ford, 1939), when Lucy Mallory's prayer seems to summon up the rescue – the cavalry, God's scourge, validating White supremacy. Here bugle call and prayer are also juxtaposed, but in reverse. The last moments of the sequence show Rukeyser responding to his apparent rescue by praising God ('God, yours is all the praise and all the glory!') as he leaves the house and the frame, before the restrained but devastating cut to the cavalry and a bugle, unused, dangling from a saddle. The meanings produced also reverse those of *Stagecoach*. In undercutting generic motif and expectation, the film operates a critique of the unthinking tradition of White supremacy represented in the Western by the last-minute rescue, a critique underlined by Rukeyser's appalling death, a hideous punishment for a character who has been created with great sympathy and dignity. As well as its implied rebuke to the audience, the sequence comments on the tactical skill and flexibility of the Apaches in using a bugle to bring Rukeyser out, on the inadequacy of the cavalry (they're never there in time to save the lives of the settlers they are supposed to protect), and on Christianity which, however deeply rooted individual faith may be, is made to seem irrelevant and out of place here.

The sequence is remarkable in a number of ways. It insists, as the film in general does, on the profound interlock between Christian theology and White military power and equally on the contradictions and confusions this nexus produces. But in a sequence that could easily invite both complacent superiority to the cavalry and to Rukeyser, and gross indulgence in violence, neither are in evidence, even though the violence, as an accomplished fact, is graphically depicted. Robert Aldrich and Alan Sharp maintain the difficult balance between sympathetic response to the human context (particularly here to Rukeyser) and clarity of viewpoint. Intelligence and responsibility, tact and discretion are qualities easier to assert than to demonstrate, but in these respects one might compare *Ulzana's Raid* with the superficially similar *Chato's Land* (Michael Winner, 1972), especially the Ruykeyser sequence with the discovery by the posse of Chato's family, which seems to have been included solely as a mechanism to allow Chato's wife to be multiply raped and her naked body displayed.

In *Ulzana's Raid* the violence (some of it cut in British prints) is extreme but neither gratuitous nor exploited for purely local effect. Its point is that, as the focus for the challenge to White civilisation, it must be so appalling that it can hardly be conceived from the White point of view as the acts of human beings so that, as the patrol goes on, responses to the violence further erode the credibility of the cavalry and of White values. After the death of Ulzana's son, some of the soldiers mutilate the boy's body, incoherently imitating the Apaches ('Apaches don't like it if you do this to their dead – kind of spooks them'). It is a moment that evokes Ethan in *The Searchers* shooting out the eyes of the dead Comanche – according to Comanche beliefs, the dead man cannot enter the spirit world without his eyes but must 'wander forever between the winds'.

But where *The Searchers* implies a link between Ethan's apparently aberrant violence and the cavalry's wider social role – almost the only cavalry sequence in that film involves the aftermath of the massacre of an Indian village – *Ulzana's Raid*, by placing soldiers in Ethan's position, enforces a sense of institutional disintegration. As DeBuin's appalled response makes clear, the soldiers' action is incompatible with the 'civilised' values they are supposed to defend. DeBuin himself attempts to maintain faith

in his father's teaching, but succumbs first to hatred and later to a provoked but nevertheless irrational outburst about Apaches which leads up to his demand that Ke-Ni-Tay bury the dead settler simply because Ke-Ni-Tay is himself Apache. It is a development that fully defines the desperate confusion that results from the Apaches' challenge and the contradictions inherent in the cavalry's role.

The night scene following Rukeyser's death, when Lt DeBuin presses Ke-Ni-Tay to explain why his people mutilate and torture, makes explicit Apache beliefs for the first time, and the sequence is visually framed by the makeshift cross on Rukeyser's grave in the foreground of Aldrich's establishing shot. Ke-Ni-Tay's explanation grounds Apache practices in accommodation to the demands of the land (avoiding the seductive woolliness of Penn's 'human beings' – to the Cheyennes, everything is alive; to the Whites, everything is dead), but recognition of how inimical the land is to any human life. The Apaches are not created as extensions of the desert, in some way naturally endowed with its properties, but (in Ke-Ni-Tay's dialogue if not in observed fact) their culture has developed in response to a hostile environment. Belief in the need for masculine power ('In this land man must have power') and in its origins (the more slowly an enemy is tortured to death, the more of his power he gives up to his torturers) provides a rationale for Apache practices that is more coherent than the Whites' value system and yet remains utterly alien. The Apaches have a moral strength and conviction greater than the Whites, but their culture cannot be recuperated – it remains resolutely Other. Unlike *Little Big Man*, in which the Cheyennes are made the positive inverse of corrupt White society and become the dream of an ideal, if impossible, alternative, *Ulzana's Raid* does not in any simple way claim moral superiority for the Apaches. Their lives (or what we see of them) are more coherently lived, but involve practices which are repugnant to any familiar ethical system: their otherness provides an unanswerable challenge to White civilisation without providing an alternative to it.

It is a further strength (though it could be construed as a weakness) of the film that it respects the implications of its presentation of the Apaches in its articulation of viewpoint by largely refusing us access to their lives except through Ke-Ni-Tay's explanations. In other words, the film implicitly recognises the relationship between its overall cultural viewpoint and its manner of presenting narrative events to the audience: the otherness of the Apaches is obviously not inherent, but is a perception consequent on where we and the White characters stand, and our access to the world of the Apaches – which is potentially available to the film – is accordingly restricted.

In a way that is consistent with these decisions, Ke-Ni-Tay remains, compared to DeBuin and McIntosh, an undeveloped character, but in several respects his role is pivotal. He is a version of the generically familiar figure of the Indian scout whose narrative function in Westerns tends to be peripheral

Stills: Ulzana's Raid. *Opposite – McIntosh and the body of Rukeyser (Karl Swenson). Above – 'I ain't arguing with no Apache about horse-shit – he's the expert!' McIntosh with Ke-Ni-Tay and Lt DeBuin (Bruce Davison).*

but whose descent can be traced from the seminal figure of James Fenimore Cooper's Chingachgook. Ke-Ni-Tay's relationship with McIntosh in fact echoes that between Chingachgook and Leatherstocking, which carries in Cooper strong suggestions of an ideal meeting between the two races. Here, however, any residual echoes of such an ideal are compromised or even invalidated by the historical situation, which produces the multiple ironies of Ke-Ni-Tay's position. He considers himself bound by his word to the army ('I signed the paper') in a morally chaotic context in which honour seems an incongruity, and his word commits him to the destruction of his own people in the interests of a civilisation that has no claim to moral superiority. But most important, the White characters, including McIntosh, would be lost without Ke-Ni-Tay – they depend almost totally on his skill in reading signs and his predictions of Ulzana's likely moves.

Even McIntosh defers consistently to Ke-Ni-Tay. Although Ke-Ni-Tay does not control the narrative, the film, by giving him the skills which unlock its development, further emphasises the helplessness and incompetence of the Whites – even McIntosh. There is no parallel to this, it is worth noting, in *Fort Apache*, in which soldiers with experience of the

West are able to read signs and predict Indian tactics. The centrality of Ke-Ni-Tay's role culminates in a further inversion of generic pattern in which he does assume control of events. In a way that parallels Martin Pawley's rescue of Debbie and killing of Scar in *The Searchers*, Ke-Ni-Tay not only finds Ulzana but kills him in what is presented as a variant of the traditional face-off. At this point, McIntosh is dying after the ambush, and the cavalry's tactics, misconceived from the outset (they leave to rescue McIntosh and the decoy wagon too early but still arrive too late), have conspicuously failed. It is a moment that displaces the White protagonists from the centre of the film and undercuts the values traditionally associated with the hero. Not that the confrontation between Ulzana and Ke-Ni-Tay *is* a traditional face-off. When Ke-Ni-Tay produces the bugle that had belonged to his dead son, Ulzana, in acknowledgement, perhaps, that his line how has no future, offers no resistance and resigns himself to death. Ke-Ni-Tay allows him to sing the death song, then executes him.

If Ke-Ni-Tay is a descendant of Chingachgook, McIntosh is clearly a Leatherstocking figure, but completely shorn of Cooper's mythic dimension of moral immutability. He stands like Leatherstocking between the two races but, rather than embodying the ideal principle of mediation that such a position might imply, he manifests at best some degree of understanding and acceptance. Although he is closer to the Apaches than are the other Whites, he remains aware of his distance from them. Here the

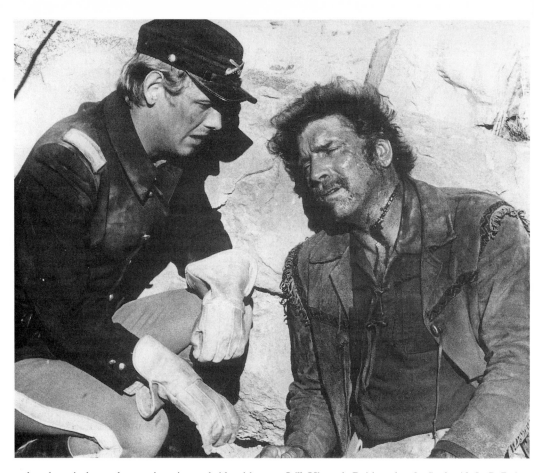

Still: Ulzana's Raid – *after the final raid, Lt DeBuin with the fatally wounded McIntosh.*

cultural gap is, beyond a certain point, unbridgeable. This is suggested throughout in Burt Lancaster's performance: not unlike Leatherstocking in 'The Prairie', the tale in which Natty dies, McIntosh has an air of weariness, of resignation, which almost suggests that the situation in which he finds himself is meaningless to him. This is clearest in the tired way in which he goes through moves that he knows may have little meaning – for instance, in the early scene in which he questions two old reservation Apaches about Ulzana ('Half of what they say is lies, the rest ain't true'); and in his repeated 'Just saying my say'. What is positive in McIntosh's attitude is his acceptance of the Apaches' otherness, but just as the historical situation presented by the film neutralises any residual generic connotations of mediation in the figures of McIntosh and Ke-Ni-Tay, so McIntosh's acceptance has nowhere to go. His role commits him to helping the Whites eradicate or at best confine the Apaches; at the end of the film, McIntosh is dying.

The ending is very uncomfortable. The film makes a moral choice between the two races impossible, but at the same time offers no support for a position of comfortable disengagement from what is presented as an intractable situation: it attempts to confront rather than evade the problem of individual action in a context of military absurdity and moral collapse. Part of its answer (insofar as it offers one) lies in its own attempt to perceive and communicate

its perceptions clearly, and specifically to discriminate between different forms of resignation – perhaps the film's crucial issue – which could easily blur into one. McIntosh is placed somewhere between Ulzana's fanatical commitment to his beliefs, confirmed even in the resignation of his death, and Major Cartwright's total lack of personal conviction. His form of engaged, stoical resignation, which involves following the rules ('Remember the rules, Lieutenant, first one to make a mistake gets to bury some people'), is perhaps the nearest to a positive that the film offers – a position quite close to that of 'The Unnameable' in Beckett's novel: 'I can't go on I must go on I'll go on.' Such an attitue is bleak and unreassuring, and politically it is hardly progressive, but, however limited, it is produced here not out of the combination of sentimentality and undiscriminating despair that characterises *Little Big Man*, but clearsightedly, part of a view of a complex situation which, as the film presents it, will allow of no simple responses.

Note: Differences in the various versions of *Ulzana's Raid*, one of which is referred to above, are usefully described in *Monthly Film Bulletin*, vol.49, nos.582 and 583, July and August 1982.

PAT GARRETT & BILLY THE KID

Brad Stevens

The relationship of *Pat Garrett & Billy the Kid* (Sam Peckinpah, 1973) to classical Hollywood cinema is clearly a complex one: part continuation, part contradiction. Peckinpah represents the answer to the vision in postwar John Ford films of the building of America; we have progressed from the dance on the church floor in *My Darling Clementine* (Ford, 1946) to the murder of Billy the Kid (Kris Kristofferson) in the crumbling fort of Peckinpah's film. The image of the fort is central: the main action begins and ends there, and this circular structure is echoed in the structure of the fort itself, with its walls forming a circle. The film's central motif is the closed circle, an image that is developed further in the framing scenes in which we see death of Pat Garrett (James Coburn) twice and which culminate in the final shot

Still: Pat Garrett & Billy the Kid – *the opening scene. Billy (Kris Kristofferson), surrounded by his gang, shoots at partly buried chickens in Fort Sumner.*

of Garrett's dead body falling past a wagon wheel, with the wheel dominating the frame. The circle comes to represent the closing in of repressive forces, literally the gradual erosion of the frontier by Chisum (Barry Sullivan).

It is probably true to say that a sense of disturbance about the value of the capitalist system was given a focus in the American consciousness by the Vietnam war and that this sense of disturbance, which was implicit in pre-'sixties Westerns, becomes explicit in *The Wild Bunch* (Peckinpah, 1969) and the films that followed. The loss of faith in American institutions provoked by Vietnam is reflected in *Pat Garrett & Billy the Kid* in the film's attack on the figure of the charismatic hero, specifically the sheriff (exemplified by Wyatt Earp in *My Darling Clementine*), who protects, and therefore upholds, the values of a noble civilisation. Here both sheriff and civilisation are seen as irredeemably corrupt. Certain critics (notably Paul Seydor in *Peckinpah: The Western*

Films, University of Illinois Press, 1980) have rather surprisingly managed to read the film as endorsing Garrett.

Richard Combs (*Monthly Film Bulletin*, no. 668, September 1987, pp.262-265) finds Billy to be 'rather hypothetical as a character, as a figure of "freedom" – a possibility that Garrett has betrayed perhaps, but also one that he has grown beyond'. If critics have actually managed to read the film like this, it is no wonder that they consequently find it nihilistic, morbid and life-denying. Garrett has certainly passed beyond Billy's values, the 'immature' values of friendship, love, self-respect and generosity; he is characterised by his 'mature' betrayal of all his past friends, his 'mature' relationship with his wife, whom he detests, and his 'mature' association with his business partners, whom he hates as much as he loves Billy, the man he kills at their behest.

Combs supports his argument by claiming that 'Garrett's struggle with freedom and integrity, age and change, survival and adaptation, are what make him central to the film, its tragic hero'. Indeed, but what Combs fails to see is that it is a struggle that Garrett loses at every point; as a tragic hero, he is more Macbeth than Hamlet.

Garrett's ambivalent status as the film's 'hero' can best be understood by examining the scene showing his humiliation of Alias (Bob Dylan), Lemuel (Chill Wills), Beaver (Donnie Fritts) and Holly (Richard Bright), which ends in Holly's death. Paul Seydor believes that Garrett kills Holly 'mainly to demonstrate to Billy the seriousness of his resolve to hunt him down', but the scene is actually far more complex than this. Apart from a certain sadistic satisfaction in his humiliation of the four men, Garrett clearly takes no pleasure at all in his actions, his face remaining drained and impassive throughout. The scene takes on something of the quality of Pier Paolo Pasolini's *Salò o le centoventi giornate di Sodoma*

Still: Pat Garrett & Billy the Kid – *Billy surrenders to Pat Garrett (James Coburn) at Stinking Springs.*

(1975) in which, in David Wilson's words, 'there is no pleasure for the torturers; and there is no pity'. The parallel can be usefully stressed by quoting some of Wilson's other observations about Pasolini's film: 'The film is structured after Dante, round three cycles, whose formal precision is reflected in the deadening sense of rite and regimentation. From the distance thus achieved the metaphor emerges all the more forcefully: that fascism, symbolised here by the total subjugation of the sexual victims, is merely the ultimate expression of a tendency latent (and to Pasolini ineradicable) in every power system which depends – as all power systems do – on the submission of the many to the few' (*Sight and Sound*, Autumn 1976).

Compare this with Paul Schrader's observation (in a 1970 article on *The Wild Bunch*) that 'what makes Peckinpah unique is his ability to come face to face with the fascist quality of his personality, American films, and America, and turn it into art'.

Peckinpah's use of symbolism in *Pat Garrett* is particularly rich and works on several levels. The most obvious place to begin is with Peckinpah's use of landscape and the elements. Peckinpah's autumnal settings act as a reflection of the death of the vitality that was associated with the frontier. The elements of nature, and all that they traditionally represent, provide a structuring motif. For example, the first shot of the raft episode (a shot sadly missing from the longer version) begins with a tree, stripped of leaves, silhouetted against a twilight sky. The camera moves to the left and reveals that the tree is by a river. Sitting on the bank is Garrett, next to a small fire. The shot not only contains the various components of landscape that make up the film's symbolic structure, but also unites the four elements of earth, air, fire and water. Billy has already been associated with fire: in several shots during his initial conversation with Garrett, he is framed next to a small fire, and, as he rides out of town after his escape from jail, the camera moves away from him and closes in on a furnace. Billy is the Yang (in Japanese, the active principle, corresponding to fire) to Garrett's Yin (the passive principle, corresponding to water), and the small and insignificant fire here serves to remind us of Billy and the oppressiveness of the forces ranged against him (the shot of the furnace also serves as an ironic reminder of Ollinger (R.G. Armstrong), who has previously told Billy that he is condemned to Hell; for Peckinpah, as for William Blake, the fire associated with Hell is potentially a force of liberating energy). The juxtaposition of the dying tree and the river (a symbol of life) takes us back to an earlier moment: the death of Sheriff Cullen Baker (Slim Pickens) by a river, a bare tree visible in the background. These trees form a motif throughout the film, also being seen as Billy rides back from Mexico and as Garrett and his deputies approach Fort Sumner at the climax. They provide a naturalistic symbol of the gradual spread of decay throughout America. The autumnal world provides a complex series of images, the season's connotations of death perfectly reflecting Peckinpah's theme.

Animal imagery provides another motif, a particularly prominent and complex example being the chickens which are used for target practice in the opening sequence. Like Billy and his gang, the chickens are trapped and, one by one, killed. The last chicken is shot by Garrett as he rides into the fort, the film's symmetry being completed at the end as Garrett, after murdering most of Billy's gang, kills Billy himself, but it is important to remember that Billy personally shoots a few of the chickens. This complex image underlines the fact that Billy participates in his own destruction: rather than going to Mexico, he chooses to remain at Fort Sumner to await his death, his turning back before even reaching the border being as much a suicide as the decision of the Wild Bunch to confront Mapache. Among other instances of animal imagery are the glimpses of a cockfight (Garrett and Billy pointlessly set against each other by Chisum), helpfully removed in almost their entirety from British cinema and video versions by the censor, the caged birds at the trading post and the horses in the stable that Billy glances at outside the jail. This last exemplifies the extraordinary depth of feeling that Peckinpah can achieve with a simple shot, the horses' immediate connotations of freedom being qualified by their imprisonment, the comparison with Billy being swiftly made; the shot takes on an added significance if we realise that the old Mexican who tends the horses may have been responsible for leaving the gun with which Billy escapes (although it is also possible that the gun was left by Garrett: most critics tend to opt for one or other of these explanations, failing to understand that Peckinpah has ambiguously left both possibilities open, adding great resonance to the moment when Billy tells his gang 'I saved you all a trip, or somebody did').

The film's religious imagery compares the legend of Billy the Kid's betrayal by his friend Pat Garrett with Jesus's betrayal by Judas. Billy is compared to Jesus at various points: as he surrenders to Garrett at Stinking Springs, his arms are held out and his head slightly tilted in a crucifixion pose; as he sits on a rock talking to some members of his gang, the image is reminiscent of Jesus addressing the disciples; as he talks to Alias after the departure of Paco (Emilio Fernandez), he stands next to a small picture of Jesus; finally, as he makes love to Maria, he moans 'Jesus, Jesus'. After he is shot down by Garrett, our final glimpse of Billy is in the shot of Maria sitting at the foot of the stone slab on which his body has been lain, like Mary Magdalene at the foot of the cross. (More ambiguously, as Billy prepares to kill Ollinger, he asks, 'How's Jesus look to you now Bob?', and as he comes across Chisum's men torturing Paco, one of them, on seeing Billy, exclaims 'Jesus Christ'. The use of Christian imagery is not, I believe, ironic; nor does it serve to reinforce a basically reactionary project (as in Elia Kazan's *On the Waterfront*, 1954); rather, the film's religious subtext is vitally linked to its radical politics.

The structural relationship of the male group to the film's two central characters is similar to that found in several other Peckinpah films. The structure can be laid out as follows:

1) *Ride the High Country* (1962)
Steve Judd   Gil Westrum   The Hammonds
(Joel McCrea)(Randolph Scott)

2) *Major Dundee* (1965)
Dundee   Tyreen   The Apaches
(Charlton Heston)(Richard Harris)

3) *The Wild Bunch* (1969)
Pike Bishop   Deke Thornton   The Bounty Hunters
(William Holden) (Robert Ryan)

4) *Straw Dogs* (1970)
David Sumner   Amy Sumner   The Villagers
(Dustin Hoffman) (Susan George)

5) *Pat Garrett & Billy the Kid* (1973)
Pat Garrett   Billy the Kid   Billy's Gang

6) *Cross of Iron* (1977)
Stransky   Steiner   Steiner's Platoon
(Maximilian Schell) (James Coburn)

7) *Convoy* (1978)
Dirty Lyle   Rubber Duck   The Convoy
(Ernest Borgnine) (Kris Kristofferson)

In each film, we have two characters, usually estranged friends (in *Straw Dogs* a wife who becomes estranged from her husband, in *Cross of Iron* and *Convoy* wary mutual admiration rather than friendship), and a group with some connection to the second character. In *Ride the High Country* and *Major Dundee*, this connection is ambiguous, but Gil Westrum's loose morality is clearly linked to that of the Hammonds while Tyreen is associated with the Apaches, at least in Dundee's mind (he threatens to hang Tyreen and the Apache leader Sierra Chariba – Michael Pate – 'to the same tree'). In *The Wild*

Bunch, although Deke Thornton is actually the leader of the group of, in his own words, 'gutter trash', there is more of a contrast than a similarity, while in *Straw Dogs* Amy finally turns not to her husband but to the villagers among whom she grew up. The thing that links all four of these films is that the group, while always associated with an energy and vitality denied the ostensible hero, is viewed in essentially negative terms. By the time we get to *Pat Garrett & Billy the Kid*, however, this judgement has been reversed: the 'hero', more pallid and drained of energy than any of his predecessors, has been totally discredited and the group, although still representing many of the same things as before, is unambiguously affirmed. Tellingly, the relationship between the second character and the group here becomes more solid, with Billy not only leading the gang but emotionally at one with it. *Cross of Iron* works in a similar fashion; here, however, although Stransky is treated in much the same way as Garrett, it is Steiner who actually resembles him (he is played by the same actor, James Coburn), and neither he nor the group (in the service of, though hostile to, the forces of fascism) can be affirmed, except insofar as they express the spirit of nihilism that drives the film and is characteristic of Peckinpah's later work. *Convoy* simply repeats the structure of *Pat Garrett & Billy the Kid* (again the same actor, Kris Kristofferson, is used in a similar role) without meaningfully developing it: compare, for example, Lyle's walk through the roadside diner, intercut with shots of Rubber Duck making love to a waitress, to the shots of Garrett walking through Fort Sumner, intercut with Billy making love to Maria (Rita Coolidge).

The spontaneity of the male group is best exemplified by the scene of the turkey chase, which is initiated by Billy, not in an effort to obtain food, but as an affirmation of friendship with Alias. Energy in Peckinpah's work is usually associated with violence, and it is worth noting that this scene has many of the qualities associated with the violent moments (rapid editing, slow-motion shots intercut with those at normal speed). In contrast to the final battle in *The Wild Bunch*, energy here is associated with a spontaneous aliveness, all the more powerful for occurring just before the brutal murder of Silva (Jorge Russek) by Chisum's men, themselves, like the Santa Fe Ring, forming a male group in opposition to Billy's gang.

Billy touches not only those within his group but also the common people for whom he represents an image of freedom, while, by way of contrast, the mutual contempt between Garrett and the citizens of Lincoln is clearly shown in the brief scene in which Garrett rides back into town after Billy's jailbreak: seeing Bell's body, he glances at the assembled crowd and says, 'Would some of you (pause) people get him up off the ground and into it', to which one man sarcastically replies 'Anything you say sheriff.' The most immediate point of comparison here is with the preceding scene, Billy's ride out of town after the jailbreak, during which he accepts back a blanket that he had dropped earlier but which is now offered as a token of friendship by the old Mexican who may have left the gun, the mutual respect between the two being conveyed, without dialogue, entirely through exchanged looks.

The image of the crumbling fort is again relevant to the presentation of Billy's gang. In the movement of the genre, it evokes, as I have already suggested, the church of *My Darling Clementine*, but specifically in dealing with the male group the film echoes Ford's cavalry trilogy. Whereas the soldiers of Ford's cavalry are sustained by a tradition, each man ennobled by subjugating himself to and fulfilling his function within it, the male group here live totally in the present, their relationship to each other defined not by a position within a heirarchy, but by values of mutual respect. The film here reflects the work of Howard Hawks, Peckinpah making explicit what in Hawks was implicit: that if true value resides within the group outside civilisation, then civilisation itself must be corrupt. By contrast, each of Garrett's relationships is defined in negative terms, being based on financial gain (Sheriff Cullen Baker's 'I got to the point where I don't do nothing for nobody unless there's a piece of gold attached to it'), coercion (Garrett's exploiting his past friendship with Kip McKinney, Richard Jaeckel), violence (his beating Ruthie Lee, Rutanya Alda, in order to obtain information), mutual contempt (Garrett and Poe, John Beck; Garrett and the people of Lincoln), murder (Garrett's killing of his one-time friend Black Harris, L.Q. Jones, his sadistic killing of Holly) and finally betrayal (his killing of Billy). The final distinction here is between self-respect (which inevitably leads to the group's mutual respect) and a misguided desire for fame, the misplaced respect of an impersonal society, seen here in the dying words of Alamosa Bill (Jack Elam), 'at least I'll be remembered', and Kip McKinney's 'I hope they spell my name right in the papers'. It is important to remember that Billy's gang live not in the past, as some have suggested, but in the present, while only the figures of corruption, including Garrett, make plans for the future (as in Garrett's 'this country's growing old and I aim to grow old with it' and his admission to Billy that he intends to live to be 'rich, old and grey'). The futility of living in the future while ignoring the present has its most poignant expression in the scenes involving Sheriff Baker, whom we first see building a boat and who dies by the side of a river on which he will never sail. Those who choose to live solely in the future narrow their horizons and consequently lose their free will: while Billy and his gang roam freely, Garrett, though he may wish it otherwise, has little choice in his course of action, the film's circular structure leading him inevitably back to the fort.

Bob Dylan's role as Alias seems to have confounded most commentators, but he has a clear role within the film's structure. Alias and Poe both function as reflections of the two central characters, a function made explicit through a pattern of comparisons and juxtapositions. The relationship between Garrett and Poe is underlined by the way they both resort to violence to obtain the information that Billy is hiding at Fort Sumner, Poe beating two aged prospectors, Garrett repeatedly slapping Ruthie Lee, a scene that anticipates the moment when Poe, finding Luke (Harry Dean Stanton) making love, knocks him unconscious and slaps the woman he was sleeping with. As a contrast to these connections the repetition of a passage of dialogue between Billy and Alias takes on a structural significance. After the departure of Paco from the fort, there is the following exchange:

Billy: Mexico might not be bad for a couple of months.
Alias: Depends on who are you are.
This is almost exactly repeated soon afterwards, but this time the speakers are reversed:
Alias: Mexico won't be so bad for a few months.
Billy: I guess that depends who you are.

Billy is able to relate to Alias as an equal, while Garrett, faced with the naked reflection of his true self, can only treat Poe with contempt. This carefully detailed pattern of mirror imagery provides the film with one of its most complex and resonant images: the mirror that Garrett fires into after killing Billy. Tellingly, it is only after Garrett destroys his own reflection that he is able to turn on Poe. Although Garrett functions, to some extent, as superego, his centrality to the film means that the id/superego conflict is also enacted within his own psyche, represented by, respectively, Billy and Poe. (Several other characters also represent aspects of Garrett's personality – which is to say that they are variations on a theme – notably Ollinger, Sheriff Baker, Alamosa Bill, the outlaw turned lawman, and J.W.Bell, Matt Clark, the basically decent man who fails to see that he has sold out to the forces of a corrupt progresss, as well as such minor figures as Elisha Cook's 'tired' prospector.)

The shot fired into the mirror is the key image of the film: coming between Garrett's killing of Billy and his lashing out at Poe, it represents both the destruction of everything positive within Garrett and his recognition of, and revulsion at, the dark side of his personality. His final comment to Poe (and the last line of dialogue in the film), 'What you want and what you get are two different things', makes complete sense only when we realise that he is actually talking to himself.

Bob Dylan's score for the film, in particular a song that reappears at several points, is inseparable from his portrayal of Alias. Lines from the song like 'Billy they don't like you to be so free', and lines of dialogue from Alias like 'I could live anywhere. I could leave anywhere too', reinforce Alias's function as a reflection of Billy. Billy's rootlessness, his refusal to be tied down ('I know Billy and he ain't exactly predictable', Garrett tells the Santa Fe Ring), is reflected not only in Alias's comments but also in his refusal to be tied down with a real name.

Alias's first appearance, as Billy breaks out of jail in Lincoln, emphasises their connection. As Billy looks out of the window of the jail and sings of the places he has been and the things he has done, intercut shots of Billy and Alias convey the impression that the two are looking at each other and Billy's song is intended primarily for him. The shot of Billy by the window, looking out at the town, is composed in such a way that Billy, in jail, appears free (he dominates the frame), while the town, seen through the bars, is in prison. The song, explicitly about freedom, underlines this, and it is Alias's recognition of what Billy represents that leads him to join the gang at Fort Sumner after seeing Garrett. Alias's meeting with Garrett at the barbershop shows his desire to define himself in terms other than those of respectable society: in answer to Garrett's 'Who are you?' he replies, 'That's a good question.' The refusal to be named clearly exemplifies his refusal of established definitions: Billy and Alias are totally self-defining, answering to no-one. Garrett, on the other hand, is entirely immersed in societal structures, answerable to the 'rule of the father' represented by Chisum, who is himself answerable to more powerful men, as we infer when Norris (John Chandler) tells Garrett that 'Chisum and the others have been advised to recognise their positions'. This is made explicit in the one scene in which Chisum appears. He is defined throughout the film in terms of the forceful restraint of energy; indeed, the first shot of the Chisum ranch shows one of his men attempting to control a bucking horse. Chisum's posture, sitting on a fence, serves to stress his dominance and to remind us of Billy's observation about 'all those trying to put a fence up around this country'; he strikes us, however, as someone trying to convey the impression of a power that he does not really possess (in reality, he can't even control his cook) in the way he, like Garrett, asserts his superiority to Poe (which is far from difficult). Peckinpah's approach to Chisum reflects his approach to Garrett: both condemnation and identification. Barry Sullivan's notable physical resemblance to Peckinpah helps emphasise the fact that Chisum is himself a victim of the forces he theoretically represents.

Pat Garrett & Billy the Kid is often criticised for being a life-denying film, tired and resigned to defeat. No criticism could be further from the truth – any work that elicits such a sympathy for its characters, such a powerful sense of loss at their deaths, must be motivated by a sense of human potential and positive moral value.

Children have an important, often ambivalent, function in Peckinpah. Here, they appear frequently:

1) There are children playing on the scaffold that is being prepared for Billy
2) Their presence, unobtrusively but consistently, in virtually every scene set at Fort Sumner – running to collect the dead chickens, playing in the background as Billy waits for Garrett's arrival (some of them dancing in a circle), watching Paco depart
3) Linked again with Fort Sumner is the boy who contemptuously hurls sods after the departing Garrett
4) The boy who obligingly runs an errand for Garrett
5) The children impassively watching the shoot-out at the trading post
6) The children in the raft that passes Garrett
7) The crying baby that Billy hears as he comes across Chisum's men torturing Paco.

Billy's ease and naturalness with children (for instance, the significantly feminine-looking young boy he picks up as he enters the trading post) are contrasted with Garrett's aloof behaviour towards the boy he asks to take a message for him (the fact that Garrett's marriage has remained childless is of obvious significance). Billy and his gang are linked with the children in three ways. First, by proximity: the fort that provides the gang's home is full of children. Second, by similar behaviour patterns: the children's games are echoed in the gang's playful target practice (this playfulness is immediately placed by Garrett's attempt to join in, not out of a desire to join the group, but in order to prove himself the best shot, just as the later scene of Billy shooting at bottles is answered by Garrett's aggressive attempt to outshoot the man on the raft). Third, by the desire for community: whereas Garrett prefers to ride alone, joining others only for pragmatic reasons, both Billy's gang and the children organise themselves into groups out of a desire for human contact, friendship being constantly affirmed through apparently pointless games, such as the turkey chase and the game of cards during Garrett's attack (in a scene cut by MGM, and still missing from the longer version, Garrett's wife, Ida (Aurora Clavell), expresses the wish that Billy escape; Garrett tells her that he won't because there's 'too much play in him', to which Ida responds 'and not enough in you'). The connection between the two groups helps to explain Peckinpah's appearance as a character called Will who is seen making a child's coffin in the moments before Billy is killed.

The children embody the romantic image of the child as a vision of renewal and hope for the future. The scene of the boy throwing sods of earth after Garrett therefore has a clear significance. Paul Seydor correctly identifies a parallel with the ending of *Shane*; he then, however, goes on to make an astonishing statement: 'At the last moment Stevens cuts to an alternate angle so that he can magnify Shane's stature against the verdant Wyoming range: Peckinpah, by contrast, holds us to the shot of the disillusioned boy, who turns and walks back toward town while Garrett's figure recedes in the distance as the barren New Mexico desert begins to swallow it up. Surely there is, in effect and implication, no bleaker, blacker, bitterer ending to any Western film.' An understanding of this reference to *Shane* is clearly crucial to the understanding of Peckinpah's film. Andrew Britton, commenting on the solipsism of modern American cinema (in his superb article 'Blissing out: the Politics of Reaganite Entertainment', *Movie* 31/32, Winter 1986), notes that 'the invocation of "the Western" in *Rio Bravo* or *The Man Who Shot Liberty Valance* [John Ford, 1962] subserves a critical investigation of the conditions of existence of the genre. Self-reference, in other words, is in this case a means to a more rigorous reference *outwards* – to the culture in which the Western has been a significant form.'

The nature of the reference to *Shane* is clearly of this kind. Seydor's description of it, however, is simply unacceptable. Anyone who fails to share my scepticism at his claim need only imagine the alternative way in which Peckinpah might have handled the scene: since, quite obviously, he could not at this point cut to Garrett 'magnified against the verdant range' (which would have been *really* bitter), the only other option would have been to stay with the defeated Garrett as he rides off to his inevitable death. By staying instead with the child, he conveys a powerful sense of hope, of the ability for change and growth (the scene's setting at sunrise is vitally linked to this). Though Billy is dead, his spirit lives on. When Garrett dies, there will be no-one, not even his wife, to mourn him.

An attempt to define exactly where Peckinpah sees the possibility of change and growth leading can best be approached by briefly looking at *Cross of Iron*. About halfway through this film, the central character, Steiner (James Coburn), convalescing in a hospital, decides to return to the front after seeing the naked body of his nurse, Eva (Senta Berger), whose response is to ask him, 'Do you love the war so much or are you afraid of what you'll be without it?' What Steiner is afraid he will be is homosexual. Andrew Britton has analysed the film from this perspective (*Movie 27/28*, Winter 1980/Spring 1981, p.20), and it would seem to be the area in which *Pat Garrett & Billy the Kid* may be most clearly open to radical interpretation; it is also, of necessity, the area where it is most incoherent. Any work of art, pushed far enough, will reveal areas of incoherence (as the *Cahiers du Cinéma* analysis of *Young Mr Lincoln* revealed), but the incoherence here is extremely near the surface, and the film's fractured editing reflects this. It is, however, to Peckinpah's credit that the film raises the issue of homosexuality at all. The fact that this subtext probably exists only on an unconscious level simply makes it more susceptible to critical analysis, testifying as it does to the traces of the constitutional bisexuality (as identified by Freud) which our culture represses (the principles of Yang and Yin, the relevance of which to, respectively, Billy and Garrett I mentioned earlier, correspond not only to fire and water but also to male and female).

Of the cuts made by the studio, the most damaging seems to have been the scene showing Garrett with his wife, Ida. This scene would, apparently, have established that Garrett had married in order to maintain the appearance of respectability, that there was never any love between them (Garrett is seeing her for the first time in several weeks; he makes an excuse and quickly leaves), and that there is probably no sexual relationship either: Ida's condemnation of Garrett, 'You don't touch me. You are dead inside', indicates his sterility. This scene is still missing from the longer version, but what is restored is a shot which, in a sense, sums up its entire meaning. We see Garrett returning home, walking up to a house surrounded by a white picket fence, outside which he pauses, as if steeling himself, before opening the gate. Garrett's attitude towards his wife is brilliantly summed up by this image, but what is even more revealing is its connection with a later scene. Towards the end of the film Garrett enters the house in Fort Sumner where he knows Billy is waiting. Here again, there is a white picket fence outside which Garrett pauses before opening the gate. The implication is unmistakable: that Garrett's sexual attraction to Billy has been suppressed;

barred from recognising his true sexuality, he is equally unable to respond sexually to his wife. This helps to make clear the meaning of the later scenes in which Garrett shows an interest in women: the moment in Santa Fe in which he offends the respectable businessmen present by glancing lasciviously at a waitress, and the scene in which he insists on sleeping with a number of prostitutes (including Ruthie Lee, whom he has just taken a perverse pleasure in slapping in order to obtain information, a scene strangely missing from the longer version), partly in order to prove his (hetero)sexuality to himself, partly for the benefit of Poe, whose disgust obviously pleases him, but mainly because he has just been told that the last time Billy was there 'he had four to get it up and five to get it down'. Garrett's sexual relationships are rooted in a desire to display a masculine power and control, the scene with the prostitutes being logically followed by his having them all jailed.

Garrett's insistence on seeing Ruthie Lee, after being told that she has 'been with the kid', indicates a function beyond that simply of narrative (she can tell him where Billy is) and points toward her role as intermediary between Garrett and Billy (a point that the removal of the interrogation scene from the longer version actually emphasises). Barred from sleeping with Billy, Garrett compensates by sharing one of Billy's women (her function here being similar to that of Teal Eye, Elizabeth Threatt, in Hawks's *The Big Sky*, 1952, and Linda, Meryl Streep, in Michael Cimino's *The Deer Hunter*, 1978), as is confirmed in his subsequent attempt to emulate Billy by sleeping with several prostitutes. Despite all the nudity in the restored brothel scene, the film, while not definitely establishing that Garrett does not make love to the prostitutes, certainly avoids establishing that he *does*; when Poe discovers him, all Garrett is doing is stroking their hair. This provides a further indication of Garrett's impotence, something that has been systematically defined in the film. Consider the following examples:

1) Holly tells Garrett that 'ever since you and the kid been together you been just a little short of supplies'
2) Beaver taunts Garrett with the words 'private parts'
3) Billy's amazingly explicit comment, addressed to Bell, 'Pat's lost his sand, won't come on a man'
4) Garrett instructing the prostitutes, who are removing his trousers, to 'pull hard, they've been on a long time'.

That Garrett's impotence is rooted in a feeling of extreme disgust for female sexuality (a characteristic emphasised in his mirror image Poe, notably in Poe's look of revulsion as he slaps the woman sleeping with Luke) is established early on in Billy's recollection of a 'humorous' exchange between Garrett and a prostitute which apparently ended with Garrett informing the woman that her vagina 'could use a few stitches' (note also the way Garrett protectively covers his genitals as he is being bathed by the prostitutes at the brothel).

Still: Pat Garrett & Billy the Kid – 'What you want and what you get are two different things.' Garrett contemplates Billy's dead body.

We are obviously meant to compare Garrett's relationships with women, particularly Ida, to Billy's relationship with Maria, which is based on tenderness, affection and a mutually shared sexuality, enjoyed, for its own sake, as an expression of love. It is here, however, that the film's partial incoherence emerges: since Peckinpah cannot show Billy as a homosexual without bringing to full consciousness the unconscious levels on which this subtext works, he has no choice but to define him as unambiguously heterosexual. It is at this point that we must strive to see beyond what the work is saying. If Peckinpah is unable to acknowledge Billy as gay, then the presentation of the character at least shows how this is a very real possibility, lurking just below the surface. In this respect the character of Eno (Luke Askew),

a member of Billy's gang, takes on particular importance. Ena is twice seen pointing phallic objects at Billy: the first time, as Billy returns to Fort Sumner, Eno mistakes him for an intruder and threatens him with a gun; the second time, as Billy enters the fort again, the object is a finger which Eno homourously pretends is a weapon. Eno is often seen dazing admiringly at Billy, and the images of him watching contentedly as Billy strips and slowly climbs into bed carry highly resonant implications.

Rather than being portrayed in the familiar macho terms of the Western outlaw, the characteristics that are emphasised (and hence valued) in Billy are his fragility, his gentleness and, I would claim, his ambiguous sexuality, his long hair and often semi-naked body being displayed by the film as erotically attractive; the easy, unstressed quality of his movement supports this view of the character as feminised (Kris Kristofferson's apparent refusal to take instruction on how to use a handgun authentically contributes perfectly to this, making even Billy's gun-play appear sexual). Billy is often on the receiving end of guns (although only the final one is actually fired): as Terence Butler has pointed out (in *Crucified Heroes: The Films of Sam Peckinpah*, Gordon Fraser, London, 1979), Ollinger's ramming a shot-gun into Billy's chest is 'suggestive of fellatio', and we are clearly supposed to contrast this with the moment when Eno playfully points a gun/finger at Billy. The penis, when associated with the open sexuality of the gang, becomes a shared joke, an instrument for play; when associated with Ollinger's repressive religious beliefs it becomes the aggressive phallus, an instrument of domination, and while Billy represents religion as liberation, Ollinger ('Repent you son of a bitch') represents religion as oppression.

If Ollinger is one of the film's many mirror images of Garrett, then it makes sense to see him, too, as a repressed homosexual, suppressing his sexuality in violent action (the gun pressed into Billy's chest comes as a reaction to Billy's invitation to 'kiss my ass'). This motif, linking the penis/phallus and the gun, reaches its (literal) climax as Billy, after making love to Maria, has his final orgasm in the form of a bullet from Garrett's gun. Throughout this scene, Garrett has already been a disruptive presence, the intercutting of him stalking through the fort with Billy making love conveying complex suggestions (frustrated desire, castration) that are resolved only when the unachievable nature of their sexual relationship is finally subordinated in an act of violence.

At two moments in the film the religious and sexual subtexts become connected: the image of Billy surrendering to Garrett with his arms held out to his sides, which is both Christ-like and calls up an image of a lover awaiting an embrace, and the shots of Billy making love to Maria while moaning 'Jesus, Jesus'. Billy's spirit will live on, Christ-like, after his death in the form of the child who hastens Garrett's departure. This is not, however, the spirit of religious acceptance dedicated to maintaining the status quo, but the spirit of radical change which, in connection with the free sexuality that Billy represents, has the potential to transform society.

CLASS FRONTIERS
The View through Heaven's Gate

Brian Woolland

Consider one of the most familiar of Western openings: a vast, empty landscape into which rides a solitary male figure. Perhaps he brings news of events that will pitch us into the action, maybe he is the action; often he'll be alone and pitted against an inhospitable and untamed world. Compare this with the opening of *Heaven's Gate* (Michael Cimino, 1980): a deserted street in Harvard substitutes for the empty frontier; into the street runs a solitary male figure, James Averill (Kris Kristofferson), racing to catch up with a group of university students who are raggedly following a marching band. When he eventually reaches them, his friend Billy Irvine (John Hurt) is delighted to see him, but nobody is waiting for him, and in his absence nothing would be very different. It's a strange opening for a Western.

The opening sequence of *Heaven's Gate* functions as more than just a prologue; it is central to an interpretation of the film, for it lays out value systems and patterns of behaviour that subsequently become the subject of the film's essential discourse: issues of class and ethnicity, of the role of women, and of the relationship between individual and collective action. Whilst these issues had sometimes been implicit concerns of earlier Westerns, they had never before been examined so explicitly or so critically.

A group of expensively dressed women is crowding eagerly at a window to watch the White male students (among whom, belatedly, is Averill) marching by to the tune of the Battle Hymn of the Republic. The students throng into a magnificent Lecture Theatre, where these same women watch and giggle (from balcony seats) as Irvine, the 'Class-of-'Seventy Orator' makes an irresponsible attempt to entertain his peers with a graduation speech that tellingly ends with him proclaiming that 'On the whole everything is well arranged'.

The women join the students in a magnificent swirling dance to a full off-screen orchestra playing 'The Blue Danube'. Averill snatches a young woman from a fellow student. She's delighted. He tells her, 'You're beautiful.' 'So are you', she replies. For

Still: Heaven's Gate – *the Establishment's finest. Harvard, Class of 'Seventy, with Billy Irvine (John Hurt) and James Averill (Kris Kristofferson) at front.*

wealthy young men of spirit, for men who know what they want and are prepared to go out and get it, everything does indeed seem well arranged.

The marching band returns; the beautiful young woman appears with friends at a window. Again they are looking down (as if from a picture frame) on the action below, now watching admiringly as Averill and his fellow students battle for a bouquet attached high on the trunk of a tree in the centre of the grassy area where previously they had been dancing. Averill wins; he plucks the bouquet from the tree and holds it aloft in triumph. The unnamed beauty at the window applauds. There may be bloody noses, the struggle for the bouquet may have been violent, but it's been well worth it: the women watch excitedly and wholeheartedly approve what in retrospect appears to have been a violent and elaborate courtship ritual, conducted to the strains of the Battle Hymn of the Republic. The imagery, the language and the music in this opening sequence all serve to link Averill's courtship of the unnamed Beautiful Young Woman with the values of the Establishment.

The only women we see in this opening sequence are young, beautiful, wealthy – and passive. They are allowed to express themselves only through formal dancing and by approving the antics of men; their sole means of expression is through response and reaction. The 'community' to which they belong is one that has institutionalised a form of competitive violence; privilege belongs to those who take strong individual action – even Irvine's impertinent and convoluted speech is tacitly approved as mild eccentricity.

After the sumptuous rituals of Harvard, Cimino cuts abruptly to a close-up of Averill asleep on a train, sun and shadows falling across him through a smoky atmosphere. At last, and quite unexpectedly, we're offered an image that's readily identifiable as belonging generically to the Western. But we're not on safe ground for long – there's an immediate cut to an exterior view of the train, and the familiar is disturbed: the engine (belching thick black smoke) is pulling a carriage, a flat wagon with a buggy on it, a large cattle wagon, another wagon marked EMI-GRANT CAR, and a caboose. The cattle wagon is empty, but its roof (like that of the emigrant car) is crowded with people, while Averill is alone in the only carriage on the train. All this is shown against a magnificent backdrop of the snow-capped mountains of Wyoming. The familiar image of trains in Westerns is here inextricably coupled with associations of trains in quite different contexts: Jews inside goods wagons being taken to concentration camps, peasants clinging to slow-moving trains trundling through India. We're unused to trains being used in this way in the West. By juxtaposing the celebrations of the privileged class and Averill's comfortable (and solitary) journey with this mass of unidentified humanity lurching precariously to God-knows-where, Cimino firmly establishes issues of privilege, class and community as the central concerns of the film.

The image of the train is complex and highly detailed, but Cimino does not point up its significance. We see it and move on. It's only as the film develops that we fully understand what we have seen. Soon we'll discover that the people on the roofs, denied access even to the comfort and relative security of a cattle wagon, are immigrants from Eastern Europe. Most of them are here as families, and have come because to them America is Heaven's Gate. They have been sold the dream, and they believe it: if only you have enough initiative and drive and are prepared to work hard, everything can be yours. It's the myth to which Irvine subscribes: America is 'well arranged' if you're willing to go out and get what you want. That's the dream; and that's what they're here for. They're travelling to Heaven's Gate in the hope that they might be allowed in.

This strategy of offering rich, complex juxtapositions which initially seem to stand alone is wholly in keeping with Cimino's methods throughout the film. He shows us events, but doesn't emphasise their meanings, which become clear retrospectively. Robin Wood has developed this line of argument more fully in his excellent article, 'Heaven's Gate Reopened' (Movie 31/32, Winter 1986, pp.72-83, reprinted in Hollywood, from Vietnam to Reagan, Columbia University Press, 1986), in which he asserts that Cimino appears to renounce conventional, linear systems of narrative organisation in favour of more symbolic systems in which it is often the interconnecting resonance of the imagery that gives the film its meanings.

From the image of the train there's another unexpected and disturbing cut: to the Kovach family – husband, wife and child – working together in mud and blood to cut up the carcase of a steer. In marked contrast to the women at Harvard, Kovach's wife (Gordana Rasmovich) is active, and this is her work as much as her husband's. That they are immigrants is immediately clear, for they speak Polish (the film is subtitled where necessary); or, rather, the woman speaks Polish, urging her husband to hurry, 'Faster, faster'. It could not be made clearer that these people are ethnically different: not only are they immigrants, they do not even speak English.

The shadow of an unknown gunman falls on the canvas wall of their shelter. The shadow raises a shotgun. Kovach (Aviars Smits) is felled, his stomach blown apart by a shotgun blast. The incident is shocking because it's so sudden, in such stark contrast to what has gone before, and because the killing is so brutal and so anonymous. Only when Kovach's body is lying in a pool of mud do we see the gunman, who is later identified as Nate Champion (Christopher Walken). Framed by a hole in the wall of the tent, he turns disdainfully, calmly mounts his horse and rides away.

This, at last, is the type of action we might expect of a Western. But Cimino chooses to treat the killing of Kovach not as a crucial plot point but instead almost as background detail. Like the journey across the plains, it is one incident in a catalogue of oppression. The Kovach family never assume particular importance; their significance is as immigrants, a small unit among the many who have emigrated to America from Europe. This formal strategy regularly shifts our attention away from the individual protagonists of the film (Averill, Champion, Canton

Still: Heaven's Gate – *Averill's retreat, in his room in Sweetwater.*

and Ella) to bit-players (such as Cully, the station-master) and the Sweetwater immigrants.

Class

There have been other Westerns in which a group of settlers (rarely termed immigrants – the choice of vocabulary is significant) is seen battling against greedy, oppressive cattle barons. What makes *Heaven's Gate* so unusual is that the cattle barons, personified by Canton (Sam Waterston), are so clearly identified with the ruling class; the oppression is seen to be class-based rather than motivated by individual greed.

In earlier Westerns, the frontier is frequently a place where justice needs to be established, but where the rigid legal systems of the East seem ludicrous and out of place. Before *Heaven's Gate*, those systems had rarely been explicitly identified as functioning in favour of a ruling class. What we have in *Heaven's Gate*, however, is a systematic attempt by 'Eastern speculators' – clearly identified as such by one of the more articulate members of the Sweetwater community – to crush a group of non-English-speaking working-class immigrants who want to work for themselves rather than as wage slaves. And this oppression is wholeheartedly supported by the Establishment.

Robin Wood has argued that 'the alleged Marxist content does not progress very far beyond what is implicit in the saying of Christ to which Cimino's title refers. It might better be described as adolescent idealism . . .' (Wood, 1986, p.80). Whilst the film may not present us with a sophisticated proposal

for socialism, it is far from naive politically. Events in Wyoming are all firmly placed in an economic and political context: the imagery, the juxtapositions, the resonances and reverberations, and even the dialogue constantly remind us that property and ownership are ethnic, gender and class issues. The immigrants have come to Sweetwater in order to own their means of production. Although none of them ever articulate their precise reasons for leaving Europe, it is clear that what they want in Johnson County is land on which they can raise their own cattle and the freedom to build a democratic, self-regulating community free of external interference.

When Averill's train arrives in Caspar, we find ourselves in a heavily industrialised town seething with traffic and overcast with smoke pouring from high chimneys. Cimino offers a dense and complex image of urban life – the antithesis of the sort of towns we might traditionally expect to find in a Western. The visual extravagance of the image has sometimes been remarked on pejoratively, almost as if Cimino chose it at random; but this perversely ignores its unmistakable function: to establish that industry and commerce, the solid foundations of capitalism, are already firmly in place in Wyoming; and furthermore (by implication) that the town is supported by a large wage-earning working-class population – people who do not own their means of production.

Surrounded by the intense activity of Caspar, Averill and Cully, the Irish stationmaster (Richard Masur), attempt a conversation. Cully tells Averill that the Stockgrowers' Association is carrying out summary executions of immigrants believed to be stealing cattle. Cully is embarrassed by his own inactivity. 'I can't afford to get involved,' he asserts. 'I just started this job.' The economic context for acquiescence could hardly be stated more baldly.

Earlier in the sequence he has remarked: 'If the rich could hire others to do their violence for them, the poor could make a wonderful living.' The naiveté of his assertion comes from the fact that the system depends upon the rich hiring the poor to do their violence for them – again made explicit in a subsequent sequence in which Canton seeks out additional recruits for his mercenary army.

The end of the Caspar sequence is marked by another remarkable cut, from the frenetic commercial activity of the industrialised town to the hallway of an opulently furnished mansion, into which walks a perfectly dressed butler carrying a silver tea service on a silver tray. In silence, he moves slowly towards the sound of voices. We follow him into a large room where, for the first time, we encounter Canton, who is making a speech to the Stockgrower's Association about producing wealth from land.

Cimino uses the Association meeting to relate issues of class and gender, employing the strategy of unmarked juxtaposition to draw attention to the distinction between the different roles assumed by women of the ruling and working classes. While Canton proposes placing the names of 125 immigrants on a death list, the camera watches the reactions of various members of the Association; Irvine doesn't much like what he's hearing and, in a remarkably economical revelation of character, he looks away. We follow his gaze out through the window to see two women (dressed much as the women had been in the Harvard sequence and clearly of the establishment) promenading with parasols whilst the men continue to discuss the death list. Although the action by the Stockgrowers' Association is claimed to be something that will make America a better place for all to live in, women have no part in the decision-making process – unlike the women of Sweetwater, who not only participate actively in all public meetings, but also butcher cattle, work the land, and go to battle.

After the meeting, Canton is confronted by Averill. 'You offset every effort we make to protect our property and that of your own class', says Canton. Averill replies, 'You're not of my class, Canton. You never will be.' It's impossible to tell whether Averill's scorn for Canton is motivated by snobbery or disgust at his actions. 'Not of my class' could as easily be a reference to a moral position as to Averill's opinion that Canton is not Ivy League. The productive ambiguity of the exchange arises from the question posed by Averill's behaviour here and subsequently; it is not just to do with his personal motivations, but also with his position as a highly educated US Marshal meting out justice in a town that is trying to function as a collective and seeking its own democracy.

The ambiguities of this position are developed in the brief sequence immediately after the Association meeting: Averill is driving his gig to Sweetwater; he meets a woman whose husband has been gunned down. She and her son are struggling with an enormous and crude cart (less like a settlers' covered wagon than something that Mother Courage herself might have disdained). Averill stops and talks with her sympathetically: he asks her what she's going to

do now that her husband's dead, whether she'll stay 'without a man'. She responds that they paid $150 for the land and then referring to her child: 'It's *our* land. We'll stay and work it.' As Averill drives away, Cimino cuts repeatedly between the woman and her child bent over, struggling to get the heavy cart moving and Averill sitting upright in the expensive gig – a birthday present to Ella (Isabelle Huppert). Averill has everything (as he later says to Ella, 'I could buy you anything'), the immigrant woman has next to nothing; Averill wants to leave, the immigrant wants to stay and work.

The exchange with the immigrant woman exemplifies the ambiguities of Averill's position, but it also highlights the way that the men and women of Sweetwater are seen working to gain a living from the land (the Kovach family butchering the steer carcase, tree trunks being dragged through the mud, women taking the place of oxen to pull a plough). In contrast, Canton maintains that he *owns* the land, but what we see him doing is organising others and making speeches. He cannot, however, maintain a grip on his empire without recruiting his mercenary army from amongst the wage-earning working class. The crucial meeting at which he offers a bounty for executing those on the death list takes place outside a factory. Although we don't see the nature of the work, it is characterised by harsh lighting and a soundtrack of heavy industrial machinery at work.

Here, as elsewhere in the film, the presentation of class interaction is complex and far from sentimental. Canton's reliance on the working class to do his dirty work is double-edged: the factory workers join the mercenary army for money; they show no recognition that they share anything with the people they are hired to kill. Perceptions of what is effectively a class war vary widely. The political and economic situation demands that characters act against their own wider interests in order to survive – as exemplified by Cully's initial inaction and by Nate Champion's role as a killer.

Nate Champion

Nate (himself a recent immigrant if we are to believe a conversation overheard in the Sweetwater dormitories) has been bought by Canton: 'You were hired to enforce the law. We are the law.' But Nate is presented as a complex character: he is not simply Canton's stooge. Although willing to shoot Kovach in cold blood, he contemptuously prevents another of Canton's mercenaries from killing a young immigrant (in spite of finding the 'boy' with a steer); he is hated and feared by the people of Sweetwater, and yet it is Nate who confronts Canton, accusing him of cowardice (an act that is far more dangerous than Averill's earlier altercation with Canton in the Gentleman's Club). Nate is the character who changes most in the course of the film, yet he remains curiously equivocal about his own motivation and the effects of his actions.

When Nate meets Averill in Sweetwater, we are led to expect a showdown, even a gunfight; what we get is an exchange of words: 'What do you want,

Nate?' asks Averill. 'How the Hell do I know? Get rich. Like you.' Nate doesn't know why he's doing what he is. As with the earlier exchange between Canton and Averill, this is ambiguous. It seems that for Nate there is no easy rationalisation of his actions: the materialist explanation (that he's driven into this by force of economic and political circumstances) is as unsatisfactory as attributing his motivation to personal envy.

From our knowledge of other Westerns, we might expect Nate's denunciation of Canton in the mercenary camp to contain at least the possibility of a positive resolution for the immigrants of Sweetwater, but Cimino refuses to allow individual actions to have the primacy we have become accustomed to. Whilst Nate exposes Canton as a coward, the confrontation is motivated primarily by his romantic attachment to Ella (he acts to save her, not to protect those on the death list), rather than by any growing awareness of the political realities of his situation. The shift in Nate may be set against a background in which the economics and politics of his situation are constantly stated, but it is a background to which he appears blind. After the encounter with Canton (which has forced the latter to reveal the full extent of collusion between the stockgrowers and the Establishment: 'I represent the full authority of the Government of the United States and the President . . .'), Nate returns to his newly 'wall-papered' shack and what he hopes will be domestic bliss with Ella, shutting out the political realities of their situation. Nate's actions appear to indicate that he believes individual action to be sufficient. He has confronted Canton; that will suffice . . . The charges of nihilism against *Heaven's Gate* seem to arise partly out of the film's refusal to accept the primacy of individual action, a refusal which is in itself a strong critique, not only of the Western, but also of most mainstream Hollywood films.

The change in Nate echoes an earlier shift in Cully, the stationmaster. When Averill arrives in Caspar, Cully is determined not to get involved: 'Every citizen's business is his affair – not mine dammit', he insists, unconsciously articulating an attitude which Canton and the Association rely upon (it echoes both Irvine's and Averill's) and which undermines any possibility of collective solidarity against Canton's fascist repression. But when Cully understands the scale of force that Canton is planning to use against the immigrants, he finds himself compelled to take action. He sets off with the intention of warning the people of Sweetwater that Canton's force is on its way. The subsequent killing of Cully, though less graphic than the great set-piece battle sequence near the end, is one of the most chilling moments in the film – partly because the killers turn it into a ruthless, cold-blooded game, partly because it illustrates so clearly that Canton will stop at nothing in his attempt to prevent collective action against the Association , but chiefly, I suspect, because the economic context of the killing is spelled out so explicitly: 'What do you think of my new suit here?' asks the mercenary. 'I paid $50 for it on credit. More'n likely pay it off real soon though.'

The personal nature of Nate's motivations and his failure to make the link between the limited personal view and the broader social and political context appear in a clearer perspective when seen in contrast with Cully's. Whether Nate is naive – so embedded in the complex social realities of his situation that clear-sightedness is virtually impossible – or wilfully unseeing, the 'blind spot' is even more pronounced in Ella.

Ella

Ella's bordello is a commercial undertaking (sex is a commodity for sale, barter and exchange); but whilst Ella strives for financial independence (she 'likes money'), she also frequently expresses a yearning for domesticity, for isolation from the world of commerce and capital exchange. This tension echoes those surrounding Nate. It creates the most difficult of the film's ambiguities, but also yields up its most provocative discourse. On one hand, we have Ella the hard-hearted, strong-headed businesswoman who makes Nate pay for his time with her, who insists that she can love two men equally, who is seen on several occasions working on her accounts. On the other, there is Ella who spends all day baking a pie for Averill, who is moved to tears by Nate's attempts to turn his shack into a haven of domestic bliss complete with newsprint for 'wallpaper', who wants Averill to marry her, and who allows her bordello to become a place where the men of Sweetwater can come for a sing-song with her girls.

A charge of sentimentality has been levelled against Cimino in connection with many of the scenes involving Ella; but the charge sticks only if his method in these sequences is fundamentally different to that employed elsewhere in the film. What we have in these 'sentimental' sequences is surely a series of personal visions, in some cases bids by Ella to realise her own fantasies, in others deliberate attempts to postpone a confrontation with the social and political realities of her world. The fantasy is one of independence, in which she believes she is 'free'. The irony is that she has gained her economic 'freedom' through commercial transactions with the world outside; she is dependent on it. Her refusal to acknowledge this dependence is perfectly imaged in her acceptance of stolen cattle – with all its appalling consequences – despite Nate's request that she 'stop taking steers for payment from these people'.

Consider Ella's role in the roller-skate dancing sequence – an exhilarating and joyous celebration of community in which difference and diversity appear to be tolerated. In the sequence she is not just a part of the community, she is a central figure within it. Nobody objects to her dancing publicly with Averill; she's surrounded by women who are active (who invite men to dance) and by vivacious smiling children who take an active part in all the proceedings. But the almost dream-like ending and sepia toning of the sequence offer a key to its broader function. At the end, Averill drags the drunken John Bridges (Jeff Bridges) out to sleep on a cart. We cut to a

Stills: Heaven's Gate. *Above – John Bridges (Jeff Bridges), Ella Watson (Isabelle Huppert) and Averill in the roller-skate dance. Right – Ella and Averill dance alone. Opposite – the community in turmoil. Immigrants by the Sweetwater church.*

close-up of Ella, who looks back into the hall; the other people have mysteriously disappeared. The meaning of this is not clear, but there is a strong suggestion that we should read the exhilaration of the dance as a self-consciously utopian vision, a dream of what might have been possible. More specifically, it seems to be Ella's vision as an immigrant, the American Dream of a world in which the community is strong, supportive and tolerant of difference, and in which the individual can achieve financial independence and commercial success, while enjoying all the pleasures and benefits of community life.

The fantasy is very appealing (both to Ella and to the audience), but it bears little relation to events in the rest of the film – in which Ella is *not* accepted by the community as a whole, the 'community' of Sweetwater is frequently riven with dissent, and Ella's presence is often bitterly resented. Everything she does is against a background of commerce. She lives in a world in which everything is shown in its economic context – but in which she insists that all her dealings with Nate, Averill and her other clients are her personal decisions, motivated only by her desire for personal freedom. Even after the women in her brothel have been slaughtered and she has been raped by the Association thugs, she still asserts to Averill that she wants economic independence. When Averill then leaves her, however, cattle can

be heard lowing, a poignant reminder that this independence is inextricably linked with a pattern of commerce that Canton is set on destroying. Framing Ella's actions in a manifestly critical perspective, it is the kind of understated masterstroke that characterises Cimino's methods throughout the film.

It is the tensions between the various perspectives (the Marxist, materialist view that all these events are underpinned by economic, social and political conditions and result from class-based oppression; and the liberal-humanist view of individuals struggling to do right both for themselves and for each other) that animate the film but are not resolved by it. The narrative closure is limited: the community is defeated; Nate and Ella are both gunned down in cold blood; Averill survives, but is desolate. Many questions remain unresolved; perhaps the most important is what constitutes an appropriate response to the brutal oppression seen in *Heaven's Gate*.

The Charge of Nihilism

Early tirades against the film frequently included the charge that it is a profoundly nihilistic work. Certainly, the battle, the gunning down of Ella and the epilogue are all deeply pessimistic. But pessimism and nihilism are not synonymous.

Cimino's representation of the immigrant community at Sweetwater is patently not a simple attempt to offer up a 'realistic' slice of late nineteenth-century life, but rather a complex exploration of the possibilities of diversity within a working-class immigrant group struggling to establish its identity as a community in the face of violent oppression. Although the community is ultimately defeated, the epilogue offers a telling commentary on that defeat. Averill is seen as an old man languishing with a woman – his wife? – on a steam yacht off Newport, Rhode Island. We're not given any indication of how he comes to be there. It's not important. What does matter is that he is extremely rich and that he has set himself apart from any sort of community. The only dialogue in this sequence is the woman saying: 'I'd like a cigarette.' Averill hands her one and lights it. She appears unable or unwilling to do anything for herself – in stark contrast to the world of Johnson County where women showed themselves clearly capable of accomplishing all the tasks traditionally held to be the preserve of men.

Averill's life is empty and meaningless. He has returned to a position of privilege and material wealth, and he appears to have resigned himself to the bleak implications of his class position. This is undeniably pessimistic, but those who charged Cimino with nihilism seem – quite unjustifiably – to have confused Averill's actions (which are indeed nihilistic) with

Cimino's film, which constantly frames the character's actions in a critical and broadening context. *Heaven's Gate* clearly proposes that those who have power and privilege but fail to act against repression are guilty of an appalling nihilism. This is disturbing and provocative, but is itself far from nihilistic.

It is rare for a Hollywood film, and particularly a Western, to propose any sort of alternative to individual action, let alone to articulate a proposal that individual action is an inadequate response to the sorts of oppression that we see in *Heaven's Gate*. But although the film is centrally about class-based and ethnically motivated oppression, it does not offer a panegyric in praise of the working class. Although it manifestly proposes the need for collective action and is highly critical of those who renege on their individual responsibilities to a community, it veers between examination of the effects of economic, social and political conditions and an account of events in which actions are seen to be driven by individual acts of personal loyalty or betrayal. It is this tension between the materialist and the liberal-humanist perspectives that makes the film both rich and fascinating. This tension is at the root of many other Westerns, but never before had it been explored so explicitly, or with such formal inventiveness.

That the film bombed at the box office, bankrupted a studio and finished off United Artists is common knowledge; it is the commonly accepted reason for the 'death of the Western' (reports of which have been greatly exaggerated). Might it also be that *Heaven's Gate* began a process of questioning class and gender roles, and of problematising the primacy of individual action, which no subsequent director of a Western could ignore, but which very few have been prepared to pick up and run with?

DANCES WITH WOLVES

Michael Walker

Dances with Wolves (1990) was a highly personal project for Kevin Costner. He began by encouraging his friend Michael Blake to write the novel and then the screenplay. However, Costner wanted to direct as well as star, and the major studios declined to finance an epic Western by a first-time director in which Native Americans played major roles and spoke a native language, Lakota. Nevertheless Costner persevered, forming Tig Productions with Jim Wilson to produce the film and continuing to seek finance from various sources. Eventually, through the agency of film financier Jake Eberts, Orion and the British-based Majestic Films jointly financed the film. Eberts has described his meeting with Costner and Wilson to discuss the film: 'It was one of the most impressive meetings I'd ever been to . . . Kevin was totally informed. He knew precisely which costumes and what props he wanted and what angle to shoot at and what lens to use' (Syd Field, *Four Screenplays*, Dell, New York, 1994. p.246). This confidence is apparent in the finished film: carping critics notwithstanding, one of the strongest features of *Dances with Wolves* is Costner's direction. He seems to know instinctively where to put the camera for a visually striking shot, he choreographs action with verve and he even makes effective use of point-of-view editing.

Although *Dances with Wolves* was a huge commercial success, critical opinion was strongly divided. The most carefully considered analyses I have found are nevertheless enthusiastic: *Positif* 360 (February 1991) has a dozen pages on the film by four different writers – one an expert on Native American history – and in *Film Quarterly*, Summer 1991, Edward D. Castillo, a Native American, whilst recognising that the film has historical flaws, is very positive about it. A useful summary of the film's 'contradictory positions' is provided by Robert Stam in *CineAction!* 32, Fall 1993; he argues that: 'the film constitutes a relatively progressive step 1) in its adoption of a pro-indigenous perspective, and 2) in respecting the linguistic integrity of the Native Americans; yet that 3) this progressive step is partially undermined by the traditional split portrayal of 'bad' Pawnee/good Sioux; that 4) it is further compromised by its elegiac emphasis on the remote past and 5) by the foregrounding of a Euro-American protagonist; 6) yet that this Euro-American focalisation, given the mass audience's identificatory propensities, also guaranteed the film's wide impact; and 7) that this impact indirectly helped open doors for Native American film-makers, without 8) dramatically improving the situation of most Native Americans, but also 9) altering the ways in which such films are likely to be made in the future'. Apart from point 8), which asks of the film an almost impossible achievement – how many films have changed history? – this seems to me a fair statement of the film's strengths and weaknesses: there are of course others. Although I see the film as much richer than has been generally recognised, it cannot handle all the more mythical generic material it pulls in, and on occasions resorts to some problematic ideological displacements.

In discussing the film, I shall be referring to the 234-minute longer version, released briefly in the cinema in Britain in 1992 and subsequently on video in a widescreen 'special edition'. Although it was the 180-minute version that grossed the millions and won the Oscars, the longer version is far more coherent and developed. The reduction to three hours removed much of value, including a number of the narrative's poetic correspondences. The major sections cut are noted in the admirable book published to accompany the film: *Dances with Wolves: The Illustrated Story of the Epic Film* by Costner, Blake and Wilson (Newmarket Press, New York, 1990). But dozens of smaller details disappeared, and several sequences – e.g. Dunbar's journey to the frontier – have also been re-edited, so that events occur in a different order.

From the point when Native Americans make their first appearance – about 45 minutes into the film – *Dances with Wolves* tells the relatively familiar story of a White man adopted into a Native American tribe, as in *Broken Arrow* (Delmer Daves, 1950) or, more recently, *Little Big Man* (Arthur Penn, 1970) and *A Man Called Horse* (Eliot Silverstein, 1970). The earlier part of the film, however, refers to a different generic tradition: the Vietnam war movie.

The Western as a genre all but disappeared around 1977, and the Vietnam war movie cycle, which began around this time, took over certain of the Western's concerns: the patrol through hostile territory, racist and brutal treatment of native peoples, an emphasis on male bonding and toughness. I would not wish to take the analogy too far, because these movies refer to only a fraction of the territory covered by the Western, and in one respect are markedly different: the sense of terror experienced by the soldiers in the Vietnam movie is rarely found in Westerns. The men *know* they do not belong in Vietnam, and the overall thrust of most of the movies is on getting the hell out of the country. Leslie Fiedler's notion in *The Return of the Vanishing American* (1968) that going west was linked with 'going crazy' – mentioned in my discussion of *Drum Beat* in the article on Delmer Daves in this book – is far more relevant when recast for the Vietnam movie. As Willard (Martin Sheen) journeys upriver into Vietcong territory in *Apocalypse Now* (Francis Ford Coppola, 1979), the White men he encounters are increasingly insane. Virtually every Vietnam movie portrayed the Americans in Vietnam as more or less unhinged, a comment on the insanity of the war itself. The film-makers ensured that the American servicemen registered in their minds and bodies the appalling traumas of the war.

In *Dances with Wolves*, as Lieutenant John Dunbar (Costner) makes the journey west, his route is marked by similar signs of insanity. At Fort Hays, Major Fambrough (Maury Chaykin), who scribbles out Dunbar's orders, is patently certifiable. Having sent Dunbar on his way, he pisses in his pants and shoots himself. The soldiers at the frontier post of Fort Sedgwick (unseen in the shorter version) are as spooked as the grunts upriver in *Apocalypse Now* – the enlisted men living in caves dug out of the bluff, the captain in charge barely able to communicate with them. But here, signalling one of the film's dominant themes, their craziness is specified above all in their litter, which is scattered over the bluff. They have converted their living quarters into a garbage dump, polluted the stream with the corpses of animals and are living like derelicts in filthy, improvised accommodation. They have been

Still: Dances with Wolves – *Dunbar (Kevin Costner) inured on the battlefield during the Civil War.*

reduced to this state partly through Sioux raiding parties – which have taken all their horses – but, more particularly, as a reflection of the film's ideological point that, like the American soldiers in Vietnam, they simply do not belong there. Instead of learning to live in harmony with their environment, as Dunbar will, they are being stretched to breaking point by their sense of isolation, which is focused on the failure of the US Army to resupply them. The dead animals in the stream demonstrate that there is plenty of game for them to survive on, but they seem to be almost starving. In the one scene in which we see all of them, the captain gathers them together, tells them they are getting out and 'the army can go to Hell' (the unspoken thought behind a number of the more radical Vietnam movies). In Blake's novel, they march back to Fort Hays, but there is no indication of this in the film. Indeed, the captain's final words suggest that they want nothing more to do with the army: they go off into the wilderness and oblivion.

Little Big Man and *Soldier Blue* (Ralph Nelson, 1970), both made before the Vietnam movie cycle, may be seen as Vietnam allegories, in which massacres of Native American villagers stand in for the massacres of the Vietnamese during the war. But whereas *Little Big Man* used America's murderous past (Washita River) to comment on its murderous present (My Lai), *Dances with Wolves* – consciously or not – uses associations with the Vietnam *movie* to suggest another perspective. First, the terror at being in Indian territory dramatically returns, as if to say that the soldiers here are no less aware than those in Vietnam that they do not belong in this country. This is a position suppressed in most earlier Westerns, with their confident assumption that 'America'

belonged to the Whites. (*Ulzana's Raid*, Robert Aldrich, 1972, is an exception, but it, too, may clearly be read as a Vietnam allegory – *see* Douglas Pye's article on it in this book.) Second, the pointless killing of animals and the pollution of the environment are examples of the sort of barbarism which has always appalled Native Americans about 'White civilisation'. And here, too, an analogy may be made with Vietnam: the soldiers' desecration of the countryside (the whole area of the fort is a brown scar in a verdant landscape) is the equivalent of the use of the defoliant, Agent Orange, to render the landscape infertile. By the time of *Thunderheart* (Michael Apted, 1992) – which deals with Native American issues in a modern setting – the use of the imagery and violence of the Vietnam war movie is foregrounded, the FBI villains even swooping in by helicopter to assault Native American settlements.

It thus seems significant that *Dances with Wolves* begins in the midst of war, and that its opening scene – in a Civil War field hospital, with the hero about to suffer amputation of his foot – evokes similar scenes in the Vietnam movie, e.g. Ron Kovic (Tom Cruise) in the field hospital in *Born on the Fourth of July* (Oliver Stone, 1989). But in *Dances with Wolves* what we then see, symbolically, is the hero's 'resurrection'. Dunbar escapes from the field hospital and rides a horse in a suicidal charge on the Confederate troops. Miraculously, he survives, and the overtones of resurrection are emphasised both in his 'Forgive me, Father' before his second

Stills: Dances with Wolves. *Above – Dunbar goes with the Lakotas to hunt buffalo. Opposite – the buffalo hunt. Dunbar introduces Kicking Bird (Graham Greene) to the use of the telescope.*

charge, and in his gesture of crucifixion as he rises in the saddle to surrender to the anticipated bullets (a gesture which could even be a specific reference to Sgt Elias, Willem Dafoe, at his moment of death in *Platoon*, Oliver Stone, 1986). Taken at face value, the scene is highly unconvincing, but thematically it is crucial. In effect, Dunbar forges himself as hero in preparation for the quest to come. Accounts of the film which attack it for its lack of verisimilitude miss the point: *Dances with Wolves* is much closer – on Northrop Frye's schema as outlined in *Anatomy of Criticism* (Princeton University Press, 1957) – to romance. Frye writes, 'In romance [nature is reduced] largely to the animal and vegetable world. Much of the hero's life is spent with animals, or at any rate the animals that are incurable romantics, such as horses, dogs and falcons . . .' (p.36). During the period at Fort Sedgwick when Dunbar clears up the mess left by the soldiers – and thus tacitly establishes his credentials as concerned enough about the natural world to be acceptable to the Sioux – he lives alone with his horse Cisco and **a** visiting wolf he names Two Socks.

The film seeks to depict the lifestyle of the Lakota Sioux before the Whites had invaded their territory to the extent that their culture was all but destroyed.

The film sustains the sense of the Lakotas as living in an Arcadian world by the way that the brutality of the Whites never quite reaches them: we see it directed against the environment, the wild animals and the White hero, but the Lakotas themselves remain just out of reach. The massacres that decimate the Native American communities in *Soldier Blue* and *Little Big Man* are held at bay.

This enables the film, quite self-consciously, to show the Lakotas living in their traditional way. Parallels may be drawn with *Little Big Man*: the White hero's adoption into a Native American tribe focusing in particular on his relationship with a 'wise leader' of the tribe; a positive view of the tribe's holistic lifestyle, coupled with a negative view of the imperialist desecrations of the Whites, a perspective that the hero comes to share; his marriage to a woman within the tribe. (There is also the ideologically suspect link that both films make the Pawnees into the 'bad' Indians, and introduce them as killers before the introduction of the 'good' Indians, the Cheyennes and Sioux.) *Dances with Wolves* lacks the vividness of some of the characterisations in *Little Big Man* – such as the heemaneh (homosexual) or the contrary (a fierce warrior who, except in battle, does everything backwards) – but it nevertheless conveys a strong sense of community, seen for example in the scenes in which members of the tribe gather together in a lodge either to discuss matters of concern or to tell stories at a communal meal.

In the longer version of the film, there are various additional scenes with the Sioux. Before the heated debate in which the tribe's leaders discuss what to do about the White man who has turned up at the Fort, we see Ten Bears (Floyd Red Crow Westerman), the ageing tribal leader, questioning his wife Pretty Shield (Doris Leader Charge) about the

behaviour of Kicking Bird (Graham Greene), the shaman. He wants to know what Kicking Bird's wife, Black Shawl (Tantoo Cardinal), has to say. This appeal to women for information clearly undermines the patriarchal structure of the tribe that is presented in the shorter version. In the ensuing scene (also cut in the shorter version) Ten Bears coaxes Kicking Bird to talk about the 'sign' he has seen that is bothering him (the first sighting of Dunbar); a child is present in the early part of the scene and is affectionately held by both men in turn. These scenes serve to shift the narrative weight of the film away from Dunbar during the period when he and the Lakota are unsure of each other. We also meet Stands with a Fist (Mary McDonnell) – a White woman adopted as a girl by the Lakotas after her family was butchered by the villainous Pawnees – when the body of her husband is brought back into the camp after a raid. We thus see her distress – as well as the attempts of other women to comfort her – before her bizarre appearance on the prairie mutilating herself.

Clearly, much of the appeal of the film lies in its romantic evocation of a lost world – the hero leaves behind the horrors brought by 'White civilisation' and steps into an almost mythical past. In the pastoral world of the film's Lakotas, everyone contributes to the life and work of the community, and relationships within the tribe are based on respect and affection. Although the most significant figures in the community are men – Ten Bears, Kicking Bird and a young warrior, Wind in His Hair (Rodney A. Grant) – their presentation is by no means uncritical: both Black Shawl and Pretty Shield have scenes in which they make fun of their husbands. About halfway through the film, after Dunbar has spent some time with the tribe – including living with

them during a buffalo hunt – he records his impressions in his journal, which we hear as a voice-over: 'I never knew a people so eager to laugh, so devoted to family and so dedicated to each other, and the only word which came to mind is harmony.' The expression is novelettish, but the import of the comments is fully supported by the film.

This has led – not unreasonably – to criticism that the film idealises the Lakotas: we see only their 'life-affirming' side. When Lakota warriors go to attack a Pawnee camp, the film does not show this, but instead shows the Pawnees coming to attack the Lakota camp, so that we see only the Pawnees as aggressors. However, the longer version of the film also includes a scene which shows a darker side to the Lakotas. Shortly before the buffalo hunt, Dunbar finds the tribe celebrating the killing of the White hunters who had earlier slaughtered the buffalo for their hides and tongues. The Lakotas are waving aloft the men's scalps; even Kicking Bird is involved. Dunbar is so repelled by this behaviour that he goes outside the encampment to sleep for the night. In fact, we see him do this in the shorter version, but his voice-over explaining his action makes no sense without the preceding scene.

The film also contains an intimation of the 'magical forces' which Frye (1957) identifies as a feature of romance. On his journey west from Fort Hays, Dunbar stands in the long grass and runs his hand over it – a gesture which links him to Kicking Bird, who is introduced later making the same gesture. But in the longer version, Dunbar's gesture is followed by a sudden gust of wind – emphasised by a track in to his back – which sends him leaping into the saddle and riding off at great speed after Timmons (Robert Pastorelli), the muleskinner who is driving the army supply wagon. We may read this as Dunbar sensing the presence of Indians – about whom he has just been talking – but the effect goes further, suggesting that Dunbar's presence is disturbing the forces of nature. In his discussion of the film, Castillo (1991) suggests that it may be read subtextually as 'a shamanistic allegory of death and rebirth'. On this reading, Dunbar is killed on the battlefield at the beginning of the film, and subsequent events are part of his journey to the Land of the Dead. (The possible reference to Elias's death in *Platoon* would strengthen this reading.) Castillo mentions the link between the gestures of Dunbar and Kicking Bird, suggesting that the latter is sensing 'a new spiritual presence in his midst' (p.22), and the wind reinforces his argument in its association of Dunbar with a mysterious power. Moreover, the first appearance of Kicking Bird ends with him experiencing exactly the same fear and also leaping on his horse and galloping off. But in his case, it is Dunbar himself, striding up to him naked (to stop him taking Cisco), who provokes the flight; in other words, it is Dunbar who possesses the power.

The ecological concerns of the film are also introduced during the journey to the frontier. After Dunbar's voice-over has commented on his travelling companion, 'He was quite possibly the foulest man I have ever met', Timmons signals his foulness by littering the prairie, throwing away an empty tin. (This, too, is cut in the shorter version.) In view of the number of times in John Ford's Westerns that John Wayne – with a suitably macho sweep – hurled empty canteens and bottles into the distance in Monument Valley, this is revisionist stuff. (I used to wonder whether some poor gofer was sent to retrieve the canteens; the bottles, of course, always smashed.) Timmons's smell leads Dunbar to make most of the journey at some distance from him – either on the back wagon or on his horse – and he recoils in repugnance when he accidentally rolls over to lie next to Timmons in his sleep.

The most powerful statement of the Whites' desecration of the environment occurs late in the movie, in another scene cut from the shorter version. Kicking Bird takes Dunbar to a holy site – according to legend, the place in the woods from which all animals originated. But they find that the site has been desecrated by White trappers and hunters who have left their litter – and the remnants of the animals they have killed – scattered over the woodland. The Whites bring both death and pollution.

When Dunbar is woken by Timmons's smell, he arouses the man by poking him in the buttocks with an arrow. On the return journey, Timmons is ambushed by Pawnee warriors, and the leader, who kills him, fires his first arrow to hit Timmons in precisely the same place. The connection is extremely significant, since it suggests a link between Dunbar and the Pawnee leader, a character referred to in the credits simply as Toughest Pawnee (Wes Studi). The Pawnees find Timmons because they see the smoke from his fire. But the film's narrative here deliberately misleads us: Costner cuts from the black smoke produced by Dunbar's fire to the Pawnees seeing smoke – naturally, we assume that it is Dunbar's. Given that Dunbar's smoke was produced by burning the waste left by the soldiers, and given that Timmons is characterised as 'foul', it seems that he is being killed in place of Dunbar. The link between the two assaults on Timmons then takes this further: it suggests that the Pawnee leader is acting for Dunbar, like his alter ego, killing Timmons because of the man's foulness. We note that this foulness is restated at the moment of Timmons's death: as the leader is about to scalp him, another Pawnee reacts with disgust at the smell of his blanket.

It is doubtful if such a subversive view of the hero was intended. I see it arising, rather, as a consequence of the need to purge Dunbar of the impulse to kill that his background – as a White man and a soldier – has planted in him. In the scene after Timmons's death, Dunbar sees the wolf for the first time. His reflex is to shoot it – twice he raises his rifle – but he desists, no longer automatically reacting as a killer. It's as if the Pawnee leader carries away Dunbar's inner violence. Not until the Pawnee attack on the Lakota village, two-thirds of the way through the film, do we see Dunbar kill, and here it is in defence of the village which at this point is mainly occupied by women, children and old men.

The Pawnee attack on the village is led by the same highly aggressive warrior. (Wes Studi moved

Still: Dances with Wolves – *Stands with a Fist (Mary McDonnell) and Dunbar.*

on to play Magua in *The Last of the Mohicans*, Michael Mann, 1992, and Geronimo in *Geronimo: An American Legend*, Walter Hill, 1994.) He is killed during the attack, and one would expect, if the sense of him as Dunbar's alter ego were to be sustained, that it would be Dunbar who killed him. In fact, an earlier scene in the film provides a far more remarkable connection. As Dunbar rides to and fro in front of the Confederate troops, he is shadowed, on horseback, by their leader, Tucker (Frank P. Constanza), riding parallel to him behind the soldiers. Although Tucker's men are firing and missing, it is not until the end of Dunbar's second pass that Tucker gives the order for a marksman to shoot him: it's as if Tucker wants first to see just what Dunbar is going to do. Dunbar is saved when the marksman himself is shot by the Union troops who have been mobilised by Dunbar's charge. This choreography is then repeated at the end of the Pawnee attack. First, the Pawnee leader is hit in the leg by an arrow, a wound that echoes Dunbar's at the beginning of the film. Then he rides to and fro among the Lakota villagers, seeking a way out. This leads him down to the stream on the edge of the village and, flanked on both sides by Lakotas armed with guns – structurally duplicating Dunbar's ride between the two lines of troops – he rides along the stream. Dunbar (echoing Tucker's ride) runs along the bank, shadowing him. Eventually, seeing that he is totally surrounded, the Pawnee lifts up his club, giving his

war cry – paralleling Dunbar's gesture of crucifixion – and is shot by the Sioux. Although Dunbar is by this time among the Sioux, he does not shoot, but on his forehead is a splash of blood in precisely the spot where the marksman was shot. Dunbar's charge is thus re-enacted in such a way that his alter ego is killed, and he himself is imaged as a combination of the two men who, during the charge, should have killed him: the officer who gave the order and the marksman who was about to fire. Dunbar witnesses this as if stunned, but his voice-over goes on to identify it as the moment he discovered his true identity: 'I'd never known who John Dunbar was . . . But, as I heard my Sioux name being called over and over, I knew for the first time who I really was.' It's as if, by witnessing the Pawnee leader killed as he himself had expected to die, Dunbar is finally liberated from his past and is resurrected – as Dances with Wolves.

Remarkable though this connection between White 'hero' and Indian 'villain' undoubtedly is, it is ultimately not as coherent as that between, say, Ethan (John Wayne) and Scar (Henry Brandon) in *The Searchers* (John Ford, 1956). When Scar rapes Martha (Dorothy Jordan) and kills her and the rest of her family, this may be related with some precision to Ethan's unconscious desires. But the only person we see the Pawnee leader kill during the attack on the Lakota camp is Stone Calf (Jimmy Herman), an ageing warrior and friend of Ten Bears, and there seems to be no reason why Dunbar might unconsciously wish Stone Calf dead. Indeed, the man has been entirely helpful and supportive: it is Stone Calf, for example, who elucidates Stands with a Fist's contradictory behaviour by explaining that she is in mourning for her dead husband. Logically, the figure whom Dunbar might unconsciously resent at this point would be Kicking Bird, since it is he – in decreeing how long Stands with a Fist's period of mourning must last – who prevents her affair with Dunbar being officially recognised. But it would be too disruptive of the film's project for Kicking Bird to die – so he is safely elsewhere, raiding the Pawnees – just as it would be too damaging for the harmony of the tribe if Ten Bears were killed. Stone Calf becomes the victim, in effect, by displacement.

Other ways in which Dunbar is criticised in the film are more obvious. The triteness of most of his journal entries is complemented by his drawings, which suggest those in a child's story book. There is a Bible on Dunbar's desk at Fort Sedgwick, but he is never shown reading it: that would complicate the film's project. The only thing we see him read is his journal, which thus comes to define the horizons of his thought. In an article on the film in *Wasafiri* 17 (Spring 1993), Megan Stern writes: 'His banal description of the wilderness when he first arrives at Fort Sedgwick suggests a *tabula rasa*: "The country is everything I dreamed it would be. There could be no place like this on earth" ' (p.51).

More consciously, the film is prepared to view

Dunbar comically, particularly in his early encounters with the Lakotas: appearing naked before Kicking Bird; fainting after his first confrontation with Wind in his Hair; knocking himself out when the teenage boys steal Cisco. In this last episode, his comic incompetence is echoed in that of the boys: Dunbar knocks himself out on the door lintel; Otter (Michael Spears) is yanked off his horse by Cisco and deposited ignominiously on the ground. Like the drawings in the journal, the connection links Dunbar with 'the childlike'. In a later scene (cut in the shorter version) in which Stands with a Fist is acting as interpreter, Dunbar's voice-over says of himself and Kicking Bird 'Like two children we are anxious to know more about each other' as, on the horizon, the three of them – Stands with a Fist with a degree of reluctance at this frivolousness – throw stones.

At the same time, there are events that reinforce Dunbar as hero which, particularly in the instances where he is privileged over the Sioux, suggests a White ethnocentricity which the film was unable fully to purge. Examples are the discovery of the buffalo herd and the way in which Dunbar becomes the figure who saves the Lakota camp from the Pawnees through providing the people with rifles. The former is a plot device to enable him to win the gratitude of the Lakota; the latter is more sinister, since it relies on the use of the very weapons which historically gave the Whites such military superiority over the Native American tribes. Dunbar finally realises his true identity only after having corrupted the Lakota people with White weapons of destruction.

Dunbar's giving guns to the Lakotas is nevertheless an example of the ways in which the film reverses

Stills: Dances with Wolves. *Above – Dunbar returns the wounded Stands with a Fist to the Lakota camp. Opposite – Dunbar and Stands with a Fist after first making love.*

Westerns' traditional attitude towards Native Americans. Earlier, Dunbar buried the guns in order to prevent them falling into the hands of the Sioux; now he digs them up in order to arm the Sioux. This thread running through the film begins with the familiar 'Nothing I've been told about these people is correct' and culminates in the very satisfying scene in which the hero, who has been taken prisoner by White soldiers, is rescued by the Sioux, who ruthlessly kill all the soldiers.

Stands with a Fist also goes against traditional Western representation. As a White 'captive' (the word itself betraying the ideological bias), she is entirely happy living with the Sioux; indeed, she is at first frightened by Dunbar's arrival in the vicinity because she fears that White men will come and take her away. Through Mary McDonnell's excellent performance (Castillo praises her 'authentic Lakota cadence and accent'), we get a strong sense of a woman who has integrated extremely well into Native American society – the opposite of most earlier representations of such figures: *see* Edward Countryman's entry on captivity narratives in Buscombe (1988). Her presence in the film – usually, of course,

it is a Native American woman whom the White hero falls for – is not merely a convenient device to get over the problem of communication between Dunbar and the Lakotas. It also answers those earlier representations in which White 'captive' women who actually wanted to remain with the tribe were considered deviant, e.g. Jennie McKeever (Vera Miles) in *The Charge at Feather River* (Gordon Douglas, 1953), who is killed for such deviance.

Dunbar's first meeting with Stands with a Fist is highly significant. After the Lakotas have repeatedly attempted to steal Cisco, Dunbar decides that he will ride out to confront them, and he dresses up in his full military regalia, even carrying the American flag. This is how he meets Stands with a Fist, who has gone on to the prairie to mourn the death of her husband, a mourning that includes self-mutilation with a knife. From her point of view, she is seeing Dunbar as exactly the monster she thinks he is – an American soldier. Blake and Costner even emphasise this by the striking device of having the flag blow over Dunbar's face as she first turns to see him. But, from his point of view, the state of Stands with a Fist – hands and skirt bloody – is an echo of the image of the army surgeons in the opening shots of the film (cut in the shorter version). If we can take it that this image 'haunts' Dunbar, and that its psychic meaning is the threat of castration, then the film is in effect neutralising the threat by projecting the image in all its bloodiness on to a woman who is not harming a man, but herself. The process of healing for both of them then begins when Dunbar binds her wounds and takes her back to the Lakota camp. A brilliant touch is that he uses the American flag to bind the wounds. (The film is, however, discreet enough not to show him tearing it up on-screen, which would have almost certainly have affected the box-office in middle America.)

For Stands with a Fist, the necessary healing is both emotional and physical: she needs to get over the loss of her husband and recover from her wounds. For Dunbar, it is spiritual. He has to shed all the trappings of a White military officer so that he is able to write in his journal of the Lakotas, 'I find myself drawn to them in ways stronger than my obligations to the military' (cut in the shorter version). Crucial to this is his change of costume: after the buffalo hunt, he exchanges his cavalry jacket and hat for a breastplate and knife; later, he shaves his moustache and wears feathers in his hair and a Native American shirt.

The love affair between hero and heroine completes the healing for both of them. Although it develops along fairly predictable lines – even to the extent of beginning whilst the patriarchal figure, Kicking Bird, is away from camp – it gains from the way in which the Lakotas collude in promoting the affair. Black Shawl encourages Stands with a Fist by telling her that the people 'are proud of the medicine you are making with Dances with Wolves'. When Kicking Bird returns to camp, Black Shawl tells him about the affair and so prompts him to release Stands with a Fist from her mourning. Wind in his Hair and Smiles a Lot (Nathan Lee Chasing His Horse) organise the villagers to supply Dunbar with the requisite goods, so that he can pay for his bride in the traditional manner (cut in the shorter version). Kicking Bird then conducts the wedding ceremony, for which Stands with a Fist – in a fine example of iconographic continuity displacing historical accuracy – wears a white buckskin dress remarkably similar to the wedding dress worn by Sonseeahray (Debra Paget) in Broken Arrow (Delmer Daves, 1950).

When Black Shawl first talks to Kicking Bird about the affair, he asks what people are saying. She answers, 'They like the match . . . It makes sense. They are both White.' This emphasises the film's avoidance of the issue of miscegenation, another criticism that has been levelled against it. To an extent, the criticism is fair; on the other hand, if Stands with a Fist were Native American, the film would have lacked a positive representation of a White 'captive'. However, if the ending of the film is compared with that of White Feather (Robert D. Webb, 1955), we can see that Stands with a Fist's Whiteness enables the film to focus more clearly on the racial difference in the characters' destinies. White Feather – which I discuss in my article on Daves in this book – ends with the White hero and the Native American heroine leaving the tribe and going off into White society for a 'happy ending'. Dances with Wolves shows the two equivalent figures leaving the tribe and going

off into White society for a 'tragic ending'. Dunbar says that he is going to talk to those who will listen, but the text that comes up over the last shot – which records the ensuing destruction of the way of life of the Plains Indians – tells us that, whatever he did, it was futile. The cross-cutting to the advancing American troops during the last five minutes of the film communicates the inevitability of the tribe being hunted down: the film ends, as it were, in narrative suspension. The departure of the two White characters from the tribe then emphasises the racial divide: it is possible for them, as Whites, to escape the destruction, an option unavailable to the Lakotas. Because the White society into which they are going is so discredited, it would have been particularly problematic for Stands with a Fist were she Native American. In contrast to White Feather, everything that is of value is focused on the past, in the scenes with the tribe. This gives to the ending a powerful sense of loss, and throws a shadow back over those scenes, converting them, in Frye's terms, from pastoral to elegiac.

By the time the film reaches the ending, however, it has brought into play another structure: that of the melodrama of protest. In this – see my article 'Melodrama and the American Cinema' in Movie 29/30, Summer 1982 – 'the world depicted is completely polarised, and our sympathies are enlisted unequivocally with a group of people – defined by race, nationality, class or political creed – who are "innocents", victims of persecution, exploitation or oppression. The oppressors/exploiters are usually heavily caricatured.' A key feature of the structure is 'the death of (an) 'innocent', or innocents (used) . . . as an emotional device, to rouse not just the people in the film, but those in the audience as well' (p.14). Since the publication of the article, a number of film-makers seem to have followed the formula with some care: Cry Freedom (Richard Attenborough, 1987) even goes into flashback in order to end with the deaths of its innocents (children killed in the 1976 Soweto protests).

Dances with Wolves begins to use the rhetoric of the melodrama of protest from the moment that Dunbar – returning to Fort Sedgwick to pick up his journal – rides over the hill and is fired at by army troops who have occupied the fort and assume he is an Indian. First, Cisco is killed, and then Dunbar, knocked out with a rifle butt, is taken prisoner. When he comes to, he cites his journal to explain his presence, but it has been spirited away: we later see pages being torn from it by an illiterate soldier, Spivey (Tony Pierce), as toilet paper. The major (Wayne Grace) becomes more suspicious of Dunbar – particularly when he declines to answer why he is out of uniform – and the troops get more aggressive towards him: he suffers a series of assaults that induce him to stop speaking English and to address them in Lakota. With the exception of one relatively sympathetic officer, Lieutenant Elgi (Charles Rocket), the soldiers are caricatured in the manner characteristic of the melodrama of protest, and our emotions are correspondingly manipulated against them. When Dunbar is taken in chains by wagon back to Fort Hays to be hanged as a traitor, the soldiers escorting him see Two Socks on a hilltop and shoot him, too.

What is unusual here is that the innocents who are killed are animals. At the same time, the film stresses the melodramatic connection with Dunbar in that each of the three rifle blows to the head he receives occur as a result of his concern for the animals: the first two for Cisco; the third for Two Socks. It's as if the deaths of the animals are heightened by being translated into assaults on the body of the hero. But the film goes a stage further. As Dunbar and Stands with a Fist ride away at the end, a wolf howls on a clifftop. The innocent who was earlier killed is here symbolically resurrected. This invocation of the very spirit of protest – it's as if the wolf is signalling that those who were destroyed will rise again – adds another component to the complexity of the film's ending.

In order to unravel exactly what the film is doing here, we need to look more closely at the function of the wolf. In the longer version, the wolf makes its first appearance watching the column of soldiers depart from Fort Sedgwick. From a shot of the soldiers in the distance the camera pans to the wolf on a hilltop in the foreground; here the wolf is in the place of the Native American. It reappears immediately after Dunbar has moved into the Fort and, if we relate its subsequent appearances to the other narrative events, a pattern emerges. The first time it follows Dunbar when he rides on the prairie is when he discards his saddle (cut from the shorter version). It declines to follow when he rides off to visit the Lakota camp in his military regalia. (What the wolf sees – Costner uses a point-of-view shot – is the American flag sticking up over the brow of the hill as Dunbar rides past. The wolf is obviously far too intelligent to follow that.) Later, it watches him dance Native American style around a fire at night: again Costner includes shots from the wolf's point of view. This is followed by the scene in which the wolf follows Dunbar so far towards the Lakota camp that he tries to send it back, leading into the game the wolf plays with him which, witnessed by a group of Lakota warriors, results in Dunbar being named Dances with Wolves. The first time the wolf takes food from his hand is followed by the first sex scene. At each stage, the wolf marks Dunbar's gradual shedding of his military persona and adoption of a Native American one.

When the wolf is finally shot and killed, it is once more on the high ground, overlooking the soldiers below. Behind it, out of sight on the other side of the hill, are Lakota warriors. Accordingly, their attack on the soldiers is the first manifestation of protest. On our behalf – for we have been aroused by the mistreatment of the hero and the death of the wolf – they rise up and kill the oppressors. But the association between wolf and Lakotas is purely symbolic: until this point, the wolf has invariably fled from them and, by cutting from Dunbar receiving his Lakota name to a warrior wearing a wolf's hide, Costner emphasises their very different attitudes to the animal (the characteristics of the wolf were thought to transfer to the hide's wearer). Insofar as the rhetoric of the melodrama of protest is being mobilised on behalf of the Native American, it is done by displacement: through the savage treatment meted out to the White hero and his two animals. One tends to feel that the film, here, is rather evading the issue – another example of its failure to get a complete grip on all the material that it is bringing into play. Not until the text over the last shot is the decimation of the Native Americans by the Whites explicitly referred to.

The symbolic return of the wolf at the end of the film is preceded by the physical return of the journal, which is Smiles a Lot's parting gift to Dunbar. After the Lakota attack, it fell into the river as Spivey's body was searched for booty, and we last saw it floating downstream. Its return at the end – with its text blurred but legible – again seems miraculous. Given that the journal led to Dunbar's capture and the Lakota's rescuing him prompted the military to commence their ruthless hunting down of the tribe, the journal is from one point of view a curse: the one item of Dunbar's White past he felt unable to give up. But at the same time, it is the sole record of Dunbar's experiences – in other words, it serves as a testament to the 'truth' about the Native Americans, much as the biography of Steve Biko (Denzel Washington) that Donald Woods (Kevin Kline) writes and smuggles out of South Africa in manuscript at the end of *Cry Freedom* tells the 'truth' about apartheid. A crucial feature of the melodrama of protest is the sense that, after the end of the film, the struggle will go on. In *Cry Freedom*, the film itself arises out of the manuscript, and its story represents a part of the struggle. In *Dances with Wolves*, the journal is too simplistic to function in quite the same way, but the principle is similar: the hero returns to 'civilisation' with an alternative account of the lives of the indigenous peoples, and that account is in turn embedded in the film we have seen.

For all its faults, *Dances with Wolves* – in its longer version, at least – is a highly commendable piece of work. For once, the relative blandness of Costner as star – the *tabula rasa* quality that Megan Stern refers to – works for the film, as it enables him to integrate into a predominantly Native American cast without excessively dominating. But it is the way he coordinates all the elements of the film into a whole that is his real achievement. Even if many of the film's more remarkable features seem unconscious, they are nevertheless there, a tribute to Costner pursuing his artistic vision despite the enormous problems of mounting such a production. When the Lakotas are debating what to do about the sudden appearance of a White man at the Fort, Kicking Bear says: 'When I see one White man alone without fear in our country . . . I see someone who might speak for all the White people . . . I think this is a person with whom treaties might be struck.' Recast to refer to Costner in his capacity as someone whom the Native Americans could trust to speak for them, this gives a good idea of his achievement. Whereas the journal is Dunbar's rather naive testament, the film is Costner's far more complex and powerful one.

UNFORGIVEN

Leighton Grist

In the first edition of *The BFI Companion to the Western*, Edward Buscombe tempers his observation of the Western's apparent demise by stating (with some prescience, as it turns out) that it 'may surprise us yet' (Buscombe, 1988, p.54). In 1991, *Dances with Wolves* (Kevin Costner, 1990) compounded its box-office success by becoming the first Western since *Cimarron* (Wesley Ruggles, 1931), and only the second ever, to win the Best Picture Academy Award, with its actor/director Costner winning the award for Best Director. The coup was repeated by *Unforgiven* (1992) and its actor/director Clint Eastwood at the 1993 awards. *Unforgiven* was also a sizeable commercial success, taking over $100 million at the American box office alone. The films have been followed by a spate of other Westerns, including, in 1993, *Posse* (Mario Van Peebles), *Tombstone* (George P. Cosmatos), and *The Ballad of Little Jo* (Maggie Greenwald), and, in 1994, *Geronimo: An American Legend* (Walter Hill) and *Wyatt Earp* (Lawrence Kasdan).

None of these films reproduced the box-office success of *Dances with Wolves* or *Unforgiven*, which had undoubtedly acted as a spur to their production, but, seen as a whole, the revival contains a number of serious attempts to grapple once again with the traditions of the Western. The films cited are revisionist in intention. *Dances with Wolves* and *Geronimo: An American Legend* seek to correct the genre's predominantly negative representation of Native Americans, *Posse* attempts to revise our perception of the role of Blacks in the history of the West (and the Western), *The Ballad of Little Jo* challenges the genre's representation of gender, *Tombstone* suggests that the West wasn't won by collective morality, but by greed and violence, and *Wyatt Earp* bids to de-mythicise its eponymous hero.

The previous major period of revisionism in the Western, impelled by the ideological upheavals of the 1960s and 1970s, effectively ended the genre's central role in Hollywood production. An analogous, if less seismic context may, following the reactionary 'eighties, be responsible for the 'nineties revival. Witness the incidence of increasingly overt racial and sexual tensions, the rise (for good or ill) of political correctness, and the election in 1992 on a comparatively 'progressive' platform of the first Democratic president for twelve years. Within this context, the reworking of the Western, whatever its commercial possibilities, has a certain logic. Of all the major genres, the Western is the most concerned with American history, with representing the establishment of social and national order and, crucially, with defining dramatically the terms of such an order. Challenging the conventions of the Western thus offers the opportunity to query the dominant order at its source. The history of *Unforgiven* actually links the two periods – its revisionism is rooted in David Webb Peoples's script, which was written in the 1970s. This may partly account for the film's challenge to conventional expectations and for the way it problematises the familiar ideological assumptions of the genre. Certainly, *Unforgiven* is the most rigorous and thematically cohesive of the 'nineties Westerns.

The question of order is raised immediately by *Unforgiven*'s motivating narrative disruption. After its opening credits, the film cuts to the town of Big Whiskey, Wyoming, and a brutal attack on a whore, Delilah (Anna Thomson), by a cowboy, Quick Mike (David Mucci), who slashes her face repeatedly with a knife. This is halted only when the owner of Greely's saloon-cum-whorehouse, Skinny (Anthony James), holds a cocked pistol to Quick Mike's head. Cut to Big Whiskey's dark, storm-lashed street, which the town's sheriff, Little Bill Daggett (Gene Hackman), crosses with a deputy, Clyde (Ron White), who tells Little Bill that Skinny has threatened to shoot Quick Mike and his younger partner, Davey (Rob Campbell). Standing in judgment over the bound pair, Little Bill sends Clyde for a bullwhip, only for Skinny to interject that whipping 'ain't gonna settle this'. Producing a 'lawful contract', he declares that Delilah represents 'an investment of capital', whose commodity value has been irreparably impaired by her injuries. Little Bill accordingly fines rather than whips the suspects, ordering Quick Mike, who 'did the cutting', to bring in five and Davey two horses for Skinny in the spring.

As the sequence thus moves from violence, via threats of revenge killing and corporal punishment, to material reparation, it concisely represents the shift from lawlessness to order, savagery to civilisation, that is central to the Western. Yet as the sequence similarly charts a movement from human – if bloody – justice to property rights, the terms of this order are patently problematised. More specifically, as it describes an emerging, plainly gendered collocation of money and power, the sequence offers a mordant critique of patriarchal capitalism. Not only is its establishment suggested to be circumstantially contingent, but its alienating oppressiveness is laid bare by the way the Skinny callously refers to Delilah, whom we have seen being viciously maimed, as 'damaged property'.

Seeking justice, the whores pledge their savings and future earnings to pay a hired gun $1,000 to kill Quick Mike and Davey. One of the whores, Strawberry Alice (Frances Fisher), overtly challenges the 'legal' correlation of women with property, with horses: 'Just because we let them smelly fools ride us like horses don't mean we gotta let 'em brand us like horses'. While this implies a positive, 'feminist' impulse, it also underlines the women's social, sexual and economic subordination: their decision ironically confirms their subjection to violent, exploitative masculine power. As Skinny, learning of the whores' plan and fearing their lack of funds, warns vindictively, 'The kind of people who'll come after that thousand won't tolerate you not having it. They won't just tear up your face a little.' This threat of violence again reflects negatively on Big Whiskey's presumptive order. Whereas many Westerns end with an assertion of law and the establishment of order, which imply the removal of the threat of, and the need for, violence, *Unforgiven* begins with law asserting itself but with violence barely contained.

Throughout the genre, law is related to the exclusion of otherness, whether of 'deviant' elements or of Native Americans. That Big Whiskey's embryonic patriarchy is based on exclusion is implied by Little Bill's enforcement of 'Ordinance 14' – 'No Firearms In Big Whiskey' – which is announced on a sign at the edge of town. Generically, such an ordinance tends to be an indication of the establishment of the Law, but in Big Whiskey it seems to apply only to outsiders – apart from Little Bill and his deputies having guns, Skinny has a pistol. Similarly suggestive is the rationale that Little Bill offers Strawberry Alice for merely fining Quick Mike and Davey: 'It ain't like they was tramps or loafers or bad men . . . they were just hard-working boys that was foolish.' Quick Mike and Davey aren't simply local and not 'deviant' but – like Skinny – they're male, White, and 'American'.

In the Western, the advent of civilisation is often confirmed by the coming of the railroad. This is true of *Unforgiven*, but subtly qualified in line with Big Whiskey's uncertain order and its rudimentary, one-street status: the trains do not actually pass through the town, and passengers instead have to travel from the railroad to Big Whiskey by stagecoach. While the railroad brings civilisation's benefits, it also brings its complexities. Not least, it threatens the Western's exclusionary order by affording easy access to information, thereby encouraging change and disruption. In *Unforgiven*, the railroad is explicitly represented as connecting Big Whiskey with the rest of the country. When Skinny tells Little Bill that the whores have been talking to their cowboy clients about the $1,000 bounty, Little Bill is led to ponder that as the cowboys have been riding beef 'to Kansas and Cheyenne', the 'word's probably got all the way down to Texas'. At this point, we hear the sound of a train whistle, which is followed by a shot of steam from the locomotive over some trees, a sight that utterly undermines Skinny's reassurance that 'nobody's gonna come clear from Texas'.

It is by railroad that the expatriate assassin, English Bob (Richard Harris) – an embodiment of cultural otherness – is shown travelling towards Big Whiskey and the whores' $1,000. The headline in a newspaper being read on the train announces the

Still: Unforgiven – *Little Bill Daggett (Gene Hackman) and Srawberry Alice (Frances Fisher).*

295

assassination of President Garfield, a disruption to national order which informs a dispute between English Bob and another passenger, who is angry at the suggestion that assassinations would cease if America had a monarch instead of a president. English Bob continues his monarchist tirade when he arrives at Big Whiskey. Like Little Bill's authority, English Bob's monarchism provides an asserted superiority on the basis of which he can patronise Americans or shoot Chinamen for the railroad, which is his job. English Bob's apparent civility – like that of Big Whiskey – is revealed to be a thin veneer that inadequately covers a more savage reality. Not only is he a professional killer, but he tries unsuccessfully to goad his fellow passenger into going for his gun so that he can shoot him, and when he's driven, defeated, from Big Whiskey, his measured, 'aristocratic' speech is replaced by peevish insults and a coarse Cockney accent.

Indeed, in *Unforgiven*'s refocusing of the Western's interplay of civilisation and savagery, the negation of apparent order by underlying violence is the prime narrative motif, the encapsulation of its social vision. This structures the representation of Little Bill. At first, he appears fittingly to manifest the order that he upholds. After fining Quick Mike and Davey, he tries to quieten Strawberry Alice, who wants the pair to be hanged, by saying, 'Haven't you seen enough blood for one night?' He's also, in an obvious, but still potent, expression of civilisation, building a house with a porch where he can 'sit of an evening, smoke my pipe, drink coffee, and watch the sunset'. Yet, as with the law that he embodies, tensions are implied from the start. The fines are backed up by the *threat* of whipping, while, as Clyde notes, there's not 'a straight angle in that whole goddamn porch, or in the whole house'. This is said as Clyde and Little Bill's other deputies prepare

Still: Unforgiven – *English Bob (Richard Harris) and his biographer, W.W. Beauchamp (Saul Rubinek).*

to meet English Bob, which they do with an oppressive show of force as the deputies surround English Bob and his biographer, W.W. Beauchamp (Saul Rubinek), with loaded guns. The scene ends with Little Bill beating and kicking English Bob unconscious. This violent repression of otherness is motivated less by moral principle than by the pragmatic impulse to warn off other assassins. The revelation of Little Bill's violence also ironically extends his likeness to English Bob, compounding which is his bemoaning a lack of 'dangerous men', 'like old Bob, like me', and the way that he echoes English Bob's action on the train by trying to incite the imprisoned English Bob into holding a loaded pistol so that he can shoot him.

Little Bill's treatment of English Bob is replayed when William Munny (Eastwood) arrives in Big Whiskey with his partners, Ned Logan (Morgan Freeman) and the Schofield Kid (Jaimz Woolvett), to claim the whores' bounty. While his partners are busy with the whores upstairs, Munny is left alone in the saloon. He is surrounded by armed deputies, and Little Bill attempts to bully him into drawing his pistol. Then, in another parallel with English Bod, Little Bill disarms Munny before brutally assaulting him. With Munny weak with fever, any lingering moral validation that Little Bill's authority may have held is unequivocally destroyed. This is ensured when he goes on to hit Strawberry Alice vindictively to extract information about Ned and the Kid. Reflecting both Quick Mike's initial violence against Delilah and Skinny's manhandling of Strawberry Alice to extract details of the whores' plan, it contributes to a pattern that implicates Big Whiskey's patriarchal order as a whole.

Central to *Unforgiven*, then, is the implication that any consideration of America's social order must focus on the problem of violence. This has to be seen in the context of the climate of violence in contemporary America. As Buscombe notes, moreover, 'many have argued that the pervasiveness of a "gun culture" within American society derives ultimately from the Western; that the anachronistic continuation into contemporary urban life of the frontier mentality is the main cause of America's appalling crime rate' (Buscombe, 1988, p.132). Given this, the Western would again seem to afford a prime site for ideological correction.

The national connotations of the film's social critique are foregrounded as Little Bill confronts and assaults English Bob. It is Independence Day, and Little Bill is repeatedly backed either by the Stars and Stripes or by the red, white and blue bunting that decorates the street. In its representation of an exclusionary patriarchal order, which reacts aggressively to challenge, and an oppressed subordinate group, whose sense of injustice prompts it to seek violent retribution, *Unforgiven*, while set in the 1880s and written in the 1970s, offers distinct parallels with early 1990s America. These have been heightened by the film happening to be released after the Rodney King court case and the ensuing Los Angeles riots, particularly as Little Bill's culminating atrocity in *Unforgiven* is the torturing to death of Ned, who is Black. Not only does the killing evoke a violent, destructive response, but – while we don't actually see Ned's death – the representation of his oppression relates it to the history of American racism. The means of Ned's death is whipping, a traditional punishment for runaway slaves, while his night-time arrest, lit by flaming torches, is redolent of the Ku Klux Klan or a lynch mob.

From the first, *Unforgiven* represents violence as brutal, dreadful, squalid: anything but noble or ennobling. The attack on Delilah is represented in a disturbing, rapidly edited alternation of viciousness and terror; Little Bill's assaults on English Bob and Munny are extended and graphically jarring; the Kid shoots a powerless Quick Mike who is taking a shit. This last is preceded by Davey's killing, an act which is excruciatingly drawn out as Munny takes three rifle shots to finish off the scared, injured cowboy, while the Kid panics and Davey's companions are petrified with fear. The film stresses violence's physical and emotional effects in equal measure. Physically, there are the visual marks of Delilah's scars and the pummelled faces of English Bob and Munny. Emotionally, we are given the disquieting spectacle of Munny, after being beaten up, being made to crawl, humiliated and impotent, from Greely's, and the harrowing sound of Davey calling for water after his fatal wounding. In *Unforgiven*, Peoples and Eastwood also successfully suggest the consequences of violence for the 'perpetrator as well as the victim' (Eastwood quoted by John C. Tibbetts, 'Clint Eastwood and the Machinery of Violence', *Literature/Film Quarterly*, vol.21, no.1, 1993, p.16). Little Bill's apparent enjoyment of violence emboldens him to commit ever more sadistic acts. By contrast, Ned, who, like Munny, has come out of 'retirement' from a violent past to ride to Big Whiskey, is agonisingly unable to kill Davey although he has managed to shoot Davey's horse. When Davey is finally dead, close-ups of Ned and Munny powerfully convey their horror at murdering another human.

This emphasis on the disturbing nature of violence contests its more familiar generic representation. While most Westerns deal with the ideological motivations and consequences of violence, far fewer examine the destructive reality, the actual effects of violent acts. Since the 'sixties, violence in the Western has been represented with differing degrees of explicitness, but the intention has rarely been to convey pain. This is largely true of Eastwood's preceding Westerns, in which violence can range from the cursory to – in various stylised, comic or censurable ways – the pleasurable.

Unforgiven's representation of violence is played off against Beauchamp's mythopoeia. Like Moultrie (Hurd Hatfield) in *The Left-Handed Gun* (Arthur Penn, 1958), Beauchamp is the biographer as dime novelist, a figure whose romanticised vision of the West is clearly at odds with the surrounding 'reality'. The point is made overtly when Little Bill corrects Beauchamp's floridly written description of English Bob's killing of Corky Corcoran. Where Beauchamp's account constructs English Bob as a gallant defender of women and heroically quick on the draw, Little Bill tells how a drunken English Bob had shot a powerless Corcoran in cold blood after Corcoran had shot himself in the toe and his pistol had exploded. During the attacks on English Bob and Munny and Ned's whipping, the film repeatedly cuts to Beauchamp's scared and horrified responses to the 'actuality' with which he's faced. Mythopoeia is contrastingly undercut when the Kid asks Munny whether an incident in which he was said to have shot two deputies who had him 'dead to rights' really happened 'the way they say it happened'. Munny disappoints the Kid by claiming that he doesn't 'recollect'. But if English Bob's reputation seems to have been overrated, Munny's seems to have been underrated: Ned later mentions to Munny that he remembers that Munny shot three, not two, men. By highlighting the unreliability of the tales, the film foregrounds its own revisionism; a process which, through the figure of the dime novelist, is contextualised within the history of the Western.

Consistent with its critique of patriarchal capitalism, the film links violence to money and masculinity. The whores' $1,000 is unequivocally the reason why English Bob and more ambiguously why the Kid, Munny (whose name is a homophone) and Ned travel to Big Whiskey. In turn, *Unforgiven* relates violence to destructive phallic energy and the male psychosexual urge to dominate with a explicitness seen rarely, if at all, in the genre since Anthony Mann's Westerns of the 'fifties.

The association of violence with male sexuality and assertion is introduced in the opening sequence: Quick Mike attacks Delilah because she inadvertently giggles at his 'teensy little pecker'. The appellation 'Quick' likewise suggests a comment on his sexual prowess. The film subsequently makes a familiar, but here overt, link between the phallus and firearms when Little Bill explains to Beauchamp that Corky Corcoran was known as 'Two-gun' not because he wore two pistols but because 'he had a dick that was so big it was longer than the barrel on that Walker Colt that he carried'. Similarly, when the Kid boasts that, unlike the beaten Munny, he would have drawn his pistol had he been challenged by Little Bill, Ned reminds him that, in fleeing from Greely's, he had drawn it 'out of the lady and out the goddamn window'. In this context, Little Bill's gun control and his disarming of his victims before he beats them gains added significance, as does his return of English Bob's pistol with its barrel bent.

Munny's and Ned's contrasting ability to kill between Munny and Ned is implicitly related to their differing expenditure of sexual energy. Ned asks Munny, as they ride, whether, since the death of his wife, Claudia, he ever goes into town for a woman. Munny replies in the negative, adding that Claudia, 'rest her soul, would never want me doing something like that'. This prompts Ned to ask, 'you just use your hand?' Munny says, 'I don't miss it all that much'. Immediately, he and Ned are forced from their horses by the Kid shooting, uncontrollably, in their direction, which problematises Munny's 'moral' demurrals by linking his sexual self-denial with violence.

Ned appears to have a stable, sexually active and even 'politically correct' marriage with a Native American, Sally Two Trees (Cherrilene Cardinal), whom, on his first night away from home, he complains that he's going to miss. By contrast, not only has Munny been a widower for nearly three years, but his claims that his wife has cured him of 'wickedness' and his incessant allusions to her influence and his moral transformation become a hollow litany, as if he is making a forced attempt to convince himself that he has changed. While Ned seems to have achieved a calm acceptance of his past, Munny is plagued by memories of his former life. When he speaks of a man whom he unjustly killed and of the fear that he instilled in his partners, his words imply guilt at his return to his old ways. Similarly, when Ned notes that if 'Claudia was alive, you wouldn't be doing this', Munny fixes him with an uncomfortable, hostile stare.

Underlying Munny's implied guilt and extending the film's order-violence motif is the suggestion of an inadmissible desire to return to his past life. After initially refusing the Kid's invitation to become his partner, Munny picks himself up from the mud of his pig pen to look, with telling longing, at the Kid's figure as he rides over the horizon. When Munny tells Ned that he's 'just a fella now . . . no different than anyone else', he speaks with a wistfulness that implies a nostalgic regret at his lost potency.

The suggestion of Munny's implied guilt reaches a peak when he lapses into fever and hallucinates about one of his victims. The fever occurs and heightens as he approaches Big Whiskey, externalising the increasing struggle in his conscience over his return to violence. Read psychoanalytically, this implies a conflict between the id and the super-ego, between Munny's repressed, instinctive impulses and the demands of his 'transformed' self. This association of violence with repressed impulses is underscored by its relation to whiskey. As Munny tells the Kid, 'It was whiskey done it . . . much as anything else'. Correspondingly, Munny's refusal of a shot of Ned's whiskey during the storm as the approach (the evocatively named) Big Whiskey not only exacerbated his fever, but as it ensures his continued, torturing repression, underlines the fever's figurative connotations. When Munny pushes away a glass of whiskey at Greely's, he does so while facing a foregrounded, upright, almost mockingly phallic whiskey bottle. Symbolically, the shot collapses repression, violence and sexuality, a connotation accentuated as Ned has just asked Munny whether he wouldn't care to join him upstairs with the whores. Munny answers with another hostile but self-revealing stare. Such refusal to alleviate his repression lends Munny's suffering a masochistic edge, which is reinforced when he 'allows' Little Bill to 'castrate' and beat him. Just before this, he tells Little Bill that his name is 'Hendershot', a self-abnegating identification with the victim about whom he had hallucinated. However, in a reflection of his mental conflict, Munny's masochism is evidenced by his claims, when Little Bill demands his gun, that he isn't 'drunk' (i.e. violent) or armed, while during his beating he pointedly picks up a whiskey bottle in a futile attempt to defend himself.

As Munny's fever also recalls the sickness suffered by his pigs, his barren, lonely farm is marked as a site of atonement, of penance for his sins. The film appears to place marriage to a good woman as a prime means of achieving order and curbing male excess. Both Claudia and Sally have transformed their husbands from killers into farmers, although the contrast between Munny's windswept homestead and Ned's lusher pastures once more implies their differing success. Nevertheless, while the civilising function of the good woman is a generic constant, the whores' implication in Munny and Ned's return to (phallic) violence opens the film to the charge that it's upholding a misogynistic madonna/whore dichotomy.

Little Bill's embodiment of order is further problematised by the absence from his domestic dream of any reference to a female partner. With the character, as played by Hackman, being hardly small in stature, one might also ponder why he's called 'Little'. Along with his lack of a woman, the appellation not only connects him with Quick Mike but similarly invites us to relate his violence to an overcompensating denial of male inadequacy. This is reinforced by his almost obsessive dislike of weakness and 'men of low character'. He tells Beauchamp, 'It just makes me sick . . . to see a man carrying two pistols and a Henry rifle and crying like a damn baby'. Before assaulting Munny, Little Bill goadingly constructs him as a 'no good son of a bitch and a liar' who's shitting himself 'because of a cowardly soul'. This insistence, coupled with the viciousness of the attack and Little Bill's determined

Still: Unforgiven – *William Munny (Clint Eastwood) and Ned Logan (Morgan Freeman).*

affirmation that you won't find Munny's 'kind' in Big Whiskey, suggests a forceful denial of his feared self, a reading corroborated by the way that, despite the parallels between himself and English Bob, he asserts to Beauchamp, 'I do not like assassins.'

Having made his reputation taming the tough towns of Kansas and Texas, Little Bill mirrors in his violence Munny's desire to regain his past potency. The decisive motivation of Munny's return to violence is psychoanalytically both precise and resonant. After Little Bill's attack, Munny's fever worsens to the extent that he hallucinates the 'Angel of Death'. Narratively, this can be related to his injuries. Figuratively, it implies his increasing psychological difficulty, after his beating, in repressing his violent impulses. Indeed, when his fever abates, Munny displays a calm readiness to kill. But his immediate target isn't, as narrative logic might suggest, Little Bill, but Davey and Quick Mike. This is clarified by the scene in which Munny revives from his fever. His first sight is Delilah's scarred face as she bends over him. Narratively, this confronts him with the results of Quick Mike's violence. Psychosexually, it presents a symbol of castration, a figure of the bleeding wound, suggesting why, despite her unimpaired body, Delilah is no longer a marketable prostitute. The threat that Delilah poses to Munny's masculinity is underscored not only by his position, lying powerless beneath her, but by the way in which he feels his own, scarred face and, in an acknowledgement of his own 'castration', says, 'I must look kinda like you now.' If this returns us to his suffering and humiliation at the saloon, his first words to Delilah, 'I thought you was an angel', recall his hallucination and tacitly relate Delilah, and castration – the loss of male potency – to death. Psychosexually, the scene hence 'explains' Munny's subsequent violence as a

phallic re-assertion. Hence, too, his fulfilling of the whores' contract, which, from the beginning, has offered Munny the opportunity to rediscover his 'lost' self. By contrast, after this scene Munny never *explicitly* mentions or acts upon his beating implies the corresponding repression of a disturbing memory. *Unforgiven*'s repeated representation of male violence as a denial, or even expression, of weakness adds undoubted force to its critique of patriarchal oppression.

The sense of the 'return' of Munny's repressed self is underscored by the emergence of Eastwood's familiar persona. Eastwood as a star is still, for most people, inextricably linked with the cool meanness typified by the Man with No Name or 'Dirty Harry' Callahan. As Munny, Eastwood initially seems to be playing a role that has none of the same characteristics. Early on, he can't shoot straight and has trouble mounting his horse, and he is first seen in the narrative proper scrabbling in his farm's pig pen. The Kid's words, on finding him there, articulate our surprise at seeing Eastwood in such a situation: 'You don't look like no rootin'-tootin' son-of-a-bitchin' cold-blooded assassin.' There is similar reflexiveness in Munny's references to his violent past and in his comment that he has hardly been in the saddle 'in a while' – the film was Eastwood's first Western since *Pale Rider* (1985). But 'do we believe Eastwood, the Man with No Name, in his first incarnation as a farmer?' (Richard Combs, 'Shadowing the Hero', *Sight and Sound*, vol.2, no.6, October 1992, p.15). Complementing Munny's psychic tensions, elements of Eastwood's more familiar persona keep breaking through. There are, for instance, occasional glimpses of his terse, ironic wit. Similarly, when the Kid draws on Ned, who has remarked upon the Kid's short-sightedness, Munny defuses the situation with a peremptory, unanswerable authority: 'Kid can see fifty yards . . . Fifty yards'll do just fine. Now let's move out.' The masochism implied during Munny's beating is another Eastwood staple which, from *Per un pugno di dollari* (Sergio Leone, 1964) to *The Rookie* (Eastwood, 1990), consistently informs his characters' taking of retributive violence.

With his recovery from fever, and 'release' from repression, Munny increasingly displays the Eastwood persona. Despite all the unease that the act occasions, Munny resolutely finishes off Davey and generally displays a growing, even impatient, decisiveness. On learning from the whore Little Sue (Tara Dawn Frederick) of Ned's death, Munny rides into Big Whiskey, enters Greely's, and with, in the words of Christopher Frayling, 'the famous Eastwood scowl on his face . . . spits out the words, "Who's the fella owns this shithole" ' ('Reviews', *Sight and Sound*, vol.2, no.6, October 1992, p.58).

It is, as Frayling notes, 'a great cinematic moment' – at least for anybody who has relished, however uneasily, Eastwood's particular brand of machismo. The scene in turn replays, summarises and brings to a climax many of the film's concerns. Violence again disturbs apparent order – Little Bill's organising of a posse to hunt Munny and the Kid – and is represented as brutal and, sustaining the film's revisionism, decidedly unheroic. Breaking all codes of accepted Western behaviour, Munny first shoots the unarmed Skinny in cold blood. This exceeds the savagery of even English Bob and Little Bill, who have at least had the 'decency' to try to make their opponents draw before they shoot. As Munny next trains his rifle on Little Bill, he calmly admits that he has killed 'just about everything that walked or crawled', his words again suggesting that previous accounts of his atrocities have been understated. His rifle misfires, but in contrast to Little Bill's tale of Corky Corcoran, the misfire isn't fatal for the man wielding the weapon. Munny instead throws the rifle at Little Bill, draws a pistol, badly wounds him, and kills or wounds four other men. These include three of Little Bill's deputies, one of whom, Fatty (Jefferson Mappin), is – in another breach of Western probity – shot in the back. That the incident reflects but undermines – and even renders doubtful – Little Bill's story continues the questioning of Western mythopoeia, with which Little Bill, with his notions of order and self-aggrandising recollections for Beauchamp, is plainly implicated throughout. This is underscored by the subsequent exchange between Munny and Beauchamp, who, with continued 'professional' curiosity, enquires whether Munny had followed Little Bill's dictum that when an 'experienced gunfighter' is 'confronted by superior numbers' he will 'always fire on the best shot first'. Munny denies the myth with an assertion of messy actuality: 'I was lucky in the order. But I've always been lucky when it comes to killing folks.'

With symbolic consistency, Munny's violence is fuelled by whiskey. When Little Sue tells how Ned, under torture, had revealed that his partner 'was really William Munny out of Missouri' – i.e. Munny's past/true self – we see Munny take his first shot of whiskey in the film. We later see the same whiskey bottle cast aside, empty, as Munny rides into town. In plot terms, Ned's death would, at this point, seem to afford ample justification for Munny's retribution – not least as Ned, who is captured as he rides home, is – unlike Munny or the Kid – innocent of murder. While Munny targets Little Bill for his brutality, he targets Skinny for allowing Ned's body to be disrespectfully displayed outside Greely's as a 'warning' to other assassins.

The situation can also be read as permitting Munny to take displaced revenge for his own beating and humiliation by Little Bill at Greely's. This not only parallels the problematising of Munny's motivations in revenging Delilah, but effectively deprives his violence of its redeeming imperative. Even if perpetrated in revenge for Ned's suffering, the carnage is such as to overwhelm any moral validation and constitutes perhaps the film's most significant revision of Western violence, which is thus reduced completely to a matter of power and circumstance rather than justice and right. Little Bill's death makes the point explicit. As Munny stands over Little Bill's prostrate, wounded body and takes point-blank aim with a rifle, Little Bill says, 'I don't deserve this. To die like this. I was building a house.' Munny responds, 'Deserve's got nothing to do with it', and shoots him.

Richard Slotkin writes of the Western: 'To be justifiable, the violence must be redemptive: it must produce a transformation in human affairs that is clearly "progressive" in some sense' ('Violence', in Buscombe, 1988, p.234). Yet at the end of *Unforgiven*, violence has brought only regression. Munny has returned to his past ways, and Big Whiskey has gone back to – or even beyond – its state at the film's opening. As he leaves, Munny – who has destroyed the established order – lays down his law. His shouted commands, however, are just a primitive version of the preceding power without the civilised veneer, thus laying bare its reliance upon violent male threat: 'You better not cut up nor otherwise harm no whores. Or I'll come back and kill every one of you sons of bitches.' The scene takes place during a portentous thunderstorm, which recalls the opening. Similar weather accompanies Munny's beating, creating a pattern that underpins the kinship of Little Bill's rule and that of Munny.

Munny is not punished for his sins. A closing credit somewhat incongruously states that he 'disappeared' with his children, 'some said to San Francisco, where it was rumoured he prospered in dry goods'. A chance for 'just' reckoning is offered, but passed up, when Charlie Hecker (John Pyper-Ferguson), Little Bill's sole surviving deputy, and hence the last representative of 'legitimate' order, is too scared to fire at Munny's departing figure. Right to the end, violent power dominates, a refusal of the Western's moral positivism that is as jarring as it seems depressingly real.

As the scene decisively undermines the 'morality'

of Western violence, so it lays waste the Eastwood persona. Throughout his career Eastwood has parodied, questioned or sought to extend his persona in, for example, *Bronco Billy* (Eastwood, 1980), *Tightrope* (Richard Tuggle, 1984) and *White Hunter, Black Heart* (Eastwood, 1990). In *Unforgiven*, Eastwood subjects his persona to an ideologically potent deconstruction. In the first place, its denial for much of the film makes its fulfilment all the more desired. The frustration is heightened not only by the film being a Western, the genre in which the Man with No Name was born, but also by the tantalising, increasing glimpses of the persona that we're offered. But, upon Munny's entry to Greely's, the extreme nature of his violence foregrounds unequivocally what has always been implicit – that Eastwood's popular persona is that of a vicious, implacable, fascistic killing-machine. Likewise, as *Unforgiven* raises then disturbs the expectations associated with the persona, so it invites us to question our assumptions and desires.

Nevertheless, there may be more positive notes. *Unforgiven* implies, if no more, a distinct belief in youth and, by extension, the future. Crucial with regard to this is the Kid. Initially he's represented as a young man obsessed with his violent masculine identity. He seeks Munny to partner him to Big Whiskey on the advice of his uncle, who, having ridden with Munny, considers him the 'meanest goddamn son of a bitch alive', a killer who doesn't 'have no weak nerve nor fear'. The Kid recounts this with a relish which, repeated when he talks of Munny's rumoured past, implies an adoring, emulative investment in Munny's supposed potency. He has also named himself after his 'Schofield model Smith and Wesson pistol'.

Once more, the representation suggests a destructive phallic overcompensation. Central to the implication is the Kid's 'blindness' – his extreme short-sightedness – which, given the film's Freudian suggestiveness, carries clear connotations of castration. His obsession with violence and travelling to Big Whiskey correspondingly suggest an attempt to deny this weakness, as does his firing on Munny and Ned, whom he can't really see, and the speed with which he threatens Ned, both when Ned dares to pick up the Kid's rifle and when Ned discovers that he's 'blind'. This animus toward Ned in addition implies an adherence to the broader, exclusionary White patriarchal order: when he speaks, unconvincingly, of killing five men, he makes special mention of one being a Mexican. By contrast, his deference before Munny suggests an assumed oedipal identification with a surrogate father figure. This is temporarily challenged when Munny 'lets' himself be beaten, but underscored when, as they wait to kill Quick Mike, the Kid's nervous, almost childlike impatience is met by Munny's weary, 'paternal' restraint.

Shooting Quick Mike confronts the Kid with the realities of murder. Despite his boasts, the Kid hasn't killed before and, with agonising, tearful hesitancy, he outlines what it means: 'It don't seem real. How he ain't gonna never breathe again, ever. How he's dead . . . All on account of pulling a trigger.' Munny responds: 'It's a hell of a thing killing a man. You take away all he's got, and all he's ever gonna have.' On learning of Ned's killing, Munny demands and the Kid hands over his pistol. This cements the characters' implied oedipal relationship by suggesting the Kid's acceptance of symbolic castration, the 'correction' of his transgressive phallic assertion. The Kid also declares that he'll never kill again. This prompts Munny to ask: 'What about the spectacles and the fancy clothes?' – i.e. the rewards of violence. The Kid's reply, 'I'd rather be blind and ragged than dead', is the film's most positive moment, a rejection of patriarchal contention before a humbler acceptance of flawed humanity.

Although the film's mordancy is upheld by the Kid getting his share of the bounty in the end – and hence the money for some spectacles – the association of youth with hope is underlined through the characters of Davey and Delilah. Called by Quick Mike to help in the attack on Delilah, Davey instead tries to restrain his partner. Then, when Davey returns to Big Whiskey with Quick Mike and the horses for Skinny, he also brings a horse, 'the best of the lot', for Delilah. The gesture is all the more potent as Davey is himself innocent of harming the woman. This compares favourably with the 'justice' of Little Bill and Munny, which – apart from its summary oppressiveness – is characterised as basically unfair. Delilah seems silently to accept Davey's reconciliatory gesture. By contrast, the film repeatedly cuts during scenes of tension and violence resulting from the whores' revenge to close shots of Delilah's troubled reactions, a device that lends her the function of a silent moral chorus condemning the action taken in her name.

From the first, it's stated that Delilah 'doesn't care one way or the other' whether her injuries are avenged. The impetus comes from Strawberry Alice, who also angrily rejects Davey's gift on Delilah's behalf. Like Munny's avenging of Ned, Strawberry Alice's avenging of Delilah implies a displaced revenge for her own suffering. Of all the whores, Strawberry Alice is represented as the oldest and most experienced. Against this, Delilah, who is not as obviously young as Davey or the Kid, reveals near-fatal inexperience: she laughs at Quick Mike's 'pecker' because she 'didn't know no better'.

Strawberry Alice's trust in violence crosses the gender divide to connect with that of English Bob, Little Bill and Munny. In common with some other revisionist Westerns, *Unforgiven* casts older actors, often with lengthy associations with the genre, as embodiments of traditional Western values. This tendency is perhaps most clearly demonstrated by two Sam Peckinpah films: *Ride the High Country* (1962) and *The Wild Bunch* (1969). In these films the values of the 'old' West are nostalgically mourned, but in *Unforgiven* the destructive attitudes of the older generation are forcefully attacked. Even if the film ends by asserting the realities of violence and might, the representation in its margins of Davey, Delilah and, especially, the Kid suggests an implicit faith in the future.

FOUR TOMBSTONES
1946-1994

Edward Gallafent

The titles of two recent Westerns, *Tombstone* (George P. Cosmatos, 1993) and *Wyatt Earp* (Lawrence Kasdan, 1994), evoke associations that are likely to be familiar to modern audiences and relate to a significant body of Western fact, fiction, and film-making. The films are not remakes – there is no single earlier feature that corresponds to either of them in shape – but the same incidents and characters form part of the landscape of the Western. The main landmarks are *My Darling Clementine* (John Ford, 1946) and *Gunfight at the OK Corral* (John Sturges, 1957). The characters also appear in *Frontier Marshal* (Allan Dwan, 1939), *Hour of the Gun* (John Sturges, 1967), and *Doc* (Frank Perry, 1971) – a complete listing would be much longer than this.

Part of what I am considering is whether the recent films can be thought of as having a different understanding of what being a hero, or being a villain, might mean, and how this is expressed in their structure and through their presentation of violence and of relations to women. Alongside this is the question of how the films relate to their own modernity, their sense of distance, both from the West of the nineteenth century and from the Hollywood production of the 'forties and 'fifties. How does their account of the past relate to an awareness of the present, the world that their 'nineties audience inhabits?

Common to the main versions of the story are the figures of Wyatt Earp, Doc Holliday and the Clantons. The Earps represent brotherhood, and the narrative uses the relationship of Wyatt to his brothers to illuminate his approach to law enforcement. In the different versions, a democratic ideal is embodied in the fact that Wyatt's deputies are his brothers – defence and celebration of the family meet defence of the democratic order.

This is dramatised most strongly in two scenes that recur across the films: the death of an Earp brother, whose body Wyatt touches – a point of absolute loss – and its opposite, the discovery that America contains the possibility of coming across a man who will become a brother to you. This can be dramatised in the meeting of Wyatt and Doc Holliday, as it is in *My Darling Clementine* and *Wyatt Earp*, or it can be built towards slowly and confirmed only when Doc Holliday decides to fight alongside the Earps.

Doc Holliday's detachment from settled America is represented by his abandonment of both place (Boston in *My Darling Clementine*, Georgia in *Gunfight at the OK Corral*, *Tombstone* and *Wyatt Earp*) and profession (dentist or, in *My Darling Clementine*,

doctor). His role as a professional gambler expresses this detachment, associating him with the saloon, and thus with chance, sudden violence and the sale of sexual favours, as opposed to Wyatt's association with the gaol and thus with order and the containment of violence. Doc's tuberculosis serves in some versions as an explanation of his detachment; in every case, it serves as an alibi. As he is a terminally ill man with no family, his joining with the Earps in the gunfight can be seen as an act without self-interest, a defence of an order from which he can derive no direct benefit.

The Clantons, and those associated with them, represent the opposing forces, which the Earps and Holliday will have to defeat. But the ways in which they are seen differ significantly from the earlier films to the modern ones, and an initial distinction can be made here.

Viciousness

Neither *My Darling Clementine* nor *Gunfight at the OK Corral* shows the Clantons as agents of unmotivated violence. The conversation between Wyatt Earp (Henry Fonda) and Old Man Clanton (Walter Brennan) at the beginning of *My Darling Clementine* is indicative. The soundtrack music and the ominousness of Clanton's manner are entirely sufficient to supply us with a sense of the distance between Earps and Clantons, but they are presented as figures who share a world, albeit from opposed perspectives. The conversation here can be read as a series of exchanges about the power of money, the right to buy (pleasure in a 'wide-open town', or the Earp steers) and the right to refuse to sell. The sequence needs to be considered alongside the one that follows it, a camp-fire scene with the Earps in which Ford delicately indicates exactly what can and cannot be purchased for silver and gold.

The deaths that precede the final gunfight – Billy Clanton (John Ireland), shot by Virgil Earp (Tim Holt), who is trying to bring him to justice, and Virgil shot in revenge by Old Man Clanton – are a single strand of cause and effect. Clanton's acts of viciousness are deliberate, and we are appalled by them precisely because they can be seen as the product of cold-blooded, logical thinking – the shooting of James Earp in order to rustle the steers at the beginning of the film is the exemplary case of this.

Violence also expresses itself as a kind of male rowdiness that has an instant contempt for the idea

of refinement. This is presented in the Dodge City sequence of *Gunfight at the OK Corral*, in which a corrupt dandy, 'Shanghai' Pierce (Ted de Corsia), and his boys burst in on a civilised dance and despoil it. The image is of light being extinguished as the cowboys pull down the chandelier and shoot out lamps.

Again, rather than expressing a psychotic itch to kill, this displays the tension between newer, more decorous manners and brawlers with guns, who embody the energies of an earlier stage in the settlement of the West. The plot leading up to the OK Corral sequence in Sturges's film is similar to that in Ford's – a matter of revenge for the killing of an Earp by the Clantons. The figure of Billy Clanton (Dennis Hopper), caught between his reluctance to prolong his role as a gunslinger and his loyalty to his brothers, aligns this version of the story closely with tragedy of a social order in which the society's corruption is highlighted through dramatic interest in the destruction of its younger members. This is also true of the deaths of James Earp (Don Garner) and Virgil Earp in the Ford, and of Jimmy Earp (Martin Milner) in the Sturges, all attractive young men.

It is the Ford that moves the story closest to an open acknowledgement of the myth that informs it, of the metaphorically sterile father whose corruption destroys his children. In the closing moments of the gunfight, Old Man Clanton, his sons now all dead, is condemned by Wyatt to wander the earth and is saved from this fate only by going for his gun and being killed by Morgan (Ward Bond). In both the

Ford and the Sturges the exercise of violence is seen, displayed alongside the attitudes of men towards or fantasies about women, as a stage in the process of settlement in a model that is concerned with the physical presence or absence of different kinds of women.

The pre-credits sequence of *Tombstone* has a voice-over by Robert Mitchum, in which the story of the rush for Arizona silver in 1879 is described as producing 'the earliest example of organised crime in America', and the murder rates of the boom towns are quoted as 'higher than those of modern-day New York or Los Angeles'. In the film's opening sequence, we see a gang of men ride up to a Mexican church inside which a wedding is taking place. The presentation of the indiscriminate gunplay that follows recalls the opening of Sam Peckinpah's *The Wild Bunch* (1969). The Mexican bridegroom is shot in cold blood by the leader of the gang, Curly Bill (Powers Boothe) – although a nominal reason is given for this, the stress is on the sadism of Curly Bill and his relish for the killing. The first sound that passes his lips is not language, but that important sign of the psychopath – laughter. The sequence ends with Johnny Ringo (Michael Biehn) killing a priest, who is invoking the imagery of apocalypse and the figure of the pale rider.

In *Wyatt Earp*, a sequence in which Wyatt (Kevin Costner) referees a prize-fight – violence contained within order – is followed by a fight with Ed Ross (Martin Kove), a man who wishes to kill him, 'over nothing', as Wyatt stresses in his victory speech. This can be linked with an earlier sequence in which the young Wyatt (Ian Bohen) is a bystander aghast at a gunfight in which a man is shot in the groin, after which he is given a sermon by his father (Gene Hackman) on 'men who will take part in all kinds of viciousness', and the attitude that should be taken to them: 'When you find yourself in a fight with such viciousness, hit first if you can, and when you do hit, hit to kill.'

A quality common to these sequences in the 1990s films is that they have no narrative relationship to the central confrontation. They exist entirely to establish the kind of violence that is operative, to assert its quality as psychopathic, as having little or no relation to any discernible cause. Another instance is a character in *Wyatt Earp* who wants to shoot Wyatt because he will not accept a drink. Nobody is killed for adequate logical or emotional reasons: no murder takes place in the commission of a crime, or to avenge the death of a brother, the causes that bring about the initial deaths in My *Darling Clementine* and *Gunfight at the OK Corral* respectively.

Is this shift simply a matter of accuracy, another revisionist statement about the violence of the West? Perhaps this is the wrong question, or the wrong way of phrasing it. Perhaps the issue is not what the West was like in actuality, but how the films construct or collapse the distance between their times and our own. The voice-over at the beginning of *Tombstone* draws attention to the way the old West resembles the present, as if we should give Tombstone our attention because of its murder rates, and so the nature of its violence, resemble those of our own cities. Mitchum's phrase, 'organised crime', arguably untrue of what we see in *Tombstone*, functions as a way of insisting on this link to the modern.

A final example may clarify these matters – I choose it because here the films are evidently similar, even down to details of dialogue. The townsfolk are taking cover because there is a drunk in the saloon, and it is up to the sheriff to deal with him. Both *My Darling Clementine* and *Wyatt Earp* have this scene. In *Wyatt Earp*, the drunk is simply an anonymous perpetrator of death. Nobody suggests that his

violence has an explanation – they assume the opposite, and this is what we understand: it embodies the random but deadly violence that the new sheriff (this is the start of Wyatt's career) is there to address.

Two differences stand out if we look back to *My Darling Clementine*. The drunk in Ford's film harms nobody, and an explanation for his state is given four times in the course of the sequence: he is an Indian, and so the blame for the situation lies, as Wyatt points out, with those who sell liquor to Indians. Of course, I do not wish to defend the racism of this, or to see it reproduced in a modern film. But his words of dismissal – 'Indian, get out of town and stay out' – determine something crucial about Wyatt, which enables Ford to see him as an agent of settlement: he can define what it is that he is trying to expel from the town by a name, and his identifying it is both his strength and an acknowledgment of limitation, of the energies that American 'civilisation' excludes, a central theme of Ford's work.

In the 'nineties films, there is no such thoughtful dismissal, perhaps because this theme is not available. Is it possible any longer even to propose, however tentatively, that a civilisation can be successfully constructed by running people, literally or otherwise, out of town? Here there is only the relief of physical punishment – notice the detail with which camera and soundtrack in *Wyatt Earp* record the moment when the head of the drunk crashes down several steps as he is dragged out of the saloon by Wyatt. (We may recall here the almost motherly tones of Henry Fonda: 'Put a knot on his head bigger than a turkey's egg.')

Just as there is no clear beginning to violence in the 'nineties films – that is to say no moment to which the narrative can point before the violence started – there can be almost no end to it. Both the Ford and the Sturges use the OK Corral gunfight as a climax, and the Sturges makes the death of Billy Clanton into a moment allied to classical tragedy – Billy is cornered in a photographer's shop, and refuses to surrender to Wyatt (Burt Lancaster). It is strongly implied that Wyatt, trapped by his role as metaphorical father to this boy, cannot bring himself to shoot, and will himself be killed as a result. Doc Holliday (Kirk Douglas) now kills Billy. The point, which runs through the film, is that Wyatt's limitations mean that he has continually to be saved by Holliday.

In *Tombstone* and *Wyatt Earp*, the OK Corral gunfight is presented as an occasion that ends nothing, almost as if it were, in its daylight formality, an early stage in hostilities which has to give way to other more bloody and surreptitious tactics. In these versions, the assassination of Morgan Earp (Linden Ashby) and the gunning down of Virgil Earp (Michael Madsen) in *Wyatt Earp* significantly occur after the gunfight, not before it, and lead on to montage sequences in both films, in which riders led by Wyatt pursue the Clantons across country. In neither film is the process complete – *Wyatt Earp* even includes a title before the final credits, informing us that Clantons continue to die mysteriously over the following years.

Brides, Brothers and Dangerous Women

Stills. Opposite – Wyatt (Kurt Russell) in Tombstone. *Above – the sterile family, Old Man Clanton (Walter Brennan) and his sons in* My Darling Clementine.

Part of what defines the Earp brothers in all four of the films is that their relation to women is conceived in terms of marriage, and what distinguishes Wyatt from his brothers is the film's interest in his finding a bride. Three of the films dramatise Wyatt's choices, and the women's choice of him, by offering more than one figure with whom we might imagine him. Alongside this, and linked with the differences between Wyatt and Doc, is a relationship that expresses sexual energies outside marriage: Doc Holliday and his girl. To call the roll, they are Doc (Victor Mature) and Chihuahua (Linda Darnell) in *My Darling Clementine*, Doc (Kirk Douglas) and Kate (Jo Van Fleet) in *Gunfight at the OK Corral*, Doc (Val Kilmer) and Kate (Joanna Pacula) in *Tombstone* and Doc (Dennis Quaid) and Big Nose Kate (Isabella Rossellini) in *Wyatt Earp*.

In *My Darling Clementine*, Chihuahua is explicitly erotic, sexually active and not above a little infidelity, associated with being Mexican or Indian, a saloon girl and singer. (The manner of her death, like some of her language – 'Why don't you go chase yourself up an alley' – reminds us how close this role is to that of the gangster's moll in a crime thriller or *film noir*.) Miss Clementine Carter (Cathy Downs) seems equally accessible, the girl from the East (Boston), nurse and future schoolmistress, sexually inactive or at least faithful to one man. The main events of the film's narrative do not appear to disturb these identifications. Chihuahua's death – she is shot by Billy Clanton as she confesses her unfaithfulness to Doc,

and dies after he has revived his medical skills in an effort to save her – is followed by Doc's death in the OK Corral gunfight, which leaves Clementine free to be courted by Wyatt. The possibility held out in the dance sequence of Wyatt and Clementine becoming the first married couple of Tombstone and the deaths of Doc and Chihuahua combine a myth of the progression of settlement with satisfaction of the requirements of the Production Code.

That this is not the whole story can be seen when the film dramatises and explores the quality of Wyatt's attitude to the two women. Chihuahua's first appearance is in the saloon where she displays herself to Wyatt, who stoically ignores her. This seems to suggest her superiority to a sexual awkwardness or innocence in the Fonda persona. She sings a teasing song and makes it clear through a conversation and a gesture – looking anxiously through the saloon's front windows – that her lover is absent. Suddenly Wyatt grabs her, pulls her outside, to the back of the saloon – the nominal reason is that she has been helping another player cheat him at poker. They quarrel. Wyatt's line is 'I'll run you back to the Apache reservation, where you belong.' She slaps him (surprisingly?) hard across the face. His response is to soak her to the skin by pushing her into a cattle trough, and the scene dissolves on her comic outrage. Chihuahua's speculative sexual teasing is unmistakable, but the sequence can be read as expressing Wyatt's desire for Chihuahua, of which he is not entirely conscious. Infantilising her by pushing her

305

into the trough is his way of avoiding the clinch with which the scene might otherwise have ended. His line about the reservation is similarly suggestive, in that there is no trace of any suggestion elsewhere in the film that Chihuahua is an Indian (her name is Mexican), and the words seem more like an impromptu insult, which connects the drunk Indian with another form of excitement or disruption: his impulse to expel from Tombstone what Chihuahua represents to his unconscious. The sequence can be connected with one much later in the film, just before the romance with Clementine gets fully under way, when Chihuahua is again quarrelling with Wyatt and threatening him with Doc's vengeance (with the striking image of twisting something around his heart). Wyatt, sitting on the porch outside the hotel, replies with a gesture of memorable elegance, his arms outstretched, his feet executing a kind of horizontal tap-dance on the post of the porch. A few minutes later he will be vertical, dancing with Clementine.

Compare this with Ford's treatment of the 'girl from the East'. This is not just a matter of the casting of Cathy Downs, who was much less well known than Linda Darnell. In terms both of camerawork and of her material in the script, her role is roughly equivalent to, say, that of Eliott Livingstone (John Loder) in Now, Voyager (Irving Rapper, 1942): we are interested in her mainly as an expression of the feelings of her potential partner. Ford seems to offer Clementine's lack of individual qualities – her name,

Stills. Above: Chihuahua (Linda Darnell) and Miss Clementine Carter (Cathy Downs) in My Darling Clementine. *Opposite –* Gunfight at the OK Corral; *top, Doc Holliday (Kirk Douglas) and Kate (Jo Van Fleet); bottom, Doc and Wyatt.*

on which Wyatt comments approvingly in the last line in the film, is the only unusual thing about her – as arguably what makes her attractive to Wyatt. She comes to represent not the uniqueness or disruptiveness of passion but the qualities – professional skills, fidelity, persistence – which implicitly define her as a typical product of the good, bourgeois Eastern home.

The situation in *My Darling Clementine* may be representative of Ford's interest in capturing a very early stage of settlement: the tentativeness and presumption of the attempt to bring civilisation to the wilderness. The very different condition explored in *Gunfight at the OK Corral* is embodied in an early sequence with Doc Holliday and Kate. Not only are the couple played by older actors than in the Ford, but the sequence acknowledges longer histories, old defeats and admissions, with the couple making circuits of violence, passion and self-loathing close to those of Douglas Sirk's melodramas (this film was made the year after *Written on the Wind*). A crucial motif is entrapment, here in the attenuated version of the domestic world that is a hotel bedroom, the site of all the couple's extended sequences. At the beginning of the film, Doc sits throwing knives – we see nine of them – into the bedroom door, as if

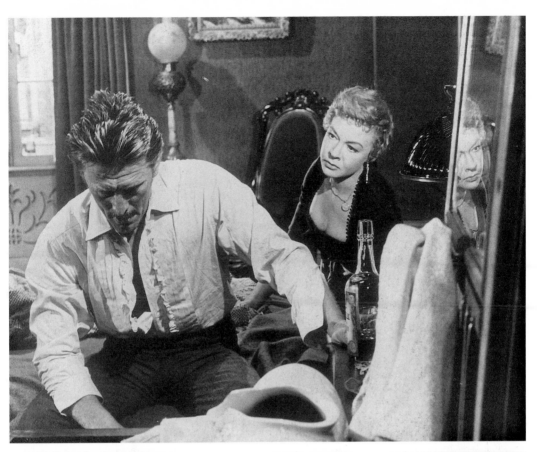

that symbol of separation from open space is what he wants to destroy.

Doc and Kate are fading dandies, marked by their sense of decline – the woman's age, the man's illness. Posed against them are Wyatt (Burt Lancaster) and the gambler Laura Denbow (Rhonda Fleming), whose attraction for each other clearly springs from the qualities they share. Both are polished professionals and successful dandies, their precision of dress hinting at concealed bodily perfection, their love scenes playing with the image of the athlete that was part of Lancaster's persona as a star. They are also associated with the open country, and all their major scenes together take place out of town. Sturges's point seems to be to emphasise the absolute division between the two couples while insisting that the Clantons can be defeated only by the combination of the qualities of both men.

Sturges is also concerned to interrogate the distance between the worlds of the Clantons and the Earps. I have already mentioned Billy Clanton's role as Wyatt's metaphorical son in this film, and Sturges presents both families through sequences showing domestic interiors and mothers – Billy's mother (Olive Carey) and Virgil's wife Betty (Joan Camden) – fearing for the future of their sons. The Clanton ranch is depicted by Sturges with the benign iconography of the family farm, in sharp contrast to Ford's presentation of Old Man Clanton's ranch as a sterile space dominated by racks of guns. Immediately before the gunfight, Sturges offers a brief montage of these apprehensive women – Ma Clanton, Kate and Betty – underlining what their situations have in common.

Part of the interest of the pairs of couples for both Ford and Sturges is in the idea that their qualities, whether faults or virtues, explain their attraction to each other. So Wyatt/Fonda and Clementine choose each other because nobody else in Tombstone has as much contact with the kind of carefulness, or indirectness, that they preserve – Wyatt/Lancaster and Laura choose each other because no other inhabitant of their world is as perfect as they are, beneath their stiff exteriors. And the same is true of apparent aversion – when Doc/Douglas comments that Kate represents 'everything I hate about Doc Holliday', he has found a way of saying that she enables him to see what he is.

In the Ford and the Sturges, a keynote of the relation to women is that the men are not consciously aware of the basis on which they make their choices, perhaps not even always aware that what they are doing is choosing and being chosen. The selection of partners here expresses the ways in which sexual energies can, and cannot, be contained in the process of settlement. In Tombstone and Wyatt Earp, such positions have been radically shifted; unconscious choice is replaced by conscious exchange. The female players in the films now function largely as a locus of overt anxieties about women, and a deliberate progression from one kind of woman to another becomes a way of defining change in the man, who discards women who are felt to be threatening.

Tombstone presents two versions of the dangerous woman. Doc's girl, Kate, is the woman as fatal, sensual temptress; we are introduced to her in a saloon sequence in which Doc celebrates her uncorseted voluptuousness, and later we see her – costumed as the scarlet woman – watch him play cards to the point of physical collapse. Earlier, Doc has compared women to devils, and the point is reprised with crude explicitness in their final scene together. The town's doctor, ministering to Doc, tells him that he should 'curb your marital impulses'. As the sequence ends, we see Kate climb on to the bed. She gives the invalid a lighted cigarette (this seems to be a common sign of corruption in 'nineties movies), and her other actions indicate her intention of sexually arousing him. With this definitive confirmation of her sexuality as almost literally murderous, Kate's role in the film is complete, and she does not appear again. (A further scene in which Doc leaves her was apparently removed from the film during editing.) Perhaps the Earp story is no longer able to focus our interest around the issue of the importance of marriage versus the erotics of cohabitation, and the dramatic force of the Doc/Kate couple can be maintained only by making the figures representative of an extreme of sexual excess. In Wyatt Earp, Kate/Rossellini's role has been reduced virtually to a cameo.

Other anxieties cohere around a figure who can now, under the changed censorship considerations of the 'nineties, be retrieved from the historical source material. This is Mattie Earp (Dana Wheeler-Nicholson), the wife of Wyatt (Kurt Russell) at the start of Tombstone. Mattie is addicted to opiates, suggesting a retreat into privacy that is also expressed in her resentment of Wyatt's public role. But the analysis stops at the substance itself – 'that stuff'll kill you' – rather than invoking any articulation of a previous history. Mattie's condition is posed against the conventionally supportive roles played by the wives of the other brothers, further emphasising her state as unique and unrepresentative, designed to be read as unexplained and self-induced.

In Tombstone, she is displaced by a woman whose qualities are felt to signify acceptable modernity, Josie Marcus (Dana Delany). Her first major scene with Wyatt is in the open air, a meeting on horseback that echoes Wyatt/Lancaster's meeting with Laura in Gunfight at the OK Corral. The association of Josie with health contrasts with the presentation of Mattie's condition as physical debility, and this is related to a movement between private and public worlds. Josie is shown first as an actor, then as a singer; her ease in public contexts is underlined in her exchange with Wyatt/Russell on the subject of their ideal futures. Wyatt's haltingly offered vision of family is countered by Josie's ideal of unfettered adventure, symbolised for her in the words 'room service'. The film makes its preference for this model of the couple very clear by following up their outdoor sequence with an bedroom scene, in which Wyatt puts the idea of 'room service' to a uncomprehending Mattie. Josie's role is to be reunited with Wyatt, constructing the film's happy ending around the rightness of the new couple. The final voice-over speaks of Mattie's death from her addiction and Wyatt and Josie's 47 years of marriage.

We are offered in *Tombstone* a man's flight from one woman associated with privacy and dependence (on a husband, on a chemical) to another associated with movement and freedom – a traditional American trajectory. We see Wyatt's abandonment of the social order that he has been defending, while Josie offers an alternative to both excessive privacy and erotic abandon. But the couple is also strikingly vacuous: Josie and Wyatt are free of the past, of place and time, and seem haunted neither by violence nor by heroism. Having begun by stressing the similarity of the old West to the present day, the film seems to argue that the couple can simply walk away from the past into a different world, one defined by the supposed modernity of the relationship between the couple.

The opening sequences of *Wyatt Earp* deal exclusively with men, starting with the young Wyatt's knowledge that his older brothers are away fighting the Civil War, and his attempt to run off to the war, which is thwarted by his father. The return of the brothers is a moment of ritual thanksgiving shared only by these four men; Kasdan shows the porch of the family homestead, but no Earp woman greets the returned sons. This mood is continued in the subsequent sequence at the family dinner table. The women are certainly present, but the script and Kasdan's direction emphasise the father's role as dominant patriarch with the credo that 'Nothing counts so much as blood, the rest are just strangers'.

The importance of this credo can be gauged in the Wyoming sequence, in which we first see Costner as the adult Wyatt, poised between the physical attractions of saloon girl Sally (Tea Leoni) and the memory of his glimpses of the perfect virgin bride, a version of Clementine Carter, who is safely distant in Lamar, Missouri: 'I seen her three times back in '63, and the third time she smiled at me just right.' Such a man has to be indifferent to Sally: he returns to Missouri, courts and marries Urilla (Annabeth Gish), the smiling virgin of his memory, and she duly becomes pregnant. But Urilla contracts typhoid and dies, and the distraught Wyatt burns their home to the ground and flees.

It might be thought that this is a story about the past that insists on the modernity of its viewpoint – Kasdan's way of reminding us that the perfect world of nineteenth-century bourgeois mid-America was always a fantasy, liable to disruption by disease or other causes. The sequence of marriage followed by loss is not, however, presented in the film just as a random mischance. There are a number of ways in which the film interrogates the marriage, and Wyatt's motivation for choosing his bride.

We are shown the obsessive quality of Wyatt's courtship, his absolute conviction of their rightness for each other. Her blood can be thought of as unpolluted in terms of both her virginity and her social class. To marry her is to subscribe to his father's values and to immerse himself further in them, substituting the patriarchal Judge Earp (Giorgio E. Tripoli), with whom he is studying law in Lamar, for his father, and abandoning the adventures of the West for a life of urban domestic pleasures. Commenting on this is Kasdan's presentation of Wyatt's and Urilla's marital home, which is organised around the different associations attached to interior and exterior spaces. The exterior can be benign, the site of a conversation about the West between the newlyweds, in which Wyatt expresses his contentment with his domestic lot while the two tend their garden. The ominous interior is first shown when the couple are house-hunting – its drab, empty space is the background for a strikingly intense embrace, but the progression from this to the moment when their sexual fulfilment can be celebrated in a restored domestic context is suggestively absent. We see warm yellow light from the windows as Wyatt takes his bride inside, but almost nothing more: there is a very brief sequence of the couple in bed in bitter winter weather. Later, a quarrelsome exchange inside the house expresses the strain imposed on Wyatt by Urilla's pregnancy and the dawning knowledge that she is ill. The next sequence seems to be a grim but clear substitution for the celebration of the couple's sexuality, as Urilla's body is finally bared only to expose her sores, and the sweat and intensity indicate not an erotic experience, but Urilla's dying minutes. The death is followed by a telling reprise of an earlier image. For an unlikely moment, as Wyatt sets the house alight, the yellow flames in its windows recall to the entry into the house on the wedding night.

(The Lamar sequence of *Wyatt Earp* can be compared to the Sicily sequence in *The Godfather*, Francis Ford Coppola, 1972, which also shatters a fantasy of perfect love. In Coppola's film, the marriage of Michael Corleone (Al Pacino) to Apollonia (Simonetta Stefanelli), which ends with her violent death, is also associated with an environment that is alien to the man, rural southern Europe as opposed to the Corleones' New York. The two films, both built around a central group of male blood relatives and an uneasy relation to the inescapability of violence, to ideas of heroism and to the roles of women, are clearly comparable in a number of important respects.)

Wyatt's insistence on the peerlessness of his love – Urilla dies pronouncing his name – can be related to his need to repress any negative feeling about his choice of woman or world. His mourning is expressed in a desire for degradation and death, a situation from which, significantly, he is released by the intervention of his father. The anxieties surrounding a birth, associated with the domestic, with marriage and the prospect of motherhood, are replaced by the rebirth of Wyatt, associated with the West and the figure of the father – an intertitle gives the period of his immersion in a state of grief as nine months.

Kasdan follows through the logic of Wyatt's withdrawal from passion by offering another model for relations between the sexes, based on exchange, in which marriage is understood as a transaction in the same sense as a prostitute's relation to her client. Wyatt discovers that Bessie (JoBeth Williams), the wife of James Earp (David Andrews), supplements

the couple's income by working as a prostitute. This prepares the ground for Wyatt's relation to Mattie (Mare Winningham), in which it is clear that he can bear to accept her only by defining her in a related way. We see him making a point of leaving money on her dresser, and later he will use the language of financial transaction: he 'owes her' the right to use his name, but children aren't 'part of the bargain'.

This thinking informs Wyatt's attitude to his brothers and their wives as the film moves to Dodge City and then Tombstone. His loyalty to the ideal of brotherhood – his version of the father's 'nothing counts so much as blood' – cannot be extended to the wives, who in his eyes always remain contingent figures, a loose alliance of women who cannot be given the same status as the Earp men. He finally tells them, 'Wives come and go, that's the plain truth of it, they run off, they die.' Given Wyatt's history, this sounds like an empirical claim, but it can be read as a definition of all he can allow marriage to mean and as part of his insistence on sticking to what he calls 'plain truth'. (The evident unbearability of this position for the woman is one of the differences between *Wyatt Earp* and *Tombstone*. In *Tombstone*, Mattie's drug addiction was an anomaly that distinguished her from the other wives, but in *Wyatt Earp*, it is offered as an understandable response to living with a man who conceives of wives as Wyatt does. A line from Virgil's wife about how much laudanum she would need to survive marriage to Wyatt makes the point.)

Wyatt Earp shares with *Tombstone* the displacement of Mattie by Josie Marcus, and both films end by footnoting their 47-year marriage. Josie (Joanna Going) in *Wyatt Earp* is again associated with youth

and health, but the treatment of the subject reflects the deeply seated anxieties displayed in Kasdan's film. Part of Josie's role is obviously to answer the premature death of Urilla, to be the woman who does not die. She knows this – hence her line about wanting to be lying next to him when they are both eighty and her cri de coeur to him 'I won't die on you, 1 swear it'.

This line cannot be a literal assurance; it is a lover's vow, coupled with the promise of fertility – 'I'll give you children' – in the same speech. Earlier, in a seduction scene in the fertile countryside (essentially the same setting as for comparable scenes in *Gunfight at the OK Corral* and *Tombstone*), the couple have talked about the stories that circulate about Wyatt, stories that are central to their feeling for each other. Josie, in this respect Desdemona to Wyatt's Othello, loves him for the dangers he has lived through, and when Wyatt questions the accuracy of the tales, Josie tells him that 'stories are always better'. At the end of the film, a young man recalls, now in flashback, the exact episode of Wyatt's past that Josie had quoted to him in the seduction scene. In response to Wyatt's questioning of it – 'Some people say it didn't happen that way' – Josie tells him, 'Never mind them, Wyatt, it happened that way.' The couple have just been talking about the gold rush, sharing the dream of instant riches taken without pain from the land – a neat emblem of American utopian fantasy.

Josie represents the quality, not of accurate prediction – although she lives to a great age, she does not have children – but of belief in a world of the heroic, or the ideal, as opposed to the 'plain truth of it' that dogs Wyatt, his uneasy awareness of the gap between the legend of Wyatt Earp and his actual performance, or between his father's faith in blood ties and his own anxieties about women. Wyatt first sees Josie in the chorus of *HMS Pinafore*. It has just been put to him that his role as lawman is the only one he is really capable of playing, when we see him transfixed by the sight of a performer who can respond to a mishap on stage with a laugh. Josie's assertiveness, effectively presented in Joanna Going's intense performance, replaces what Wyatt cannot feel: his heroism and their ideal marriage exist through her faith, her announcement of them.

Wyatt Earp shares with *Tombstone* a sense of the difficulty and exhaustion entailed in ending the violence of its world, and Kasdan's film also leaves the couple in retreat from the West, on board ship off the coast of Alaska. The interest in the social world that will replace the world of settlement is more complex. The suppressed anxieties of the Lamar sequence are echoed in Josie's vow to Wyatt, in the same speech as her promises of fertility and health, 'We'll make our own place, where no-one will find us.' *Wyatt Earp* can be read as a film in which Lamar, the world which is closest to a recognisable modern America, is associated with domestic entrapment and with the promises of the settled world, which disintegrate in the face of conditions beyond the reach of medical science – a recognisable image of our own times.

Deliberation and Freedom

Wyatt Earp can be distinguished from *Tombstone* in its treatment of the heroic ideal around which Wyatt's mental life revolves. This is clear from very early in Kasdan's film – the young Wyatt aiming his gun at the moon is echoed in the metaphorical shooting of the stars (literally they are fireworks) after the adult Wyatt has triumphed over Ed Ross, when, significantly, he is quite unconscious of the attractions of the girl next to him. His ideal is symbolised by the need for a response to his name that will express this unique self to others. With Urilla, with Doc and with Josie, much is made of the speaking of his Christian name, as if the word were a magic charm. The denial of its force can also be a form of curse, as in Wyatt's exchange with Ed Ross, and in his encounter with the Clements gang in Dodge City, in which his naming of himself is greeted with a line that, in breaking a convention, draws attention to its modernity and the possibility of the loss of heroic status: 'Who the fuck is Wyatt Earp?' Compare this to the moment in *My Darling Clementine* in which Wyatt announces to Old Man Clanton that he is staying on in Tombstone as sheriff. This news is greeted with implied derision, until the conversation brings out the words 'Wyatt Earp', and then it is clear that the Clantons know by these two words who this man is.

It may not be coincidental that, in the Clements gang sequence of *Wyatt Earp*, Kasdan has photographed Costner from an angle which seems to stress his resemblance to Gary Cooper. (Kasdan has made a related connection in an interview in *Projections* 3, ed. John Boorman and Walter Donohue, Faber, London, 1994, p.136). One of Costner's important qualities as a star is his isolation, or what might be called his besetting seriousness. As Wyatt Earp, it is what he calls being a 'deliberate' man; he recognises its opposite in the character of Ed Masterson (Bill Pullman), 'You're not a deliberate man. I don't sense that about you, you're too affable.' This quality of deliberation dominates the character when he is being the 'Wyatt Earp' of legend, most evidently immediately before the OK Corral gunfight in the saloon sequence that forms the pre-credits sequence of Kasdan's movie.

It is clear from the scene with the Clantons in *My Darling Clementine* that Wyatt's name is emblematic of his power. But Ford knows that this also symbolises his burden, the solemnity and gravitas from which he must be redeemed. This is the work of comedy, of Cupid, in the shape of the town barber, spraying perfume on the sheriff. Wyatt smells like honeysuckle, like home, like nature; it is a condition of his redemption that he must be embarrassed by this and that the embarrassment must be met, in the right way, by the woman he will marry. I take the exchange between them here to be central in their mutual definition: Clementine, 'The air's so clean and clear. The scent of the desert flowers . . .' Wyatt, 'That's me. Barber . . .' (An audience which has seen *The Lady Eve*, *The Awful Truth*, or *Ball of Fire* will follow this; it depends on the richness of the years of Hollywood sound comedy that preceded it, the redemption of the seriousness of men played by Gary Cooper, Henry Fonda, or Cary Grant by women, played by the likes of Barbara Stanwyck, Irene Dunne, and Claudette Colbert.) If we look in *Wyatt Earp* for Costner's redemption from his deliberateness, we find that Josie can only reassure Wyatt about his heroic persona, not redeem him from it. There is a recurrent awareness, registered most strongly by the other Earp wives and by Doc's ironies, that some part of Wyatt's self-imposed role as stiff-necked patriarch is intolerable. But there is no equivalent here of the perfume sequence (or, to give another example, of the bloomers sequence in *Rio Bravo,* Howard Hawks, 1959), no ritual delivery of the hero from his heroism.

It might occur to us that the young man who accosts Wyatt and Josie on the boat at the end of *Wyatt Earp* with his 'flashback' to Wyatt's past is a reminder of a crucial figure for modern cinema: the young male viewer who represents an important typical target audience for a modern Western. The young man produces his belief in the Earp legend, the moment of perfect heroic action; Wyatt interrogates it; Josie brushes the interrogation aside. No one of these positions is preferred – although Josie has the last word, the camera is on her back, not her face. We are left with an exchange about the assertion, denial, and affirmation of legend. The energy of this debate, this interestedness, is Kasdan's final offering on the value of the Western. Perhaps it has to be, because the question – was this the way it was? – is something we still feel able to understand, when other elements of the world of the Western are becoming increasingly difficult to interrogate.

Stills: Wyatt Earp. Opposite – the language of financial transaction; Wyatt with Mattie (Mare Winningham). Below – the legendary marriage; Wyatt and Josie (Joanna Going).

INDEX